Lecture Notes in Computer Science 9938

Commenced Publication in 1973
Founding and Former Series Editors:
Gerhard Goos, Juris Hartmanis, and Jan van Leeuwen

More information about this series at http://www.springer.com/series/7408

Cyrille Artho · Axel Legay
Doron Peled (Eds.)

Automated Technology for Verification and Analysis

14th International Symposium, ATVA 2016
Chiba, Japan, October 17–20, 2016
Proceedings

 Springer

Editors
Cyrille Artho
AIST
Osaka
Japan

Doron Peled
Bar Ilan University
Ramat Gan
Israel

Axel Legay
Inria Rennes
Rennes
France

ISSN 0302-9743 ISSN 1611-3349 (electronic)
Lecture Notes in Computer Science
ISBN 978-3-319-46519-7 ISBN 978-3-319-46520-3 (eBook)
DOI 10.1007/978-3-319-46520-3

Library of Congress Control Number: 2016951981

LNCS Sublibrary: SL2 – Programming and Software Engineering

This Springer imprint is published by Springer Nature
The registered company is Springer International Publishing AG
The registered company address is: Gewerbestrasse 11, 6330 Cham, Switzerland

Preface

This volume contains the papers presented at ATVA 2016, the 14th International Symposium on Automated Technology for Verification and Analysis held during October 17–20 in Chiba, Japan. The purpose of ATVA is to promote research on theoretical and practical aspects of automated analysis, verification, and synthesis by providing an international forum for interaction among researchers in academia and industry.

ATVA attracted 82 submissions in response to the call for papers. Each submission was assigned to at least four reviewers of the Program Committee. The Program Committee discussed the submissions electronically, judging them on their perceived importance, originality, clarity, and appropriateness to the expected audience. The Program Committee selected 31 papers for presentation, leading to an acceptance rate of 38 %.

The program of ATVA also included three invited talks and three invited tutorial given by Prof. Tevfik Bultan (University of Santa Barbara), Prof. Javier Esparza (Technical University of Munich), and Prof. Masahiro Fujita (Fujita Laboratory and the University of Tokyo).

The chairs would like to thank the authors for submitting their papers to ATVA 2016. We are grateful to the reviewers who contributed to nearly 320 informed and detailed reports and discussions during the electronic Program Committee meeting. We also sincerely thank the Steering Committee for their advice. Finally, we would like to thank the local organizers, Prof. Mitsuharu Yamamoto and Prof. Yoshinori Tanabe, who devoted a large amount of their time to the conference. ATVA received financial help from the National Institute of Advanced Industrial Science and Technology (AIST), Springer, Chiba Convention Bureau and International Center (CCB-IC), and Chiba University.

July 2016

Cyrille Artho
Axel Legay
Doron Peled

Organization

Program Committee

Toshiaki Aoki	JAIST, Japan
Cyrille Artho	AIST, USA
Christel Baier	Technical University of Dresden, Germany
Armin Biere	Johannes Kepler University, Austria
Tevfik Bultan	University of California at Santa Barbara, USA
Franck Cassez	Macquarie University, Australia
Krishnendu Chaterjee	Institute of Science and Technology (IST)
Allesandro Cimatti	FBK-irst, Italy
Rance Cleaveland	University of Maryland, USA
Deepak D'Souza	Indian Institute of Science, Bangalore, India
Bernd Finkbeiner	Saarland University, Germany
Radu Grosu	Stony Brook University, USA
Klaus Havelund	Jet Propulsion Laboratory, California Institute of Technology, USA
Marieke Huisman	University of Twente, The Netherlands
Ralf Huuck	UNSW/SYNOPSYS, Australia
Moonzoo Kim	KAIST, South Korea
Marta Kwiatkowska	University of Oxford, UK
Kim Larsen	Aalborg University, Denmark
Axel Legay	IRISA/Inria, Rennes, France
Tiziana Margaria	University of Limerick, Ireland
Madhavan Mukund	Chennai Mathematical Institute, India
Anca Muscholl	LaBRI, Université Bordeaux, France
Doron Peled	Bar-Ilan University, Israel
Andreas Podelski	University of Freiburg, Germany
Geguang Pu	East China Normal University, China
Sven Schewe	University of Liverpool, UK
Oleg Sokolsky	University of Pennsylvania, USA
Marielle Stoelinga	University of Twente, The Netherlands
Bow-Yaw Wang	Academia Sinica, Taiwan
Chao Wang	Virginia Tech, USA
Farn Wang	National Taiwan University, Taiwan
Wang Yi	Uppsala University, Sweden
Naijun Zhan	Institute of Software, Chinese Academy of Sciences, China

Lijun Zhang   Institute of Software, Chinese Academy of Sciences,
                                        China
Huibiao Zhu   Software Engineering Institute, East China Normal
                                        University, China

Additional Reviewers

Bacci, Giorgio
Bacci, Giovanni
Barbot, Benoit
Barnat, Jiri
Basset, Nicolas
Ben Sassi, Mohamed Amin
Blom, Stefan
Bogomolov, Sergiy
Bollig, Benedikt
Ceska, Milan
Chen, Yu-Fang
Chiba, Yuki
Doyen, Laurent
Engelhardt, Kai
Fang, Huixing
Feng, Lu
Forejt, Vojtech
Frehse, Goran
Gario, Marco
Gburek, Daniel
Gerhold, Marcus
Gerke, Michael
González De Aledo, Pablo
Griggio, Alberto
Guck, Dennis
Guo, Shengjian
Hahn, Ernst Moritz
Hansen, Zaza Nadja Lee
Heizmann, Matthias
Hoenicke, Jochen
Hoffmann, Philipp
Huang, Xiaowei
Ishii, Daisuke
Jacob, Jeremy
Jaksic, Stefan

Jensen, Peter Gjøl
Kim, Hyunwoo
Kim, Jin Hyun
Kim, Yunho
Klein, Felix
Komondoor, Raghavan
Kusano, Markus
Lahijanian, Morteza
Li, Jianwen
Li, Yangjia
Liu, Bing
Liu, Jiang
Liu, Wanwei
Lodaya, Kamal
Lombardy, Sylvain
Lukina, Anna
Mariegaard, Anders
Mattarei, Cristian
McIver, Annabelle
Meijer, Jeroen
Micheli, Andrea
Müller, David
Müller-Olm, Markus
Nouri, Ayoub
Nutz, Alexander
Park, Junkil
Penelle, Vincent
Perez, Guillermo A.
Petri, Gustavo
Pinto, João Sousa
Pous, Damien
Praveen, M.
Quilbeuf, Jean
Ratasich, Denise
Rodionova, Alena

Rogalewicz, Adam
Ruijters, Enno
Sankur, Ocan
Santos, Gabriel
Schilling, Christian
Seidl, Martina
Sergey, Ilya
Sharma, Subodh
Song, Fu
Stoelinga, Marielle
Su, Ting
Summers, Alexander J.
Sung, Chungha
Suresh, S.P.
Sutre, Grégoire
Taankvist, Jakob Haahr
Tentrup, Leander
Tomita, Takashi
Torfah, Hazem
Traonouez, Louis-Marie
Tsai, Ming-Hsien
Turrini, Andrea
van Dijk, Tom
Villa, Tiziano
Wang, Xu
Wu, Meng
Wu, Xi
Wu, Zhilin
Xia, Mingji
Xue, Bingtian
Zhang, Min
Zhang, Naling
Zhang, Teng
Zhao, Hengjun
Zimmermann, Martin

Contents

Parallelism, Concurrency

Complexity, Decidability

Synthesis, Refinement

Keynote

Synthesizing and Completely Testing Hardware Based on Templates Through Small Numbers of Test Patterns

Masahiro Fujita[✉]

The University of Tokyo, Tokyo, Japan
fujita@ee.t.u-tokyo.ac.jp

Abstract. Here we first introduce Quantified Boolean Formula (QBF) based approaches to logic synthesis and testing in general including automatic corrections of designs. It is formulated as: If some appropriate values are assigned to what we call programmable variables, the resulting circuits behaves as our intentions for all possible input values, that is, they become the ones whose logic functions are the intended ones. In this paper we only target combinational circuits and sequential circuits which are time-frame expanded by fixed times. The QBF problems are solved by repeatedly applying SAT solvers, not QBF solvers, with incremental additions of new constraints for each iteration which come from counter examples for the SAT problems. The required numbers of iterations until solutions are obtained are experimentally shown to be pretty small (in the order of tens) even if there are hundreds of inputs, regardless of the fact that they have exponentially many value combinations. Then the applications of the proposed methodology to logic synthesis, logic debugging, and automatic test pattern generations (ATPG) for multiple faults are discussed with experimental results. In the case of ATPG, a test pattern is generated for each iteration, and programmable variables can represent complete sets of functional and multiple faults, which are the most general faults models.

1 QBF Formulation

In general the synthesis of partial missing portions of the circuits can be formulated as Quantified Boolean Formula (QBF) problems. Here missing portions can be any sets of sub-circuits or single gates, and their synthesis covers logic synthesis/optimization, logic debugging/Engineering Change Order (ECO), and automatic test pattern generation (ATPG) for general multiple faults. In this paper we deal with combinational circuits or sequential circuits with fixed numbers of time-frame expansions. By modelling the missing portions with Look Up Table (LUT) or some kind of programmable circuits, their synthesis, verification, and testing problems can be formulated as QBF problems as follows.

When the portion to be filled is just one, the problem is illustrated in Fig. 1. In the figure, on the top there is a target circuit which has a missing portion, $C1$. On the bottom, there is a corresponding specification which could be another

© Springer International Publishing AG 2016
C. Artho et al. (Eds.): ATVA 2016, LNCS 9938, pp. 3–10, 2016.
DOI: 10.1007/978-3-319-46520-3_1

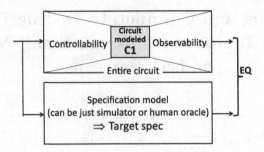

Fig. 1. The target problem: most simple case

circuit or some sorts of logical specification. The problem here is to find out an appropriate circuit for $C1$ which makes the entire target circuit logically equivalent to the specification. There can be two situations: One is when a logical specification as well as a formal equivalence checker which certifies the correctness of the target circuit with $C1$ and can generate a counter example in the case of non-equivalence. The other situation we consider is when only simulation models are available and no formal verifiers are available. We present an extended technique which can certify the correctness of the target with $C1$ even just with simulations.

If the inputs to the sub-circuit, $C1$, are fixed as shown in Fig. 1, $C1$ can be generally represented as Look Up Table (LUT). By appropriately programming the LUT, if we can make the entire target circuits equivalent to the specification, we say that the problem is successfully resolved.

As can be seen from [1], the problems can be formulated as Quantified Boolean Formula (QBF). That is, the problem is formulated as:

"Under appropriate programs for LUTs (existentially quantified), the circuit behaves correctly for all possible input values (universally quantified)".

More recently, a new improved algorithm, which our work is also based on, has been proposed [2,3]. By utilizing ideas from Counter Example Guided Abstraction Refinement (CEGAR) in formal verification fields, QBF problems can be efficiently solved by repeatedly applying SAT solvers based on CEGAR paradigm [4]. By utilizing this idea, much larger problems related to PPC can be processed as shown in [2,3].

Although in [2,3] two SAT problems are solved in one iteration, the first one is always a very simple one (as most of inputs are getting constant values) and can be solved very quickly whereas the second one can be more efficiently performed with combinational equivalence checkers. There had been significant research on combinational equivalence checkers which are based on not only powerful SAT solvers but also identification of internal equivalence points for problem decompositions. Now they are commercialized and successfully used for industrial designs having more than one million gates. We show that by utilizing such combinational equivalence checkers, even if sizes of entire circuits is more than 100,000 gates, if the portions to be partially synthesized ($C1$ in Fig. 1) are not large, we can successfully synthesize.

Most of these techniques as well as the ones for test pattern generation, which will be discussed in the next section, have been implemented on top of the logic synthesis and verification tool, ABC from UCB [5].

Moreover, we also show techniques which can work for cases where only simulation models are available. In this case, we cannot use formal equivalence checkers since no usable logical specification is available. As simulation models are available, however, if we can generate two solution candidates, we can check which one is correct or both are incorrect by simulation. By repeating this process, if there is only one solution candidate existing, we may be able to conclude that candidate is actually a real solution. We show by experiments that with reasonably small numbers of iterations (hundreds), correct circuits can be successfully synthesized.

2 The Base Algorithm

For easiness of explanation, in this paper, we assume the number of output for the target buggy circuit is one. That is, one logic function in terms of primary inputs can represent the logic function for the entire circuit. This makes the notations much simpler, and also extension for multiple outputs is straightforward. Also, variables in this paper are mostly vectors of individual ones.

As there is only one output in the design, a specification can be written as one logic function with the set of primary inputs as inputs to the function. For a given specification $SPEC(x)$ and an implementation with programmable circuits $IMPL(x, v)$, where x denotes the set of primary input variables and v denotes the set of variables to configure programmable circuits inside, the problem is to find a set of appropriate values for v satisfying that $SPEC$ and $IMPL$ are logically equivalent. This problem can be described as QBF (Quantified Boolean Formula) problem as follows:

$$\exists v. \forall x. SPEC(x) = IMPL(x, v).$$

That is, with appropriate values for v, regardless of input values (values of x), the circuits must be equivalent to the specification (i.e., the output values are the same), which can be formulated as the equivalence of the two logic functions for the specification and the implementation. There are two nested quantifiers in the formula above, that is, existential quantifiers are followed by universal quantifiers, which are called QBF in general. Normal SAT formulae have only existential quantifiers and no universal ones.

In [2,3], CEGAR (Counter-Example Guided Abstraction Refinement) based QBF solving method is applied to the circuit rectification problem. Here, we explain the method using 2-input LUT for simplicity, although LUT having any numbers of inputs can be processed in a similar way. Logic functions of a 2-input LUT can be represented by introducing four variables, $v_{00}, v_{01}, v_{10}, v_{11}$, each of which corresponds to the value of one row of the truth table. Those

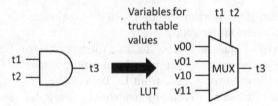

Fig. 2. LUT is represented with multiplexed four variables as truth table values.

four variables are multiplexed with the two inputs of the original gate as control variables, as shown in Fig. 2. In the figure a two-input AND gate is replaced with a two-input LUT. The inputs, t_1, t_2, of the AND gate becomes the control inputs to the multiplexer. With these control inputs, the output is selected from the four values, $v_{00}, v_{01}, v_{10}, v_{11}$. If we introduce M of 2-input LUTs, the circuit has $4 \times M$ more variables than the variables that exist in the original circuit. We represent those variables as v_{ij} or simply v which represents a vector of v_{ij}. v variables are treated as pseudo primary inputs as they are programmed (assigned appropriate values) before utilizing the circuit. t variables in the figure correspond to intermediate variables in the circuit. They appear in the CNF of the circuits for SAT/QBF solvers.

If the logic function at the output of the circuit is represented as $f_I(v, x)$ where x is an input variable vector and v is a program variable vector, after replacements with LUTs, the QBF formula to be solved becomes:

$$\exists v. \forall x. f_I(v, x) = f_S(x),$$

where f_S is the logic function that represents the specification to be implemented. Under appropriate programming of LUTs (assigning appropriate values to v), the circuit behaves exactly the same as specification for all input value combinations.

Although this can simply be solved by any QBF solvers theoretically, only small circuits or small numbers of LUTs can be successfully processed [2,3]. Instead of doing that way, we here like to solve given QBF problems by repeatedly applying normal SAT solvers using the ideas shown in [4,9].

Basically we solve the QBF problem only with normal SAT solvers in the following way. Instead of checking all value combinations on the universally quantified variables, we just pick up some small numbers of value combinations and assign them to the universally quantified variables. This would generate SAT formulae which are just necessary conditions for the original QBF formulae. Note that here we are dealing with only two-level QBF, and so if universally quantified variables get assigned actual values (0 or 1), the resulting formulae simply become SAT formulae. The overall flow of the proposed method is shown in Fig. 3. For example, if we assign two combinations of values for x variables, say $a1$ and $a2$, the resulting SAT formula to be solved becomes like: $\exists v. (f_I(v, a1) = f_S(a1)) \wedge (f_I(v, a2) = f_S(a2))$. Then we can just apply any SAT solvers to them. If there is no solution, we can conclude that the original QBF

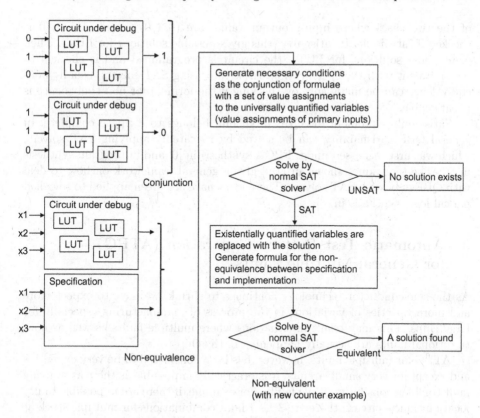

Fig. 3. Overall flow of the rectification method in [2,3].

formulae do not have solution neither. If there is a solution found, we need to make sure that it is a real solution for the original QBF formula. Because we have a solution candidate $v_{assigns}$ (these are the solution found by SAT solvers) for v, we simply make sure the following:

$$\forall x. f_I(v_{assigns}, x) = f_S(x).$$

This can be solved by either usual SAT solvers or combinational equivalence checkers. In the latter case, circuits with tens of millions of gates may be processed, as there have been conducted significant amount of researches for combinational equivalence checkers which utilize not only state-of-the-art SAT techniques but also various analysis methods on circuit topology. If they are actually equivalent, then the current solution is a real solution of the original QBF formula. But if they are not equivalent, a counterexample, say x_{sol}, is generated and is added to the conditions for the next iteration:

$$\exists v. (f_I(v, a1) = f_S(a1)) \wedge (f_I(v, a2) = f_S(a2)) \wedge (f_I(v, x_{sol}) = f_S(x_{sol})).$$

This solving process is repeated until we have a real solution or we prove the non-existence of solution. In the left side of Fig. 3, as an example, the conjunction of the two cases where inputs/output values are $(0,1,0)/1$ and $(1,1,0)/0$ is checked if satisfiable. If satisfiable, this gives possible solutions for LUTs. Then using those solutions for LUTs, the circuit is programmed and is checked to be equivalent with the specification. As we are using SAT solvers, usually non-equivalence can be made sure by checking if the formula for non-equivalence is unsatisfiable.

Satisfiability problem for QBF in general belongs to P-Space complete. In general QBF satisfiability can be solved by repeatedly applying SAT solvers, which was first discussed under FPGA synthesis in [6] and in program synthesis in [7]. The techniques shown in [4,9] give a general framework on how to deal with QBF only with SAT solvers. These ideas have also been applied to so called partial logic synthesis in [3].

3   Automatic Test Pattern Generation (ATPG) for General Multiple Faults

As the semiconductor technology continues to shrink, we have to expect more and more varieties of variations in the process of manufacturing especially for large chips. This may result in situations where multiple faults as well as non-traditional faults are actually happening in the chips.

ATPG for multiple faults, however, has been considered to be very expensive and except for very small circuits, it is practically impossible as there as so many fault combinations for multiple faults. For example, if there are m possibly faulty locations in the circuit, there are $3^m - 1$ fault combinations for multiple stuck-at faults. If m is 10,000, there are $3^{10,000} - 1 \approx 10^{4771}$ fault combinations. If we check whether each fault can be detected by the current set of test patterns, that process will take almost forever.

Traditionally ATPG processes include pattern generation as well as fault simulation in order to eliminate detectable faults with the current sets of test patterns from the sets of target faults. The problem here is the fact that fault simulators represent all faults explicitly. Therefore, fault simulators do not work if the numbers of fault combinations becomes exponentially large which is the case if we target all of multiple fault combinations.

We can resolve this problem by representing fault lists "implicitly" and combine the detectable fault elimination process with test pattern generation process as incremental SAT (Satisfiability checking) problems.

Moreover, in order to deal with varieties of fault models, functional modeling methods for faults in general are introduced. That is, various faults for each gate in the circuit are represented as resulting faulty logic functions. When fault happens in the gate, such logic functions show which kind of functionality can be found at the inputs and output of the faulty gate. This is realized with what we call "parameter" variables. Basically if values of the parameter variables are all zero, there is no fault in the gate. If some or all variables are non-zero, however, there are corresponding faulty functions defined by the logic functions with parameter variables.

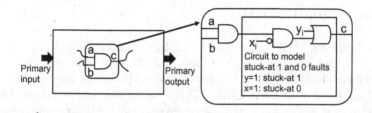

Fig. 4. Modeling stuck-at faults at the inputs and the output of a gate

For example, if we like to model stuck-at 0 fault at the output of a gate and stuck-at 1 faults at the inputs of a gate, we introduce the logic circuit (or logic function) with parameter variables, p, q, r as shown in Fig. 4. Here the target gate is an AND gate and its output is replaced with the circuit shown in the figure. That is, the output of the AND gate, c is replaced with $((a \lor p) \land (b \lor q)) \land \neg r$, which becomes 0 (corresponding to stuck-at 1 on signal c) when $r = 1$, b (corresponding to stuck-at 1 fault on signal a) when $p = 1, q = r = 0$, and a (corresponding to stuck-at 1 fault on signal b) when $q = 1, p = r = 0$. When a stuck-at 1 fault happens on the input signal a, that value becomes 1 and so the logic function observed at the output, c is b assuming that there is no more fault in this gate. If all of p, q, r are 0, the behavior remains the same as original AND function which is non-faulty.

Stuck-at faulty behaviors for each location are realized with these additional circuits. That is, circuits with additional ones can simulate the stuck-at 1 and 0 effects by appropriately setting the values of $p, q, r, \ldots$. For m possibly faulty locations, we use m of $p, q, r, \ldots$ variables. As we deal with multiple faults, these circuits for modeling various faults should be inserted into each gate in the circuit. By introducing appropriate circuit (or logic functions) with parameter variables, varieties of multiple faults can be formulated in a uniform way.

The ATPG problems can be naturally formulated as QBF (Quantified Boolean Formula). The ATPG methods have been implemented on top of ABC tool [5]. Experimental results show that we can perform ATPG for all combinations of various multiple faults for all ISCAS89 circuits. As shown in the experiments, complete sets of test vectors (exclusive of redundant faults) are successfully generated for several fault models for all ISCAS89 circuits.

The fault models defined through their resulting logic functions can be considered to be transformations of gates. That is, under faults, each gate change its behavior, which are represented by the logic functions and correspond to circuit transformations. By interpreting this way, the proposed methods can also be used for logic synthesis based on circuit transformations. If there are p transformations possible on a gate and there are in total m gates in the circuit, logic synthesis based on the proposed method can search synthesized circuits out of p^m possible multiple transformations. Although this is a very interesting topic, we reserve it for a future research topic.

4   Concluding Remarks

We have shown an ATPG framework for multiple various faults with user-define fault models and implicit representation of fault lists. The problems can be naturally formulated as QBF (Quantified Boolean Formula), but solved through repeated application of SAT solvers. There have been works in this direction [4,6,7]. From the discussion in this paper we may say that those problems could also be processed as incremental SAT problems instead of QBF problem, and those incremental SAT problems can essentially be solved as single (unsatisfiable) SAT problems allowing additional constraints in the fly, which could be much more efficient.

The experimental results shown in this paper are very preliminary. Although complete sets of test patterns for various multiple faults have been successfully generated, which is, as long as we know, the first time ever, there are lots of rooms in the proposed methods to be improved and to be extended. One of them is to try to compact the test pattern sets. Also use of the proposed methods for verification rather than testing is definitely one of the future topics.

References

1. Mangassarian, H., Yoshida, H., Veneris, A.G., Yamashita, S., Fujita, M.: On error tolerance and engineering change with partially programmable circuits. In: The 17th Asia and South Pacific Design Automation Conference (ASP-DAC 2012), pp. 695–700 (2012)
2. Jo, S., Matsumoto, T., Fujita, M.: SAT-based automatic rectification and debugging of combinational circuits with LUT insertions. In: Asian Test Symposium (ATS), pp. 19–24, November 2012
3. Fujita, M., Jo, S., Ono, S., Matsumoto, T.: Partial synthesis through sampling with and without specification. In: International Conference on Computer Aided Design (ICCAD), pp. 787–794, November 2013
4. Janota, M., Klieber, W., Marques-Silva, J., Clarke, E.: Solving QBF with counterexample guided refinement. In: Cimatti, A., Sebastiani, R. (eds.) SAT 2012. LNCS, vol. 7317, pp. 114–128. Springer, Heidelberg (2012). doi:10.1007/978-3-642-31612-8_10
5. Brayton, R., Mishchenko, A.: ABC: an academic industrial-strength verification tool. In: Touili, T., Cook, B., Jackson, P. (eds.) CAV 2010. LNCS, vol. 6174, pp. 24–40. Springer, Heidelberg (2010). doi:10.1007/978-3-642-14295-6_5
6. Ling, A., Singh, D.P., Brown, S.D.: FPGA logic synthesis using quantified boolean satisfiability. In: Bacchus, F., Walsh, T. (eds.) SAT 2005. LNCS, vol. 3569, pp. 444–450. Springer, Heidelberg (2005). doi:10.1007/11499107_37
7. Solar-Lezama, A., Tancau, L., Bodik, R., Seshia, S.A., Saraswat, V.A.: Combinatorial sketching for finite programs. In: ASPLOS 2006, pp. 404–415 (2006)
8. Jain, J., Mukherjee, R., Fujita, M.: Advanced verification techniques based on learning. In: The 32nd Annual ACM/IEEE Design Automation Conference, pp. 420–426 (1995)
9. Janota, M., Marques-Silva, J.: Abstraction-based algorithm for 2QBF. In: Sakallah, K.A., Simon, L. (eds.) SAT 2011. LNCS, vol. 6695, pp. 230–244. Springer, Heidelberg (2011). doi:10.1007/978-3-642-21581-0_19

Markov Models, Chains, and Decision Processes

Approximate Policy Iteration for Markov Decision Processes via Quantitative Adaptive Aggregations

Alessandro Abate[1], Milan Češka[1,2]([✉]), and Marta Kwiatkowska[1]

[1] Department of Computer Science, University of Oxford, Oxford, UK
[2] Faculty of Information Technology, Brno University of Technology,
Brno, Czech Republic
ceskam@fit.vutbr.cz

Abstract. We consider the problem of finding an optimal policy in a Markov decision process that maximises the expected discounted sum of rewards over an infinite time horizon. Since the explicit iterative dynamical programming scheme does not scale when increasing the dimension of the state space, a number of approximate methods have been developed. These are typically based on value or policy iteration, enabling further speedups through lumped and distributed updates, or by employing succinct representations of the value functions. However, none of the existing approximate techniques provides general, explicit and tunable bounds on the approximation error, a problem particularly relevant when the level of accuracy affects the optimality of the policy. In this paper we propose a new approximate policy iteration scheme that mitigates the state-space explosion problem by adaptive state-space aggregation, at the same time providing rigorous and explicit error bounds that can be used to control the optimality level of the obtained policy. We evaluate the new approach on a case study, demonstrating evidence that the state-space reduction results in considerable acceleration of the policy iteration scheme, while being able to meet the required level of precision.

1 Introduction

Dynamic programming (DP) is one of the most celebrated algorithms in computer science, optimisation, control theory, and operations research [3]. Applied to reactive models with actions, it allows synthesising optimal policies that optimise a given reward function over the state space of the model. According to Bellman's principle of optimality, the DP algorithm is a recursive procedure over value functions. Value functions are defined over the whole state and action spaces and over the time horizon of the decision problem. They are updated backward-recursively by means of locally optimal policies and, evaluated at the

This work has been partially supported by the ERC Advanced Grant VERIWARE, the EPSRC Mobile Autonomy Programme Grant EP/M019918/1, the Czech Grant Agency grant No. GA16-17538S (M. Češka), and the John Fell Oxford University Press (OUP) Research Fund.

© Springer International Publishing AG 2016
C. Artho et al. (Eds.): ATVA 2016, LNCS 9938, pp. 13–31, 2016.
DOI: 10.1007/978-3-319-46520-3_2

initial time point or in steady-state, yield the optimised global reward and the associated optimal policy. By construction, the DP scheme is prone to issues related to state-space explosion, otherwise known as the "curse of dimensionality". An active research area [5,6] has investigated approaches to mitigate this issue: we can broadly distinguish two classic approaches.

Sample-based schemes approximate the reward functions by sampling over the model's dynamics [6,14], either by regressing the associated value function over a given (parameterised) function class, or by synthesising upper and lower bounds for the reward function. As such, whilst in principle avoiding exhaustive exploration of the state space, they are associated to known limitations: they often require much tuning or selection of the function class; they are not always associated with quantitative convergence properties or strong asymptotic statistical guarantees; and they are prone to requiring naïve search of the action space, and hence scale badly over the non-determinism. In contrast to the state-space aggregation scheme presented in this paper, they compute the optimal policy only for the explored states, which can be in many cases insufficient.

Numerical schemes perform the recursion step for DP in a computationally enhanced manner. We distinguish two known alternatives. Value iteration updates backward-recursively value functions embedding the policy computation within each iteration. The iteration terminates once a non-linear equation (the familiar "Bellman equation") is verified. On the other hand, policy iteration schemes [4] distinguish two steps: policy update, where a new policy is computed; and policy evaluation, where the reward function associated to the given policy is evaluated (this boils down to an iteration up to convergence, or to the solution of a linear system of equations). Convergence proofs for both schemes are widely known and discussed in [5]. Both approaches can be further simplified by means of approximate schemes: for instance, the value iteration steps can be performed with distributed iterations attempting a modularisation, or via approximate value updates. Similarly to policy iteration, policy updates can be approximated and, for instance, run via prioritised sweeping over specific parts of the state space; furthermore, policy evaluations can be done optimistically (over a finite number of iterations), or by approximating the associated value functions.

In this work, we focus on the following modelling context: we deal with finite-state, discrete-time stochastic models, widely known as Markov decision processes (MDP) [16], and with γ-discounted, additive reward decision problems over an infinite time horizon. We set up an optimisation problem, seeking the optimal policy maximising the expected value of the given (provably bounded) reward function. We formulate the solution of this problem by means of a numerical approximate scheme.

Key Contributions. In this work we present a number of accomplishments:

- We put forward a modified policy iteration scheme which, while retaining the policy update step on the original MDP, performs an approximate policy evaluation by clustering the state space of the model.

- We derive explicit error bounds on the approximate policy evaluation step, which depend on the model dynamics, on the reward structure, and on the chosen state-space aggregation.
- We develop an automated policy iteration scheme, which adaptively updates the model aggregation at each policy evaluation step, according to the computed explicit error bounds.
- We argue that, unlike cognate literature, our quality certificates on the approximate policy evaluations only depend on manipulations of the abstract model.
- We argue that, whilst in the developed scheme the policy update is played out over the original (concrete) MDP, our approach can be extended to encompass an approximate policy update over the abstract model.
- With a case study, we show that the automated scheme does indeed improve the performance of the explicit policy iteration scheme, both in terms of state-space reduction and time.

Related Work. With emphasis on reward-based decision problems over MDP models, we can relate our contribution to the two alternative approaches discussed above, and quantitatively compare our scheme to existing numerical ones; note that sample-based approaches lack strong quantitative guarantees and therefore cannot be fairly compared.

Numerical and approximate schemes are discussed in [4] in detail. Specifically, with regards to policy iteration via approximate and optimistic policy updates, we argue that we provide certificates that only depend on manipulations of the abstract model and reward function, and that the approximation steps can be automatically embedded within the global policy iteration scheme.

Sample-based schemes are discussed in [6]; they differ from the numerical schemes in that they rarely provide guarantees. One exception is bounded real-time dynamical programming, for which precise bounds on approximation errors have been proposed, including policy synthesis for stochastic shortest path problems [14] and verification of quantitative specifications [7]. Further related work can be found in [9,15].

Finally, our work can be related to approaches which resort to uncertain (interval-based) MDPs as an abstraction framework and aim at providing lower and upper bounds on the probability of quantitative specifications. The work in [11] generates abstractions for MDPs using stochastic two-player games that can be further refined. The method computes lower and upper bounds on the minimum and maximum probability, which serve as a measure of the quality of the abstraction. Interval-based Markov chains have been used to obtain three-valued abstraction for discrete-space probabilistic systems [10], as well as to abstract continuous-space stochastic systems. In [2,8] the approximation error of the continuous dynamics is explicitly computed and can be tuned through different partitioning of the state space. In [13] bounded-parameter MDPs are used to abstract switched discrete-time stochastic systems.

2   Notations and Problem Setup

Model Syntax. We work with discrete-time Markov decision processes (MDP), with full state observations [3,16]. Formally, an MDP is defined as a triple (S, A, P), where

- $S = \{s_1, \ldots, s_n\}$ is the finite state space of size n;
- $A = \{a_1, \ldots, a_l\}$ is the finite action (input) space of size l;
- $P_{(\cdot)} : S \times A \times S \to [0, 1]$ is the transition probability matrix, which is such that $\forall i \in S, \forall a \in A : \sum_{j=1}^{n} P_a(i, j) = 1$.

We have assumed, for the sake of simplifying the notation, that all actions are available at any state s: this could be generalised by defining state-dependent sets $A(s), s \in S$, which are such that $A(s) \subseteq A$.

In order to characterise a run (a path) of the MDP, we consider finite or infinite strings of actions of the form $(a_0, a_1, a_2, \ldots), a_i \in A$. Of interest to this work, we structure actions as feedback functions from the model states S to the action space A, namely for any $k \geq 0, a_k$ takes the shape of a function $\mu_k : S \to A$. Further, we consider infinite strings of such feedback actions $\mu = (\mu_0, \mu_1, \mu_2, \ldots)$, which we denote as policies. We restrict to policies μ that are memoryless (Markovian) and deterministic (non-randomised), and denote with $\mu \in \mathcal{M}$ the set of all such admissible policies. For the problems of interest in this work, we seek to compute time-homogeneous policies, namely of the form $\mu = (\bar{\mu}, \bar{\mu}, \bar{\mu}, \ldots)$.

Model Semantics. Consider the model (S, A, P) and a given policy μ. The model is initialised via distribution $\pi_0 : S \to [0, 1]$, where $\sum_{s \in S} \pi_0(s) = 1$, and its transient probability distribution at time step $k \geq 0$ is

$$\pi_{k+1}(s) = \sum_{s' \in S} \pi_k(s') P_{\mu_k}(s', s) = P_{\mu_k}^T \pi_k, \tag{1}$$

or more concisely as $\pi_{k+1} = \pi_k P_{\mu_k}$ (where the π_k's are row vectors), and where of course $P_{\mu_k}(s', s) = P_{\mu_k(s')}(s', s)$.

The work in [1] has studied the derivation of a compact representation and an efficient computation of the vectors π_k for a Markov chain, which is an MDP under a time-homogeneous policy.

Decision Problem and Optimal Policy Synthesis. Consider a time-homogeneous reward function $g : S \times A \to \mathbb{R}_0^+$, which we assume to be bounded, and a discount factor $\gamma \in (0, 1)$. Consider the following decision problem

$$J^*(s) := \sup_{\mu \in \mathcal{M}} \mathbb{E} \left[\sum_{k=0}^{\infty} \gamma^k g(s, \mu_k) \right],$$

for any $s \in S$, and where $\mathbb{E}$ denotes the expected value of a function of the process (as in the previous formula). Notice that in this setup the reward function unfolds over an infinite time horizon; however, it is bounded in view of the presence of the discounting factor γ and the assumption on function g. We are also interested in deriving the optimal policy attaining the supremum, namely

$$\mu^*(s) := \arg\sup_{\mu \in \mathcal{M}} \mathbb{E}\left[\sum_{k=0}^{\infty} \gamma^k g(s, \mu_k)\right].$$

It is well known [3] that the class $\mathcal{M}$ of policies is sufficient to characterise the optimal policy given an MDP model and the additive optimisation setup above, namely we need not seek beyond this class (say, to randomised or non-Markovian policies). Further, the optimal policy is necessarily stationary (homogeneous in time).

Remark 1. It is likewise possible to consider decision problems where cost functions (similar in shape as those considered above) are infimised. Whilst in this work we focus on the first setup, our results are directly applicable to this second class of optimisation problems.   □

Optimal Policy Synthesis: Characterisation via Dynamic Programming. Consider the class $\mathcal{F}$ of bounded functions $f : S \to \mathbb{R}_0^+$. In order to characterise the solution of the decision problem above as a recursive dynamic programming (DP) scheme, let us introduce operators (or mappings) $T, T_a : \mathcal{F} \to \mathcal{F}, a \in A$, such that

$$(T_a f)(s) = g(s, a) + \gamma \sum_{s' \in S} P_a(s, s') f(s'),$$

$$(T f)(s) = \sup_{a \in A} \left\{ g(s, a) + \gamma \sum_{s' \in S} P_a(s, s') f(s') \right\}.$$

In a more succinct vector form, we can express $T_a f = g_a + \gamma P_a f$, and further the condition $f_a = T_a f_a = g_a + \gamma P_a f_a$, so that $f_a = (I - \gamma P_a)^{-1} g_a$, which is a system of linear equations [3] that is relevant below (also in the form depending on the operator T). Further, the sequential application of this operator k times, where $k > 0$, is denoted as $(T_a^k f)(s) = (T_a(T_a^{k-1} f))(s), s \in S$ (and similarly for operator T).

Consider an initial value function $J_0 : S \to \mathbb{R}_0^+$. The DP algorithm hinges on the Bellman recursion which, for $s \in S$, operates as

$$(T^{k+1} J_0)(s) = \sup_{a \in A} \left\{ g(s, a) + \gamma \sum_{s' \in S} P_a(s, s')(T^k J_0)(s') \right\}. \tag{2}$$

At the limit, the optimal value function satisfies the following fix-point equation:

$$J^*(s) = \sup_{a \in A} \left\{ g(s, a) + \gamma \sum_{s' \in S} P_a(s, s') J^*(s') \right\}, \tag{3}$$

which is succinctly expressed as $J^* = TJ^*$ and known as the Bellman equation
[3]. Given a non-trivial initial value function $J_0 : S \to \mathbb{R}_0^+$, the following convergence result holds: $J^*(s) = \lim_{k\to\infty}(T^k J_0)(s), s \in S$. The results above, focused
on the characterisation of the optimal value function, also lead to the optimal
policy μ^*.

The numerical solution of the discussed infinite-horizon decision problem
hinges on the computation of the iterations in (2), or on the solution of the
non-linear optimisation problem in (3), both of which can be computationally
expensive when the cardinality of the state space $| S |$ is large. Several approaches
have been developed to facilitate the numerical computation of optimal value
functions and policies [5]. Two main schemes can be distinguished: value and
policy iteration.

Value iteration boils down to iteratively computing applications of the optimal operator T, and exploiting monotonicity properties of the obtained value
functions (in view of the operator's contractivity) to establish conditions for the
convergence of the quantity $\lim_{k\to\infty} T^k J_0(s), s \in S$. Variants based on distributed and approximate iterations have also been developed [5]. We next focus on
the alternative *policy iteration* scheme.

DP via Policy Iteration, Exact and Approximate. The policy iteration
algorithm, which is proven to find the optimal policy in a finite number of steps,
works as follows. Assume an initial (non-trivial) value function $J_0 : S \to \mathbb{R}_0^+$.
Compute the corresponding optimal policy μ_0, which is such that $T_{\mu_0} J_0 = T J_0$,
namely compute

$$\mu_0(s) = \arg\sup_{a \in A} \left\{ g(s,a) + \gamma \sum_{s' \in S} P_a(s,s') J_0(s') \right\}.$$

This is known as the *policy update* step. The obtained policy μ_0 can be successively *evaluated* over a fully updated value function J_{μ_0}, which is such that
$J_{\mu_0} = g_{\mu_0} + \gamma P_{\mu_0} J_{\mu_0}$ (as mentioned above). The scheme proceeds further by
updating the policy as $\mu_1 : T_{\mu_1} J_{\mu_0} = T J_{\mu_0}$; by later evaluating it via value
function J_{μ_1}; and so forth until finite-step convergence.

We stress that the value update involved with the policy evaluation is in
general quite expensive, and can be performed either as a recursive numerical
scheme, or as a numerical solution of a linear system of equations. *Approximate
policy iteration* schemes introduce approximations either in the policy update
or in the policy evaluation steps, and are shown to attain suboptimal policies
whilst ameliorating the otherwise computationally expensive exact scheme [4].

3   New Approximate Policy Iteration

We propose to speed up the above standard policy iteration scheme by accelerating the policy update step. The approach is inspired by recent work in [1],
where a sequential and adaptive aggregation approach allows us to quantifiably

approximate the forward computation of the probability distribution in time (namely, the transient distribution) of a given Markov chain. In this work, we tailor this related work to the backward DP scheme, based on the fact that the policy evaluation steps work on a closed-loop model (indeed, a Markov chain obtained by selecting the currently optimal policy).

3.1 State-Space Aggregation for MDPs

We aggregate the MDP (S, A, P) into the abstract model $(\bar{S}, A, \bar{P})$ by a procedure that is inspired by our work in [1]. We partition $S = \cup_{i=1}^{m} S_i$, where the cardinality index m has been selected so that $m << n$, where again $n = |S|$. We denote the *abstract (aggregated) state space* as $\bar{S}$ and its elements (the *abstract states*) with $\phi_i, i = 1, \ldots, m$. Introduce the abstraction and refinement maps as $\alpha : S \rightarrow \bar{S}$ and $A : \bar{S} \rightarrow 2^S$, respectively – the first takes concrete points into abstract ones, whereas the latter relates abstract states to concrete partitioning sets. We argue that no abstraction of actions is needed at this stage, namely the aggregation of the MDP is performed for a given feedback function $\mu : S \rightarrow A$. For any pair of indices $i, j = 1, \ldots, m$, define the abstract transition probability matrix as

$$\bar{P}_\mu(\phi_i, \phi_j) \doteq \frac{\sum_{s \in A(\phi_i)} \sum_{s' \in A(\phi_j)} P_{\mu(s)}(s, s')}{|S_i|}.$$

This transition probability matrix can be de-aggregated piecewise constantly over the state space, as:

$$\forall s \in S_i, s' \in S_j, \quad \tilde{P}_\mu(s, s') = \frac{1}{|S_i|} \bar{P}_\mu(\phi_i, \phi_j).$$

Given an initial function $J_0(s), s \in S_i$, cluster it into $\bar{J}_0(\phi_i) = \frac{1}{|A(\phi_i)|} \sum_{s \in A(\phi_i)} J_0(s)$, where $\phi_i = \alpha(s)$, and de-cluster it into $\tilde{J}_0(s) = \bar{J}_0(\phi_i)$, for all $s \in A(\alpha(s))$. Similarly, given an initial policy μ_0, cluster the running reward function $g(s, \mu_0(s))$ (which is evaluated under a selected policy and thus only state dependent) into $\bar{g}(\phi_i) = \frac{1}{|A(\phi_i)|} \sum_{s \in A(\phi_i)} g(s, \mu_0(s))$, and later de-cluster it as $\tilde{g}(s) = \bar{g}(\phi_i)$. Given these definitions, the operators T_μ, T can then immediately aggregated as $\bar{T}_\mu, \bar{T}$.

Remark 2. The aggregation scheme described above can be alternatively implemented by selecting an arbitrary representative point within each partition $s^\star \in S_i$: $\bar{P}_\mu(\phi_i, \phi_j) \doteq \sum_{s' \in A(\phi_j)} P_{\mu(s^\star)}(s^\star, s')$. This leads to formal connections with the notion of (forward) approximate probabilistic bisimulation [8]. $\square$

3.2 Approximate Policy Iteration: Quantification and Use of Error Bounds

Approximate Policy Iteration. Algorithm 1 summarises the approximate policy iteration scheme. On line 2 the procedure performs an initial spatial aggregation based on an initial value function which, in the absence of alternatives,

---

Algorithm 1. Adaptive aggregation scheme for approximate policy iteration

---

Require: Finite MDP $M = (S, A, P)$, reward function g, initial policy μ_0, allowable
   error θ
Ensure: $\forall s \in S$ global error $\vec{E}(s) \leq \theta$
1: $policyTerm \leftarrow$ false; $valueTerm \leftarrow$ false; $\mu \leftarrow \mu_0$; $J \leftarrow g$
2: $(\bar{S}, \bar{P}_\mu, \bar{g}, \bar{J}, \vec{X}, \vec{Y}, Z) \leftarrow$ initAggregation (S, P_μ, g, J)
3: **while** (!$policyTerm$) **do**
4:     **while** (!$valueTerm$) **do**   ▷ Approximated policy evaluation
5:         $(\bar{J}, \vec{E}, valueTerm) \leftarrow$ updateValues$(\bar{S}, \bar{P}_\mu, \bar{g}, \bar{J}, \vec{X}, \vec{Y}, Z)$
6:         **if** $\vec{E} \geq \theta$ **then**   ▷ Maximal error has been reached
7:             $(\bar{S}, \bar{P}_\mu, \bar{g}, \vec{X}, \vec{Y}, Z) \leftarrow$ reAggregation $\left(S, P_\mu, g, \bar{J}, \vec{E}\right)$
8:             $\bar{J} \leftarrow$ aggregate$(\bar{S}, J)$ ▷ Restart the policy iteration
9:             $valueTerm \leftarrow$ false
10:    $J \leftarrow$ deAggregation$(\bar{J})$; $valueTerm \leftarrow$ false
11:    $(\mu, policyTerm) \leftarrow$ updatePolicy(P, J, μ) ▷ Policy update step
12:    $(\bar{P}_\mu, \bar{g}, \vec{X}, \vec{Y}, Z) \leftarrow$ updateAggregatedSystem $(\bar{S}, P_\mu, g)$

---

is taken to be equal to the reward function, $J_0 = g$, and on an initial policy μ_0
(the choice of which is also quite arbitrary). The procedure builds the aggregated
system comprising state space $\bar{S}$, transition matrix $\bar{P}_{\mu_0}$, value function $\bar{J}_0$, and
reward function $\bar{g}$. The procedure also updates auxiliary data structures (for the
quantities $\vec{X}, \vec{Y}$ and Z, to be introduced in Sect. 3.3) that are required for the
computation of the error bounds $\vec{E}$. Further, the procedure named updateValues
(line 5) performs policy evaluation by means of value function updates, namely
it updates the aggregated value function based on the current aggregated policy.
Note that this procedure introduces an approximation error (as further elabo-
rated in the next section): as such, it also updates the vector of error bounds $\vec{E}$
and checks if the termination criterion for the value iteration is reached.

If the max allowable error bound θ has been exceeded before the termination criterion is met, the closed-loop MDP is re-aggregated (based on the error,
as per line 7) and the policy evaluation step is restarted. Note that the adaptive re-aggregation step employs the current value function $\bar{J}$ and the current
error $\vec{E}$, both of which reflect the model dynamics and the specific optimisation
problem. In particular, the re-aggregation refines every cluster ϕ_i for which the
current error $\vec{E}(\phi_i)$ is above the bound θ, and the new clustering takes $\bar{J}$ into
consideration. The value function is reset using the values J corresponding to
the last policy update.

If the value iterations terminate before the maximal error is reached, the
final value function $\bar{J}$ is de-aggregated into J (line 9). Afterwards, the procedure
updatePolicy updates the policy using the obtained J, and checks if a termination
criterion over the policy update has been met. If not, before the next policy
evaluation the aggregated system has to be updated: we retain the clustering $\bar{S}$
from the previous step, and thus only refresh (in view of the updated policy) the
transition matrix, the reward function g, and the auxiliary data structures.

Approximate Policy Evaluation: Quantification of Error Bounds. Having obtained policy μ_k, its k-th step, policy evaluation performs the operation $\bar{J}_{k+1} := \bar{J}_k^{m_k}$, where $\bar{J}_k^{m_k} = \bar{T}_{\mu_k}^{m_k} \bar{J}_k$, and where m_k is a finite integer number accounting for the optimistic evaluation over the aggregated closed-loop operator $\bar{T}_{\mu_k}$. This update introduces two errors: the first is due to the aggregated computation; the second is due to the finite number of update steps (m_k). We then interpolate the obtained $\bar{J}_k^{m_k}(\bar{s})$ piecewise constantly over the concrete state space S, obtaining $\tilde{J}_k^{m_k}(s)$. We aim at comparing the following:

$$\left| \tilde{J}_k^{m_k}(s) - J_{\mu_k}(s) \right| \leq \left| \tilde{J}_k^{m_k}(s) - T_{\mu_k}^{m_k} J_k(s) \right| + \left| T_{\mu_k}^{m_k} J_k(s) - J_{\mu_k}(s) \right|. \tag{4}$$

Error bounds on the approximate evaluation of the current policy resort to the Bellman iteration. We introduce a number of terms $(\zeta_i^j(s), \xi_i(s), y_i(s)$, and the corresponding aggregated terms $Z^j, X, Y)$, which help in succinctly expressing parts of this iteration.

Definition 1. *Consider an MDP (S, A, P) with a fixed policy $\mu_k : S \to A$, and the aggregated MDP $(\bar{S}, A, \bar{P}_{\mu_k})$. Introduce the following quantities, $\forall s \in S_i, i \in \{1, \ldots, m\}$:*

$$\left| P_{\mu_k}(s, S_j) - \bar{P}_{\mu_k}(\phi_i, \phi_j) \right| = \zeta_i^j(s),$$

$$\left| J_k(s) - \tilde{J}_k(s) \right| = \left| J_k(s) - \frac{1}{|A(\alpha(s))|} \sum_{s' \in A(\alpha(s))} J_k(s') \right| \leq \xi_i(s),$$

$$\left| g(s, \mu_k(s)) - \tilde{g}(s) \right| = \left| g(s, \mu_k(s)) - \frac{1}{A(\alpha(s))} \sum_{s' \in A(\alpha(s))} g(s', \mu_k(s')) \right| \leq y_i(s),$$

and further introduce

$$Z_i^j = \max_{s \in S_i} \zeta_i^j(s), \qquad\qquad Z^j = \max_{i=1,\ldots,m} Z_i^j,$$

$$X_i = \max_{s \in S_i} \xi_i(s), \qquad\qquad X = \max_{i=1,\ldots,m} X_i,$$

$$Y_i = \max_{s \in S_i} y_i(s), \qquad\qquad Y = \max_{i=1,\ldots,m} Y_i.$$

Theorem 1 (Error Bounds on Approximate Evaluation of a Given Policy). *A bound for Eq. (4) is the following:*

$$\left| \tilde{J}_k^{m_k}(s) - J_{\mu_k}(s) \right| \leq 2\mathcal{B}(m_k) + \mathcal{B}(m_k - 1) + (\tilde{J}_k^{m_k}(s) - \tilde{J}_k^{m_k-1}(s)),$$

where

$$\mathcal{B}(m_k) = \sum_{i=0}^{m_k} \alpha^i Y + \alpha^{m_k} X + \sum_{i=0}^{m_k} \alpha^{m_k-i} \sum_{j=1}^{m} \bar{J}_k^i(\phi_j) Z^j.$$

Proof (Sketch). The desired upper bound on the error is obtained by first splitting it into two contributions:

$$\left|\tilde{J}_k^{m_k}(s) - J_{\mu_k}(s)\right| \le \left|\tilde{J}_k^{m_k}(s) - T_{\mu_k}^{m_k} J_k(s)\right| + \left|T_{\mu_k}^{m_k} J_k(s) - J_{\mu_k}(s)\right|.$$

The first term results from performing the evaluation of policy μ_k over the aggregated model, and an upper bound is obtained from the three contributions, accounting respectively for the difference between concrete and aggregated running costs, initial value functions, and dynamics (namely transition probability matrices).

On the other hand, the second term results from an optimistic policy evaluation, iterating over value functions only a finite (m_k) number of times. The error can be obtained from [5, Chapter 1] and, importantly, fully computed over the abstract model. □

Remark 3. We comment on the asymptotics of the two contributions to the total error. The first contribution to the error in the previous proposition is bounded as the number of steps m_k grows, whereas the second term decreases exponentially. It might be meaningful to seek an empirical tradeoff, namely a parameter m_k minimising their sum. □

Within a single iteration of the policy iteration scheme, Theorem 1 has established an explicit bound on the approximate policy evaluation part. We are interested in assessing the sub-optimality of the policy obtained upon convergence of the approximate policy iteration scheme.

Theorem 2 (Bounds on Sub-optimality of Approximate Policy Iteration). *Assume that after a finite number of steps p a steady-state policy μ_p is obtained. Compute the upper bound δ on the error related to the approximate policy evaluation steps, namely $\delta = \max_{k=0,\ldots,p} \left|\tilde{J}_k^{m_k}(s) - J_{\mu_k}(s)\right|$. We obtain the following sub-optimality bound:*

$$\left|\tilde{J}_p^{m_p}(s) - J^*(s)\right| \le \frac{2\gamma\delta}{1-\gamma},$$

where $\tilde{J}_p^{m_p}(s)$ is obtained from $\bar{J}_p^{m_p}$, and where $\bar{J}_p^{m_p} = \bar{T}_{\mu_p}^{m_p} \bar{J}_p$.

Proof. It follows from a straightforward adaptation of the results in [4, Section 3]. □

Remark 4. As a generalisation (relaxation of the assumptions) of the previous theorem, if no steady-state policy is attained, we obtain the following bound $\frac{2\gamma\delta}{(1-\gamma)^2}$. □

Remark 5. As a side remark notice that, within the iterative policy-update evaluation scheme, we do not need to account for a re-aggregation error (as in [1]), since this is already taken care by the initialisation of the policy evaluation scheme and the error terms X. Alternatively, we can avoid restarting the policy evaluation, which would reduce the re-aggregation overhead, and introduce a re-aggregation error as in [1]. □

Remark 6. Beyond policy evaluation, we can also perform an approximate version of policy update, and account for a global error, according to [5, Proposition 1.3.6].   □

3.3 Tighter and Computationally Faster Matrix Bounds

The error bounds given by Theorem 1 can be coarse, and thus not very useful in practice, since they may not adequately reflect the true empirical errors. The reason is that the error $\mathcal{B}(m_k)$ corresponding to the aggregation is state independent, and employs the global quantities X, Y and Z^j. In this section we will first improve the error bounds, then show how to approximate their computation to obtain a scheme that can speed up the overall DP algorithm.

As before we focus on the first iteration of policy evaluation. Define the matrix $Z \in \mathbb{R}^{m \times m}, Z_{ij} = Z_i^j$ and the column vector $\vec{X}(i) = X_i$. Then, of course, $\forall s \in S_i$ the third error (for the first value iteration) can be encompassed by $\gamma Z_i \cdot \bar{J}_0^0$, where $\bar{J}_0^0$ is a column vector and Z_i is the i-th row of matrix Z. This leads to

$$\left| \tilde{J}_0^1(s) - J_0^1(s) \right| \leq Y_i + \gamma P_{\mu_0}(s, \cdot)\vec{X} + \gamma Z_i \cdot \bar{J}_0^0$$

$$\text{(uniformly over } s) \ \leq Y_i + \gamma \bar{P}(\phi_i, \cdot)\vec{X} + \gamma Z_i \cdot \bar{J}_0^0,$$

At the next (second) iteration, the error is

$$\left| \tilde{J}_0^2(s) - J_0^2(s) \right| \leq (1 + \alpha)Y_i + \gamma^2 \sum_{k=1}^m P_{\mu_0}^2(s, S_k)X_k + \gamma^2 \sum_{k=1}^m \bar{J}_0^0(\phi_k)Z^k + \gamma \sum_{j=1}^m \bar{J}_0^1(\phi_j)Z^j$$

$$\leq (1 + \alpha)Y_i + \gamma^2 P_{\mu_0}^2(s, \cdot)\vec{X} + \gamma^2 P_{\mu_0}(s, \cdot)Z\bar{J}_0^0 + \gamma Z_i \cdot \bar{J}_0^1$$

$$\text{(unif. over } s) \ \leq (1 + \gamma)Y_i + \gamma^2 \bar{P}^2(\phi_i, \cdot)\vec{X} + \alpha^2 \bar{P}(\phi_i, \cdot)Z\bar{J}_0^0 + \gamma Z_i \cdot \bar{J}_0^1.$$

Now, uniformising over $s \in S_j$ (i.e. over j-th cluster), we can directly write

$$\sup_{s \in S_j} \left| \tilde{J}_0^{m_0}(s) - J_0^{m_0}(s) \right| \leq \sum_{i=0}^{m_0} \gamma^i Y_j + \gamma^{m_0} \bar{P}^{m_0}(\phi_j, \cdot)\vec{X} + \sum_{i=0}^{m_0-1} \gamma^{m_0-i} \bar{P}^{m_0-i-1}(\phi_j, \cdot)Z\bar{J}_0^i,$$

$$(5)$$

where we have imposed that $\bar{P}^0(\phi_j, \cdot)Z = Z_j$.

Whilst providing tighter bounds, the computation of these formulas can be expensive due to the last term representing a number of matrix-matrix multiplications that is linear with the number of value function updates. We therefore introduce an approximate computation of the bounds, which combines the coarse and uniform bounds that can be easily computed, with the improved but expensive matrix bounds. The new computation attempts to make the approximate policy iteration practically useful, namely to provide considerable speedup of the computation whilst, at the same time, deriving informative bounds on the approximation error.

Define vectors $\vec{E}$ and $\vec{Y}$ such that $\vec{E}(j) = \sup_{s \in S_j} \left| \tilde{J}_0^{m_0}(s) - J_0^{m_0}(s) \right|$ and $\vec{Y}(j) = Y_j$. Based on Eq. (5) we obtain that

$$\vec{E} \leq \sum_{i=0}^{m_0} \gamma^i \vec{Y} + \gamma^{m_0} \bar{P}^{m_0} \vec{X} + \sum_{i=0}^{m_0-1} \gamma^{m_0-i} \bar{P}^{m_0-i-1} Z \tilde{J}_0^i, \tag{6}$$

where $\leq$ is defined element-wise. These three terms can be approximated as follows:

$$\left(\sum_{i=0}^{m_0} \gamma^i \vec{Y} \right)(j) \leq \left(\sum_{i=0}^{B_1} \gamma^i \vec{Y} \right)(j) + \sum_{B_1+1}^{m_0} \gamma^i Y$$

$$\left(\gamma^{m_0} \bar{P}^{m_0} \vec{X} \right)(j) \leq \gamma^{m_0} X \ (\text{if } m_0 \geq B_2)$$

$$\sum_{i=0}^{m_0-1} \gamma^{m_0-i} \bar{P}^{m_0-i-1} Z \tilde{J}_0^i \leq \sum_{i=m_0-B_3+1}^{m_0-1} \gamma^{m_0-i} \bar{P}^{m_0-i-1} Z \tilde{J}_0^i$$

$$+ \sum_{i=0}^{m_0-B_3} \gamma^{m_0-i} \bar{P}^{B_3-1} Z \tilde{J}_0^{m_0-B_3}$$

$$\leq \sum_{i=m_0-B_3+1}^{m_0-1} \gamma^{m_0-i} \bar{P}^{m_0-i-1} Z \tilde{J}_0^i$$

$$+ (m_0 - B_3 + 1) \gamma^{B_3} \bar{P}^{B_3-1} Z \tilde{J}_0^{m_0-B_3},$$

where B_i for $i \in 1, 2, 3$ denotes three thresholds that affect the precision and time complexity of the computations. The approximation allows us to make the number of constant-vector, matrix-vector and matrix-matrix multiplications, required by the error computations, independent from the number of value function updates. Intuitively increasing these thresholds increases the precision, but also the time complexity. In our experimental evaluation we set $B_1 = B_2 = 10$ and $B_3 = 5$.

The first inequality holds, since $Y = \max_{i=1,\ldots,m} \vec{Y}(i)$. The second inequality holds, since $X = \max_{i=1,\ldots,m} \vec{X}(i)$ and P^{m_0} is a stochastic matrix. The third term in Eq. (6) is approximated as detailed next. The error related to the last, most significant, $B_3 - 1$ iterations is computed using the tighter matrix bounds (the first term in the right hand side of the last inequality). The error related to the first $k = m_0 - B_3 + 1$ iterations is approximated using a single vector obtained from the k-th iteration (the second term). The correctness follows from the monotonicity of J_0^k, i.e. $J_0^k \leq J_0^{k+1}$ (element-wise).

Finally, note that the computation of the bounds, as well as the policy evaluation itself, can be rewritten such that the expensive matrix-matrix multiplication can be replaced by matrix-vector multiplications.

4 Experimental Evaluation

We have developed a prototype implementation of the approximate policy iteration in PRISM [12]. Both the aggregated and the non-aggregated implementation use the explicit engine of PRISM for model construction and manipulation; however, the models are then translated into a sparse and fixed matrix representation, that is, a similar data structure as that used in the sparse engine, which is the fastest PRISM engine. We have run all experiments on a MackBook Pro™ with 2.9 GHz Intel Core i5 and 8 GB 1866 MHz RAM. Alongside memory usage, in the following experiments we report and compare runtimes for the policy iteration scheme, whereas the runtimes associated to the model construction, which are the same for aggregated and non-aggregated computations and hinge on the chosen engine in PRISM, are not included.

The practical performance of the proposed approximate policy iteration scheme depends on several related aspects. In our evaluation we attempt to dissect these aspects and identifying scenarios where our approach can achieve significant acceleration over the explicit algorithm, and, on the other hand, where it experiences practical performance limitations. We divide the experiments into two parts: (1) evaluation of the method for a fixed number of policy iterations (namely, policy updates/evaluations); and (2) evaluation of the convergence of the scheme.

We consider a case study from robot motion planning. The MDP model describes a finite two-dimensional discrete grid (say defined over integer variables $-D \leq x, y \leq D$), and deals with a robot moving over this map. The size of the state space thus is $|S| = (2D + 1)^2$. The robot dynamics is affected via 5 actions (up, down, left, right, stay), which are not associated to fully deterministic moves, namely, there is a probability that performing a given action might result in an undesired output (e.g., for an action up the robot actually moves, say, to the right, as explained below).

We are interested in synthesising a policy that steers the robot to a specific point on the grid. We consider a reward function, which we seek to maximise over the infinite horizon over the available actions, that attains its maximum over the desired goal point. The reward function (which in this instance is independent of the actions) is embedded within a discounted, additive objective, of which we compute the expected value. As discussed earlier, the DP scheme will yield a memoryless, deterministic, and homogeneous policy as a function of the state space.

4.1 Fixed Number of Policy Updates and Evaluations

The required number of policy updates and evaluations (the latter obtained as value function updates) is key in the performance of the policy iteration scheme. This number depends on the structure of the system dynamics, which is affected by the aggregation procedure, and on parameters controlling the termination of the computations, which usually check the relative difference between consecutive updates. As such, we first assume that the number of the updates is the same for both standard and approximate policy iterations, which allows us to assess the performance of the proposed aggregation scheme with respect to the following key aspects: (1) the number of value function updates, (2) the size of the model, (3) the discounting factor, and (4) the shape of the reward function. Later we evaluate how the state-space aggregation influences the convergence of the policy and value function updates.

We consider the following instance of the robotic case study (denoted as *Robotic 1*), where the actions are structured as follows: there is an 80 % chance of performing the intended action, i.e. moving to a position (x, y) and the remaining probability is uniformly distributed over four undesired local moves, namely $(x + 1, y)$, $(x, y + 1)$, $(x - 1, y)$, and $(x, y - 1)$. The reward function is defined as $g(x, y) = e^{-\frac{x^2 + y^2}{\rho}}$, over a bounded range of integers x, y. Note that the parameter ρ affects the stiffness of the reward function. We have also added some obstacles to the map, and our experiments indicate that the map modification does not have a noticeable impact on the performance of the method, which demonstrates its robustness with respect to different motion planning scenarios.

Figures 1 and 2 illustrate the experimental outcomes. The curves display how the memory reduction factor and time speedup vary for different maximal error bounds. The maximal bound represents the threshold that controls the model re-aggregations, as per line 6 in Algorithm 1: whenever this threshold is reached, a model re-clustering is performed and the value function iterations for the policy evaluation are restarted.

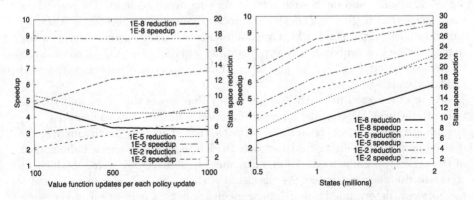

Fig. 1. Robotic 1 setup with the discounting factor $\gamma = 0.8$ and stiffness $\rho = 100$. **Left:** Fixed state space $|S| = 0.5\mathrm{M}$ and 50 policy updates. The figure shows results for different numbers of value function updates for a given policy update. The runtimes for non-aggregated computations over 100, 500 and 1000 value function updates are 137, 732 and 1174 s, respectively. **Right:** 50 policy updates and 1000 value function updates for a given policy update. The figure shows results for different sizes of the state space. The runtimes for non-aggregated computations over a model with $|S| = 0.5\mathrm{M}$, 1M and 2M states are 1174, 2560 and 5571 s, respectively.

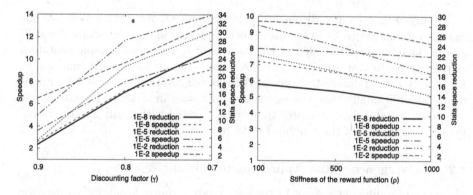

Fig. 2. Robotic 1 setup with $|S| = 2M$, 50 policy updates, 1000 value function updates per single policy update. **Left:** fixed stiffness $\rho = 100$: the figure shows results for different discounting factors γ. **Right:** fixed $\gamma = 0.8$: the figure shows results for different values ρ. Since the parameters γ and ρ have only a negligible impact on the runtimes of the non-aggregated computation, we report the runtime for the choice $\gamma = 0.8$, $\rho = 100$, which is 5571 s.

Figure 1 (left) shows how the average number of value function updates for a given policy update affect both the state-space reduction and the speedup. Since both the empirical errors and error bounds grow with increasing number of value function updates, we can observe a small decrease of the reduction factor. However, the trend becomes negligible later, likely in view of the convergence of the policy and value function updates. On the other hand, the speedup steadily increases, despite the decreasing state-space reduction: this is because the overhead related to every policy update, including updating the aggregated transition matrix and other data structures, becomes less relevant. Note that the number of re-aggregations decreases with number of policy updates, which also increases the speedup. For this case study the speedup saturates around 50 policy updates and 2000 value function updates per each policy update.

Figure 1 (right) confirms the scalability of our approach with respect to the state space size. Both the state reduction factor and the time speedup considerably grow with the increasing size of the model.

Figure 2 (left) illustrates the effect of the discounting factor γ on the policy iteration scheme. As expected, as the factor gets closer to the max value 1.0, both the empirical errors and the error bounds grow, and thus both the reduction factor and the speedup decrease. Factors above 0.9 limit the performance of our method, especially if a high precision is required: the current implementation of the aggregated scheme requires a high number of re-aggregations, which increases the overhead and results in a poor overall speedup. On the other hand, we do not consider factors below 0.7 since the model would converge too fast (faster than the 50/1000 policy/value function updates): still, the results indicate that better reduction factors would be achieved.

Finally, Fig. 2 (right) displays the robustness of our aggregation scheme against varying shapes of the reward function, where in our case study the stiffness of the reward is controlled by the parameter ρ. The current implementation of the aggregation strategy uses the average value of the reward function to adequately handle different shapes of the function. Note that for stiff functions we could additionally tune the aggregation strategy in order to provide better reduction and speedup, by states that are associated with small rewards (away from the maximum of the function) in large clusters.

4.2 Convergence of the Approximate Scheme

We consider a different variant of the case study (named *Robotic 2*), where for each action there is an 80 % probability that the robot does not move, a 15 % probability that the action has the intended effect, and the remaining probability is uniformly distributed over the four undesired outputs, similarly as in the previous variant of the model. The *Robotic 2* model displays slower dynamics and convergence to the optimum in the decision problem, and thus allows us to better evaluate how the state-space aggregation performs in time.

For both the aggregated and the non-aggregated computations, we use same termination criteria based on the difference between successive updates. In particular, the value function iteration (for policy evaluation) terminates if the values for all states in successive iterations differ by at most 1E-6, whereas the policy iteration terminates if there is no policy update in successive iterations, or if policy updates improve the value function by at most 1E-12. Note that these are the standard convergence thresholds used in PRISM for the numerical policy iteration scheme, and by decreasing them we slow down the overall convergence. This would improve the speedup of the adaptive scheme, due to a higher number of the value function updates and the policy updates: recall the result in Fig. 1 (left). The sub-optimality bounds for the non-aggregated computation are thus obtained as $\frac{2\gamma 1E-6}{1-\gamma}$, as per Theorem 2. Also note that there can be more than one optimal action over a state, so the difference in the policy does not necessarily correspond to an actual error.

Table 1 depicts the results for the discounting factor $\gamma = 0.85$ (top batch) and $\gamma = 0.95$ (bottom batch). The columns have the following meaning (from left to right): threshold on the maximal error bound $\mathcal{B}_{\mathrm{max}}$ for policy evaluation; maximal error bound $\mathcal{B}_{max}$; maximal empirical error $\mathcal{J}_{max}$ for policy evaluation; number of states that result in a different optimal action; global error bound $\mathcal{G}_{max}$ given by Theorem 2; reduction factor for memory usage; total number of policy updates and value function updates, respectively; and time speedup. We can see that, in all cases, decreasing the error bounds improves both the empirical errors and the optimality of the policy.

The top batch of the table demonstrates that, although the state-space reduction factor remains high for all three error thresholds, the overall time speedup is limited due to the low average number of value function updates (which can be run over the aggregated model) per policy update. As such, since in this case the convergence (overall number of iterations) is not affected by the reduction factor,

Table 1. Top: Robotic 2 setup with $|S| = 1\text{M}$, $\rho = 100$ and $\gamma = 0.85$: the non-aggregated computation has required 12/1.3K policy/value function updates, with a sub-optimality bound of 1.1E-5, and has taken 73 s. **Bottom:** Robotic 2 setup with $|S| = 1\text{M}$, $\rho = 100$ and $\gamma = 0.95$: the non-aggregated computation has required 55/11K policy/value function updates, with a sub-optimality bound of 3.8E-5, and has taken 674 s.

Errors					Aggregation		
Threshold	$\mathcal{B}_{max}$	$\mathcal{J}_{max}$	Policy	$\mathcal{G}_{max}$	Reduction	Iterations	Speedup
1E-2	2.6E-3	1.1E-5	10.5K	5.8E-2	33.7	13/1.3K	5.7
1E-5	7.9E-6	3.7E-8	4.5K	1.9E-4	30.1	10/1.1K	4.5
1E-8	6.1E-9	5.3E-11	0.5K	1.1E-5	27.4	15/1.6K	3.0
1E-2	9.5E-3	8.6E-6	36.5K	7.2E-1	22.2	22/8.6K	13.6
1E-5	7.2E-6	3.5E-8	11.9K	5.4E-4	13.2	44/21.5K	4.0
1E-8	7.9E-9	2.5E-11	1.3K	3.8E-5	8.1	55/31.0K	1.9

also the overall performance (i.e. the speedup with respect to the non-aggregated computation) is relatively stable.

The bottom part of the table shows that for a discounting factor closer to 1.0 the situation is different. In particular, both the reduction factor and the performance of the approximate policy iteration scheme downgrade with decreasing error bounds, whilst remaining faster than the iterations over the concrete model. In particular, for the error threshold 1E-2, the aggregation provides more than a 13-fold speedup, since the reduction factor is high and the approximate scheme converges faster (i.e. considerably fewer policy/value function updates are required). However, for lower error bounds both the reduction factor and the convergence speed decrease, which results in smaller speedups.

4.3 Discussion of the Experimental Results

Our experimental evaluation dissects important aspects of the DP algorithm that impact the performance metrics (i.e. reduction factors, convergence, precision, overall speedup) of the proposed approximate scheme. The experimental results clearly indicate that, for complex instances running over large state spaces and requiring a high number of policy and value function updates, our approximate scheme provides significant reduction of the computation time, while providing explicit bounds on the approximation errors. The maximal permissible error is specified by users and controls the tradeoff between the state-space reduction, which directly affects the speedup, and the precision of the computation in the form of maximal error of the value function.

The experiments further show that the overall performance of the method considerably depends on the aggregation strategy, namely, on a set of parameters and thresholds that control the aggregation. Intuitively, there is a tradeoff between the reduction vs. precision ratio and the overhead related to the re-aggregations. To provide a fair comparison we have run all experiments with the same setting (except for the thresholds on the maximal error bounds). However, our observations show that a fine tuning of the parameters for a certain problem can lead to additional performance improvements.

The overhead related to updating the aggregated model (by means of its transition matrix), proved to have a significant impact on the overall performance. Therefore, a dynamic data structure implementing the model can improve the performance. Such a dynamic representation supports efficient local updates that are faster than global updates required by a static representation, and reduces the number of operations over the non-aggregated matrix. On the other hand, certain computations over dynamic structures (i.e. value function updates) might require additional overhead with respect to a static representation.

5 Conclusions and Future Work

In this article we have proposed a new approximate policy iteration scheme that mitigates the state-space explosion problem by adaptive state-space aggregation, at the same time providing rigorous and explicit error bounds that can be used to control the optimality level of the obtained policy.

The discussed approximate policy iteration scheme, and its associated error bounds, can be extended to approximate policy updates. This, on the one hand, would naturally incur an additional approximation error, but, on the other, would allow for a computational scheme completely based on aggregated (abstract) models.

References

1. Abate, A., Brim, L., Češka, M., Kwiatkowska, M.: Adaptive aggregation of Markov chains: quantitative analysis of chemical reaction networks. In: Kroening, D., Păsăreanu, C.S. (eds.) CAV 2015. LNCS, vol. 9206, pp. 195–213. Springer, Heidelberg (2015). doi:10.1007/978-3-319-21690-4_12
2. Abate, A., D'Innocenzo, A., Benedetto, M.D.: Approximate abstractions of stochastic hybrid systems. IEEE Trans. Autom. Control 56(11), 2688–2694 (2011)
3. Bertsekas, D.: Dynamic Programming and Optimal Control, vol. I. Athena Scientific, Belmont (1995)
4. Bertsekas, D.: Approximate policy iteration: a survey and some new methods. J. Control Theor. Appl. 9(3), 310–335 (2011)
5. Bertsekas, D.: Dynamic Programming and Optimal Control, Vol. II: Approximate Dynamic Programming. Athena Scientific, Belmont (2012)
6. Bertsekas, D.: Tsitsiklis: Neuro-Dynamic Programming. Athena Scientific, Belmont (1996)
7. Brázdil, T., Chatterjee, K., Chmelík, M., Forejt, V., Křetínský, J., Kwiatkowska, M., Parker, D., Ujma, M.: Verification of Markov decision processes using learning algorithms. In: Cassez, F., Raskin, J.-F. (eds.) ATVA 2014. LNCS, vol. 8837, pp. 98–114. Springer, Heidelberg (2014). doi:10.1007/978-3-319-11936-6_8
8. D'Innocenzo, A., Abate, A., Katoen, J.-P.: Robust PCTL model checking. In: Proceedings of the HSCC 2012, pp. 275–285. ACM (2012)

9. Haesaert, S., Babuska, R., Abate, A.: Sampling-based approximations with quantitative performance for the probabilistic reach-avoid problem over general Markov processes. arXiv (2014). arXiv:1409.0553
10. Katoen, J.-P., Klink, D., Leucker, M., Wolf, V.: Three-valued abstraction for probabilistic systems. J. Logic Algebraic Program. **81**(4), 356–389 (2012)
11. Kattenbelt, M., Kwiatkowska, M., Norman, G., Parker, D.: A game-based abstraction-refinement framework for Markov decision processes. Formal Methods Syst. Des. **36**(3), 246–280 (2010)
12. Kwiatkowska, M., Norman, G., Parker, D.: PRISM 4.0: verification of probabilistic real-time systems. In: Gopalakrishnan, G., Qadeer, S. (eds.) CAV 2011. LNCS, vol. 6806, pp. 585–591. Springer, Heidelberg (2011). doi:10.1007/978-3-642-22110-1_47
13. Lahijanian, M., Andersson, S.B., Belta, C.: Formal verification and synthesis for discrete-time stochastic systems. IEEE Trans. Autom. Control **60**(8), 2031–2045 (2015)
14. McMahan, H.B., Likhachev, M., Gordon, G.J.: Bounded real-time dynamic programming: RTDP with monotone upper bounds and performance guarantees. In: Proceedings of the ICML, pp. 569–576. ACM (2005)
15. Munos, R., Szepesvari, C.: Finite time bounds for fitted value iteration. J. Mach. Learn. Res. **9**, 815–857 (2008)
16. Puterman, M.: Markov Decision Processes: Discrete Stochastic Dynamic Programming. John Wiley and Sons, Hoboken (2005)

Optimizing the Expected Mean Payoff in Energy Markov Decision Processes

Tomáš Brázdil[1], Antonín Kučera[1], and Petr Novotný[2(✉)]

[1] Faculty of Informatics MU, Botanická 68a, 602 00 Brno, Czech Republic
{brazdil,kucera}@fi.muni.cz
[2] IST Austria, Klosterneuburg, Austria
petr.novotny@ist.ac.at

Abstract. Energy Markov Decision Processes (EMDPs) are finite-state Markov decision processes where each transition is assigned an integer counter update and a rational payoff. An EMDP configuration is a pair $s(n)$, where s is a control state and n is the current counter value. The configurations are changed by performing transitions in the standard way. We consider the problem of computing a safe strategy (i.e., a strategy that keeps the counter non-negative) which maximizes the expected mean payoff.

1 Introduction

Resource-aware systems are systems that consume/produce a discrete resource, such as (units of) time, energy, or money, along their runs. This resource is *critical*, i.e., if it is fully exhausted along a run, a severe runtime error appears, so such a situation should be avoided. Technically, resource-aware systems are modelled as finite-state programs operating over an integer counter representing the resource. A *configuration* is a pair $s(n)$ where s is the current control state and n is the number of currently available resource units. Each transition is assigned an integer *update* modelling the consumption/production of the resource caused by performing the transition.

Our Contribution. In this paper, we concentrate on the *long-run average optimization problem* for resource-aware systems with both controllable and stochastic states. That is, we assume that the finite control of our resource-aware system is a finite-state Markov decision process (MDP), and each transition is assigned (in addition to the integer counter update) a rational *payoff*[1]. The resulting model is called *energy Markov decision process (EMDP)*. Intuitively, given an

---

The research was funded by the Czech Science Foundation Grant No. P202/12/G061 and by the People Programme (Marie Curie Actions) of the European Union's Seventh Framework Programme (FP7/2007-2013) under REA grant agreement no [291734].

[1] The payoff may correspond to some independent performance measure, or it can reflect the use of the critical resource represented by the counter.

© Springer International Publishing AG 2016
C. Artho et al. (Eds.): ATVA 2016, LNCS 9938, pp. 32–49, 2016.
DOI: 10.1007/978-3-319-46520-3_3

EMDP and its initial configuration, the task is to compute a *safe* strategy maximizing the *expected mean payoff*. Here, a strategy is safe if it ensures that the counter stays non-negative along all runs. The *value* of a given configuration $s(n)$, denoted by $Val(s(n))$, is the supremum of all expected mean payoffs achievable by a safe strategy, and a strategy is *optimal* for $s(n)$ if it is safe and achieves the value. Observe that $Val(s(n)) \geq Val(s(m))$ whenever $n \geq m$, and hence we can also define the *limit value* of s, denoted by $Val(s)$, as $\lim_{n \to \infty} Val(s(n))$.

Since optimal safe strategies may not exists in general, the first natural question is the following:

[Q1]. *Can we determine a "reasonable" condition under which an optimal strategy exists?*

By "reasonable" we mean that the condition should be decidable (with low complexity) and tight in the sense that we should provide counterexamples witnessing that optimal strategies do not necessarily exist if the condition is violated. Further, there are two basic algorithmic questions.

[Q2]. *Can we compute $Val(s(n))$ for a given configuration $s(n)$? If not, can we at least approximate the value up to a given absolute error $\varepsilon > 0$? Can we compute/approximate $Val(s)$ for a given state s? What is the complexity of these problems?*

To show that computing an ε-approximation of $Val(s(n))$ is computationally hard, we consider the following *gap threshold problem*: given a configuration $t(k)$ of a given EMDP and numbers x, ε, where $\varepsilon > 0$, such that either $Val(t(k)) \geq x$ or $Val(t(k)) \leq x - \varepsilon$, decide which of these two alternatives holds[2]. Note that if the gap threshold problem is X-hard for some complexity class X, then $Val(s(n))$ cannot be ε-approximated in polynomial time unless X = P.

[Q3]. *Can we compute (a finite description of) an optimal strategy for a given configuration (if it exists)? For a given $\varepsilon > 0$, can we compute an ε-optimal strategy? How much memory is required by these strategies? What is the complexity of the strategy synthesis problems?*

Before formulating our answers to the above questions, we need to briefly discuss the relationship between EMDPs and *energy games* [4,14,15].

The problems of **[Q2]** and **[Q3]** subsume the question whether a given configuration of a given EMDP is safe. This problem can be solved by algorithms for 2-player non-stochastic energy games [14], where we treat the stochastic vertices as if they were controlled by an adversarial player. The correctness of this approach stems from the fact that keeping the energy level non-negative is an objective whose violation is witnessed by a finite prefix of a run. Let EG (Energy Games) be the problem of deciding whether a given configuration in a given energy game is safe. A $\mathsf{P^{EG}}$ algorithm is a deterministic polynomial-time algorithm which inputs an EMDP $\mathcal{E}$ (and possibly some initial configuration $s(n)$ of $\mathcal{E}$) and uses an oracle which freely decides the safety problem for the configurations of $\mathcal{E}$. We assume that the counter updates and rewards used in $\mathcal{E}$, and the n in $s(n)$, are encoded as (fractions of) binary numbers. The size of

---

[2] Formally, the decision algorithm answers "yes" iff, say, first possibility holds.

$\mathcal{E}$ and $s(n)$ is denoted by $\|\mathcal{E}\|$ and $\|s(n)\|$, respectively. It is known that EG is solvable in pseudo-polynomial time, belongs to NP ∩ coNP, and it is at least as hard as the parity game problem. From this we immediately obtain that every decision problem solvable by a P^{EG} algorithm belongs to NP ∩ coNP, and every P^{EG} algorithm runs in pseudo-polynomial time, i.e., in time polynomial in $\|\mathcal{E}\|$, $\|s(n)\|$, and $M_{\mathcal{E}}$, where $M_{\mathcal{E}}$ is the maximal absolute value of a counter update in $\mathcal{E}$. We say that a decision problem X is EG-*hard* if there is a polynomial-time reduction from EG to X.

Our results (answers to [**Q1**]–[**Q3**]) can be formulated as follows:

[**A1**]. We show that an optimal strategy is guaranteed to exist in a configuration $s(n)$ if the underlying EMDP is *strongly connected and pumpable*. An EMDP is strongly connected if its underlying graph is strongly connected, and pumpable if for every safe configuration $t(m)$ there exists a safe strategy σ such that the counter value is unbounded in almost all runs initiated in $t(m)$.

The problem whether a given EMDP is strongly connected and pumpable is in P^{EG} and EG-hard. Further, an optimal strategy in $s(n)$ does not necessarily exist if just one of these two conditions is violated. We use SP-EMDP to denote the subclass of strongly connected and pumpable EMDPs.

[**A2, A3**]. If a given EMDP belongs to the SP-EMDP subclass, the following holds:

- The value of every safe configuration is the same and computable by a P^{EG} algorithm (consequently, the limit value of all states is also the same and computable by a P^{EG} algorithm). The gap threshold problem is EG-hard.
- There exists a strategy σ which is optimal in every configuration. In general, σ may require infinite memory. A finite description[3] of σ is computable by a P^{EG} algorithm. The same holds for ε-optimal strategies where $\varepsilon > 0$, except that ε-optimal strategies require only finite memory.

Note that since the gap threshold problem is EG-hard, approximating the value is not much easier than computing the value precisely for SP-EMDPs.

For general EMDPs, optimal strategies are not guaranteed to exist. Still, for every EMDP $\mathcal{E}$ we have the following:

- The value of every configuration $s(n)$ can be approximated up to an arbitrarily small given $\varepsilon > 0$ in time polynomial in $\|\mathcal{E}\|$, $\|s(n)\|$, $M_{\mathcal{E}}$, and $1/\varepsilon$. The limit value of each control state is computable in time polynomial in $\|\mathcal{E}\|$ and $M_{\mathcal{E}}$.
- For a given $\varepsilon > 0$, there exists a strategy σ which is ε-optimal in every configuration. In general, σ may require infinite memory. A finite description of σ is computable in time polynomial in $\|\mathcal{E}\|$, $M_{\mathcal{E}}$, and $1/\varepsilon$.
- The gap threshold problem is PSPACE-hard.

The above results are non-trivial and based on detailed structural analysis of EMDPs. As a byproduct, we yield a good intuitive understanding on what

---

[3] Under a finite description we can imagine a program with unbounded integer variables encoding the strategy's execution.

can actually happen when we wish to construct a (sub)optimal strategy in a given EMDP configuration. The main steps are sketched below (we also explain where and how we employ the existing ideas, and where we need to invent new techniques). The details and examples illustrating the discussed phenomena are given later in Sect. 3.

The core of the problem is the analysis of maximal end components of a given EMDP, so let us suppose that our EMDP is strongly connected (but not necessarily pumpable). First, we check whether there exists *some* strategy such that the average change of the counter per transition is positive (this can be done by linear programming) and distinguish two possibilities:

If there is such a strategy, then we try to optimize the mean payoff under the constraint that the average change of the counter is non-negative. This can be formulated by a linear program whose solution allows to construct finitely many randomized memoryless strategies and an appropriate "mixing ratio" for these strategies that produces an optimal mean payoff. This part is inspired by the technique used in [6] for the analysis of MDPs with multiple mean-payoff objectives. However, here we cannot implement the optimal mixing ratio "immediately" because we also need to ensure that the resulting strategy is safe. We can solve this problem using two different methods, depending on whether the EMDP is pumpable or not. If it is not pumpable, then, since we aim at constructing an ε-optimal strategy, we can always slightly modify the mix, adding, in a right proportion, the aforementioned strategy which increases the counter. If the counter becomes too low, we permanently switch to some safe strategy (which may produce a low mean payoff). Since the counter has a tendency to increase, we can set everything up so that the probability of visiting low counter values is very small if we start with a sufficiently large initial counter value. Hence, for configurations with a sufficiently large counter value, we play ε-optimally. For the configurations with "low" counter value, we compute a suboptimal strategy by "cutting" the counter when it reaches a large value (where we already know how to play) and applying the algorithm for finite-state MDPs.

More interesting is the case when the EMDP *is* pumpable. Here, instead of switching to *some* safe strategy, we switch to a *pumping* strategy, i.e. a safe strategy that is capable of increasing the counter above any threshold with probability 1. Once the pumping strategy increases the counter to some sufficiently high value, we can switch back to playing the aforementioned "mixture." To obtain an optimal strategy in this way, we need to extremely carefully set up the events which trigger "(de-)activation" of the pumping strategy, so as to ensure that it keeps the counter sufficiently high and at the same time assure that it does not negatively affect the mean payoff. We innovatively use the martingale techniques designed in [8] to accomplish this delicate task.

If there is no such strategy, we need to analyze our EMDP differently. We prove that *every* safe strategy then satisfies the following: almost all runs end by an infinite suffix where all visited configurations with the same control state have the same counter value. This implies that only finitely many configurations are visited in the suffix, and we can analyze the associated mean payoff by methods for finite-state MDPs.

Omitted proofs can be found in [9]. Let us note that some of the presented ideas can be easily extended even to multi-energy MDPs. Since a full analysis of EMDPs is rather lenghty and complicated, we leave this extension for future work.

Related Work. MDPs with mean payoff objectives have been heavily studied since the 60s (see, e.g., [26,30]). Several algorithms for computing optimal values and strategies have been developed for both finite-state systems (see e.g. [6,17, 22,30]) and various types of infinite-state MDPs typically related to queueing systems (see, e.g., [28]). For an extensive survey see [30]. Various logics were developed for reasoning about mean payoff and other reward-based properties [3]. Model checking MDPs against specifications in these logics is supported by state of the art tools [23].

MDPs with energy objectives have been studied in [7] as one-counter MDPs. Subsequently, several papers concerned MDPs with counters (resources) have been published (for a survey see [29], for recent work see e.g. [2]). A closely related paper [15] studies MDPs with combined energy-parity and mean-payoff-parity objectives (however, the combination of energy with mean payoff is not studied in [15]).

A considerable amount of attention has been devoted to non-stochastic turn-based games with energy objectives [4,14]. Solving energy games belongs to NP∩coNP but no polynomial time algorithm is known. Energy games are poly-nomially equivalent to mean-payoff games [4]. Several papers are concerned with complexity of energy games (or equivalent problems, see e.g. [11,20,24,32]). For a more detailed account of results on energy games see [19]. Games with vari-ous combinations of objectives as well as multi-energy objectives have also been studied (see e.g. [1,5,10,15,16,27,31]), as well as energy constraints in automata setting [13].

Our work is closely related to the recent papers [12,21] where the combina-tion of expected and worst-case mean-payoff objectives is considered. In particu-lar, [21] considers a problem of optimizing the expected multi-dimensional mean-payoff under the condition that the mean-payoff in the first component is positive for all runs. At first glance, one may be tempted to "reduce" **[Q2]** and **[Q3]** to results of [21] as follows: Ask for a strategy which ensures that the mean-payoff in the first counter is non-negative for all runs, and then try to optimize the expected mean-payoff of the second counter. However, this approach does not work for several reasons. First, a strategy achieving non-negative mean-payoff in the first counter may still decrease the counter arbitrarily deep. So no matter what initial value of the counter is used, the zero counter value may be reached with positive probability. Second, the techniques developed in [21] do not work in the case of "balanced" EMDPs. Intuitively, balanced EMDPs are those where we inevitably need to employ strategies that balance the counter, i.e., the expected average change of the counter per transition is zero. In the framework of sto-chastic counter systems, the balanced subcase is often more difficult than the other subcases when the counters have a tendency to "drift" in some direction. In our case, the balanced EMDPs also require a special (and non-trivial) proof techniques based on martingales and some new "structural" observations. We believe that these tools can be adapted to handle the "balanced subcase" in even more general problems related to systems with more counters, MDPs over vector addition systems, and similar models.

2   Preliminaries

We use $\mathbb{Z}$, $\mathbb{N}$, $\mathbb{N}^+$, $\mathbb{Q}$, and $\mathbb{R}$ to denote the set of all integers, non-negative integers, positive integers, rational numbers, and real numbers, respectively. We assume familiarity with basic notions of probability theory, e.g., *probability space*, *random variable*, or the *expected value*. A *probability distribution* over a finite or countably infinite set A is a function $f : A \to [0,1]$ such that $\sum_{a \in A} f(a) = 1$. We call f *positive* if $f(a) > 0$ for each $a \in A$, *rational* if $f(a) \in \mathbb{Q}$ for each $a \in A$, and *Dirac* if $f(a) = 1$ for some $a \in A$.

Definition 1 (MDP). *A* Markov decision process (MDP) *is a tuple* $\mathcal{M} = (S, (S_\square, S_\bigcirc), T, Prob, r)$, *where* S *is a finite set of* states, $(S_\square, S_\bigcirc)$ *is a partitioning of* S *into the sets* $S_\square$ *of* controllable states *and* $S_\bigcirc$ *of* stochastic states, *respectively,* $T \subseteq S \times S$ *is a* transition relation, *Prob is a function assigning to every stochastic state* $s \in S_\bigcirc$ *a positive probability distribution over its outgoing transitions, and* $r : T \to \mathbb{Q}$ *is a reward function. We assume that* T *is total, i.e., for each* $s \in S$ *there is* $t \in S$ *such that* $(s, t) \in T$.

We use $Prob(s, t)$ as an abbreviation for $(Prob(s))(s, t)$, i.e., $Prob(s, t)$ is the probability of taking the transition (s, t) in s. For a state s we denote by $out(s)$ the set of transitions outgoing from s. A *finite path* is a sequence $w = s_0 s_1 \cdots s_n$ of states such that $(s_i, s_{i+1}) \in T$ for all $0 \le i < n$. We write $len(w) = n$ for the length of the path. A *run* (or an *infinite path*) is an infinite sequence ω of states such that every finite prefix of ω is a finite path. For a finite path w, we denote by $Run_\mathcal{M}(w)$ the set of all runs having w as a prefix.

An *end component* of $\mathcal{M}$ is a pair (S', T'), where $S' \subseteq S$, $T' \subseteq S' \times S' \cap T$, satisfying the following conditions: (1) for every $s \in S'$, we have that $out(s) \cap T' \ne \emptyset$; (2) if $s \in S' \cap S_\bigcirc$, then $out(s) \subseteq T'$; (3) the graph determined by (S', T') is strongly connected. Note that every end component of $\mathcal{M}$ can be seen as a strongly connected MDP (obtained by restricting the states and transitions of $\mathcal{M}$). A *maximal end component (MEC)* is an end component which is maximal w.r.t. pairwise inclusion. The MECs of a given MDP $\mathcal{M}$ are computable in polynomial time [18].

A *strategy* (or a *policy*) in an MDP $\mathcal{M}$ is a tuple $\sigma = (M, m_0, update, next)$ where M is a set of memory elements, $m_0 \in M$ is an initial memory element, $update : M \times S \to M$ a memory-update function, and $next$ is a function which to every pair $(s, m) \in S_\square \times M$ assigns a probability distribution over $out(s)$. The function $update$ is extended to finite sequences of states in the natural way. We say that σ is *finite-memory* if M is finite, and *memoryless* if M is a singleton. Further, we say that σ is *deterministic* if $next(s,m)$ is Dirac for all $(s,m) \in S_\square \times M$. Note that σ determines a function which to every finite path in $\mathcal{M}$ of the form ws, where $s \in S_\square$, assigns the probability distribution $next(s,m)$, where $m = update(m_0, w)$. Slightly abusing the notation, we use σ to denote this function.

Fixing a strategy σ and an initial state s, we obtain the standard probability space $(Run_\mathcal{M}(s), \mathcal{F}, \mathbb{P}_s^\sigma)$ of all runs starting at s, where $\mathcal{F}$ is the σ-field generated by all *basic cylinders* $Run_\mathcal{M}(w)$, where w is a finite path starting at s, and $\mathbb{P}_s^\sigma : \mathcal{F} \to [0,1]$ is the unique probability measure such that for all finite paths $w = s_0 \cdots s_n$ it holds $\mathbb{P}_s^\sigma(Run_\mathcal{M}(w)) = \prod_{i=1}^n x_i$, where each x_i is either $\sigma(s_0 \cdots s_{i-1})(s_{i-1}, s_i)$, or $Prob(s_{i-1}, s_i)$, depending on whether s_{i-1} is controllable or stochastic (the empty product evaluates to 1). We denote by $\mathbb{E}_s^\sigma$ the expectation operator of this probability space.

We say that a run $\omega = s_0 s_1 \cdots$ is *compatible* with a strategy σ if $\sigma(s_0 \cdots s_i)(s_i, s_{i+1}) > 0$ for all $i \geq 0$ such that $s_i \in S_\square$.

Definition 2 (EMDP). *An* energy MDP (EMDP) *is a tuple* $\mathcal{E} = (\mathcal{M}, E)$, *where $\mathcal{M}$ is a finite MDP and E is a function assigning to every transition of $\mathcal{M}$ an integer update.*

We implicitly extend all MDP-related notions to EMDPs, i.e., for $\mathcal{E} = (\mathcal{M}, E)$ we speak about runs and strategies in $\mathcal{E}$ rather than about runs and strategies in $\mathcal{M}$. A *configuration* of $\mathcal{E}$ is an element of $S \times \mathbb{Z}$ written as $s(n)$.

Given an EMDP $\mathcal{E} = (\mathcal{M}, E)$ and a configuration $s(n)$ of $\mathcal{E}$, we use $\|\mathcal{E}\|$ and $\|s(n)\|$ to denote the encoding size of $\mathcal{E}$ and $s(n)$, respectively, where the counter updates and rewards used in $\mathcal{E}$, as well as the n in $s(n)$, are written as (fractions of) binary numbers. We also use $M_\mathcal{E}$ to denote the maximal non-negative integer u such that u or $-u$ is an update assigned by E to some transition.

Given a finite or infinite path $w = s_0 s_1 \cdots$ in $\mathcal{E}$ and an *initial configuration* $s_0(n_0)$, we define the *energy level* after i steps of w as $Lev_{n_0}^{(i)}(w) = n_0 + \sum_{i=0}^{i-1} E(s_i, s_{i+1})$ (the empty sum evaluates to zero). A configuration of $\mathcal{E}$ after i steps of w is then the configuration $s_i(n_i)$, where $n_i = Lev_{n_0}^{(i)}(w)$. Note that for all n and $i \geq 0$, $Lev_n^{(i)}$ can be understood as a random variable.

We say that a run ω initiated in s_0 is *safe* in a configuration $s_0(n_0)$ if $Lev_{n_0}^{(i)}(\omega) \geq 0$ for all $i \geq 0$. A strategy σ is safe in $s_0(n_0)$ if all runs compatible with σ are safe in $s_0(n_0)$. Finally, a configuration $s_0(n_0)$ is safe if there is at least one strategy safe in $s_0(n_0)$. The following lemma is straightforward.

Lemma 1. *If $s(n)$ is safe and $m \geq n$, then $s(m)$ is safe.*

To every run $\omega = s_0 s_1 \cdots$ in $\mathcal{E}$ we assign a mean payoff $MP(\omega)$ collected along ω defined as $MP(\omega) := \liminf_{n \to \infty} (\sum_{i=1}^n r(s_{i-1}, s_i))/n$. The function MP can be seen as a random variable, and for every strategy σ and initial state s we denote by $\mathbb{E}_s^\sigma[MP]$ its expected value (w.r.t. $\mathbb{P}_s^\sigma$).

Definition 3 (Energy-Constrained Value). *Let $\mathcal{E} = (\mathcal{M}, E)$ be an EMDP and $s(n)$ its configuration. The* energy-constrained mean-payoff value *(or simply* *the* value*) of $s(n)$ is defined by $Val(s(n)) := \sup \{\mathbb{E}_s^\sigma[MP] \mid \sigma$ is safe in $s(n)\}$. For every state s we also put $Val(s) := \lim_{n\to\infty} Val(s(n))$.*

Note that the value of every unsafe configuration is $-\infty$. We say that a strategy σ is ε-*optimal* in $s(n)$, where $\varepsilon \geq 0$, if σ is safe in $s(n)$ and $Val(s(n)) - \mathbb{E}_s^\sigma[MP] \leq \varepsilon$. A 0-optimal strategy is called *optimal*.

3   The Results

In this section we precisely formulate and prove the results about EMDPs announced in Sect. 1. Let $\mathcal{E} = (\mathcal{M}, E)$ be an EMDP. For every state s of $\mathcal{E}$, let *min-safe*(s) be the least $n \in \mathbb{N}$ such that $s(n)$ is a safe configuration. If there is no such n, we put *min-safe*$(s) = \infty$. The following lemma follows from the standard results on one-dimensional energy games [14].

Lemma 2. *There is a P^{EG} algorithm which computes, for a given EMDP $\mathcal{E} = (\mathcal{M}, E)$ and its state s, the value min-safe(s).*

Next, we present a precise definition of strongly connected and pumpable EMDPs. We say that $\mathcal{E}$ is *strongly connected* if for each pair of states s, t there is a finite path starting in s and ending in t. The pumpability condition is more specific.

Definition 4. *Let $\mathcal{E}$ be an EMDP and $s(n)$ a configuration of $\mathcal{E}$. We say that a strategy σ is pumping in $s(n)$ if σ is safe in $s(n)$ and $\mathbb{P}_s^\sigma(\sup_{i\geq 0} Lev_n^{(i)} = \infty) = 1$. Further, we say that $s(n)$ is pumpable if there is a strategy pumping in $s(n)$, and $\mathcal{E}$ is pumpable if every safe configuration of $\mathcal{E}$ is pumpable.*

The subclass of strongly connected pumpable EMDPs is denoted by SP-EMDP. Clearly, if $s(n)$ is pumpable, then every $s(m)$, where $m \geq n$, is also pumpable. Hence, for every $s \in S$, we define *min-pump*(s) as the least n such that $s(n)$ is pumpable. If there is no such n, we put *min-pump*$(s) = \infty$.

Intuitively, the condition of pumpability allows to increase the counter to an arbitrarily high value whenever we need.

Lemma 3. *For every EMDP $\mathcal{E}$ there exist a memoryless globally pumping strategy σ, i.e. a strategy that is pumping in every pumpable configuration of $\mathcal{E}$. Further, there is a P^{EG} algorithm which computes the strategy σ and the value min-pump$(s) \leq 3 \cdot |S| \cdot M_\mathcal{E}$ for every state s of $\mathcal{E}$. The problem whether a given configuration of $\mathcal{E}$ is pumpable is EG-hard.*

Now we can state our results about SP-EMDPs.

Theorem 1. *For the subclass of SP-EMDPs, we have the following:*

1. *The problem whether a given EMDP $\mathcal{E}$ belongs to SP-EMDP is EG-hard and solvable by a P^{EG} algorithm.*

2. *The value of all safe configurations of a given SP-EMDP $\mathcal{E}$ is the same. Moreover, there is a P^{EG} algorithm which computes this value.*
3. *For every SP-EMDP $\mathcal{E}$ and every configuration $s(n)$ of $\mathcal{E}$, there is a strategy σ optimal in $s(n)$. In general, σ may require infinite memory, and there is a P^{EG} algorithm which computes a finite description of this strategy.*
4. *For every SP-EMDP $\mathcal{E}$, every configuration $s(n)$ of $\mathcal{E}$, and every $\varepsilon > 0$, there is a finite-memory strategy which is ε-optimal in $s(n)$. Further, there is a P^{EG} algorithm which computes a finite description of this strategy.*
5. *The gap threshold problem for SP-EMDPs is EG hard.*

In particular, note that ε-optimal strategies in SP-EMDPs require only finite memory (4), but they are not easier to compute than optimal strategies (5).

The following theorem summarizes the results for general EMDPs.

Theorem 2. *For general EMDPs, we have the following:*

1. *Optimal strategies may not exist in EMDPs that are either not strongly connected or not pumpable.*
2. *Given an EMDP $\mathcal{E}$, a configuration $s(n)$ of $\mathcal{E}$, and $\varepsilon > 0$, the value of $s(n)$ can be approximated up to the absolute error ε in time which is polynomial in $\|\mathcal{E}\|$, $\|s(n)\|$, $M_{\mathcal{E}}$, and $1/\varepsilon$.*
3. *Given an EMDP $\mathcal{E}$ and a state s of $\mathcal{E}$, the limit value $Val(s)$ is computable in time polynomial in $\|\mathcal{E}\|$ and $M_{\mathcal{E}}$.*
4. *Let $\mathcal{E}$ be an EMDP, $s(n)$ a configuration of $\mathcal{E}$, and $\varepsilon > 0$. An ε-optimal strategy in $s(n)$ may require infinite memory. A finite description of a strategy σ which is ε-optimal in $s(n)$ is computable in time polynomial in $\|\mathcal{E}\|$, $M_{\mathcal{E}}$, and $1/\varepsilon$.*
5. *The gap threshold problem for EMDPs is in $\mathsf{EXPTIME}$ and PSPACE-hard.*

Before proving Theorems 1 and 2, we introduce several tools that are useful for the analysis of strongly connected EMDPs. For the rest of this section, we fix a *strongly connected* EMDP $\mathcal{E} = (\mathcal{M}, E)$ where $\mathcal{M} = (S, (S_\square, S_\circ), T, Prob, r)$.

The key component for the analysis of $\mathcal{E}$ is the linear program $\mathcal{L}_{\mathcal{E}}$ shown in Fig. 1 (left). The program is a modification of a one used in [6] for multi-objective mean-payoff optimization. For each transition e of $\mathcal{E}$ we have a non-negative variable f_e that intuitively represents the long-run frequency of traversals of e under some strategy (the fact that f_e's can be given this interpretation is ensured by the *flow constraints* in the first three lines). The constraint in the fourth line then ensures that a strategy that visits each transition e with frequency f_e achieves a non-negative long-run change of the energy level, i.e. it ensures that the energy level does not have a tendency to decrease.

Intuitively, the optimal value of $\mathcal{L}_{\mathcal{E}}$ is the maximal expected mean payoff achievable under the constraint that the long-run average change (or *trend*) of the energy level is non-negative. Every safe strategy has to satisfy this constraint, because otherwise the probability of visiting a configuration with negative counter would be positive. Thus, using the methods adopted from [6], we get the following.

Lemma 4. *If there is a strategy σ that is safe in some configuration $s(n)$ of $\mathcal{E}$, then the linear program $\mathcal{L}_\mathcal{E}$ has a solution whose objective value is at least $\mathbb{E}_s^\sigma[MP]$.*

On the other hand, even if a strategy achieves a non-negative (or even positive) counter trend, it can still be unsafe in all configurations of $\mathcal{E}$. To see this, consider the EMDP in Fig. 1 (right). There is only one strategy (the empty function), and it is easy to verify that assigning $1/4$ to each variable in $\mathcal{L}_\mathcal{E}$ solves the linear program with $\sum_{e \in T} f_e \cdot E(e) = \frac{1}{4}$. However, for every m there is a positive probability that the decrementing loop on t is taken at least m times, and thus the strategy is not safe.

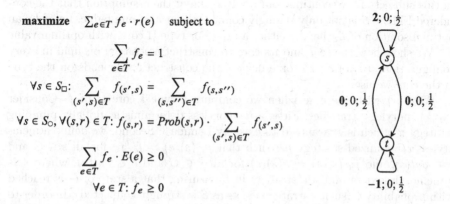

maximize $\sum_{e \in T} f_e \cdot r(e)$ subject to

$$\sum_{e \in T} f_e = 1$$

$$\forall s \in S_\square: \sum_{(s',s) \in T} f_{(s',s)} = \sum_{(s,s'') \in T} f_{(s,s'')}$$

$$\forall s \in S_\bigcirc, \forall (s,r) \in T: f_{(s,r)} = Prob(s,r) \cdot \sum_{(s',s) \in T} f_{(s',s)}$$

$$\sum_{e \in T} f_e \cdot E(e) \geq 0$$

$$\forall e \in T: f_e \geq 0$$

Fig. 1. A linear program $\mathcal{L}_\mathcal{E}$ with non-negative variables f_e, $e \in T$ (left), and an EMDP where the strategy corresponding to the solution of $\mathcal{L}_\mathcal{E}$ is not safe (right). Each transition is labelled by the associated counter update (in boldface), reward, and probability

Although the program $\mathcal{L}_\mathcal{E}$ does not directly yield a safe strategy optimizing the mean payoff, it is still useful for obtaining certain "building blocks" of such a strategy. To this end we introduce additional terminology.

Let $f = (f_e)_{e \in T}$ be an optimal solution of $\mathcal{L}_\mathcal{E}$, and let f^* be the corresponding optimal value of the objective function. A *flow graph* of f is a digraph G_f whose vertices are the states of $\mathcal{E}$, and there is an edge (s,t) in G_f iff there is a transition $e = (s,t)$ with $f_e > 0$. A *component* of f is a maximal set C of states that forms a strongly connected subgraph of G_f. The set T_C consists of all $(s,t) \in T$ such that $s \in C$ and $f_{(s,t)} > 0$. A *frequency* of a component C is the number $f_C = \sum_{e \in T_C} f_e$. Finally, a *trend* and *mean-payoff* of a component C are the numbers $trend_C = \sum_{e \in T_C} (f_e/f_C) \cdot E(e)$ and $mp_C = \sum_{e \in T_C} (f_e/f_C) \cdot r(e)$.

Intuitively, the components of f are those families of states that are visited infinitely often by a certain strategy that maximizes the mean payoff while ensuring that the counter trend is non-negative. We show that our analysis can be simplified by considering only certain components of f. We define a *type I core* and *type II core* of f as follows:

- A type I core of f is a component C of f such that $trend_C > 0$ and $mp_C \geq f^*$.
- A type II core of f is a pair C_1, C_2 of its components such that $trend_{C_1} \geq 0$, $trend_{C_2} \leq 0$, $f_{C_1} \cdot trend_{C_1} + f_{C_2} \cdot trend_{C_2} \geq 0$ and $f_{C_1} \cdot mp_{C_1} + f_{C_2} \cdot mp_{C_2} \geq f^*$.

The following lemma is easy.

Lemma 5. *From each optimal solution f' of $\mathcal{L}_\mathcal{E}$ one can compute, in polynomial time, an optimal solution f that has a type I or a type II core. Moreover, a core of f (of some type) can be also found in polynomial time.*

3.1   Strongly Connected and Pumpable EMDPs

In this subsection, we continue our analysis under the assumption that the considered EMDP $\mathcal{E}$ is not only strongly connected but also pumpable. Let f be an optimal solution of $\mathcal{L}_\mathcal{E}$ having either a type I or type II core, with optimal value f^*. We show how to use f and its core to construct a strategy optimal in every configuration $s(n)$ of $\mathcal{E}$. To some degree, the construction depends on the type of the core we use.

We start with the case when we compute a type I core C of f. Consider two memoryless strategies: First, a memoryless deterministic globally pumping strategy π which is guaranteed to exist by Lemma 3. Second, we define a memoryless randomized strategy μ_C such that $\mu_C(s)(e) = f_e/f_C$ for all $s \in C$ and $e \in out(s)$, and $\mu_C(s)(e) = \kappa(s)(e)$ for all $s \notin C$ and $e \in out(s)$, where κ is a memoryless deterministic strategy in $\mathcal{E}$ ensuring that a state of C is reached with probability 1 (such a strategy exists as $\mathcal{E}$ is strongly connected). In order to combine these two strategies, we define a function low_n which assigns to a finite path w a value 1 if and only if there is $0 \leq j \leq len(w)$ such that $Lev_n^{(j)}(w) \leq L := M_\mathcal{E} + \max_{s \in S} min\text{-}pump(s)$ and $Lev_n^{(i)}(w) \leq H := L + |S| + 2|S|^2 \cdot M_\mathcal{E}$ for all $j \leq i \leq len(w)$; otherwise, $low_n(w) = 0$. We then define a strategy σ_n^* as follows:

$$\sigma_n^*(w)(e) = \begin{cases} \mu_C(last(w))(e) & \text{if } low_n(w) = 0 \\ \pi(last(w))(e) & \text{if } low_n(w) = 1. \end{cases}$$

Proposition 1. *Let $s(n)$ be a configuration of $\mathcal{E}$. Then σ_n^* is optimal in $s(n)$.*

Let us summarize the intuition behind the proof of Proposition 1. If the counter value is sufficiently high, we play the strategy μ prescribed by $\mathcal{L}_\mathcal{E}$ (i.e., we strive to achieve the mean payoff value f^*) until the counter becomes "dangerously low", in which case we switch to a pumping strategy that increases the counter to a sufficiently high value, where we again switch to μ_C. The positive counter trend achieved by μ_C ensures that if we start with a sufficiently high counter value, the probability of the counter *never* decreasing to dangerous levels is bounded away from zero. Moreover, once we switch to the pumping strategy π, with probability 1 we again pump the counter above H and thus switch back to μ_C. Hence, with probability 1 we eventually switch to strategy μ_C and use this strategy forever, and thus achieve mean payoff f^*.

Let us now consider the case where we compute a type II core of f. The overall idea is similar as in the type I case. We try to execute a strategy that has non-negative counter trend and achieves the value f^* computed by $\mathcal{L}_\mathcal{E}$. This amounts to periodical switching between components C_1 and C_2, in such a way that the ratio of time spent in C_i tends to f_{C_i}. As in [6], this is done by fixing a large number N and fragmenting the play into infinitely many iterations: in the k-th iteration, we spend roughly $k \cdot N \cdot f_{C_1}$ steps in C_1, then move to C_2 and spend $k \cdot N \cdot f_{C_2}$ steps in C_2, then move back to C_1 and initialize the $(k+1)$-th iteration. Inside the component C_i we use the strategy μ_{C_i} defined above, until it either is time to switch to C_{3-i} or the counter becomes dangerously low. If the latter event happens, we immediately end the current iteration, switch to a pumping strategy, wait until a counter increases to a sufficient height, and then begin the $(k+1)$-th iteration. However, as the trend of μ_{C_2} is negative, the energy level tends to return to the value to which we increase the level during the pumping phase: it is thus no longer possible to prove that we eventually stop hitting dangerously low levels. To overcome this problem, we use *progressive pumping*: the height to which we increase the counter after the "pumping mode" is switched on in the k-th iteration must increase with k, and it must increase asymptotically faster than $\sqrt{k}$. If this technical requirement is satisfied, we can use martingale techniques to show that progressive pumping decreases, with each iteration, the probability of drops towards dangerous levels. However, it also lengthens the time spent on pumping once such a period is initiated. To ensure that the fraction of time spent on pumping still tends to zero, we have to ensure that the threshold to which we pump increases *sublinearly* in k. We set the bound to roughly $k^{\frac{3}{4}}$ in order to satisfy both of the aforementioned constraints. More details in [9].

Proposition 2. *Each type II core of f yields a strategy optimal in $s(n)$.*

3.2   General EMDPs

In this section we prove Theorem 2. The two counterexamples required to prove part (1.) of the theorem are given in Fig. 2. On the left, there is a strongly connected but not pumpable EMDP (note that $t(0)$ is safe but not pumpable) where $Val(s(0)) = 5$, but there is no optimal strategy. It can be shown that *every* strategy achieving a positive mean-payoff requires infinite memory [9]. Hence, this example also demonstrates that ε-optimal strategies may require infinite memory, as stated in part (4) of Theorem 2. On the right, there is a pumpable but not strongly connected EMDP where $Val(a(0)) = 5$, but no optimal strategy exists in $a(0)$.

For the rest of this section, we fix an EMDP $\mathcal{E} = (\mathcal{M}, E)$. For simplicity, we assume that *for every $s \in S$ there is some $n \in \mathbb{N}$ such that the configuration $s(n)$ is safe*. The other control states can be easily recognized and eliminated (see Lemma 2).

Since $\mathcal{E}$ is not necessarily strongly connected, we start by identifying and constructing the MECs of $\mathcal{E}$ (this can be achieved in time polynomial in $\|\mathcal{E}\|$). Recall that each MEC of $\mathcal{E}$ can be seen as an EMDP, and each run eventually stays

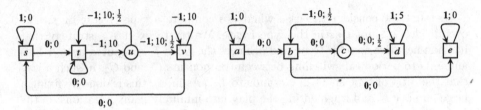

Fig. 2. Examples of EMDPs where optimal strategies do not exist in some configurations. Probabilities are pictured only for stochastic states u and c.

in some MEC [3]. Hence, we start by analyzing the individual MECs separately. Technically, we first assume that $\mathcal{E}$ is strongly connected.

The Case when $\mathcal{E}$ is Strongly Connected. Consider a linear program $\mathcal{T}_{\mathcal{E}}$ which is the same as the program $\mathcal{L}_{\mathcal{E}}$ of Fig. 1 except for its objective function which is set to **maximize** $\sum_{t \in T} f_t \cdot E(t)$. In other words, $\mathcal{T}_{\mathcal{E}}$ tries to maximize the long-run average change of the energy level under the constraints given in $\mathcal{L}_{\mathcal{E}}$. Let $\boldsymbol{g} = (g_e)_{e \in T}$ be an optimal solution of $\mathcal{T}_{\mathcal{E}}$, and let g^* be the corresponding optimal value of the objective function. Now we distinguish two cases, which require completely different proof techniques.

Case A. $g^* > 0$.
Case B. $g^* = 0$.

We start with **Case A**. Note that if $g^* > 0$, then there exists a component D of $\boldsymbol{g}$ such that $trend_D \geq g^* > 0$. We proceed by solving the linear program $\mathcal{L}_{\mathcal{E}}$ of Fig. 1, and identifying the core of an optimal solution $\boldsymbol{f}$ of $\mathcal{L}_{\mathcal{E}}$. Recall that $\boldsymbol{f}$ can have either a type I core C, or a type II core C_1, C_2. In the first case, we set $E_1 := C$ and $E_2 := C$, and in the latter case we set $E_1 := C_1$ and $E_2 := C_2$. Let us fix some $\varepsilon > 0$. We compute positive rationals α_1, α_2 such

- $\alpha_1 + \alpha_2 = 1$
- $\alpha_1 \cdot mp_{E_1} + \alpha_2 \cdot mp_{E_2} \geq f^* - \varepsilon/2$
- $\alpha_1 \cdot trend_{E_1} + \alpha_2 \cdot trend_{E_2} > 0$.

Observe that we can compute α_1, α_2 so that the length of the binary encoding of all of the above numbers is polynomial in $\|\mathcal{E}\|$ and $\|\varepsilon\|$. Now we construct a strategy which is safe and ε-optimal in every configuration with a sufficiently high counter value. Intuitively, we again just combine the two memoryless randomized strategies extracted from $\boldsymbol{f}$ (and possibly $\boldsymbol{g}$) in the ratio given by α_1 and α_2. Since the counter now has a tendency to increase under such a strategy, the probability of visiting a "dangerously low" counter value can be made arbitrarily small by starting sufficiently high (exponential height is sufficient for the probability to be smaller than ε). Hence, when such a dangerous situation occurs, we can permanently switch to *any* safe strategy (this is where our approach bears resemblance to [21]). For the finitely many configurations where the counter height is not "sufficiently large," the ε-optimal strategy can be computed

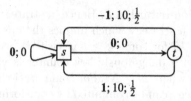

Fig. 3. An EMDP where the solution of $\mathcal{L}_\mathcal{E}$ is irrelevant. For the sake of succinctness we relax the definition of MDP and allow two transitions from t to s.

by encoding these configurations into a finite MDP and optimizing mean-payoff in this MDP using standard methods.

Now consider **Case B**. If $g^* = 0$, the solution of $\mathcal{L}_\mathcal{E}$ is irrelevant, and we need to proceed in a completely different way. To illustrate this, consider the simple EMDP of Fig. 3. Here, the optimal solution f of $\mathcal{L}_\mathcal{E}$ produces $f^* = 5$ and assigns $\frac{1}{2}$ to the transition (s, t). Clearly, we have that $Val(s(n)) = 0$ for an arbitrarily large n, so we cannot aim at approaching f^*. Instead, we show that if $g^* = 0$, then almost all runs produced by a safe strategy are *stable* in the following sense. We say that $s \in S$ is *stable at* $k \in \mathbb{Z}$ in a run $\omega = s_0 s_1 \cdots$ if there exists $i \in \mathbb{N}$ such that for every $j \geq i$ we have that $s_j = s$ implies $Lev_0^{(j)} = k$. Further, we say that s is *stable* in ω if s is stable at k in ω for some k. Note that the initial value of the counter does not influence the (in)stability of s in ω. Intuitively, s is stable in ω if it is visited finitely often, or it is visited infinitely often but from some point on, the energy level is the same in each visit. We say that a *run* is stable if each control state is stable in the run.

The next proposition represents another key insight into the structure of EMDPs. The proof is non-trivial and can be found in [9].

Proposition 3. *Suppose that* $g^* = 0$*, and let* σ *be a strategy which is safe in* $s(n)$*. Then*

$$\mathbb{P}_s^\sigma(\{\omega \in Run(s) \mid \omega \text{ is stable }\}) = 1.$$

Due to Proposition 3, we can analyze the configurations of $\mathcal{E}$ in the following way. We construct a finite-state MDP where the states are the configurations of $\mathcal{E}$ with a non-negative counter value bounded by $|S| \cdot M_\mathcal{E}$. Transition attempting to decrease the counter below zero or increase the counter above $|S| \cdot M_\mathcal{E}$ lead to a special sink state with a self-loop whose reward is strictly smaller than the minimal reward used in $\mathcal{E}$. Then, we apply the standard polynomial-time algorithm for finite-state MDPs to compute the values in the constructed MDP, and identify a configuration $r(\ell)$ with the largest value. By applying Proposition 3, we obtain that $Val(t) = Val(r(\ell))$ for *every* $t \in S$. For every $\varepsilon > 0$, we can easily compute a bound $N_\varepsilon \in \mathbb{N}$ polynomial in $\|\mathcal{E}\|$, $M_\mathcal{E}$, and $1/\varepsilon$, and a memoryless strategy ϱ such that for every configuration $t(m)$ where $m \geq N_\varepsilon$ we have that the $\mathbb{P}_t^\varrho$ probability of all runs initiated in $t(m)$ that visit a configuration $r(k)$ for some $k \geq \ell$ without a prior visit to a configuration where the counter is "dangerously low" is at least $1 - (\varepsilon/2R)$, where R is the difference between the maximal and the minimal transition reward in $\mathcal{E}$. Hence, a strategy which behaves like ϱ and "switches" either to a strategy which mimics the optimal behaviour in $r(\ell)$ (when a configuration $r(k)$ for some $k \geq \ell$ is visited) or to some safe strategy (when a configuration with dangerously low counter is visited) is ε-optimal in every configuration $t(m)$ where $m \geq N_\varepsilon$. For configurations with smaller counter value, an ε-optimal strategy can be computed by transforming the configurations with a non-negative counter value bounded by N_ε into a finite-state MDP and optimizing mean payoff in this finite-state MDP.

The Case when $\mathcal{E}$ is not Strongly Connected. We finish by considering the general case when $\mathcal{E}$ is not strongly connected. Here, we again rely on standard methods for finite-state MDPs (see [30]). More precisely, we transform $\mathcal{E}$ into a finite-state MDP $\mathcal{M}[\mathcal{E}]$ in the following way. The states $\mathcal{M}[\mathcal{E}]$ consist of those states of $\mathcal{E}$ that do not appear in any MEC of $\mathcal{E}$, and for each MEC M of $\mathcal{E}$ we further add a fresh controllable state r_M to $\mathcal{M}[\mathcal{E}]$. The transitions of $\mathcal{M}[\mathcal{E}]$ are constructed as follows. For each r_M we add a self-loop whose reward is the limit value of the states of the MEC M when M is taken as a stand-alone EMDP (see the previous paragraph). Further, for every state s of $\mathcal{E}$, let $\hat{s}$ be either the state s of $\mathcal{M}[\mathcal{E}]$ or the state r_M of $\mathcal{M}[\mathcal{E}]$, depending on whether s belongs to some MEC M of $\mathcal{E}$ or not, respectively. For every transition (s, t) of $\mathcal{E}$ where s, t do *not* belong to the same MEC, we add a transition $(\hat{s}, \hat{t})$ to $\mathcal{M}[\mathcal{E}]$. The rewards for all transitions, except for the self-loops on r_M, can be chosen arbitrarily.

Now we solve the standard mean-payoff optimization problem for $\mathcal{M}[\mathcal{E}]$, which can be achieved in polynomial time by constructing a suitable linear program [30]. The program also computes a *memoryless and deterministic* strategy σ which achieves the optimal mean-payoff $MP(s)$ in every state s of $\mathcal{M}[\mathcal{E}]$. Note that $MP(r_M)$ is *not* necessarily the same as the limit value of the states of M computed by considering M as a "standalone EMDP", because some other MEC with a better mean payoff can be reachable from M. However, the strategy σ eventually "stays" in some target r_M almost surely, and the probability of executing a path of length k before reaching a target r_M decays exponentially in k. Hence, for every $\delta > 0$, one can compute a bound L_δ such that the probability of reaching a target r_M in at most L_δ steps is at least $1 - \delta$. Moreover, L_δ is polynomial in $\|\mathcal{E}\|$ and $1/\delta$.

Now we show that $MP(s) = Val(t)$ for every state t of $\mathcal{E}$ where $\hat{t} = s$. Further, we show that for every $\varepsilon \geq 0$, we can compute a sufficiently large $N_\varepsilon \in \mathbb{N}$ (still polynomial in $\|\mathcal{E}\|$, $M_\mathcal{E}$, and $1/\varepsilon$) and a strategy ϱ such that for every initial configuration $t(m)$, where $m \geq N_\varepsilon$, we have that ϱ is safe in $t(m)$ and $\mathbb{E}_t^\varrho[MP] \geq MP(s) - \varepsilon$, where $\hat{t} = s$. The strategy ϱ "mimics" the strategy σ and eventually switches to some other strategy (temporarily or forever) in the following way:

- Whenever a configuration with a "dangerously low" counter value is encountered, ϱ switches to a safe strategy permanently.
- In a controllable state t of $\mathcal{M}$ which does not belong to any MEC of $\mathcal{E}$, ϱ selects a transition (t, u) such that $(t, \hat{u})$ is the transition selected by σ. In

particular, if σ selects a transition (t, r_M), then ϱ selects a transition leading from t to a state of M.

- In a controllable state t of a MEC M, ϱ mimics σ in the following sense. If σ selects the transition (r_M, r_M), then ϱ permanently switches to the $\varepsilon/2$-optimal strategy for M constructed in the previous paragraph. If σ selects a different transition, then there must be a transition (s, t) of $\mathcal{E}$ where $s \in M$ such that $(r_M, \hat{t})$ is the transition selected by σ. Then ϱ temporarily switches to a strategy which strives to reach the control state s. When s is reached, ϱ restarts mimicking σ. Note that for every $\delta > 0$, one can compute a bound M_δ polynomial in $\|\mathcal{E}\|$ and $1/\delta$ such that the probability of reaching s in at most M_δ steps is at least $1 - \delta$.

We choose N_ε sufficiently large (with the help of the L_δ and M_δ introduced above) so that the probability of all runs initiated in $t(m)$, where $m \geq N_\varepsilon$, that reach a target MEC M with a counter value above the threshold computed for M and $\varepsilon/2$ by the methods of the previous paragraph, is at least $1 - \frac{\varepsilon}{2R}$, where R is the difference between the maximal and the minimal transition reward in $\mathcal{E}$. Hence, ϱ is ε-optimal in every $t(m)$ where $m \geq N_\varepsilon$. For configuration with smaller initial counter value, we compute an ε-optimal strategy as before.

Finally, let us note that Theorem 2 (5) can be proven by reducing the following *cost problem* which is known to be PSPACE-hard [25]: Given an acyclic MDP $\mathcal{M} = (S, (S_\square, S_\bigcirc), T, Prob, r)$, i.e., an MDP whose graph does not contain an oriented cycle, a non-negative cost function c (which assigns costs to transitions), an initial state s_0, a target state s_t, a probability threshold x, and a bound B, decide whether there is a strategy which with probability at least x visits s_t in such a way that the total cost accumulated along the path is at most B. The reduction is straightforward and hence omitted.

References

1. Abdulla, P.A., Mayr, R., Sangnier, A., Sproston, J.: Solving parity games on integer vectors. In: DArgenio, P.R., Melgratti, H. (eds.) CONCUR 2013. LNCS, vol. 8052, pp. 106–120. Springer, Heidelberg (2013). doi:10.1007/978-3-642-40184-8_9
2. Abdulla, P.A., Ciobanu, R., Mayr, R., Sangnier, A., Sproston, J.: Qualitative analysis of VASS-induced MDPs. In: Jacobs, B., et al. (eds.) FOSSACS 2016. LNCS, vol. 9634, pp. 319–334. Springer, Heidelberg (2016). doi:10.1007/978-3-662-49630-5_19
3. de Alfaro, L.: Formal verification of probabilistic systems. Ph.D. thesis, Stanford University, Stanford, CA, USA (1998)
4. Bouyer, P., Fahrenberg, U., Larsen, K.G., Markey, N., Srba, J.: Infinite runs in weighted timed automata with energy constraints. In: Cassez, F., Jard, C. (eds.) FORMATS 2008. LNCS, vol. 5215, pp. 33–47. Springer, Heidelberg (2008). doi:10.1007/978-3-540-85778-5_4
5. Bouyer, P., Markey, N., Randour, M., Larsen, K.G., Laursen, S.: Average-energy games. In: Proceedings of GandALF 2015, pp. 1–15 (2015)
6. Brázdil, T., Brožek, V., Chatterjee, K., Forejt, V., Kučera, A.: Two views on multiple mean-payoff objectives in Markov decision processes. In: Proceedings of LICS 2011, pp. 33–42 (2011)

7. Brázdil, T., Brozek, V., Etessami, K., Kučera, A., Wojtczak, D.: One-counter Markov decision processes. In: Proceedings of SODA 2010, pp. 863–874. SIAM (2010)
8. Brázdil, T., Kiefer, S., Kučera, A.: Efficient analysis of probabilistic programs with an unbounded counter. J. ACM **61**(6), 41:1–41:35 (2014)
9. Brázdil, T., Kučera, A., Novotný, P.: Optimizing the Expected Mean Payoff in Energy Markov Decision Processes. CoRR abs/1607.00678 (2016)
10. Brenguier, R., Cassez, F., Raskin, J.F.: Energy and mean-payoff timed games. In: Proceedings of the 17th International Conference on Hybrid Systems: Computation and Control, HSCC 2014, pp. 283–292. ACM, New York (2014)
11. Brim, L., Chaloupka, J., Doyen, L., Gentilini, R., Raskin, J.: Faster algorithms for mean-payoff games. Formal Methods Syst. Des. **38**(2), 97–118 (2011)
12. Bruyère, V., Filiot, E., Randour, M., Raskin, J.F.: Meet your expectations with guarantees: beyond worst-case synthesis in quantitative games. In: Mayr, E.W., Portier, N. (eds.) STACS 2014. Leibniz International Proceedings in Informatics (LIPIcs), vol. 25, pp. 199–213. Schloss Dagstuhl–Leibniz-Zentrum fuer Informatik, Dagstuhl, Germany (2014)
13. Cachera, D., Fahrenberg, U., Legay, A.: An omega-algebra for real-time energy problems. In: Proceedings of FSTTCS 2015. LIPIcs, vol. 45, pp. 394–407. Schloss Dagstuhl–Leibniz-Zentrum fuer Informatik, Dagstuhl, Germany (2015)
14. Chakrabarti, A., Alfaro, L., Henzinger, T.A., Stoelinga, M.: Resource interfaces. In: Alur, R., Lee, I. (eds.) EMSOFT 2003. LNCS, vol. 2855, pp. 117–133. Springer, Heidelberg (2003). doi:10.1007/978-3-540-45212-6_9
15. Chatterjee, K., Doyen, L.: Energy parity games. In: Abramsky, S., Gavoille, C., Kirchner, C., Meyer auf der Heide, F., Spirakis, P.G. (eds.) ICALP 2010. LNCS, vol. 6199, pp. 599–610. Springer, Heidelberg (2010). doi:10.1007/978-3-642-14162-1_50
16. Chatterjee, K., Doyen, L., Henzinger, T., Raskin, J.: Generalized mean-payoff and energy games. In: Proceedings of FST & TCS 2010. LIPIcs, vol. 8, pp. 505–516. Schloss Dagstuhl–Leibniz-Zentrum fuer Informatik (2010)
17. Chatterjee, K., Komárková, Z., Křetínský, J.: Unifying two views on multiple mean-payoff objectives in Markov decision processes. In: Proceedings of LICS 2015, pp. 244–256 (2015)
18. Chatterjee, K., Henzinger, M.: Efficient and dynamic algorithms for alternating Büchi games and maximal end-component decomposition. J. ACM **61**(3), 15:1–15:40 (2014)
19. Chatterjee, K., Henzinger, M., Krinninger, S., Nanongkai, D.: Polynomial-time algorithms for energy games with special weight structures. Algorithmica **70**(3), 457–492 (2014)
20. Chatterjee, K., Randour, M., Raskin, J.F.: Strategy synthesis for multi-dimensional quantitative objectives. Acta Informatica **51**(3–4), 129–163 (2014)
21. Clemente, L., Raskin, J.F.: Multidimensional beyond worst-case and almost-sure problems for mean-payoff objectives. In: Proceedings of LICS 2015, pp. 257–268. IEEE Computer Society, Washington (2015)
22. Filar, J., Vrieze, K.: Competitive Markov Decision Processes. Springer-Verlag New York Inc., New York (1996)
23. Forejt, V., Kwiatkowska, M., Norman, G., Parker, D.: Automated verification techniques for probabilistic systems. In: Bernardo, M., Issarny, V. (eds.) SFM 2011. LNCS, vol. 6659, pp. 53–113. springer, Heidelberg (2011). doi:10.1007/978-3-642-21455-4_3

24. Gurvich, V., Karzanov, A., Khachiyan, L.: Cyclic games and an algorithm to find minimax cycle means in directed graphs. USSR Comput. Math. Math. Phys. **28**(5), 85–91 (1990)

25. Haase, C., Kiefer, S.: The odds of staying on budget. In: Halldórsson, M.M., Iwama, K., Kobayashi, N., Speckmann, B. (eds.) ICALP 2015. LNCS, vol. 9135, pp. 234–246. Springer, Heidelberg (2015). doi:10.1007/978-3-662-47666-6_19

26. Howard, R.: Dynamic Programming and Markov Processes. MIT Press, New York (1960)

27. Juhl, L., Guldstrand Larsen, K., Raskin, J.-F.: Optimal bounds for multiweighted and parametrised energy games. In: Liu, Z., Woodcock, J., Zhu, H. (eds.) Theories of Programming and Formal Methods. LNCS, vol. 8051, pp. 244–255. Springer, Heidelberg (2013). doi:10.1007/978-3-642-39698-4_15

28. Kitaev, M., Rykov, V.: Controlled Queueing Systems. CRC Press, Boca Raton (1995)

29. Kučera, A.: Playing games with counter automata. In: Finkel, A., Leroux, J., Potapov, I. (eds.) RP 2012. LNCS, vol. 7550, pp. 29–41. Springer, Heidelberg (2012). doi:10.1007/978-3-642-33512-9_4

30. Puterman, M.L.: Markov Decision Processes. Wiley-Interscience, Hoboken (2005)

31. Velner, Y., Chatterjee, K., Doyen, L., Henzinger, T., Rabinovich, A., Raskin, J.: The complexity of multi-mean-payoff and multi-energy games. Inf. Comput. **241**, 177–196 (2015)

32. Zwick, U., Paterson, M.: The complexity of mean payoff games on graphs. Theor. Comput. Sci. **158**(1&2), 343–359 (1996)

Parameter Synthesis for Markov Models: Faster Than Ever

Tim Quatmann[1], Christian Dehnert[1], Nils Jansen[2],
Sebastian Junges[1(✉)], and Joost-Pieter Katoen[1]

[1] RWTH Aachen University, Aachen, Germany
sebastian.junges@rwth-aachen.de
[2] University of Texas at Austin, Austin, USA

Abstract. We propose a conceptually simple technique for verifying probabilistic models whose transition probabilities are parametric. The key is to replace parametric transitions by nondeterministic choices of extremal values. Analysing the resulting parameter-free model using off-the-shelf means yields (refinable) lower and upper bounds on probabilities of regions in the parameter space. The technique outperforms the existing analysis of parametric Markov chains by several orders of magnitude regarding both run-time and scalability. Its beauty is its applicability to various probabilistic models. It in particular provides the first sound and feasible method for performing parameter synthesis of Markov decision processes.

1 Introduction

The key procedure in probabilistic model checking is computing reachability probabilities: What is the probability to reach some target state? For models exhibiting nondeterminism, such as Markov decision processes (MDPs), the probability to reach a state is subject to resolving the nondeterminism, and one considers minimal and maximal reachability probabilities. Model checkers support these procedures, e. g., PRISM [1] and iscasMc [2]. Successful applications to models of hundreds of millions of states have been reported, and extensions to stochastic games exist [3].

This paper treats *parameter synthesis* in Markov models. Given a model whose transition probabilities are (polynomials over) variables, and a reachability specification—e.g., the likelihood to reach a bad state should be below 10^{-6}—the parameter synthesis problem aims at finding all parameter values for which the parametric model satisfies the specification. In practise, this amounts to partition the parameter space into *safe* and *unsafe* regions with a large (say, >95 %) coverage. For a system in which components are subject to random failures, parameter synthesis is thus able to obtain the maximal tolerable failure probability of the components while ensuring the system's specification.

Parametric probabilistic models have various applications as witnessed by several recent works. Model repair [4] exploits parametric Markov chains (MCs) to tune the parameters of the model. In quality-of-service analysis of software,

C. Artho et al. (Eds.): ATVA 2016, LNCS 9938, pp. 50–67, 2016.
DOI: 10.1007/978-3-319-46520-3_4

parameters are used to model the unquantified estimation errors in log data [5]. Ceska *et al.* [6] consider the problem of synthesising rate parameters in stochastic biochemical networks. Parametric probabilistic models are also used to rank patches in the repair of software [7] and for computing perturbation bounds [8, 9]. The main problem though is that current parametric probabilistic model-checking algorithms cannot cope with the complexity of these applications. Their scalability is restricted to a couple of thousands of states and a few (preferably independent) parameters, and models with nondeterminism are out of reach. (The only existing algorithm [10] for parametric MDPs uses an unsound heuristic in its implementation to improve scalability.)

We present an algorithm that overcomes all these limitations: It is scalable to millions of states, several (dependent) parameters, and—perhaps most importantly—provides the first sound and feasible technique to do parameter synthesis of parametric MDPs.

The key technique used so far is computing a rational function (in terms of the parameters) expressing the reachability probability in a parametric MC. Tools like PARAM [11], PRISM [1], and PROPhESY [12] exploit (variants of) the state elimination approach by Daws [13] to obtain such a function which conceptually allows for many types of analysis. While state elimination is feasible for millions of states [12], it does not scale well in the number of different parameters. Moreover, the size of the obtained functions often limits the practicability as analysing the (potentially large) rational function via SMT solving [12] is often not feasible.

This paper takes a completely different approach: *Parameter lifting*. Consider the parametric MC in Fig. 1(a) modelling two subsequent tosses of a biased coin, where the probability for *heads* is x. Inspired by an observation made in [14] on continuous time Markov chains, we first equip each state with a fresh parameter, thus removing parameter dependencies; the outcome (referred to as *relaxation*) is depicted in Fig. 1(b). Now, for each function over these state parameters, we compute *extremal values*, i. e., maximal and minimal probabilities. The key idea is to replace the (parametric) probabilistic choice at each state by a *nondeterministic choice* between these extremal values; we call this *substitution*. This is exemplified in Fig. 1(c), assuming *heads* has a likelihood in $[0.3, 0.6]$. The resulting (non-parametric) model can be verified using off-the-shelf, efficient algorithms. Applying this procedure to a parametric MC (as in the example) yields a parameter-free MDP. Parameter lifting thus boils down to verify an MDP and

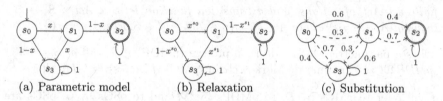

(a) Parametric model   (b) Relaxation   (c) Substitution

Fig. 1. Two biased coin tosses and the specification "First *heads* then *tails*".

avoids computing rational functions and SMT solving. The beauty of this technique is that it can be applied to parametric MDPs without much further ado. Parameter lifting of a parametric MDP yields a parameter-free two-player stochastic game (SG). SGs and MDPs can be solved using techniques such as value and policy iteration. Note that the theoretical complexity for solving MDPs is lower than for SGs.

This paper presents the details of parameter lifting, and proves the correctness for parametric Markov models whose parameters are given as *multi-affine polynomials*. This covers a rich class of models, e. g., the diverse set of parametric benchmarks available at the `PARAM` webpage are of this form. Experiments demonstrate the feasibility: The parameter lifting approach can treat Markov models of millions of states with thousands of parametric transitions. This applies to parametric MCs as well as MDPs. Parameter lifting achieves a parameter space coverage of at least 95% rather quickly. This is out of reach for competitive techniques such as SMT-based [12] and sampling-based [10] parameter synthesis.

2   Preliminaries

Let V be a finite set of *parameters* over the domain $\mathbb{R}$ ranged over by x, y, z. A *valuation* for V is a function $u\colon V \to \mathbb{R}$. Let $\mathbb{Q}_V$ denote the set of *multi-affine multivariate polynomials* f over V satisfying $f = \sum_{i \le m} a_i \cdot \prod_{x \in V_i} x$ for suitable $m \in \mathbb{N}$, $a_i \in \mathbb{Q}$, and $V_i \subseteq V$ (for $i \le m$). $\mathbb{Q}_V$ does not contain polynomials where a variable has a degree greater than 1, e. g., $x \cdot y \in \mathbb{Q}_V$ but $x^2 \notin \mathbb{Q}_V$. We write $f = 0$ if f can be reduced to 0, and $f \ne 0$ otherwise. Applying the valuation u to $f \in \mathbb{Q}_V$ results in a real number $f[u] \in \mathbb{R}$, obtained from f by replacing each occurrence of variable x in f by $u(x)$.

2.1   Probabilistic Models

We consider different types of parametric (discrete) probabilistic models. They can all be seen as transition systems (with a possible partition of the state space into two sets) where the transitions are labeled with polynomials in $\mathbb{Q}_V$.

Definition 1 (Parametric Probabilistic Models). *A parametric stochastic game (pSG) is a tuple $\mathfrak{M} = (S, V, s_I, Act, \mathcal{P})$ with a finite set S of states such that $S = S_\circ \uplus S_\square$, a finite set V of parameters over $\mathbb{R}$, an initial state $s_I \in S$, a finite set Act of actions, and a transition function $\mathcal{P}\colon S \times Act \times S \to \mathbb{Q}_V$ satisfying: $Act(s) \ne \emptyset$ where $Act(s) = \{\alpha \in Act \mid \exists s' \in S. \mathcal{P}(s, \alpha, s') \ne 0\}$.*

- *$\mathfrak{M}$ is a parametric Markov decision process (pMDP) if $S_\circ = \emptyset$ or $S_\square = \emptyset$.*
- *pMDP $\mathfrak{M}$ is a parametric Markov chain (pMC) if $|Act(s)| = 1$ for all $s \in S$.*

We will refer to pMCs by $\mathcal{D}$, to pMDPs by $\mathcal{M}$ and to pSGs by $\mathcal{G}$. pSGs are two-player parametric stochastic games involving players $\circ$ and $\square$ with states

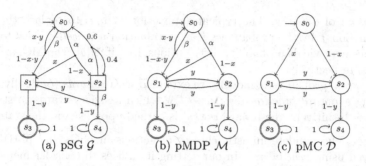

Fig. 2. The considered types of parametric probabilistic models.

in $S_\circ$ and $S_\square$, respectively, whose transition probabilities are represented by polynomials from $\mathbb{Q}_V$. The players *nondeterministically* choose an action at each state and the successors are intended to be determined *probabilistically* as defined by the transition function. $Act(s)$ is the set of *enabled* actions at state s. As $Act(s)$ is non-empty for all $s \in S$, there are no deadlock states. For state s and action α, we set $V_s^\alpha = \{x \in V \mid x \text{ occurs in } \mathcal{P}(s, \alpha, s') \text{ for some } s' \in S\}$.

pMDPs and pMCs are one- and zero-player parametric stochastic games, respectively. As pMCs have in fact just a single enabled action at each state, we omit this action in the notation and just write $\mathcal{P}(s, s')$ and V_s.

Example 1. Figure 2 depicts (a.) a pSG, (b.) a pMDP, and (c.) a pMC with parameters $\{x, y\}$. The states of the players $\circ$ and $\square$ are depicted with circles and rectangles, respectively. The initial state is indicated by an arrow; target states have double lines. We draw a transition from state s to s' and label it with α and $\mathcal{P}(s, \alpha, s')$ whenever $\mathcal{P}(s, \alpha, s') \neq 0$. If $|Act(s)| = 1$, the action is omitted.

Remark 1. In the literature [12, 15], the images of transition functions (of pMCs) are rational functions, i.e., fractions of polynomials. This is mainly motivated by the usage of state elimination for computing functions expressing reachability probabilities. As our approach does not rely on state elimination, the set of considered functions can be simplified. The restriction to polynomials in $\mathbb{Q}_V$ is realistic; *all* benchmarks from the PARAM webpage [16] are of this form. We will exploit this restriction in our proof of Theorem 1.

Definition 2 (Stochastic Game). *A pSG $\mathcal{G}$ is a* stochastic game (SG) *if $\mathcal{P}: S \times Act \times S \to [0, 1]$ and $\sum_{s' \in S} \mathcal{P}(s, \alpha, s') = 1$ for all $s \in S$ and $\alpha \in Act(s)$.*

Analogously, MCs and MDPs are defined as special cases of pMCs and pMDPs. Thus, a model is *parameter-free* if all transition probabilities are constant.

Valuations and Rewards. Applying a *valuation* u to parametric model $\mathfrak{M}$, denoted $\mathfrak{M}[u]$, replaces each polynomial f in $\mathfrak{M}$ by $f[u]$. We call $\mathfrak{M}[u]$ the *instantiation* of $\mathfrak{M}$ at u. The typical application of u is to replace the transition function f by the probability $f[u]$. A valuation u is *well-defined* for $\mathfrak{M}$ if the replacement yields probability distributions, i. e., if $\mathfrak{M}[u]$ is an MC, an MDP, or an SG, respectively.

Parametric probabilistic models are extended with *rewards* (or dually, costs) by adding a *reward function* rew: $S \to \mathbb{Q}_V$ which assigns rewards to states of the model. Intuitively, the reward $\text{rew}(s)$ is earned upon leaving the state s.

Schedulers. The nondeterministic choices of actions in pSGs and pMDPs can be resolved using *schedulers*[1]. In our setting it suffices to consider memoryless deterministic schedulers [17]. For more general definitions we refer to [18].

Definition 3 (Scheduler). *A scheduler for pMDP* $\mathcal{M} = (S, V, s_I, Act, \mathcal{P})$ *is a function* $\sigma: S \to Act$ *with* $\sigma(s) \in Act(s)$ *for all* $s \in S$.

Let $\mathfrak{S}(\mathcal{M})$ denote the set of all schedulers for $\mathcal{M}$. Applying a scheduler to a pMDP yields an *induced parametric Markov chain*, as all nondeterminism is resolved, i. e., the transition probabilities are obtained w. r. t. the choice of actions.

Definition 4 (Induced pMC). *For pMDP* $\mathcal{M} = (S, V, s_I, Act, \mathcal{P})$ *and scheduler* $\sigma \in \mathfrak{S}(\mathcal{M})$, *the pMC induced by* $\mathcal{M}$ *and* σ *is* $\mathcal{M}^\sigma = (S, V, s_I, \mathcal{P}^\sigma)$ *where*

$$\mathcal{P}^\sigma(s, s') = \mathcal{P}(s, \sigma(s), s') \quad \text{for all } s, s' \in S .$$

Resolving nondeterminism in an SG requires to have individual schedulers for each player. For $S_\circ$ and $S_\square$ we need schedulers $\sigma \in \mathfrak{S}_\circ(\mathcal{G})$ and $\rho \in \mathfrak{S}_\square(\mathcal{G})$ of the form $\sigma: S_\circ \to Act$ and $\rho: S_\square \to Act$. The induced pMC $\mathcal{G}^{\sigma,\rho}$ of a pSG $\mathcal{G}$ with schedulers σ and ρ for both players is defined analogously to the one for pMDPs.

Example 2. Reconsider the models $\mathcal{G}$, $\mathcal{M}$, and $\mathcal{D}$ as shown in Fig. 2. For schedulers σ, ρ with $\sigma(s_0) = \alpha$ and $\rho(s_2) = \beta$, the induced pMCs satisfy $\mathcal{G}^{\sigma,\rho} = \mathcal{M}^\rho = \mathcal{D}$.

2.2 Properties of Interest

As specifications we consider *reachability properties* and *expected reward properties*. We first define these properties on MCs and then discuss the other models.

Properties on MCs. For MC $\mathcal{D}$ with state space S, let $\text{Pr}_s^{\mathcal{D}}(\Diamond T)$ denote the probability to reach a set of target states $T \subseteq S$ from state $s \in S$ within $\mathcal{D}$; simply $\text{Pr}^{\mathcal{D}}(\Diamond T)$ refers to this specific probability for the initial state s_I. We use a standard probability measure on infinite paths through an MC as defined in [18, Ch. 10]. For threshold $\lambda \in [0, 1]$, the *reachability property* asserting that a target state is to be reached with probability at most λ is denoted $\varphi_{reach} = \mathbb{P}_{\leq\lambda}(\Diamond T)$. The property is satisfied by $\mathcal{D}$, written $\mathcal{D} \models \varphi_{reach}$, iff $\text{Pr}^{\mathcal{D}}(\Diamond T) \leq \lambda$. (Comparisons like $<$, $>$, and $\geq$ are treated in a similar way.)

---

[1] Also referred to as adversaries, strategies, or policies.

The reward of a path through an MC $\mathcal{D}$ until T is the sum of the rewards of the states visited along on the path before reaching T. The expected reward of a finite path is given by its probability times its reward. Given $\mathrm{Pr}^{\mathcal{D}}(\Diamond T) = 1$, the expected reward of reaching $T \subseteq S$, is the sum of the expected rewards of all paths to reach T. An expected reward property is satisfied if the expected reward of reaching T is bounded by a threshold $\kappa \in \mathbb{R}$. Formal definitions can be found in e.g., [18, ch. 10].

Properties on Nondeterministic Models. In order to define a probability measure for MDPs and SGs, the nondeterminism has to be resolved. A reachability property $\mathbb{P}_{\leq \lambda}(\Diamond T)$ is satisfied for an MDP $\mathcal{M}$ iff it holds for all induced MCs:

$$\mathcal{M} \models \mathbb{P}_{\leq \lambda}(\Diamond T) \iff \left(\max_{\sigma \in \mathfrak{S}(\mathcal{M})} \mathrm{Pr}^{\mathcal{M}^{\sigma}}(\Diamond T) \right) \leq \lambda.$$

Satisfaction of a property φ for an SG $\mathcal{G}$ depends on the objectives of both players. We write $\mathcal{G} \models_{\triangle} \varphi$ iff players in $\triangle \subseteq \{\circ, \square\}$ can enforce that φ holds, e. g.,

$$\mathcal{G} \models_{\{\circ\}} \mathbb{P}_{\leq \lambda}(\Diamond T) \iff \left(\min_{\sigma \in \mathfrak{S}_{\circ}(\mathcal{G})} \max_{\rho \in \mathfrak{S}_{\square}(\mathcal{G})} \mathrm{Pr}^{\mathcal{G}^{\sigma, \rho}}(\Diamond T) \right) \leq \lambda.$$

Computing the maximal (or minimal) probability to reach a set of target states from the initial state can be done using standard techniques, such as linear programming, value iteration or policy iteration [19].

The satisfaction relation for expected reward properties is defined analogously. As usual, we write $\mathfrak{M} \models \neg \varphi$ whenever $\mathfrak{M} \not\models \varphi$.

3   Regional Model Checking of Markov Chains

In the following, we consider sets of valuations that map each parameter to a value within a given interval. We present an approximative approach to check all instantiations of a pMC with respect to a valuation in such a set. This consists of three steps: Formalising regions and the considered problem, construction of the sound over-approximation, and reduction to an MDP problem.

3.1   Regions

Definition 5 (Region). *Given a set of parameters $V = \{x_1, \ldots x_n\}$ and rational parameter bounds $B(x_i) = \{b_1, b_2\}$. The parameter bounds induce a parameter interval $I(x_i) = [b_1, b_2]$ with $b_1 \leq b_2$. The set of valuations $\{u \mid \forall x_i \in V. u(x_i) \in I(x_i)\}$ is called a region (for V).*

The regions we consider correspond to $\times_{x \in V} I(x)$, i. e., they are *hyperrectangles*.

We aim to identify sets of instantiated models by regions. That is, regions represent instantiations $\mathfrak{M}[u]$ of a parametric model $\mathfrak{M}$. As these instantiations are only well-defined under some restrictions, we lift these restrictions to regions.

Definition 6 (Well-Defined Region). *Let $\mathfrak{M}$ be a parametric model. A region r for V is well-defined for $\mathfrak{M}$ if for all $u \in r$ it holds that u is well-defined for $\mathfrak{M}$, and for all polynomials f in $\mathfrak{M}$ either $f = 0$ or $f[u] > 0$.*

The first condition says that $\mathfrak{M}[u]$ is a probabilistic model (SG, MC, or MDP) while the second one ensures that $\mathfrak{M}[u]$ and $\mathfrak{M}$ have the same topology.

Example 3. Let $\mathcal{D}$ be the pMC in Fig. 3(a), the region $r = [0.1, 0.8] \times [0.4, 0.7]$ and the valuation $u = (0.8, 0.6) \in r$. Figure 3(b) depicts the instantiation $\mathcal{D}[u]$, which is an MC as defined in Sect. 2.1 with the same topology as $\mathcal{D}$. As this holds for all possible instantiations $\mathcal{D}[u']$ with $u' \in r$, region r is well-defined. The region $r' = [0, 1] \times [0, 1]$ is not well-defined as, e. g., the valuation $(0, 0) \in r'$ results in an MC that has no transition from s_1 to s_2.

Our aim is to prove that a property φ holds *for all instantiations* of a parametric model $\mathfrak{M}$ which are represented by a region r, i. e., $\mathfrak{M}, r \models \varphi$ defined as follows.

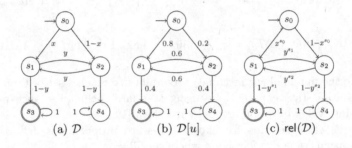

Fig. 3. A pMC $\mathcal{D}$, some instantiation $\mathcal{D}[u]$ and the relaxation $\mathrm{rel}(\mathcal{D})$.

Definition 7 (Satisfaction Relation for Regions). *For a parametric model $\mathfrak{M}$, a well-defined region r, and a property φ, the relation $\models$ is defined as*

$$\mathfrak{M}, r \models \varphi \iff \mathfrak{M}[u] \models \varphi \text{ for all } u \in r.$$

Notice that $\mathfrak{M}, r \not\models \varphi$ implies $\mathfrak{M}[u] \not\models \varphi$ for *some* $u \in r$. This differs from $\mathfrak{M}, r \models \neg\varphi$ which implies $\mathfrak{M}[u] \not\models \varphi$ for *all* $u \in r$. If $\mathfrak{M}$ and φ are clear from the context, we will call region r *safe* if $\mathfrak{M}, r \models \varphi$ and *unsafe* if $\mathfrak{M}, r \models \neg\varphi$.

Let $\mathcal{D} = (S, V, s_I, \mathcal{P})$ be a pMC, r a region that is *well-defined* for $\mathcal{D}$, and $\varphi_{reach} = \mathbb{P}_{\leq\lambda}(\Diamond T)$ a reachability property. We want to infer that r is safe (or unsafe). We do this by considering the *maximal (or minimal) possible reachability probability* over all valuations u from r. We give the equivalences for safe regions:

$$\mathcal{D}, r \models \varphi_{reach} \iff \left(\max_{u \in r} \Pr^{\mathcal{D}[u]}(\Diamond T) \right) \leq \lambda$$

$$\mathcal{D}, r \models \neg\varphi_{reach} \iff \left(\min_{u \in r} \Pr^{\mathcal{D}[u]}(\Diamond T) \right) > \lambda$$

Remark 2. As shown in [13], $\Pr^{\mathcal{D}[u]}(\lozenge T)$ can be expressed as a rational function $f = g_1/g_2$ with polynomials g_1, g_2. As r is well-defined, $g_2(u) \neq 0$ for all $u \in r$. Therefore, f is continuous on the closed set r. Hence, there is always a valuation that induces the maximal (or minimal) reachability probability:

$$\sup_{u \in r} \Pr^{\mathcal{D}[u]}(\lozenge T) = \max_{u \in r} \Pr^{\mathcal{D}[u]}(\lozenge T)$$

$$\text{and } \inf_{u \in r} \Pr^{\mathcal{D}[u]}(\lozenge T) = \min_{u \in r} \Pr^{\mathcal{D}[u]}(\lozenge T) \, .$$

Example 4. Reconsider the pMC $\mathcal{D}$ in Fig. 3(a) and region $r = [0.1, 0.8] \times [0.4, 0.7]$. We look for a valuation $u \in r$ that maximises $\Pr^{\mathcal{D}[u]}(\lozenge\{s_3\})$, i.e., the probability to reach s_3 from s_0. Notice that s_4 is the only state from which we cannot reach s_3, furthermore, s_4 is only reachable via s_2. Hence, it is best to avoid s_2. For the parameter x it follows that the value $u(x)$ should be as high as possible, i.e., $u(x) = 0.8$. Consider state s_1: As we want to reach s_3, the value of y should be preferably low. On the other hand, from s_2, y should be assigned a high value as we want to avoid s_4. Thus, it requires a thorough analysis to find an optimal value for y, due to the trade-off for the reachability probabilities from s_1 and s_2.

3.2   Relaxation

The idea of our approach, inspired by [14], is to drop these dependencies by means of a *relaxation* of the problem in order to ease finding an optimal valuation.

Definition 8 (Relaxation). *The* relaxation *of pMC $\mathcal{D} = (S, V, s_I, \mathcal{P})$ is the pMC* $rel(\mathcal{D}) = (S, rel_{\mathcal{D}}(V), s_I, \mathcal{P}')$ *with* $rel_{\mathcal{D}}(V) = \{x_i^s \mid x_i \in V, s \in S\}$ *and* $\mathcal{P}'(s, s') = \mathcal{P}(s, s')[x_1, \ldots, x_n/x_1^s, \ldots, x_n^s]$.

Intuitively, the relaxation $rel(\mathcal{D})$ arises from $\mathcal{D}$ by equipping each state with its own parameters and thereby eliminating parameter dependencies. We extend a valuation u for $\mathcal{D}$ to the *relaxed valuation* $rel_{\mathcal{D}}(u)$ for $rel(\mathcal{D})$ by $rel_{\mathcal{D}}(u)(x_i^s) = u(x_i)$ for every s. We have that for all u, $\mathcal{D}[u] = \mathcal{D}[rel_{\mathcal{D}}(u)]$. We lift the relaxation to regions such that $B(x_i^s) = B(x_i)$ for all s, i.e., $rel_{\mathcal{D}}(r) = {\times}_{x_i^s \in rel_{\mathcal{D}}(V)} B(x_i)$. We drop the subscript $\mathcal{D}$, whenever it is clear from the context.

Example 5. Fig. 3(c) depicts the relaxation $rel(\mathcal{D})$ of the pMC $\mathcal{D}$ from Fig. 3(a). For $r = [0.1, 0.8] \times [0.4, 0.7]$ and $u = (0.8, 0.6) \in r$ from Example 3, we obtain $rel(r) = [0.1, 0.8] \times [0.4, 0.7] \times [0.4, 0.7]$ and $rel(u) = (0.8, 0.6, 0.6)$. The instantiation $rel(\mathcal{D})[rel(u)]$ corresponds to $\mathcal{D}[u]$ as depicted in Fig. 3(b). Notice that the relaxed region $rel(r)$ contains also valuations, e.g., $(0.8, 0.5, 0.6)$ which give rise to instantiations which are not realisable by valuations in r.

For a pMC $\mathcal{D}$ and a region r that is well-defined for $\mathcal{D}$, notice that $\{\mathcal{D}[u] \mid u \in r\} \subseteq \{rel(\mathcal{D})[u] \mid u \in rel(r)\}$. Due to the fact that $rel(\mathcal{D})$ is an over-approximation of $\mathcal{D}$, the maximal reachability probability over all instantiations of $\mathcal{D}$ within r is at most as high as the one for all instantiations of $rel(\mathcal{D})$ within $rel(r)$.

Lemma 1. *For pMC $\mathcal{D}$ and well-defined region r, we have*

$$\max_{u \in r}\left(\Pr^{\mathcal{D}[u]}(\Diamond T)\right) = \max_{u \in r}\left(\Pr^{rel(\mathcal{D})[rel(u)]}(\Diamond T)\right) \leq \max_{u \in rel(r)}\left(\Pr^{rel(\mathcal{D})[u]}(\Diamond T)\right).$$

Thus, if the relaxation satisfies a reachability property, so does the original pMC.

Corollary 1. *Given a pMC $\mathcal{D}$ and a well-defined region r it holds that*

$$\max_{u \in rel(r)}\left(\Pr^{rel(\mathcal{D})[u]}(\Diamond T)\right) \leq \lambda \; implies \; \mathcal{D}, r \models \mathbb{P}_{\leq \lambda}(\Diamond T).$$

Note that the relaxation does not aggravate the problem for our setting. In fact, although $rel(\mathcal{D})$ has (usually) much more parameters than $\mathcal{D}$, it is intuitively easier to find a valuation $u \in rel(r)$ that maximises the reachability probability: For some $x_i^s \in rel(V)$, we can always pick a value in $I(x_i^s)$ that maximises the probability to reach T from state s. There is no (negative) effect for the reachability probability at the remaining states as x_i^s only occurs at s.

Recall that the functions f occurring in $rel(\mathcal{D})$ are of the form $f = \sum_{i \leq m} a_i \cdot \prod_{x \in V_i} x$ (with $a_i \in \mathbb{Q}$ and $V_i \subseteq rel(V)$). Finding a valuation that maximises the reachability probability becomes especially easy for this setting: We only need to consider valuations u that set the value of each parameter to either the lowest or highest possible value, i.e., $u(x_i^s) \in B(x_i^s)$ for all $x_i^s \in rel(V)$. This important result is stated as follows.

Theorem 1. *Let $\mathcal{D}$ be a pMC, r be a well-defined region, and $T \subseteq S$ be a set of target states. There is a valuation $u' \in rel(r)$ satisfying $u'(x_i^s) \in B(x_i^s)$ for all $x_i^s \in rel(V)$ such that $\Pr^{rel(\mathcal{D})[u']}(\Diamond T) = \max_{u \in rel(r)} \Pr^{rel(\mathcal{D})[u]}(\Diamond T)$.*

We prove this by showing that any valuation which assigns some variable to something other than its bound can be modified such that the variable is assigned to its bound, without decreasing the induced reachability probability. The full proof including an illustrating example is given in [20].

3.3 Substituting Parameters with Nondeterminism

We have now seen that, in order to determine $\max_{u \in rel(r)} \Pr^{rel(\mathcal{D})[u]}(\Diamond T)$, we have to make a discrete choice over valuations $v \colon rel(V) \to \mathbb{R}$ with $v(x_i^s) \in B(x_i)$. This choice can be made locally at every state, which brings us to the key idea of *constructing a (non-parametric) MDP out of the pMC $\mathcal{D}$ and the region r*, where nondeterministic choices represent all valuations that need to be considered.

Definition 9 (Substitution-pMC). *An MDP $sub_r(\mathcal{D}) = (S, s_I, Act_{sub}, \mathcal{P}_{sub})$ is the (parameter-)substitution of a pMC $\mathcal{D} = (S, V, s_I, \mathcal{P})$ and a region r if $Act_{sub} = \biguplus_{s \in S}\{v \colon V_s \to \mathbb{R} \mid v(x_i) \in B(x_i)\}$ and*

$$\mathcal{P}_{sub}(s, v, s') = \begin{cases} \mathcal{P}(s, s')[v] & if \; v \in Act(s), \\ 0 & otherwise. \end{cases}$$

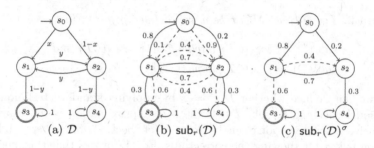

Fig. 4. Illustrating parameter-substitution.

Thus, choosing action v in s corresponds to assigning the extremal values $B(x_i)$ to the parameters x_i^s. The number of outgoing actions for s is therefore $2^{|V_s|}$.

Example 6. Consider pMC $\mathcal{D}$ – depicted in Fig. 4(a) – with $r = [0.1, 0.8] \times [0.4, 0.7]$ as before. The substitution of $\mathcal{D}$ on r is shown in Fig. 4(b). In $\mathcal{D}$, each outgoing transition of states s_0, s_1, s_2 is replaced by a nondeterministic choice in $\mathsf{sub}_r(\mathcal{D})$. That is, we either pick the upper or lower bound for the corresponding variable. The solid (dashed) lines depict transitions that belong to the action for the upper (lower) bound. For the states s_3 and s_4 there is no choice, as their outgoing transitions in $\mathcal{D}$ are constant. Figure 4(c) depicts the MC $\mathsf{sub}_r(\mathcal{D})^\sigma$ which is induced by the scheduler σ on $\mathsf{sub}_{\mathcal{D}}(r)$ that chooses the upper bounds at s_0 and s_2, and the lower bound at s_1. Notice that $\mathsf{sub}_r(\mathcal{D})^\sigma$ coincides with $\mathsf{rel}(\mathcal{D})[v]$ for a suitable valuation v, as depicted in Fig. 3(c).

First, observe that the nondeterministic choices introduced by the substitution only depend on the values $B(x_i)$ of the parameters x_i in r. Since the ranges of the parameters x_i^s in $\mathsf{rel}(r)$ agree with the range of x_i in r, we have

$$\mathsf{sub}_{\mathsf{rel}(r)}(\mathsf{rel}(\mathcal{D})) = \mathsf{sub}_r(\mathcal{D}) \quad \text{for all well-defined } r. \tag{1}$$

Second, note that the substitution encodes the local choices for a relaxed pMC. That is, for an arbitrary pMC, there is a one-to-one correspondence between schedulers $\sigma \in \mathfrak{S}(\mathsf{sub}_{\mathsf{rel}(r)}(\mathsf{rel}(\mathcal{D})))$ and valuations $v \in \mathsf{rel}(r)$ for $\mathsf{rel}(\mathcal{D})$ with $v(x_i^s) \in B(x_i)$. Combining the observations with Theorem 1, yields the following.

Corollary 2. *For a pMC $\mathcal{D}$, a well-defined region r and a set of target states T of $\mathcal{D}$:*

$$\max_{u \in r} \mathrm{Pr}^{\mathcal{D}[u]}(\lozenge T) \leq \max_{\sigma \in \mathfrak{S}} \mathrm{Pr}^{\mathsf{sub}_{\mathsf{rel}(r)}(\mathsf{rel}(\mathcal{D}))^\sigma}(\lozenge T) = \max_{\sigma \in \mathfrak{S}} \mathrm{Pr}^{\mathsf{sub}_r(\mathcal{D})^\sigma}(\lozenge T)$$

$$\min_{u \in r} \mathrm{Pr}^{\mathcal{D}[u]}(\lozenge T) \geq \min_{\sigma \in \mathfrak{S}} \mathrm{Pr}^{\mathsf{sub}_{\mathsf{rel}(r)}(\mathsf{rel}(\mathcal{D}))^\sigma}(\lozenge T) = \min_{\sigma \in \mathfrak{S}} \mathrm{Pr}^{\mathsf{sub}_r(\mathcal{D})^\sigma}(\lozenge T)$$

As a direct consequence of this, we can state Theorem 2.

Theorem 2. *Let $\mathcal{D}$ be a pMC, r be a well-defined region. Then*

$$sub_r(\mathcal{D}) \models \mathbb{P}_{\leq\lambda}(\lozenge T) \text{ implies } \mathcal{D}, r \models \mathbb{P}_{\leq\lambda}(\lozenge T) \text{ and}$$
$$sub_r(\mathcal{D}) \models \mathbb{P}_{>\lambda}(\lozenge T) \text{ implies } \mathcal{D}, r \models \neg\mathbb{P}_{\leq\lambda}(\lozenge T).$$

Hence, we can deduce whether $\mathcal{D}, r \models \varphi$ by applying standard techniques for MDP model checking to $sub_r(\mathcal{D})$. If the over-approximation is too coarse for a conclusive answer, regions can be refined (cf. Sect. 5). Moreover, while the relaxation is key for showing the correctness, Eq. (1) proves that this step does not actually need to be performed.

Example 7. Reconsider Example 6. From $sub_r(\mathcal{D})$ in Fig. 4(b), we can derive $\max_{\sigma\in\mathfrak{S}} \Pr^{sub_r(\mathcal{D})^\sigma}(\lozenge T) = {}^{47}/_{60}$ and, by Theorem 2, $\mathcal{D}, r \models \mathbb{P}_{\leq 0.8}(\lozenge T)$ follows. Despite the large considered region, we were able to establish a non-trivial upper bound on the reachability probability over all valuations in r.

Expected Reward Properties. The notions above can be applied to perform regional model checking of pMCs and expected reward properties. Regions have to be further restricted such that: $\Pr^{\mathcal{D}[u]}(\lozenge T) = 1$ for all $u \in r$ – to ensure that the expected reward is defined – and, for transition-rewards, reward-parameters and probability-parameters have to be disjoint. We can then generalise relaxation and substitution to the reward models, and obtain analogous results.

4   Regional Checking of Models with Nondeterminism

In the last section we showed how to bound reachability probabilities of pMCs from below and above. Introducing nondeterministic choices between these bounds enabled to utilise standard MDP model checking for the parameter synthesis. This approach can readily be generalised to systems originally exhibiting nondeterminism. In particular, for pMDPs this adds choices over valuations (inherent to parameters) to the choices over actions (inherent to MDPs). This new nondeterminism leads to a game with two players: One for the nondeterminism of the MDP and one for the abstracted parameters, yielding a stochastic game.

In the following, let $\mathcal{M} = (S, V, s_I, Act, \mathcal{P})$ be a pMDP and r a well-defined region for $\mathcal{M}$. We want to analyse r for all scheduler-induced pMCs $\mathcal{M}^\sigma$ of $\mathcal{M}$.

Example 8. Consider the pMDP $\mathcal{M}$ in Fig. 5(a), where state s has two enabled actions α and β. The scheduler σ given by $\{s \mapsto \alpha\}$ applied to $\mathcal{M}$ yields a pMC, which is subject to substitution, cf. Fig. 3(b).

The parameter substitution of a pMDP (cf. Fig. 5(a)) yields an SG—as in Fig. 5(d). It represents, for all schedulers of the pMDP, the substitution of each induced pMC. For the construction of the substitution, we first introduce intermediate states to separate nondeterministic actions from probabilistic choices in two steps:

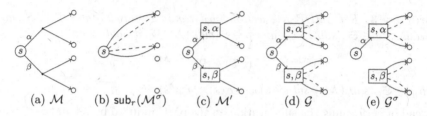

(a) $\mathcal{M}$ (b) $\mathsf{sub}_r(\mathcal{M}^\sigma)$ (c) $\mathcal{M}'$ (d) $\mathcal{G}$ (e) $\mathcal{G}^\sigma$

Fig. 5. Illustration of the substitution of a pMDP.

- Split each state $s \in S$ into $\{s\} \uplus \{\langle s, \alpha \rangle \mid \alpha \in Act(s)\}$.
- For $s \in S$ and $\alpha \in Act(s)$, add a transition with probability one from s to $\langle s, \alpha \rangle$ and move the probabilistic choice at s w.r.t. α to $\langle s, \alpha \rangle$.

We obtain a pMDP as in Fig. 5(c) where state s has pure *nondeterministic* choices leading to states of the form $\langle s, \alpha \rangle$ with pure *probabilistic* choices. The subsequent substitution on the probabilistic states yields the stochastic game, where one player represents the nondeterminism of the original pMDP, while the other player decides whether parameters should be set to their lower or upper bound. Formally, the game $\mathcal{G} = \mathsf{sub}_r(\mathcal{M})$ is defined as follows.

Definition 10 (Substitution-pMDP). *Given a pMDP $\mathcal{M} = (S, V, s_I, Act, \mathcal{P})$ and a region r, an SG $\mathsf{sub}_r(\mathcal{M}) = (S_\circ \uplus S_\square, s_I, Act_{sub}, \mathcal{P}_{sub})$ with $S_\circ = S$ and $S_\square = \{\langle s, \alpha \rangle \mid \alpha \in Act(s)\}$ is the* (parameter-)substitution *of $\mathcal{M}$ and r if $Act_{sub} = Act \uplus \left(\biguplus_{\langle s, \alpha \rangle \in S_\square} Act_s^\alpha \right)$ with $Act_s^\alpha = \{v \colon V_s^\alpha \to \mathbb{R} \mid v(x_i) \in B(x_i)\}$ and*

$$\mathcal{P}_{sub}(t, \beta, t') = \begin{cases} 1 & \text{if } t \in S_\circ \text{ and } t' = \langle t, \beta \rangle \in S_\square, \\ \mathcal{P}(s, \alpha, t')[\beta] & \text{if } t = \langle s, \alpha \rangle \in S_\square, \beta \in Act_s^\alpha, \text{ and } t' \in S_\circ, \\ 0 & \text{otherwise.} \end{cases}$$

We now relate the obtained stochastic game $\mathcal{G} = \mathsf{sub}_r(\mathcal{M})$ under different schedulers for player $\circ$ with the substitution in the scheduler-induced pMCs of $\mathcal{M}$. We observe that the schedulers $\sigma \in \mathfrak{S}_\circ(\mathcal{G})$ for player $\circ$ coincide with the schedulers in $\mathcal{M}$. Consider $\mathcal{G}^\sigma$ with $\sigma \in \mathfrak{S}_\circ(\mathcal{G})$ which arises from $\mathcal{G}$ by erasing transitions not agreeing with σ, i.e., we set all $\mathcal{P}_\mathcal{G}(s, \alpha, \langle s, \alpha \rangle)$ with $s \in S_\circ$ and $\alpha \neq \sigma(s)$ to zero. Note that $\mathcal{G}^\sigma$ is an MDP as at each state of player $\circ$, only one action is enabled and therefore only player $\square$ has nondeterministic choices.

Example 9. Continuing Example 8, applying scheduler σ to $\mathcal{G}$ yields $\mathcal{G}^\sigma$, see Fig. 5(e). The MDP $\mathcal{G}^\sigma$ matches the MDP $\mathsf{sub}_r(\mathcal{M}^\sigma)$ apart from intermediate states of the form $\langle s, \alpha \rangle$: The state s in $\mathsf{sub}_r(\mathcal{M}^\sigma)$ has the same outgoing transitions as the state $\langle s, \alpha \rangle$ in $\mathcal{G}^\sigma$ and $\langle s, \alpha \rangle$ is the unique successor of s in $\mathcal{G}^\sigma$.

Note that $\mathcal{G}^\sigma$ and $\mathsf{sub}_r(\mathcal{M}^\sigma)$ induce the same reachability probabilities. Formally:

Corollary 3. *For pMDP $\mathcal{M}$, well-defined region r, target states $T \subseteq S$, and schedulers $\sigma \in \mathfrak{S}_\circ(sub_r(\mathcal{M}))$ and $\rho \in \mathfrak{S}(sub_r(\mathcal{M}^\sigma))$, it holds that*

$$\mathrm{Pr}^{(sub_r(\mathcal{M}^\sigma))^\rho}(\Diamond T) = \mathrm{Pr}^{sub_r(\mathcal{M})^{\sigma,\widehat{\rho}}}(\Diamond T)$$

with $\widehat{\rho} \in \mathfrak{S}_\square(sub_r(\mathcal{M}))$ satisfies $\widehat{\rho}(\langle s, \sigma(s)\rangle) = \rho(s)$.

Instead of performing the substitution on the pMC induced by $\mathcal{M}$ and σ, we can perform the substitution on $\mathcal{M}$ directly and preserve the reachability probability.

Theorem 3. *Let $\mathcal{M}$ be a pMDP, r be a well-defined region. Then*

$$sub_r(\mathcal{M}) \models_\emptyset \mathbb{P}_{\leq\lambda}(\Diamond T) \ implies \ \mathcal{M}, r \models \mathbb{P}_{\leq\lambda}(\Diamond T), \ and$$
$$sub_r(\mathcal{M}) \models_{\{\circ\}} \mathbb{P}_{>\lambda}(\Diamond T) \ implies \ \mathcal{M}, r \models \neg\mathbb{P}_{\leq\lambda}(\Diamond T).$$

Therefore, analogously to the pMC case (cf. Theorem 2), we can derive whether $sub_r(\mathcal{M}) \models \varphi$ by analysing a stochastic game. The formal proof is in [20].

5   Parameter Synthesis

In this section we briefly discuss how the regional model checking is embedded into a complete parameter space partitioning framework as, e. g., described in [12]. The goal is to partition the parameter space into *safe* and *unsafe* regions (cf. Sect. 3.1). From a practical point of view, yielding a 100 % coverage of the parameter space is not realistic; instead a large coverage (say, 95 %) is aimed at.

We discuss the complete chain for a pMDP $\mathcal{M}$ and a property φ. In addition, a well-defined region R is given which serves as *parameter space*. Recall that a region $r \subseteq R$ is safe or unsafe if $\mathcal{M}, r \models \varphi$ or $\mathcal{M}, r \models \neg\varphi$, respectively. Note that parameter space partitioning is also applicable if only parts of R are well-defined, as well-definedness of a region is effectively decidable and such (sub-)regions can simply be tagged as *not defined* and treated as being inconclusive.

As a *preprocessing* step, the input model is simplified by reducing its state space. First, *bisimulation minimisation* for parametric probabilistic models [15] is used. Then, *state elimination* [13] is applied to all states with $V_s^\alpha = \emptyset$ and $|Act(s)| = 1$. We then construct the parameter-substitution of the model. As the topology of the substitution is independent of the region, for checking multiple regions we simply substitute the probabilities according to the region of interest.

Now, using a heuristic from the parameter space partitioning framework, we determine a candidate region. A naive heuristic would be to start with R, and then to split inconclusive regions along each dimension recursively – as in [10], thereby reducing the over-approximation. More evolved heuristics apply some instantiations of the model to construct candidate regions [12].

For a candidate region $r \subseteq R$, regional model checking (Sects. 3 and 4) determines it to be safe or unsafe. Moreover, the result for a region may be *inconclusive*, which might occur if r is neither safe nor unsafe, but also if the approximation was too coarse. The procedure stops as soon as a sufficiently large area of the parameter space R has been classified into safe and unsafe regions.

6   Experimental Evaluation

We implemented and analysed the *parameter lifting algorithm* (PLA) as described in Sects. 3 and 4. Moreover, we connected the implementation with the parameter synthesis framework PROPhESY [12].

Setup. We implemented PLA in C++. Solving the resulting non-parametric systems is done via value iteration (using sparse matrices) with a precision of $\varepsilon = 10^{-6}$. We evaluated the performance and compared it to parameter space partitioning in PARAM and in PRISM, both based on [10] and using an unsound heuristic in the implementation. The experiments were conducted on an HP BL685C G7, 48 cores, 2.0 GHz each, and 192 GB of RAM. We restricted the RAM to 30 GB and set a time-out of one hour for all experiments. Our PLA implementation used a single core only. We consider the well-known pMC and pMDP benchmarks from [16]. We additionally translated existing MDPs for a semi-autonomous vehicle [21] and the zeroconf protocol [22] into pMDPs, cf. [20]. For each instance, we analysed the parameter space $R = [10^{-5}, 1-10^{-5}]^{\#\mathrm{pars}}$ until 95 % is classified as safe or unsafe. Regions for which no decisive result was found were split into equally large regions, thus mimicking the behaviour of [10]. We also compared PLA to the SMT-based synthesis for pMCs in [12]. However, using naive heuristics for determining region candidates, the SMT solver often spent too much time for checking certain regions. For the desired coverage of 95 %, this led to timeouts for all tested benchmarks.

Results. The results are summarised in Table 1, listing the benchmark set and the particular instance. Further columns reflect whether a reachability or an expected reward property was checked ($\mathbb{P}$ vs. $\mathbb{E}$) and the number of *parameters*, *states* and *transitions*. We used the properties as given in their sources, for details see [20]. We ran PLA in two different settings: With strong bisimulation minimisation (*bisim*) and without (*direct*). We list the number of considered *regions*, i. e., those required to cover >95 % of the parameter space, and the required run time in seconds for the complete verification task, including model building and preprocessing. For PRISM, we give the fastest run time producing a correct result out of 30 different possible configurations, differing in the performed bisimulation minimisation (none, strong, weak), how inconclusive regions are split (each or longest edge), and the order of states (all except "random"). The PRISM implementation was superior to the PARAM implementation in all cases. The sound variant of PRISM and PARAM would require SMT calls similar to [12], decreasing their performance.

To evaluate the approximation quality, we additionally ran PLA for 625 equally large regions that were not refined in the case of indecisive results. We depict detailed results for a selection in Table 2, where we denote model, instance, property type, number of parameters, states and transitions as in Table 2. Column *#par trans* lists the number of transitions labeled with a non-constant function. Running times are given in column t. Next, we show the percentage of regions that our approach could conclusively identify as safe or unsafe. For the remaining regions, we sampled the model at the corner points to analyse the

Table 1. Runtimes of synthesis on different benchmark models.

	Benchmark	Instance	φ	#Pars	#States	#Trans	PLA #Regions	Direct	Bisim	PRISM Best
pMC	brp	(256,5)	$\mathbb{P}$	2	19 720	26 627	37	**6**	14	TO
		(4096,5)	$\mathbb{P}$	2	315 400	425 987	13	**233**	TO	TO
		(256,5)	$\mathbb{E}$	2	20 744	27 651	195	**8**	15	TO
		(4096,5)	$\mathbb{E}$	2	331 784	442 371	195	502	**417**	TO
		(16,5)	$\mathbb{E}$	4	1 304	1 731	1 251 220	2 764	**1 597**	TO
		(32,5)	$\mathbb{E}$	4	2 600	3 459	1 031 893	TO	**2 722**	TO
		(256,5)	$\mathbb{E}$	4	20 744	27 651	–	TO	TO	TO
	crowds	(10,5)	$\mathbb{P}$	2	104 512	246 082	123	17	**6**	2038
		(15,7)	$\mathbb{P}$	2	8 364 409	25 108 729	116	1 880	**518**	TO
		(20,7)	$\mathbb{P}$	2	45 421 597	164 432 797	119	TO	**2 935**	TO
	nand	(10,5)	$\mathbb{P}$	2	35 112	52 647	469	**22**	30	TO[a]
		(25,5)	$\mathbb{P}$	2	865 592	1 347 047	360	**735**	2 061	TO
pMDP	brp	(256,5)	$\mathbb{P}$	2	40 721	55 143	37	**35**	3 359	TO
		(4096,5)	$\mathbb{P}$	2	647 441	876 903	13	**3 424**	TO	TO
	consensus	(2,2)	$\mathbb{P}$	2	272	492	119	**<1**	<1	31[a]
		(2,32)	$\mathbb{P}$	2	4 112	7 692	108	**113**	141	TO[a]
		(4,2)	$\mathbb{P}$	4	22 656	75 232	6 125	**1 866**	2 022	TO[a]
		(4,4)	$\mathbb{P}$	4	43 136	144 352	–	TO	TO	TO[a]
	sav	(6,2,2)	$\mathbb{P}$	2	379	1 127	162	**<1**	<1	TO[a]
		(100,10,10)	$\mathbb{P}$	2	1 307 395	6 474 535	37	**1 612**	TO	TO
		(6,2,2)	$\mathbb{P}$	4	379	1 127	621 175	944	**917**	TO[a]
		(10,3,3)	$\mathbb{P}$	4	1 850	6 561	–	TO	TO	TO[a]
	zeroconf	(2)	$\mathbb{P}$	2	88 858	203 550	186	**86**	1 295	TO
		(5)	$\mathbb{P}$	2	494 930	1 133 781	403	**2 400**	TO	TO

[a]The fastest PRISM configuration gave an incorrect answer

Table 2. Results for classification of a constant number of regions.

		Instance	φ	#Pars	#States	#Trans	#Par trans	t	Safe	Unsafe	Neither	Unkn
pMC	Brp	(256,5)	$\mathbb{E}$	2	20 744	27 651	13 814	**51**	14.9 %	79.2 %	**5.8%**	0.2%
		(256,5)	$\mathbb{E}$	4	20 744	27 651	13 814	**71**	7.5 %	51.0 %	**40.6%**	0.8%
	Crowds	(10,5)	$\mathbb{P}$	2	104 512	246 082	51 480	**44**	54.4 %	41.1 %	**4.2%**	0.3%
	Nand	(10,5)	$\mathbb{P}$	2	35 112	52 647	25 370	**21**	21.4 %	68.5 %	**6.9%**	3.2%
pMDP	brp	(256,5)	$\mathbb{P}$	2	40 721	55 143	27 800	**153**	6.6 %	90.4 %	**3.0%**	0.0%
	Consensus	(4,2)	$\mathbb{P}$	4	22 656	75 232	29 376	**357**	2.6 %	87.0 %	**10.4%**	0.0%
	Aav	(6,2,2)	$\mathbb{P}$	4	379	1 127	552	**2**	44.0 %	15.4 %	**35.4%**	5.3%
	Zeroconf	(2)	$\mathbb{P}$	2	88 858	203 550	80 088	**186**	16.6 %	77.3 %	**5.6%**	0.5%

approximation error. Column *neither* gives the percentage of regions for which the property is neither always satisfied, nor always violated (as obtained from the sampling). In these cases, the inconclusive result is not caused by the approximation error but by the region selection. Finally, the fraction of the remaining regions for which it is still unknown if they are safe, unsafe or neither is given in column *unkn*.

Observations. PLA outperforms existing approaches by several orders of magnitude. We see two major reasons. First, the approach exploits the structure of parametric models, in which transition probabilities are usually described by simple functions. This is a major benefit over state-elimination based approaches where any structure is lost. Secondly, the approach benefits from the speed of the numerical approaches used in non-parametric probabilistic verification. However, it is well known that problems due to numerical instability are an issue here. Furthermore, when checking a single region, the number of parameters has only a minor influence on the runtime; more important is the number of states and the graph-structure. However, the number of required regions grows exponentially in the number of parameters. Therefore, investigating good heuristics for the selection of candidate regions proves to be essential. Nevertheless, already the naive version used here yields a superior performance.

Table 2 shows that the over-approximation of PLA is sufficiently tight to immediately cover large parts of the parameter space. In particular, for all benchmark models with two parameters, we can categorise more than 89 % of the parameter space as safe/unsafe within less than four minutes. For four parameters, we cannot cover as much space due to the poor choice of regions: A lot of regions cannot be proven (un)safe, because they are in fact neither (completely) safe nor unsafe and not because of the approximation. This is tightly linked with the observed increase in runtime for models with four parameters in Table 1 since it implies that regions have to be split considerably before a decision can be made. The minimal number of regions depends only on the property and the threshold used, as in [10] and in [12]. PLA might need additional regions (although empirically, this is not significant), this corresponds to the practical case in [12] when regions are split just due to a time-out of the SMT-solver.

7   Conclusion

This paper presented parameter lifting, a new approach for parameter synthesis of Markov models. It relies on replacing parameters by nondeterminism, scales well, and naturally extends to treating parametric MDPs.

Acknowledgement. This work was supported by the Excellence Initiative of the German federal and state government, and the CDZ project CAP (GZ 1023).

References

1. Kwiatkowska, M., Norman, G., Parker, D.: PRISM 4.0: verification of probabilistic real-time systems. In: Gopalakrishnan, G., Qadeer, S. (eds.) CAV 2011. LNCS, vol. 6806, pp. 585–591. Springer, Heidelberg (2011). doi:10.1007/978-3-642-22110-1_47
2. Hahn, E.M., Li, Y., Schewe, S., Turrini, A., Zhang, L.: ISCASMC: a web-based probabilistic model checker. In: Jones, C., Pihlajasaari, P., Sun, J. (eds.) FM 2014. LNCS, vol. 8442, pp. 312–317. Springer, Heidelberg (2014). doi:10.1007/978-3-319-06410-9_22
3. Chen, T., Forejt, V., Kwiatkowska, M., Parker, D., Simaitis, A.: PRISM-games: a model checker for stochastic multi-player games. In: Piterman, N., Smolka, S.A. (eds.) TACAS 2013. LNCS, vol. 7795, pp. 185–191. Springer, Heidelberg (2013). doi:10.1007/978-3-642-36742-7_13

4. Bartocci, E., Grosu, R., Katsaros, P., Ramakrishnan, C.R., Smolka, S.A.: Model repair for probabilistic systems. In: Abdulla, P.A., Leino, K.R.M. (eds.) TACAS 2011. LNCS, vol. 6605, pp. 326–340. Springer, Heidelberg (2011). doi:10.1007/978-3-642-19835-9_30

5. Calinescu, R., Ghezzi, C., Johnson, K., Pezze, M., Rafiq, Y., Tamburrelli, G.: Formal verification with confidence intervals: a new approach to establishing the quality-of-service properties of software systems. IEEE Trans. Rel. **65**(1), 107–125 (2016)

6. Češka, M., Dannenberg, F., Kwiatkowska, M., Paoletti, N.: Precise parameter synthesis for stochastic biochemical systems. In: Mendes, P., Dada, J.O., Smallbone, K. (eds.) CMSB 2014. LNCS, vol. 8859, pp. 86–98. Springer, Heidelberg (2014). doi:10.1007/978-3-319-12982-2_7

7. Long, F., Rinard, M.: Automatic patch generation by learning correct code. In: Bodik, R., Majumdar, R., eds. POPL, pp. 298–312. ACM (2016)

8. Su, G., Rosenblum, D.S.: Nested reachability approximation for discrete-time Markov chains with univariate parameters. In: Cassez, F., Raskin, J.-F. (eds.) ATVA 2014. LNCS, vol. 8837, pp. 364–379. Springer, Heidelberg (2014). doi:10.1007/978-3-319-11936-6_26

9. Su, G., Rosenblum, D.S., Tamburrelli, G.: Reliability of run-time quality-of-service evaluation using parametric model checking. In: ICSE. ACM (2016, to appear)

10. Hahn, E.M., Han, T., Zhang, L.: Synthesis for PCTL in parametric Markov decision processes. In: Bobaru, M., Havelund, K., Holzmann, G.J., Joshi, R. (eds.) NFM 2011. LNCS, vol. 6617, pp. 146–161. Springer, Heidelberg (2011). doi:10.1007/978-3-642-20398-5_12

11. Hahn, E.M., Hermanns, H., Wachter, B., Zhang, L.: PARAM: a model checker for parametric Markov models. In: Touili, T., Cook, B., Jackson, P. (eds.) CAV 2010. LNCS, vol. 6174, pp. 660–664. Springer, Heidelberg (2010). doi:10.1007/978-3-642-14295-6_56

12. Dehnert, C., Junges, S., Jansen, N., Corzilius, F., Volk, M., Bruintjes, H., Katoen, J.P., Ábrahám, E.: PROPhESY: a probabilistic parameter synthesis tool. In: Kroening, D., Păsăreanu, C.S. (eds.) CAV. LNCS, vol. 9206, pp. 214–231. Springer, Heidelberg (2015)

13. Daws, C.: Symbolic and parametric model checking of discrete-time Markov chains. In: Liu, Z., Araki, K. (eds.) ICTAC 2004. LNCS, vol. 3407, pp. 280–294. Springer, Heidelberg (2005). doi:10.1007/978-3-540-31862-0_21

14. Brim, L., Češka, M., Dražan, S., Šafránek, D.: Exploring parameter space of stochastic biochemical systems using quantitative model checking. In: Sharygina, N., Veith, H. (eds.) CAV 2013. LNCS, vol. 8044, pp. 107–123. Springer, Heidelberg (2013). doi:10.1007/978-3-642-39799-8_7

15. Hahn, E.M., Hermanns, H., Zhang, L.: Probabilistic reachability for parametric Markov models. STTT **13**(1), 3–19 (2010)

16. PARAM Website: (2015). http://depend.cs.uni-sb.de/tools/param/

17. Vardi, M.Y.: Automatic verification of probabilistic concurrent finite-state programs. In: FOCS, pp. 327–338, IEEE CS (1985)

18. Baier, C., Katoen, J.P.: Principles of Model Checking. The MIT Press, Cambridge (2008)

19. Puterman, M.L.: Markov Decision Processes: Discrete Stochastic Dynamic Programming. Wiley, Hoboken (1994)

20. Quatmann, T., Dehnert, C., Jansen, N., Junges, S., Katoen, J.P.: Parameter synthesis for Markov models: faster than ever. CoRR abs/1602.05113 (2016)

21. Junges, S., Jansen, N., Dehnert, C., Topcu, U., Katoen, J.-P.: Safety-constrained reinforcement learning for MDPs. In: Chechik, M., Raskin, J.-F. (eds.) TACAS 2016. LNCS, vol. 9636, pp. 130–146. Springer, Heidelberg (2016). doi:10.1007/978-3-662-49674-9_8
22. Kwiatkowska, M., Norman, G., Parker, D., Sproston, J.: Performance analysis of probabilistic timed automata using digital clocks. FMSD **29**, 33–78 (2006)

Bounded Model Checking
for Probabilistic Programs

Nils Jansen[2]([✉]), Christian Dehnert[1], Benjamin Lucien Kaminski[1],
Joost-Pieter Katoen[1], and Lukas Westhofen[1]

[1] RWTH Aachen University, Aachen, Germany
[2] University of Texas at Austin, Austin, USA
njansen@utexas.edu

Abstract. In this paper we investigate the applicability of standard model checking approaches to verifying properties in probabilistic programming. As the operational model for a standard probabilistic program is a potentially infinite parametric Markov decision process, no direct adaption of existing techniques is possible. Therefore, we propose an on–the–fly approach where the operational model is successively created and verified via a step–wise execution of the program. This approach enables to take key features of many probabilistic programs into account: nondeterminism and conditioning. We discuss the restrictions and demonstrate the scalability on several benchmarks.

1 Introduction

Probabilistic programs are imperative programs, written in languages like C, Scala, Prolog, or ML, with two added constructs: (1) the ability to draw values at random from probability distributions, and (2) the ability to condition values of variables in a program through observations. In the past years, such programming languages became very popular due to their wide applicability for several different research areas [1]: Probabilistic programming is at the heart of *machine learning* for describing distribution functions; *Bayesian inference* is pivotal in their analysis. They are central in *security* for describing cryptographic constructions (such as randomized encryption) and security experiments. In addition, probabilistic programs are an active research topic in *quantitative information flow*. Moreover, *quantum programs* are inherently probabilistic due to the random outcomes of quantum measurements. All in all, the simple and intuitive syntax of probabilistic programs makes these different research areas accessible to a broad audience.

However, although these programs typically consist of a few lines of code, they are often hard to understand and analyze; bugs, for instance *non–termination* of a program, can easily occur. It seems of utmost importance to be able to

This work has been partly funded by the awards AFRL # FA9453-15-1-0317, ARO # W911NF-15-1-0592 and ONR # N00014-15-IP-00052 and is supported by the Excellence Initiative of the German federal and state government.

C. Artho et al. (Eds.): ATVA 2016, LNCS 9938, pp. 68–85, 2016.
DOI: 10.1007/978-3-319-46520-3_5

automatically prove properties like *"Is the probability for termination of the program at least 90 %"* or *"Is the expected value of a certain program variable at least 5 after successful termination?"*. Approaches based on the simulation of a program to show properties or infer probabilities have been made in the past [2,3]. However, to the best of our knowledge there is no work which exploits well-established *model checking algorithms* for probabilistic systems such as Markov decision processes (MDP) or Markov chains (MCs), as already argued to be an interesting avenue for the future in [1].

As the operational semantics for a probabilistic program can be expressed as a (possible infinite) MDP [4], it seems worthwhile to investigate the opportunities there. However, probabilistic model checkers like PRISM [5], iscasMc [6], or MRMC [7] offer efficient methods only for *finite models*.

We make use of the simple fact that for a finite unrolling of a program the corresponding operational MDP is also finite. Starting from a profound understanding of the (intricate) probabilistic program semantics—including features such as observations, unbounded (and hence possibly diverging) loops, and nondeterminism—we show that with each unrolling of the program both conditional reachability probabilities and conditional expected values of program variables increase monotonically. This gives rise to a *bounded model-checking approach* for verifying probabilistic programs. This enables for a user to write a program and automatically verify it against a desired property without further knowledge of the programs semantics.

We extend this methodology to the even more complicated case of *parametric probabilistic programs*, where probabilities are given by functions over parameters. At each iteration of the bounded model checking procedure, parameter valuations violating certain properties are guaranteed to induce violation at each further iteration.

We demonstrate the applicability of our approach using five well-known benchmarks from the literature. Using efficient model building and verification methods, our prototype is able to prove properties where either the state space of the operational model is infinite or consists of millions of states.

Related Work. Besides the tools employing probabilistic model checking as listed above, one should mention the approach in [8], where *finite abstractions* of the operational semantics of a program were verified. However, this was defined for programs without parametric probabilities or observe statements. In [9], verification on partial operational semantics is theoretically discussed for termination probabilities.

The paper is organized as follows: In Sect. 2, we introduce the probabilistic models we use, the probabilistic programming language, and the structured operational semantics (SOS) rules to construct an operational (parametric) MDP. Section 3 first introduces formal concepts needed for the finite unrollings of the program, then shows how expectations and probabilities grow monotonically, and finally explains how this is utilized for bounded model checking. In Sect. 4, an extensive description of used benchmarks, properties and experiments is given before the paper concludes with Sect. 5.

2 Preliminaries

2.1 Distributions and Polynomials

A *probability distribution* over a finite or countably infinite set X is a function $\mu\colon X \to [0, 1] \subseteq \mathbb{R}$ with $\sum_{x \in X} \mu(x) = 1$. The set of all distributions on X is denoted by $Distr(X)$. Let V be a finite set of *parameters* over $\mathbb{R}$. A *valuation* for V is a function $u\colon V \to \mathbb{R}$. Let $\mathbb{Q}[V]$ denote the set of multivariate *polynomials* with rational coefficients and $\mathbb{Q}_V$ the set of *rational functions* (fractions of polynomials) over V. For $g \in \mathbb{Q}[V]$ or $g \in \mathbb{Q}_V$, let $g[u]$ denote the evaluation of g at u. We write $g = 0$ if g can be reduced to 0, and $g \neq 0$ otherwise.

2.2 Probabilistic Models

First, we introduce parametric probabilistic models which can be seen as transition systems where the transitions are labelled with polynomials in $\mathbb{Q}[V]$.

Definition 1 (pMDP and pMC). *A* parametric Markov decision process *(pMDP) is a tuple* $\mathcal{M} = (S, s_I, Act, \mathcal{P})$ *with a countable set S of states, an initial state $s_I \in S$, a finite set Act of actions, and a transition function* $\mathcal{P}\colon S \times Act \times S \to \mathbb{Q}[V]$ *satisfying for all $s \in S$: $Act(s) \neq \emptyset$, where V is a finite set of parameters over $\mathbb{R}$ and $Act(s) = \{\alpha \in Act \mid \exists s' \in S.\,\mathcal{P}(s, \alpha, s') \neq 0\}$. If for all $s \in S$ it holds that $|Act(s)| = 1$, $\mathcal{M}$ is called a* parametric discrete-time Markov chain *(pMC), denoted by $\mathcal{D}$.*

At each state, an action is chosen *nondeterministically*, then the successor states are determined *probabilistically* as defined by the transition function. $Act(s)$ is the set of *enabled* actions at state s. As $Act(s)$ is non-empty for all $s \in S$, there are no deadlock states. For pMCs there is only one single action per state and we write the transition probability function as $\mathcal{P}\colon S \times S \to \mathbb{Q}[V]$, omitting that action. *Rewards* are defined using a *reward function* rew$\colon S \to \mathbb{R}$ which assigns rewards to states of the model. Intuitively, the reward rew(s) is earned upon *leaving* the state s.

Schedulers. The nondeterministic choices of actions in pMDPs can be resolved using *schedulers*[1]. In our setting it suffices to consider memoryless deterministic schedulers [10]. For more general definitions we refer to [11].

Definition 2 (Scheduler). *A scheduler for pMDP* $\mathcal{M} = (S, s_I, Act, \mathcal{P})$ *is a function* $\mathfrak{S}\colon S \to Act$ *with* $\mathfrak{S}(s) \in Act(s)$ *for all $s \in S$.*

Let $Sched^{\mathcal{M}}$ denote the set of all schedulers for $\mathcal{M}$. Applying a scheduler to a pMDP yields an *induced parametric Markov chain*, as all nondeterminism is resolved, i.e., the transition probabilities are obtained w.r.t. the choice of actions.

Definition 3 (Induced pMC). *Given a pMDP* $\mathcal{M} = (S, s_I, Act, \mathcal{P})$, *the pMC induced by* $\mathfrak{S} \in Sched^{\mathcal{M}}$ *is given by* $\mathcal{M}^{\mathfrak{S}} = (S, s_I, Act, \mathcal{P}^{\mathfrak{S}})$, *where*

$$\mathcal{P}^{\mathfrak{S}}(s, s') = \mathcal{P}(s, \mathfrak{S}(s), s'), \quad \text{for all } s, s' \in S.$$

---

[1] Also referred to as adversaries, strategies, or policies.

Valuations. Applying a *valuation* u to a pMDP $\mathcal{M}$, denoted $\mathcal{M}[u]$, replaces each polynomial g in $\mathcal{M}$ by $g[u]$. We call $\mathcal{M}[u]$ the *instantiation* of $\mathcal{M}$ at u. A valuation u is *well-defined* for $\mathcal{M}$ if the replacement yields *probability distributions* at all states; the resulting model $\mathcal{M}[u]$ is a Markov decision process (MDP) or, in absence of nondeterminism, a Markov chain (MC).

Properties. For our purpose we consider *conditional reachability properties* and *conditional expected reward properties* in MCs. For more detailed definitions we refer to [11, Chap. 10]. Given an MC $\mathcal{D}$ with state space S and initial state s_I, let $\Pr^{\mathcal{D}}(\neg \Diamond U)$ denote the probability *not* to reach a set of undesired states U from the initial state s_I within $\mathcal{D}$. Furthermore, let $\Pr^{\mathcal{D}}(\Diamond T \mid \neg \Diamond U)$ denote the conditional probability to reach a set of target states $T \subseteq S$ from the initial state s_I within $\mathcal{D}$, given that no state in the set U is reached. We use the standard probability measure on infinite paths through an MC. For threshold $\lambda \in [0, 1] \subseteq \mathbb{R}$, the reachability property, asserting that a target state is to be reached with conditional probability at most λ, is denoted $\varphi = \mathbb{P}_{\leq \lambda}(\Diamond T \mid \neg \Diamond U)$. The property is satisfied by $\mathcal{D}$, written $\mathcal{D} \models \varphi$, iff $\Pr^{\mathcal{D}}(\Diamond T \mid \neg \Diamond U) \leq \lambda$. This is analogous for comparisons like $<$, $>$, and $\geq$.

The reward of a path through an MC $\mathcal{D}$ until T is the sum of the rewards of the states visited along on the path before reaching T. The expected reward of a finite path is given by its probability times its reward. Given $\Pr^{\mathcal{D}}(\Diamond T) = 1$, the conditional expected reward of reaching $T \subseteq S$, given that no state in set $U \subseteq S$ is reached, denoted $\mathrm{ER}^{\mathcal{D}}(\Diamond T \mid \neg \Diamond U)$, is the expected reward of all paths accumulated until hitting T while not visiting a state in U in between divided by the probability of not reaching a state in U (i.e., divided by $\Pr^{\mathcal{D}}(\neg \Diamond U)$). An expected reward property is given by $\psi = \mathbb{E}_{\leq \kappa}(\Diamond T \mid \neg \Diamond U)$ with threshold $\kappa \in \mathbb{R}_{\geq 0}$. The property is satisfied by $\mathcal{D}$, written $\mathcal{D} \models \psi$, iff $\mathrm{ER}^{\mathcal{D}}(\Diamond T \mid \neg \Diamond U) \leq \kappa$. Again, this is analogous for comparisons like $<$, $>$, and $\geq$. For details about conditional probabilities and expected rewards see [12].

Reachability probabilities and expected rewards for MDPs are defined on induced MCs for specific schedulers. We take here the conservative view that a property for an MDP has to hold for *all possible schedulers*.

Parameter Synthesis. For pMCs, one is interested in *synthesizing* well-defined valuations that induce satisfaction or violation of the given specifications [13]. In detail, for a pMC $\mathcal{D}$, a rational function $g \in \mathbb{Q}_V$ is computed which— when instantiated by a well-defined valuation u for $\mathcal{D}$—evaluates to the actual reachability probability or expected reward for $\mathcal{D}$, i.e., $g[u] = \Pr^{\mathcal{D}[u]}(\Diamond T)$ or $g[u] = \mathrm{ER}^{\mathcal{D}[u]}(\Diamond T)$. For pMDPs, schedulers inducing *maximal* or *minimal* probability or expected reward have to be considered [14].

2.3   Conditional Probabilistic Guarded Command Language

We first present a programming language which is an extension of Dijkstra's guarded command language [15] with a binary probabilistic choice operator, yielding the *probabilistic guarded command language* (pGCL) [16]. In [17], pGCL was endowed with *observe statements*, giving rise to conditioning. The syntax of this *conditional probabilistic guarded command language* (cpGCL) is given by

$$\mathcal{P} ::= \texttt{skip} \mid \texttt{abort} \mid x := E \mid \mathcal{P}; \mathcal{P} \mid \texttt{if } G \texttt{ then } \mathcal{P} \texttt{ else } \mathcal{P}$$
$$\mid \{\mathcal{P}\} \, [g] \, \{\mathcal{P}\} \mid \{\mathcal{P}\} \,\square\, \{\mathcal{P}\} \mid \texttt{while} \, (G) \, \{\mathcal{P}\} \mid \texttt{observe}(G)$$

Here, x belongs to the set of *program variables* $\mathcal{V}$; E is an arithmetical expression over $\mathcal{V}$; G is a *Boolean expression* over arithmetical expressions over $\mathcal{V}$. The *probability* is given by a polynomial $g \in \mathbb{Q}[V]$. Most of the cpGCL instructions are self–explanatory; we elaborate only on the following: For cpGCL-programs P and Q, $\{P\} \, [g] \, \{Q\}$ is a *probabilistic choice* where P is executed with probability g and Q with probability $1-g$; analogously, $\{P\} \,\square\, \{Q\}$ is a *nondeterministic choice* between P and Q; abort is syntactic sugar for the diverging program while (true) {skip}. The statement observe(G) for the Boolean expression G *blocks* all program executions violating G and induces a *rescaling* of probability of the remaining execution traces so that they sum up to one. For a cpGCL-program P, the set of *program states* is given by $\mathbb{S} = \{\sigma \mid \sigma \colon \mathcal{V} \to \mathbb{Q}\}$, i.e., the set of all variable valuations. We assume all variables to be assigned zero prior to execution or at the start of the program. This initial variable valuation $\sigma_I \in \mathbb{S}$ with $\forall x \in \mathcal{V}. \, \sigma_I(x) = 0$ is called the *initial state* of the program.

Example 1. Consider the following cpGCL-program with variables x and c:

```
1  while (c = 0) {
2      { x := x + 1 } [0.5] { c := 1 }
3  };
4  observe "x is odd"
```

While c is 0, the loop body is iterated: With probability $1/2$ either x is incremented by one or c is set to one. After leaving the loop, the event that the valuation of x is odd is *observed*, which means that all program executions where x is even are blocked. Properties of interest for this program would, e.g., concern the termination probability, or the expected value of x after termination. $\triangle$

2.4   Operational Semantics for Probabilistic Programs

We now introduce an operational semantics for cpGCL-programs which is given by an MDP as in Definition 1. The structure of such an operational MDP is schematically depicted below.

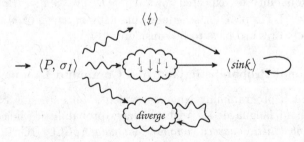

Squiggly arrows indicate reaching certain states via possibly multiple paths and states; the clouds indicate that there might be several states of the particular kind. $\langle P, \sigma_I \rangle$ marks the initial state of the program P. In general the states of the operational MDP are of the form $\langle P', \sigma' \rangle$ where P' is the program that is left to be executed and σ' is the current variable valuation.

All runs of the program (paths through the MDP) are either *terminating* and eventually end up in the $\langle sink \rangle$ state, or are *diverging* (thus they never reach $\langle sink \rangle$). Diverging runs occur due to non–terminating computations. A terminating run has either terminated successfully, i.e., it passes a $\downarrow$–state, or it has terminated due to a *violation of an observation*, i.e., it passes the $\langle \notz \rangle$–state. Sets of runs that eventually reach $\langle \notz \rangle$, or $\langle sink \rangle$, or diverge are pairwise disjoint.

The $\downarrow$–labelled states are the *only ones* with positive reward, which is due to the fact that we want to capture probabilities of events (respectively expected values of random variables) occurring at *successful termination* of the program.

The random variables of interest are $\mathbb{E} = \{f | f \colon \mathbb{S} \to \mathbb{R}_{\geq 0}\}$. Such random variables are referred to as post–expectations [16]. Formally, we have:

Definition 4 (Operational Semantics of Programs). *The* operational semantics *of a* cpGCL *program P with respect to a post–expectation $f \in \mathbb{E}$ is the MDP $\mathcal{M}^f[\![P]\!] = (S, \langle P, \sigma_I \rangle, Act, \mathcal{P})$ together with a reward function* rew, *where*

- $S = \{\langle Q, \sigma \rangle, \langle \downarrow, \sigma \rangle | Q$ is a cpGCL program, $\sigma \in \mathbb{S}\} \cup \{\langle \notz \rangle, \langle sink \rangle\}$ *is the countable set of states,*
- $\langle P, \sigma_I \rangle \in S$ *is the initial state,*
- $Act = \{left, right, none\}$ *is the set of actions, and*
- $\mathcal{P}$ *is the smallest relation defined by the SOS rules given in Fig.* 1.

The reward function is rew$(s) = f(\sigma)$ *if $s = \langle \downarrow, \sigma \rangle$, and* rew$(s) = 0$, *otherwise.*

A state of the form $\langle \downarrow, \sigma \rangle$ indicates successful termination, i.e., no commands are left to be executed. These terminal states and the $\langle \notz \rangle$–state go to the $\langle sink \rangle$ state. skip without context terminates successfully. abort self–loops, i.e., diverges. $x := E$ alters the variable valuation according to the assignment then terminates successfully. For the concatenation, $\langle \downarrow; Q, \sigma \rangle$ indicates successful termination of the first program, so the execution continues with $\langle Q, \sigma \rangle$. If for $P; Q$ the execution of P leads to $\langle \notz \rangle$, $P; Q$ does so, too. Otherwise, for $\langle P, \sigma \rangle \longrightarrow \mu$, μ is lifted such that Q is concatenated to the support of μ. For more details on the operational semantics we refer to [4].

If for the conditional choice $\sigma \models G$ holds, P is executed, otherwise Q. The case for while is similar. For the probabilistic choice, a distribution ν is created according to probability p. For $\{P\} \square \{Q\}$, we call P the *left* choice and Q the *right* choice for actions $left, right \in Act$. For the observe statement, if $\sigma \models G$ then observe acts like skip. Otherwise, the execution leads directly to $\langle \notz \rangle$ indicating a violation of the observe statement.

(terminal) $\dfrac{}{\langle\downarrow,\sigma\rangle \;\longrightarrow\; \langle\mathsf{sink}\rangle}$ **(skip)** $\dfrac{}{\langle\mathtt{skip},\sigma\rangle \;\longrightarrow\; \langle\downarrow,\sigma\rangle}$ **(abort)** $\dfrac{}{\langle\mathtt{abort},\sigma\rangle \;\longrightarrow\; \langle\mathtt{abort},\sigma\rangle}$

(undesired) $\dfrac{}{\langle\frac{1}{2}\rangle \;\longrightarrow\; \langle\mathsf{sink}\rangle}$ **(assign)** $\dfrac{}{\langle x := E,\sigma\rangle \;\longrightarrow\; \langle\downarrow,\sigma[x \leftarrow [\![E]\!]_\sigma]\rangle}$

(observe1) $\dfrac{\sigma \models G}{\langle\mathtt{observe}\,G,\sigma\rangle \;\longrightarrow\; \langle\downarrow,\sigma\rangle}$ **(observe2)** $\dfrac{\sigma \not\models G}{\langle\mathtt{observe}\,G,\sigma\rangle \;\longrightarrow\; \langle\frac{1}{2}\rangle}$

(concatenate1) $\dfrac{}{\langle\downarrow;Q,\sigma\rangle \;\longrightarrow\; \langle Q,\sigma\rangle}$ **(concatenate2)** $\dfrac{\langle P,\sigma\rangle \;\longrightarrow\; \langle\frac{1}{2}\rangle}{\langle P;Q,\sigma\rangle \;\longrightarrow\; \langle\frac{1}{2}\rangle}$

(concatenate3) $\dfrac{\langle P,\sigma\rangle \;\longrightarrow\; \mu}{\langle P;Q,\sigma\rangle \;\longrightarrow\; \nu}$, where $\forall P'.\,\nu(\langle P';Q,\sigma'\rangle) := \mu(\langle P',\sigma'\rangle)$

(if1) $\dfrac{\sigma \models G}{\langle\mathtt{ite}\,(G)\,\{P\}\,\{Q\},\sigma\rangle \;\longrightarrow\; \langle P,\sigma\rangle}$ **(if2)** $\dfrac{\sigma \not\models G}{\langle\mathtt{ite}\,(G)\,\{P\}\,\{Q\},\sigma\rangle \;\longrightarrow\; \langle Q,\sigma\rangle}$

(while1) $\dfrac{\sigma \models G}{\langle\mathtt{while}\,(G)\,\{P\},\sigma\rangle \;\longrightarrow\; \langle P;\mathtt{while}\,(G)\,\{P\},\sigma\rangle}$ **(while2)** $\dfrac{\sigma \not\models G}{\langle\mathtt{while}\,(G)\,\{P\},\sigma\rangle \;\longrightarrow\; \langle\downarrow,\sigma\rangle}$

(prob) $\dfrac{}{\langle\{P\}\,[p]\,\{Q\},\sigma\rangle \;\longrightarrow\; \nu}$, where $\nu(\langle P,\sigma\rangle) := p,\ \nu(\langle Q,\sigma\rangle) := 1 - p$

(nondet1) $\dfrac{}{\langle\{P\}\,\Box\,\{Q\},\sigma\rangle \;\xrightarrow{\;left\;}\; \langle P,\sigma\rangle}$ **(nondet2)** $\dfrac{}{\langle\{P\}\,\Box\,\{Q\},\sigma\rangle \;\xrightarrow{\;right\;}\; \langle Q,\sigma\rangle}$

Fig. 1. SOS rules for constructing the operational MDP of a cpGCL program. We use $s \longrightarrow t$ to indicate $\mathcal{P}(s, none, t) = 1$, $s \longrightarrow \mu$ for $\mu \in Distr(S)$ to indicate $\forall t \in S: \mathcal{P}(s, none, t) = \mu(t)$, $s \xrightarrow{\;left\;} t$ to indicate $\mathcal{P}(s, left, t) = 1$, and $s \xrightarrow{\;right\;} t$ to indicate $\mathcal{P}(s, right, t) = 1$.

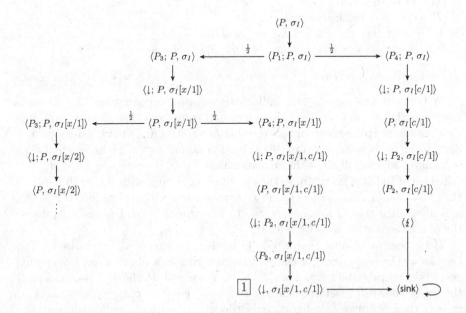

Fig. 2. Partially unrolled operational semantics for program P

Example 2. Reconsider Example 1, where we set for readability $P_1 = \{x :=$ $x + 1\}$ $[0.5]$ $\{c := 1\}$, $P_2 = \text{observe}(\text{"}x \text{ is odd"})$, $P_3 = \{x := x + 1\}$, and $P_4 = \{c := 1\}$. A part of the operational MDP $\mathcal{M}^f[\![P]\!]$ for an arbitrary initial variable valuation σ_I and post–expectation x is depicted in Fig. 2.[2] Note that this MDP is an MC, as P contains no nondeterministic choices. The MDP has been unrolled until the second loop iteration, i.e., at state $\langle P, \sigma_I[x/2]\rangle$, the unrolling could be continued. The only terminating state is $\langle \downarrow, \sigma_I[x/1, c/1]\rangle$. As our post-expectation is the value of variable x, we assign this value to terminating states, i.e., reward $\boxed{1}$ at state $\langle \downarrow, \sigma_I[x/1, c/1]\rangle$, where x has been assigned 1. At state $\langle P, \sigma_I[c/1]\rangle$, the loop condition is violated as is the subsequent observation because of x being assigned an even number. $\qquad\qquad\triangle$

3   Bounded Model Checking for Probabilistic Programs

In this section we describe our approach to model checking probabilistic programs. The key idea is that satisfaction or violation of certain properties for a program can be shown by means of a *finite unrolling* of the program. Therefore, we introduce the notion of a partial operational semantics of a program, which we exploit to apply standard model checking to prove or disprove properties.

First, we state the correspondence between the satisfaction of a property for a cpGCL-program P and for its operational semantics, the MDP $\mathcal{M}^f[\![P]\!]$. Intuitively, a program satisfies a property if and only if the property is satisfied on the operational semantics of the program.

Definition 5 (Satisfaction of Properties). *Given a* cpGCL *program P and a (conditional) reachability or expected reward property φ. We define*

$$P \models \varphi \quad \text{iff} \quad \mathcal{M}^f[\![P]\!] \models \varphi.$$

This correspondence on the level of a denotational semantics for cpGCL has been discussed extensively in [17]. Note that there only schedulers which minimize expected rewards were considered. Here, we also need maximal schedulers as we are considering both upper and lower bounds on expected rewards and probabilities. Note that satisfaction of properties is solely based on the operational semantics and induced maximal or minimal probabilities or expected rewards.

We now introduce the notion of a partial operational MDP for a cpGCL–program P, which is a finite approximation of the full operational MDP of P. Intuitively, this amounts to the successive application of SOS rules given in Fig. 1, while not all possible rules have been applied yet.

Definition 6 (Partial Operational Semantics). *A partial operational semantics for a* cpGCL*–program P is a sub-MDP $\mathcal{M}^f[\![P]\!]' = (S', \langle P, \sigma_I\rangle, Act, \mathcal{P}')$ of the operational semantics for P (denoted $\mathcal{M}^f[\![P]\!]' \subseteq \mathcal{M}^f[\![P]\!]$) with $S' \subseteq S$. Let $S_{exp} = S' \setminus \{\langle Q, \sigma\rangle \in S' \mid Q \neq \downarrow, \exists s \in S \setminus S' \exists \alpha \in Act \colon \mathcal{P}(\langle Q, \sigma\rangle, \alpha, s) > 0\}$*

---

[2] We have tacitly overloaded the variable name x to an expectation here for readability. More formally, by the "expectation x" we actually mean the expectation $\lambda\sigma.\sigma(x)$.

be the set of expandable states. *Then the transition probability function $\mathcal{P}'$ is for $s, s' \in S'$ and $\alpha \in Act$ given by*

$$\mathcal{P}'(s, \alpha, s') = \begin{cases} 1, & \text{if } s = s' \text{ for } s, s' \in S_{exp}, \\ \mathcal{P}(s, \alpha, s'), & \text{otherwise.} \end{cases}$$

Intuitively, the set of non–terminating *expandable states* describes the states where there are still SOS rules applicable. Using this definition, the only transitions leaving expandable states are self-loops, enabling to have a well-defined probability measure on partial operational semantics. We will use this for our method, which is based on the fact that both (conditional) reachability probabilities and expected rewards for certain properties will always monotonically increase for further unrollings of a program and the respective partial operational semantics. This is discussed in what follows.

3.1   Growing Expectations

As mentioned before, we are interested in the probability of termination or the expected values of expectations (i.e. random variables ranging over program states) after successful termination of the program. This is measured on the operational MDP by the set of paths *reaching $\langle sink \rangle$ from the initial state conditioned on not reaching $\langle \frac{\ell}{4} \rangle$* [17]. In detail, we have to compute the conditional expected value of post–expectation f after successful termination of program P, given that no observation was violated along the computation. For nondeterministic programs, we have to compute this value either under a minimizing or maximizing scheduler (depending on the given property). We focus our presentation on expected rewards and minimizing schedulers, but all concepts are analogous for the other cases. For $\mathcal{M}^f[\![P]\!]$ we have

$$\inf_{\mathfrak{S} \in Sched^{\mathcal{M}^f[\![P]\!]}} \mathrm{ER}^{\mathcal{M}^f[\![P]\!]^{\mathfrak{S}}}(\Diamond \langle sink \rangle \mid \neg \Diamond \langle \tfrac{\ell}{4} \rangle).$$

Recall that $\mathcal{M}^f[\![P]\!]^{\mathfrak{S}}$ is the induced MC under scheduler $\mathfrak{S} \in Sched^{\mathcal{M}^f[\![P]\!]}$ as in Definition 3. Recall also that for $\neg \Diamond \langle \tfrac{\ell}{4} \rangle$ all paths not eventually reaching $\langle \tfrac{\ell}{4} \rangle$ either diverge (collecting reward 0) or pass by a $\downarrow$–state and reach $\langle sink \rangle$. More importantly, all paths that *do* eventually reach $\langle \tfrac{\ell}{4} \rangle$ also collect reward 0. Thus:

$$\inf_{\mathfrak{S} \in Sched^{\mathcal{M}^f[\![P]\!]}} \mathrm{ER}^{\mathcal{M}^f[\![P]\!]^{\mathfrak{S}}}(\Diamond \langle sink \rangle \mid \neg \Diamond \langle \tfrac{\ell}{4} \rangle)$$

$$= \inf_{\mathfrak{S} \in Sched^{\mathcal{M}^f[\![P]\!]}} \frac{\mathrm{ER}^{\mathcal{M}^f[\![P]\!]^{\mathfrak{S}}}(\Diamond \langle sink \rangle \cap \neg \Diamond \langle \tfrac{\ell}{4} \rangle)}{\mathrm{Pr}^{\mathcal{M}^f[\![P]\!]^{\mathfrak{S}}}(\neg \Diamond \tfrac{\ell}{4})}$$

$$= \inf_{\mathfrak{S} \in Sched^{\mathcal{M}^f[\![P]\!]}} \frac{\mathrm{ER}^{\mathcal{M}^f[\![P]\!]^{\mathfrak{S}}}(\Diamond \langle sink \rangle)}{\mathrm{Pr}^{\mathcal{M}^f[\![P]\!]^{\mathfrak{S}}}(\neg \Diamond \tfrac{\ell}{4})}.$$

Finally, observe that the probability of not reaching $\langle \xi \rangle$ is one minus the probability of reaching $\langle \xi \rangle$, which gives us:

$$= \inf_{\mathfrak{S} \in Sched^{\mathcal{M}^f[\![P]\!]}} \frac{ER^{\mathcal{M}^f[\![P]\!]^{\mathfrak{S}}}(\Diamond\langle sink \rangle)}{1 - Pr^{\mathcal{M}^f[\![P]\!]^{\mathfrak{S}}}(\Diamond \xi)}. \qquad \dagger$$

Regarding the quotient minimization we assume "$\frac{0}{0} < 0$" as we see $\frac{0}{0}$—being undefined—to be less favorable than 0. For programs without nondeterminism this view agrees with a weakest–precondition–style semantics for probabilistic programs with conditioning [17].

It was shown in [18] that *all strict lower bounds* for $ER^{\mathcal{M}^f[\![P]\!]^{\mathfrak{S}}}(\Diamond\langle sink \rangle)$ are in principle computably enumerable in a monotonically non–decreasing fashion. One way to do so, is to allow for the program to be executed for an increasing number of k steps, and collect the expected rewards of all execution traces that have lead to termination within k computation steps. This corresponds naturally to constructing a partial operational semantics $\mathcal{M}^f[\![P]\!]' \subseteq \mathcal{M}^f[\![P]\!]$ as in Definition 6 and computing minimal expected rewards on $\mathcal{M}^f[\![P]\!]'$.

Analogously, it is of course also possible to monotonically enumerate all strict lower bounds of $Pr^{\mathcal{M}^f[\![P]\!]^{\mathfrak{S}}}(\Diamond \xi)$, since—again—we need to just collect the probability mass of all traces that have led to $\langle \xi \rangle$ within k computation steps. Since probabilities are quantities bounded between 0 and 1, a lower bound for $Pr^{\mathcal{M}^f[\![P]\!]^{\mathfrak{S}}}(\Diamond \xi)$ is an upper bound for $1 - Pr^{\mathcal{M}^f[\![P]\!]^{\mathfrak{S}}}(\Diamond \xi)$.

Put together, a lower bound for $ER^{\mathcal{M}^f[\![P]\!]^{\mathfrak{S}}}(\Diamond\langle sink \rangle)$ and a lower bound for $Pr^{\mathcal{M}^f[\![P]\!]^{\mathfrak{S}}}(\Diamond \xi)$ yields a lower bound for (†). We are thus able to enumerate all lower bounds of $ER^{\mathcal{M}^f[\![P]\!]^{\mathfrak{S}}}(\Diamond\langle sink \rangle \mid \neg\Diamond\langle \xi \rangle)$ by inspection of a finite sub–MDP of $\mathcal{M}^f[\![P]\!]$. Formally, we have:

Theorem 1. *For a cpGCL program P, post–expectation f, and a partial operational MDP $\mathcal{M}^f[\![P]\!]' \subseteq \mathcal{M}^f[\![P]\!]$ it holds that*

$$\inf_{\mathfrak{S} \in Sched^{\mathcal{M}^f[\![P]\!]'}} ER^{\mathcal{M}^f[\![P]\!]'^{\mathfrak{S}}}(\Diamond\langle sink \rangle \mid \neg\Diamond\langle \xi \rangle)$$

$$\leq \inf_{\mathfrak{S} \in Sched^{\mathcal{M}^f[\![P]\!]}} ER^{\mathcal{M}^f[\![P]\!]^{\mathfrak{S}}}(\Diamond\langle sink \rangle \mid \neg\Diamond\langle \xi \rangle).$$

3.2 Model Checking

Using Theorem 1, we transfer satisfaction or violation of certain properties from a partial operational semantics $\mathcal{M}^f[\![P]\!]' \subseteq \mathcal{M}^f[\![P]\!]$ to the full semantics of the program. For an upper bounded conditional expected reward property $\varphi = \mathbb{E}_{\leq\kappa}(\Diamond T \mid \neg\Diamond U)$ where $T, U \in \mathbb{S}$ we exploit that

$$\mathcal{M}^f[\![P]\!]' \not\models \varphi \quad \Longrightarrow \quad P \not\models \varphi. \tag{1}$$

That means, if we can prove the violation of φ on the MDP induced by a finite unrolling of the program, it will hold for all further unrollings, too. This is because all rewards and probabilities are positive and thus further unrolling can only increase the accumulated reward and/or probability mass.

Dually, for a lower bounded conditional expected reward property $\psi = \mathbb{E}_{\geq \lambda}(\lozenge T \mid \lozenge U)$ we use the following property:

$$\mathcal{M}^f [\![P]\!]' \models \psi \quad \Longrightarrow \quad P \models \varphi. \tag{2}$$

The preconditions of Implication (1) and Implication (2) can be checked by probabilistic model checkers like PRISM [5]; this is analogous for conditional reachability properties. Let us illustrate this by means of an example.

Example 3. As mentioned in Example 1, we are interested in the *probability of termination*. As outlined in Sect. 2.4, this probability can be measured by

$$\Pr(\lozenge \langle \mathit{sink} \rangle \mid \neg \lozenge \langle \mathnormal{\ell} \rangle) = \frac{\Pr(\lozenge \langle \mathit{sink} \rangle \wedge \neg \lozenge \langle \mathnormal{\ell} \rangle)}{\Pr(\lozenge \langle \mathnormal{\ell} \rangle)}.$$

We want this probability to be at least $1/2$, i.e., $\varphi = \mathbb{P}_{\geq 0.5}(\lozenge \langle \mathit{sink} \rangle \mid \neg \lozenge \langle \mathnormal{\ell} \rangle)$. Since for further unrollings of our partially unrolled MDP this probability never decreases, the property can already be verified on the partial MDP $\mathcal{M}^f [\![P]\!]'$ by

$$\Pr^{\mathcal{M}^f [\![P]\!]'}(\lozenge \langle \mathit{sink} \rangle \mid \neg \lozenge \langle \mathnormal{\ell} \rangle) = \frac{1/4}{1/2} = \frac{1}{2},$$

where $\mathcal{M}^f [\![P]\!]'$ is the sub-MDP from Fig. 2. This finite sub-MDP $\mathcal{M}^f [\![P]\!]'$ is therefore a witness of $\mathcal{M}^f [\![P]\!] \models \varphi$. △

Algorithmically, this technique relies on suitable heuristics regarding the size of the considered partial MDPs. Basically, in each step k states are expanded and the corresponding MDP is model checked, until either the property can be shown to be satisfied or violated, or no more states are expandable. In addition, heuristics based on shortest path searching algorithms can be employed to favor expandable states that so far induce high probabilities.

Note that this method is a *semi-algorithm* when the model checking problems stated in Implications (1) and (2) are considering strict bounds, i.e. $< \kappa$ and $> \kappa$. It is then guaranteed that the given bounds are finally exceeded.

Consider now the case where we want to show *satisfaction* of $\varphi = \mathbb{E}_{\leq \kappa}(\lozenge T \mid \neg \lozenge U)$, i.e., $\mathcal{M}^f [\![P]\!]' \models \varphi \Rightarrow P \models \varphi$. As the conditional expected reward will monotonically increase as long as the partial MDP is expandable, the implication is only true if there are no more expandable states, i.e., the model is fully expanded. This is analogous for the violation of upper bounded properties. Note that many practical examples actually induce finite operational MDPs which enables to build the full model and perform model checking.

It remains to discuss how this approach can be utilized for parameter synthesis as explained in Sect. 2.2. For a partial operational pMDP $\mathcal{M}^f [\![P]\!]'$ and a property $\varphi = \mathbb{E}_{\leq \kappa}(\lozenge T \mid \neg \lozenge U)$ we use tools like PROPhESY [13] to determine for which parameter valuations φ is violated. For each valuation u with $\mathcal{M}^f [\![P]\!]'[u] \not\models \varphi$ it holds that $\mathcal{M}^f [\![P]\!][u] \not\models \varphi$; each parameter valuation violating a property on a partial pMDP also violates it on the fully expanded MDP.

4 Evaluation

Experimental Setup. We implemented and evaluated the bounded model checking method in C++. For the model checking functionality, we use the stochastic model checker Storm, developed at RWTH Aachen University, and PROPhESY [19] for parameter synthesis.

We consider five different, well-known benchmark programs, three of which are based on models from the PRISM benchmark suite [5] and others taken from other literature (see [20] for some examples). We give the running times of our prototype on several instances of these models. Since there is — to the best of our knowledge — no other tool that can analyze cpGCL programs in a purely automated fashion, we cannot meaningfully compare these figures to other tools. As our technique is restricted to establishing that lower bounds on reachability probabilities and the expectations of program variables, respectively, exceed a threshold λ, we need to fix λ for each experiment. For all our experiments, we chose λ to be 90 % of the actual value for the corresponding query and choose to expand 10^6 states of the partial operational semantics of a program between each model checking run.

We ran the experiments on an HP BL685C G7 machine with 48 cores clocked with 2.0 GHz each and 192 GB of RAM while each experiment only runs in a single thread with a time–out of one hour. We ran the following benchmarks[3]:

Crowds Protocol [21]. This protocol aims at anonymizing the sender of R messages by routing them probabilistically through a crowd of N hosts. Some of these hosts, however, are corrupt and try to determine the real sender by observing the host that most recently forwarded a message. For this model, we are interested in (a) the probability that the real sender is observed more than $R/10$ times, and (b) the expected number of times that the real sender is observed.

We also consider a variant (crowds-obs) of the model in which an observe statement ensures that after all messages have been delivered, hosts different from the real sender have been observed at least $R/4$ times. Unlike the model from the PRISM website, our model abstracts from the concrete identity of hosts different from the sender, since they are irrelevant for properties of interest.

Herman Protocol. In this protocol [22], N hosts form a token-passing ring and try to steer the system into a stable state. We consider the probability that the system eventually reaches such a state in two variants of this model where the initial state is either chosen probabilistically or nondeterministically.

Robot. The robot case-study is loosely based on a similar model from the PRISM benchmark suite. It models a robot that navigates through a bounded area of an unbounded grid. Doing so, the robot can be blocked by a janitor that is moving probabilistically across the whole grid. The property of interest is the probability that the robot will eventually reach its final destination.

---

[3] All input programs and log files of the experiments can be downloaded at moves.rwth-aachen.de/wp-content/uploads/conference_material/pgcl_atva16.tar.gz.

Predator. This model is due to Lotka and Volterra [23, p. 127]. A predator and a prey population evolve with mutual dependency on each other's numbers. Following some basic biology principles, both populations undergo periodic fluctuations. We are interested in (a) the probability of one of the species going extinct, and (b) the expected size of the prey population after one species has gone extinct.

Coupon Collector. This is a famous example[4] from textbooks on randomized algorithms [24]. A collector's goal is to collect all of N distinct coupons. In every round, the collector draws three new coupons chosen uniformly at random out of the N coupons. We consider (a) the probability that the collector possesses all coupons after N rounds, and (b) the expected number of rounds the collector needs until he has all the coupons as properties of interest. Furthermore, we consider two slight variants: in the first one (coupon-obs), an observe statement ensures that the three drawn coupons are all different and in the second one (coupon-classic), the collector may only draw one coupon in each round.

Table 1 shows the results for the probability queries. For each model instance, we give the number of explored states and transitions and whether or not the

Table 1. Benchmark results for probability queries.

Program	Instance	#states	#trans	Full?	λ	Result	Actual	Time
Crowds	(100, 60)	877370	1104290	yes	0.29	0.33	0.33	109
	(100, 80)	10^6	1258755	no	0.30	0.33	0.33	131
	(100, 100)	$2 \cdot 10^6$	2518395	no	0.30	0.33	0.33	354
Crowds-obs	(100, 60)	878405	1105325	yes	0.23	0.26	0.26	126
	(100, 80)	10^6	1258718	no	0.23	0.25	0.26	170
	(100, 100)	$3 \cdot 10^6$	3778192	no	0.23	0.26	0.26	890
Herman	(17)	10^6	1136612	no	0.9	0.99	1	91
	(21)	10^6	1222530	no	0.9	0.99	1	142
Herman-nd	(13)	1005945	1112188	yes	0.9	1	1	551
	(17)	–	–	no	0.9	0	1	TO
Robot	-	181595	234320	yes	0.9	1	1	24
Predator	-	10^6	1234854	no	0.9	0.98	1	116
Coupon	(5)	10^6	1589528	no	0.75	0.83	0.83	11
	(7)	$2 \cdot 10^6$	3635966	no	0.67	0.72	0.74	440
	(10)	–	–	no	0.57	0	0.63	TO
Coupon-obs	(5)	10^6	1750932	no	0.85	0.99	0.99	11
	(7)	10^6	1901206	no	0.88	0.91	0.98	15
	(10)	–	–	no	0.85	0	0.95	TO
Coupon-classic	(5)	10^6	1356463	no	3.4e-3	3.8e-3	3.8e-3	9
	(7)	10^6	1428286	no	5.5e-4	6.1e-4	6.1e-4	9
	(10)	–	–	no	3.3e-5	0	3.6e-5	TO

---

[4] https://en.wikipedia.org/wiki/Coupon_collector%27s_problem.

model was fully expanded. Note that the state number is a multiple of 10^6 in case the model was not fully explored, because our prototype always expands 10^6 states before it does the next model checking call. The next three columns show the probability bound (λ), the result that the tool could achieve as well as the actual answer to the query on the full (potentially infinite) model. Due to space constraints, we rounded these figures to two significant digits. We report on the time in seconds that the prototype took to establish the result (TO = 3600 s).

We observe that for most examples it suffices to perform few unfolding steps to achieve more than 90 % of the actual probability. For example, for the largest crowds-obs program, $3 \cdot 10^6$ states are expanded, meaning that three unfolding steps were performed. Answering queries on programs including an observe statement can be costlier (crowds vs. crowds-obs), but does not need to be (coupon vs. coupon-obs). In the latter case, the observe statement prunes some paths early that were not promising to begin with, whereas in the former case, the observe statement only happens at the very end, which intuitively makes it harder for the search to find target states. We are able to obtain non-trivial lower bounds for all but two case studies. For herman-nd, not all of the (nondeterministically chosen) initial states were explored, because our exploration order currently does not favour states that influence the obtained result the most. Similarly, for the largest coupon collector examples, the time limit did not allow for finding one target state. Again, an exploration heuristic that is more directed towards these could potentially improve performance drastically.

Table 2 shows the results for computing the expected value of program variables at terminating states. For technical reasons, our prototype currently cannot

Table 2. Benchmark results for expectation queries.

Program	Instance	#states	#trans	Full?	Result	Actual	Time
Crowds	(100, 60)	877370	1104290	yes	5.61	5.61	125
	(100, 80)	10^6	1258605	no	7.27	7.47	176
	(100, 100)	$2 \cdot 10^6$	2518270	no	9.22	9.34	383
Crowds-obs	(100, 60)	878405	1105325	yes	5.18	5.18	134
	(100, 80)	10^6	1258569	no	6.42	6.98	206
	(100, 100)	$2 \cdot 10^6$	2518220	no	8.39	8.79	462
Predator	–	$3 \cdot 10^6$	3716578	no	99.14	?	369
Coupon	(5)	10^6	1589528	no	4.13	4.13	15
	(7)	$3 \cdot 10^6$	5379492	no	5.86	6.38	46
	(10)	–	–	no	0	10.1	TO
Coupon-obs	(5)	10^6	1750932	no	2.57	2.57	13
	(7)	$2 \cdot 10^6$	3752912	no	4.22	4.23	30
	(10)	–	–	no	0	6.96	TO
Coupon-classic	(5)	10^6	1356463	no	11.41	11.42	15
	(7)	10^6	1393360	no	18.15	18.15	21
	(10)	–	–	no	0	29.29	TO

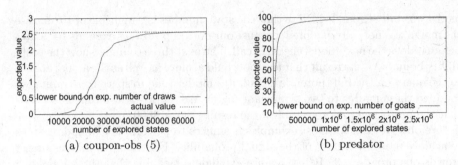

(a) coupon-obs (5)   (b) predator

Fig. 3. The obtained values approach the actual value from below.

perform more than one unfolding step for this type of query. To achieve meaningful results, we therefore vary the number of explored states until 90 % of the actual result is achieved. Note that for the predator program, the actual value for the query is not known to us, so we report on the value at which the result only grows very slowly. The results are similar to the probability case in that most often a low number of states suffices to show meaningful lower bounds. Unfortunately — as before — we can only prove a trivial lower bound for the largest coupon collector examples.

Figure 3 illustrates how the obtained lower bounds approach the actual expected value with increasing number of explored states for two case studies. For example, in the left picture one can observe that exploring 60000 states is enough to obtain a very precise lower bound on the expected number of rounds the collector needs to gather all five coupons, as indicated by the dashed line.

Finally, we analyze a parametric version of the crowds model that uses the parameters f and b to leave the probabilities (i) for a crowd member to be corrupt (b) and (ii) of forwarding (instead of delivering) a message (f) unspecified. In each iteration of our algorithm, we obtain a rational function describing a lower bound on the actual probability of observing the real sender of the message more than once *for each parameter valuation*. Figure 4 shows the regions of

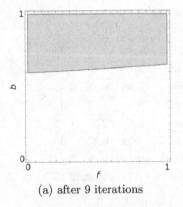
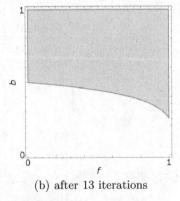

(a) after 9 iterations   (b) after 13 iterations

Fig. 4. Analyzing parametric models yields violating parameter instances.

the parameter space in which the protocol was determined to be unsafe (after iterations 9 and 13, respectively) in the sense that the probability to identify the real sender exceeds $\frac{1}{2}$. Since the results obtained over different iterations are monotonically increasing, we can conclude that all parameter valuations that were proved to be unsafe in some iteration are in fact unsafe in the full model. This in turn means that the blue area in Fig. 4 grows in each iteration.

5 Conclusion and Future Work

We presented a direct verification method for probabilistic programs employing probabilistic model checking. We conjecture that the basic idea would smoothly translate to reasoning about recursive probabilistic programs [25]. In the future we are interested in how loop invariants [26] can be utilized to devise complete model checking procedures preventing possibly infinite loop unrollings. This is especially interesting for reasoning about covariances [27], where a mixture of invariant–reasoning and successively constructing the operational MC would yield sound over- and underapproximations of covariances. To extend the gain for the user, we will combine this approach with methods for counterexamples [28], which can be given in terms of the programming language [19,29]. Moreover, it seem promising to investigate how approaches to automatically *repair* a probabilistic model towards satisfaction of properties [30,31] can be transferred to programs.

References

1. Gordon, A.D., Henzinger, T.A., Nori, A.V., Rajamani, S.K.: Probabilistic programming. In: FOSE, pp. 167–181. ACM Press (2014)
2. Sankaranarayanan, S., Chakarov, A., Gulwani, S.: Static analysis for probabilistic programs: inferring whole program properties from finitely many paths. In: PLDI, pp. 447–458. ACM (2013)
3. Claret, G., Rajamani, S.K., Nori, A.V., Gordon, A.D., Borgström, J.: Bayesian inference using data flow analysis. In: ESEC/SIGSOFT FSE, pp. 92–102. ACM Press (2013)
4. Gretz, F., Katoen, J.P., McIver, A.: Operational versus weakest pre-expectation semantics for the probabilistic guarded command language. Perform. Eval. **73**, 110–132 (2014)
5. Kwiatkowska, M., Norman, G., Parker, D.: PRISM 4.0: verification of probabilistic real-time systems. In: Gopalakrishnan, G., Qadeer, S. (eds.) CAV 2011. LNCS, vol. 6806, pp. 585–591. Springer, Heidelberg (2011). doi:10.1007/978-3-642-22110-1_47
6. Hahn, E.M., Li, Y., Schewe, S., Turrini, A., Zhang, L.: ISCASMC: a web-based probabilistic model checker. In: Jones, C., Pihlajasaari, P., Sun, J. (eds.) FM 2014. LNCS, vol. 8442, pp. 312–317. Springer, Heidelberg (2014). doi:10.1007/978-3-319-06410-9_22
7. Katoen, J.P., Zapreev, I.S., Hahn, E.M., Hermanns, H., Jansen, D.N.: The ins and outs of the probabilistic model checker MRMC. Perform. Eval. **68**(2), 90–104 (2011)

8. Kattenbelt, M.: Automated quantitative software verification. Ph.D. thesis, Oxford University (2011)
9. Sharir, M., Pnueli, A., Hart, S.: Verification of probabilistic programs. SIAM J. Comput. **13**(2), 292–314 (1984)
10. Vardi, M.Y.: Automatic verification of probabilistic concurrent finite-state programs. In: FOCS, pp. 327–338. IEEE Computer Society (1985)
11. Baier, C., Katoen, J.P.: Principles of Model Checking. The MIT Press, Cambridge (2008)
12. Baier, C., Klein, J., Klüppelholz, S., Märcker, S.: Computing conditional probabilities in Markovian models efficiently. In: Ábrahám, E., Havelund, K. (eds.) TACAS 2014. LNCS, vol. 8413, pp. 515–530. Springer, Heidelberg (2014). doi:10. 1007/978-3-642-54862-8_43
13. Dehnert, C., Junges, S., Jansen, N., Corzilius, F., Volk, M., Bruintjes, H., Katoen, J., Ábrahám, E.: PROPhESY: a probabilistic parameter synthesis tool. In: Kroening, D., Pâsâreanu, C.S. (eds.) CAV 2015. LNCS, vol. 9206, pp. 214–231. Springer, Berlin (2015)
14. Quatmann, T., Dehnert, C., Jansen, N., Junges, S., Katoen, J.: Parameter synthesis for Markov models: faster than ever. In: Nelson, S.P., Meyer, V. (eds.) ATVA 2016. LNCS, vol. 9938, pp. xx–yy. Springer, Heidelberg (2016). CoRR abs/1602.05113
15. Dijkstra, E.W.: A Discipline of Programming. Prentice Hall, Englewood Cliffs (1976)
16. McIver, A., Morgan, C.: Abstraction, Refinement and Proof for Probabilistic Systems. Springer, Berlin (2004)
17. Jansen, N., Kaminski, B.L., Katoen, J., Olmedo, F., Gretz, F., McIver, A.: Conditioning in probabilistic programming. Electr. Notes Theoret. Comput. Sci. **319**, 199–216 (2015)
18. Kaminski, B.L., Katoen, J.-P.: On the hardness of almost–sure termination. In: Italiano, G.F., Pighizzini, G., Sannella, D.T. (eds.) MFCS 2015. LNCS, vol. 9234, pp. 307–318. Springer, Heidelberg (2015)
19. Dehnert, C., Jansen, N., Wimmer, R., Ábrahám, E., Katoen, J.-P.: Fast debugging of PRISM models. In: Cassez, F., Raskin, J.-F. (eds.) ATVA 2014. LNCS, vol. 8837, pp. 146–162. Springer, Heidelberg (2014). doi:10.1007/978-3-319-11936-6_11
20. Jansen, N., Dehnert, C., Kaminski, B.L., Katoen, J., Westhofen, L.: Bounded model checking for probabilistic programs. In: Nelson, S.P., Meyer, V. (eds.) ATVA 2016. LNCS, vol. 9938, pp. xx–yy. Springer, Heidelberg (2016). CoRR abs/1605.04477
21. Reiter, M.K., Rubin, A.D.: Crowds: anonymity for web transactions. ACM Trans. Inf. Syst. Secur. **1**(1), 66–92 (1998)
22. Herman, T.: Probabilistic self-stabilization. Inf. Process. Lett. **35**(2), 63–67 (1990)
23. Brauer, F., Castillo-Chavez, C.: Mathematical Models in Population Biology and Epidemiology. Texts in Applied Mathematics. Springer, New York (2001)
24. Erds, P., Rnyi, A.: On a classical problem of probability theory. Publ. Math. Inst. Hung. Acad. Sci. Ser. A **6**, 215–220 (1961)
25. Olmedo, F., Kaminski, B., Katoen, J.P., Matheja, C.: Reasoning about recursive probabilistic programs. In: LICS (2016, to appear)
26. Gretz, F., Katoen, J.-P., McIver, A.: PRINSYS—on a quest for probabilistic loop invariants. In: Joshi, K., Siegle, M., Stoelinga, M., D'Argenio, P.R. (eds.) QEST 2013. LNCS, vol. 8054, pp. 193–208. Springer, Heidelberg (2013)
27. Kaminski, B.L., Katoen, J.-P., Matheja, C.: Inferring covariances for probabilistic programs. In: Agha, G., Houdt, B. (eds.) QEST 2016. LNCS, vol. 9826, pp. 191–206. Springer, Heidelberg (2016). doi:10.1007/978-3-319-43425-4_14

28. Ábrahám, E., Becker, B., Dehnert, C., Jansen, N., Katoen, J.-P., Wimmer, R.: Counterexample generation for discrete-time Markov models: an introductory survey. In: Bernardo, M., Damiani, F., Hähnle, R., Johnsen, E.B., Schaefer, I. (eds.) SFM 2014. LNCS, vol. 8483, pp. 65–121. Springer, Heidelberg (2014). doi:10.1007/978-3-319-07317-0_3

29. Wimmer, R., Jansen, N., Abraham, E., Katoen, J.P.: High-level counterexamples for probabilistic automata. Log. Methods Comput. Sci. **11**, 1–15 (2015)

30. Bartocci, E., Grosu, R., Katsaros, P., Ramakrishnan, C.R., Smolka, S.A.: Model repair for probabilistic systems. In: Abdulla, P.A., Leino, K.R.M. (eds.) TACAS 2011. LNCS, vol. 6605, pp. 326–340. Springer, Heidelberg (2011). doi:10.1007/978-3-642-19835-9_30

31. Pathak, S., Ábrahám, E., Jansen, N., Tacchella, A., Katoen, J.-P.: A greedy approach for the efficient repair of stochastic models. In: Havelund, K., Holzmann, G., Joshi, R. (eds.) NFM 2015. LNCS, vol. 9058, pp. 295–309. Springer, Heidelberg (2015). doi:10.1007/978-3-319-17524-9_21

Counter Systems, Automata

How Hard is It to Verify Flat Affine Counter Systems with the Finite Monoid Property?

Radu Iosif[1] and Arnaud Sangnier[2]($\boxtimes$)

[1] Verimag, Université Grenoble Alpes, CNRS, Grenoble, France
[2] IRIF, Université Paris Diderot, CNRS, Paris, France
`sangnier@liafa.univ-paris-diderot.fr`

Abstract. We study several decision problems for counter systems with guards defined by convex polyhedra and updates defined by affine transformations. In general, the reachability problem is undecidable for such systems. Decidability can be achieved by imposing two restrictions: (1) the control structure of the counter system is *flat*, meaning that nested loops are forbidden, and (2) the multiplicative monoid generated by the affine update matrices present in the system is finite. We provide complexity bounds for several decision problems of such systems, by proving that reachability and model checking for Past Linear Temporal Logic stands in the second level of the polynomial hierarchy Σ_2^P, while model checking for First Order Logic is PSPACE-complete.

1 Introduction

Counter systems are finite state automata extended with integer variables, also known as counter automata or counter machines. These are Turing-complete models of computation, often used to describe the behavior of complex real-life systems, such as embedded/control hardware and/or software systems. Because many verification problems, of rather complex systems, can be reduced to decision problems for counter systems, it is important to understand the difficulties faced by potential verification algorithms designed to work with the latter.

Due to their succinctness and expressive power, most decision problems, such as reachability, termination and temporal logic model-checking, are undecidable for counter systems, even when the operations on the counters are restricted to increment, decrement and zero-test [24]. This early negative result motivated the search for subclasses with decidable decision problems. Such classes include *one-counter systems* [14], *vector addition systems with states* [22], *reversal-bounded counter machines* [15] and *flat counter systems* [4,12].

Flat counter systems are defined by a natural syntactic restriction, which requires that no state occurs in more than one simple cycle in the control flow graph of the system. Decidability results on the verification of reachability problems for flat counter systems have been obtained by proving that, under certain restrictions on the logic that defines the transition rules, the set of reachable

R. Iosif—Supported by the French ANR project VECOLIB (ANR-14-CE28-0018).

C. Artho et al. (Eds.): ATVA 2016, LNCS 9938, pp. 89–105, 2016.
DOI: 10.1007/978-3-319-46520-3_6

configurations is semilinear and effectively definable in Presburger arithmetic [4,6,12]. Even though flatness is an important restriction (few counter systems modeling real-life hardware and software artifacts are actually flat), this class provides the grounds for a useful method that under-approximates the set of behaviors of a non-flat counter system by larger and larger sets of paths described by flat counter systems. This method is currently used by model checking tools, such as FAST [2] and FLATA [19], and has been applied to improve the results of static analysis [13], as well as the convergence of counterexample-driven abstraction refinement algorithms [17]. Moreover, several works define classes of *flattable* counter systems, for which there exist flat unfoldings of the system with identical reachability sets. Such is the case of timed automata [7] and of 2-dimensional vector addition systems with states [3,21]. For these systems, the method of under-approximations by flat unfoldings is guaranteed to terminate.

In general, the flatness restriction is shown to reduce the computational complexity of several decision problems, such as reachability or temporal logic model checking. For instance, in the case of Kripke structures, flatness reduces the complexity of the model-checking of Linear Temporal Logic (LTL) from PSPACE to NP [20]. When considering flat counter systems whose updates are described by translations, the complexity of these problems drops from undecidable to NP-complete [10], while model checking for First Order Logic (FO) is coined to be PSPACE-complete [8]. For branching time temporal logics, flatness yields decidable problems, but with less remarkable complexity bounds [9].

In this work, we focus on the model of affine counter systems, in which each transition is labeled with (i) a guard defined by (a disjunction of) convex polyhedra, i.e. linear systems of inequalities of the form $C \cdot x \leq d$, and (ii) a deterministic update defined by an affine transformations $f(x) = A \cdot x + b$ where $A, C \in \mathbb{Z}^{n \times n}$ are square matrices with integer entries, $b, d \in \mathbb{Z}^n$ are vectors of integer constants and $x = [x_1, \ldots, x_n]$ is a vector of counters. For such systems, the set of reachable configurations is semilinear (thus reachability is decidable), provided that the multiplicative monoid generated by the matrices used in update functions is finite. This condition is also known as the *finite monoid property* [4,12]. Moreover, it has been shown that the model-checking of such systems, for an extended version of the branching time logic CTL* is decidable, also by reduction to the satisfiability of a Presburger formula, of size exponential in the size of the counter system [11].

In this work, we show that for flat affine counter systems with the finite monoid property, reachability and model checking for Past LTL are Σ_2^P, whereas model checking for FO is PSPACE-complete. Our result generalizes the results for flat counter systems with translations [8,10], since these systems are a strict subclass of flat affine counter systems with the finite monoid property. For instance, a transfer of values between different counters can be done in one step with an affine counter system, whereas a translating counter system would need a cycle to implement such operations. Our proof technique is based on an analysis of the behavior of the sequence of matrix powers in a finite multiplicative monoid, and adapts several techniques for translating counter systems to this more general case.

Due to lack of space, omitted proofs can be found in [18].

2   Counter Systems and Their Decision Problems

We denote by $\mathbb{N}$ and $\mathbb{Z}$ the sets of natural and integer numbers, respectively. We write $[\ell, u]$ for the integer interval $\{\ell, \ell + 1, \ldots, u\}$, where $\ell \leq u$, and $\text{abs}(n)$ for the absolute value of the integer $n \in \mathbb{Z}$. The cardinality of a finite set S is denoted by $\|S\|$.

We denote by $\mathbb{Z}^{n \times m}$ the set of matrices with n rows and m columns, where $\boldsymbol{A}[i]$ is the i-th column and $\boldsymbol{A}[i][j]$ is the entry on the i-th row and j-th column of $\boldsymbol{A} \in \mathbb{Z}^{n \times m}$, for each $i \in [1, n]$ and $j \in [1, m]$. If $n = m$, we call this number the *dimension* of A, and we denote by $\mathbf{I}_n$ the identity matrix in $\mathbb{Z}^{n \times n}$. For $\boldsymbol{A} \in \mathbb{Z}^{n \times m}$ and $\boldsymbol{B} \in \mathbb{Z}^{m \times p}$, we denote by $\boldsymbol{A} \cdot \boldsymbol{B} \in \mathbb{Z}^{n \times p}$ the matrix product of $\boldsymbol{A}$ and $\boldsymbol{B}$. For a matrix $\boldsymbol{A} \in \mathbb{Z}^{n \times n}$, we define $\boldsymbol{A}^0 = \mathbf{I}_n$ and $\boldsymbol{A}^i = \boldsymbol{A}^{i-1} \cdot \boldsymbol{A}$, for all $i > 0$.

We write $\mathbb{Z}^n$ for $\mathbb{Z}^{n \times 1}$ in the following. Each $\boldsymbol{v} \in \mathbb{Z}^n$ is a column vector, where $\boldsymbol{v}[i]$ is the entry on its i-th row. For a vector $\boldsymbol{x}$ of variables of length n and a matrix $\boldsymbol{A} \in \mathbb{Z}^{m \times n}$, the product $\boldsymbol{A} \cdot \boldsymbol{x}$ is the vector of terms $(\boldsymbol{A} \cdot \boldsymbol{x})[i] = \sum_{j=1}^{n} \boldsymbol{A}[i][j] \cdot \boldsymbol{x}[j]$, for all $i \in [1, m]$. A row vector is denoted by $\boldsymbol{v} = [v_1, \ldots, v_n] \in \mathbb{Z}^{1 \times n}$. For a row vector $\boldsymbol{v}$, we denote its transpose by $\boldsymbol{v}^\top$.

For a vector $\boldsymbol{v} \in \mathbb{Z}^n$, we consider the standard infinity $\| \boldsymbol{v} \|_\infty = \max_{i=1}^{n} \text{abs}(\boldsymbol{v}[i])$ norm . Given $\boldsymbol{A} \in \mathbb{Z}^{m \times n}$, consider the induced $\| \boldsymbol{A} \|_\infty = \max_{i=1}^{m} \sum_{j=1}^{n} \text{abs}(\boldsymbol{A}[i][j])$, and the maximum $\| \boldsymbol{A} \|_{\max} = \max_{i=1}^{m} \max_{j=1}^{n} \text{abs}(\boldsymbol{A}[i][j])$ norms. The size of a matrix is $size(\boldsymbol{A}) = \sum_{i=1}^{m} \sum_{j=1}^{n} \log_2(\boldsymbol{A}[i][j] + 1)$, with integers encoded in binary.

2.1   Counter Systems

Let $\mathsf{X}_n = \{x_1, x_2, \ldots, x_n\}$ be a finite set of integer variables, called *counters*, $\boldsymbol{x}$ be the vector such that $\boldsymbol{x}[i] = x_i$, for all $i \in [1, n]$, and $\mathsf{AP} = \{\mathsf{a}, \mathsf{b}, \mathsf{c}, \ldots\}$ be a countable set of Boolean *atomic propositions*. A *guard* is either true, denoted by $\top$, or a disjunction of systems of inequalities, denoted by $\bigvee_{i=1}^{k} \boldsymbol{C}_i \cdot \boldsymbol{x} \leq \boldsymbol{d}_i$ where $\boldsymbol{C}_i \in \mathbb{Z}^{m \times n}$ and $\boldsymbol{d}_i \in \mathbb{Z}^m$ for all $i \in [1, k]$. A guard is said to be without disjunction if it is either true or it consists of a single system of inequalities.

An integer vector $\boldsymbol{v} \in \mathbb{Z}^n$ *satisfies* the guard g, written $\boldsymbol{v} \models \mathsf{g}$, if either (i) $\mathsf{g} := \top$, or (ii) $\mathsf{g} := \bigvee_{i=1}^{k} \boldsymbol{C}_i \cdot \boldsymbol{x} \leq \boldsymbol{d}_i$ and $\boldsymbol{v}$ is a solution of a system $\boldsymbol{C}_i \cdot \boldsymbol{x} \leq \boldsymbol{d}_i$, for some $i \in [1, k]$. The set of guards using X_n is denoted by $\mathsf{CG}(\mathsf{X}_n)$. An *affine function* $f : \mathbb{Z}^n \to \mathbb{Z}^n$ is a pair $(\boldsymbol{A}, \boldsymbol{b}) \in \mathbb{Z}^{n \times n} \times \mathbb{Z}^n$. Given a vector $\boldsymbol{v} \in \mathbb{Z}^n$, the result of the function $f = (\boldsymbol{A}, \boldsymbol{b})$ applied to $\boldsymbol{v}$ is $f(\boldsymbol{v}) = \boldsymbol{A} \cdot \boldsymbol{v} + \boldsymbol{b}$. We denote by Aff_n the set of affine functions over $\mathbb{Z}^n$. An affine function $(\boldsymbol{A}, \boldsymbol{b})$ where $\boldsymbol{A} = \mathbf{I}_n$ is called a *translation*.

Definition 1 *(Affine Counter System). For an integer $n \geq 0$, an* affine counter system of dimension n *(shortly a* counter system*) is a tuple $S = \langle Q, \mathsf{X}_n, \Delta, \Lambda \rangle$,* where: *(i) Q is a finite set of* control states, *(ii) $\Lambda : Q \to 2^{AP}$ is a* labeling function, *and (iii) $\Delta \subseteq Q \times \mathsf{CG}(\mathsf{X}_n) \times \mathsf{Aff}_n \times Q$ is a finite set of* transition rules *labeled by guards and affine functions (updates).*

A counter system is said to be *disjunction free* if all its guards are without disjunction. For a transition rule $\delta = \langle q, \mathsf{g}, f, q' \rangle \in \Delta$, we use the notations $source(\delta) = q$, $guard(\delta) = \mathsf{g}$, $update(\delta) = f$ and $target(\delta) = q'$. A *path* π of S is a non-empty sequence of transition rules $\delta_1 \ldots \delta_m$ such that $source(\delta_{i+1}) = target(\delta_i)$ for all $i \in [1, m-1]$. The path π is a *simple cycle* if $\delta_1 \ldots \delta_m$ are pairwise distinct and $source(\delta_1) = target(\delta_m)$. In this case, we denote $source(\pi) = target(\pi) = source(\delta_1)$. A counter system S is *flat* if for each control state $q \in Q$ there exists at most one simple cycle π such that $source(\pi) = q$. In such a system any path leaving a simple cycle cannot revisit it.

Example 1. Figure 1 shows a flat counter system whose control states q_0, q_1, q_2, q_3 are labeled by the atomic propositions $\mathsf{a}, \mathsf{b}, \mathsf{c}, \mathsf{d}$, respectively. From the initial state q_0 with all counters equal to 0, this system begins with incrementing x_1 a certain number of times by a transition δ_0 then, with δ_1, it transfers the value of the counter x_1 to x_3 and resets x_1; the loop labeled by δ_2 increments both x_1 and x_2 until they both reach the value of x_3 and finally the loop labeled by δ_4 is used to decrement x_2 and increment x_1 until the value of x_1 is twice the value of x_3. As a consequence, when the system reaches q_3 the value of x_1 is twice the value of x_3 and the value of x_2 is equal to 0. Hence, any run reaching q_3 visits the state q_1 exactly the same number of times as the state q_2.   ∎

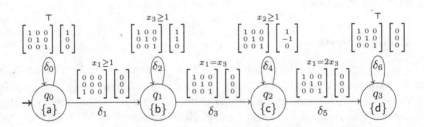

Fig. 1. A flat affine counter system

The size of a counter system S is $size(S) = \sum_{\delta \in \Delta} size(\delta) + \sum_{q \in Q} \|\Lambda(q)\|$, where $size(\delta) = 1 + size(guard(\delta)) + size(update(\delta))$, for a guard $\mathsf{g} := \bigvee_{i=1}^{k} \boldsymbol{C}_i \cdot \boldsymbol{x} \leq \boldsymbol{d}_i$ we have $size(g) = \sum_{i=1}^{k} size(\boldsymbol{C}_i) + size(\boldsymbol{d}_i)$, and for an update $f = (\boldsymbol{A}, \boldsymbol{b})$, $size(f) = size(\boldsymbol{A}) + size(\boldsymbol{b})$.

A counter system of dimension $n = 0$ is called a *Kripke structure*. We denote by KS and KS$_\mathsf{f}$ the sets of Kripke structures and flat Kripke structures, respectively. A counter system of dimension $n \geq 1$ is *translating* if all updates labeling the transition rules are pairs $(\mathbf{I}_n, \boldsymbol{b})$. Let TS and $\mathsf{TS_f}$ denote the sets of translating and flat translating counter systems of any dimension $n \geq 1$.

For a counter system S of dimension $n \geq 1$, we consider $\mathcal{M}_S \subseteq \mathbb{Z}^{n \times n}$ to be the smallest set of matrices, closed under product, which contains $\mathbf{I}_n$ and each matrix $\boldsymbol{A}$ occurring in an update $(\boldsymbol{A}, \boldsymbol{b})$ of a transition rule in S. Clearly, $\mathcal{M}_S$ forms a monoid with the matrix product and identity $\mathbf{I}_n$. We say that S has the *finite monoid property* if the set $\mathcal{M}_S$ is finite. Let $\mathsf{AS_{fm}}$ be the set of flat counter systems with the finite monoid property and $\mathsf{AS_{fm}^{df}}$ its restriction to disjunction free systems. These latter classes are the main focus of this paper.

A *configuration* of the counter system $S = \langle Q, \mathsf{X}_n, \Delta, \Lambda \rangle$ is a pair $(q, \boldsymbol{v}) \in Q \times \mathbb{Z}^n$, where q is the current control state and $\boldsymbol{v}[i]$ is the value of the counter x_i, for all $i \in [1, n]$. Given two configurations $\gamma = (q, \boldsymbol{v})$ and $\gamma' = (q', \boldsymbol{v}')$ and a transition rule δ, we write $\gamma \xrightarrow{\delta} \gamma'$ iff $q = source(\delta)$, $q' = target(\delta)$, $\boldsymbol{v} \models guard(\delta)$ and $\boldsymbol{v}' = update(\delta)(\boldsymbol{v})$. We use the notation $\gamma \to \gamma'$ when there exists a transition rule δ such that $\gamma \xrightarrow{\delta} \gamma'$. A *run* of S is then an infinite sequence of the form $\rho : \gamma_0 \xrightarrow{\delta_0} \gamma_1 \xrightarrow{\delta_1} \gamma_2 \xrightarrow{\delta_2} \dots$. We say that such a run starts at configuration γ_0, furthermore we denote by $trans(\rho) = \delta_0 \delta_1 \delta_2 \dots$ the infinite sequence of transition rules seen during ρ. Without loss of generality we consider *deadlock-free* counter systems only, where for each configuration $\gamma \in Q \times \mathbb{Z}^n$, there exists a configuration γ' such that $\gamma \to \gamma'$.[1]

Example 2. The sequence below is a run of the counter system from Fig. 1:

$$\left(q_0, \begin{bmatrix} 0 \\ 0 \\ 0 \end{bmatrix} \right) \xrightarrow{\delta_0} \left(q_0, \begin{bmatrix} 1 \\ 0 \\ 0 \end{bmatrix} \right) \xrightarrow{\delta_1} \left(q_1, \begin{bmatrix} 0 \\ 0 \\ 1 \end{bmatrix} \right) \xrightarrow{\delta_2} \left(q_1, \begin{bmatrix} 1 \\ 1 \\ 1 \end{bmatrix} \right) \xrightarrow{\delta_3} \left(q_2, \begin{bmatrix} 1 \\ 1 \\ 1 \end{bmatrix} \right)$$

$$\xrightarrow{\delta_4} \left(q_2, \begin{bmatrix} 2 \\ 0 \\ 1 \end{bmatrix} \right) \xrightarrow{\delta_5} \left(q_3, \begin{bmatrix} 2 \\ 0 \\ 1 \end{bmatrix} \right) \xrightarrow{\delta_6} \left(q_3, \begin{bmatrix} 2 \\ 0 \\ 1 \end{bmatrix} \right) \xrightarrow{\delta_6} \left(q_3, \begin{bmatrix} 2 \\ 0 \\ 1 \end{bmatrix} \right) \xrightarrow{\delta_6} \dots \blacksquare$$

2.2 Decision Problems

The *reachability problem* for a class of counter systems $\mathcal{C}$, denoted by $\textsc{Reach}(\mathcal{C})$, can then be stated as follows: given a counter system S in $\mathcal{C}$, an initial configuration γ_0, and a control state q_f, does S have a run starting in γ_0 and containing a configuration $(q_f, \boldsymbol{v})$, for some $\boldsymbol{v} \in \mathbb{Z}^n$? It is well known that $\textsc{Reach}(\mathsf{TS})$ is undecidable for non-flat counter systems, even for only 2 counters with zero test guards, and increment/decrement updates [24].

In this work we also consider *model checking* problems for two specification logics, namely Past Linear Temporal Logic (PLTL) and First Order Logic (FO).

---

[1] We ensure deadlock-freedom by adding a sink state σ to S, with a self-loop $\sigma \xrightarrow{\top} \sigma$, and a transition $q \xrightarrow{\top} \sigma$ from each state $q \in Q$.

The formulae of PLTL are defined by the grammar: $\phi ::= p \mid \neg\phi \mid \phi \wedge \phi \mid X\phi \mid \phi U\phi \mid X^{-1}\phi \mid \phi S\phi$, where $p \in AP$. As usual, we consider the derived modal operators $F\phi := \top U\phi$ and $G\phi := \neg F\neg\phi$. Given a run ρ: $\gamma_0 \xrightarrow{\delta_0} \gamma_1 \xrightarrow{\delta_1} \gamma_2 \xrightarrow{\delta_2} \ldots$ of a counter system S and a PLTL formula ϕ, the semantics of PLTL is defined by an inductive forcing relation $\rho, i \models_{\text{PLTL}} \phi$, where for all $i \geq 0$: $\rho, i \models_{\text{PLTL}} p \Leftrightarrow \gamma_i = (q, v)$ and $p \in \Lambda(q)$; $\rho, i \models_{\text{PLTL}} X\phi \Leftrightarrow \rho, i+1 \models_{\text{PLTL}} \phi$; $\rho, i \models_{\text{PLTL}} \phi U\psi \Leftrightarrow \rho, j \models_{\text{PLTL}} \psi$ for some $j \geq i$ and $\rho, k \models_{\text{PLTL}} \phi$ for all $i \leq k < j$; $\rho, i \models_{\text{PLTL}} X^{-1}\phi \Leftrightarrow i > 0$ and $\rho, i-1 \models_{\text{PLTL}} \phi$; $\rho, i \models_{\text{PLTL}} \phi S\psi \Leftrightarrow \rho, j \models_{\text{PLTL}} \psi$ for some $0 \leq j \leq i$ and $\rho, k \models_{\text{PLTL}} \phi$ for all $j < k \leq i$. The semantics of the Boolean connectives $\wedge$ and $\neg$ is the usual one. We write $\rho \models_{\text{PLTL}} \phi$ for $\rho, 0 \models_{\text{PLTL}} \phi$. For instance, each run of the counter system from Fig. 1 satisfies $G((b \wedge Xb \wedge Fd) \rightarrow F(c \wedge Xc))$, because each run visiting q_3 sees the same number of b's and c's.

The formulae of FO are defined by the grammar: $\phi ::= p(z) \mid z < z' \mid \neg\phi \mid \phi \wedge \phi \mid \exists z.\phi$, where $p \in AP$ and z belongs to a countable set of *logical variables* Var. The semantics is given by a forcing relation $\rho \models_{\text{FO}} \phi$ between runs ρ of S and closed formulae ϕ, with no free variables, which interprets the quantified variables $z \in$ Var as positive integers denoting positions in the run. With this convention, the semantics of FO is standard. For instance, each run of the counter system from Fig. 1 satisfies the FO property: $\forall x \forall x'.(x < x' \wedge b(x) \wedge b(x') \wedge \exists z.d(z)) \rightarrow \exists y \exists y' . c(y) \wedge c(y')$, which differs from the previous PLTL formula only in that x and x' (y and y') are not necessarily consecutive moments in time. For both of these logics, we consider the size of a formula as its number of subformulae.

The model-checking problem for counter systems in a class $\mathcal{C}$ with specification language $\mathcal{L}$ (in this work either PLTL or FO), denoted by $\text{MC}_{\mathcal{L}}(\mathcal{C})$, is defined as follows: given a counter system S in $\mathcal{C}$, an initial configuration γ_0, and a formula ϕ of $\mathcal{L}$, does there exist a run ρ of S starting in γ_0 such that $\rho \models_{\mathcal{L}} \phi$.

Table 1. Known results

	KS	KS$_f$	TS	TS$_f$	AS$_{fm}$
Reach	NLOGSPACE	NLOGSPACE	Undec. [24]	NP-c. [10]	4EXPTIME [12]
MC$_{PLTL}$	PSPACE-c. [25]	NP-c. [10,20]	Undec.	NP-c. [10]	4EXPTIME [11]
MC$_{FO}$	NONELEM. [26]	PSPACE-c. [8]	Undec.	PSPACE-c. [8]	Decid. [11]

Table 1 gives an overview of the known complexity bounds for the previously mentioned decision problems looking at different classes of counter systems. For flat Kripke structures, it is proved in [10,20] that $\text{MC}_{PLTL}(KS_f)$ is NP-complete and in [8] that $\text{MC}_{FO}(KS_f)$ is PSPACE-complete, whereas $\text{MC}_{PLTL}(KS)$ is PSPACE-complete and $\text{MC}_{FO}(KS)$ is non-elementary. As explained in [8,10], the complexity of these two last problems does not change if one considers flat translating counter systems. For what concerns flat counter systems with the finite monoid property, it has been shown that one can compute a Presburger formula which characterizes the reachability set, which entails the decidability of Reach(AS$_{fm}$) [12]. Later on, in [11], the authors have shown that the model-checking of an extension of the branching time logic CTL* is decidable. Hence we know that $MC_{PLTL}(AS_{fm})$ and $MC_{FO}(AS_{fm})$ are decidable, however no precise complexity for these problems is known. We only can deduce from the proofs in [5, 11, 12] that for $REACH(AS_{fm})$ and $MC_{PLTL}(AS_{fm})$ there exists a reduction to the satisfiability problem for Presburger arithmetic where the built formula is exponentially bigger than the size of the model, this leads to an upper bound in 4EXPTIME (the satisfiability problem for Presburger arithmetic can in fact be solved in 3EXPTIME, see e.g. [16]).

In this work, we aim at improving the complexity for the problems related to affine counter systems with the finite monoid property. Note that for the presented results, the counter systems were manipulating natural numbers instead of integers, but considering the latter option does not change the stated results.

3   A Hardness Result

In this section we prove that the reachability problem for flat affine counter systems with the finite monoid property is Σ_2^P-hard, by reduction from the validity problem for the $\exists^*\forall^*$ fragment of quantified boolean formulae (Σ_2-QBF), which is a well-known Σ_2^P-complete problem [1, Sect. 5.2]. Let us consider a formula $\Phi := \exists y_1 \ldots \exists y_p \forall z_1 \ldots \forall z_q . \Psi(\boldsymbol{y}, \boldsymbol{z})$, where $\boldsymbol{y} = \{y_1, \ldots, y_p\}$ and $\boldsymbol{z} = \{z_1, \ldots, z_q\}$ are non-empty sets of boolean variables, and Ψ is a quantifier-free boolean formula. We shall build, in polynomial time, a flat counter system S_Φ, with the finite monoid property, such that Φ is valid if and only if S_Φ has a run reaching q_f which starts in $(q_0, \boldsymbol{v}_0)$ for a certain valuation $\boldsymbol{v}_0$ of its counters.

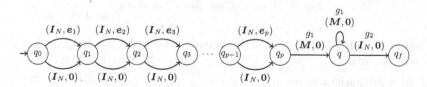

Fig. 2. The counter system S_Φ corresponding to the Σ_2-QBF Φ

Let π_n denote the n-th prime number, i.e. $\pi_1 = 2, \pi_2 = 3, \pi_3 = 5$, etc. Formally, $S_\Phi = \langle Q, \mathsf{X}_N, \Delta, \Lambda \rangle$, where $Q = \{q_0, \ldots, q_p, q, q_f\}$, $N = p + \sum_{n=1}^q \pi_n$, and Λ is the function associating to each state an empty set of propositions. We recall that π_n is a polynomial in the size of n, hence N is as well polynomial in the size of n. The transition rules Δ are depicted in Fig. 2. Intuitively, each existentially quantified boolean variable y_i of Φ is modeled by the counter x_i in S_Φ, each universally quantified variable z_j of Φ is modeled by the counter $x_{p+\sum_{n=1}^j \pi_n}$, and the rest are working counters. All counters range over the set $\{0, 1\}$, with the obvious meaning (0 stands for false and 1 for true).

The counter system S_Φ works in two phases. The first phase, corresponding to transitions $q_0 \to \ldots \to q_p$, initializes the counters $x_1, \ldots, x_p$ to some values from the set $\{0, 1\}$, thus mimicking a choice of boolean values for the existentially quantified variables $y_1, \ldots, y_p$ from Φ. Here $\mathbf{I}_N \in \mathbb{Z}^{N \times N}$ is the identity matrix, and $\boldsymbol{e}_i \in \{0, 1\}^N$ is the unit vector such that $\boldsymbol{e}_i[j] = 0$ if $j \neq i$ and $\boldsymbol{e}_i[i] = 1$.

The second phase checks that Φ is valid for each choice of $z_1, \ldots, z_q$. This is done by the cycle $q \to q$, which explores all combinations of 0's and 1's for the counters $x_{p + \sum_{n=1}^{j} \pi_n}$, corresponding to z_j, for all $j \in [1, q]$. To this end, we use the permutation matrix $\boldsymbol{M}$, which consists of $\mathbf{I}_p$ and q rotation blocks $\boldsymbol{M}_{\pi_j} \in \{0, 1\}^{\pi_j \times \pi_j}$ (Fig. 3). The valuation $\boldsymbol{v}_0$ ensures that the initial value of $x_{p + \sum_{n=1}^{j} \pi_n}$ is 1, for all $j \in [1, q]$, the other counters being 0 initially (Fig. 3).

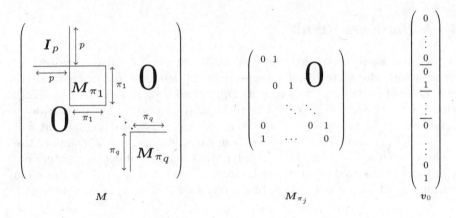

Fig. 3. Matrix $\boldsymbol{M}$ and initial vector $\boldsymbol{v}_0$

Intuitively, after n iterations of the affine function $(\boldsymbol{M}, \boldsymbol{0})$, labeling the cycle $q \to q$ in S_Φ, we have $x_{p + \sum_{n=1}^{j} \pi_n} = 1$ iff n is a multiple of π_j. This fact guarantees that all combinations of 0's and 1's for $z_1, \ldots, z_q$ have been visited in $\Pi_{j=1}^{q} \pi_j$ iterations of the cycle. The guard g_1, labeling the cycle, tests that, at each iteration, the formula Ψ is satisfied, using a standard encoding of the formula Ψ. Namely, each variable y_i is encoded as the term $x_i \geq 1$ and each z_j is encoded as $x_{p + \sum_{n=1}^{j} \pi_n} \geq 1$.

For instance, the formula $y_1 \vee \neg z_2$ is encoded as $x_1 \geq 1 \vee \neg(x_{p + \pi_1 + \pi_2} \geq 1))$ which is equivalent to $x_1 \geq 1 \vee x_{p + \pi_1 + \pi_2} < 1$. Finally, the guard g_2 simply checks that $x_{\pi_1} = \ldots = x_{\pi_1 + \ldots + \pi_q} = 1$, ensuring that the loop has been iterated sufficiently many times. This allows us to deduce the following result.

Lemma 1. REACH($\mathsf{AS}_{\mathrm{fm}}$) *is* Σ_2^P*-hard.*

4   Bounding the Number of Cycle Iterations

In this section we prove a crucial property of counter systems from the $\mathsf{AS}_{\mathrm{fm}}^{\mathrm{df}}$ class, namely that there exists a polynomial function $\mathrm{Poly}(x)$ such that, for each run ρ starting at γ_0 of the considered counter system, there exists another run ρ' starting at γ_0, using the same transition rules as ρ, in exactly the same order, and which iterates each simple cycle at most $2^{\mathsf{Poly}(size(S)+size(\gamma_0))}$ times.

In the rest of this section, we fix a flat disjunction free affine counter system $S = \langle Q, \mathsf{X}_n, \Delta, \Lambda \rangle$ with the finite monoid property. We recall here that the set of runs of a flat counter system can be captured by a finite (though exponential) number of *path schemas* [8]. Formally, a path schema is a non-empty finite sequence $P := u_1 \ldots u_N$, where u_i is either a transition rule from Δ or a simple cycle, such that (i) $u_1, \ldots, u_N$ are pairwise distinct, (ii) u_N is a simple cycle, called *terminal*, and (iii) $target(u_i) = source(u_{i+1})$, for all $i \in [1, N-1]$. All simple cycles on P, except for u_N, are called *nonterminal*. We use then the following notations: $len(P)$ for N, $P[i]$ for u_i with $i \in [1, N]$, and $size(P)$ is the sum of the sizes of all transition rules occurring in P.

Intuitively a path schema P represents a set of infinite paths obtained by iterating the non-terminal cycles a certain number of times. We can hence represent such a path by an associated path schema and an iteration vector. Formally, an *iterated path schema* is a pair $\langle P, \boldsymbol{m} \rangle$, such that P is a path schema, and $\boldsymbol{m} \in \mathbb{N}^{len(P)-1}$ is a vector, where for all $i \in [1, len(P) - 1]$, $\boldsymbol{m}[i] \geq 1$ and $\boldsymbol{m}[i] > 1$ implies that $P[i]$ is a cycle. An iterated path schema defines a unique infinite word over Δ, denoted by $trans(P, \boldsymbol{m}) = P[1]^{\boldsymbol{m}[1]} P[2]^{\boldsymbol{m}[2]} \cdots P[len(P) - 1]^{\boldsymbol{m}[len(P)-1]} P[len(P)]^{\omega}$. We recall the following result:

Lemma 2 [10]. *Let S be a flat affine counter system. Then:*

1. *the length and the size of a path schema of S are polynomial in $size(S)$;*
2. *for any run ρ of S, there exists an iterated path schema $\langle P, \boldsymbol{m} \rangle$ such that $trans(\rho) = trans(P, \boldsymbol{m})$.*

For a run ρ, we consider the set $ips(\rho) = \{\langle P, \boldsymbol{m} \rangle \mid trans(\rho) = trans(P, \boldsymbol{m})\}$. Observe that $ips(\rho) \neq \emptyset$ for any run ρ of S, due to Lemma 2 (2). Moreover, as a consequence of Lemma 2 (2), the number of path schemas is bounded by a simple exponential in the size of S. Note that $ips(\rho)$ is not necessarily a singleton: if a run enters and exits a loop in different states then, in the path schema, the loop may begin either from the entering state or from the exiting state.

We fix a run ρ of S starting at γ_0, and $\langle P, \boldsymbol{m} \rangle \in ips(\rho)$ an iterated path schema corresponding to ρ. We consider a simple cycle $c = \delta_0 \ldots \delta_{k-1}$ of P, whose transition rules are $\delta_i = \langle q_i, \boldsymbol{C}_i \cdot x \leq \boldsymbol{d}_i, (\boldsymbol{A}_i, \boldsymbol{b}_i), q_{i+1} \rangle$, for all $i \in [0, k-1]$, and $q_k = q_0$. Let $f_c = (\boldsymbol{A}_c, \boldsymbol{b}_c)$ be the update of the entire cycle c, where $\boldsymbol{A}_c = \boldsymbol{A}_{k-1} \cdots \boldsymbol{A}_1 \cdot \boldsymbol{A}_0$, denoted $\prod_{i=k-1}^{0} \boldsymbol{A}_i$, and $\boldsymbol{b}_c = \sum_{i=0}^{k-1} \prod_{j=k-1}^{i+1} \boldsymbol{A}_j \cdot \boldsymbol{b}_i$. Since S has the finite monoid property, the set $\mathcal{M}_c = \{ \boldsymbol{A}_c^i \mid i \in \mathbb{N} \}$ is finite. Then there exist two integer constants $\alpha, \beta \in \mathbb{N}$, such that $0 \leq \alpha + \beta \leq \|\mathcal{M}_c\| + 1$, and $\boldsymbol{A}_c^{\alpha} = \boldsymbol{A}_c^{\alpha+\beta}$. Observe that, in this case, we have $\mathcal{M}_c = \{ \boldsymbol{A}_c^0, \ldots, \boldsymbol{A}_c^{\alpha}, \ldots, \boldsymbol{A}_c^{\alpha+\beta-1} \}$.

Our goal is to exhibit another run ρ' of S and an iterated path schema $\langle P, \boldsymbol{m}' \rangle \in ips(\rho')$, such that $\| \boldsymbol{m}' \|_{\infty} \leq 2^{\mathsf{Poly}(size(S)+size(\gamma_0))}$, for a polynomial function $\mathsf{Poly}(x)$. Because $c = \delta_0 \ldots \delta_{k-1}$ is a simple cycle of P and $\langle P, \boldsymbol{m} \rangle \in ips(\rho)$, there exists a (possibly infinite) contiguous subsequence of ρ, let us call it $\theta = (q_0, v_0) \xrightarrow{\tau_0} (q_1, v_1) \xrightarrow{\tau_1} \ldots$ that iterates c, i.e. $\tau_i = \delta_{(i \bmod k)}$, for all $i \geq 0$. In the following, we call any subsequence of a run an *execution*.

The main intuition now is that θ can be decomposed into a prefix of length $(\alpha + \beta)k$ and k infinite sequences of translations along some effectively computable vectors $w_0, \ldots, w_{k-1}$. More precisely, all valuations v_i of θ, for $i \geq (\alpha + \beta)k$, that are situated at distance βk one from another, differ by exactly the same vector. We refer to Fig. 4 for an illustration of this idea.

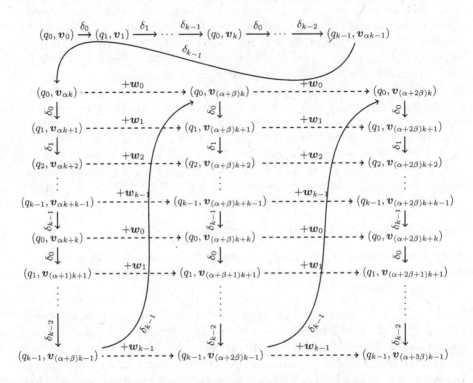

Fig. 4. Behavior of an execution which iterates $\alpha + 3\beta$ times the cycle $c = \delta_0 \ldots \delta_{k-1}$

Lemma 3. *Given an execution* $(q_0, v_0) \xrightarrow{\delta_0} \ldots \xrightarrow{\delta_{k-1}} (q_k, v_k) \xrightarrow{\delta_0} \ldots$ *of* S *that iterates a simple cycle* $c = \delta_0 \ldots \delta_{k-1}$, *there exist* $w_0, \ldots, w_{k-1} \in \mathbb{Z}^n$, *such that* $v_{(\alpha+p\beta+r)k+q} = v_{(\alpha+r)k+q} + p \cdot w_q$, *for all* $p \geq 0, r \in [0, \beta - 1]$ *and* $q \in [0, k-1]$, *where* $f_c = (A_c, b_c)$ *is the update of* c *and* $\alpha, \beta \geq 0$ *are such that* $A_c^\alpha = A_c^{\alpha+\beta}$.

We distinguish now the case when c is a nonterminal cycle of P, iterated finitely many times, from the case when c is terminal, thus iterated ad infinitum. We consider first the case when c is a nonterminal cycle, taken a finite number of times. Viewing the sequence of counter valuations, that occur during the unfolding of a simple loop, as a set of translations by vectors $w_0, \ldots, w_{k-1}$, prefixed by an initial sequence, allows us to reduce the problem of checking the validity of the guards along this sequence to checking the guards only in the beginning and in the end of each translation by $\boldsymbol{w}_q$, for $q \in [0, k-1]$. This is possible because the counter systems is disjunction free and hence each guard in the loop is defined by a convex vector set $\{\boldsymbol{v} \in \mathbb{Z}^n \mid \boldsymbol{C} \cdot \boldsymbol{v} \leq \boldsymbol{d}\}$, for a matrix $\boldsymbol{C} \in \mathbb{Z}^{m \times n}$ and a vector $\boldsymbol{d} \in \mathbb{Z}^m$, thus a sequence of vectors produced by a translation cannot exit and then re-enter the same guard, later on. This crucial observation, needed to prove the upper bound, is formalized below.

We consider the relaxed transition relation $\rightsquigarrow \subseteq (Q \times \mathbb{Z}^n) \times \Delta \times (Q \times \mathbb{Z}^n)$, defined as $(q, \boldsymbol{v}) \overset{\delta}{\rightsquigarrow} (q', \boldsymbol{v}')$ iff $source(\delta) = q$, $\boldsymbol{v}' = update(\delta)(\boldsymbol{v})$ and $target(\delta) = q'$. Hence, $\rightsquigarrow$ allows to move from one configuration to another as in $\rightarrow$, but without testing the guards. In the following, we fix a sequence of configurations $\theta' = (q_0, \boldsymbol{v}_0) \overset{\tau_0}{\rightsquigarrow} (q_1, \boldsymbol{v}_1) \overset{\tau_1}{\rightsquigarrow} \ldots$ called a *pseudo-execution*. We assume, moreover, that θ' iterates the simple cycle $c = \delta_0, \ldots, \delta_{k-1}$ a finite number of times, i.e. $\tau_i := \delta_{i \bmod k}$, for all $i \geq 0$. To check whether θ' is a real execution, it is enough to check the guards in the first $\alpha + \beta + 1$ and the last β iterations of the cycle, as shown by the following lemma:

Lemma 4. *For any $m > (\alpha+\beta+1)k$, given a finite pseudo-execution $(q_0, \boldsymbol{v}_0) \overset{\tau_0}{\rightsquigarrow} \ldots \overset{\tau_{m-1}}{\rightsquigarrow} (q_m, \boldsymbol{v}_m)$ of S, that iterates a nonterminal simple cycle $c = \delta_0 \ldots \delta_{k-1}$, $(q_0, \boldsymbol{v}_0) \overset{\tau_0}{\longrightarrow} \ldots \overset{\tau_{m-1}}{\longrightarrow} (q_m, \boldsymbol{v}_m)$ is an execution of S iff $\boldsymbol{v}_i \models guard(\tau_i)$, for all $i \in [0, (\alpha + \beta + 1)k - 1] \cup [m - \beta k, m - 1]$.*

The next step is to show that if a cycle is iterated ℓ times with $\ell = \alpha + \beta + p\beta + r$ for some $p > 0$ and $r \in [0, \beta - 1]$, starting with values $\boldsymbol{v} \in \mathbb{Z}^n$, then $[\boldsymbol{v}[1], \ldots, \boldsymbol{v}[n], p]^\top$ is the solution of a system of inequations $\boldsymbol{M}_c \cdot [\boldsymbol{y}; z]^\top \leq \boldsymbol{n}_c$, where $[\boldsymbol{y}; z] = [y_1, \ldots, y_n, z]$ is a vector of $n + 1$ variables. The bound on the number of iterations follows from the theorem below, by proving that the sizes of the entries of $\boldsymbol{M}_c$ and $\boldsymbol{n}_c$ (in binary) are bounded by a polynomial in $size(S)$.

Theorem 1. *Given $\boldsymbol{A} \in \mathbb{Z}^{m \times n}$ and $\boldsymbol{b} \in \mathbb{Z}^m$, for $n \geq 2$, the system $\boldsymbol{A} \cdot \boldsymbol{x} \leq \boldsymbol{b}$ has a solution in $\mathbb{N}^n$ iff it has a solution such that $\|\boldsymbol{x}\|_\infty \leq m^{2n} \cdot \|\boldsymbol{A}\|_{\max}^n \cdot \|\boldsymbol{b}\|_\infty$.*

We recall that $c = \delta_0, \ldots, \delta_{k-1}$, where $guard(\delta_i) := \boldsymbol{C}_i \cdot \boldsymbol{x} \leq \boldsymbol{d}_i$, $update(\delta_i) := (\boldsymbol{A}_i, \boldsymbol{b}_i)$, and that $f_c = (\boldsymbol{A}_c, \boldsymbol{b}_c)$ is the affine function defining the update of the entire cycle. For any $j > 0$, we define $\boldsymbol{b}_c^j = \Sigma_{i=0}^{j-1} \boldsymbol{A}_c^i \cdot \boldsymbol{b}_c$, hence $f_c^\ell = (\boldsymbol{A}_c^\ell, \boldsymbol{b}_c^\ell)$ is the update corresponding to ℓ iterations of the cycle for a fixed integer constant $\ell > 0$. The following set of inequalities expresses the fact that all guards are satisfied within the ℓ-th iteration of the cycle starting at $\boldsymbol{v} \in \mathbb{Z}^n$:

$$\boldsymbol{C}_p \cdot \left(\prod_{i=p-1}^{0} \boldsymbol{A}_i \cdot (\boldsymbol{A}_c^{\ell-1} \cdot \boldsymbol{v} + \boldsymbol{b}_c^{\ell-1}) + \sum_{i=0}^{p-1} \boldsymbol{A}_{p-1} \cdots \boldsymbol{A}_{i+1} \cdot \boldsymbol{b}_i \right) \leq \boldsymbol{d}_p, \text{ for all } p = 0, \ldots, k-1$$

In the sequel, we define $\boldsymbol{M}_\ell$ as the matrix obtained by vertically stacking the matrices $\boldsymbol{C}_j \cdot \prod_{i=j-1}^{0} \boldsymbol{A}_i \cdot \boldsymbol{A}_c^{\ell-1}$ for $j = 0, \ldots, k-1$, with $\boldsymbol{C}_0 \cdot \boldsymbol{A}_c^{\ell-1}$ on top. Also,

n_ℓ is the column vector with rows $n_\ell[j] = d_j - \left(C_j \cdot \prod_{i=j-1}^{0} A_i \cdot b_c^{\ell-1} + C_j \cdot \left(\sum_{i=0}^{j-1} A_{j-1} \cdots A_{i+1} \cdot b_i \right) \right)$, for $j = 0, \ldots, k-1$. For technical reasons that will be made clear next, we do not need to consider the case when the loop is iterated less than $\alpha + 2\beta + 1$ times. We know, from Lemma 4, that checking whether a given cycle c can be iterated $\ell > \alpha + 2\beta + 1$ times from v, reduces to checking the validity of the guards during the first $\alpha + \beta + 1$ and the last β iterations only. This condition is encoded by the union of the linear inequality systems below:

$$\begin{bmatrix} M_1 \\ \cdots \\ M_{\alpha+\beta+1} \end{bmatrix} \cdot v \leq \begin{bmatrix} n_1 \\ \cdots \\ n_{\alpha+\beta+1} \end{bmatrix} \qquad \begin{bmatrix} M_1 \\ \cdots \\ M_\beta \end{bmatrix} \cdot f_c^{\ell-\beta}(v) \leq \begin{bmatrix} n_1 \\ \cdots \\ n_\beta \end{bmatrix}$$

Since we assumed that $\ell > \alpha + 2\beta + 1$, it follows that $\ell - \beta = \alpha + p\beta + r$ for some $p > 0$ and $r \in [0, \beta-1]$, thus $f_c^{\ell-\beta}(v) = f_c^{\alpha+r}(v) + p \cdot w_0 = A_c^{\alpha+r} \cdot v + b_c^{\alpha+r} + p \cdot w_0$, by Lemma 3. Then, for any finite execution starting with v, and consisting of $\alpha + p\beta + r$ iterations of c, we have that the column vector $[v[1], \ldots, v[n], p]^\top$ is a solution of the linear system $M_{c,r} \cdot [y; z]^\top \leq n_{c,r}$, where:

$$M_{c,r} = \begin{bmatrix} M_1 & 0 \\ \cdots & \\ M_{\alpha+\beta+1} & 0 \\ M_1 \cdot A_c^{\alpha+r} & M_1 \cdot w_0 \\ \cdots & \\ M_\beta \cdot A_c^{\alpha+r} & M_\beta \cdot w_0 \end{bmatrix} \qquad n_{c,r} = \begin{bmatrix} n_1 \\ \cdots \\ n_{\alpha+\beta+1} \\ n_1 - M_1 \cdot b_c^{\alpha+r} \\ \cdots \\ n_\beta - M_\beta \cdot b_c^{\alpha+r} \end{bmatrix}$$

We now consider the case when the simple cycle $c = \delta_0 \ldots \delta_{k-1}$ is terminal and let $w_0, \ldots, w_{k-1} \in \mathbb{Z}^n$ be the vectors from Lemma 3. We say that c is *infinitely iterable* iff for all $i \in [0, k-1]$, we have $C_i \cdot w_i \leq 0$. Since $w_0, \ldots, w_{k-1}$ are effectively computable vectors[2], this condition is effective. The next lemma reduces the existence of an infinite iteration of the cycle to the existence of an integer solution of a linear inequation system.

Lemma 5. *Given an infinite pseudo-execution* $(q_0, v_0) \overset{\tau_0}{\leadsto} (q_1, v_1) \overset{\tau_1}{\leadsto} \ldots$ *of* S, *that iterates a terminal simple cycle* $c = \delta_0 \ldots \delta_{k-1}$, $(q_0, v_0) \overset{\tau_0}{\longrightarrow} (q_1, v_1) \overset{\tau_1}{\longrightarrow} \ldots$ *is an infinite execution of* S *iff* c *is infinitely iterable and* $v_i \models guard(\tau_i)$, *for all* $i \in [0, (\alpha + \beta + 1)k - 1]$.

As a consequence, for an infinitely iterable cycle c, the existence of an execution that iterates c infinitely often is captured by the linear system $M_{c,\omega} \cdot y \leq n_{c,\omega}$, where $M_{c,\omega}$ and $n_{c,\omega}$ are obtained by stacking the matrices $M_1, \ldots, M_{\alpha+\beta+1}$ and vectors $n_1, \ldots, n_{\alpha+\beta+1}$, respectively.

We have now all the ingredients needed to bound the number of cycle iterations within the runs of a flat disjunction free affine counter system having the finite monoid property. The argument used in the proof relies on the result of Theorem 1, namely that the size of a minimal solution of a linear system of inequalities is polynomially bounded in the maximum absolute value of its

---

[2] They are defined in the proof of Lemma 3.

coefficients, and the number of rows, and exponentially bounded in the number of columns. Since the number of rows depends on the maximum size of the monoids of the update matrices in the counter system, we use the result from [18, Lemma 13, Sect. B.1], namely that the size of a finite monoid of a square matrix is simply exponential in the dimension of that matrix.

Theorem 2.   *Given a flat disjunction free affine counter system $S = \langle Q, X_n, \Delta, \Lambda \rangle$, with the finite monoid property, for any run ρ of S, starting in (q_0, v_0), and any iterated path schema $\langle P, m \rangle \in ips(\rho)$, there exists a run ρ', starting in (q_0, v_0), and an iterated path schema $\langle P, m' \rangle \in ips(\rho')$, such that $\|m'\|_\infty \leq 2^{\mathsf{Poly}(size(S)+size(v_0))}$, for a polynomial function $\mathsf{Poly}(x)$.*

5   The Complexities of Decision Problems for AS_{fm}^{df}

In this section, we will prove that the previous reasoning on iterated path schemas allows us to deduce complexity bounds of the reachability problems and of model-checking with PLTL and FO formulae for disjunction free flat counter systems with the finite monoid property.

5.1   Reachability is Σ_2^P

In this section we give the first upper bound, for the reachability problem and show that $\mathrm{REACH}(\mathsf{AS}_{fm}^{df})$ is Σ_2^P. Even if this upper bound holds only for disjunction free counter system, we believe we could extend it to all the class AS_{fm} by adapting the method presented in [10] to eliminate the disjunctions. This would allow us to match the lower bound from Sect. 3. However we did not wish to enter into the heavy details of eliminating disjunctions in this work, in order to focus more on the specific aspects of affine counter systems. Anyway the provided result improves the 4EXPTIME upper bound from Table 1. The crux of the proof is based on the result provided by Theorem 2 and it follows the following reasoning: we use a polynomial-time bounded nondeterministic Turing machine that guesses an iterated path schema and then a NP oracle to check whether a guard has been violated. This gives us an $\mathrm{NP}^{\mathrm{NP}}$ algorithm for $\mathrm{REACH}(\mathsf{AS}_{fm}^{df})$, which then lies in Σ_2^P. Theorem 2 ensures us the soundness of the Algorithm and the correctness is provided by the fact that if, in an iterated path schema, no guard is violated then it corresponds necessarily to a run.

Let us now explain how our NP oracle works. The next lemma is based on the fact that any power A^k of a finite monoid matrix A can be computed in time polynomial in $size(A)$ and $\log_2 k$, using matrix exponentiation by squaring. The reason is that the value of an entry of any power of a finite monoid matrix A is bounded by an exponential in $size(A)$, thus the size of its binary representation is polynomially bounded by $size(A)$, and each step of the squaring algorithm takes polynomial time [18, Lemma 14, Sect. B.1].

Lemma 6.   *Given an iterated path schema $\langle P, m \rangle$ of a counter system with the finite monoid property S and an initial configuration γ_0, checking whether there is no run ρ starting at γ_0 such that $\langle P, m \rangle \in ips(\rho)$ is in NP.*

The next theorem gives the main result of this section.

Theorem 3. REACH($\text{AS}_{\text{fm}}^{\text{df}}$) *is* Σ_2^P.

5.2 PLTL Model Checking is Σ_2^P

For a PLTL formula ϕ, its temporal depth $td(\phi)$ is defined as the maximal nesting depth of temporal operators in ϕ, and the size of ϕ is its number of subformulae. In [10, Theorem 4.1], the authors have proved a *stuttering* theorem for PLTL stating that if an ω-word $w = w_1 w_2^M w_3$ over the alphabet 2^{AP} with $w_2 \neq \epsilon$ satisfies a PLTL formula ϕ (i.e. $w, 0 \models_{\text{PLTL}} \phi$) and if $M \geq 2td(\phi) + 5$ then all ω-words $w' = w_1 w_2^{M'} w_3$ with $M' \geq 2td(\phi) + 5$ are such that $w', 0 \models_{\text{PLTL}} \phi$. In other words, to verify if an ω-word with some repeated infix words satisfies a PLTL formula it is enough to verify the property for the ω-words where each infix is repeated at most $2td(\phi) + 5$ times. This allows to deduce that the model-checking of PLTL for flat translating counter systems is NP-complete. We rewrite now in our terminology the main proposition which leads to this result.

In the sequel we consider a flat disjunction free counter system $S = \langle Q, \mathsf{X}_n, \Delta, \Lambda \rangle$ with the finite monoid property. For a finite sequence of transitions $\delta_1 \ldots \delta_k$, we denote by $\Lambda(\delta_1 \ldots \delta_k) = \Lambda(source(\delta_1)) \ldots \Lambda(source(\delta_k))$ the finite word labeling the sequence with sets of atomic propositions. We lift this definition to iterated path schemas $\langle P, \boldsymbol{m} \rangle$ as $\Lambda(P, \boldsymbol{m}) = \Lambda(P[1])^{m[1]}$ $\Lambda(P[2])^{m[2]} \cdots \Lambda(P[len(P) - 1])^{m[len(P)-1]}[0]\Lambda(P[len(P)])^{\omega}$. Observe that, for a run ρ of a counter system, if $\langle P, \boldsymbol{m} \rangle \in ips(\rho)$ is an iterated path schema, we have by definition of the semantics of PLTL that $\rho \models_{\text{PLTL}} \phi$ iff $\Lambda(P, \boldsymbol{m}), 0 \models_{\text{PLTL}} \phi$[3] for all PLTL formulae ϕ. Moreover, for each $m \in \mathbb{N}$, we define the function ξ_m mapping each vector $\boldsymbol{v} \in \mathbb{N}^k$ to $\xi_m(\boldsymbol{v}) \in \mathbb{N}^k$, where, for all $i \in [1, k]$: $\xi_m(\boldsymbol{v})[i] = \boldsymbol{v}[i]$ if $\boldsymbol{v}[i] < m$ and $\xi_m(\boldsymbol{v})[i] = m$ otherwise. Let us now recall the main technical propositions established in [10], which are a consequence of the stuttering theorem for PLTL and of the result on the complexity of model-checking ultimately periodic path with PLTL given in [23].

Lemma 7. *Let* $\langle P, \boldsymbol{m} \rangle$ *be an iterated path schema and* ϕ *a* PLTL *formula, then:*

1. [10, Proposition 5.1] $\Lambda(P, \boldsymbol{m}), 0 \models_{\text{PLTL}} \phi$ *iff* $\Lambda(P, \xi_{2td(\phi)+5}(\boldsymbol{m})), 0 \models_{\text{PLTL}} \phi$,
2. [23, Theorem 3.2] *Given finite words* u *and* v, *checking* $uv^{\omega}, 0 \models_{\text{PLTL}} \phi$ *can be done in time polynomial in the sizes of* uv *and* ϕ.

We need furthermore a version of Theorem 2 above, which ensures that given an iterated path schema and a PLTL formula ϕ, we do not change the number of times a loop is iterated if this one is less than $2.td(\phi) + 5$. The proof of the next result can in fact be deduced by adapting the proof of Theorem 2 by unfolding the loop which are iterated less than $2.td(\phi) + 5$ for a given formula ϕ. As a consequence of Lemma 7, the new run ρ', obtained in the next lemma, is such that $\rho \models_{\text{PLTL}} \phi$ iff $\rho' \models_{\text{PLTL}} \phi$ for the considered PLTL formula ϕ.

---

[3] We take here the classical semantics of PLTL over infinite words.

Lemma 8. *For a run ρ of S starting in $(q_0, \boldsymbol{v}_0)$, an iterated path schema $\langle P, \boldsymbol{m} \rangle \in ips(\rho)$ and a PLTL formula ϕ, there exists a run ρ' starting in $(q_0, \boldsymbol{v}_0)$, and an iterated path schema $\langle P, \boldsymbol{m}' \rangle \in ips(\rho')$, such that $\|\boldsymbol{m}'\|_\infty \le 2^{\mathsf{Poly}(size(S) + size(v_0) + td(\phi))}$ for a polynomial $\mathsf{Poly}(x)$ and $\xi_{2td(\phi)+5}(\boldsymbol{m}) = \xi_{2td(\phi)+5}(\boldsymbol{m}')$.*

We can now explain why the model-checking of flat counter systems with the finite monoid property with PLTL formulae is in Σ_2^P. Given a flat counter system S with the finite monoid property, an initial configuration γ_0, and a PLTL formula ϕ, we guess an iterated path schema $\langle P, \boldsymbol{m} \rangle$ of polynomial size in the size of S, γ_0 and ϕ and we check whether $\Lambda(P, \xi_{2td(\phi)+5}(\boldsymbol{m})), 0 \models_{\mathsf{PLTL}} \phi$. This check can be done in polynomial time in the size of P and ϕ thanks to Lemma 7. Finally, we use the NP algorithm of Lemma 6 to verify that there exists a run ρ starting at γ_0, such that $\langle P, \boldsymbol{m} \rangle \in ips(\rho)$. This gives us a Σ_2^P algorithm whose correctness is ensured by Lemmas 2 and 8.

Theorem 4. $\mathsf{MC}_{\mathsf{PLTL}}(\mathsf{AS}_{\mathsf{fm}}^{\mathsf{df}})$ *is* Σ_2^P.

5.3 FO Model Checking is PSPACE-complete

For a FO formula ϕ, its quantifier height $qh(\phi)$ is the maximal nesting depth of its quantifiers, and the size of ϕ is its number of subformulae. Similarly, as for the PLTL case, in [8, Theorem 6], a stuttering theorem for FO is provided, which says that that two ω-words $w = w_1 w_2^M w_3$ and $w = w_1 w_2^{M'} w_3$ with $w \ne \epsilon$ are indistinguishable by a FO formula ϕ if M and M' are strictly bigger than $2^{qh(\phi)+2}$. The main difference with PLTL is that this provides an exponential bound in the maximum number of times an infix of an ω-word needs to be repeated to satisfy a FO formula. In the sequel we consider a flat counter system $S = \langle Q, \mathsf{X}_n, \Delta, \Lambda \rangle$ with the finite monoid property and we reuse the notations introduced in the previous section. The results of [8] can be restated as follows.

Lemma 9. *Given an iterated path schema $\langle P, \boldsymbol{m} \rangle$ and a FO formula ϕ, then:*

1. *[8, Lemma 7] $\Lambda(P, \boldsymbol{m}) \models_{\mathsf{FO}} \phi$ iff $\Lambda(P, \xi_{2^{qh(\phi)+2}}(\boldsymbol{m})) \models_{\mathsf{FO}} \phi$,*
2. *[8, Theorem 9] Checking $\Lambda(P, \boldsymbol{m}), 0 \models_{\mathsf{FO}} \phi$ can be done in space polynomial in the sizes of $\langle P, \boldsymbol{m} \rangle$ and ϕ.*

As for the PLTL case, this allows us to deduce a NPSPACE algorithm for the model-checking problem of flat counter system with the finite monoid property with FO formulae. Since the problem is already PSPACE-hard for flat translating counter systems [8, Theorem 9], we conclude by the following theorem.

Theorem 5. $\mathsf{MC}_{\mathsf{FO}}(\mathsf{AS}_{\mathsf{fm}}^{\mathsf{df}})$ *is* PSPACE-*complete*.

References

1. Arora, S., Barak, B.: Computational Complexity: A Modern Approach. Cambridge University Press, Cambridge (2009)

2. Bardin, S., Finkel, A., Petrucci, J.L.L.: FAST: fast acceleration of symbolic transition systems. http://tapas.labri.fr/trac/wiki/FASTer
3. Blondin, M., Finkel, A., Göller, S., Haase, C., McKenzie, P.: Reachability in two-dimensional vector addition systems with states is PSPACE-complete. CoRR abs/1412.4259 (2014). http://arxiv.org/abs/1412.4259
4. Boigelot, B.: Symbolic methods for exploring infinite state spaces. Ph.D., Univ. de Liège (1999)
5. Bozga, M., Iosif, R., Konecný, F.: Deciding conditional termination. Log. Methods Comput. Sci. **10**(3), 1–61 (2014)
6. Bozga, M., Iosif, R., Konečný, F.: Fast acceleration of ultimately periodic relations. In: Touili, T., Cook, B., Jackson, P. (eds.) CAV 2010. LNCS, vol. 6174, pp. 227–242. Springer, Heidelberg (2010)
7. Comon, H., Jurski, Y.: Timed automata and the theory of real numbers. In: Baeten, J.C.M., Mauw, S. (eds.) CONCUR 1999. LNCS, vol. 1664, pp. 242–257. Springer, Heidelberg (1999)
8. Demri, S., Dhar, A.K., Sangnier, A.: On the complexity of verifying regular properties on flat counter systems. In: Fomin, F.V., Freivalds, R., Kwiatkowska, M., Peleg, D. (eds.) ICALP 2013, Part II. LNCS, vol. 7966, pp. 162–173. Springer, Heidelberg (2013)
9. Demri, S., Dhar, A.K., Sangnier, A.: Equivalence between model-checking flat counter systems and Presburger arithmetic. In: Ouaknine, J., Potapov, I., Worrell, J. (eds.) RP 2014. LNCS, vol. 8762, pp. 85–97. Springer, Heidelberg (2014)
10. Demri, S., Dhar, A.K., Sangnier, A.: Taming past LTL and flat counter systems. Inf. Comput. **242**, 306–339 (2015)
11. Demri, S., Finkel, A., Goranko, V., van Drimmelen, G.: Model-checking CTL* over flat Presburger counter systems. J. Appl. Non-Class. Log. **20**(4), 313–344 (2010)
12. Finkel, A., Leroux, J.: How to compose Presburger-accelerations: applications to broadcast protocols. In: Agrawal, M., Seth, A.K. (eds.) FSTTCS 2002. LNCS, vol. 2556, pp. 145–156. Springer, Heidelberg (2002)
13. Gawlitza, T.M., Monniaux, D.: Invariant generation through strategy iteration in succinctly represented control flow graphs. Logical Methods Comput. Sci. **8**(3) (2012)
14. Göller, S., Haase, C., Ouaknine, J., Worrell, J.: Model checking succinct and parametric one-counter automata. In: Abramsky, S., Gavoille, C., Kirchner, C., Meyer auf der Heide, F., Spirakis, P.G. (eds.) ICALP 2010. LNCS, vol. 6199, pp. 575–586. Springer, Heidelberg (2010)
15. Gurari, E.M., Ibarra, O.H.: The complexity of decision problems for finite-turn multicounter machines. J. Comput. Syst. Sci. **22**, 220–229 (1981)
16. Haase, C.: Subclasses of Presburger arithmetic and the weak EXP hierarchy. In: CSL-LICS 2014, pp. 47:1–47:10. ACM (2014)
17. Hojjat, H., Iosif, R., Konečný, F., Kuncak, V., Rümmer, P.: Accelerating interpolants. In: Chakraborty, S., Mukund, M. (eds.) ATVA 2012. LNCS, vol. 7561, pp. 187–202. Springer, Heidelberg (2012)
18. Iosif, R., Sangnier, A.: How hard is it to verify flat affine counter systems with the finite monoid property? CoRR abs/1605.05836 (2016). http://arxiv.org/abs/1605.05836
19. Konecny, F., Iosif, R., Bozga, M.: FLATA: a verification toolset for counter machines (2009). http://nts.imag.fr/index.php/Flata
20. Kuhtz, L., Finkbeiner, B.: Weak Kripke structures and LTL. In: Katoen, J.-P., König, B. (eds.) CONCUR 2011. LNCS, vol. 6901, pp. 419–433. Springer, Heidelberg (2011)

21. Leroux, J., Sutre, G.: On flatness for 2-Dimensional vector addition systems with states. In: Gardner, P., Yoshida, N. (eds.) CONCUR 2004. LNCS, vol. 3170, pp. 402–416. Springer, Heidelberg (2004)
22. Lipton, R.J.: The reachability problem is exponential-space-hard. Technical report 62, Department of Computer Science, Yale University (1976)
23. Markey, N., Schnoebelen, P.: Model checking a path. In: Amadio, R.M., Lugiez, D. (eds.) CONCUR 2003. LNCS, vol. 2761, pp. 251–265. Springer, Heidelberg (2003)
24. Minsky, M.: Computation: Finite and Infinite Machines. Prentice-Hall, Upper Saddle River (1967)
25. Sistla, A., Clarke, E.: The complexity of propositional linear temporal logic. J. ACM **32**(3), 733–749 (1985)
26. Stockmeyer, L.J.: The complexity of decision problems in automata and logic. Ph.D. thesis, MIT (1974)

Solving Language Equations Using Flanked Automata

Florent Avellaneda[1], Silvano Dal Zilio[2(✉)], and Jean-Baptiste Raclet[3]

[1] CRIM, Montreal, Canada
[2] LAAS-CNRS, Université de Toulouse, CNRS, Toulouse, France
dalzilio@laas.fr
[3] IRIT, Université de Toulouse, CNRS, Toulouse, France

Abstract. We define a new subclass of nondeterministic finite automata for prefix-closed languages called *Flanked Finite Automata* (FFA). Our motivation is to provide an efficient way to compute the quotient and inclusion of regular languages without the need to determinize the underlying automata. These operations are the building blocks of several verification algorithms that can be interpreted as language equation solving problems. We provide a construction for computing a FFA accepting the quotient and product of languages that is compositional and that does not incur an exponential blow up in size. This makes flanked automata a good candidate as a formalism for compositional design and verification of systems.

1 Introduction

A very common problem in system design is to solve equations of the form $C \parallel X \preceq G$, where C is the specification of a given system and G is the overall behavior (the goal) that we want to implement. The objective is to compute a subsystem X that, when composed with C, produces a system which conforms to the specification G. We are generally interested in the maximal solution. When it exists, this solution is denoted G/C, also called the quotient of G by C.

Solving language equations is a problem that appears in many different domains, with different choices for the composition operator ($\parallel$) and for the conformance relation ($\preceq$). For example, this problem has been studied by the discrete-event systems community under the name *controller synthesis* [19]. In other works, finding X is sometimes referred to as computing a *protocol converter* or an *adaptor* [24]. In this context, the goal is to correct some mismatches between a set of n interacting subsystems in order to satisfy a compatibility property (deadlock freeness, for instance) specified by G. Likewise, the quotient G/C can be seen as the implementation of a subsystem that needs to realize a given specification G while reusing a trustworthy *off-the-shelf* component C [18]. Finally, computing the language quotient is a stepping stone to verify contract satisfaction [6]. The links between all these problems has been clearly highlighted in the literature [11,23].

Our interest in the quotient operator is motivated by our interest in contract-based design. Contracts have recently been identified as a key element for the

C. Artho et al. (Eds.): ATVA 2016, LNCS 9938, pp. 106–121, 2016.
DOI: 10.1007/978-3-319-46520-3_7

modular design of complex systems [7]. Fundamentally, a contract for a system S can be viewed as a pair (A, G) of two specification requirements, where A is an assumption on the environment where S executes and G is a guarantee on the behavior of the system (given that the assumptions in A are met). Namely, with our notations, the pair (A, G) is a contract for S if and only if $A \parallel S \preceq G$. In this case, when we fix the guarantee G, the best possible assumption is given by the quotient G/S.

Contracts, and the use of the quotient operator, arises naturally in the context of compositional verification. For example, when we consider the simplest instance of the Assume-Guarantee law (see for example [12]):

$$\frac{A \parallel P_1 \preceq G \qquad P_2 \preceq A}{P_1 \parallel P_2 \preceq G}$$

then a natural choice for the assumption A is to find a contract of the form (A, G) for P_1. Also, the quotient operator is central when computing the contract of a compound system $P_1 \parallel P_2$. Indeed, if (A_1, G_1) and (A_2, G_2) are contracts for the processes P_1, P_2, then a sensible contract for $P_1 \parallel P_2$ is given by the pair $(A_1/G_2 \wedge A_2/G_1, G_1 \parallel G_2)$. As a consequence, it is clear that any tool based on the use of contract theory needs to compute quotients efficiently.

In this paper, we propose a new method to compute the quotient and composition of two or more specifications in a compositional way. We describe our approach by choosing the simplest possible instantiation for the language equation problem. We consider that the semantics of a system is given by a regular and prefix-closed set of traces. Likewise, we use language intersection for the composition of systems ($\parallel$) and language inclusion for conformance ($\preceq$). In this simple context, the quotient of two prefix-closed regular languages G/C can be defined as the biggest prefix-closed language included in $G \cup \overline{C}$, where $\overline{C}$ is the complement of language C. While we concentrate on regular languages in this paper, our approach can be extended to more general composition operators, like synchronous product, and to more complex formalisms.

Contributions. Since we want to solve a problem on regular languages, the simplest choice would be to select either deterministic (DFA) or nondeterministic finite automata (NFA); but this is not satisfying. While the problems of checking universality or language inclusion are known to be computationally easy for DFA, they are PSPACE-complete for NFA. On the other hand, the size of a NFA can be exponentially smaller than the size of an equivalent minimal DFA. This gap in complexity between the two models can be problematic in practice. This is the case when using finite state automata for system verification, where we need to manipulate a very large number of states.

To solve this problem, we need an extension of finite automata that share the same complexity properties as DFA while being, as much as possible, as succinct as NFA. In this paper, we define a new class of finite state automata called *Flanked Finite Automata* (FFA) that has good complexity and closure properties. With our approach, it is possible to efficiently compute the quotient of two languages without relying on the use of deterministic automata or on the determinization of automata. We also prove that FFA can be exponentially more succinct than an equivalent DFA. We give some examples of the gain of performance brought by this new approach with a simple use case (Sect. 6).

In Sect. 3, we show that the universality problem for FFA is in linear-time while testing the language inclusion between two FFA $\mathcal{A}$ and $\mathcal{B}$ is in time $O(|\mathcal{A}| \cdot |\mathcal{B}|)$. In Sect. 4, we define several operations on FFA. In particular we describe how to compute a flanked automaton for the intersection, union and quotient of two languages defined by FFA. The benefit of our encoding is that the composition of two FFA, $\mathcal{A}$ and $\mathcal{B}$, has always less than $(|\mathcal{A}| + 1) \cdot (|\mathcal{B}| + 1)$ states. Moreover the resulting automaton is still flanked. Therefore it is possible to compute the successive composition and quotient of different specifications $\mathcal{A}_1, \ldots, \mathcal{A}_n$ in time $O(|\mathcal{A}_1| \cdot \ldots \cdot |\mathcal{A}_n|)$.

Finally, we prove that FFA are strictly more concise than DFA. Indeed, on the one hand, every DFA can be easily extended into a FFA with the same set of states and transitions. On the other hand, in Sect. 5, we give an example of (a family of) regular languages that can be accepted by FFA which are exponentially more succinct than their equivalent minimal DFA.

Our main motivation for introducing a new extension of NFA is to provide an efficient way to compute the quotient of two regular languages. We believe that our work provides the first algorithm for computing the quotient of two regular languages without using determinization and without suffering from an exponential blow up of the result. Our approach can be slightly modified to support other kinds of composition operators, like for instance the synchronous product of languages, instead of simply language intersection. It can also be easily extended to take into account the addition of modalities [18]. We also believe that the notion of "flanked relation" can be easily applied to other settings, like for example tree automata. For instance, the prototype implementation of our algorithms can also handle trace languages generated by "flanked" Petri nets.

2   Notations and Definitions

A finite automaton is a tuple $\mathcal{A} = (Q, \Sigma, E, Q_{in})$ where: Q is a finite set of states; Σ is the alphabet of $\mathcal{A}$ (that is a finite set of symbols); $E \subseteq Q \times \Sigma \times Q$ is the transition relation; and $Q_{in} \subseteq Q$ is the set of initial states. In the remainder of this text, we assume that every state is final, hence we do not need a distinguished subset of accepting states. Without loss of generality, we also assume that every state in Q is reachable in $\mathcal{A}$ from Q_{in} following a sequence of transitions in E.

For every word $u \in \Sigma^*$ we denote $\mathcal{A}(u)$ the subset of states in Q that can be reached when trying to accept the word u from an initial state in the automaton. We can define the set $\mathcal{A}(u)$ by induction on the word u. We assume that ϵ is the empty word and we use the notation $u\,a$ for the word obtained from u by concatenating the symbol $a \in \Sigma$. Then $\mathcal{A}(\epsilon) = Q_{in}$ and $\mathcal{A}(u\,a) = \{q' \mid \exists q \in \mathcal{A}(u).(q, a, q') \in E\}$. By extension, we say that a word u is accepted by $\mathcal{A}$, denoted $u \in \mathcal{A}$, if the set $\mathcal{A}(u)$ is not empty.

Definition 1. *A Flanked Finite Automaton (FFA) is a pair $(\mathcal{A}, F)$ where $\mathcal{A} = (Q, \Sigma, E, Q_{in})$ is a finite automaton and $F : Q \times \Sigma$ is a "flanking relation" that associates symbols of Σ to states of $\mathcal{A}$. We also require the following relation between $\mathcal{A}$ and F:*

$$\forall u \in \Sigma^*, a \in \Sigma. \left((u \in \mathcal{A} \wedge u\,a \notin \mathcal{A}) \Leftrightarrow \exists q \in \mathcal{A}(u).(q,a) \in F \right) \qquad \text{(F\star)}$$

We will often use the notation $q \xrightarrow{a} q'$ when $(q,a,q') \in E$. Likewise, we use the notation $q \xrightarrow{a}\!\!\!\!\!\! {\scriptstyle/}\;\,$ when $(q,a) \in F$.

With our condition that every state of an automaton is final, the relation $q \xrightarrow{a} q'$ states that every word u "reaching" q in $\mathcal{A}$ can be extended by the symbol a, meaning that $u\,a$ is also accepted by $\mathcal{A}$. Conversely, the relation $q \xrightarrow{a}\!\!\!\!\!\! {\scriptstyle/}\;\,$ states that the word $u\,a$ is not accepted. Therefore, in a FFA $(\mathcal{A}, F)$, when $q \in \mathcal{A}(u)$ and $(q, a) \in F$, then we know that the word u cannot be extended with a. In other words, the flanking relation gives information on the "frontier" of a prefix-closed language—the extreme limit over which words are no longer accepted by the automaton—hence the use of the noun *flank* to describe this class.

In the rest of the paper, we simply say that the pair $(\mathcal{A}, F)$ is *flanked* when condition (F$\star$) is met. We also say that the automaton $\mathcal{A}$ is *flankable* if there exist a flanking relation F such that $(\mathcal{A}, F)$ is flanked.

Testing if a Pair $(\mathcal{A}, F)$ is Flanked. We can use the traditional Rabin-Scott powerset construction to test whether F flanks the automaton $\mathcal{A} = (Q, \Sigma, E, Q_{in})$. We build from $\mathcal{A}$ the "powerset automaton" $\wp(\mathcal{A})$, a DFA with alphabet Σ and with states in 2^Q (also called classes) that are the sets of states in Q reached after accepting a given word prefix; that is all the sets of the form $\mathcal{A}(u)$. The initial state of $\wp(\mathcal{A})$ is the class $\mathcal{A}(\epsilon) = Q_{in}$. Finally, we have that $C \xrightarrow{a} C'$ in $\wp(\mathcal{A})$ if and only if there is $q \in C$ and $q' \in C'$ such that $q \xrightarrow{a} q'$.

Let $F^{-1}(a)$ be the set $\{q \mid q \xrightarrow{a}\!\!\!\!\!\! {\scriptstyle/}\;\,\}$ of states that "forbids" the symbol a after a word accepted by $\mathcal{A}$. Then the pair $(\mathcal{A}, F)$ is flanked if, for every possible symbol $a \in \Sigma$ and for every reachable class $C \in \wp(\mathcal{A})$ we have: $C \cap F^{-1}(a) \neq \emptyset$ if and only if there is no class C' such that $C \xrightarrow{a} C'$.

This construction suggests that checking if a pair $(\mathcal{A}, F)$ is flanked should be a costly operation, that is, it should be as complex as exploring a deterministic automaton equivalent to $\mathcal{A}$. In Sect. 3 we prove that this problem is actually PSPACE-complete.

Testing if a NFA is Flankable. It is easy to show that the class of FFA includes the class of deterministic finite state automata; meaning that every DFA is flankable. If an automaton $\mathcal{A}$ is deterministic, then it is enough to choose the "flanking relation" F such that, for every state q in Q, we have $q \xrightarrow{a}\!\!\!\!\!\! {\scriptstyle/}\;\,$ if and only if there are no transitions of the form $q \xrightarrow{a} q'$ in $\mathcal{A}$. DFA are a proper subset of FFA; indeed we give examples of NFA that are flankable in Sect. 5.

On the other hand, if an automaton is not deterministic, then in some cases it is not possible to define a suitable flanking relation F. For example, consider

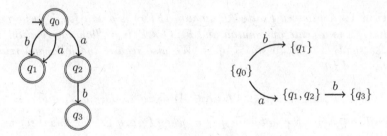

Fig. 1. A non-flankable NFA (left) and its associated Rabin-Scott powerset construction (right).

the automaton from Fig. 1 and assume, by contradiction, that we can define a flankable relation F for this automaton. The word b is accepted by $\mathcal{A}$ but the word bb is not, so by definition of FFA (see eq. (F⋆)), there must be a state $q \in \mathcal{A}(b)$ such that $q \overset{b}{\nrightarrow}$. Hence, because q_1 is the only state in $\mathcal{A}(b)$, we should necessarily have $q_1 \overset{b}{\nrightarrow}$. However, this contradicts the fact that the word ab is in $\mathcal{A}$, since q_1 is also in $\mathcal{A}(a)$.

More generally, it is possible to define a necessary and sufficient condition for the existence of a flanking relation; this leads to an algorithm for testing if an automaton $\mathcal{A}$ is flankable. Let $\mathcal{A}^{-1}(a)$ denote the set of states reachable by words that can be extended by the symbol a (remember that we consider prefix-closed languages): $\mathcal{A}^{-1}(a) = \bigcup\{\mathcal{A}(u) \mid ua \in \mathcal{A}\}$.

It is possible to find a flanking relation F for the automaton $\mathcal{A}$ if and only if, for every word $u \in \mathcal{A}$ such that $ua \notin \mathcal{A}$, the set $\mathcal{A}(u) \setminus \mathcal{A}^{-1}(a)$ is not empty. Indeed, in this case, it is possible to choose F such that $(q, a) \in F$ as soon as there exists a word u with $q \in \mathcal{A}(u) \setminus \mathcal{A}^{-1}(a)$. Conversely, an automaton $\mathcal{A}$ is not flankable if we can find a word $u \in \mathcal{A}$ such that $ua \notin \mathcal{A}$ and $\mathcal{A}(u) \subseteq \mathcal{A}^{-1}(a)$. For example, for the automaton in Fig. 1, we have $\mathcal{A}^{-1}(b) = \{q_0, q_1, q_2\}$ while $bb \notin \mathcal{A}$ and $\mathcal{A}(b) = \{q_1\}$. As in the previous section, this condition can be checked directly using the powerset construction.

3   Complexity Results for Basic Problems

In this section we give some results on the complexity of basic operations over FFA. Complete proofs can be found in an extended version of this paper [2].

Theorem 1. *The universality problem for FFA is decidable in linear time.*

Proof. It is enough to prove that a FFA $(\mathcal{A}, F)$ is universal if and only if the relation F is empty; meaning that for all states $q \in Q$ it is not possible to find a symbol $a \in \Sigma$ such that $q \overset{a}{\nrightarrow}$. As a consequence, to test whether $\mathcal{A}$ is universal, it is enough to check whether there is a state $q \in Q$ that is mapped to a non-empty set of symbols in F. Note that, given a different encoding of F, this operation could be performed in constant time.   □

We can use this result to settle the complexity of testing if an automaton is flankable.

Theorem 2. *Given an automaton $\mathcal{A} = (Q, \Sigma, E, Q_{in})$ and a relation $F \in Q \times \Sigma$, the problem of testing if $(\mathcal{A}, F)$ is a flanked automaton is PSPACE-complete when there are at least two symbols in Σ.*

Proof. We can define a simple nondeterministic algorithm for testing if $(\mathcal{A}, F)$ is flanked. We recall that the relation $F^{-1}(a)$ stands for the set $\{q \mid q \overset{a}{\not\rightarrow}\}$ of states that "forbid" the symbol a. As stated in Sect. 2, to test if $(\mathcal{A}, F)$ is flanked, we need, for every symbol $a \in \Sigma$, to explore the classes C in the powerset automaton of $\mathcal{A}$ and test whether $C \overset{a}{\rightarrow} C'$ in $\wp(\mathcal{A})$ and whether $C \cap F^{-1}(a) = \emptyset$ or not. These tests can be performed using $|Q|$ bits since every class C and every set $F^{-1}(a)$ is a subset of Q. Moreover there are at most $2^{|Q|}$ classes in $\wp(\mathcal{A})$. Hence, using Savitch's theorem, the problem is in PSPACE.

On the other way, we can reduce the problem of testing the universality of a NFA $\mathcal{A}$ to the problem of testing if a pair $(\mathcal{A}, \emptyset)$ is flanked (where $\emptyset$ stands for the "empty" flanking relation over $Q \times \Sigma$). The universality problem is known to be PSPACE-hard when the alphabet Σ is of size at least 2, even if all the states of $\mathcal{A}$ are final [16]. Hence our problem is also PSPACE-hard. □

To conclude this section, we prove that the complexity of checking language inclusion between a NFA and a FFA is in polynomial time. We say that the language of $\mathcal{A}_1$ is included in $\mathcal{A}_2$, simply denoted $\mathcal{A}_1 \subseteq \mathcal{A}_2$, if all the words accepted by $\mathcal{A}_1$ are also accepted by $\mathcal{A}_2$.

Theorem 3. *Given a NFA $\mathcal{A}_1$ and a FFA $(\mathcal{A}_2, F_2)$, we can test whether $\mathcal{A}_1 \subseteq \mathcal{A}_2$ in polynomial time.*

Proof. Without loss of generality, we can assume that $\mathcal{A}_1 = (Q_1, \Sigma, E_1, I_1)$ and $\mathcal{A}_2 = (Q_2, \Sigma, E_2, I_2)$ are two NFA over the same alphabet Σ. We define a variant of the classical product construction between $\mathcal{A}_1$ and $\mathcal{A}_2$ that also takes into account the "pseudo-transitions" $q \overset{a}{\not\rightarrow}$ defined by the flanking relations.

We define the product of $\mathcal{A}_1$ and $(\mathcal{A}_2, F_2)$ as the NFA $\mathcal{A} = (Q, \Sigma, E, I)$ such that $I = I_1 \times I_2$ and $Q = (Q_1 \times Q_2) \cup \{\bot\}$. The extra state $\bot$ will be used to detect an "error condition", that is a word that is accepted by $\mathcal{A}_1$ and not by $\mathcal{A}_2$. The transition relation of $\mathcal{A}$ is such that:

- if $q_1 \overset{a}{\rightarrow} q_1'$ in $\mathcal{A}_1$ and $q_2 \overset{a}{\rightarrow} q_2'$ in $\mathcal{A}_2$ then $(q_1, q_2) \overset{a}{\rightarrow} (q_1', q_2')$ in $\mathcal{A}$;
- if $q_1 \overset{a}{\rightarrow} q_1'$ in $\mathcal{A}_1$ and $q_2 \overset{a}{\not\rightarrow}$ in $\mathcal{A}_2$ then $(q_1, q_2) \overset{a}{\rightarrow} \bot$ in $\mathcal{A}$

The result follows from the fact that $\mathcal{A}_1$ is included in $\mathcal{A}_2$ if and only if the state $\bot$ is not reachable in $\mathcal{A}$. (Actually, we can prove that any word u such that $\bot \in \mathcal{A}(u)$ is a word accepted by $\mathcal{A}_1$ and not by $\mathcal{A}_2$.) Since we cannot generate more than $|Q_1| \cdot |Q_2|$ reachable states in $\mathcal{A}$ before finding the error $\bot$, this algorithm is solvable in polynomial time. □

4   Closure Properties of Flanked Automata

In this section, we study how to compute the composition of flanked automata. We prove that the class of FFA is closed by language intersection and by the "intersection adjunct", also called quotient. On a negative side, we show that the class is not closed by non-injective relabeling.

We consider the problem of computing a flanked automaton accepting the intersection of two prefix-closed, regular languages. More precisely, given two FFA $(\mathcal{A}_1, F_1)$ and $(\mathcal{A}_2, F_2)$, we want to compute a FFA $(\mathcal{A}, F)$ that recognizes the set of words accepted by both $\mathcal{A}_1$ and $\mathcal{A}_2$, denoted simply $\mathcal{A}_1 \cap \mathcal{A}_2$.

Theorem 4. *Given two FFA $(\mathcal{A}_1, F_1)$ and $(\mathcal{A}_2, F_2)$, we can compute a FFA $(\mathcal{A}, F)$ for the language $\mathcal{A}_1 \cap \mathcal{A}_2$ in polynomial time. The NFA $\mathcal{A}$ has size less than $|\mathcal{A}_1| \cdot |\mathcal{A}_2|$.*

Proof. We define a classical product construction between $\mathcal{A}_1$ and $\mathcal{A}_2$ and show how to extend this composition on the flanking relations. We assume that $\mathcal{A}_i$ is an automaton (Q_i, Σ, E_i, I_i) for $i \in \{1, 2\}$.

The automaton $\mathcal{A} = (Q, \Sigma, E, I)$ is defined as the synchronous product of $\mathcal{A}_1$ and $\mathcal{A}_2$, that is: $Q = Q_1 \times Q_2$; $I = I_1 \times I_2$; and the transition relation is such that $(q_1, q_2) \xrightarrow{a} (q_1', q_2')$ in $\mathcal{A}$ if both $q_1 \xrightarrow{a} q_1'$ in $\mathcal{A}_1$ and $q_2 \xrightarrow{a} q_2'$ in $\mathcal{A}_2$. It is a standard result that $\mathcal{A}$ accepts the language $\mathcal{A}_1 \cap \mathcal{A}_2$.

The *flanking relation* F is defined as follows: for each accessible state $(q_1, q_2) \in Q$, we have $(q_1, q_2) \xslashed{a}$ if and only if $q_1 \xslashed{a}$ in $\mathcal{A}_1$ or $q_2 \xslashed{a}$ in $\mathcal{A}_2$. What is left to prove is that $(\mathcal{A}, F)$ is flanked, that is, we show that condition (F$\star$) is correct:

- assume u is accepted by $\mathcal{A}$ and $u\,a$ is not; then there is a state $q = (q_1, q_2)$ in $\mathcal{A}$ such that $q \in \mathcal{A}(u)$ and $(q, a) \in F$. By definition of $\mathcal{A}$, we have that u is accepted by both $\mathcal{A}_1$ and $\mathcal{A}_2$, while the word $u\,a$ is not accepted by at least one of them. Assume that $u\,a$ is not accepted by $\mathcal{A}_1$. Since F_1 is a flanking relation for $\mathcal{A}_1$, we have by equation (F$\star$) that there is at least one state $q_1 \in \mathcal{A}_1$ such that $(q_1, a) \in F_1$; and therefore $(q, a) \in F$, as required.
- assume there is a reachable state $q = (q_1, q_2)$ in $\mathcal{A}$ such that $q \in \mathcal{A}(u)$ and $(q, a) \in F$; then u is accepted by $\mathcal{A}$. We show, by contradiction, that $u\,a$ cannot be accepted by $\mathcal{A}$, that is $u\,a \notin \mathcal{A}_1 \cap \mathcal{A}_2$. Indeed, if so, then $u\,a$ will be accepted both by $\mathcal{A}_1$ and $\mathcal{A}_2$ and therefore we will have $(q_1, a) \notin F_1$ and $(q_2, a) \notin F_2$, which contradicts the fact that $(q, a) \in F$. $\square$

Next we consider the adjunct of the intersection operation, denoted $\mathcal{A}_1 / \mathcal{A}_2$. This operation, also called *quotient*, is defined as the biggest prefix-closed language X such that $\mathcal{A}_2 \cap X \subseteq \mathcal{A}_1$. Informally, X is the solution to the following question: what is the biggest set of words x such that x is either accepted by $\mathcal{A}_1$ or not accepted by $\mathcal{A}_2$. Therefore the language $\mathcal{A}_1 / \mathcal{A}_2$ is always defined (and not empty, since it contains at least the empty word ϵ). Actually, the quotient can be interpreted as the biggest prefix-closed language included in the set $\mathcal{L}_1 \cup \bar{\mathcal{L}}_2$, where $\mathcal{L}_1$ is the language accepted by $\mathcal{A}_1$ and $\bar{\mathcal{L}}_2$ is the complement of the language of $\mathcal{A}_2$.

The quotient operation can also be defined by the following two axioms:

$$(\text{Ax1}) \quad \mathcal{A}_2 \cap (\mathcal{A}_1/\mathcal{A}_2) \subseteq \mathcal{A}_1$$
$$(\text{Ax2}) \quad \forall X.\, \mathcal{A}_2 \cap X \subseteq \mathcal{A}_1 \Rightarrow X \subseteq \mathcal{A}_1/\mathcal{A}_2$$

The quotient operation is useful when trying to solve *language equations problems* [22] and has applications in the domain of system verification and synthesis. For instance, we can find a similar operation in the contract framework of Benveniste et al. [6] or in the contract framework of Bauer et al. [4].

Our results on FFA can be used for the simplest instantiation of these frameworks that considers a simple trace-based semantics where the behavior of systems is given as a regular set of words; composition is language intersection; and implementation conformance is language inclusion. Our work was motivated by the fact that there are no known efficient methods to compute the quotient. Indeed, to the best of our knowledge, all the approaches rely on the determinization of NFA, which is very expensive in practice [18,22].

Our definitions of quotient could be easily extended to replace language intersection by synchronous product and to take into account the addition of modalities [18].

Theorem 5. *Given two FFA* $(\mathcal{A}_1, F_1)$ *and* $(\mathcal{A}_2, F_2)$, *we can compute a FFA* $(\mathcal{A}, F)$ *for the quotient language* $\mathcal{A}_1/\mathcal{A}_2$ *in polynomial time. The NFA* $\mathcal{A}$ *has size less than* $|\mathcal{A}_1| \cdot |\mathcal{A}_2| + 1$

Proof. Without loss of generality, we can assume that $\mathcal{A}_1 = (Q_1, \Sigma, E_1, I_1)$ and $\mathcal{A}_2 = (Q_2, \Sigma, E_2, I_2)$ are two NFA over the same alphabet Σ. Like in the construction for testing language inclusion, we define a variant of the classical product construction between $\mathcal{A}_1$ and $\mathcal{A}_2$ that also takes into account the flanking relations.

We define the product of $(\mathcal{A}_1, F_1)$ and $(\mathcal{A}_2, F_2)$ as the NFA $\mathcal{A} = (Q, \Sigma, E, I)$ such that $I = I_1 \times I_2$ and $Q = (Q_1 \times Q_2) \cup \{\top\}$. The extra state $\top$ will be used as a sink state from which every suffix can be accepted. The transition relation of $\mathcal{A}$ is such that:

- if $q_1 \xrightarrow{a} q_1'$ in $\mathcal{A}_1$ and $q_2 \xrightarrow{a} q_2'$ in $\mathcal{A}_2$ then $(q_1, q_2) \xrightarrow{a} (q_1', q_2')$ in $\mathcal{A}$;
- if $q_2 \xrightarrow{a}\!\!\!\!\!/\ $ in $\mathcal{A}_2$ then $(q_1, q_2) \xrightarrow{a} \top$ in $\mathcal{A}$ for all states $q_1 \in Q_1$
- $\top \xrightarrow{a} \top$ for every $a \in \Sigma$

Note that we do not have a transition rule for the case where $q_1 \xrightarrow{a}\!\!\!\!\!/\ $ in $\mathcal{A}_1$ and $q_2 \xrightarrow{a} q_2'$; this models the fact that a word "that can be extended" in $\mathcal{A}_2$ but not in $\mathcal{A}_1$ cannot be in the quotient $\mathcal{A}_1/\mathcal{A}_2$. It is not difficult to show that $\mathcal{A}$ accepts the language $\mathcal{A}_1/\mathcal{A}_2$. We give an example of the construction in Fig. 2.

Next we show that $\mathcal{A}$ is flankable and define a suitable flanking relation. Let F be the relation in $Q \times \Sigma$ such that $(q_1, q_2) \xrightarrow{a}\!\!\!\!\!/\ $ if and only if $q_1 \xrightarrow{a}\!\!\!\!\!/\ $ in F_1 and $q_2 \xrightarrow{a} q_2'$ in $\mathcal{A}_2$. That is, the symbol a is forbidden exactly in the case that was ruled out in the transition relation of $\mathcal{A}$. What is left to prove is that $(\mathcal{A}, F)$ is flanked, that is, we show that condition (F$\star$) is correct:

- Assume u is accepted by $\mathcal{A}$ and $u\,a$ is not. Since $u\,a$ is not accepted, it must be the case that $q \neq \top$. Therefore there is a state $q = (q_1, q_2)$ in $\mathcal{A}$ such that $q_1 \in \mathcal{A}_1(u)$ and $q_2 \in \mathcal{A}_2(u)$. Also, since there is no transition with label a from q, then necessarily $q_1 \overset{a}{\nrightarrow}$ in $\mathcal{A}_1$ and $q_2 \overset{a}{\rightarrow} q_2'$. This is exactly the case where $(q, a) \in F$, as required.
- Assume there is a reachable state q in $\mathcal{A}$ such that $q \in \mathcal{A}(u)$ and $(q, a) \in F$. Since $(q, a) \in F$, we have $q \neq \top$ and therefore $q = (q_1, q_2)$ with $q_1 \in \mathcal{A}_1(u)$, $q_1 \overset{a}{\nrightarrow}$ in F_1, $q_2 \in \mathcal{A}_2(u)$ and $q_2 \overset{a}{\rightarrow}$ in F_2. Next, we show by contradiction that $u\,a$ cannot be accepted by $\mathcal{A}$. Indeed, if it was the case, then we would have either $q_1 \overset{a}{\rightarrow}$ in F_1 or both $u\,a \notin \mathcal{A}_1$ and $u\,a \notin \mathcal{A}_2$. □

We give an example of the construction of the "quotient" FFA in Fig. 2. If we look more closely at the construction used in Theorem 5 that defines an automaton for the quotient of two FFA $(\mathcal{A}_1, F_1)$ and $(\mathcal{A}_2, F_2)$, we see that the flanking relation F_1 is used only to compute the flanking relation of the result. Therefore, as a corollary, it is not difficult to prove that we can use the same construction to build a quotient automaton for $\mathcal{A}_1/\mathcal{A}_2$ from an arbitrary NFA $\mathcal{A}_1$ and a FFA $(\mathcal{A}_2, F_2)$. However the resulting automaton may not be flankable.

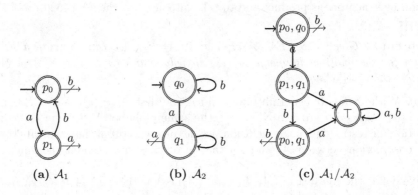

(a) $\mathcal{A}_1$ **(b)** $\mathcal{A}_2$ **(c)** $\mathcal{A}_1/\mathcal{A}_2$

Fig. 2. Construction for the quotient of two FFA.

We can also prove that flankability is preserved by language union (see [2]): given two FFA $(\mathcal{A}_1, F_1)$ and $(\mathcal{A}_2, F_2)$, we can compute a FFA $(\mathcal{A}, F)$ that recognizes the set of words accepted by $\mathcal{A}_1$ or by $\mathcal{A}_2$, denoted $\mathcal{A}_1 \cup \mathcal{A}_2$. (Operations corresponding to the Kleene star closure or to the adjunct of the union are not interesting in our case.)

Even though the class of FFA enjoys interesting closure properties, there are operations that, when applied to a FFA, may produce a result that is not flankable. This is for example the case with "(non-injective) relabeling", that is the operation of applying a substitution over the symbols of an automaton. The same can be observed if we consider an erasure operation, in which we can replace all transitions with a given symbol by an ϵ-transition. Informally, it appears that the property flankable can be lost when applying an operation that increases the non-determinism of the transition relation.

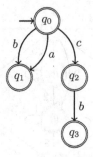

Fig. 3. Example of a FFA not flankable after relabeling c to a.

We can prove this result by exhibiting a simple counterexample, see the automaton in Fig. 3. This automaton with alphabet $\Sigma = \{a, b, c\}$ is deterministic, so we can easily define an associated flanking relation. For example we can choose $F = \{(q_1, a), (q_1, b), (q_1, c), (q_2, a), (q_2, c), (q_3, a), (q_3, b), (q_3, c)\}$. However, if we substitute the symbol c with a, we obtain the non-flankable automaton described in Sect. 2 (see Fig. 1).

5   Succinctness of Flanked Automata

In this section we show that a flankable automaton can be exponentially more succinct than its equivalent minimal DFA. This is done by defining a language over an alphabet of size $2n$ that can be accepted by a linear size FFA but that corresponds to a minimal DFA with an exponential number of states. This example is due to Colcombet.

At first sight, this result may seem quite counterintuitive. Indeed, even if a flanked automata is built from a NFA, the combination of the automaton and the flanking relation contains enough information to "encode" both a language and its complement. This explains the good complexity results on testing language inclusion for example. Therefore we could expect worse results concerning the relative size of a FFA and an equivalent DFA.

Theorem 6. *For every integer n, we can find a FFA $(\mathcal{A}_n, F)$ such that $\mathcal{A}_n$ has $2n+2$ states and that the language of $\mathcal{A}_n$ cannot be accepted by a DFA with less than 2^n states.*

Proof. We consider two alphabets with n symbols: $\Pi_n = \{1, \dots, n\}$ and $\Theta_n = \{\sharp_1, \sharp_2, \dots, \sharp_n\}$. We define the language L_n over the alphabet $\Pi_n \cup \Theta_n$ as the smallest set of words such that:

- all words in Π_n^* are in L_n, that is all the words that do not contain a symbol of the kind $\sharp_i$;
- a word of the form $(u\,\sharp_i)$ is in L_n if and only if u is a word of Π_n^* that contains at least one occurrence of the symbol i. That is L_n contains all the words of the form $\Pi_n^* \cdot i \cdot \Pi_n^* \cdot \sharp_i$ for all $i \in 1..n$. We denote L_n^i the regular language consisting of the words of the form $\Pi_n^* \cdot i \cdot \Pi_n^* \cdot \sharp_i$.

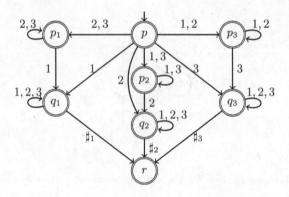

Fig. 4. Flankable NFA for the language L_3.

Clearly the language L_n is the union of $n+1$ regular languages; $L = \Pi_n^* \cup L_n^1 \cup \cdots \cup L_n^n$. It is also easy to prove that L_n is prefix-closed, since the set of prefixes of the words in L_n^i is exactly Π_n^* for all $i \in 1..n$.

A DFA accepting the language L_n must have at least 2^n different states. Indeed it must be able to record the subset of symbols in Π_n that have already been seen before accepting $\natural_i$ as a final symbol; to accept a word of the form $u \natural_i$ the DFA must know whether i has been seen in u for all possible $i \in 1..n$.

Next we define a flankable NFA $\mathcal{A}_n = (Q_n, \Pi_n \cup \Theta_n, E_n, \{p\})$ with $2n+2$ states that can recognize the language L_n. We give an example of the construction in Fig. 4 for the case $n = 3$. The NFA $\mathcal{A}_n$ has a single initial state, p, and a single sink state (a state without outgoing transitions), r. The set Q_n also contains two states, p_i and q_i, for every symbol i in Π.

The transition relation E_n is the smallest relation that contains the following triplets for all $i \in 1..n$:

- the 3 transitions $p \xrightarrow{i} q_i$; $p_i \xrightarrow{i} q_i$; and $q_i \xrightarrow{i} q_i$;
- for every index $j \neq i$, the 3 transitions $p \xrightarrow{j} p_i$; $p_i \xrightarrow{j} p_i$; and $q_i \xrightarrow{j} q_i$;
- and the transition $q_i \xrightarrow{\natural_i} r$.

Intuitively, a transition from p to p_i or q_i will select non-deterministically which final symbol $\natural_i$ is expected at the end of the word (which sub-language L_n^i we try to recognize). Once a symbol in Θ has been seen—in one of the transition of the kind $q_i \xrightarrow{\natural_i} r$—the automaton is stuck on the state r. It is therefore easy to prove that $\mathcal{A}_n$ accepts the union of the languages L_n^i and their prefixes.

Finally, the NFA $\mathcal{A}_n$ is flankable. It is enough to choose, for the flanking relation, the smallest relation on $Q \times \Theta_n$ such that $p_i \overset{\natural_i}{\nrightarrow}$ and $p \overset{\natural_i}{\nrightarrow}$ for all $i \in 1..n$; and such that $r \overset{a}{\nrightarrow}$ for all the symbols $a \in \Pi_n \cup \Theta_n$. Indeed, it is not possible to accept the symbol $\natural_i$ from the initial state, p, or from a word that can reach p_i; that is, it is not possible to extend a word without any occurrence of the symbol i with the symbol $\natural_i$. Also, it is not possible to extend a word that can reach the state r in $\mathcal{A}_n$. It is easy to prove that this covers all the possible words not accepted by $\mathcal{A}_n$.   □

6 A Simple Use Case for FFA

In this section, we study a simple example related to controller synthesis in a component-based system. We use our approach to compute a controller, G, for a system obtained from the parallel composition of n copies of the same components: $(S_1 \parallel \cdots \parallel S_n)$. The architecture of this system is given in Fig. 5. We use this example to study the performance of our approach when compared to traditional techniques.

Each component S_k can receive messages from two different channels: a public channel i, shared by everyone, which represents the main input channel of the whole system; and a private channel d_k that can be used to disable the component S_k. While the component is active, it can emit a message on its output channel, r_k, after receiving the two messages i_1 and i_2, in this order, over the channel i. Once disabled, the component does not interact with its environment. The overall behavior of the system is given by the automaton in Fig. 5-(c). We expect the system to emit a message on channel o when it receives two messages on channel i. Even though this behavior is very simple, the task of the controller G is made difficult by the fact that it cannot listen on the channel i. The component G can only observe the output of the components on the channels r_i, for $i \in 1..n$, and the disabling messages.

By definition, the semantics of the controller G is the biggest solution (for G) of the language equation $(S_1 \parallel \cdots \parallel S_n \parallel G) \subseteq A$, hence: $G = A/(S_1 \parallel \cdots \parallel S_n)$.

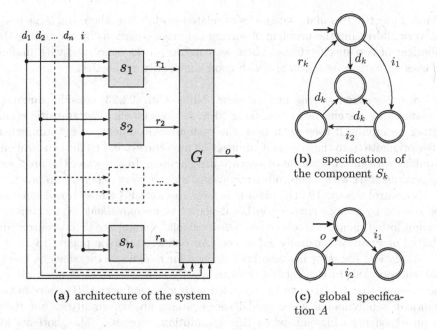

(a) architecture of the system

(b) specification of the component S_k

(c) global specification A

Fig. 5. Architecture and specification of a simple voting network.

We have used this example to compare the time necessary to compute G with two approaches; first using the tool MoTraS [17], then using a prototype implementation based on FFA. MoTraS is a tool for modal transition systems that implements all the standard operations for specification theories, such as language quotient. The results are given in the table below, where we give the performance when varying the number of components in the system (the value of the parameter n). These results were obtained on a desktop computer with 8 GB of RAM.

n	7	8	9	100	200	500	1000	2000
MoTraS time (s) (memory)	8 s (750 MB)	27 s (1.5 GB)	190 s (2 GB)	— —	— —	— —	— —	— —
FFA time (s) (memory)	<0.01 s (1.3 MB)	<0.01 s (1.3 MB)	<0.01 s (1.3 MB)	0.05 s (2.4 MB)	0.2 s (3.5 MB)	1.5 s (6.5 MB)	5.8 s (13 MB)	30 s (23 MB)

We observe that it is not possible to compute G for values of n greater than 10 using a classical approach. These results are similar to what we obtained using our own prototype implementation based on DFA. On the opposite, when we use flanked automata, we are able to compute the quotient for up to several thousand components.

7   Related Work

We can identify two main categories of related work. First, there is a large body of work addressing the problem of solving language equations by computing the quotient of two specifications. Then, we consider works concerned with finding classes of finite state automata with good complexity properties.

Work on equation solving and quotient. Villa et al. [22,23] consider language equations for systems described using NFA. Actions labeling the transitions can either be inputs, if they stem from the system environment, or outputs, when they originate from the system. Composition may correspond to the synchronous product with internalization of synchronized actions. In any case, the proposed algorithms start with a determinization step, which is very expensive in practice.

In control theory [19], the plant is in most cases a DFA whose transitions can be labeled by actions that are either declared as *uncontrollable* (the controller cannot forbid them) or *unobservable* (the controller cannot *see* their occurrence). Partial observation naturally led to consider nondeterministic plants [13].

A quotient operator has also been defined for modal specifications by one of the authors [18]. In this setting, we can specify that it *may* or it *must* always be the case that a trace can be extended with a certain action. The size of the quotient is polynomial when modal specifications are deterministic, but there is an exponential blow-up when this assumption is relaxed [5]. Quotients for extensions of modal specifications to capture timed and quantitative languages have also been recently considered [3,9,10].

Work on Finite State Automata. Several works have tried to find classes of finite automata that retain the same complexity as DFA on some operations while still being more succinct than the minimal DFA. One such example is the class of Unambiguous Finite Automata (UFA) [20,21]. Informally, an UFA is a finite state automaton such that, if a word is accepted, then there is a unique run which witnesses this fact, that is a unique sequence of states visited when accepting the word. Like with DFA, the problems of universality and inclusion for UFA is in polynomial-time. Unfortunately, UFA are difficult to complement. (Actually, finding the exact complexity of complementation for UFA is still an open problem [8].) Therefore they are not a good choice for computing quotients.

Another problem lies in the use of UFA for prefix-closed languages. In this paper, we restrict our study to automata recognizing prefix-closed languages. More precisely, we assume that all the states of the automaton are final (which is equivalent). This restriction is very common when using NFA for the purpose of system verification. For instance, Kripke structures used in model-checking algorithms are often interpreted as finite state automata where all states are final. It is easy to see that, with this restriction, an UFA is necessarily deterministic.

In the context of automata on infinite words, we can also mention the *safety automata* of Isaak and Löding [14]. A safety (or looping) automaton can be viewed as a Büchi automaton in which all states are accepting, except for possibly one rejecting sink state. For unambiguous safety automata, the problems of inclusion, equivalence, and universality can be solved in polynomial time. We show similar complexity results for our class of automata (on finite words). Moreover, a FFA can also be described, superficially, as a safety automaton without the Büchi acceptance condition. Nonetheless, without the use of the flanking relation, it is not clear how to define the quotient operation for safety automata, especially if we want a compositional construction that does not involve determinization.

It should be stressed that our problem is not made simpler by the choice to restrict to prefix-closed languages. Indeed, all the classical complexity results on NFA are still valid in this context. For instance, given a NFA $\mathcal{A}$ with all its states final, checking the universality of $\mathcal{A}$ is PSPACE-hard [16]. Likewise for the minimization problem. Indeed, there are examples of NFA with n states, all final, such that the minimal equivalent DFA has 2^n states. We provide such an example in Sect. 5 of this paper. Intuitively, it is always possible to view a regular language L, over the alphabet Σ, as the prefix closed-language containing words of the form $w\sharp$, where w is in L and $\sharp$ is some new (terminal) symbol not used in Σ.

8 Conclusion

We define a new subclass of NFA for prefix-closed languages called flanked automata. Intuitively, a FFA $(\mathcal{A}, F)$ is a simple extension of NFA where we add in the relation F extra information that can be used to check (non-deterministically) whether a word is not accepted by $\mathcal{A}$. Hence a FFA can be used both to test whether a word is in the language associated with $\mathcal{A}$ or in its complement. As a consequence, we obtain good complexity results for several interesting problems such as universality and language inclusion. This idea of adding extra information to encode both a language and its complement seems to be new. It is also quite different from existing approaches used to define subclasses of NFA with good complexity properties, like unambiguity for example.

Our work could be extended in several ways. First, we have implemented all our proposed algorithms and constructions and have found that—for several examples coming from the system verification domain—it was often easy to define a flanking relation for a given NFA (even though we showed in Sect. 2 that it is not always possible). More experimental work is still needed, and in particular the definition of a good set of benchmarks.

Next, we have used the powerset construction multiple times in our definitions. Most particularly as a way to test if a FFA is flanked or if a NFA is flankable. Other constructions used to check language inclusion or simulation between NFA could be useful in this context like, for example, the antichain-based method [1].

Finally, we still do not know how to compute a "succinct" flanked automaton from a NFA that is not flankable. At the moment, our only solution is to compute a minimal equivalent DFA (since DFA are always flankable). While it could be possible to subsequently simplify the DFA—which is known to be computationally hard [15]—it would be interesting to have a more direct construction.

Acknowledgments. We thank Denis Kuperberg, Thomas Colcombet, and Jean-Eric Pin for providing their expertise and insight and for suggesting the example that led to the proof of Theorem 6.

References

1. Abdulla, P.A., Chen, Y.-F., Holík, L., Mayr, R., Vojnar, T.: When simulation meets antichains. In: Esparza, J., Majumdar, R. (eds.) TACAS 2010. LNCS, vol. 6015, pp. 158–174. Springer, Heidelberg (2010)
2. Avellaneda, F., Dal Zilio, S., Raclet, J.: On the complexity of flanked finite state automata. CoRR abs/1509.06501 (2015)
3. Bauer, S.S., Fahrenberg, U., Juhl, L., Larsen, K.G., Legay, A., Thrane, C.R.: Weighted modal transition systems. Formal Methods Syst. Des. **42**(2), 193–220 (2013)
4. Bauer, S.S., David, A., Hennicker, R., Guldstrand Larsen, K., Legay, A., Nyman, U., Wąsowski, A.: Moving from specifications to contracts in component-based design. In: Lara, J., Zisman, A. (eds.) Fundamental Approaches to Software Engineering. LNCS, vol. 7212, pp. 43–58. Springer, Heidelberg (2012)
5. Beneš, N., Delahaye, B., Fahrenberg, U., Křetínský, J., Legay, A.: Hennessy-Milner logic with greatest fixed points as a complete behavioural specification theory. In: D'Argenio, P.R., Melgratti, H. (eds.) CONCUR 2013 – Concurrency Theory. LNCS, vol. 8052, pp. 76–90. Springer, Heidelberg (2013)

6. Benveniste, A., Caillaud, B., Ferrari, A., Mangeruca, L., Passerone, R., Sofronis, C.: Multiple viewpoint contract-based specification and design. In: Boer, F.S., Bonsangue, M.M., Graf, S., Roever, W.-P. (eds.) FMCO 2007. LNCS, vol. 5382, pp. 200–225. Springer, Heidelberg (2008). Revised Lectures
7. Benveniste, A., Caillaud, B., Nickovic, D., Passerone, R., Raclet, J.B., Reinkemeier, P., Sangiovanni-Vincentelli, A., Damm, W., Henzinger, T., Larsen, K.G.: Contracts for system design (2012)
8. Colcombet, T.: Forms of determinism for automata. In: Symposium on Theoretical Aspects of Computer Science (STACS), vol. 14, pp. 1–23 (2012)
9. David, A., Larsen, K.G., Legay, A., Nyman, U., Wasowski, A.: Timed I/O automata: a complete specification theory for real-time systems. In: HSCC, pp. 91–100. ACM (2010)
10. Fahrenberg, U., Křetínský, J., Legay, A., Traonouez, L.-M.: Compositionality for quantitative specifications. In: Lanese, I., Madelaine, E. (eds.) FACS 2014. LNCS, vol. 8997, pp. 306–324. Springer, Heidelberg (2015)
11. Gierds, C., Mooij, A.J., Wolf, K.: Reducing adapter synthesis to controller synthesis. IEEE Trans. Serv. Comput. 5(1), 72–85 (2012)
12. Henzinger, T.A., Qadeer, S., Rajamani, S.K.: You assume, we guarantee: methodology and case studies. In: Hu, A.J., Vardi, M.Y. (eds.) Computer Aided Verification. LNCS, vol. 1427, pp. 440–451. Springer, Heidelberg (1998)
13. Heymann, M., Lin, F.: Discrete-event control of nondeterministic systems. IEEE Trans. Autom. Control 43(1), 3–17 (1998)
14. Isaak, D., Löding, C.: Efficient inclusion testing for simple classes of unambiguous ω-automata. Inf. Process. Lett. 112, 14–15 (2012)
15. Jiang, T., Ravikumar, B.: Minimal NFA problems are hard. SIAM J. Comput. 22(6), 1117–1141 (1993)
16. Kao, J.Y., Rampersad, N., Shallit, J.: On NFAs where all states are final, initial, or both. Theor. Comput. Sci. 410(4749), 5010–5021 (2009)
17. Kretínský, J., Sickert, S.: MoTraS: a tool for modal transition systems and their extensions. In: 11th International Symposium Automated Technology for Verification and Analysis (ATVA) (2013)
18. Raclet, J.B.: Residual for component specifications. ENTCS 215, 93–110 (2008). Workshop on Formal Aspects of Component Software (FACS)
19. Ramadge, P., Wonham, W.: The control of discrete event systems. Proc. IEEE 77(1), 81–98 (1989)
20. Schmidt, E.M.: Succinctness of description of context-free, regular and unambiguous languages. Ph.D. thesis, Cornell University (1978)
21. Stearns, R.E., Hunt III, H.B.: On the equivalence and containment problems for unambiguous regular expressions, regular grammars and finite automata. SIAM J. Comput. 14(3), 598–611 (1985)
22. Villa, T., Petrenko, A., Yevtushenko, N., Mishchenko, A., Brayton, R.: Component-based design by solving language equations. Proc. IEEE 99, 1–16 (2015)
23. Villa, T., Yevtushenko, N., Brayton, R.K., Mishchenko, A., Petrenko, A., Sangiovanni-Vincentelli, A.: The Unknown Component Problem: Theory and Applications. Springer, Heidelberg (2011)
24. Yellin, D., Strom, R.: Protocol specifications and component adaptors. ACM Trans. Programm. Lang. Syst. (TOPLAS) 19(2), 292–333 (1997)

Spot 2.0 — A Framework for LTL and ω-Automata Manipulation

Alexandre Duret-Lutz[✉], Alexandre Lewkowicz, Amaury Fauchille,
Thibaud Michaud, Étienne·Renault, and Laurent Xu

LRDE, EPITA, Kremlin-Bicêtre, France
spot@lrde.epita.fr

Abstract. We present Spot 2.0, a C++ library with Python bindings
and an assortment of command-line tools designed to manipulate LTL
and ω-automata in batch. New automata-manipulation tools were introduced in Spot 2.0; they support arbitrary acceptance conditions, as
expressible in the Hanoi Omega Automaton format. Besides being useful
to researchers who have automata to process, its Python bindings can
also be used in interactive environments to teach ω-automata and model
checking.

1 Introduction

Spot is a C++ library of model-checking algorithms that was first presented in
2004 [15]. It contains algorithms to perform the usual tasks in the automata-
theoretic approach to LTL model checking [36]. It was purely a library until
Spot 1.0, when we started distributing command-line tools for LTL manipulation [13] and translation of LTL to some generalizations of Büchi Automata.

Spot 2.0 is a very large rewrite of the core of the library, in C++11, with a
focus on supporting automata with arbitrary acceptance conditions as described
in the Hanoi Omega Automata format (HOA) [6]. Those acceptance conditions
are expressed as positive Boolean formulas over terms such as $\mathsf{Inf}(n)$ and $\mathsf{Fin}(n)$,
which indicate respectively that some set S_n of states or transitions should be visited infinitely or finitely often. Traditional acceptance conditions look as follows
in this formalism:

Büchi:	$\mathsf{Inf}(0)$	generalized-Büchi:	$\mathsf{Inf}(0) \wedge \mathsf{Inf}(1) \wedge \mathsf{Inf}(2) \wedge \ldots$
co-Büchi:	$\mathsf{Fin}(0)$	generalized-co-Büchi:	$\mathsf{Fin}(0) \vee \mathsf{Fin}(1) \vee \mathsf{Fin}(2) \vee \ldots$
Rabin:	$(\mathsf{Fin}(0) \wedge \mathsf{Inf}(1)) \vee (\mathsf{Fin}(2) \wedge \mathsf{Inf}(3)) \vee \ldots$		
Streett:	$(\mathsf{Fin}(0) \vee \mathsf{Inf}(1)) \wedge (\mathsf{Fin}(2) \vee \mathsf{Inf}(3)) \wedge \ldots$		

Parity acceptance, generalized-Rabin [5,24], and any Boolean combination of
the above can be expressed as well. The use of HOA as default format makes
it easy to chain Spot's command-line tools, and interact with other tools that
implement HOA, regardless of the actual acceptance condition used.

© Springer International Publishing AG 2016
C. Artho et al. (Eds.): ATVA 2016, LNCS 9938, pp. 122–129, 2016.
DOI: 10.1007/978-3-319-46520-3_8

Additionally, Spot 2.0 ships with Python bindings usable in interactive environments such as IPython/Jupyter [29], easing development, experimentation, and teaching.

Spot is a free software and can be obtained from https://spot.lrde.epita.fr/. The reader who wants to try Spot without installing it is invited to visit http://spot-sandbox.lrde.epita.fr/ where a live installation of Jupyter and Spot allows all examples (command lines or Python) of this paper to be replayed.

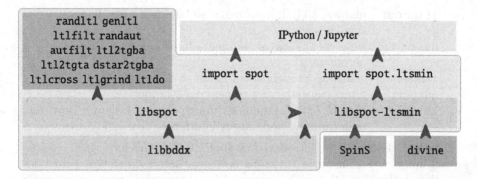

Fig. 1. Architecture of Spot. C++ libraries are in orange boxes, binaries in red, and Python packages in blue. The outlined area is what Spot distributes. (Color figure online)

Figure 1 shows that Spot is actually split in three libraries. `libbddx` is a customized version de BuDDy [26] for representing Binary Decision Diagrams [10] which we use to label transitions in automata, and to implement a few algorithms [4,14]. `libspot` is the main library containing all data structures and algorithms. `libspot-ltsmin` contains code to interface with state-spaces generated as shared libraries by LTSmin [20].

In the rest of this article, we highlight some of the features of Spot by presenting the command-line tools and the Python bindings built on top of these libraries. The reader should keep in mind that everything that we illustrate as shell command or in Python can be performed directly in C++; in fact our web site gives several examples of tasks implemented with each of these three interfaces.

2   Command-Line Tools

Spot 2.0 installs the following eleven command-line tools, that are designed to be combined as traditional Unix tools.

	randltl	generates random LTL/PSL formulas
	genltl	generates LTL formulas from scalable patterns
	ltlfilt	filter, converts, and transforms LTL/PSL formulas
[13]	ltl2tgba	translates LTL/PSL formulas into generalized Büchi automata [14], or deterministic parity automata (new in 2.0)
	ltl2tgta	translates LTL/PSL formulas into Testing automata [8]
	ltlcross	cross-compares LTL/PSL-to-automata translators to find bugs (works with arbitrary acceptance conditions since Spot 2.0)
	ltlgrind	mutates LTL/PSL formulas to help reproduce bugs on smaller ones
	dstar2tgba	converts ltl2dstar automata into Generalized Büchi automata [1]
	randaut	generates random ω-automata
	autfilt	filters, converts, and transforms ω-automata
	ltldo	runs LTL/PSL formulas through other translators, providing uniform input and output interfaces

The first six tools were introduced in Spot 1.0 [13], and have since received several updates. For instance ltl2tgba now uses better simulation reductions and degeneralization [4], and it now provides a way to output deterministic automata using transition-based parity acceptance; ltlfilt has learned to decide stutter-invariance of any LTL/PSL formula using an automaton-based check that is independent on the actual logic used [27]; and ltlcross can now perform precise equivalence checks of automata in addition to supporting arbitrary acceptance conditions—it has been used by the authors of ltl3dra [5], ltl2dstar [21,22], and Rabinizer 3 [23] to test recent releases of their respective tools.

The dstar2tgba tool was introduced in Spot 1.2 while working on the minimization of deterministic generalized Büchi automata using a SAT-solver [1]. It implements algorithms that translate deterministic Rabin automata into Büchi automata, preserving determinism if possible [25], as well as conversion from Streett to generalized Büchi. These two different kinds of input correspond to the possible outputs of ltl2dstar. In Spot 2.0, these specialized acceptance conversions have been preserved, but they are supplemented with more general transformations that input automata with arbitrary acceptance conditions, and transform them into automata with "Fin-less" acceptance, or with (Generalized) Büchi acceptance. These acceptance transformations are essential to a few core algorithms that cannot cope with arbitrary acceptance: for instance currently Spot can only check the emptiness of automata with Fin-less acceptance (all SCC-based emptiness-checks [11,12,31] are compatible with that), so more complex acceptances are transformed when needed.

All these acceptance transformations, as well as other automata transformations are available through the autfilt tool. This command can input a stream of automata in 4 different formats (HOA [6], LBTT's format [33], never claims [19], or ltl2dstar's format [22]), and can output automata, maybe after filtering or transformation, in some other format (including GraphViz's dot format [17] for display).

As an example of transformation and format conversion, consider:

```
% spin -f'[]<>a' | autfilt --complement --dot=abr | dot -Tpng >aut.png
```

This command translates the LTL formula GFa into a Büchi automaton using spin [19], the resulting never claim is then fed into autfilt for complementation, and the complemented automaton is output into GraphViz's format for graphical rendering with dot. The arguments a, b, and r passed to --dot cause the acceptance condition to be displayed, and the acceptance marks to be shown as colored bullets.

In the above example the input to autfilt happens to be a deterministic Büchi automaton, so the complementation is as simple as changing the acceptance condition into co-Büchi. If a Büchi output is desired instead, the above command should be changed to autfilt --complement --ba and will output a non-deterministic Büchi automaton. This of course works with arbitrary acceptance conditions as input.

Complementation of non-deterministic automata is done via determinization. Our determinization algorithm inputs transition-based Büchi automata (so we may have some preprocessing to do if the input has a different acceptance), and outputs automata with transition-based Parity acceptance. It mixes the construction of Redziejowski [30] with some optimizations of ltl2dstar [21,22] and a few of our own.

The ltldo command wraps third-party LTL translators and provides them with inputs and outputs that are compatible with the Spot tool-suite. In particular it allows using "single-shot" translators in a pipeline. For instance spin can only translate one formula at a time to produce a never claim. The command ltldo spin will process multiple formulas (in any syntax supported by Spot [13]), translate them all using spin, and output all results in any supported automaton format (HOA by default). For instance the following command uses Spin to translate 10 random LTL formulas into Büchi automata in the HOA format:

```
% randltl -n 10 a b | ltldo spin --name=%f
```

Option --name=%f requests input formulas to be used as the "name:" field in the HOA format. This field could then be used to retrieve the original formula after further processing: autfilt --stats=%M can be used to print the name of each input automaton.

As a more complex example, the following pipeline finds 10 formulas for which ltl3ba [3] produces a deterministic Büchi automaton, but ltl2ba [18] does not.

```
% randltl -n -1 a b |
  ltldo ltl3ba --name=%f | autfilt --is-deterministic --stats=%M |
  ltldo ltl2ba --name=%f | autfilt -v --is-deterministic --stats=%M -n 10
```

This creates an infinite (-n -1) stream of LTL formulas over atomic propositions a and b, translates them using ltl3ba, retains those that were translated
to deterministic automata, translate them with ltl2ba and retains the non-
deterministic ones (-v inverts matches, as with grep). With the final -n 10, the
pipeline is eventually killed once the last command has found 10 matches.

The autfilt tool provides access to other ω-automata algorithms such
as product, emptiness checks, language inclusion or equivalence, language-
preserving simplifications of automata, refinement of labels [9], strength-based
decompositions [32], SAT-based minimization of deterministic automata with
arbitrary input and output acceptance [2], or conversion from transition-based
acceptance to state-based acceptance. Most algorithms work with arbitrary
acceptance conditions, except a few (emptiness checks, determinization) that
currently have to reduce the acceptance conditions upfront.

3   The Python Interface

Similar tasks can be performed in a more "algorithm-friendly" environment using
the Python interface. Combined with the IPython/Jupyter notebook [29] (a web
application for interactive programming), this provides a nice environment for
experiments, where automata and formulas are automatically displayed. Figure 2
shows two examples that we used in a practical lecture on model checking with
students from EPITA.

The first example illustrates how LTL formulas can be parsed
(spot.formula()), and then translated (using translate()) into automata
with transition-based generalized Büchi acceptance. Using product, negation,
and emptiness check, a student can define a procedure to test the equivalence of
two LTL formulas and then use it to explore her understanding of LTL.

The second example illustrates the classical automata-theoretic approach to
explicit LTL model checking [36]. Spot can read the shared-libraries used to
represent state spaces in the LTSmin project [20]. Those can be compiled from
Promela models using SpinS [35], or from DiVinE models using LTSmin's modified version of DiVinE 2 [7]. In this example the %%dve keyword is used to specify
a short DiVinE model called adding (this model comes from the BEEM database [28]) which is immediately compiled and loaded as a shared library. Printing
the adding Python variable reveals that it is an object using the LTSmin interface, and lists the variables that can be used to build atomic proposition on this
model. A Kripke structure can be instantiated from the model by providing a list
of atomic propositions that should be valuated on each state. Displaying large
Kripke structures is of course not very practical: by default Spot displays only the
50 first states (this can be changed using for instance the max_states argument
in the first cell). With this interface, we can now easily write a model_check()
procedure that inputs a model and a formula, instanciates a Kripke structure
from the model using all the atomic propositions that appear in the formula,
translates the negation of the formula into an automaton, and tests the emptiness of the product between the Kripke structure and this automaton. Note that

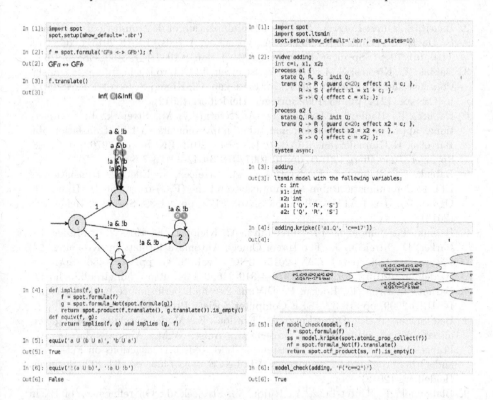

Fig. 2. Two examples of using the Python bindings of Spot in the Jupyter notebook.

`otf_product()` performs an on-the-fly product: the state-space and the product are constructed as needed by the emptiness check algorithm.

4   Model Checkers Built Using Spot

At the C++ level, the interface with LTSmin demonstrated above wraps the LTSmin state-space as a subclass of Spot's Kripke structure class. This class basically just specifies the initial state and how to find the successors of a state, therefore allowing on-the-fly exploration. Model checkers like ITS-Tools [34] or Neco [16] have been implemented in the same way (both have been recently updated to Spot 2.0).

References

1. Baarir, S., Duret-Lutz, A.: Mechanizing the minimization of deterministic generalized Büchi automata. In: Ábrahám, E., Palamidessi, C. (eds.) FORTE 2014. LNCS, vol. 8461, pp. 266–283. Springer, Heidelberg (2014). doi:10.1007/978-3-662-43613-4_17

2. Baarir, S., Duret-Lutz, A.: SAT-based minimization of deterministic ω-automata. In: Davis, M., Fehnker, A., McIver, A., Voronkov, A. (eds.) LPAR 2015. LNCS, vol. 9450, pp. 79–87. Springer, Heidelberg (2015). doi:10.1007/978-3-662-48899-7_6

3. Babiak, T., Křetínský, M., Řehák, V., Strejček, J.: LTL to Büchi automata translation: fast and more deterministic. In: Flanagan, C., König, B. (eds.) TACAS 2012. LNCS, vol. 7214, pp. 95–109. Springer, Heidelberg (2012)

4. Babiak, T., Badie, T., Duret-Lutz, A., Křetínský, M., Strejček, J.: Compositional approach to suspension and other improvements to LTL translation. In: Bartocci, E., Ramakrishnan, C.R. (eds.) SPIN 2013. LNCS, vol. 7976, pp. 81–98. Springer, Heidelberg (2013). doi:10.1007/978-3-642-39176-7_6

5. Babiak, T., Blahoudek, F., Křetínský, M., Strejček, J.: Effective translation of LTL to deterministic Rabin automata: beyond the (F,G)-fragment. In: Hung, D., Ogawa, M. (eds.) ATVA 2013. LNCS, vol. 8172, pp. 24–39. Springer, Heidelberg (2013)

6. Babiak, T., Blahoudek, F., Duret-Lutz, A., Klein, J., Křetínský, J., Müller, D., Parker, D., Strejček, J.: The Hanoi Omega-Automata format. In: Kroening, D., Păsăreanu, C.S. (eds.) CAV 2015. LNCS, vol. 9206, pp. 479–486. Springer, Heidelberg (2015). doi:10.1007/978-3-319-21690-4_31. http://adl.github.io/hoaf/

7. Barnat, J., Brim, L., Rockai, P.: DiVinE 2.0: high-performance model checking. In: HiBi 2009, pp. 31–32. IEEE Computer Society Press (2009)

8. Ben Salem, A.-E., Duret-Lutz, A., Kordon, F.: Model checking using generalized testing automata. In: Jensen, K., Aalst, W.M., Ajmone Marsan, M., Franceschinis, G., Kleijn, J., Kristensen, L.M. (eds.) Transactions on Petri Nets and Other Models of Concurrency VI. LNCS, vol. 7400, pp. 94–122. Springer, Heidelberg (2012)

9. Blahoudek, F., Duret-Lutz, A., Rujbr, V., Strejček, J.: On refinement of Büchi automata for explicit model checking. In: Fischer, B., Geldenhuys, J. (eds.) SPIN 2015. LNCS, vol. 9232, pp. 66–83. Springer, Heidelberg (2015). doi:10.1007/978-3-319-23404-5_6

10. Bryant, R.E.: Graph-based algorithms for boolean function manipulation. IEEE Trans. Comput. 35(8), 677–691 (1986)

11. Couvreur, J.-M.: On-the-fly verification of linear temporal logic. In: Wing, J.M., Woodcock, J. (eds.) FM 1999. LNCS, vol. 1708, pp. 253–271. Springer, Heidelberg (1999)

12. Couvreur, J.-M., Duret-Lutz, A., Poitrenaud, D.: On-the-fly emptiness checks for generalized Büchi automata. In: Godefroid, P. (ed.) SPIN 2005. LNCS, vol. 3639, pp. 169–184. Springer, Heidelberg (2005). doi:10.1007/11537328_15

13. Duret-Lutz, A.: Manipulating LTL formulas using Spot 1.0. In: Hung, D., Ogawa, M. (eds.) ATVA 2013. LNCS, vol. 8172, pp. 442–445. Springer, Heidelberg (2013). doi:10.1007/978-3-319-02444-8_31

14. Duret-Lutz, A.: LTL translation improvements in Spot 1.0. Int. J. Crit. Comput. Based Syst. 5(1–2), 31–54 (2014)

15. Duret-Lutz, A., Poitrenaud, D.: SPOT: an extensible model checking library using transition-based generalized Büchi automata. In: MASCOTS 2004, pp. 76–83. IEEE Computer Society Press (2004)

16. Fronc, Ł., Duret-Lutz, A.: LTL model checking with Neco. In: Hung, D., Ogawa, M. (eds.) ATVA 2013. LNCS, vol. 8172, pp. 451–454. Springer, Heidelberg (2013). doi:10.1007/978-3-319-02444-8_33. https://github.com/Lvyn/neco-net-compiler

17. Gansner, E.R., North, S.C.: An open graph visualization system and its applications to software engineering. Softw. Pract. Exp. 30(11), 1203–1233 (2000)

18. Gastin, P., Oddoux, D.: Fast LTL to Büchi automata translation. In: Berry, G., Comon, H., Finkel, A. (eds.) CAV 2001. LNCS, vol. 2102, pp. 53–65. Springer, Heidelberg (2001). doi:10.1007/3-540-44585-4_6

19. Holzmann, G.J.: The Spin Model Checker: Primer and Reference Manual. Addison-Wesley, Boston (2003)

20. Kant, G., Laarman, A., Meijer, J., van de Pol, J., Blom, S., van Dijk, T.: LTSmin: high-performance language-independent model checking. In: Baier, C., Tinelli, C. (eds.) TACAS 2015. LNCS, vol. 9035, pp. 692–707. Springer, Heidelberg (2015)

21. Klein, J., Baier, C.: Experiments with deterministic ω-automata for formulas of linear temporal logic. Theoret. Comput. Sci. 363(2), 182–195 (2006)

22. Klein, J., Baier, C.: On-the-fly stuttering in the construction of deterministic ω-automata. In: Holub, J., Žďárek, J. (eds.) CIAA 2007. LNCS, vol. 4783, pp. 51–61. Springer, Heidelberg (2007)

23. Komárková, Z., Křetínský, J.: Rabinizer 3: safraless translation of LTL to small deterministic automata. In: Cassez, F., Raskin, J.-F. (eds.) ATVA 2014. LNCS, vol. 8837, pp. 235–241. Springer, Heidelberg (2014)

24. Křetínský, J., Esparza, J.: Deterministic automata for the (F,G)-fragment of LTL. In: Madhusudan, P., Seshia, S.A. (eds.) CAV 2012. LNCS, vol. 7358, pp. 7–22. Springer, Heidelberg (2012)

25. Krishnan, S.C., Puri, A., Brayton, R.K.: Deterministic ω-automata vis-a-vis deterministic Büchi automata. In: Du, D.-Z., Zhang, X.-S. (eds.) ISAAC 1994. LNCS, vol. 834, pp. 378–386. Springer, Heidelberg (1994)

26. Lind-Nielsen, J., Cohen, H.: BuDDy: Binary Decision Diagram Package. https://sourceforge.net/projects/buddy/. Accessed 2 Apr 2014

27. Michaud, T., Duret-Lutz, A.: Practical stutter-invariance checks for ω-regular languages. In: Fischer, B., Geldenhuys, J. (eds.) SPIN 2015. LNCS, vol. 9232, pp. 84–101. Springer, Heidelberg (2015). doi:10.1007/978-3-319-23404-5_7

28. Pelánek, R.: BEEM: benchmarks for explicit model checkers. In: Bošnački, D., Edelkamp, S. (eds.) SPIN 2007. LNCS, vol. 4595, pp. 263–267. Springer, Heidelberg (2007)

29. Pérez, F., Granger, B.E.: IPython: a system for interactive scientific computing. Comput. Sci. Eng. 9(3), 21–29 (2007). http://ipython.org

30. Redziejowski, R.: An improved construction of deterministic omega-automaton using derivatives. Fundam. Informaticae 119(3–4), 393–496 (2012)

31. Renault, E., Duret-Lutz, A., Kordon, F., Poitrenaud, D.: Three SCC-based emptiness checks for generalized Büchi automata. In: McMillan, K., Middeldorp, A., Voronkov, A. (eds.) LPAR 2013. LNCS, vol. 8312, pp. 668–682. Springer, Heidelberg (2013). doi:10.1007/978-3-642-45221-5_44

32. Renault, E., Duret-Lutz, A., Kordon, F., Poitrenaud, D.: Strength-based decomposition of the property Büchi automaton for faster model checking. In: Piterman, N., Smolka, S.A. (eds.) TACAS 2013. LNCS, vol. 7795, pp. 580–593. Springer, Heidelberg (2013). doi:10.1007/978-3-642-36742-7_42

33. Tauriainen, H., Heljanko, K.: Testing LTL formula translation into Büchi automata. STTT 4(1), 57–70 (2002)

34. Thierry-Mieg, Y.: Symbolic model-checking using ITS-tools. In: Baier, C., Tinelli, C. (eds.) TACAS 2015. LNCS, vol. 9035, pp. 231–237. Springer, Heidelberg (2015)

35. van der Berg, F.I., Laarman, A.W.: SpinS: extending LTSmin with Promela through SpinJa. In: PDMC 2012. ENTCS, vol. 296, pp. 95–105. Elsevier (2012)

36. Vardi, M.Y.: An automata-theoretic approach to linear temporal logic. In: Moller, F., Birtwistle, G. (eds.). LNCS, vol. 1043, pp. 238–266. Springer, Heidelberg (1996). doi:10.1007/3-540-60915-6_6

MoChiBA: Probabilistic LTL Model Checking Using Limit-Deterministic Büchi Automata

Salomon Sickert[✉] and Jan Křetínský

Technische Universität München, Munich, Germany
{sickert,jan.kretinsky}@in.tum.de

Abstract. The limiting factor for quantitative analysis of Markov decision processes (MDP) against specifications given in linear temporal logic (LTL) is the size of the generated product. As recently shown, a special subclass of limit-deterministic Büchi automata (LDBA) can replace deterministic Rabin automata in quantitative probabilistic model checking algorithms. We present an extension of PRISM for LTL model checking of MDP using LDBA. While existing algorithms can be used only with minimal changes, the new approach takes advantage of the special structure and the smaller size of the obtained LDBA to speed up the model checking. We demonstrate the speed up experimentally by a comparison with other approaches.

1 Introduction

Linear temporal logic (LTL) [30] is a prominent specification language and has been proven useful in industrial practice. The key to efficient LTL model checking is the automata-theoretic approach [38]: first, a given LTL formula is translated into an automaton; second, a product of the system and the automaton is constructed and analysed. Since real systems are huge, it is crucial to construct *small automata* in order to avoid a large size increase of the product.

LTL is typically translated into non-deterministic Büchi automata (NBA) [2,8,10,11,14,15,17,18,36]. However, for probabilistic models such as Markov decision processes (MDP) non-deterministic automata are not applicable [3] and the standard solution is to *determinise* them using Safra's construction [22,29, 32,33,37]. This approach is implemented in the most widespread probabilistic model checker PRISM [27]. However, the determinisation step is costly and often increases the size of automata dramatically. Therefore, *direct translations of LTL to deterministic automata* have been proposed [1,13,25,26], implemented [5,16,24], and shown to be more efficient for probabilistic model checking [6]. Nevertheless, despite more sophisticated acceptance conditions, such as generalized Rabin [26], the imposed determinism inevitably increases the size of the automata.

This naturally raises the question whether fully deterministic automata are necessary or whether restricted forms of determinism are sufficient. For instance, in the setting of games where NBA are not applicable either, a weaker notion of determinism called *good-for-games automata* is sufficient [20]. It has been proven sufficient also for probabilistic model checking, but practically "did not improve on the standard approach" [23]. Further, *unambiguous automata* can be

C. Artho et al. (Eds.): ATVA 2016, LNCS 9938, pp. 130–137, 2016.
DOI: 10.1007/978-3-319-46520-3_9

used [9] for model checking Markov chains, but not for MDPs. Moreover, *limit-deterministic* Büchi automata (LDBA) [7,38] can be used for probabilistic model checking MDPs in the qualitative case (deciding whether a property holds with probability 1). This idea has been further explored also in the quantitative setting (computing the probability of satisfaction) and an algorithm constructing products with several (limit-)deterministic automata proposed [19]. Although LDBA cannot in general be used for probabilistic model checking, a recent translation [35] of LTL produces LDBA, which can be used in the standard algorithm based on the construction of a single product. It also discusses the subclass of LDBA that can be used for this task. Note that there is also an exponentially better translation [21] (based on [25]) of a fragment of LTL called $LTL_{\setminus \mathbf{GU}}$ into LDBA and that there is also an efficient complementation procedure for LDBA [4].

In this paper, we provide the first implementation of the probabilistic model checking procedure proposed in [35] based on LDBA. Apart from smaller sizes of LDBA, another advantage of the Büchi acceptance condition is a faster analysis of maximal end components (MECs), compared to the standard repetitive recomputation for each Rabin pair. We also present several crucial optimizations, which make our implementation outperform other approaches on many formulas. We illustrate this on experimental results. The tool as well as the explanation of its name can be found on https://www7.in.tum.de/~sickert/projects/mochiba/.

2   Overview of the Algorithm

In order to present our implementation and optimizations, we have to sketch how an MDP $\mathcal{M}$ is checked against an LTL formula φ by the algorithm of [35]. First, φ is translated into an LDBA $\mathcal{A}(\varphi)$. Second, $\mathcal{M}$ is checked against $\mathcal{A}(\varphi)$ using a straightforward extension of the standard algorithm.

LDBA Construction. An LDBA is a (possibly generalised) Büchi automaton partitioned into an *initial* and an *accepting* part, where the initial part contains no accepting transitions and the accepting part is deterministic. Moreover, the construction of [35] produces LDBA with the initial part deterministic except for ε-transitions into the accepting part.

We illustrate the translation on $\varphi = a \wedge \mathbf{X}(\mathbf{FG}a \vee \mathbf{FG}b)$. Each state in the initial part is labeled with a formula. The words accepted from a state are exactly those satisfying the formula. Observe that $\mathbf{FG}a \vee \mathbf{FG}b$ holds iff eventually we reach a point where $\mathbf{G}a$ holds or $\mathbf{G}b$ holds. We non-deterministically guess this point and take the ε-transition to the accepting part, where we check the guess.

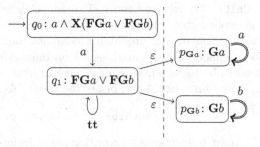

Fig. 1. LDBA $\mathcal{A}(\varphi)$ with the initial part on the left and the accepting on the right.

For this formula `spot` (2.0) produces a deterministic Rabin automaton with 4 states, too, but adding two more disjuncts **FG**c and **FG**d increases the size to 26 states. In contrast, our LDBA requires only two extra states.

Product Construction and Analysis. We proceed according to the standard algorithm:

1. Construct the product $\mathcal{P} = \mathcal{M} \times \mathcal{A}(\varphi)$.
2. Compute maximal end-components (MECs) of $\mathcal{P}$.
3. Compute the maximum probability to reach winning MECs. A MEC is winning if it satisfies the acceptance condition of $\mathcal{A}(\varphi)$: here, if it contains an accepting transition for each Büchi condition.

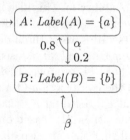

Fig. 2. An MDP $\mathcal{M}$.

The standard product of an MDP and a deterministic automaton defines the transitions (in the usual notation) by $P(\langle s,q \rangle, \alpha, \langle s',q' \rangle) = P(s,\alpha,s')$ if $q' = \delta(q, Label(s'))$ and otherwise equals 0. We extend the procedure to handle also non-deterministic ε-transitions by additional actions: let $q_1, \ldots, q_n$ be the successors of q under ε, then for each $i = 1, \ldots, n$ we add a new action called ε_{q_i} and define $P(\langle s,q \rangle, \varepsilon_{q_i}, \langle s,q_i \rangle) = 1$ (note that s does not move here).

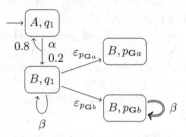

Fig. 3. The product $\mathcal{M} \times \mathcal{A}(\varphi)$.

Figure 3 illustrates the construction by a product of the system of Fig. 2 and the automaton of Fig. 1. A crucial optimization used here is that it is sufficient to take ε-transitions only from states in MECs of $\mathcal{M} \times \mathcal{N}(\varphi)$ (which are exactly MECs of the product of $\mathcal{M}$ and the initial part of $\mathcal{A}(\varphi)$). Hence no ε-transitions have to be produced in the initial state here.

3   Implementation and Optimizations

`MoChiBA` [34] replaces the LTL model-checker and the MEC computation in the explicit-state model-checker of PRISM, while other infrastructure (parsing, model construction, probability computation) are inherited from PRISM. The tool cannot be configured — all optimizations are enabled — and does not need to be installed. It reads a model (given as an MDP, `.nm`) and a property specification (`.pctl`) and prints the results to `stdout`:

```
./mochiba.sh model.nm properties.pctl
```

Apart from taking ε-transitions only from states in MECs of $\mathcal{M} \times \mathcal{N}(\varphi)$ as mentioned above, we implement the following optimizations:

Transition-based acceptance leads to smaller automata, compared to state-based acceptance. Consequently, it is used by many translators, for instance [1, 11, 24]. However, PRISM translates all automata to state-based, thus increasing the size of the product. Our procedure avoids this and constructs and analyses directly the transition-based product.

Generalised Büchi acceptance condition allows for more efficient analysis than (generalised) Rabin, Streett, or parity conditions. Indeed, for the latter conditions expensive re-computations of MECs are necessary to handle different sets to be visited finitely often. In contrast, we compute MECs only once and check whether each set to be visited infinitely often intersects the MEC.

A single trap state is present in the product. Should the product enter any state from which the automaton component can never accept, the exploration of this part stops and redirects the transition to the single trap state.

Primitive data structures such as arrays are used instead of the more flexible Java collections, since they are more memory efficient, as boxing into objects is not necessary.

Sparse bit sets have proven more memory efficient for our approach than plain bit sets with a mapping table.

MEC decomposition is performed locally on disconnected accepting parts (corresponding to different ε-transitions). Together with the use of sparse bit sets, MECs are computed faster and using less memory.

4   Experimental Evaluation

We evaluate our novel approach in the setting of [6, 19]: we consider the Pneuli-Zuck randomised mutual exclusion protocol [31] of the PRISM benchmark suite [28] and also the same previously considered formulas (see lines 1–10 of Table 1). Additionally, lines 11–14 consider the deeply nested formulas of [35]. Finally, complementary to the **GF**-, **FG**- and fairness-like properties, lines 15–16 include simple reachability properties, which lie in the focus of the traditional methods.

The experiments were performed on a 2.5 GHz Intel Core i7 (I7-4870HQ) and granted 12 GB RAM and 1 h computing time for model checking each property (given the model already in the memory). We denote time-outs and mem-outs by "-". We compare the following tools

- **MoChiBA** (1.0) [34] is our implementation based on the LDBA translation of [35] and the explicit model checker of PRISM.
- **PRISM** (4.3) [27] with the symbolic engine, which is the fastest here, and with the following translators:
    - Built-in LTL to deterministic Rabin automaton translation, re-implementing ltl2dstar [22].
    - **Rabinizer** (3.1) [24] using the Safra-less direct translation into generalised Rabin automata, which are now supported by PRISM.
- **IscasMC** (unofficial, unversioned) implements the lazy approach of [19], using SPOT 1.2.6 [12] to translate LTL to non-deterministic Büchi automaton. We used the two fastest configurations as listed in [19]:
    - Multi-breakpoint (**BP**) construction with the explicit engine.
    - Rabin (**R**) construction with the explicit engine.

Table 1. Runtime comparison on model checking these properties on the Pneuli-Zuck randomised mutual exclusion protocol [31].

Property	n	MoChiBA	PRISM	Rabinizer	IscasMC-BP	IscasMC-R
			Time (rounded, in seconds)			
(1) $\mathbb{P}_{max=?}[\begin{smallmatrix}\mathbf{GF}p1=10\wedge\mathbf{GF}p2=10\\ \wedge\mathbf{GF}p3=10\end{smallmatrix}]$	4	< 1	16	< 1	< 1	< 1
	5	2	230	< 1	12	11
(2) $\mathbb{P}_{max=?}[\begin{smallmatrix}\mathbf{GF}p1=10\wedge\mathbf{GF}p2=10\\ \wedge\mathbf{GF}p3=10\wedge\mathbf{GF}p4=10\end{smallmatrix}]$	4	< 1	26	< 1	1	< 1
	5	2	345	< 1	12	12
(3) $\mathbb{P}_{min=?}[\begin{smallmatrix}\mathbf{GF}p1=10\wedge\mathbf{GF}p2=10\\ \wedge\mathbf{GF}p3=10\wedge\mathbf{GF}p4=10\end{smallmatrix}]$	4	1	3552	33	1	22
	5	11	-	572	18	641
(4) $\mathbb{P}_{max=?}[\begin{smallmatrix}(\mathbf{GF}p1=0\vee\mathbf{FG}p2\neq0)\\ \wedge(\mathbf{GF}p2=0\vee\mathbf{FG}p3\neq0)\end{smallmatrix}]$	4	1	684	18	2	4
	5	15	-	293	19	50
(5) $\mathbb{P}_{max=?}[\begin{smallmatrix}(\mathbf{GF}p1=0\vee\mathbf{FG}p1\neq0)\\ \wedge(\mathbf{GF}p2=0\vee\mathbf{FG}p2\neq0)\end{smallmatrix}]$	4	< 1	< 1	23	1	4
	5	1	< 1	403	17	59
(6) $\mathbb{P}_{max=?}[\begin{smallmatrix}(\mathbf{GF}p1=0\vee\mathbf{GF}p2\neq0)\\ \wedge(\mathbf{GF}p2=0\vee\mathbf{FG}p3\neq0)\\ \wedge(\mathbf{GF}p3=0\vee\mathbf{FG}p1\neq0)\end{smallmatrix}]$	4	< 1	78	9	3	10
	5	10	1293	137	29	143
(7) $\mathbb{P}_{max=?}[\begin{smallmatrix}(\mathbf{GF}p1=0\vee\mathbf{GF}p1\neq0)\\ \wedge(\mathbf{GF}p2=0\vee\mathbf{FG}p2\neq0)\\ \wedge(\mathbf{GF}p3=0\vee\mathbf{FG}p3\neq0)\end{smallmatrix}]$	4	< 1	< 1	61	2	18
	5	1	< 1	1077	27	277
(8) $\mathbb{P}_{min=?}[\begin{smallmatrix}(\mathbf{GF}p1\neq10\vee\mathbf{GF}p1=0\vee\mathbf{GF}p1=1)\\ \wedge\mathbf{GF}p1\neq0\wedge\mathbf{GF}p1=1\end{smallmatrix}]$	4	< 1	8	8	1	1
	5	1	145	190	16	21
(9) $\mathbb{P}_{max=?}[\begin{smallmatrix}(\mathbf{G}p1\neq10\vee\mathbf{G}p2\neq10\vee\mathbf{G}p3\neq10)\\ \wedge[\mathbf{FG}p1\neq1\vee\mathbf{GF}p2=1\vee\mathbf{GF}p3=1)\\ \wedge(\mathbf{FG}p2\neq1)\vee\mathbf{GF}p1=1\vee\mathbf{GF}p3=1)\end{smallmatrix}]$	4	**5**	-	1195	8	871
	5	**99**	-	-	125	-
(10) $\mathbb{P}_{min=?}[\begin{smallmatrix}\mathbf{FG}p1\neq0\vee\mathbf{FG}p2=0\\ \vee\mathbf{GF}p3=0\vee(\mathbf{FG}p1\neq10\\ \wedge\mathbf{GF}p2=10\wedge\mathbf{GF}p3=10)\end{smallmatrix}]$	4	1	728	33	79	6
	5	**24**	-	486	-	77
(11) $\mathbb{P}_{min=?}[f_{0,0}]=\mathbb{P}_{min=?}[\begin{smallmatrix}(\mathbf{GF}p1=10)\mathbf{U}\\(p2=10)\end{smallmatrix}]$	4	< 1	17	40	2	2
	5	11	257	715	23	54
(12) $\mathbb{P}_{max=?}[f_{0,4}]=\mathbb{P}_{max=?}[\begin{smallmatrix}(\mathbf{GF}p1=10)\mathbf{U}\\(\mathbf{XXXX}p2=10)\end{smallmatrix}]$	4	< 1	3	< 1	1	15
	5	5	20	2	20	2381
(13) $\mathbb{P}_{min=?}[f_{1,0}]=\mathbb{P}_{min=?}[\begin{smallmatrix}(\mathbf{GF}p1=10)\mathbf{U}\\(\mathbf{G}((\mathbf{GF}p2=10)\mathbf{U}\\(p3=10)))\end{smallmatrix}]$	4	< 1	909	22	314	4
	5	13	-	436	-	59
(14) $\mathbb{P}_{max=?}[f_{1,4}]=\mathbb{P}_{max=?}[\begin{smallmatrix}(\mathbf{GF}p1=10)\mathbf{U}\\(\mathbf{G}((\mathbf{GF}p2=10)\mathbf{U}\\(\mathbf{XXXX}p3=10)))\end{smallmatrix}]$	4	< 1	-	18	2	2
	5	12	-	285	24	25
(15) $\mathbb{P}_{max=?}[p1=0\;\mathbf{U}\;p2=10]$	4	< 1	< 1	< 1	< 1	< 1
	5	< 1	< 1	< 1	7	7
(16) $\mathbb{P}_{max=?}[\mathbf{XXXXXX}p1=0]$	4	< 1	< 1	< 1	1	< 1
	5	3	< 1	< 1	19	16

5   Conclusion

We have implemented a novel approach for probabilistic LTL model checking using a subclass of non-deterministic Büchi automata. Since the experimental results for the explicit state-space implementation are encouraging, we plan to extend the approach to a symbolic one. Further, a parellelisation of the product construction and MECs analysis, as well as dedicated constructions for the *Release*-operator or various LTL fragments could lead to further speed ups.

Acknowledgements. This work is partially funded by the DFG Research Training Group "PUMA: Programm- und Modell-Analyse" (GRK 1480) and by the Czech Science Foundation, grant No. 15-17564S.

The authors want to thank Ernst Moritz Hahn and Andrea Turrini for providing a private version of IscasMC to compare to and for assistance in using it.

References

1. Babiak, T., Blahoudek, F., Křetínský, M., Strejček, J.: Effective translation of LTL to deterministic Rabin automata: beyond the (F, G)-fragment. In: ATVA, pp. 24–39 (2013)
2. Babiak, T., Křetínský, M., Řehák, V., Strejček, J.: LTL to Büchi automata translation: fast and more deterministic. In: Flanagan, C., König, B. (eds.) TACAS 2012. LNCS, vol. 7214, pp. 95–109. Springer, Heidelberg (2012). doi:10.1007/978-3-642-28756-5_8
3. Baier, C., Katoen, J.: Principles of Model Checking. MIT Press, Cambridge (2008)
4. Blahoudek, F., Heizmann, M., Schewe, S., Strejček, J., Tsai, M.-H.: Complementing semi-deterministic Büchi automata. In: Chechik, M., Raskin, J.-F. (eds.) TACAS 2016. LNCS, vol. 9636, pp. 770–787. Springer, Heidelberg (2016). doi:10.1007/978-3-662-49674-9_49
5. Blahoudek, F., Křetínský, M., Strejček, J.: Comparison of LTL to deterministic Rabin automata translators. In: McMillan, K., Middeldorp, A., Voronkov, A. (eds.) LPAR 2013. LNCS, vol. 8312, pp. 164–172. Springer, Heidelberg (2013). doi:10.1007/978-3-642-45221-5_12
6. Chatterjee, K., Gaiser, A., Křetínský, J.: Automata with generalized Rabin pairs for probabilistic model checking and LTL synthesis. In: Sharygina, N., Veith, H. (eds.) CAV 2013. LNCS, vol. 8044, pp. 559–575. Springer, Heidelberg (2013). doi:10.1007/978-3-642-39799-8_37
7. Courcoubetis, C., Yannakakis, M.: The complexity of probabilistic verification. J. ACM **42**(4), 857–907 (1995)
8. Couvreur, J.-M.: On-the-fly verification of linear temporal logic. In: Wing, J.M., Woodcock, J., Davies, J. (eds.) FM 1999. LNCS, vol. 1708, pp. 253–271. Springer, Heidelberg (1999). doi:10.1007/3-540-48119-2_16
9. Couvreur, J.-M., Saheb, N., Sutre, G.: An optimal automata approach to LTL model checking of probabilistic systems. In: Vardi, M.Y., Voronkov, A. (eds.) LPAR 2003. LNCS (LNAI), vol. 2850, pp. 361–375. Springer, Heidelberg (2003). doi:10.1007/978-3-540-39813-4_26
10. Daniele, M., Giunchiglia, F., Vardi, M.Y.: Improved automata generation for linear temporal logic. In: Halbwachs, N., Peled, D. (eds.) CAV 1999. LNCS, vol. 1633, pp. 249–260. Springer, Heidelberg (1999). doi:10.1007/3-540-48683-6_23
11. Duret-Lutz, A.: Manipulating LTL formulas using Spot 1.0. In: Hung, D., Ogawa, M. (eds.) ATVA 2013. LNCS, vol. 8172, pp. 442–445. Springer, Heidelberg (2013). doi:10.1007/978-3-319-02444-8_31
12. Duret-Lutz, A.: LTL translation improvements in Spot 1.0. IJCCBS **5**(1–2), 31–54 (2014)
13. Esparza, J., Křetínský, J.: From LTL to deterministic automata: a safraless compositional approach. In: Biere, A., Bloem, R. (eds.) CAV 2014. LNCS, vol. 8559, pp. 192–208. Springer, Heidelberg (2014). doi:10.1007/978-3-319-08867-9_13

14. Etessami, K., Holzmann, G.J.: Optimizing Büchi automata. In: Palamidessi, C. (ed.) CONCUR 2000. LNCS, vol. 1877, pp. 153–168. Springer, Heidelberg (2000). doi:10.1007/3-540-44618-4_13

15. Fritz, C.: Constructing Büchi automata from linear temporal logic using simulation relations for alternating Büchi automata. In: Ibarra, O.H., Dang, Z. (eds.) CIAA 2003. LNCS, vol. 2759, pp. 35–48. Springer, Heidelberg (2003). doi:10.1007/3-540-45089-0_5

16. Gaiser, A., Křetínský, J., Esparza, J.: Rabinizer: small deterministic automata for LTL(F, G). In: ATVA, pp. 72–76 (2012)

17. Gastin, P., Oddoux, D.: Fast LTL to Büchi automatatranslation. In: CAV, pp. 53–65 (2001). http://www.lsv.ens-cachan.fr/~gastin/ltl2ba/

18. Giannakopoulou, D., Lerda, F.: From states to transitions: improving translation of LTL formulae to Büchi automata. In: Peled, D.A., Vardi, M.Y. (eds.) FORTE 2002. LNCS, vol. 2529, pp. 308–326. Springer, Heidelberg (2002). doi:10.1007/3-540-36135-9_20

19. Hahn, E.M., Li, G., Schewe, S., Turrini, A., Zhang, L.: Lazyprobabilistic model checking without determinisation. In: CONCUR. LIPIcs, vol. 42, pp. 354–367 (2015)

20. Henzinger, T.A., Piterman, N.: Solving games without determinization. In: Ésik, Z. (ed.) CSL 2006. LNCS, vol. 4207, pp. 395–410. Springer, Heidelberg (2006). doi:10.1007/11874683_26

21. Kini, D., Viswanathan, M.: Limit deterministic and probabilistic automata for LTL \ GU. In: Baier, C., Tinelli, C. (eds.) TACAS 2015. LNCS, vol. 9035, pp. 628–642. Springer, Heidelberg (2015)

22. Klein, J.: ltl2dstar - LTL to deterministic Streett and Rabinautomata. http://www.ltl2dstar.de/

23. Klein, J., Müller, D., Baier, C., Klüppelholz, S.: Are good-for-games automata good for probabilistic model checking? In: Dediu, A.-H., Martín-Vide, C., Sierra-Rodríguez, J.-L., Truthe, B. (eds.) LATA 2014. LNCS, vol. 8370, pp. 453–465. Springer, Heidelberg (2014). doi:10.1007/978-3-319-04921-2_37

24. Komárková, Z., Křetínský, J.: Rabinizer 3: safraless translation of LTL to small deterministic automata. In: Cassez, F., Raskin, J.-F. (eds.) ATVA 2014. LNCS, vol. 8837, pp. 235–241. Springer, Heidelberg (2014). doi:10.1007/978-3-319-11936-6_17

25. Křetínský, J., Ledesma-Garza, R.: Rabinizer 2: small deterministic automata for LTL\GU. In: ATVA, pp. 446–450 (2013)

26. Křetínský, J., Esparza, J.: Deterministic automata for the (F, G)-fragment of LTL. In: CAV, pp. 7–22 (2012)

27. Kwiatkowska, M., Norman, G., Parker, D.: PRISM 4.0: verification of probabilistic real-time systems. In: Gopalakrishnan, G., Qadeer, S. (eds.) CAV 2011. LNCS, vol. 6806, pp. 585–591. Springer, Heidelberg (2011). doi:10.1007/978-3-642-22110-1_47

28. Kwiatkowska, M.Z., Norman, G., Parker, D.: The PRISM benchmark suite. In: QEST, pp. 203–204 (2012)

29. Piterman, N.: From nondeterministic Büchi and Streett automata to deterministic parity automata. In: LICS, pp. 255–264 (2006)

30. Pnueli, A.: The temporal logic of programs. In: FOCS, pp. 46–57 (1977)

31. Pnueli, A., Zuck, L.D.: Verification of multiprocess probabilistic protocols. Distrib. Comput. 1(1), 53–72 (1986). doi:10.1007/BF01843570

32. Safra, S.: On the complexity of omega-automata. In: FOCS, pp. 319–327 (1988)

33. Schewe, S.: Tighter bounds for the determinisation of Büchi automata. In: Alfaro, L. (ed.) FoSSaCS 2009. LNCS, vol. 5504, pp. 167–181. Springer, Heidelberg (2009). doi:10.1007/978-3-642-00596-1_13

34. Sickert, S.: MoChiBA. https://www7.in.tum.de/~sickert/projects/mochiba/
35. Sickert, S., Esparza, J., Jaax, S., Křetínský, J.: Limit-deterministic Büchi automata for linear temporal logic. In: Chaudhuri, S., Farzan, A. (eds.) CAV 2016. LNCS, vol. 9780, pp. 312–332. Springer, Heidelberg (2016). doi:10.1007/978-3-319-41540-6_17
36. Somenzi, F., Bloem, R.: Efficient Büchi automata from LTL formulae. In: Emerson, E.A., Sistla, A.P. (eds.) CAV 2000. LNCS, vol. 1855, pp. 248–263. Springer, Heidelberg (2000). doi:10.1007/10722167_21
37. Tsai, M.-H., Tsay, Y.-K., Hwang, Y.-S.: GOAL for games, omega-automata, and logics. In: Sharygina, N., Veith, H. (eds.) CAV 2013. LNCS, vol. 8044, pp. 883–889. Springer, Heidelberg (2013). doi:10.1007/978-3-642-39799-8_62
38. Vardi, M.Y., Wolper, P.: An automata-theoretic approach to automatic program verification (preliminary report). In: LICS, pp. 332–344 (1986)

Parallelism, Concurrency

Synchronous Products of Rewrite Systems

Óscar Martín[✉], Alberto Verdejo, and Narciso Martí-Oliet

Facultad de Informática, Universidad Complutense de Madrid, Madrid, Spain
{omartins,jalberto,narciso}@ucm.es

Abstract. We present a concept of module composition for rewrite systems that we call synchronous product, and also a corresponding concept for doubly labeled transition systems (as proposed by De Nicola and Vaandrager) used as semantics for the former. In both cases, synchronization happens on states and on transitions, providing in this way more flexibility and more natural specifications. We describe our implementation in Maude, a rewriting logic-based language and system. A series of examples shows their use for modular specification and hints at other possible uses, including modular verification.

1 Introduction

In this paper we propose a composition of rewrite systems [19] by means of synchronous products with the aim of using it for modular specification of systems. We also define a synchronous product for doubly labeled transition systems (L^2TS) as defined in [7]. We use the latter to semantically ground the former.

Our concept of synchronous product is akin to the one from automata theory, whence it borrows its name, but also to the composition of processes in CCS [22], to request-wait-block threads in behavioral programming [13], and to other formalisms for module composition. Most of these formalisms rely on action identifiers for synchronization, that is, actions with the same name in both component systems execute simultaneously. Some, like [16], synchronize states: the ones simultaneously visited by the component systems must agree on the atomic propositions they satisfy: if $s_1 \models p$ and $s_2 \models \neg p$ for some proposition p, then $\langle s_1, s_2 \rangle$ is not even a state of the composed system.

As explained in several papers [8,14,18,21], state-only based or action-only based settings are often not enough for a natural specification of systems and temporal properties. In some cases, we are interested in the propositions of the states; in other cases, it is the action that took the system to that state that matters. In many cases, the combined use of propositions on states and on transitions results in more natural formulas. For instance, the formula

$$\square \lozenge \, \texttt{enabled-a} \rightarrow \square \lozenge \, \texttt{taking-a}$$

Partially supported by MINECO Spanish projects StrongSoft (TIN2012–39391–C04–04) and TRACES (TIN2015–67522–C3–3–R), Comunidad de Madrid program N-GREENS Software (S2013/ICE-2731), and UCM-Santander grant GR3/14.

C. Artho et al. (Eds.): ATVA 2016, LNCS 9938, pp. 141–156, 2016.
DOI: 10.1007/978-3-319-46520-3_10

(from [21]) expresses fairness for action a: if action a is infinitely often enabled, then it is infinitely often taken. Here, enabled-a is a property of states (that they allow the execution of a on them), but taking-a is a property of the transition taking place. In the same spirit, this paper suggests that composition of modules is better approached by synchronizing both states and actions. The papers [18,21] show how it is always possible to *cook* a system so that all relevant information about transitions is included in states. Thus, strictly speaking, action synchronization is not needed, but is most convenient.

L^2TSs are a kind of amalgamation of LTSs (labeled transition systems) and Kripke structures: they label states with sets of propositions (as Krikpe structures do), and transitions with action identifiers (as LTSs do). They are state- and action-based, and are appropriate for our discussion.

The theoretical contribution of this paper is the definition of the synchronous product for both L^2TSs and rewrite systems. States synchronize based on their atomic propositions, and transitions based on their action identifiers or rule labels. We show how rewrite systems (and their synchronous product) can be given semantics on L^2TSs (and their own synchronous product).

As a more practical contribution, the aim of our definitions is to allow the modular specification of rewrite systems. This is shown in the examples. We foresee that this would make modular verification possible. Also, as a composed system only has the behaviors that are possible in both component systems, it can be used as a means to control a system with another one tailored for that purpose. We see this as a possible implementation of strategies for rewrite systems—and one suited to modular verification. These two possibilities are work in progress and are just hinted at in the examples.

The rest of this paper is divided into six sections. Section 2 recalls L^2TSs and defines their synchronous product. Section 3 focuses on the synchronous product for rewrite systems and on their semantics. Section 4 shows some examples of modular specification. Section 5 discusses some issues having to do with the prototype implementation of the synchronous product that we have developed in Maude. Section 6 proposes directions for future work and mentions, at the same time, related literature. Section 7 summarizes the conclusions of the paper.

There is an extended version of this paper available at our website: http:// maude.sip.ucm.es/syncprod. The Maude code for our implementation and the examples can also be found there.

2   Synchronous Products of L^2TSs

We start at the semantic level, presenting the particular kind of transition systems convenient to our discussion, and showing how they can be composed by the operation we call *synchronous product*.

2.1 L^2TS: Doubly Labeled Transition Systems

Doubly labeled transition systems were introduced by De Nicola and Vaandrager in [7] with the aim of comparing properties of Kripke structures and of labeled transition systems (LTSs). Indeed, L^2TSs join in a single object the characteristics of these different structures. That is, their states are labeled by sets of atomic propositions (the ones that hold true in the state) and their transitions are labeled by action identifiers. The original definition from [7] includes invisible actions, but we will not need them.

Formally, an L^2TS is defined as a tuple $(S, \Lambda, \rightarrow, \mathrm{AP}, L)$, where S is a set of states, Λ is an alphabet of action identifiers, $\rightarrow \subseteq S \times \Lambda \times S$ is a transition relation (denoted as $s \xrightarrow{\lambda} s'$), AP is a set of atomic propositions, and $L : S \rightarrow 2^{\mathrm{AP}}$ is a labeling function, that assigns to each state the atomic propositions that hold true on it.

2.2 Synchronous Products

The synchronous product of two systems is a way to make them evolve in parallel, making sure that they agree at each step and in every moment. Given two L^2TSs $\mathcal{L}_i = (S_i, \Lambda_i, \rightarrow_i, \mathrm{AP}_i, L_i)$, we define next their synchronous product $\mathcal{L}_1 \,\|\, \mathcal{L}_2 = (S, \Lambda, \rightarrow, \mathrm{AP}, L)$. The synchronization is specified by relating properties and actions common to both structures, that is, existing with the same name in both. For a state $s_1 \in S_1$ to be visited by $\mathcal{L}_1$ at the same time as $s_2 \in S_2$ is visited by $\mathcal{L}_2$ it is necessary that, for each common atomic proposition $p \in \mathrm{AP}_1 \cap \mathrm{AP}_2$, we have that p holds for s_1 iff it holds for s_2; more formally: $L_1(s_1) \cap \mathrm{AP}_2 = L_2(s_2) \cap \mathrm{AP}_1$. We denote this by $s_1 \approx s_2$ and say that s_1 and s_2 are *compatible* or that the pair $\langle s_1, s_2 \rangle$ is compatible. For a transition $s_1 \xrightarrow{\lambda_1}_1 s_1'$ to occur in $\mathcal{L}_1$ simultaneously with $s_2 \xrightarrow{\lambda_2}_2 s_2'$ in $\mathcal{L}_2$ it is necessary that $\lambda_1 = \lambda_2$ (in addition to $s_1 \approx s_2$ and $s_1' \approx s_2'$). However, actions existing only in one of the systems can execute by themselves. This is the definition of $\mathcal{L}_1 \,\|\, \mathcal{L}_2 = (S, \Lambda, \rightarrow, \mathrm{AP}, L)$:

- $S := S_1 \times S_2$;
- $\Lambda := \Lambda_1 \cup \Lambda_2$;
- regarding transitions (assuming $s_1 \approx s_2$):
  - $\langle s_1, s_2 \rangle \xrightarrow{\lambda} \langle s_1', s_2' \rangle$ iff $s_1 \xrightarrow{\lambda} s_1'$ and $s_2 \xrightarrow{\lambda} s_2'$ and $s_1' \approx s_2'$,
  - $\langle s_1, s_2 \rangle \xrightarrow{\lambda} \langle s_1', s_2 \rangle$ iff $s_1 \xrightarrow{\lambda} s_1'$ and $\lambda \notin \Lambda_2$ and $s_1' \approx s_2$,
  - $\langle s_1, s_2 \rangle \xrightarrow{\lambda} \langle s_1, s_2' \rangle$ iff $s_2 \xrightarrow{\lambda} s_2'$ and $\lambda \notin \Lambda_1$ and $s_1 \approx s_2'$;
- $\mathrm{AP} := \mathrm{AP}_1 \cup \mathrm{AP}_2$;
- $L(\langle s_1, s_2 \rangle) := L_1(s_1) \cup L_2(s_2)$.

Some notes on the definition and its consequences are in order:

- We let the space state S include non-compatible pairs. However, only transitions going into compatible states are allowed, so that all states reachable from a compatible initial state are compatible.
- The resulting composed system includes all the propositions and action identifiers from both component systems (we take their unions), but for synchronization only the ones that are common are taken into account (their intersections).

- Renaming of propositions and actions in a structure can be done with no harm to get equal names in both structures as needed for synchronization.
- When the two systems being composed have no common propositions and no common actions ($AP_1 \cap AP_2 = \emptyset$ and $\Lambda_1 \cap \Lambda_2 = \emptyset$), they progress with no consideration to each other: any state can pair with any other, and each action is executed by itself.
- A system controls the actions the other one can perform. Consider the situation where the composed system is in state $\langle s_1, s_2 \rangle$ (with $s_1 \approx s_2$) and $\mathcal{L}_1$ can execute action λ from s_1 ($s_1 \xrightarrow{\lambda} s_1'$). There are three possibilities to consider in $\mathcal{L}_2$:
  - if $\lambda \notin \Lambda_2$, the action can be run in $\mathcal{L}_1$ by itself: $\langle s_1, s_2 \rangle \xrightarrow{\lambda} \langle s_1', s_2 \rangle$ (provided $s_1' \approx s_2$);
  - if $\lambda \in \Lambda_2$, but it cannot be executed from s_2, then λ cannot be executed in the composed system at the moment;
  - if $\lambda \in \Lambda_2$ and can be executed from s_2 in $\mathcal{L}_2$ ($s_2 \xrightarrow{\lambda} s_2'$), then λ can only be executed simultaneously in both systems: $\langle s_1, s_2 \rangle \xrightarrow{\lambda} \langle s_1', s_2' \rangle$ (provided $s_1' \approx s_2'$).

3   Synchronous Products of Rewrite Systems

Our aim is to implement and practically use synchronous products for modular specification. Thus, we now reflect the abstract definitions above in the more concrete realm of rewrite systems.

3.1   Rewrite Systems

Rewriting logic takes on the concept of term rewriting and tailors it to the specification of concurrent and non-deterministic systems. It was introduced as such by Meseguer in [19]. Maude [5] is a language (and system) for specification and programming based on this idea. A specification in rewriting logic contains equations and rewrite rules. Equations work much like in functional programming; rules describe the way in which a system state evolves into a different one.

Maude's flavor of rewriting logic is based on order-sorted equational logic—membership equational logic indeed [20], but we are not using such a feature in this paper. Thus, a rewrite system has the form $\mathcal{R} = (\Sigma, E \cup Ax, R)$, where: Σ is a signature containing declarations for sorts, subsorts, and operators; E is a set of equations; Ax is a set of equational axioms for operators, such as commutativity and associativity; and R is a set of labeled rewrite rules of the form $[\ell]\, s \to s'$.

In Sect. 3.2 below, we show a way to compose and synchronize rewrite systems. Synchronization on states happens on coincidence on their common propositions. For that to be meaningful, we need a way to handle propositions, which are not, in principle, an ingredient of rewrite systems. Thus, we require of each rewrite system $\mathcal{R} = (\Sigma, E \cup Ax, R)$ the following:

- the sort in Σ that represents the states of the system is called State;
- Σ includes a sort Prop, representing atomic propositions, composed by a finite amount of constants (this requirement is needed in Sect. 3.2 to define the synchronous product);
- $\mathcal{R}$ includes the definition of a theory of the Booleans declaring, in particular, the sort Bool, and the constants true and false;
- Σ includes an infix relation symbol _ $\models$ _ : State $\times$ Prop $\rightarrow$ Bool, and E includes equations that completely define $\models$, that is, each expression $s \models p$ is reduced to true or false by $E \cup Ax$.

These conventions are a standard way to introduce propositions in rewrite systems. It is the setting needed to use Maude's LTL model checker [10], for instance. However, we are using propositions only for synchronization. Even if model checking were performed on any of these systems, the propositions used for that need not be the same ones used for synchronization.

We have one additional technical requirement: the system has to be *topmost*. A topmost rewrite system is one in which all rewrites happen on the whole state term—not on its subterms. (Formally, this is guaranteed by requiring that all rules involve terms of sort State, and that the sort State is not an argument of any constructor, so that no term of sort State can be subterm of another term of the same sort). The aim of this requirement is that rules preserve their meaning after composition. For instance, the non-topmost rule $a \rightarrow a'$ would rewrite the term $f(a)$ to $f(a')$, because a is a subterm of $f(a)$; but the composed rule $\langle a, t \rangle \rightarrow \langle a', t' \rangle$ would not rewrite the composed term $\langle f(a), s \rangle$, whatever s and t could be, because $\langle a, t \rangle$ is not a subterm of $\langle f(a), s \rangle$. Many rewrite systems are topmost or can be easily transformed into an equivalent one that is formally similar and topmost [11].

3.2   Synchronous Products

Given two rewrite systems as above, $\mathcal{R}_i = (\Sigma_i, E_i \cup Ax_i, R_i)$, for $i = 1, 2$, their *synchronous product*, denoted $\mathcal{R}_1 \parallel \mathcal{R}_2$, is a new rewrite system $\mathcal{R} = (\Sigma, E \cup Ax, R)$ as specified below.

A technical detail is needed about names and namespaces. The conditions in Sect. 3.1 require that each system includes some sorts and operators: State, $\models$, and so on. This does not mean that sorts with the same name in different systems are the same sort. Indeed, we consider that each system has implicit its own namespace. Names for sorts, constants, and the other elements must be understood within the namespace of their respective systems. When needed, we qualify a name with a prefix showing the system it belongs to or where it originated: $\mathcal{R}$.State. We omit the prefix whenever there is no danger of confusion. Sometimes we say that something is true "in $\mathcal{R}$" to avoid cluttering the text with prefixes for each element that would need it.

We refer as *naked names* to the ones without the qualifying prefixes. These are needed for synchronization, as it is done on coincidence of naked names, and those names remain as such in the product system, with different qualification.

For instance, the value of $\mathcal{R}_1.p$ has to be the same as the one of $\mathcal{R}_2.p$ and both give rise to $\mathcal{R}.p$.

With this convention about namespaces, signatures Σ_1 and Σ_2 are naturally disjoint, as are the sets of equations, axioms, and rule labels. Equations, in particular, are included verbatim from each system into the synchronous product, according to the definition below; any equational deduction valid in one of the systems is still valid in the product. Rules, instead, are not included verbatim from the component systems, but synchronized as formalized below.

As also mentioned in Sect. 2.2, we assume that renaming has previously taken place as needed, so that synchronization happens on the set of rule labels and the set of atomic propositions whose naked names are common to both systems.

This is the rather long definition of the synchronous product:

- $\Sigma := \Sigma_1 \uplus \Sigma_2 \uplus \Sigma'$, where Σ' contains:
  - declarations for sorts $\mathcal{R}.\texttt{State}$ and $\mathcal{R}.\texttt{Prop}$;
  - declarations for $\mathcal{R}.\texttt{Bool}$, $\mathcal{R}.\texttt{true}$, and $\mathcal{R}.\texttt{false}$;
  - a declaration for the operator $\mathcal{R}.\models\ :\mathcal{R}.\texttt{State} \times \mathcal{R}.\texttt{Prop} \to \mathcal{R}.\texttt{Bool}$;
  - a new constructor symbol $\langle \_ , \_ \rangle : \mathcal{R}_1.\texttt{State} \times \mathcal{R}_2.\texttt{State} \to \mathcal{R}.\texttt{State}$;
  - a set of declarations for operators to make $\mathcal{R}.\texttt{Prop}$ the union of $\mathcal{R}_1.\texttt{Prop}$ and $\mathcal{R}_2.\texttt{Prop}$, that is:

$$\{\mathcal{R}.p : \mathcal{R}.\texttt{Prop} \mid \mathcal{R}_1.p : \mathcal{R}_1.\texttt{Prop} \in \Sigma_1 \text{ or } \mathcal{R}_2.p : \mathcal{R}_2.\texttt{Prop} \in \Sigma_2 \text{ or both}\};$$

  - a declaration for the predicate: $\mathcal{R}.\approx\ :\mathcal{R}_1.\texttt{State} \times \mathcal{R}_2.\texttt{State} \to \mathcal{R}.\texttt{Bool}$.
- $E := E_1 \uplus E_2 \uplus E'$, where E' contains:
  - equations for a theory of the Booleans;
  - equations to reduce $s_1 \approx s_2$ to $\texttt{true}$ in $\mathcal{R}$ iff ($s_1 \models p = \texttt{true}$ in $\mathcal{R}_1 \iff s_2 \models p = \texttt{true}$ in $\mathcal{R}_2$, for every proposition whose naked name p exists in both systems), and to $\mathcal{R}.\texttt{false}$ otherwise;
  - for each p such that $\mathcal{R}_1.p : \mathcal{R}_1.\texttt{Prop} \in \Sigma_1$, the equation:

$$\langle x_1, x_2 \rangle\ \mathcal{R}.\models\ \mathcal{R}.p = x_1\ \mathcal{R}_1.\models\ \mathcal{R}_1.p,$$

  - for each p not in the previous item but such that $\mathcal{R}_2.p : \mathcal{R}_2.\texttt{Prop} \in \Sigma_2$, the equation:

$$\langle x_1, x_2 \rangle\ \mathcal{R}.\models\ \mathcal{R}.p = x_2\ \mathcal{R}_2.\models\ \mathcal{R}_2.p.$$

In these equations x_1 and x_2 are variables of sorts $\mathcal{R}_1.\texttt{State}$ and $\mathcal{R}_2.\texttt{State}$, respectively. Because of the conditions on the rules below, only compatible pairs $\langle x_1, x_2 \rangle$ are reachable. And only for such pairs we will need to use some of the last two equations above. Thus, for a proposition p whose naked name exists in both systems, we have arbitrarily but harmlessly chosen to use the value from the first system.

- $Ax := Ax_1 \uplus Ax_2$.
- R is composed of the following set of rules:
  - for each rule label ℓ that exists in both systems, say $[\ell]\ s_i \to s_i' \in R_i$, we have in R the conditional rule $[\ell]\ \langle s_1, s_2 \rangle \to \langle s_1', s_2' \rangle$ if $s_1' \approx s_2'$;

- for each rule label ℓ that exists in R_1 but not in R_2, say $[\ell]\, s_1 \to s_1' \in R_1$, we have in R the conditional rule $[\ell]\, \langle s_1, x_2 \rangle \to \langle s_1', x_2 \rangle$ if $s_1' \approx x_2$ (with x_2 a variable of sort $R_2.\texttt{State}$);
- correspondingly for rule labels in R_2 but not in R_1.

In these three kinds of rules, the condition guarantees that only compatible states are reached.

Several items above include universal quantification on atomic propositions. This could be problematic, and it is the reason why we require the sorts $\texttt{Prop}$ to consist only of a finite amount of constants.

3.3 Semantics

Given a rewrite system as above, $\mathcal{R} = (\Sigma, E \cup Ax, R)$, its semantics is an L^2TS $\mathcal{L} = (S, \Lambda, \to, \text{AP}, L)$, based on the usual term-algebra semantics (see [19], for instance) in this way:

- $S := T_{\Sigma/E \cup Ax, \texttt{State}}$, the set of terms of sort $\texttt{State}$ modulo equations;
- Λ is the set of rule labels in R;
- $\to$ corresponds to the transition relation generated by rewriting with the rules from R [19], that is, $s \xrightarrow{\lambda} s'$ iff there is a rule in R with label λ that allows rewriting s to s' in one step within $\mathcal{R}$;
- $\text{AP} := T_{\Sigma/E \cup Ax, \texttt{Prop}}$, the set of terms of sort $\texttt{Prop}$ modulo equations;
- $L(s) := \{p \in \text{AP} \mid s \models p = \texttt{true} \text{ modulo } E \cup Ax\}$.

Let "sem" denote the *semantics operator*, which assigns to each rewrite system an L^2TS as just explained. All previous definitions have been chosen so that the following result holds.

Theorem. *For any rewrite systems $\mathcal{R}_1$ and $\mathcal{R}_2$, we have that $\text{sem}(\mathcal{R}_1 \parallel \mathcal{R}_2)$ is isomorphic to $\text{sem}(\mathcal{R}_1) \parallel \text{sem}(\mathcal{R}_2)$. The isomorphism is in the sense that there exist bijections between their sets of states, between their sets of actions, and between their sets of atomic propositions that preserve the transition relation and the labeling.*

4   Examples

We present examples of synchronous products of rewrite systems. Many of them show systems made up to control others. They are coded in Maude [5], the rewriting based language and system we have used to develop our implementation of the synchronous product. They should be easily understood by anyone acquainted with rewriting logic or algebraic programming. All the examples are downloadable from our website: http://maude.sip.ucm.es/syncprod. Many of the examples build on previous ones. The first one involves no synchronization, but it uses modular specification, and serves as basis for subsequent ones.

4.1   Modular Specification: Two Railways

Consider this sketchy implementation of a railway in Maude:

```
mod RAILWAY1 is
   including BOOL .
   including SATISFACTION .   --- declares State, Prop, and |=.
   ops waiting crossing to-station in-station from-station : -> State .
   rl [t1wc] : waiting => crossing .
   rl [t1ct] : crossing => to-station .
   rl [t1ti] : to-station => in-station .
   rl [t1if] : in-station => from-station .
   rl [t1fw] : from-station => waiting .
endm
```

Modules BOOL and SATISFACTION are conveniently predefined in Maude. We can picture the system as a closed loop railway with a station and a crossing with another railway. Indeed, we model this other railway in the same way and call it RAILWAY2. The rule names in this new system have a 2 instead of a 1 (our framework does not allow for parametric modules).

The whole system is given by RAIL := RAILWAY1 ‖ RAILWAY2, with rules like:

```
rl [t1wc] : < waiting, T2 > => < crossing, T2 > .
```

with T2 a variable of sort RAILWAY2.State. No synchronization is possible, because all rule labels are different and there are no propositions, but the modular specification is simpler and more natural than a monolithic one would be.

With this specification, both trains are allowed, but not mandated, to wait before the crossing. They need to be controlled to avoid crashes.

4.2   Synchronizing Actions: Safety Control

We want to control the whole system so as to ensure that trains do not cross simultaneously. Consider this controller system:

```
mod SAFETY is
   including BOOL .
   including SATISFACTION .   --- declares State, Prop, and |=.
   ops none-crossing one-crossing : -> State .
   rl [t1wc] : none-crossing => one-crossing .
   rl [t2wc] : none-crossing => one-crossing .
   rl [t1ct] : one-crossing => none-crossing .
   rl [t2ct] : one-crossing => none-crossing .
endm
```

Note that the rule labels used are some of the ones appearing in RAILWAY1 and RAILWAY2. The rules ensure that from state one-crossing only transitions out of the crossing are allowed. The system RAIL ‖ SAFETY behaves as desired. The rules of this composed system have, for example, this shape:

```
rl [t1wc] : < < waiting, T2 >, none-crossing > =>
            < < crossing, T2 >, one-crossing > .
```

This is certainly equivalent to

```
crl [t1wc] : < waiting, T2 > => < crossing, T2 > if T2 =/= crossing .
```

But, to obtain this latter one, we would need to modify RAIL—not extending, but overwriting it. The advantage of modularity, in this case, is that it allows an external, non-intrusive control.

This example showed synchronization on actions; the next focuses on states.

4.3   Synchronizing States: Alternative Safety Control

In more complex implementations of the RAIL system, controlling all the ways in which trains can get into the crossing can be involved. For instance, both trains could be allowed to move into the crossing at the same time, so that controlling individual isolated movements as above would not be enough. In such cases, it can be easier to base the control on the states.

We extend the system RAIL with the following lines, declaring and defining the atomic proposition safe to hold when at least one train is out of the crossing:

```
mod RAIL-EXT is
    including RAILWAY1 || RAILWAY2 .
    op safe : -> Prop .
    eq < crossing, crossing > |= safe = false .
    eq < T1, T2 > |= safe = true [owise] .
endm
```

The new controller system we propose, SAFETY2, has a single state, named o, that satisfies the proposition safe, and no rules:

```
mod SAFETY2 is
    including BOOL .
    including SATISFACTION .
    op o : -> State .
    op safe : -> Prop .
    eq o |= safe = true .
endm
```

Consider RAIL-EXT || SAFETY2. A typical rule in this composed system is

```
crl [t1wc] : < < waiting, T2 >, X > => < < crossing, T2 >, X >
    if compatible(< crossing, T2 >, X) .
```

It is not too different from the previous t1wc, except for the compatibility condition. As o is always safe, also < crossing, T2 > must be safe for the rule to be applied. So, SAFETY2 restricts RAIL-EXT to visit only safe states, as desired.

Note again the advantage of a modular specification: once RAIL-EXT is given, we can easily choose the control that fits better, either SAFETY or SAFETY2 or some other given module with the same purpose.

4.4   Repeated Composition: Controlling Performance

Now that safety is guaranteed, experts have decided that for a better performance of the public transport network, it is worth letting two trains pass through way 1 for each one passing through way 2. This can be achieved by a synchronous product of RAIL || SAFETY with this new system:

```
mod PERFORMANCE is
   including BOOL .
   including SATISFACTION .
   ops 0cross 1cross 2cross : -> State .
   rl [t1wc] : 0cross => 1cross .
   rl [t1wc] : 1cross => 2cross .
   rl [t2wc] : 2cross => 0cross .
endm
```

This *accumulated control* is possible because synchronized rules in RAIL ∥ SAFETY keep their names and are still visible from the outside.

Note that the product SAFETY ∥ PERFORMANCE is meaningful by itself: it is a system that, when composed with any uncontrolled implementation of the railway crossing (using the same rule labels), guarantees both safety and performance.

4.5   Instrumentation: Counting Crossings

Instrumentation is the technique of adding to the specification of a system some code in order to get information about the system's execution: number of steps, timing, sequence of actions, etc. To some extent, it can be done by using synchronous products.

This time we want to keep track of the number of crossings for each train. For RAILWAY1 we propose this very simple system:

```
mod COUNT1 is
   including BOOL .
   including SATISFACTION .
   including NAT .
   subsort Nat < State .
   var N : Nat .
   rl [t1wc] : N => N + 1 .
endm
```

A state of RAILWAY1 ∥ COUNT1 is a pair whose second component is the counter. The initial state must be < in-station, 0 > (if in-station was the initial state for RAILWAY1). The same can be done to RAILWAY2. Then, the instrumented systems can be controlled in any of the ways described above.

4.6   Separation of Concerns: Dekker's Algorithm

Consider this new module:

```
mod DEKKER is
   including BOOL .
   including SATISFACTION .
   sorts Waiting Turn .
   ops 0w 1w 2w : -> Waiting .
   ops t1 t2 : -> Turn .
   op (_,_) : Waiting Turn -> State .
   var T : Turn .
   rl [t1wc] : (1w,T)  => (0w,t2) .    rl [t2wc] : (1w,T)  => (0w,t1) .
   rl [t1wc] : (2w,t1) => (1w,t2) .    rl [t2wc] : (2w,t2) => (1w,t1) .
   rl [t1fw] : (0w,T)  => (1w,T) .     rl [t2fw] : (0w,T)  => (1w,T) .
```

```
|    rl [t1fw] : (1w,T)  => (2w,T) .    rl [t2fw] : (1w,T)  => (2w,T) .
| endm
```

This module can be used to ensure absence of starvation in the controlled system, that is, that no process waits indefinitely. The `Waiting` component of the state stores how many processes are waiting to enter the critical section: both, one, or none. The `Turn` component stores whose turn is next, in case both processes are waiting (if only one process is waiting, it can just go on).

Usual presentations of Dekker's algorithm also include mutual exclusion control. Our module `DEKKER` does not control when processes exit the critical section so it cannot ensure mutual exclusion by itself. In our case, the combined control is achieved by the product `SAFETY ‖ DEKKER`. Separation of different concerns in different modules is made possible by the synchronous product construction.

4.7 State and Rule Synchronization: Two Trains in a Linear Railway

As an example that sometimes synchronization is convenient on states and on transitions in the same system, consider this one, taken from [6], told again in terms of train traffic. There is a single linear railway divided into tracks, and there are two trains going along it from track to track, always in the same direction—to the right, say. Each train can move at any time from one track to the next, but they can never be at the same time on the same track. Thus, whenever the trains are in adjacent tracks, only the rightmost one can move. This is the specification for the train on the left:

```
| mod LTRAIN is
|    including BOOL .
|    including SATISFACTION .
|    including NAT .
|    subsort Nat < State .
|    var Track : Nat .
|    rl [lmove] : Track => Track + 1 .
| endm
```

The one on the right is specified in module `RTRAIN` which is the same as above except that the rule is called `rmove`. The controller we need has to detect when the trains are in adjacent tracks, and this is a property on the states of `LTRAIN ‖ RTRAIN`. To make the control possible, we extend this composed system with the declaration of the proposition `adjacent`:

```
| mod TRAINS-EXT is
|    including LTRAIN || RTRAIN .
|    op adjacent : -> Prop .
|    vars T T' : Nat .
|    eq < T, T + 1 > |= adjacent = true .
|    eq < T, T' > |= adjacent = false [owise] .
| endm
```

The controller is this:

```
| mod CONTROL is
|    including BOOL .
```

```
    including SATISFACTION .
    ops adj nonadj : -> State .
    var S : State .
    rl [lmove] : nonadj => nonadj .
    rl [lmove] : nonadj => adj .
    rl [rmove] : S => nonadj .
    op adjacent : -> Prop .
    eq adj |= adjacent = true .
    eq nonadj |= adjacent = false .
endm
```

Only the movement of the train on the left can take the system to a configuration with adjacency. When it does, the controller remembers it in its state, and the next movement can only be made by the train on the right. Note that both kinds of synchronization, on states and on transitions, are present in this example, and that using only one of them would result in a more involved specification.

5   Notes on the Implementation

Our prototype implementation of the synchronous product in Maude can be downloaded from our website: http://maude.sip.ucm.es/syncprod. The extended version of this paper contains a brief appendix with instructions. The implementation largely follows the explanations in Sect. 3.2. Some details, however, could be appreciated by those familiar with Maude or rewriting logic.

Choice of Tools. We want a program that takes as arguments two Maude modules and produces a new one containing their synchronous product. Our program has to handle rules, equations, labels and so on. Even complete modules have to be treated as objects by the program we seek. It turns out that Maude itself is a very convenient tool for this second-order programming task.

Rewriting logic is reflective, and that implies in particular that constructs of the language can be represented and handled as terms [5]. Maude provides a set of metalevel functions for this purpose. The function getRls, to name just an example, takes as argument a module and returns its set of rules. Modules, rules, and the rest of Maude's syntactic constructs must be *meta-represented* for these metalevel functions to be able to handle them. That is, they cease to be Maude code and become terms of sorts Module, Rule, and so on. Maude also provides functions to perform such meta-representation. We have chosen this as the natural way to the implementation. We have coded a Maude function syncprod that receives two terms of sort Module and produces one representing their synchronous product.

But that function can only be invoked at the metalevel, feeding it with two terms of sort Module, not with two Maude modules. A decent implementation must allow a simpler use. For those acquainted with Maude, the tool of choice for such a task is Full Maude. Full Maude [5,9] is a re-implementation of the Maude interpreter using Maude itself. It is adaptable and extensible, and allows the definition of new module expressions, as we need. We have extended Full

Maude to include an operator || on modules to represent the synchronous product. A module containing **including MODULE1 || MODULE2** can refer to any of the constructs of the synchronous product, like pairs of states, propositions inherited from the operand systems, and so on.

Name Clashes. We discussed in Sect. 3.1 that names **State**, **Prop**, **Bool**, and so on are required to appear in each operand system, and in the resulting system as well. In the theoretical description we assumed each occurrence of them to be qualified by its namespace. In practice, there are three cases to be considered:

- Sorts such as **Bool** and **Nat**, and their operators, are most probably going to be defined and used in the same way in every system. Keeping several copies of them would not harm, but is pointless.
- The sort **State** for the resulting system is defined as pairs of operand **States**. Thus, all three **State** sorts need to be present in the resulting system, with different names. The same applies to the operator |=, whose definition uses the corresponding operators from each system.
- The sort **Prop** is somewhat special in that we identify elements with the same name in the three systems. Having just one sort **Prop** makes things easier.

This is what our implementation does: First, for each operand module, it renames its sort **State** to **ModName.State**, if **ModName** is the name of the module; also, it renames the satisfaction symbol from |= to **ModName.**|=. Once this is done for both operand modules, their union is computed, thus leaving only one sort **Prop**, and also one sort **Bool**, and so on. A fresh sort **State** and a fresh operator |= are then declared. The just mentioned union affects declarations and equations, but not rules, that are individually computed in their composed forms.

6   Related and Future Work

Some of the proposals of this paper set the ground on which interesting work is already being done. Let's be more concrete.

Egalitarian Synchronization. In [18] we presented a class of transition systems called *egalitarian structures*. They are egalitarian in the sense that they treat states and transition as equals. In particular, they allow using atomic propositions on transitions. That paper also showed how rewrite systems are egalitarian in nature, because transitions are represented by proof terms in the same way as states are represented by terms of the appropriate sort.

As pointed in the introduction and also in [18], the expression of temporal properties by formulas benefits from an egalitarian view. Composition of systems should benefit in the same way. An egalitarian synchronous product would allow transitions to synchronize not just on labels, but on their common propositions (depending, in particular, on variable instantiations).

Strategies. The examples have shown how it is possible to control a system with another one made up for that purpose. It is fair to call *strategic* this kind of control. Indeed, we see the synchronous product as a means to implement strategies for rewrite systems. As also shown in [18], strategies can also benefit from an egalitarian treatment. We expect to be able to develop automatic translations from some strategy languages to equivalent Maude modules, although the precise power of such a technique is still to be seen.

From its origin in games, the concept of strategy, under different names and in different flavors, has become pervasive, particularly in relation to rewriting (see the recent and excellent survey [15]). Maude [5] includes flexible strategies for the evaluation of terms (like lazy, innermost and so on), and external implementations have been proposed in [17] and in [25]. ELAN [2], Tom [1], and Stratego [26] include strategies built-in. They also appear in graph rewriting systems (see references in [15] and also [23], where they are called just *programs*). The same concept is used in theorem provers: it allows the user to guide the system towards the theorem, or to represent the whole proof once found.

Modularity for Specification and Verification. Modular systems are easier to write, read, and verify. For the writing phase, the separation of concerns among modules has great simplifying power: one module implements the base system, another ensures mutual exclusion, another deals just with starvation.

Model checking [3] performed in a modular way can be more efficient, given that the size of the state space of the composed system is of the order of the product of the individual sizes. An attractive possibility is that of providing the specifier with a library of pre-manufactured and pre-verified modules ready to be used (through synchronous product) for specific tasks. For ensuring mutual exclusion, for instance, one could readily choose among SAFETY or SAFETY2 or some other. Care is needed, however, as it is not always the case that a composed system preserves the properties of the components.

Much work already exists on modular model checking and verification, but not many tools allow for it and, to the best of our knowledge, no implementation on rewriting logic has been developed. The papers [4,16], among many others, show techniques for drawing conclusions compositionally. Adapting such techniques to our framework is pending work.

Composition of modules can generate new deadlocks in cases where the components do not agree on a common next step. The system SAFETY2 from Sect. 4.3 is a very simple example: as it constrains the base system to visit only safe states, absence of new deadlocks is only guaranteed assuming that in the base system, RAIL-EXT, a safe state is always reachable in one step. This is the same assume-guarantee paradigm proposed in [16] for modular model checking.

We are particularly interested in model checking strategically controlled systems. Once the concept of control through synchronous products is in place, existing tools can be used, ideally in a modular way (particularly, for us, Maude's LTL model checker [10]). The nearest works on this we are aware of are GP 2, that includes Hoare-style verification in the context of graph rewriting [24], and the BPmc prototype tool for model checking behavioral programs in Java [12].

Behavioral Programming. Based on the idea that a system can be decomposed into several synchronized threads, each of them implementing a behavior of the system, behavioral programming [13] bears many similarities with our proposal. Formally, it uses the *request-wait-block* paradigm. According to it, at each synchronization point, each thread declares three sets of events: the ones it requests (it needs one of them to go on), the ones it does not request, but wants to be informed when they happen, and the ones it blocks. An external scheduler chooses an event requested by some thread and blocked by none, and so the system goes on to the next synchronization point. Although there is not a perfect fit between their formalization and ours, the resulting settings are very similar, and the examples in [12, 13] are easily translatable to synchronized Maude modules.

7   Conclusions

The concept of synchronous product can be extended from automata theory to the specification of systems, where it represents composition of modules. It can be equivalently defined on abstract transition systems (namely, L^2TSs) and on rewrite systems. For more flexible and natural specifications, it is possible and convenient to synchronize at the same time on states and on transitions. We have used atomic propositions to synchronize states, but just rule labels (or action names) for transitions. We intend to generalize this in the near future.

The examples (to be run in our implementation in Maude) show how the synchronous product makes modular specifications easier in rewriting logic. We expect that it will also make possible the implementation of some kind of strategies and the modular verification of systems, even after they have been controlled by strategies. All this is work in progress.

References

1. Balland, E., Brauner, P., Kopetz, R., Moreau, P.-E., Reilles, A.: Tom: piggybacking rewriting on Java. In: Baader, F. (ed.) RTA 2007. LNCS, vol. 4533, pp. 36–47. Springer, Heidelberg (2007)
2. Borovanský, P., Kirchner, C., Kirchner, H., Moreau, P.E.: ELAN from a rewriting logic point of view. Theor. Comput. Sci. **285**(2), 155–185 (2002)
3. Clarke, E.M., Grumberg, O., Peled, D.: Model Checking. MIT Press, Cambridge (2001)
4. Clarke, E.M., Long, D., McMillan, K.: Compositional model checking. In: Proceedings of Logic in Computer Science, LICS 1989, pp. 353–362 (1989)
5. Clavel, M., Durán, F., Eker, S., Lincoln, P., Martí-Oliet, N., Meseguer, J., Talcott, C.: All About Maude - A High-Performance Logical Framework. LNCS, vol. 4350. Springer, Heidelberg (2007)
6. De Nicola, R., Fantechi, A., Gnesi, S., Ristori, G.: An action-based framework for verifying logical and behavioural properties of concurrent systems. Comput. Netw. ISDN Syst. **25**(7), 761–778 (1993)
7. De Nicola, R., Vaandrager, F.: Three logics for branching bisimulation. J. ACM **42**(2), 458–487 (1995)

8. De Nicola, R., Vaandrager, F.: Action versus state based logics for transition systems. In: Guessarian, I. (ed.) LITP 1990. LNCS, vol. 469, pp. 407–419. Springer, Heidelberg (1990)

9. Durán, F., Meseguer, J.: The Maude specification of Full Maude (1999). Manuscript, Computer Science Laboratory, SRI International. http://maude.cs.uiuc.edu/papers

10. Eker, S., Meseguer, J., Sridharanarayanan, A.: The Maude LTL model checker. In: Gadducci, F., Montanari, U. (eds.) Proceedings of WRLA 2002. (Electron. Notes Theor. Comput. Sci. **71**, 162–187 (2004). Elsevier)

11. Escobar, S., Meseguer, J.: Symbolic model checking of infinite-state systems using narrowing. In: Baader, F. (ed.) RTA 2007. LNCS, vol. 4533, pp. 153–168. Springer, Heidelberg (2007)

12. Harel, D., Lampert, R., Marron, A., Weiss, G.: Model-checking behavioral programs. In: Proceedings of EMSOFT 2011. ACM (2011)

13. Harel, D., Marron, A., Weiss, G.: Behavioral programming. Commun. ACM **55**(7), 90–100 (2012)

14. Kindler, E., Vesper, T.: ESTL: a temporal logic for events and states. In: Desel, J., Silva, M. (eds.) ICATPN 1998. LNCS, vol. 1420, pp. 365–384. Springer, Heidelberg (1998)

15. Kirchner, H.: Rewriting strategies and strategic rewrite programs. In: Martí-Oliet, N., Ölveczky, P.C., Talcott, C. (eds.) Meseguer Festschrift. LNCS, vol. 9200, pp. 380–403. Springer, Heidelberg (2015)

16. Kupferman, O., Vardi, M.Y.: An automata-theoretic approach to modular model checking. ACM Trans. Program. Lang. Syst. **22**(1), 87–128 (2000)

17. Martí-Oliet, N., Meseguer, J., Verdejo, A.: A rewriting semantics for Maude strategies. In: Roşu, G. (ed.) Proceedings of WRLA 2008. (Electron. Notes Theor. Comput. Sci. **238**(3), 227–247 (2009). Elsevier)

18. Martín, Ó., Verdejo, A., Martí-Oliet, N.: Egalitarian state-transition systems. In: Lucanu, D. (ed.) WRLA 2016. LNCS, vol. 9942, pp. 98–117. Springer, Heidelberg (2016)

19. Meseguer, J.: Conditional rewriting logic as a unified model of concurrency. Theor. Comput. Sci. **96**(1), 73–155 (1992)

20. Meseguer, J.: Membership algebra as a logical framework for equational specification. In: Parisi-Presicce, F. (ed.) WADT 1997. LNCS, vol. 1376, pp. 18–61. Springer, Heidelberg (1998)

21. Meseguer, J.: The temporal logic of rewriting: a gentle introduction. In: Degano, P., Nicola, R., Meseguer, J. (eds.) Concurrency, Graphs and Models. LNCS, vol. 5065, pp. 354–382. Springer, Heidelberg (2008)

22. Milner, R.: A Calculus of Communicating Systems. LNCS, vol. 92. Springer, Heidelberg (1980)

23. Plump, D.: The design of GP 2. In: Escobar, S. (ed.) Proceedings of WRS 2011. (Electron. Proc. Theor. Comput. Sci. **82**, 1–16 (2011))

24. Poskitt, C.M., Plump, D.: Hoare-style verification of graph programs. Fundam. Inform. **118**(1–2), 135–175 (2012)

25. Roldán, M., Durán, F., Vallecillo, A.: Invariant-driven specifications in Maude. Sci. Comput. Program. **74**(10), 812–835 (2009)

26. Visser, E.: A survey of rewriting strategies in program transformation systems. In: WRS 2001 (Electron. Notes Theor. Comput. Sci. **57**, 109–143 (2001))

Specifying and Verifying Secrecy in Workflows with Arbitrarily Many Agents

Bernd Finkbeiner[1], Helmut Seidl[2], and Christian Müller[2（✉）]

[1] Universität des Saarlandes, 66123 Saarbrücken, Germany
finkbeiner@cs.uni-saarland.de
[2] TU München, 80333 München, Germany
{seidl,christian.mueller}@in.tum.de

Abstract. Web-based workflow management systems, like EasyChair, HealthVault, Ebay, or Amazon, often deal with confidential information such as the identity of reviewers, health data, or credit card numbers. Because the number of participants in the workflow is in principle unbounded, it is difficult to describe the information flow policy of such systems in specification languages that are limited to a fixed number of agents. We introduce a first-order version of HyperLTL, which allows us to express information flow requirements in workflows with arbitrarily many agents. We present a bounded model checking technique that reduces the violation of the information flow policy to the satisfiability of a first-order formula. We furthermore identify conditions under which the resulting satisfiability problem is guaranteed to be decidable.

1 Introduction

Web-based workflow management systems allow diverse groups of users to collaborate efficiently on complex tasks. For example, conference management systems like EasyChair let authors, reviewers, and program committees collaborate on the organization of a scientific conference; health management systems like HealthVault let family members, doctors, and other health care providers collaborate on the management of a patient's care; shopping sites like Amazon or Ebay let merchants, customers, as well as various other agents responsible for payment, customer service, and shipping, collaborate on the purchase and delivery of products.

Since the information maintained in such systems is often confidential, the workflows must carefully manage who has access to what information in a particular stage of the workflow. For example, in a conference management system, PC members must declare conflicts of interest, and they should only see reviews of papers where no conflict exists. Authors eventually get access to reviews of their papers, but only when the process has reached the official notification stage, and without identifying information about the reviewers.

It is difficult to characterize the legitimate information flow in such systems with standard notions of secrecy. Classic information flow policies are often too strong. For example, *noninterference* [12] requires that the PC member cannot

© Springer International Publishing AG 2016
C. Artho et al. (Eds.): ATVA 2016, LNCS 9938, pp. 157–173, 2016.
DOI: 10.1007/978-3-319-46520-3_11

observe any difference when classified input, such as the reviews of papers where the PC member has a conflict of interest, is removed. This strong requirement is typically violated, because another PC member might, for example, nondeterministically post a message in a discussion about a paper where they both have no conflict. Weaker information flow policies, on the other hand, often turn out too weak. *Nondeducibility* [19], for example, only requires that an agent cannot deduce, i.e., conclusively determine, the classified information. The problem is that a piece of information is considered nondeducible already if, in the entire space of potential behaviors, there exists some other explanation. In reality, however, not all agents exhibit the full set of potentially possible behaviors, and an actual agent might be able to deduce far more than expected (cf. [15]).

Temporal logics for the specification of information flow [10] are an important step forward, because they make it possible to customize the secrecy properties. HyperLTL [7] is the linear-time representative of this class of logics. As an extension of linear-time temporal logic (LTL), HyperLTL can describe the precise circumstances under which a particular information flow policy must hold. While standard linear or branching-time logics, like LTL or CTL*, can only reason about the observations at a single computation trace at a time, and can thus, by themselves, not specify information flow, HyperLTL formulas use trace quantifiers and trace variables to simultaneously refer to multiple traces. For example, HyperLTL can directly express information flow properties like "for any pair of traces π, π', if the low-security observer sees the same inputs on π and π', then the low-security observer must also see the same outputs on π and π'". The key limitation of HyperLTL for the specification of workflows is that it is a propositional logic. It is, hence, impossible to specify the information flow in workflows unless the number of agents is fixed *a-priori*. In this paper, we overcome this limitation.

We introduce a framework for the specification and verification of secrecy in workflows with arbitrarily many agents. Our framework consists of a workflow description language, a specification language, and a verification method. Our *workflow description language* gives a precise description of the behavior of workflow management systems with an arbitrary number of agents. Figure 1 shows a simple example workflow of a conference management system. The workflow manipulates several relations over the unbounded domain of agents, that each characterize a particular relationship between the agents: for example, a pair (x, p) in *Conf* indicates that PC member x has declared a conflict with paper p, a triple (x, y, p) in *Comm* indicates that PC member x has received from PC member y a message about paper p. As a *specification language* for the information flow policies in such workflows, we introduce a first-order version of HyperLTL. We extend HyperLTL with first-order quantifiers, allowing the formulas to refer to an arbitrary number of agents. We show that the new logic can be used to specify precise assumptions on the behavior of the agents, such as *causality*: while a nondeterministic agent can take *any* action, the actions of a causal agent can only reveal *information the agent has actually observed*. Restricting the behaviors of the agents to the causal behavior allows us to

(1) **forall** x, p. **may** $true \rightarrow Conf \mathrel{+}= (x, p)$
      % PC members declare conflicts of interest
(2) **forall** x, p. **may** $\neg Conf(x, p) \rightarrow A \mathrel{+}= (x, p)$
      % PC chair makes paper assignments taking into account the conflicts
(3) **forall** x, p, r. $A(x, p) \land Oracle(p, r) \rightarrow Read \mathrel{+}= (x, p, r)$
      % PC members without conflicts read reviews
(4) **forall** y, x, p. **may** $A(x, p) \land A(y, p) \rightarrow Comm \mathrel{+}= (x, y, p)$
      % PC discussion among members assigned to the same paper

Fig. 1. Example workflow from a conference management system.

quantify universally over the actions of the agents, as in classic notions of secrecy like noninterference, and, at the same time, eliminate the false positives of these notions. Finally, we introduce a *verification method*, which translates the verification problem of workflows with arbitrarily many agents and specifications in first-order HyperLTL to the satisfiability problem of first-order logic. While first-order logic is in general undecidable, we identify conditions under which the satisfiability problem for the particular formulas in the verification of the workflows is guaranteed to be decidable.

2   Workflows with Arbitrarily Many Agents

Symbolic Transition Systems. As the formal setting for the specification and verification of our workflows, we chose symbolic transition systems, where the states are defined as the valuations of a set of first-order predicates $\mathcal{P}$. The initial states and the transitions between states are described symbolically using an assertion logic over $\mathcal{P}$. For the purpose of describing workflows, we use first-order predicate logic (PL) with equality as the assertion language.

A *symbolic transition system* $\mathcal{S} = (\mathcal{P}, \Theta, \Delta)$ consists of a set of predicates $\mathcal{P}$, an *initial condition* Θ, and a *transition relation* Δ. The initial condition Θ is given as a formula of the assertion language over the predicates $\mathcal{P}$. The transition relation $\Delta(P_1, \ldots, P_k; P_1', \ldots, P_k')$ is given as a formula over the predicates $\mathcal{P} = \{P_1, \ldots, P_k\}$, which indicate the interpretation of the predicates in the present state, and the set of primed predicates $\mathcal{P}' = \{P_1', \ldots, P_k'\}$, which indicate the interpretation of the predicates in the next state.

Let U be some arbitrary universe. In the case of the workflows, U is the set of agents participating in the workflow. Let $\mathcal{P}^n$ denote the set of predicates with arity n. A *state* $s : \bigcup_{n \geq 0} \mathcal{P}^n \times U^n \rightarrow \mathbb{B}$ is then an evaluation of the predicates over U. A *trace* is an infinite sequence of states $s_0, s_1, \ldots$ such that (1) s_0 satisfies Θ (*initiation*), and (2) for each $i \geq 0$, the transition relation Δ is satisfied by the consecutive states s_i and s_{i+1}, where the predicates in $\mathcal{P}$ are evaluated according to s_i and the predicates in $\mathcal{P}'$ are evaluated according to s_{i+1}. We denote the set of all traces of a transition system $\mathcal{S}$ as $Traces(\mathcal{S})$.

The Workflow Language. We define a language to specify workflows. A workflow is structured into multiple *blocks*. Each block specifies the behaviour of a group of agents. A block is made of several statements which add (or remove) specific tuples from a given relation depending on a guard clause.

$$
\begin{array}{llll}
p & ::= & block; p \mid \epsilon & // \quad \text{workflow program} \\
block & ::= & \textbf{forall } x_0, \ldots, x_k.\{stmts\} & \\
& & \mid \textbf{forall } x_0, \ldots, x_k.\ \textbf{may } \{stmts\} & // \quad \text{block} \\
stmts & ::= & \theta \rightarrow R \mathrel{+}= (t_1, \ldots, t_n); stmts & \\
& & \mid \theta \rightarrow R \mathrel{-}= (t_1, \ldots, t_n); stmts & \\
& & \mid \epsilon & // \quad \text{updates} \\
t & ::= & x_j \mid c & // \quad \text{terms}
\end{array}
$$

Here, terms $t_1, \ldots, t_n$ are either agent variables $x_0, \ldots, x_k$ or constant values c, R denotes a predicate symbol, and θ is a *guard* clause that needs to be met before performing the update. If the guard is not met, no update occurs. Guards can be arbitrary formulas from first-order predicate logic (PL). The set of predicate symbols contains a special symbol *Oracle* denoting the environment input. In order to specify deterministic/nondeterministic behaviour, we use two different kinds of statements. In a normal block, all agents execute the block, i.e., the listed sequence of guarded updates. In a **may** block, only a subset of tuples of agents may decide to execute the block. Note that guarded remove to a predicate R of the form $\theta \rightarrow R \mathrel{-}= (t_0, \ldots, t_n)$ can be simulated by a guarded addition to a fresh predicate R'. For that, we define: $R(t_0, \ldots, t_n) \wedge \neg\theta \rightarrow R' \mathrel{+}= (t_0, \ldots, t_n)$ and subsequently, replace uses of R with uses of R'.

Semantics. In the following, we give a semantics for workflow $w = b_1 \ldots b_T$ as a transition system. The set of variables then consists of the universe U of agents participating in the workflow, together with a finite set of relations or predicates over U. In order to control the transitions between system states, we require one predicate $Choice_i$ for the i-th **may** statement to control the subset of tuples of agents choosing to execute the statement. Furthermore, let $Count_0, \ldots, Count_T$ denote a sequence of boolean flags indicating the current program point. Iteration of the workflow from 0 to T is expressed by the formula Φ_{Count} given by:

$$
Count_T \rightarrow (Count'_T \wedge \bigwedge_{l' \neq T} \neg Count'_{l'}) \wedge \bigwedge_{l=0}^{T-1} Count_l \rightarrow (Count'_{l+1} \wedge \bigwedge_{l' \neq l+1} \neg Count'_{l'})
$$

Initially, all predicates are *false*, except for the designated relation *Oracle* that provides input data to the workflow and the relations $Choice_i$ that provide the agent behaviour. Moreover, all flags $Count_l$, but $Count_0$ are *false*. An execution of the workflow program then is completely determined by the initial value of *Oracle* together with the choices of the agents as provided by the relations $Choice_i$. W.l.o.g., we assume that within a statement, every relation R is updated at most once. For every k-ary relation R and program point l, we construct a formula $\Phi_{R,l}(y_1, \ldots, y_k)$ using free variables $y_1, \ldots, y_k$, so that $R(y_1, \ldots, y_k)$ holds after execution of block b_l iff $\Phi_{R,l}(y_1, \ldots, y_k)$ holds before the execution of b_l. The transition relation is defined by the conjunction of Φ_{Count} together with the conjunction over all formulas

$$
\bigwedge_{l=0}^{T-1} Count_l \rightarrow \forall y_1, \ldots, y_k.\ R'(y_1, \ldots, y_k) \leftrightarrow \Phi_{R,l}(y_1, \ldots, y_k) \wedge
$$
$$
\forall y_1, \ldots, y_k.\ Count_T \rightarrow R'(y_1, \ldots, y_k) \leftrightarrow R(y_1, \ldots, y_k)
$$

where R' denotes the value of R after the transition. Thus, we assume that after the last step, the workflow *stutters*, i.e., the last state is repeated indefinitely. For defining the formulas $\Phi_{R,l}(y_1,\ldots,y_k)$, consider a block b_l of the form:

$$\textbf{forall } x_0,\ldots,x_m \ \{$$
$$\theta_1 \rightarrow R_1 += (t_{11},\ldots,t_{1k_1});$$
$$\ldots$$
$$\theta_r \rightarrow R_r += (t_{r1},\ldots,t_{rk_r});$$
$$\}$$

Then for $j = 1,\ldots,r$, $\Phi_{R_j,l}(y_1,\ldots,y_k)$ is $\Phi_{R_j,l}(y_1,\ldots,y_k) \vee \exists x_0,\ldots,x_m.\ \bar{\theta}_j \wedge (y_1 = t_{j1}) \wedge \ldots \wedge (y_{k_j} = t_{jk_j})$, where $\bar{\theta}_j$ is obtained from θ_j by replacing every literal $R_i(s_1,\ldots,s_{k_i})$ with the corresponding formula $\Phi_{R_i,l}(s_1,\ldots,s_{k_i})$. For all other predicates R, $\Phi_{R,l}(y_1,\ldots,y_k) \equiv \Phi_{R,l}(y_1,\ldots,y_k)$. If b_l is the n-th **may** block and of the form:

$$\textbf{forall } x_0,\ldots,x_m \ \textbf{may} \ \{$$
$$\theta_1 \rightarrow R_1 += (t_{11},\ldots,t_{1k_1});$$
$$\ldots$$
$$\theta_r \rightarrow R_r += (t_{r1},\ldots,t_{rk_r});$$
$$\}$$

we proceed analogously, but add the choice relation $Choice_n(x_0,\ldots,x_m)$ as an additional condition to the θ_j. Thus for $j = 1,\ldots,r$, $\Phi_{R_j,l}(y_1,\ldots,y_k)$ is given by:

$$\Phi_{R_j,l}(y_1,\ldots,y_k) \vee \exists x_1,\ldots,x_k.\ \bar{\theta}_j \wedge Choice_n(x_0,\ldots,x_m) \wedge$$
$$(y_1 = t_{j1}) \wedge \ldots \wedge (y_{k_j} = t_{jk_j})$$

where $\bar{\theta}_j$ is obtained from θ_j by replacing every literal $R_i(s_1,\ldots,s_{k_i})$ with the corresponding formula $\Phi_{R_i,l}(s_1,\ldots,s_{k_i})$. For all other predicates R, $\Phi_{R,l}(y_1,\ldots,y_k) \equiv \Phi_{R,l}(y_1,\ldots,y_k)$.

We remark that, by successive substitution of the formulas $\Phi_{R,l}$, we obtain for every prefix of the workflow of length l and for every predicate R, a formula $\bar{\Phi}_{R,l}$ which expresses the value of R in terms of the predicates at program start and the predicates $Choice_i$ only.

Example 1. Consider a variation of the conference management workflow given in the introduction, where a set of all PC members that do not have a conflict with any paper is collected.

(s_1) **forall** x,p **may** $true \ \rightarrow \ Conf \ += \ (x,p)$
(s_2) **forall** $x,p \ \neg Conf(x,p) \ \rightarrow \ S \ += \ (x)$

Then for (s_1), $\bar{\Phi}_{Conf,1}(x,p) \equiv \bar{\Phi}_{Conf,2}(x,p)$ is given by $\exists x_1,p_1.\ Choice_1(x_1,p_1) \wedge (x_1 = x) \wedge (p_1 = p)$, which is equivalent to $Choice_1(x,p)$. Accordingly for (s_2), $\bar{\Phi}_{S,2}$ is given by: $\exists x_2,p_2.\ \neg\bar{\Phi}_{Conf,1}(x_2,p_2) \wedge (x_2 = x)$ which can be simplified to $\exists p_2.\ \neg\bar{\Phi}_{Conf,1}(x,p_2)$. Altogether, we obtain:

$$\bar{\Phi}_{Conf,2}(x,p) \equiv Choice_1(x,p)$$
$$\bar{\Phi}_{S,2}(x) \quad\equiv \exists p_2.\ \neg Choice_1(x,p_2)$$

Example 2. Consider the workflow (WF1), shown in Fig. 1 in the introduction. Within this workflow, every statement updates exactly one predicate, and each predicate *Conf, A, Read* and *Comm* is updated only once. Accordingly, we can drop the extra index t and write $\bar{\Phi}_{Conf}, \bar{\Phi}_A, \bar{\Phi}_{Read}, \bar{\Phi}_{Comm}$ for the corresponding predicates after their respective updates. We have:

$$
\begin{aligned}
\bar{\Phi}_{Conf}(y_1, y_2) &\equiv Choice_1(y_1, y_2) \\
\bar{\Phi}_A(y_1, y_2) &\equiv \neg Choice_1(y_1, y_2) \wedge Choice_2(y_1, y_2) \\
\bar{\Phi}_{Read}(y_1, y_2, y_3) &\equiv \neg Choice_1(y_1, y_2) \wedge Choice_2(y_1, y_2) \wedge Oracle(y_2, y_3) \\
\bar{\Phi}_{Comm}(y_1, y_2, y_3) &\equiv \neg Choice_1(y_1, y_3) \wedge Choice_2(y_1, y_3) \wedge \\
&\quad \neg Choice_1(y_2, y_3) \wedge Choice_2(y_2, y_3) \wedge Choice_3(y_2, y_1, y_3)
\end{aligned}
$$

□

3   Specifying Secrecy with First-Order HyperLTL

HyperLTL [7] is a recent extension of linear-time temporal logic (LTL) with *trace variables* and *trace quantifiers*. HyperLTL can express noninterference and other information flow policies by relating multiple traces, which are each identified by a separate trace variable. Since HyperLTL was introduced as a propositional logic, it cannot express properties about systems with an arbitrary number of agents. We now present *first-order* HyperLTL, which extends propositional HyperLTL with first-order quantifiers. In the following, we will refer to first-order HyperLTL simply as HyperLTL.

HyperLTL Syntax. Let $\mathcal{P}$ be a set of predicates, $\mathcal{V}$ be a set of first-order variables, and Π be a set of *trace variables*. We call the set $\mathcal{P}_\Pi = \{P_\pi \mid P \in \mathcal{P}, \pi \in \Pi\}$ the set of *indexed predicates*. Our logic builds on the assertion language used in the description of the symbolic transition systems. In the case of the workflows, this is first-order predicate logic (PL) with equality. The *atomic formulas* of HyperLTL are formulas of the assertion language over the indexed predicates $\mathcal{P}_\Pi$ and the variables $\mathcal{V}$. HyperLTL *formulas* are then generated by the following grammar (with initial symbol ψ):

$$
\begin{aligned}
\psi &::= \exists \pi.\, \psi \mid \exists \pi.\, \varphi \mid \neg \psi \\
\varphi &::= \Psi \mid \neg \varphi \mid \varphi \wedge \varphi \mid \exists x.\, \varphi \mid \bigcirc \varphi \mid \varphi\, \mathcal{U}\, \varphi,
\end{aligned}
$$

where Ψ is an atomic formula, $\pi \in \Pi$ is a trace variable, and $x \in \mathcal{V}$ is a first-order variable. HyperLTL formulas thus start with a prefix of trace quantifiers consisting of at least one quantifier and then continue with a subformula that contains only first-order quantifiers, no trace quantifiers. Universal trace quantification is defined as $\forall \pi.\varphi \equiv \neg \exists \pi.\neg \varphi$. $\mathcal{U}$ and $\bigcirc$ are the usual Until and Next modalities from LTL. We also consider the usual derived Boolean operators and the derived temporal operators *Eventually* $\Diamond \varphi \equiv true\, \mathcal{U}\, \varphi$, *Globally* $\Box \varphi \equiv \neg \Diamond \neg \varphi$, and *Weak Until* $\varphi\, \mathcal{W}\, \psi \equiv \varphi\, \mathcal{U}\, \psi \vee \Box \varphi$.

HyperLTL Semantics. The semantics of a HyperLTL formula ψ is given with respect to a set of traces $\mathcal{T}$, an evaluation $\alpha : \mathcal{V} \to U$ of the first-order variables, and an evaluation $\beta : \Pi \to \mathcal{T}$ of the trace variables. Let $\sigma(n)$ denote the n-*th element* in a trace σ, and let $\sigma[n, \infty] = \sigma(n)\sigma(n + 1)\ldots$ denote the n-*th suffix* of σ. We lift the suffix operation from traces to trace assignments and define $\beta[n, \infty](\sigma) := \beta(\sigma)[n, \infty]$. The *update* of an evaluation of the first-order or trace variables is defined as follows: $\gamma[x \mapsto a](x) = a$ and $\gamma[x \mapsto a](y) = \gamma(x)$ for $x \neq y$. The *satisfaction* of a HyperLTL formula ψ, denoted by $\alpha, \beta \models_{\mathcal{T}} \psi$, is then defined as follows:

$$
\begin{aligned}
\alpha, \beta &\models_{\mathcal{T}} \exists \pi.\, \psi &\quad \text{iff} \quad& \exists t \in \mathcal{T}.\ \alpha, \beta[\pi \mapsto t] \models_{\mathcal{T}} \psi, \\
\alpha, \beta &\models_{\mathcal{T}} \neg \psi &\quad \text{iff} \quad& \alpha, \beta \not\models_{\mathcal{T}} \psi, \\
\alpha, \beta &\models_{\mathcal{T}} \Psi &\quad \text{iff} \quad& \alpha, \delta \models \Psi, \\
\alpha, \beta &\models_{\mathcal{T}} \varphi_1 \wedge \varphi_2 &\quad \text{iff} \quad& \alpha, \beta \models_{\mathcal{T}} \varphi_1 \text{ and } \alpha, \beta \models_{\mathcal{T}} \varphi_2, \\
\alpha, \beta &\models_{\mathcal{T}} \exists x.\, \varphi &\quad \text{iff} \quad& \exists a \in U.\ \alpha[x \mapsto a], \beta \models_{\mathcal{T}} \varphi, \\
\alpha, \beta &\models_{\mathcal{T}} \bigcirc \varphi &\quad \text{iff} \quad& \alpha, \beta[1, \infty] \models_{\mathcal{T}} \varphi, \\
\alpha, \beta &\models_{\mathcal{T}} \varphi_1 \,\mathcal{U}\, \varphi_2 &\quad \text{iff} \quad& \exists i \geq 0 :\ \alpha, \beta[i, \infty] \models_{\mathcal{T}} \varphi_2 \text{ and} \\
& & & \forall 0 \leq j < i :\ \alpha, \beta[j, \infty] \models_{\mathcal{T}} \varphi_1,
\end{aligned}
$$

where ψ, φ_1, and φ_2 are HyperLTL formulas, Ψ is an atomic formula, and $\alpha, \delta \models \Psi$ denotes the satisfaction of the formula Ψ of the assertion logic in the valuation α of the first-order variables and the interpretation δ of the indexed predicates. The interpretation $\delta(P_\pi)$ of an indexed predicate P_π is defined as the interpretation $\delta(P_\pi) = \beta(\pi)(0)(P)$ of P provided by the first state of the trace assigned to π. A formula without free first-order and trace variables is called *closed*. A closed formula ψ is *satisfied* by a transition system $\mathcal{S}$, denoted by $\mathcal{S} \models \psi$, iff $\alpha, \beta \models_{\mathcal{T}} \psi$ for the empty assignments α and β and the set $\mathcal{T} = Traces(\mathcal{S})$ of traces of the transition system. HyperLTL formulas in which all trace quantifiers are universal are called *universal formulas*. In the remainder of the paper, we will only consider universal formulas. This fragment contains many information flow properties of practical interest.

Noninterference. Secrecy properties like noninterference are based on a classification of the inputs and outputs of a system into either *low*, meaning not confidential, or *high*, meaning highly confidential. A system has the *noninterference* property [12] if in any pair of traces where the low inputs are the same, the low outputs are the same as well, regardless of the high inputs. When we are interested in the noninterference property of a single agent, it is possible to model the low and high inputs and the low and high outputs of the system (as seen by the agent) using separate predicates, for example, as I_l, I_h, O_l, O_h, respectively. Noninterference can then be expressed as the HyperLTL formula

$$
\forall \pi. \forall \pi'.\ \square(I_{l,\pi} \leftrightarrow I_{l,\pi'}) \ \to\ \square(O_{l,\pi} \leftrightarrow O_{l,\pi'}),
$$

which states that all traces π and π' that have the same low input I_l at all times, must also have the same low output O_l at all times.

In a workflow, the inputs or outputs of different agents may be collected in the same predicate. In the conference management example from the introduction, the low outputs observed by a PC member x consist of the pairs (x, p, r) for some paper p in the *Read* relation and, additionally, of the tuples (x, y, p) for some PC member y and a paper p in the *Comm* relation. The low input provided by agent x is given by the tuples of the *Choice* predicates that begin with x. Additionally, the system has high input in the form of the *Oracle* predicate.

Generalizing from the example, we assume there is one or more predicates of the form $O_l(x, \boldsymbol{y})$, modeling *low output* observed by the agents from the system, and one or more predicates of the form $I_l(x, \boldsymbol{y})$ modeling *low inputs* provided by the agents to the system. An output is observable by agent x whenever x occurs in the first position of the tuple. Likewise, an input is controllable by agent x whenever x occurs in the first position of the tuple. The remaining components of the tuple are denoted by the vector $\boldsymbol{y} = y_1, y_2, \ldots$. Noninterference is then expressed as the HyperLTL formula

$$\forall \pi, \pi'. \forall x.\ \Box(\forall \boldsymbol{y}\ .\ I_{l,\pi}(x, \boldsymbol{y}) \leftrightarrow I_{l,\pi'}(x, \boldsymbol{y}))\ \rightarrow\ \Box(\forall \boldsymbol{y}.\ O_{l,\pi}(x, \boldsymbol{y}) \leftrightarrow O_{l,\pi'}(x, \boldsymbol{y}))$$

which states that, for all agents x, if the low input provided by agent x on traces π and π' is the same, then the low output read by x on π and π' must be the same as well.

Declassification. Declassification [18] becomes necessary when the functionality of the system makes it unavoidable that some information is leaked. In the conference management example, a PC member x is supposed to read the reviews of the papers assigned to x. This is legitimate as long as x has not declared a conflict of interest with those papers. We assume that, in addition to the input and output predicates, there is a *declassification condition* $D(x, \boldsymbol{y})$, which indicates that agent x is allowed to learn about the high input $I_h(x, \boldsymbol{y})$. Noninterference with Declassification is then expressed as the HyperLTL formula

$$\forall \pi, \pi'. \forall x.\ \Box(\forall \boldsymbol{y}.\ I_{l,\pi}(x, \boldsymbol{y}) \leftrightarrow I_{l,\pi'}(x, \boldsymbol{y})\ \wedge\ (D(x, \boldsymbol{y}) \rightarrow (I_{h,\pi}(x, \boldsymbol{y}) \leftrightarrow I_{h,\pi'}(x, \boldsymbol{y}))))$$
$$\rightarrow \Box(\forall \boldsymbol{y}.\ (O_{l,\pi}(x, \boldsymbol{y}) \leftrightarrow O_{l,\pi'}(x, \boldsymbol{y}))),$$

which expresses that on all pairs of traces where the low inputs are the same and, additionally, the high inputs are the same whenever the declassification condition is true, the low outputs must be the same.

Example 3. In the conference management example, we specify the information flow policy that an agent should not receive information regarding papers where a conflict of interest has been declared as a noninterference property:

$$\forall \pi, \pi'. \forall x.\ \Box(\forall \boldsymbol{y}. \bigwedge_{i=1}^{3}(Choice_{i,\pi}(x, \boldsymbol{y}) \leftrightarrow Choice_{i,\pi'}(x, \boldsymbol{y})) \wedge$$
$$(\forall p, r.\ (\neg Conf_\pi(x, p) \wedge \neg Conf_{\pi'}(x, p)) \rightarrow (Oracle_\pi(p, r) \leftrightarrow Oracle_{\pi'}(p, r)))) \rightarrow$$
$$\Box(\forall p, r.\ (Read_\pi(x, p, r) \leftrightarrow Read_{\pi'}(x, p, r)) \wedge (\forall y, p.\ Comm_\pi(x, y, p) \leftrightarrow Comm_{\pi'}(x, y, p)))$$
$$\Box$$

Causality Assumptions on Agents. In the workflow from Fig. 1, it is easy to see that no PC member can directly read the reviews of papers where a conflict of interest has been declared: the PC member can only read a review if the PC member was assigned to the paper, which, in turn, can only happen if no conflict of interest was declared. It is much more difficult to rule out an indirect flow of information via a message sent by another PC member. So far, neither the description of the workflow, nor the HyperLTL specification would prevent other PC members to add such messages to *Comm*. To rule out messages that would leak information about papers where a PC member has a conflict, we must make assumptions about the possible behaviors of the *other* agents.

Stubborn Agents. A radical restriction on the behavior of the other agents is to require that they always, stubbornly, produce the same input, independently of their own observations. We assume that the input is represented by one or more predicates of the form $I(x, y)$, where an input is controllable by agent x whenever x occurs in the first position of the tuple. The requirement for traces π, π' that all agents are *stubborn* can be specified by the HyperLTL formula:

$$\forall x. \ \Box(\forall y. \ I_\pi(x, y) \leftrightarrow I_{\pi'}(x, y)).$$

Causal Agents. A more natural restriction on the behavior of the other agents is to require that they act causally, i.e., they only provide different inputs if they, themselves, have previously observed different outputs. The *causality* of agents w.r.t. traces π, π' can be described by the HyperLTL formula:

$$\forall x. \ (\forall y. \ I_\pi(x, y) \leftrightarrow I_{\pi'}(x, y)) \ \mathcal{W} \ (\exists y. \ O_\pi(x, y) \not\leftrightarrow O_{\pi'}(x, y))$$

which states that, for all agents x the inputs provided on two traces are the same *until* a difference in the outputs observed by x occurs.

Example 4. In the conference management example, stubbornness for traces π, π' can be specified as the HyperLTL formula $\forall x. \ \Box(\forall y. \ Choice_{1,\pi}(x, y) \leftrightarrow Choice_{1,\pi'}(x, y) \land \ldots)$. The requirement of causality for π, π' is specified as the HyperLTL formula

$$\forall x. \ (\forall y. \ Choice_{1,\pi}(x, y) \leftrightarrow Choice_{1,\pi'}(x, y) \land \ldots) \ \mathcal{W}$$
$$((\exists p, r. \ Read_\pi(x, p, r) \not\leftrightarrow Read_{\pi'}(x, p, r)) \lor (\exists y, p. \ Comm_\pi(x, y, p) \not\leftrightarrow Comm_{\pi'}(x, y, p))).$$
$\Box$

Combining the agent assumptions with the specification of noninterference (and possibly declassification), we obtain a formula of the form

$$\forall \pi_1, \ldots, \pi_n. \ \varphi_{\mathsf{causal}} \rightarrow \varphi$$

where $\varphi_{\mathsf{causal}}$ describes the agent assumption on all pairs of paths in $\pi_1, \ldots, \pi_n$.

4 Verifying Secrecy

We now present a bounded model checking method for symbolic transition systems and HyperLTL specifications. The approach reduces the violation of a HyperLTL formula on the prefix of a trace of a given symbolic transition system to the satisfiability of a formula of the assertion language. For workflows, it suffices to consider prefixes of bounded length, because the workflow terminates (and then stutters forever) after a fixed number of steps. Since the assertion language in the description of the workflows is first-order predicate logic, satisfiability of the resulting formula is not necessarily decidable. We return to this issue in Sect. 5, where we identify conditions under which decidability is guaranteed.

Bounded Satisfaction. Bounded model checking is based on a restricted notion of HyperLTL satisfaction where only trace prefixes of length n, for some fixed bound n, are considered. Let $\mathcal{T}$ be a set of traces, $\alpha : \mathcal{V} \to U$ an evaluation of the first-order variables, and $\beta : \Pi \to \mathcal{T}$ an evaluation of the trace variables. The n-*bounded satisfaction* of a HyperLTL formula ψ, denoted by $\alpha, \beta \models_{\mathcal{T}}^{n} \psi$, is then defined as follows:

$$
\begin{aligned}
\alpha, \beta &\models_{\mathcal{T}}^{n} \exists \pi.\ \psi &\text{iff}\quad& \exists t \in \mathcal{T}.\ \alpha, \beta[\pi \mapsto t] \models_{\mathcal{T}}^{n} \psi, \\
\alpha, \beta &\models_{\mathcal{T}}^{n} \neg\psi &\text{iff}\quad& \alpha, \beta \not\models_{\mathcal{T}}^{n} \psi, \\
\alpha, \beta &\models_{\mathcal{T}}^{n} \Psi &\text{iff}\quad& \alpha, \delta \models \Psi, \\
\alpha, \beta &\models_{\mathcal{T}}^{n} \varphi_1 \wedge \varphi_2 &\text{iff}\quad& \alpha, \beta \models_{\mathcal{T}}^{n} \varphi_1 \text{ and } \alpha, \beta \models_{\mathcal{T}}^{n} \varphi_2, \\
\alpha, \beta &\models_{\mathcal{T}}^{n} \exists x.\ \varphi &\text{iff}\quad& \exists a \in U.\ \alpha[x \mapsto a], \beta \models_{\mathcal{T}}^{n} \varphi, \\
\alpha, \beta &\models_{\mathcal{T}}^{n} \bigcirc\varphi &\text{iff}\quad& \alpha, \beta[1, \infty] \models_{\mathcal{T}}^{n-1} \varphi,\ \text{for } n > 0, \\
\alpha, \beta &\models_{\mathcal{T}}^{0} \bigcirc\varphi &\text{iff}\quad& \alpha, \beta \models_{\mathcal{T}} \varphi, \\
\alpha, \beta &\models_{\mathcal{T}}^{n} \varphi_1\, \mathcal{U}\, \varphi_2 &\text{iff}\quad& \exists i \geq 0 :\ \alpha, \beta[i, \infty] \models_{\mathcal{T}}^{n-i} \varphi_2 \text{ and} \\
&&& \forall 0 \leq j < i :\ \alpha, \beta[j, \infty] \models_{\mathcal{T}}^{n-j} \varphi_1,\ \text{for } n > 0, \\
\alpha, \beta &\models_{\mathcal{T}}^{0} \varphi_1\, \mathcal{U}\, \varphi_2 &\text{iff}\quad& \alpha, \beta[i, \infty] \models_{\mathcal{T}}^{0} \varphi_2,
\end{aligned}
$$

where $\psi, \varphi, \varphi_1,$ and φ_2 are HyperLTL formulas, Ψ is an atomic formula, and $\delta(P_\pi) = \beta(\pi)(0)(P)$. A closed formula ψ is n-*bounded satisfied* by a transition system $\mathcal{S}$, denoted by $\mathcal{S} \models^n \psi$, iff $\alpha, \beta \models_{\mathcal{T}}^{n} \psi$ for the empty assignments α and β and the set $\mathcal{T} = Traces(\mathcal{S})$ of traces of the transition system.

For workflows, satisfaction and bounded satisfaction coincide.

Theorem 1. *Let $\mathcal{S}$ be the transition system representing a workflow with n blocks. For all HyperLTL formulas ψ, it holds that $\mathcal{S} \models \psi$ iff $\mathcal{S} \models^n \psi$.*

Bounded Model Checking. We now translate a transition system $\mathcal{S}$ and a given universal HyperLTL formula for a given bound n into a formula $\Psi_{\mathcal{S}, \neg\psi}$ of the assertion language such that $\Psi_{\mathcal{S}, \neg\psi}$ is satisfiable iff $\mathcal{S} \not\models^n \psi$. Since ψ is universal, its negation is of the form $\exists \pi_1, \ldots, \pi_k.\ \varphi$, where φ does not contain any more trace quantifiers. Let the set of predicates $\mathcal{P}$ be given as $\mathcal{P} = \{P_1, \ldots, P_m\}$. In $\Psi_{\mathcal{S}, \neg\psi}^{n}$, we use for every predicate P_i several copies $P_{i,\pi,l}$, one per trace variable $\pi \in \{\pi_1, \ldots, \pi_k\}$ and position l, $0 \leq l \leq n$. The formula $\Psi_{\mathcal{S}, \neg\psi}^{n} = [\mathcal{S}]^n \wedge [\varphi]_0^n$ is a conjunction of two formulas of the assertion language, the unfolding $[\mathcal{S}]^n$ of the transition system $\mathcal{S}$ and the unfolding $[\varphi]_0^n$ of the HyperLTL formula φ.

For a symbolic transition system $\mathcal{S}$ and a bound $n \geq 0$, the *unfolding* $[\mathcal{S}]^n$ is defined as follows:

$$
[\mathcal{S}]^n = \bigwedge_{\pi \in \{\pi_1, \ldots, \pi_k\}} \Theta(P_{1,\pi,0}, \ldots P_{m,\pi,0}) \wedge \bigwedge_{l=0}^{n-1} \Delta(P_{1,\pi,l}, \ldots, P_{k,\pi,l}; P_{1,\pi,l+1}, \ldots, P_{m,\pi,l+1})
$$

For a HyperLTL formula φ without trace quantifiers and a bound $n \geq 0$, the *unfolding* $[\![\varphi]\!]_l^n$ is defined as follows:

$$
\begin{aligned}
[\![\neg\varphi]\!]_l^n &= \neg[\![\varphi]\!]_l^n, \\
[\![\varPsi]\!]_l^n &= \varPsi_l, \\
[\![\varphi_1 \wedge \varphi_2]\!]_l^n &= [\![\varphi_1]\!]_l^n \wedge [\![\varphi_2]\!]_l^n, \\
[\![\exists x.\ \varphi]\!]_l^n &= \exists x.\ [\![\varphi]\!]_l^n, \\
[\![\bigcirc\varphi]\!]_l^n &= [\![\varphi]\!]_{l+1}^{n-1} \text{ for } n > 0, \\
[\![\bigcirc\varphi]\!]_l^0 &= [\![\varphi]\!]_l^0, \\
[\![\varphi_1 \,\mathcal{U}\, \varphi_2]\!]_l^n &= [\![\varphi_2]\!]_l^n \vee ([\![\varphi_1]\!]_l^n \wedge [\![\varphi_1 \,\mathcal{U}\, \varphi_2]\!]_{l+1}^{n-1}) \text{ for } n > 0, \\
[\![\varphi_1 \,\mathcal{U}\, \varphi_2]\!]_l^0 &= [\![\varphi_2]\!]_l^0
\end{aligned}
$$

where φ, φ_1, and φ_2 are HyperLTL formulas, $\varPsi$ is a formula of the assertion language over indexed predicates $P_{i,\pi}$ and $\varPsi_l$ is the same formula with all occurrences of an indexed predicate $P_{i,\pi}$ replaced by the predicate $P_{i,\pi,l}$.

Theorem 2. *For a symbolic transition system S, a universal HyperLTL formulas ψ, and a bound $n \geq 0$, it holds that $S \models^n \psi$ iff $\varPsi_{S,\neg\psi}^n$ is unsatisfiable.*

Combining Theorems 1 and 2, we obtain the corollary that bounded model checking is a complete verification technique for workflows.

Corollary 1. *Let S be the transition system representing a workflow with T blocks. For all HyperLTL formulas ψ, it holds that $S \models \psi$ iff $\varPsi_{S,\neg\psi}^T$ is unsatisfiable.* □

5   Decidability

We now identify cases where the satisfiability of the predicate logic formulas constructed by the verification method of the previous section are decidable. For background on PL and decidable subclasses, we refer to the textbook [6].

Theorem 3. *Consider a workflow consisting of T blocks where all agents are stubborn, and every predicate R encountered by the workflow after l blocks, is characterized by a quantifier-free formula $\bar{\varPhi}_{R,l}$.*

Let $\forall \pi_1, \ldots, \pi_r . \varphi_{\mathsf{stubborn}} \rightarrow \varphi$ denotes a HyperLTL formula where $\varPsi' \equiv [\![\neg\varphi]\!]_0^T$ is a Bernays-Schönfinkel formula, i.e., the prenex form of $\varPsi'$ has a quantifier sequence of the form $\exists^*\forall^*$. Then it is decidable whether $\forall \pi_1, \ldots, \pi_r . \varphi_{\mathsf{stubborn}} \rightarrow \varphi$ holds.

Proof. For every predicate R, let $\bar{\varPhi}_{R,\pi_j,l}$ denote the formula which characterizes $R_{\pi_j,l}$, i.e., the value of R after l blocks along the execution of π_j. The formula $\bar{\varPhi}_{R,\pi_j,l}$ is obtained from $\bar{\varPhi}_{R,l}$ by replacing the occurrences of $Choice_i$, $Oracle$ with $Choice_{i,\pi_j}$ and $Oracle_{\pi_j}$, respectively. Let $\bar{\varPsi}'$ denote the formula obtained from $\varPsi'$ by first replacing every occurrence of a literal $R_{\pi_j,l}(s_1, \ldots, s_k)$ with $\bar{\varPhi}_{R,\pi_j,l}(s_1, \ldots, s_k)$. As all agents are stubborn, the predicates $Choice_{i,\pi_j}$ are equivalent for $j = 1, \ldots, r$. Accordingly, we may replace all $Choice_{i,\pi_j}(s_1, \ldots, s_k)$

with $Choice_{i,\pi_1}(s_1, \ldots, s_k)$. The resulting formula is still a Bernays-Schönfinkel formula. It is unsatisfiable iff $\forall \pi_1, \ldots, \pi_r$. $\varphi_{\text{stubborn}} \rightarrow \varphi$ is universally true. Satisfiability of $\bar{\Psi}'$, however, is decidable — which thus implies the the theorem.

□

Theorem 3 can be extended also to more general classes of workflows, given that the predicates $R_{\pi_j,l}$ occur only positively or only negatively in Ψ'. Non-interference, however, amounts to stating that (under certain conditions) no distinction is observable between some $R_{\pi_j,l}$ and $R_{\pi_{j'},l}$. Logically, indistinguishability is expressed by equivalence, which thus results in both positive and negative occurrences of the predicates in question.

Theorem 4. *Consider a workflow consisting of T blocks where all agents are causal, and every predicate R encountered by the workflow after l blocks, is characterized by a quantifierfree formula $\bar{\Phi}_{R,l}$. Assume that $\forall \pi_1, \ldots, \pi_r$. $\varphi_{\text{causal}} \rightarrow \varphi$ is a temporal formula where the prenex form of $\Psi' \equiv [\![\neg \varphi]\!]_0^T$ is purely existential. Then it is decidable whether $\forall \pi_1, \ldots, \pi_r$. $\varphi_{\text{causal}} \rightarrow \varphi$ holds.*

Proof. The argument for causal agents is somewhat more complicated and accordingly leads to decidability only for a smaller fragment of HyperLTL formulas. Removal of the temporal operators and skolemization of the formula φ_{causal} describing causality yields a conjunction of clauses in one of the forms (∗): $S(x, f_1(x), \ldots, f_r(x)) \vee Choice_{i,\pi_{j_1}}(x, \mathbf{z}) \vee \neg Choice_{i,\pi_j}(x, \mathbf{z})$, or $S(x, f_1(x), \ldots, f_r(x)) \vee \neg Choice_{i,\pi_{j_2}}(x, \mathbf{z}) \vee Choice_{i,\pi_j}(x, \mathbf{z})$ for $j_1, j_2 < j$, where the disjunction S refers to predicates which depend on $Choice_{i',\_}$ for $i' < i$ only. To perform ordered resolution, we order predicates so that $Choice_{i,\pi_j}$ receives a higher priority than $Choice_{i',\pi_{j'}}$ if $i' < i$ or, if $i = i'$, $j' < j$. All predicates in S have lower priorities than the $Choice$ predicates. Accordingly, the highest priority literal in each clause of φ_{causal} contains all free variables of the clause.

Let us first consider the case $r = 2$. Then resolution of two clauses with a positive and negative occurrence of the same highest-priority literal will result in a tautology and therefore is useless. As in the proof of Theorem 3, let $\bar{\Psi}'$ denote the formula obtained from Ψ' by replacing each occurrence of a predicate $R_{\pi_j,l}(s_1, \ldots, s_k)$ with the formulas $\bar{\Phi}_{R,\pi_j,l}(s_1, \ldots, s_k)$ $(j = 1, 2)$. According to our assumption on Ψ', the clauses obtained from $\bar{\Psi}'$ are all ground. Resolution of such a clause with a clause of φ_{causal} for some $Choice_{i,\pi_2}$ will again return a ground formula. By substituting the semantic formulas $\bar{\Phi}_{R,\pi_j,l}$ we obtain a set of new ground clauses, this time, however, with occurrences of predicates $Choice_{i',\pi_{j'}}$, $i' < i$, only. As a consequence, for every i, there is a bounded number of new clauses derivable by means of clauses from φ_{causal} with highest priority predicate $Choice_{i,\pi_2}$. Altogether, we therefore obtain only a bounded number of ground clauses which are derivable by means of ordered resolution. Hence, it is decidable whether a contradiction is derivable or not. This concludes the proof.

The argument for $r > 2$ is similar, only that resolution of any two such clauses originating from φ_{causal} with $j_1 \neq j_2$ upon the literal $Choice_{i,\pi_j}(x, \mathbf{z})$ will again result in a clause of the given form. In particular, no further literals are introduced. Therefore, saturation of φ_{causal} by ordered resolution will eventually terminate. Then the argument for termination proceeds analogously to the case $r = 2$ where φ_{causal} is replaced with the saturation of φ_{causal}. $\qquad\square$

Theorem 4 can be extended to formulas φ where $\bar{\Psi}'$ obtained from $[\![\neg\varphi]\!]_0^T$ is a Bernays-Schönfinkel formula at least in restricted cases. Consider the clauses of the form $(*)$ as obtained from φ_{causal} after skolemization. In case that the disjunction S is empty, we call the corresponding clause *simple*, otherwise *complex*. Now assume that complex clauses from the saturation of φ_{causal} are always resolved with clauses (originating from the skolemization of $\bar{\Psi}'$) upon a *ground* literal. Then the same argument as in the proof of Theorem 4 applies to show that saturation by resolution will eventually terminate.

6   Completing the Conference Management Example

We now complete the verification of our running example, that no PC member learns about the reviews of a paper for which he has declared a conflict. As already discussed in Sect. 3, it is easy to see that no PC member can directly read the reviews of papers where a conflict of interest has been declared. To prove the noninterference property in Example 3, it remains to show that the communication received from the other agents is the same on two traces π and π' whenever the Oracle for the papers with a conflict are the same on π and π'. For both stubborn and causal agents, the predicates $Conf_\pi(x, p)$ and $A_\pi(y, p)$ coincide with their counterparts in π'. Furthermore, for stubborn agents, the *Choice* predicates do not depend on the execution paths. As the predicates $Comm_\pi$ and $Comm_{\pi'}$ only depend on *Choice* predicates, the equivalence in the conclusion is trivially true. Hence, the property holds under the assumption that the agents are stubborn. The situation is different for causal agents. The causality assumption φ_{causal} (given in Sect. 3) states that the other PC members only send different communications if there was a different observation on the two traces. Since causality already implies that $Choice_1$ and $Choice_2$ are equal on all paths, this can be omitted from the antecedent of the requirement. The negation of the remaining property is then given by the following formula:

$$\exists \pi, \pi'. \varphi_{\text{causal}} \land \forall x. \Box (\forall y, p.\ Choice_3(x, y, p) \leftrightarrow Choice_3(x, y, p) \land$$
$$(\forall p, r.\ (\neg Conf_\pi(x, p) \land \neg Conf_{\pi'}(x, p)) \rightarrow Oracle_\pi(p, r) \leftrightarrow Oracle_{\pi'}(p, r))) \land$$
$$\Diamond (\exists y, p.\ Comm_\pi(x, y, p) \nleftrightarrow Comm_{\pi'}(x, y, p))$$

Due to the causality assumption, when we unroll $\mathcal{W}$ and replace *Read* with its semantics formula $\bar{\Phi}_{Read}$, we obtain that $Choice_1$ and $Choice_2$ are always equal and $Choice_3$ could differ on π and π' if there is a difference in the oracle.

$$\varphi_{\text{causal}} = \bigwedge\nolimits_{i=1}^{2} \forall x, p.\ Choice_{i,\pi}(x, p) \leftrightarrow Choice_{i,\pi'}(x, p) \land$$
$$\forall x, y, p, r.\ (Oracle_\pi(p, r) \leftrightarrow Oracle_{\pi'}(p, r)) \rightarrow$$
$$(Choice_{3,\pi}(x, y, p) \leftrightarrow Choice_{3,\pi'}(x, y, p))$$

Since in our example, the relation *Comm* is only assigned once, the $\Diamond$ operator is unrolled to a large disjunction that is false everywhere before the last step, since

Comm is empty on both paths. By unrolling $\neg\Psi$ and subsequently simplifying the formula with the causal equalities for $Choice_1$ and $Choice_2$, we obtain:

$$\neg\bar{\Psi} = \exists\pi,\pi'.\bar{\varphi}_{\mathsf{causal}} \wedge \exists x.(\forall p,r.\ Choice_{1,\pi}(x,p) \vee Oracle_\pi(p,r) \leftrightarrow Oracle_{\pi'}(p,r))$$
$$\wedge\ \exists y,p'.\ Choice_{3,\pi}(y,x,p') \not\leftrightarrow Choice_{3,\pi'}(y,x,p')$$

Note that all literals $Choice_{3,\pi}(y,x,p')$, $Choice_{3,\pi'}(y,x,p')$ contain existentially quantified variables only. Therefore, the assumptions of (the extension of) Theorem 4 are met. For the given formula, no contradiction can be derived. Instead, a model can be constructed as follows:

$$
\begin{aligned}
U &= \{x,y,p_1,p_2,r\}, \\
Oracle_\pi &= \{(p_1,r)\} & Oracle_{\pi'} &= \emptyset \\
Choice_{1,\pi} &= \{(x,p_1)\} & Choice_{1,\pi'} &= \{(x,p_1)\}, \\
Choice_{2,\pi} &= \{(x,p_2),(y,p_1),(y,p_2)\} & Choice_{2,\pi'} &= \{(x,p_2),(y,p_1),(y,p_2)\}, \\
Choice_{3,\pi} &= \{(y,x,p_1)\} & Choice_{3,\pi'} &= \emptyset
\end{aligned}
$$

Suppose the PC member x who has a conflict with paper p is assigned to a paper q where he does not have a conflict, and another PC member y, who does not have a conflict with either paper, is assigned to both p and q. Then y can communicate with x and therefore leak the review on paper p to x. To repair the problem, we let the PC chair remove the assignment of PC member y to paper q in such situations. Let (WF2) be (WF1) with the new line (2a) added in-between lines (2) and (3):

(2a) **forall** $x,y,p,q.\ Conf(x,p) \wedge \neg Conf(y,p) \wedge A(x,q) \wedge A(y,q) \rightarrow A \mathbin{-}= (y,q)$
    % PC chair removes assignments that might cause leaks

For the resulting workflow (WF2), we obtain a new formula $\bar{\Phi}_{A'}$, which in turn affects the formulas $\bar{\Phi}_{Read}$ and $\bar{\Phi}_{Comm}$ for *Read* and *Comm*:

$$\bar{\Phi}_{A'}(y,q) = \neg Choice_1(y,q) \wedge Choice_2(y,q) \wedge$$
$$\forall x,p.\ (Choice_1(x,q) \vee \neg Choice_2(x,q) \vee \neg Choice_1(x,p) \vee Choice_1(y,p))$$

The resulting formula after substitution of the semantics formulas and simplification is similar to $\neg\bar{\Psi}$, but adds two conjunctions with the $\forall$-clause of $\bar{\Phi}_{A'}$ instantiated for (x,p') and (y,p') on both sides of the inequivalence. The resulting formula is a Bernays-Schönfinkel formula where again the decision procedure of Theorem 4 can be applied. That procedure now derives a contradiction. Intuitively, the reason is that on both paths, x has declared a conflict with p_1. Since y is assigned to p_1, x and y cannot be assigned jointly to the same paper. Thus, both sides of the inequivalence collapse to *false* — implying that for (WF2) requirement (2) is satisfied and thus (WF2) is indeed noninterferent.   □

7 Related Work

There is a vast body of work on information flow policies and associated verification techniques. We mention Goguen and Meseguer's seminal work on *noninterference* [12], Zdancewic and Myer's *observational determinism* [20], Sutherland's *nondeducability* [19], and Halpern and O'Neill's *secrecy maintenance* [13] as representative examples. See Kanav *et al.* [15] for a recent overview with a detailed discussion of the most relevant notions for the verification of workflows. Our approach is based on the temporal logic HyperLTL [7]. HyperLTL has been applied in the verification of hardware systems, such as an Ethernet controller with 20000 latches [11]. Other logical approaches to information flow control include SecLTL [8], the polyadic modal μ-calculus [2] and the epistemic temporal logics [9]. While standard linear-time temporal logic has been extended with first-order quantifiers [16], our first-order extension of HyperLTL is the first temporal logic for the specification of information flow in systems with arbitrarily many agents. In terms of practical verification efforts, there has been a lot of recent interest in proving secrecy in web-based workflow management systems. For example, for the ConfiChair conference management system it was proven that the system provider cannot learn the contents of papers [3]. For CoCon, another conference management system, it was proven that various groups of users, such as authors, reviewers, and PC members cannot deduce certain content, such as reviews, unless certain declassification triggers, such as being a PC member without a conflict of interest, are met [15]. For the verification of an eHealth system, Bhardwaj and Prasad [5] assume that all agents are known at analysis time. Based on this information, the authors construct a dedicated security lattice and then apply techniques from universal information flow [1,14]. Our verification method is based on a reduction to the satisfiability problem of first-order predicate logic. First-order logic has many applications in verification. Most related, perhaps, is recent work on the verification of software defined networks [4,17]. There, a network controller is translated into a first order formula and either a theorem prover or an SMT-solver is used to determine properties of the topology so that the controller satisfies a given invariant.

8   Conclusion

We have presented a formalization of fine-grained security properties for workflow systems with an unbounded number of agents. HyperLTL is the first approach to specify hyperproperties for systems without a fixed set of agents. For the verification of HyperLTL formulas, we have provided a bounded model checking algorithm that translates the problem of verifying such a property for a given workflow to the satisfiability of first-order predicate logic. We have also provided a non-trivial fragment of properties and workflows so that the corresponding decision problem is decidable. As an example we considered noninterference for a simple workflow of a conference management system. Unexpectedly, our method exhibited a subtle form of indirect information flow. We also indicated how that deficiency can be cured. All corresponding proving took place within our benevolent fragments. Various problems remain for future work. Further decidable fragments are of major concern. Also, our work should be extended to more complex and thus more expressive forms of workflows.

Acknowledgment. This work was partially supported by the German Research Foundation (DFG) under the project "SpAGAT" (grant no. FI 936/2-1) in the priority program "Reliably Secure Software Systems "RS3" and the doctorate program "Program and Model Analysis - PUMA" (no. 1480).

References

1. Amtoft, T., Banerjee, A.: Information flow analysis in logical form. In: Giacobazzi, R. (ed.) SAS 2004. LNCS, vol. 3148, pp. 100–115. Springer, Heidelberg (2004)
2. Andersen, H.R.: A polyadic modal μ-calculus. Technical report, Danmarks TekniskeUniversitet (1994)
3. Arapinis, M., Bursuc, S., Ryan, M.: Privacy supporting cloud computing: ConfiChair, a case study. In: Degano, P., Guttman, J.D. (eds.) Principles of Security and Trust. LNCS, vol. 7215, pp. 89–108. Springer, Heidelberg (2012)
4. Ball, T., Bjørner, N., Gember, A., Itzhaky, S., Karbyshev, A., Sagiv, M., Schapira, M., Valadarsky, A.: Vericon: towards verifying controller programs in software-defined networks. In: ACM SIGPLAN Notices, vol. 49, pp. 282–293. ACM (2014)
5. Bhardwaj, C., Prasad, S.: Parametric information flow control in ehealth. Proc. HealthCom **2015**, 102–107 (2015)
6. Börger, E., Grädel, E., Gurevich, Y.: The Classical Decision Problem. Perspectives in Mathematical Logic. Springer, Heidelberg (1997)
7. Clarkson, M.R., Finkbeiner, B., Koleini, M., Micinski, K.K., Rabe, M.N., Sánchez, C.: Temporal logics for hyperproperties. In: Abadi, M., Kremer, S. (eds.) POST 2014 (ETAPS 2014). LNCS, vol. 8414, pp. 265–284. Springer, Heidelberg (2014)
8. Dimitrova, R., Finkbeiner, B., Kovács, M., Rabe, M.N., Seidl, H.: Model checking information flow in reactive systems. In: Kuncak, V., Rybalchenko, A. (eds.) VMCAI 2012. LNCS, vol. 7148, pp. 169–185. Springer, Heidelberg (2012)
9. Fagin, R., Halpern, J.Y., Moses, Y., Vardi, M.Y.: Reasoning About Knowledge. MIT Press, Cambridge (1995)
10. Finkbeiner, B., Rabe, M.N.: The linear-hyper-branching spectrum of temporal logics. IT - Inf. Technol. **56**(6), 273–279 (2014)
11. Finkbeiner, B., Rabe, M.N., Sánchez, C.: Algorithms for Model Checking Hyper-LTL and HyperCTL*. In: Kroening, D., Păsăreanu, C.S. (eds.) CAV 2015. LNCS, vol. 9206, pp. 30–48. Springer, Heidelberg (2015)
12. Goguen, J.A., Meseguer, J.: Security policies and security models. In: IEEE Symposium on Security and Privacy, pp. 11–20 (1982)
13. Halpern, J.Y., O'Neill, K.R.: Secrecy in multiagent systems. ACM Trans. Inf. Syst. Secur. **12**(1), 5:1–5:47 (2008)
14. Hunt, S., Sands, D.: On flow-sensitive security types. In: Morrisett, J.G., Jones, S.L.P. (eds.) Proceedings of POpPL 2006, pp. 79–90 (2006)
15. Kanav, S., Lammich, P., Popescu, A.: A conference management system with verified document confidentiality. In: Biere, A., Bloem, R. (eds.) CAV 2014. LNCS, vol. 8559, pp. 167–183. Springer, Heidelberg (2014)
16. Manna, Z., Pnueli, A.: Verification of Concurrent Programs: The Temporal Framework. The Correctness Problem in Computer Science, pp. 215–273. Academic Press, London (1981)

17. Padon, O., Immerman, N., Karbyshev, A., Lahav, O., Sagiv, M., Shoham, S.: Decentralizing SDN policies. In: ACM SIGPLAN Notices, vol. 50, pp. 663–676. ACM (2015)
18. Sabelfeld, A., Sands, D.: Dimensions and principles of declassification. In: Proceedings CSFW 2005, pp. 255–269. IEEE Computer Society (2005)
19. Sutherland, D.: A model of information. In: Proceedings of the 9th National Computer Security Conference, pp. 175–183. DTIC Document (1986)
20. Zdancewic, S., Myers, A.C.: Observational determinism for concurrent program security. In: Proceedings CSFW 2003 (2003)

Lazy Sequentialization for the Safety Verification of Unbounded Concurrent Programs

Truc L. Nguyen[1]([✉]), Bernd Fischer[2], Salvatore La Torre[3],
and Gennaro Parlato[1]

[1] Electronics and Computer Science, University of Southampton, Southampton, UK
tnl2g10@soton.ac.uk
[2] Computer Science, Stellenbosch University, Stellenbosch, South Africa
[3] Informatica, Università degli Studi di Salerno, Fisciano, Italy

Abstract. Lazy sequentialization has emerged as one of the most promising approaches for concurrent program analysis but the only efficient implementation given so far works just for bounded programs. This restricts the approach to bug-finding purposes. In this paper, we describe and evaluate a new lazy sequentialization translation that does not unwind loops and thus allows to analyze unbounded computations, even with an unbounded number of context switches. In connection with an appropriate sequential backend verification tool it can thus also be used for the safety verification of concurrent programs, rather than just for bug-finding. The main technical novelty of our translation is the simulation of the thread resumption in a way that does not use gotos and thus does not require that each statement is executed at most once. We have implemented this translation in the UL-CSeq tool for C99 programs that use the pthreads API. We evaluate UL-CSeq on several benchmarks, using different sequential verification backends on the sequentialized program, and show that it is more effective than previous approaches in proving the correctness of the safe benchmarks, and still remains competitive with state-of-the-art approaches for finding bugs in the unsafe benchmarks.

1 Introduction

Concurrent programming is becoming more important as concurrent computer architectures such as multi-core processors are becoming more common. However, the automated verification of concurrent programs remains a difficult problem. The main cause of the difficulties is the large number of possible ways in which the different elements of a concurrent program can interact with each other, e.g., the number of different thread schedules. This in turn makes it difficult and time-consuming to build effective concurrent program verification tools, either from scratch or by extending existing sequential program verification tools.

Partially supported by EPSRC grant No. EP/M008991/1, and MIUR-FARB 2013-2016 grants.

C. Artho et al. (Eds.): ATVA 2016, LNCS 9938, pp. 174–191, 2016.
DOI: 10.1007/978-3-319-46520-3_12

An alternative approach is to translate the concurrent program into a nondeterministic sequential program that *simulates* the original program, and then to reuse an existing sequential program verification tool as a black-box backend to verify this simulation program. This approach is also known as *sequentialization* [15,19,23]. It has been used successfully both for bug-finding purposes [3,12,25] and for the verification of reachability properties [7,16,17]. Its main advantage is that it separates the concurrency aspects from the rest of the verification tool design and implementation. This has several benefits. First, it simplifies the concurrency handling, which can be reduced to one (usually simple) source-to-source translation. Second, it makes it thus also easier to experiment with different concurrency handling techniques; for example, we have already implemented a number of different translations such as [5,12,25] within our CSeq framework [11]. Third, it makes it easier to integrate different sequential backends. Finally, it reduces the overall development effort, because the sequential program aspects and tools can be reused.

The most widely used sequentialization (implemented in Corral [18], Smack [24], and LR-CSeq [5]) by Lal and Reps [19] uses additional copies of the shared variables for the simulation and guesses their values (*eager* sequentialization). This makes the schema unsuitable to be extended for proof finding: it can handle only a bounded number of context switches, and the unconstrained variable guesses lead to over-approximations that are too coarse and make proofs infeasible in practice. *Lazy* sequentializations [15], on the other hand, do not over-approximate the data, and thus maintain the concurrent program's invariants and simulate only feasible computations. They are therefore in principle more amenable to be extended for correctness proofs although efficient implementations exist only for bounded programs [16,17].

Here, we develop and implement a lazy sequentialization that can handle programs with unbounded loops and an unbounded number of context switches, and is therefore suitable for program verification (both for correctness and bugfinding). The main technical novelty of our translation is the simulation of the thread resumption in a way that does not require that each statement is executed at most once and does (unlike Lazy-CSeq [11–13]) not rely on gotos to reposition the execution. Instead, we maintain a single scalar variable that determines whether the simulation needs to skip over a statement or needs to execute it. Our first contribution in this paper is the description of the corresponding source-to-source translation in Sect. 3. As a second contribution, we have implemented this sequentialization in the UL-CSeq tool (within our CSeq framework) for C99 programs that use the pthreads API (see Sect. 4). We have evaluated, as a third contribution, UL-CSeq on a large set of benchmarks from the literature and the concurrency category of the software verification competition SV-COMP, using different sequential verification backends on the sequentialized program. We empirically demonstrate, also in Sect. 4, that our approach is surprisingly efficient in proving the correctness of the safe benchmarks and improves on existing techniques that are specifically developed for concurrent programs. Furthermore, we show that our solution is competitive with state-of-the-art approaches for finding bugs in the unsafe benchmarks. We present related work in Sect. 5 and conclude in Sect. 6.

2   Multi-threaded Programs

In this paper, we use a simple multi-threaded imperative language to illustrate our approach. It includes dynamic thread creation and join, and mutex locking and unlocking operations for thread synchronization. However, our approach can easily be extended to full-fledged programming languages, and our implementation can handle full C99.

$$
\begin{array}{rcl}
P & ::= & (dec;)^* \ (typ \ p \ (\langle dec,\rangle^*) \ \{(dec;)^* stm\})^* \\[4pt]
dec & ::= & typ \ z \\[4pt]
typ & ::= & \texttt{bool} \mid \texttt{int} \mid \texttt{mutex} \mid \texttt{void} \\[4pt]
stm & ::= & seq \mid con \mid \{\langle stm;\rangle^*\} \\[4pt]
seq & ::= & \texttt{assume}\,(b) \mid \texttt{assert}\,(b) \mid x\texttt{=}e \mid p\,(\langle e,\rangle^*) \mid \textbf{return}\ e \\
 & & \mid \ \textbf{if}(b)\ stm\ [\textbf{else}\ stm] \mid \textbf{while}(b)\ \textbf{do}\ stm \mid l\colon seq \mid \textbf{goto}\ l \\[4pt]
con & ::= & x\texttt{=}y \mid y\texttt{=}x \mid t\texttt{=}\textbf{create}\ p\,(\langle e,\rangle^*) \mid \textbf{join}\ t \\
 & & \mid \ \textbf{init}\ m \mid \ \textbf{lock}\ m \mid \ \textbf{unlock}\ m \mid \ \textbf{destroy}\ m \mid l\colon con
\end{array}
$$

Fig. 1. Syntax of multi-threaded programs.

Syntax. The syntax of multi-threaded programs is defined by the grammar shown in Fig. 1. x denotes a local variable, y a shared variable, m a mutex, t a thread variable and p a procedure name. All variables involved in a sequential statement are local. We assume expressions e to be local variables, constants, that can be combined using mathematical operators. Boolean expressions b can be **true** or **false**, or Boolean variables, which can be combined using standard Boolean operations.

A *multi-threaded* program P consists of a list of *global* variable declarations (i.e., *shared* variables), followed by a list of procedures. Each procedure has a list of zero or more typed parameters, and its body has a declaration of *local* variables followed by a statement. A statement *stm* is either a sequential, or a concurrent statement, or a sequence of statements enclosed in braces.

A *sequential statement seq* can be an **assume**- or **assert**-statement, an assignment, a call to a procedure that takes multiple parameters (with an implicit call-by-reference parameter passing semantics), a **return**-statement, a conditional statement, a **while**-loop, a labelled sequential statement, or a jump to a label. Local variables are considered uninitialised right after their declaration, which means that they can take any value from their respective domains. Therefore, until not explicitly set by an appropriate assignment statement, they can non-deterministically assume any value allowed by their type. We also use the symbol * to denote the expression that non-deterministically evaluates to any possible value; for example, with x = * we mean that x is assigned any possible value of its type domain.

A *concurrent statement con* can be a concurrent assignment, a call to a thread routine, such as a thread creation, a join, or a mutex operation (i.e., init, lock, unlock, and destroy), or a labelled concurrent statement. A concurrent assignment assigns a shared (resp. local) variable to a local (resp. shared) one. Unlike local variables, global variables are always assumed to be initialised to a default value. A thread creation statement $t = \mathtt{create}\ p(e_1, \ldots, e_n)$ spawns a new thread from procedure p with expressions $e_1, \ldots, e_n$ as arguments. A thread join statement, $\mathtt{join}\ t$, pauses the current thread until the thread identified by t *terminates* its execution. Lock and unlock statements respectively acquire and release a mutex. If the mutex is already acquired, the lock operation is blocking for the thread, i.e., the thread is suspended until the mutex is released and can then be acquired.

We assume that a valid program P satisfies the usual well-formedness and type-correctness conditions. We also assume that P does not contain direct or indirect recursive function calls but contains a procedure $\mathtt{main}$, which is the starting procedure of the only thread that exists in the beginning. We call this the *main thread*. We further assume that there are no calls to $\mathtt{main}$ in P and no other thread can be created that uses $\mathtt{main}$ as starting procedure. Finally, our programs are not *parameterized*, in the sense that we allow only for a bounded number of thread creations.

Semantics. We assume a C-like semantics for each thread execution and a standard semantics by interleaving for the concurrent executions. At any given time of a computation, only one thread is executing (*active*). In the beginning only the main thread is active and no other thread exists; new threads can be spawned by a thread creation statement and are added to the pool of *enabled* threads. At a *context switch* the currently active thread is suspended and becomes enabled, and one of the enabled threads is resumed and becomes the new active thread. When a thread is resumed its execution continues either from the point where it was suspended or, if it becomes active for the first time, from the beginning.

All threads share the same address space: they can write to or read from global (*shared*) variables of the program to communicate with each other. We assume the *sequential consistency* memory model: when a shared variable is updated its new valuation is immediately visible to all the other threads [20]. We further assume that each statement is atomic. This is not a severe restriction, as it is always possible to decompose a statement into a sequence of statements, each involving at most one shared variable.

```
mutex m1,m2; int c;
void P(int b) {          void C() {              void main() {
    int l=b;                 L: lock m2;             c=0;
    lock m1;                 if(c<1) {               init m1;
    if(c>0) c=c+1            unlock m2;              init m2;
    else {                   goto L;                 int p0,p1,c0,c1;
        c=0;                 }                       p0=create P(5);
        while(l>0) do {      c=c-1;                  p1=create P(1);
            c=c+1;           assert(c>=0);           c0=create C();
            l=l-1;           unlock m2;              c1=create C();
        }                }                       }
    }
    unlock m1;
}
```

Fig. 2. Producer-consumer multi-threaded program containing a reachable assertion failure. In the `main` thread, functions P and C are both used twice to spawn a thread.

Example. The program shown in Fig. 2 models a producer-consumer system, with two shared variables, two mutexes m1 and m2, an integer c that stores the number of items that have been produced but not yet consumed.

The `main` function initializes the mutex and spawns two threads executing P (*producer*) and two threads executing C (*consumer*). Each producer acquires m1, increments c if it is positive or copies over the initial value "one-by-one", and terminates by releasing m1. Each consumer first acquires m2, then checks whether all the elements have been consumed; if so, it releases m2 and restarts from the beginning (goto-statement); otherwise, it decrements c, checks the assertion $c \geq 0$, releases m2 and terminates.

At any point of the computation, mutex m1 ensures that at most one producer is operating and mutex m2 ensures that only one consumer is attempting to decrement c. Therefore the assertion cannot be violated (*safe instance* of the Producer-Consumer program). However, by removing the consumers' synchronization on mutex m2, the assertion could be violated since the behavior of the two consumer threads now can be freely interleaved: with $c = 1$, both consumers can decrement c and one of them will write the value -1 back to c, and thus violate the assertion (*unsafe instance* of the Producer-Consumer program). □

3 Unlimited Lazy Sequentialization

In this section we present a code-to-code translation from a multi-threaded program P to a sequential program P^{seq} that simulates all executions of P.

We assume that P consists of $n+1$ functions $f_0, \ldots, f_n$, where f_0 is the `main` function, and that there are no function calls and each `create` statement (1) is executed at most once in any execution and (2) is associated with a distinct start function f_i. Consequently, the number of threads is bounded, and threads and functions can be identified. For ease of presentation, we also assume that thread functions have no arguments. We adopt the convention that each statement in P is annotated with a (unique) numerical label: the first statement of each function is labelled by 0, while its following statements are labelled with consecutive numbers increasing in the text order. This ordering on the numerical labels is used by our translation for controlling the simulation of the starting program in the resulting sequential program. These restrictions are used only to simplify the presentation.

P^{seq} simulates P in a *round-robin* fashion. Each computation of P is split into rounds. Each *round* is an execution of zero or more statements from each thread in the order $f_0, \ldots, f_n$. Note that this suffices to capture any possible execution since we allow for unboundedly many rounds and we can arbitrarily skip the execution of a thread in any round (i.e., execute zero statements). The `main` of P^{seq} is a driver formed by an infinite `while`-loop that simulates one round of P in each iteration, by repeatedly calling the thread simulation function f_i^{seq} of each thread f_i.

Each simulation function f_i^{seq} can non-deterministically exit at any statement to simulate a context switch. Thus, for each thread f_i, P^{seq} maintains in a global variable pc_i the numerical label at which the context switch was simulated in the previous round and where the computation must thus resume from in the next round. The local variables of f_i are made persistent in f_i^{seq} (i.e., changed to `static`) such that we do not need to recompute them on resuming suspended executions. Each f_i^{seq} is essentially f_i with few lines of injected control code for each statement that guard its execution, and the thread routines (i.e., `create`, `join`, `init`, `lock`, `unlock`, `destroy`) are replaced with calls to corresponding simulation functions. The execution of each call to a function f_i^{seq} goes through the following modes:

RESUME: the control is stepping through the lines of code without executing any actual statements of f_i until the label stored in pc_i is reached; this mode is entered every time the function f_i^{seq} is called.

EXECUTE: the execution of f_i has been resumed (i.e., the label stored in pc_i has been reached) and the actual statements of f_i are now executing.

SUSPEND: the execution has been blocked and the control returns to the main function; hence, no actual statements of f_i are executed in this mode. It is entered non-deterministically from the EXECUTE mode; on entering it, the numerical label of the current f_i statement (the one to be executed next) is stored in pc_i.

Code-to-Code Translation

We now describe our translation in a top-down fashion and convey an informal correctness argument as we go along. The entire translation is formally described by the recursive code-to-code translation function $[\![\cdot]\!]$ defined by the rewrite rules given in Fig. 3. Rule 1 gives the outer structure of P^{seq}: it adds the declarations of the global auxiliary variables, replaces each thread function f_i with the corresponding simulation function f_i^{seq}, adds the code stubs for the thread routines, and then the main function. The remaining rules give the transformation for all

1.
$$\left[\begin{array}{l}(dec;)^* \\ (\\ \quad \text{void } f_i\,() \\ \quad \{(dec;)^* stm\} \\ )_{i=0,\dots,n}\end{array}\right] \stackrel{\text{def}}{=} \begin{array}{l}\text{bool created}_0=1,\text{created}_1,\dots,\text{created}_n; \\ \text{int s, pc}_0,\dots,\text{pc}_n; \\ (dec;)^*\ (\text{void } f_i^{seq}\,()\,\{(\text{static } dec;)^*\,[\![stm]\!]_i\})_{i=0,\dots,n} \\ \text{seq\_create(int t, int arg)\{\dots\}} \\ \text{seq\_join(int t)\{\dots\}} \\ \text{seq\_init(int m)\{\dots\}}\quad\text{seq\_destroy(int m)\{\dots\}} \\ \text{seq\_lock(int m)\{\dots\}}\quad\text{seq\_unlock(int m)\{\dots\}} \\ \text{main()\{\dots\}}\end{array}$$

2. $[\![stm]\!]_i \stackrel{\text{def}}{=} \text{CONTR}(l)\ l\colon [\![seq]\!]_i \mid \text{CONTR}(l)\ l\colon \text{EXEC}([\![con]\!]_i) \mid \{\langle[\![stm]\!]_i;\rangle^*\}$

3. $[\![seq]\!]_i \stackrel{\text{def}}{=} \begin{array}{l}\text{EXEC(assume}(b)) \mid \text{EXEC(assert}(b)) \mid \text{EXEC}(x{=}e) \mid \\ \text{EXEC(return }e) \mid [\![\text{if}(b)\ stm\ [\text{else } stm]]\!]_i \mid \\ [\![\text{while}(b)\ \text{do } stm]\!]_i \mid \text{EXEC(goto }l)\end{array}$

4. $[\![con]\!]_i \stackrel{\text{def}}{=} \begin{array}{l}x{=}y \mid y{=}x \mid [\![t := \textbf{create } f_j()]\!]_i \mid [\![\text{join } t]\!]_i \\ \mid [\![\text{init } m]\!]_i \mid [\![\text{lock } m]\!]_i \mid [\![\text{unlock } m]\!]_i \mid [\![\text{destroy } m]\!]_i\end{array}$

5.
$$\left[\!\!\left[\begin{array}{l}\text{if } (b)\ \{\dots l_1:stm_1\} \\ [\text{ else } \{\dots l_2:stm_2\}\ ]\end{array}\right]\!\!\right]_i \stackrel{\text{def}}{=} \begin{array}{l}\text{if ((s==RESUME \&\& pc}_i \text{ <=}l_1) \mid\mid \text{(s==EXECUTE \&\& } b)\text{)} \\ \quad [\![\{\dots l_1:stm\}]\!]_i \\ \text{else if ((s==RESUME \&\& pc}_i \text{<=}l_2) \mid\mid \text{(s==EXECUTE))} \\ \quad [\![\{\dots l_2:stm\}]\!]_i;\end{array}$$

6. $[\![\text{while }(b)\ \text{do }\{\dots l_1:stm\}]\!]_i \stackrel{\text{def}}{=} \begin{array}{l}\text{while(}\quad\text{(s == RESUME \&\& pc}_i \text{ <= } l_1) \\ \quad\mid\mid \text{ (s == EXECUTE \&\& } b\text{)) do} \\ \quad [\![\{\dots l_1 : stm\}]\!]_i;\end{array}$

7. $[\![t := \textbf{create } f_j()]\!]_i \stackrel{\text{def}}{=} \{\ t := j;\ \text{seq\_create}(e, j)\ \}$

8. $[\![\text{join } t]\!]_i \stackrel{\text{def}}{=} \text{seq\_join}(t)$

9. $[\![\text{init } m]\!]_i \stackrel{\text{def}}{=} \text{seq\_init}(m)$

10. $[\![\text{lock } m]\!]_i \stackrel{\text{def}}{=} \text{seq\_lock}(m)$

11. $[\![\text{unlock } m]\!]_i \stackrel{\text{def}}{=} \text{seq\_unlock}(m)$

12. $[\![\text{destroy } m]\!]_i \stackrel{\text{def}}{=} \text{seq\_destroy}(m)$

$$\text{CONTR}(l) \stackrel{\text{def}}{=} \begin{array}{l}\text{if(s == RESUME \&\& pc}_i \text{ == } l)\ \text{s = EXECUTE;} \\ \text{if(s == EXECUTE \&\& *) \{ pc}_i{=}l;\ \text{s = SUSPEND;\}}\end{array}$$

$$\text{EXEC}(x) \stackrel{\text{def}}{=} \text{if(s == EXECUTE) }\{x;\ \};$$

Fig. 3. Rewriting rules for the lazy sequentialization.

statement types in our grammar; we will return to this in the description of the translation of each thread function f_i into the corresponding simulation function f_i^{seq}.

We start by describing the global auxiliary variables used in the translation. Then, we give the details of function **main** of P^{seq}, and illustrate the translation from f_i into f_i^{seq}. Finally, we discuss how the thread routines are simulated.

Auxiliary Variables. Let N denote the maximal number of threads in the program other than the main thread. We statically assign a distinct identifier to each thread of P from the interval $[0, \text{N}]$; the identifier assigned to **main** is 0. During the simulation of P, P^{seq} maintains the following auxiliary variables, for $i \in [0, \text{N}]$:

- bool $created_i$ tracks whether the thread with identifier i has ever been created. Initially, only $created_0$ is set to true since f_0^{seq} simulates the main function of P.
- int pc_i stores the numerical label of the last context switch point for thread i. All the variables pc_i are initialized to 0 that is the numerical label of the first statement of all thread functions.
- int s tracks the simulation mode as described above. It can only assume the values RESUME, EXECUTE, or SUSPEND.

Main Driver. The new main of P^{seq} (see Fig. 4) consists of an infinite loop that calls at each iteration the thread functions of the active threads.

```
int main(void){
  while(true) do {
    s = RESUME; /* set mode to RESUME before thread simulation */
    f₀();                    /* main thread simulation */

    s = RESUME;
    if (created₁) f₁();      /* simulation of thread with id 1 */
    ...
    s = RESUME;
    if (createdₙ) fₙ();   /* simulation of thread with id n */
  }
}
```

Fig. 4. The main function of P^{seq}.

Thread Simulation Functions. Each function f_i representing a thread in P is translated into the thread simulation function f_i^{seq} in P^{seq} as follows. First, the local variables of f_i are declared as static in f_i^{seq} to make them *persistent* between consecutive invocations of f_i^{seq}. Then, $[\![\cdot]\!]_i$ is applied recursively to the statements in the body of f_i^{seq} (see Rule 1 of Fig. 3).

For each statement we inject a few lines of code that implement the control of the simulation, i.e., make decisions on mode transitions in the simulation and, depending on the current mode, execute or skip the guarded statement. Specifically, every original statement is preceded by the code of the macro CONTR defined in Fig. 3 that takes as input the label l of the statement (see Rule 2). The injected code allows to set the mode to EXECUTE if the simulation is in RESUME mode and the old context switch point is reached. After that, if the simulation is in EXECUTE mode, it can non-deterministically transit into SUSPEND, and if so the label l is stored into pc_i. Note that, to skip the execution of a thread in a round, we need first to switch from RESUME to EXECUTE and then to SUSPEND before the simulation of the original statement. Furthermore, except for if- and while-statements, all the other statements are guarded by an if-statement injected by the macro EXEC that prevents their simulation unless the mode of the simulation is EXECUTE.

We need to (partially) simulate the if- and while-statements even if we are in RESUME mode, in order to position the execution back to the resumption point stored in pc_i. We achieve this by modifying their respective control flow guards. For the if-statement (see Rule 3), we check whether pc_i is in either of the then- or else-branch (note that if pc_i was less then the label of the current if-statement, we must already be in the EXECUTE mode and so we need to compare only against l_1 and l_2 which are respectively the labels of the last statements in the then- and else branches). If so, we go into the corresponding branch, independent of the *current* valuation of the condition b; we do this because we are only repositioning, and our resumption point reflects the *previous* valuation of the condition that held when the context switch occurred. Of course, if we are in EXECUTE mode, we need to check the condition. We follow a similar approach for while-statements. Note that here we only need one iteration over the loop's body to find the resumption point, so we do not need to check the condition in the RESUME mode. Finally, each call to a thread routine is also translated into a call to the corresponding simulation function (Rules 7–12).

Figure 5 shows the thread simulation function resulting from sequentializing the thread P shown in Fig. 2.

```
void P (int b){ static int 1;
    if (s == RESUME && pc == 0) s = EXECUTE;
    if (s == EXECUTE && *) {pc = 0; s = SUSPEND;}
    if (s == EXECUTE) { 1 = b; }
    if (s == RESUME && pc == 1) s = EXECUTE;
    if (s == EXECUTE && *) {pc = 1; s = SUSPEND;}
    if (s == EXECUTE) { seq_lock(m1); }
    if (s == RESUME && pc == 2) s = EXECUTE;
    if (s == EXECUTE && *) {pc = 2; s = SUSPEND;}
    if ((s == RESUME && pc <= 3) || (s == EXECUTE && (c > 0))){
        if (s == RESUME && pc == 3) s = EXECUTE;
        if (s == EXECUTE && *) {pc = 3; s = SUSPEND;}
        if (s == EXECUTE && LOCKED(m1)) { c = c + 1; }}
    else if ((s == RESUME && pc <= 6) || (s == EXECUTE)) {
        if (s == RESUME && pc == 4) s = EXECUTE;
        if (s == EXECUTE && *) {pc = 4; s = SUSPEND;}
        if (s == EXECUTE && LOCKED(m1)) { c = 0; }
        if (s == RESUME && pc == 5) s = EXECUTE;
        if (s == EXECUTE && *) {pc = 5; s = SUSPEND;}
        while ((s == RESUME && pc <= 6) || ((s == EXECUTE) && (1 > 0))) do {
            if (s == RESUME && pc == 6) s = EXECUTE;
            if (s == EXECUTE && *) {pc = 6; s = SUSPEND;}
            if (s == EXECUTE && LOCKED(m1)) { c = c + 1; }
            if (s == EXECUTE && LOCKED(m1)){ 1 = 1 - 1; }}}
    if (s == RESUME && pc == 7) s = EXECUTE;
    if (s == EXECUTE && *) {pc = 7; s = SUSPEND;}
    if (s == EXECUTE && LOCKED(m1)) { seq_unlock(m1); }
    if (s == EXECUTE || (s == RESUME && pc == 8)){ pc = 8; s = SUSPEND; }
}
```

Fig. 5. Translation of thread P from Fig. 2.

Simulation of the Thread Routines. For each thread routine we provide a verification stub, i.e., a simple standard C function that replaces the original implementation for verification purposes. The verification stubs are identical to those used by Lazy-CSeq. Below, we informally describe how they work; full details are given in [12]. In `seq_create` we simply set the thread's `created` flag. Note that we do not need to store the thread start function, as the `main` driver calls all thread simulation functions explicitly and `seq_create` uses an additional integer argument that serves as thread identifier that is statically determined in the call.

According to the semantics of the `join`-statement, a thread executing `join` t should be blocked until thread t is terminated (i.e., the corresponding pc variable is set to `LAST_LABEL` that is a statically defined constant larger than any other label in P). We choose to not implement in P^{seq} any notion of blocking or unblocking a thread; instead `seq_join` uses an `assume`-statement with the condition `pc_t == LAST_LABEL` to prune away any simulation that corresponds to a blocking join. We can then see that this pruning does not alter the thread reachability properties of the original program. Assume that the joining thread t terminates after the execution of `join` t. The invoking thread should be unblocked then but the simulation has already been pruned. However, this execution can be captured by another simulation in which a context switch is simulated right before the execution of this `join`-statement, and the invoking thread is scheduled to run only after t has terminated, hence avoiding the pruning as above.

For mutexes we need to know whether they are free or already destroyed, or which thread holds them otherwise. For this, in the corresponding functions, we use two constants `FREE` and `DESTROY`. On initializing or destroying a mutex we assign it the appropriate constant. In `seq_lock`, we assert that the mutex is not destroyed and then check whether it is free before assigning it the index of the thread that has invoked the function. As in the case of the `join`-statement we block the simulation if the lock is held by another thread. In `seq_unlock`, we first assert that the lock is held by the invoking thread and then set it to `FREE`. We also support re-entrant mutexes.

Correctness. The correctness of our construction is quite straightforward.

For the *completeness*, assume any non-empty execution ρ of P that creates at most N threads. Let $\rho = \rho_0 \ldots \rho_k$ be split into maximal execution contexts (i.e., each ρ_i is non-empty and has statements only from one thread and ρ_i and ρ_{i+1} are from different threads). Clearly, ρ_0 is a context of the main thread of P that is the only one existing in the beginning. P^{seq} starts the execution from the driver `main` and then calls f_0^{seq} (i.e., the simulation function of the main thread of P). At the first injected control code, since s evaluates to `RESUME` and pc_0 evaluates to 0 (since s is always set to `RESUME` in the driver before calling a simulation function and all the pc_i's are initialized to 0), and since we do not context switch yet, s is updated to `EXECUTE` and the original statement of P is executed (see Fig. 3). The simulation of the remaining statements in ρ_0 is done similarly. On context-switching from ρ_0 to ρ_1, at the second `if`-statement of the macro `CONTR` injected to control the first statement in ρ_1, since we are in the `EXECUTE` mode, we can select to context-switch and thus pc_0 is updated with the label of this statement (that is the next to execute when the thread will be resumed) and change the simulation mode to `SUSPEND`. From this point to the end of f_0^{seq} the control code will skip the execution of all the remaining statements of f_0, and thus the control returns to the main function of P^{seq} after the call to f_0^{seq}. Now, assume that ρ_1 is a context of a thread f_j, $j \neq 0$. Clearly, the thread must have been created in ρ_0, thus created$_j$ must hold true. Thus in the main driver we skip all calls to f_i for $i < j$, either because created$_i$ is false (i.e., the thread has not been created yet) or because we context-switch out immediately when calling f_i^{seq}. Then, we call f_j^{seq} and repeat the same argument as for ρ_0. To complete this part we need just to handle the case when we execute a context ρ_j of thread f_i that is not its first context. In this case, since the simulation mode is set to RESUME in the main driver, the control code forces to skip all the statement of P until we reach the label stored in pc$_i$. Since all the local variables are declared static and there are no function calls besides the call to the thread routine stubs, the local state of f_i is exactly as it was when the thread was pre-empted last time. Therefore, we can simulate ρ_j as observed above and we are done.

The *soundness* argument is a direct consequence of the fact that P^{seq} executes statements of P and the injected control code just positions the control for the simulation of context-switching. Thus, from each execution ρ of P^{seq} we can extract an execution of P by simply projecting out the auxiliary variables and the control code statements.

Therefore, we get that P^{seq} violates an assertion if and only if P does and the following theorem holds:

Theorem 1. *A concurrent program P violates an assertion in at least one of its executions with at most N thread creations if and only if P^{seq} violates the same assertion.*

4   Implementation and Experiments

4.1   Implementation

We have implemented in UL-CSeq v0.2[1] the schema discussed in Sect. 3 as a code-to-code transformation for sequentially-consistent concurrent C programs with POSIX threads (pthreads). This implementation is slightly optimized compared to the version that participated (using the CPAchecker backend) in SV-COMP16 [22].

UL-CSeq is implemented as a chain of modules within the CSeq framework [5, 6]. The sequentialized program is obtained from the original program through transformations, which (i) insert boilerplate code for simulating the pthreads API; (ii) unwind any loops that create threads; (iii) create multiple copies of the thread start functions, and inline all other function calls; (iv) implement the translation rules, as shown in Fig. 3; and (v) insert code for the main driver, and finalize the translation by adding backend-specific instrumentation.

---

[1] http://users.ecs.soton.ac.uk/gp4/cseq/files/ul-cseq-0.2_64bit.tar.gz.

4.2 Experiments

We experimentally evaluated the capabilities and performance of our UL-CSeq implementation (as sketched above) for both verification and bug-finding purposes. We mainly used the benchmark set from the Concurrency category of the TACAS Software Verification Competition (SV-COMP16) [2]. These are widespread benchmarks, and many state-of-the-art analysis tools have been trained on them. They offer a good coverage of the core features of the C programming language as well as of the basic concurrency mechanisms. In addition, we also used two smaller benchmark collections from the literature [7,27]. For all benchmarks we unwound thread-creating loops twice. Since we executed the verification and the bug-finding experiments on different machines and benchmark subsets, we report on them separately.

Verification. Here, we used UL-CSeq in combination with four different sequential backends (SeaHorn, Ultimate Automizer, CPAchecker, and VVT), and compared it with four different verification tools with built-in concurrency handling (Impara, Satabs, Threader, and VVT). These were chosen to cover a range of different sequential and concurrent verification techniques. Please note that we cannot compare to the top tools of the SV-COMP because all three medal winners are based on bounded model checking and do not produce proofs but simply claim benchmarks to be safe if they do not find a bug with their chosen settings.

Experimental Setup. For the verification experiments, we used the 221 safe benchmarks from the SV-COMP collection as well as the 13 safe benchmarks from [7,27]. The total size of the benchmarks was approximately 37 K lines of code. We ran the experiments on a large compute cluster of Xeon E5-2670 2.6 GHz processors with 16 GB of memory each, running a Linux operating system with 64-bit kernel 2.6.32. We set a 15 GB memory limit and a 900 s timeout for the analysis of each benchmark. We used SeaHorn [9] (v0.1.0),[2] an LLVM-based [21] framework for verification of safety properties of programs using Horn Clause solvers; Ultimate Automizer [10] (SV-COMP16),[3] an automata-based software model checker that is implemented in the Ultimate software analysis framework; CPAchecker (v1.4 with predicate abstraction),[4] a tool for configurable software verification that supports a wide range of techniques, including predicate abstraction, and shape and value analysis; Impara (v0.2),[5] a tool that implements an algorithm that combines a symbolic form of partial-order reduction and lazy abstraction with interpolants for concurrent programs; Satabs

---

[2] https://github.com/seahorn/seahorn/releases/download/v0.1.0/SeaHorn-0.1.0-Linuxx8664.tar.gz.

[3] http://ultimate.informatik.uni-freiburg.de/downloads/svcomp2016/UltimateAutomizer.zip.

[4] http://cpachecker.sosy-lab.org/CPAchecker-1.4-unix.tar.bz2.

[5] http://www.cprover.org/concurrent-impact/impara-linux64-0.2.tgz.

Table 1. Performance comparison of different verification tools on safe benchmarks: UL-CSeq with different sequential backends (top); other tools with built-in concurrency handling (bottom). Each row corresponds to a sub-category of the SV-COMP16 benchmarks, or to one of the benchmark sets from the literature; we report the number of files and the total number of lines of code. *pass* denotes the number of correctly verified safe benchmarks (i.e., proofs found), *fail* the number of benchmarks where the tool found a spurious error or crashed (including running out of memory), *t.o.* the number of benchmarks on which the tool exceeded the given time limit, and *time* is the average proof time (i.e., excluding failed attempts).

| | | | UL-CSeq + | | | | | | | | | | | | | | | |
| | | | SeaHorn | | | | Automizer | | | | CPAchecker | | | | VVT | | | |
Sub-category	Files	l.o.c.	pass	fail	t.o.	time	pass	fail	t.o.	time	pass	fail	t.o.	time	pass	fail	t.o.	time
pthread	15	1285	3	2	10	67.3	3	2	10	390.8	2	3	10	204.9	5	3	7	247.3
pthread-atomic	9	1136	6	1	2	167.9	3	1	5	456.7	5	0	4	352.6	5	0	4	171.8
pthread-ext	45	3679	27	0	18	199.1	12	2	31	226.5	15	0	30	214.6	16	5	24	179.7
pthread-lit	8	427	3	0	5	23.3	1	0	7	544.9	3	0	5	164.1	3	2	3	79.8
pthread-wmm	144	29426	144	0	0	32.5	60	0	84	421.6	26	0	118	271.3	141	0	3	275.3
[27]	7	542	5	0	2	51.1	3	1	3	238.6	4	0	3	244.7	4	1	2	133.1
[7]	6	290	6	0	0	5.7	5	0	1	181.8	5	0	1	44.9	6	0	0	17.2
Totals	234	36785	194	3	37	59.9	87	6	141	376.2	60	3	171	235.7	180	11	43	248.2

| | | | Impara | | | | Satabs | | | | Threader | | | | VVT | | | |
Sub-category	Files	l.o.c.	pass	fail	t.o.	time	pass	fail	t.o.	time	pass	fail	t.o.	time	pass	fail	t.o.	time
pthread	15	1285	5	2	8	12.2	3	8	4	308.7	6	8	1	128.4	5	1	9	7.3
pthread-atomic	9	1136	5	0	4	61.8	4	3	2	1.3	7	0	2	24.4	7	1	1	143.7
pthread-ext	45	3679	30	0	15	8.7	15	13	17	34.6	36	1	8	104.8	38	1	6	66.2
pthread-lit	8	427	2	0	6	0.4	2	5	1	8.1	0	7	1	N/A	5	1	2	7.3
pthread-wmm	144	29426	24	0	120	9.0	100	22	22	312.2	0	144	0	N/A	130	0	14	222.2
[27]	7	542	6	0	1	0.5	4	1	2	1.0	5	1	1	27.5	4	3	0	154.7
[7]	6	290	5	1	0	2.7	6	0	0	0.8	3	3	0	58.2	3	3	0	8.8
Totals	234	36785	77	3	154	11.2	134	52	48	244.0	57	164	13	88.2	192	10	30	172.6

(v3.2),[6] a verification tool based on predicate abstraction; and Threader (SV-COMP14), a tool that uses compositional reasoning with regards to the thread structure of concurrent programs based on abstraction refinement. VVT (SV-COMP16), a tool that can both verify programs using IC3 and predicate abstraction also can find bugs using bounded model checking. We ran each tool with its default configuration.

Results. Table 1 summarizes the results. It demonstrates that our approach is (with suitable backends) surprisingly effective: using SeaHorn, we can prove 194 out of the 234 benchmarks, and just edge out victory over VVT, the best-performing tool with built-in concurrency handling. However, note that UL-CSeq's performance varies widely with the applied backend, and using Automizer or CPAchecker produces noticeably worse results. Proof times are difficult to compare in aggregate, but overall UL-CSeq's proof times are within the range of the other tools, indicating that the sequentialization does not introduce too much complexity. This is further corroborated by the fact that the combination of UL-CSeq and VVT (which finds 180 proofs) is only slightly weaker than VVT relying on its built-in concurrency handling (which finds 192 proofs).

---

[6] http://www.cprover.org/satabs/download/satabs-3-2-linux-32.tgz.

Table 2. Performance comparison of different tools on the unsafe instances of the SV-COMP16 *Concurrency category*. Each row corresponds to a sub-category of the SV-COMP16 benchmarks; we report the number of files and the total number of lines of code. *pass* now denotes the number of correctly identified unsafe benchmarks (i.e., counterexamples found) and *t.o.* the number of benchmarks on which the tool exceeded the given time limit, and *time* the average time to find a bug. None of the tools reported any spurious counterexample.

Sub-category	Files	l.o.c	UL-CSeq + CBMC			Lazy-CSeq + CBMC			CBMC			CIVL			Smack		
			pass	t.o	time	pass	t.o	time	pass	t.o	time	pass	t.o	time	pass	t.o	time
pthread	17	4085	14	3	12.2	17	0	19.4	16	1	63.1	17	0	14.9	8	9	84.2
pthread-atomic	2	204	2	0	1.4	2	0	1.0	2	0	0.4	2	0	3.4	2	0	15.0
pthread-ext	8	780	8	0	1.0	8	0	0.3	7	1	12.0	8	0	0.3	8	0	47.2
pthread-lit	3	148	3	0	1.4	3	0	1.3	2	1	0.2	3	0	2.7	1	2	11.1
pthread-wmm	754	237700	754	0	1.1	754	0	1.2	754	0	0.5	754	0	6.1	753	1	78.1
Total	784	242917	781	3	1.4	784	0	1.6	781	3	2.9	784	0	6.2	772	12	77.6

Bug-Finding. Here, we used UL-CSeq in combination with CBMC as sequential backend, and compared it with four different bug-finding tools, Lazy-CSeq, CBMC, CIVL, and Smack. All four are (ultimately) based on bounded model checking, and have performed very well in the recent SV-COMP verification competitions: both Lazy-CSeq and CIVL scored full marks. Note that the verifiers we used in the experiments described in the previous section performed noticeably worse.

Experimental Setup. For the bug-finding experiments, we used the 784 unsafe benchmarks from the SV-COMP collection. The total size of the benchmarks was approximately 240 K lines of code. We ran the experiments on an otherwise idle machine with an Intel i7-3770 CPU 3.4 GHz and 16 GB of memory, running a Linux operating system with 64-bit kernel 4.4.0. We also set a 15 GB memory limit and a 900 s timeout for the analysis of each benchmark.

We used CBMC [4] (v5.4)[7] both as sequential backend (for UL-CSeq and Lazy-CSeq) and stand-alone bug-finding tool. It is a mature SAT-based bounded software model checker that uses a partial-order approach [1] to handle concurrent programs. We further used Lazy-CSeq [12] (v1.0),[8] a lazy sequentialization for bounded programs; CIVL [28] (v1.5),[9] a framework that uses a combination of explicit model checking and symbolic execution for verification; and SMACK [24] (v1.5.2),[10] a bounded software model checker that verifies programs up to a given bound on loop iterations and recursion depth. For all tools we used as loop unwinding and round bounds the (same) minimum values necessary to find all bugs in the given sub-category.

Results. Table 2 summarizes the results. We can see that our *proof*-oriented sequentialization does not actually impact negatively on our tool's *bug-finding*

---

[7] http://www.cprover.org/cbmc/download/cbmc-5-4-linux-64.tgz.

[8] http://users.ecs.soton.ac.uk/gp4/cseq/files/lazy-cseq-1.0.tar.gz.

[9] http://vsl.cis.udel.edu/lib/sw/civl/1.5/svcomp16/CIVL-1.5_2739_svcomp16.tgz.

[10] http://soarlab.org/smack/smack-1.5.2-64.tgz.

performance. UL-CSeq solves 781 of the 784 benchmarks, only three fewer than Lazy-CSeq (whose sequentialization specifically exploits the structure of bounded programs) or CIVL, and more than Smack. Analysis times are comparable across all tools, with the exception of the noticeably slower Smack. These results indicate that unwinding and lazy sequentialization can effectively be applied in either order.

The UL-CSeq source code, static Linux binaries and benchmarks are available at http://users.ecs.soton.ac.uk/gp4/cseq/atva16.zip.

5   Related Work

There is a wide range of approaches to verify concurrent programs. However, here we focus on more closely related sequentialization approaches. The idea of sequentialization was originally proposed by Qadeer and Wu [23]. The first scheme for an arbitrary but bounded number of context switches was given in [19]. Since then, several algorithms and implementations have been developed (see [3,5,14,15,18]).

Lazy sequentialization schemes have played an important role in the development of efficient tools. Their main feature is that they do not guess the original program's data but just its schedules and so induce less non-determinism and often simpler verification conditions. They also only explore reachable states of the original program, thus preserving the local invariants. This last property makes them suitable for static analysis [19]. The first such sequentialization was given in [15] for bounded context switching and extended to unboundedly many threads in [16,17]. These schemes avoid the cross-product of the local states (since only one thread is tracked at any time of a computation) but require their recomputation at each context-switch. This is a major drawback when such a sequentialization is used in combination with bounded model-checking (see [8]). The scheme Lazy-CSeq [12] avoids such recomputations by flattening the programs and making the locals persistent, and achieves efficiency by handling context-switches with a very lightweight and decentralized control code.

All sequentializations mentioned above yield under-approximations of the multi-threaded programs and thus (except for [16] that gives a sufficient condition to test completeness of the reached state space) are designed mainly for bug-finding. The new lazy sequentialization that we have designed in this paper is similar in spirit to Lazy-CSeq in that it injects lightweight control code to reposition the program counter on simulating a thread resumption but the injected control code itself is completely different. The main limitation of Lazy-CSeq's approach is that it assumes that each thread program counter uniquely identify its local state (which can be guaranteed for loop-free bounded programs), whereas our approach can handle a wider class of programs. First, we do not unwind loops and thus we allow for an exact simulation of unbounded loops. Second, we do not bound the number of context-switches in any explored computation. Our experiments show that the new control code is almost as effective as the goto-based control code used in Lazy-CSeq when using UL-CSeq with a bounded model checking backend, and performs very well when used to prove correctness of programs.

The only sequentialization that can be used to prove correctness of multithreaded programs is [7], but its approach is quite different from ours. It is closely related to the rely-guarantee style proofs and is aimed to avoid the cross-product of the thread-local states. Only the valuation of some local variables of the other threads (forming the abstraction for the assume-guarantee relation) is retained when simulating a thread. For this, frequent recomputations of the thread local states are required (in particular, whenever a context switch needs to be simulated in the construction of the rely-guarantee relations) which introduces control non-determinism and recursive function calls even if the original program does not contain any recursive calls. Moreover, the resulting sequentialization yields an overapproximation of the original program and thus cannot be used for bug-finding.

6   Conclusions and Future Work

We have presented a new sequentialization of concurrent programs that does not need to bound the number of context-switches or to unwind the loops. We only bound the number of threads and do not allow unbounded function call recursion. Noticeably, the resulting sequential program preserves all local invariants of the original program. In combination with suitable sequential verification tools it can thus be used both to find bugs (i.e., prove assertion violations) and prove concurrent programs safe.

We have implemented this sequentialization in the tool UL-CSeq within our framework CSeq and provided support for several backends. We have conducted a large set of experiments which have shown that UL-CSeq performs almost as efficiently as the best performing tools for bug-finding, and is very competitive for proving correctness. To the best of our knowledge this is the first approach that works well both as bug finder and to prove correctness for concurrent programs.

UL-CSeq is a first prototype implementation and has wide margins for improvements with fine tuning and optimizations. As future work, we plan to extend the range of programs that UL-CSeq can handle. We will modify the translation to lift some of the restrictions (e.g., the bounded number of thread creations), and will support new language features (e.g., other thread synchronization and communication primitives). We will also integrate further backends. Finally, we are working to extend our approach to support weak memory models implemented in modern architectures [26].

References

1. Alglave, J., Kroening, D., Tautschnig, M.: Partial orders for efficient bounded model checking of concurrent software. In: Sharygina, N., Veith, H. (eds.) CAV 2013. LNCS, vol. 8044, pp. 141–157. Springer, Heidelberg (2013)
2. Beyer, D.: Reliable and reproducible competition results with BenchExec and witnesses (report on SV-COMP 2016). In: Chechik, M., Raskin, J.-F. (eds.) TACAS 2016. LNCS, vol. 9636, pp. 887–904. Springer, Heidelberg (2016). doi:10.1007/978-3-662-49674-9_55
3. Chaki, S., Gurfinkel, A., Strichman, O.: Time-bounded analysis of real-time systems. In: FMCAD, pp. 72–80 (2011)
4. Clarke, E., Kroening, D., Lerda, F.: A tool for checking ANSI-C programs. In: Jensen, K., Podelski, A. (eds.) TACAS 2004. LNCS, vol. 2988, pp. 168–176. Springer, Heidelberg (2004). doi:10.1007/978-3-540-24730-2_15
5. Fischer, B., Inverso, O., Parlato, G.: CSeq: a concurrency pre-processor for sequential C verification tools. In: ASE, pp. 710–713 (2013)
6. Fischer, B., Inverso, O., Parlato, G.: CSeq: a sequentialization tool for C - (competition contribution). In: Piterman, N., Smolka, S.A. (eds.) TACAS 2013 (ETAPS 2013). LNCS, vol. 7795, pp. 616–618. Springer, Heidelberg (2013)
7. Garg, P., Madhusudan, P.: Compositionality entails sequentializability. In: Abdulla, P.A., Leino, K.R.M. (eds.) TACAS 2011. LNCS, vol. 6605, pp. 26–40. Springer, Heidelberg (2011). doi:10.1007/978-3-642-19835-9_4
8. Ghafari, N., Hu, A.J., Rakamarić, Z.: Context-bounded translations for concurrent software: an empirical evaluation. In: Pol, J., Weber, M. (eds.) Model Checking Software. LNCS, vol. 6349, pp. 227–244. Springer, Heidelberg (2010)
9. Gurfinkel, A., Kahsai, T., Komuravelli, A., Navas, J.A.: The SeaHorn verification framework. In: Kroening, D., Păsăreanu, C.S. (eds.) CAV 2015. LNCS, vol. 9206, pp. 343–361. Springer, Heidelberg (2015). doi:10.1007/978-3-319-21690-4_20
10. Heizmann, M., Christ, J., Dietsch, D., Ermis, E., Hoenicke, J., Lindenmann, M., Nutz, A., Schilling, C., Podelski, A.: Ultimate automizer with SMTInterpol - (competition contribution). In: Piterman, N., Smolka, S.A. (eds.) TACAS 2013. LNCS, vol. 7795, pp. 641–643. Springer, Heidelberg (2013). doi:10.1007/978-3-642-36742-7_53
11. Inverso, O., Nguyen, T.L., Fischer, B., La Torre, S., Parlato, G.: Lazy-CSeq: a context-bounded model checking tool for multi-threaded C-programs. In: ASE, pp. 807–812 (2015)
12. Inverso, O., Tomasco, E., Fischer, B., La Torre, S., Parlato, G.: Bounded model checking of multi-threaded C programs via lazy sequentialization. In: Biere, A., Bloem, R. (eds.) CAV 2014. LNCS, vol. 8559, pp. 585–602. Springer, Heidelberg (2014). doi:10.1007/978-3-319-08867-9_39
13. Inverso, O., Tomasco, E., Fischer, B., La Torre, S., Parlato, G.: Lazy-CSeq: a lazy sequentialization tool for C - (competition contribution). In: Havelund, K., Ábrahám, E. (eds.) TACAS 2014 (ETAPS). LNCS, vol. 8413, pp. 398–401. Springer, Heidelberg (2014)
14. La Torre, S., Madhusudan, P., Parlato, G.: Analyzing recursive programs using a fixed-point calculus. In: PLDI, pp. 211–222 (2009)
15. Torre, S., Madhusudan, P., Parlato, G.: Reducing context-bounded concurrent reachability to sequential reachability. In: Bouajjani, A., Maler, O. (eds.) CAV 2009. LNCS, vol. 5643, pp. 477–492. Springer, Heidelberg (2009). doi:10.1007/978-3-642-02658-4_36

16. La Torre, S., Madhusudan, P., Parlato, G.: Model-checking parameterized concurrent programs using linear interfaces. In: Touili, T., Cook, B., Jackson, P. (eds.) CAV 2010. LNCS, vol. 6174, pp. 629–644. Springer, Heidelberg (2010)

17. La Torre, S., Madhusudan, P., Parlato, G.: Sequentializing parameterized programs. In: FIT, pp. 34–47 (2012)

18. Lal, A., Qadeer, S., Lahiri, S.K.: A solver for reachability modulo theories. In: Madhusudan, P., Seshia, S.A. (eds.) CAV 2012. LNCS, vol. 7358, pp. 427–443. Springer, Heidelberg (2012). doi:10.1007/978-3-642-31424-7_32

19. Lal, A., Reps, T.W.: Reducing concurrent analysis under a context bound to sequential analysis. Formal Methods Syst. Des. **35**(1), 73–97 (2009)

20. Lamport, L.: A new approach to proving the correctness of multiprocess programs. ACM Trans. Program. Lang. Syst. **1**(1), 84–97 (1979)

21. Lattner, C., Adve, V.: LLVM: a compilation framework for lifelong program analysis & transformation. In: CGO, pp. 75–86. IEEE (2004)

22. Nguyen, T.L., Fischer, B., La Torre, S., Parlato, G.: Unbounded Lazy-CSeq: a lazy sequentialization tool for C programs with unbounded context switches - (competition contribution). In: Baier, C., Tinelli, C. (eds.) TACAS 2015. LNCS, vol. 9035, pp. 461–463. Springer, Heidelberg (2015)

23. Qadeer, S., Wu, D.: KISS: keep it simple and sequential. In: PLDI, pp. 14–24 (2004)

24. Rakamarić, Z., Emmi, M.: SMACK: decoupling source language details from verifier implementations. In: Biere, A., Bloem, R. (eds.) CAV 2014. LNCS, vol. 8559, pp. 106–113. Springer, Heidelberg (2014)

25. Tomasco, E., Inverso, O., Fischer, B., Torre, S., Parlato, G.: Verifying concurrent programs by memory unwinding. In: Baier, C., Tinelli, C. (eds.) TACAS 2015. LNCS, vol. 9035, pp. 551–565. Springer, Heidelberg (2015). doi:10.1007/978-3-662-46681-0_52

26. Tomasco, E., Nguyen, T.L., Inverso, O., Fischer, B., La Torre, S., Parlato, G.: Lazy sequentialization for TSO and PSO via shared memory abstractions. In: FMCAD (2016, to appear). http://eprints.soton.ac.uk/397759/

27. Wachter, B., Kroening, D., Ouaknine, J.: Verifying multi-threaded software with impact. In: FMCAD, pp. 210–217 (2013)

28. Zheng, M., Edenhofner, J.G., Luo, Z., Gerrard, M.J., Rogers, M.S., Dwyer, M.B., Siegel, S.F.: CIVL: applying a general concurrency verification framework to C/Pthreads programs (competition contribution). In: Chechik, M., Raskin, J.-F. (eds.) TACAS 2016. LNCS, vol. 9636, pp. 908–911. Springer, Heidelberg (2016)

Parallel SMT-Based Parameter Synthesis with Application to Piecewise Multi-affine Systems

Nikola Beneš, Luboš Brim, Martin Demko,
Samuel Pastva, and David Šafránek[✉]

Systems Biology Laboratory, Faculty of Informatics, Masaryk University,
Botanická 68a, 602 00 Brno, Czech Republic
{xbenes3,brim,xdemko,xpastva,xsafran1}@fi.muni.cz

Abstract. We propose a novel scalable parallel algorithm for synthesis of interdependent parameters from CTL specifications for non-linear dynamical systems. The method employs a symbolic representation of sets of parameter valuations in terms of the first-order theory of the reals. To demonstrate its practicability, we apply the method to a class of piecewise multi-affine dynamical systems representing dynamics of biological systems with complex non-linear behaviour.

1 Introduction

Complex dynamical phenomena arising in real-world systems such as biological, biophysical processes, or networks involving economic and social interactions are typically formalised by means of *dynamical systems* employing the framework of non-linear ordinary differential equations that are highly parameterised. In most cases, the model complexity and the number of *unknown parameters* do not allow to analyse the systems analytically. Computer-aided analysis of complex dynamical systems and their models is a necessary precursor for design of reliable cyber-physical and cyber-biological systems such as synthetic design and control of living cells [21,32] or safe medical treatment [1].

Phenomena occurring in the time domain of systems dynamics can be encoded in *temporal logics* (TL). TL have the advantage of rigorous and abstract representation of sequences (or even branching structures) of desired observable events in systems dynamics including quantitative bounds on time and variable values [8,10,31] and can be also combined with frequency-domain analysis [19].

In this paper, we target the problem of *global parameter synthesis* (extended with *static constraints* over parameter space). To solve the problem means to *identify parameter valuations* that *satisfy* a given set of *TL properties* universally (regardless of specific initial conditions) provided that the specified *static constraints* are also satisfied. Static constraints include *a priori* known restrictions, dependencies and correlations of individual parameter valuations (e.g., restrictions on production/degradation parameters ratio [36]).

This work has been supported by the Czech Science Foundation grant GA15-11089S.

C. Artho et al. (Eds.): ATVA 2016, LNCS 9938, pp. 192–208, 2016.
DOI: 10.1007/978-3-319-46520-3_13

In general, computationally efficient (scalable) global parameter synthesis under large uncertainty of a number of unknown parameters and unrestricted initial conditions with respect to satisfaction of a given TL specification remains a challenge. Existing techniques do not sufficiently target non-quantitative branching-time properties that can efficiently cope with *decision* events and *multi-stability* arising in complex real-world systems (e.g., existence and characteristics of unstable states in chemical or electric power systems [14,28], or reachability of multiple stable states in a biological switch [24,37]). The situation is even worse if the parameters are *interdependent*.

We introduce a novel approach to global parameter synthesis based on distributed CTL model checking. In particular, parameter synthesis for a given CTL specification and the given parameter space is solved by the coloured model checking technique [3,11] extended with symbolic encoding of parameter valuations and constraints. The main principle of our new technique relies on symbolic representation of parameters. The parameter encoding relies on the first-order theory of reals for which the satisfiability can be algorithmically solved [6]. In particular, we employ *Satisfiability Modulo Theories* (SMT) as a subprocedure wrapped inside the enumerative distributed CTL model checking algorithm. This allows for every state to synthesise a first-order formula that encodes the parameter valuations for which the CTL specification is guaranteed to be satisfied in that state. A significant advantage of employing *enumerative* CTL model checking for parameter synthesis is its capability of computing integrated information in a single parallel run. In particular, the parameter valuations are synthesised for every state and every subformula of the given CTL property. This allows to compute the parameter synthesis for a set of CTL formulae at once.

The distributed algorithm is based on assumption-based CTL model checking we have introduced in [13]. Its extension to parameter synthesis for interval-representation of parameter sets has been considered in [11]. The main drawback of that approach has been the restriction to synthesis of algebraically independent parameters. By using SMT, we significantly generalise the method to parameterisations including interdependent parameters. The new algorithm retains good scaling with increasing number of computing nodes. Since the number of calls to the SMT solver is proportional to the size of the state space, distribution of the state space and related computing tasks realise efficiently the divide&conquer paradigm while minimising the number of SMT calls and parallelising their computation on independent computing nodes.

The typical application domains for our method are highly parameterised systems appearing in systems biology (e.g., dynamics of gene regulatory networks represented by Boolean networks or non-linear continuous systems [3]) or control and verification of hybrid systems [18].

Summary of Our Contribution. The main result of this paper is a new parallel algorithm for parameter synthesis from CTL specifications for dynamical systems with *interdependent* parameters. Our method is unique in combining enumerative model checking with SMT solvers for parameter synthesis. It is distinctive in the following aspects:

1. universality – the method works on a large family of finite-state discrete dynamical systems or finite-state qualitative abstractions of continuous systems in which parameterisations can be encoded in a first-order logic over reals,
2. user feedback – the resulting parameter sets are sampled from the SMT representation and further post-processed by third-party tools such as Symba [29],
3. high-performance – the method is supplied with a parallel distributed-memory algorithm that allows good scalability in a distributed environment.

In order to evaluate our approach, we apply the method to piecewise multi-affine dynamical systems where the systems dynamics is a linear function of the parameters. In the case study we use a model of a gene regulatory network.

Related Work. Monitoring-based synthesis techniques have been developed for continuous-time and discrete-time dynamical systems [4, 10, 17, 34, 35] and linear-time TL. These techniques rely on numerical solvers which are well-developed for systems with fixed parameters or small parameter spaces (perturbations). An advantage of these techniques is that they consider the function defining the systems dynamics as a black box provided that there is basically no limitation on the form of parameterisation of the system. The main drawback is the need to sample the parameter space and initial states while losing robust guarantees for the results. This drawback can be overcome by replacing numerical solvers with Satisfiability Modulo Theories (SMT) solvers that can cope with non-linear functions and real domains up to required precision [23]. However, these techniques are limited to reachability analysis [30] and their extension to work with general TL specifications is a non-trivial task yet to be explored. The method in [16] targets reachability analysis and combines guided random exploration of the state space together with sensitivity analysis.

Existing techniques for global parameter synthesis from TL specification are either based on model checking performed directly on a qualitative finite quotient of systems dynamics [3, 7, 8, 11] or on techniques from hybrid systems [9]. Typical limitation of these methods is determined by restrictions on the form of allowed parameterisations. By employing SMT, we obtain support for all parameterisations and constraints that can be encoded in a first-order logic over reals. This is a significant improvement over our previous work [11] that has been limited to algebraically independent parameters only. In [8, 26] parameter sets are encoded symbolically in terms of polytopes allowing linear dependencies only. In [25], the authors employ symbolic bounded model checking with SMT to parameter synthesis of discrete synchronous models of weighted genetic regulatory networks. To the best of our knowledge, none of these methods have been parallelised.

In [20], the authors provide a parameter synthesis algorithm for polynomial dynamical systems based on the Bernstein polynomial representation. The approach targets discrete time dynamical systems.

2   Definitions and Problem Statement

The general setting of the parameter synthesis problem is given by the notion of a parameterised Kripke structure [3]. This notion encapsulates a family of Kripke structures with the same state space but with different transitions. The existence of transitions is governed by parameter valuations.

Definition 1. *Let* AP *be a set of atomic propositions. A parameterised Kripke structure (PKS) over* AP *is a tuple* $\mathcal{K} = (\mathcal{P}, S, I, \rightarrow, L)$ *where* $\mathcal{P}$ *is a finite set of parameter valuations, S is a finite set of states, $I \subseteq S$ is the set of initial states, $L : S \rightarrow 2^{\mathrm{AP}}$ is a labelling of the states and $\rightarrow \subseteq S \times P \times S$ is a transition relation labelled with the parameter valuations. We write $s \xrightarrow{p} t$ instead of $(s, p, t) \in \rightarrow$. We assume that the PKS is total, i.e. for all s, p there exists at least one t such that $s \xrightarrow{p} t$.*

Fixing a concrete parameter valuation $p \in \mathcal{P}$ reduces the parameterised Kripke structure $\mathcal{K}$ to a standard Kripke structure $\mathcal{K}_p = (S, I, \xrightarrow{p}, L)$. We use the notation $\mathcal{P}(s, t) = \{p \in \mathcal{P} \mid s \xrightarrow{p} t\}$ to denote the set of all parameter valuations that enable the transition from s to t. A parameterised Kripke structure can be seen as a Kripke structure with labelled transitions, where the transition labels are the sets $\mathcal{P}(s, t)$.

In the following, we assume that parameter valuations of the PKS are represented symbolically. We thus assume that we are given a (first-order) theory that is interpreted over the parameter valuations; every $\mathcal{P}(s, t)$ is then described via a formula $\Phi_{s,t}$ such that $\mathcal{P}(s, t) = \{p \in \mathcal{P} \mid p \models \Phi_{s,t}\}$. The symbolic representation of a PKS can be thus seen as a Kripke structure with labelled transitions, where the transition labels are the formulae $\Phi_{s,t}$.

To express properties of interest, we employ the standard branching time logic CTL. The formulae of CTL are defined by the following abstract syntax:

$$\varphi ::= q \mid \neg\varphi \mid \varphi_1 \wedge \varphi_2 \mid \mathbf{AX}\,\varphi \mid \mathbf{EX}\,\varphi \mid \mathbf{A}(\varphi_1 \mathbf{U} \varphi_2) \mid \mathbf{E}(\varphi_1 \mathbf{U} \varphi_2)$$

where q ranges over the atomic propositions from the set AP. We use the standard abbreviations such as $\mathbf{EF}\,\varphi \equiv \mathbf{E}(\mathbf{tt}\,\mathbf{U}\,\varphi)$ and $\mathbf{AG}\,\varphi \equiv \neg\mathbf{EF}\,\neg\varphi$.

Note that there are two sets of formulae we use here: the CTL formulae that consider the states of the PKS and the formulae that are used to symbolically describe the parameter sets in the PKS. To easily distinguish between these two kinds of formulae, we shall adopt the convention to denote CTL formulae by lower-case Greek letters φ, ψ, etc., and the parameter formulae by upper-case Greek letters Φ, Ψ, etc.

The Problem Formulation. Let $\mathcal{K} = (\mathcal{P}, S, I, \rightarrow, L)$ be a parameterised Kripke structure over AP with symbolic description as explained above and let Φ_I be an initial parameter constraint, described using the same theory as the one used in the symbolic description. Let further φ be a CTL formula over AP. The *parametric synthesis problem* is, given $\mathcal{K}$, Φ_I, and φ, to find the function $\mathcal{F}$ that assigns to every state of the Kripke structure the set of parameters that ensure the satisfaction of the CTL formula. Formally, the function is described as follows:

$$\mathcal{F}(s) = \{p \in \mathcal{P} \mid p \models \Phi_I, s \models_{\mathcal{K}_p} \varphi\}. \tag{1}$$

We extend the basic parametric synthesis problem with the possibility of an optimisation criterion, given as an objective function $f : \mathcal{P} \to \mathbb{R}$ that assigns a real value to every parameter valuation. The *parametric optimisation problem* is, given $\mathcal{K}$, Φ_I, φ, and f, to find the maximal value of f over the set $\mathcal{F}(s)$ for every state s, i.e. to find the function m satisfying $m(s) = \max\{f(p) \mid p \in \mathcal{F}(s)\}$. We are also interested in the parameter valuations that realise this maximum.

3   Parallel Algorithm

We are now going to describe the distributed-memory semi-symbolic parameter synthesis algorithm that solves the parameter synthesis problem described above, i.e. finding the function $\mathcal{F}$. The parametric optimisation problem is then solved using the result of this algorithm as an input to further tools that provide SMT optimisation, such as Symba [29]. We assume that the symbolic description of the parameters is given in a decidable first-order theory.

We adapt the assumption-based distributed CTL model checking algorithm [11,13] as the basis for our work. In this approach, the algorithm is run on a cluster of n computational nodes (workstations). Each workstation owns a part of the original PKS as defined by a partition function. This part is extended with the so called *border states*. Intuitively, border states are states that in fact belong to another computational node and represent the missing parts of the state space. They serve as a proxy between two parts.

More precisely, we define a *PKS fragment* $\mathcal{K}_i$ to be a substructure of the PKS $\mathcal{K}$ satisfying the property that every state in $\mathcal{K}_i$ has either no successor in $\mathcal{K}_i$ or it has exactly the same successors as in $\mathcal{K}$. The states without any successors in $\mathcal{K}_i$ are called the *border states* of $\mathcal{K}_i$. A partition of the PKS $\mathcal{K}$ is a finite set of PKS fragments $\mathcal{K}_1, \ldots, \mathcal{K}_n$ such that every state of $\mathcal{K}$ is present in exactly one $\mathcal{K}_i$ as a non-border state; it may be present in several other $\mathcal{K}_j$ as a border state. In fact, every border state is stored several times: as original one on the node that owns it and as duplicates on nodes that own its predecessors.

To define the semantics of CTL formulae over fragments we need to adapt the standard semantic definition. To that end, we define the notion of the truth under assumptions associated with border states. We start by recalling the notion of an assumption function of [11], itself an extension of the original assumption functions of [13]. However, as we want to deal with the parameters in a symbolic way, we then adapt the notions to our semi-symbolic setting.

For a CTL formula ψ, let $cl(\psi)$ denote the set of all subformulae of ψ and let $tcl(\psi)$ denote the set of all temporal subformulae of ψ. An *assumption function* for a parameterised Kripke structure $\mathcal{K}$ and a CTL formula ψ is defined as a partial function of type $\mathcal{A} : \mathcal{P} \times S \times cl(\psi) \to Bool$. The values $\mathcal{A}(p, s, \varphi)$ are called *assumptions*. We use the notation $\mathcal{A}(p, s, \varphi) = \bot$ to say that the value of $\mathcal{A}(p, s, \varphi)$ is undefined. By $\mathcal{A}_\bot$ we denote the assumption function which is undefined for all inputs. Intuitively, $\mathcal{A}(p, s, \varphi) = \mathtt{tt}$ if we can assume that φ holds in the state s under parameter valuation p, $\mathcal{A}(p, s, \varphi) = \mathtt{ff}$ if we can assume that φ does not hold in the state s under parameter valuation p, and $\mathcal{A}(p, s, \varphi) = \bot$ if we cannot assume anything.

Instead of working with the explicit assumption functions as described in [11], we want to deal with the parameters symbolically. We thus replace the assumption functions with *symbolic assumption functions* defined as follows. A symbolic assumption $\widetilde{\mathcal{A}}$ is a function that assigns to each pair (s, φ) a pair of formulae (Φ_t, Φ_f) such that for all $p \in \mathcal{P}$: $p \models \Phi_t$ iff $\mathcal{A}(p, s, \varphi) = \mathtt{tt}$ and $p \models \Phi_f$ iff $\mathcal{A}(p, s, \varphi) = \mathtt{ff}$. Each such function thus divides the set of all parameter valuations into three sets: those parameters that ensure the satisfaction of φ (Φ_t), those that ensure that φ is not satisfied (Φ_f), and finally those parameter valuations under which the satisfaction of φ is undefined ($\neg\Phi_t \wedge \neg\Phi_f$).

To simplify some of the notation in the algorithms below, we sometimes deal with the two parts (true and false) of the symbolic assumption function separately and use the notation $(\widetilde{\mathcal{A}}^t(s, \varphi), \widetilde{\mathcal{A}}^f(s, \varphi)) = \widetilde{\mathcal{A}}(s, \varphi)$.

The main operation of the distributed algorithm is the iterative computation of the symbolic assumption functions starting from the simplest subformulae of ψ (the atomic propositions) and moving towards ψ. The algorithm takes into account the symbolic assumptions of border states, initially set to $\bot$. The symbolic assumptions for non-temporal subformulae are easily computed as follows:

$$\widetilde{\mathcal{A}}(s, p) = (\mathtt{tt}, \mathtt{ff}) \text{ if } p \in L(s), (\mathtt{ff}, \mathtt{tt}) \text{ otherwise}$$

$$\widetilde{\mathcal{A}}(s, \varphi_1 \wedge \varphi_2) = (\widetilde{\mathcal{A}}^t(s, \varphi_1) \wedge \widetilde{\mathcal{A}}^t(s, \varphi_2), \widetilde{\mathcal{A}}^f(s, \varphi_1) \vee \widetilde{\mathcal{A}}^f(s, \varphi_2))$$

$$\widetilde{\mathcal{A}}(s, \neg\varphi) = (\widetilde{\mathcal{A}}^f(s, \varphi), \widetilde{\mathcal{A}}^t(s, \varphi))$$

The symbolic assumptions for temporal subformulae are computed via Algorithms 1, 2, and 3 . Each of these algorithms assumes that all possible assumptions for all subformulae have been already computed (given the current assumptions on border states).

Algorithm 1 computes the assumptions for temporal subformulae of the form **EX** φ (existential next). Initially, the assumption function is set to "false for all parameter valuations". Then, the algorithm iteratively collects assumptions about φ and propagates the information into predecessor states. This propagation extends the set of parameters for which the assumption is true and reduces the set of parameters for which the assumption is false. This ensures that if a state under given parameter valuation has at least one successor that satisfies φ (under the same parameter valuation), this valuation is going to be included in the true assumption formula for that state. Moreover, if all successors of a state under given parameter valuation refute φ, that valuation is going to be included in the false assumption formula for that state. Finally, if a state under given parameter valuation has no successors that satisfy φ and at least one successor whose satisfaction of φ is undefined in the current assumption, this parameter valuation is not going to be included in either the true or false assumption function.

Algorithm 2 computes the assumptions for temporal subformulae of the form $\mathbf{E}(\varphi_1 \mathbf{U} \varphi_2)$ (existential until). Initially, the assumption function for all non-border states is set to the assumption for φ_2. The propagation of assumptions works similarly to the previous case, with the two differences that (a) assumptions are only changed for states that satisfy φ_1 and (b) once a state's assumptions change, the state is returned to the queue for processing. This ensures that the assumptions propagate as much as possible. To determine whether a state's assumptions have changed, we employ the SMT-solver. The convergence of this procedure is guaranteed due to the monotonicity of the computation. As there is only a finite number of states and a finite number of parameter formulae in the system, the symbolic assumptions $\widetilde{\mathcal{A}}^t(s', \psi)$ and $\widetilde{\mathcal{A}}^f(s', \psi)$, which are build out of these parameter formulae using conjunctions and disjunctions, shall eventually reach a fixed point.

The last Algorithm 3, which computes the assumptions for temporal subformulae of the form $\mathbf{A}(\varphi_1 \mathbf{U} \varphi_2)$ (universal until), is slightly more complex. Contrary to the $\mathbf{EX}\,\varphi$ and $\mathbf{E}(\varphi_1 \mathbf{U} \varphi_2)$ cases, which required at least one successor of a state to be valid in order to add assumptions to the true part, the computation of $\mathbf{A}(\varphi_1 \mathbf{U} \varphi_2)$ needs all successor states (under given parameter valuation) to be valid. In order to ensure this, we need an auxiliary formula $\mathcal{T}(s, s')$ for each pair of states s, s'. One can see this auxiliary formula as a "copy" of the transitions in the PKS. During the propagation phase, the encountered transitions are removed from $\mathcal{T}$ and only as a parameter valuation leaves $\mathcal{T}(s', s)$ for all s, it may be added to the true assumption function. Note that the formula $\widehat{\Phi}_{s'} \wedge \bigwedge_{s' \to s} \neg \mathcal{T}(s', s)$ may be interpreted as a set difference between the set of all outgoing transitions of s' and the set of those outgoing transitions of s' that remain in $\mathcal{T}$.

We are now ready to describe the main algorithm for distributed-memory parameter synthesis. In order to compute the assumption function in the distributed environment, we iteratively compute assumption functions that are defined on fragments of the system $\mathcal{K}$. The algorithm starts by partitioning the given state space of $\mathcal{K}$ among the nodes using a partition function. There are many different partition functions that can be used; one function that is often used is random partitioning.

The main idea of the entire distributed computation, summarised in Algorithm 5, is the following. Each fragment $\mathcal{K}_i$ is managed by a separate process (node) P_i. These processes are running in parallel (simultaneously on each node). Each process P_i initialises the assumption function $\mathcal{A}_i$ to the undefined assumption function $\mathcal{A}_\perp$. After initialisation, it computes the new assumption function from the initial assumption function using the algorithms described above.

Once the algorithm has finished computing the symbolic assumptions, the node exchanges information about border states with other nodes. It sends to each other node the information it has about that node's border states and receives similar information from other nodes. After this exchange is completed, the computation is restarted. These steps are repeated until the whole network reaches a fixpoint, i.e. until no new information is computed by any node.

Algorithm 1. Compute symbolic assumptions for $\mathbf{EX}\,\varphi$

Require: PKS fragment $\mathcal{K}$, CTL formula $\psi = \mathbf{EX}\,\varphi$, initial assumptions $\widetilde{\mathcal{A}}_{in}$
Ensure: new symbolic assumptions $\widetilde{\mathcal{A}}$
   $\widetilde{\mathcal{A}} := \widetilde{\mathcal{A}}_{in}$
   set $\widetilde{\mathcal{A}}(s,\psi) := (\mathbf{ff},\mathbf{tt})$ for all non-border states s
   $init := \{(s,\Phi_t,\Phi_f) \mid \widetilde{\mathcal{A}}_{in}(s,\varphi) = (\Phi_t,\Phi_f)\}$
   for (s,Φ_t,Φ_f) **in** $init$ **do**
      for $(s',\Phi_{s',s})$ **in** $pred(s)$ **do**
         $\widetilde{\mathcal{A}}^t(s',\psi) := \widetilde{\mathcal{A}}^t(s',\psi) \vee (\Phi_t \wedge \Phi_{s',s})$
         $\widetilde{\mathcal{A}}^f(s',\psi) := \widetilde{\mathcal{A}}^f(s',\psi) \wedge (\Phi_f \vee \neg\Phi_{s',s}))$

Algorithm 2. Compute symbolic assumptions for $\mathbf{E}(\varphi_1\,\mathbf{U}\,\varphi_2)$

Require: PKS fragment $\mathcal{K}$, CTL formula $\psi = \mathbf{E}(\varphi_1\,\mathbf{U}\,\varphi_2)$, initial assumptions $\widetilde{\mathcal{A}}_{in}$
Ensure: new symbolic assumptions $\widetilde{\mathcal{A}}$
   $\widetilde{\mathcal{A}} := \widetilde{\mathcal{A}}_{in}$
   set $\widetilde{\mathcal{A}}(s,\psi) := \widetilde{\mathcal{A}}_{in}(s,\varphi_2)$ for all non-border states s
   $queue := S$ (all states)
   while $queue$ not empty **do**
      select and remove s from $queue$
      for $(s',\Phi_{s',s})$ **in** $pred(s)$ **do**
         $\widetilde{\mathcal{A}}^t(s',\psi) := \widetilde{\mathcal{A}}^t(s',\psi) \vee \left(\widetilde{\mathcal{A}}^t(s',\varphi_1) \wedge \widetilde{\mathcal{A}}^t(s,\psi) \wedge \Phi_{s',s} \right)$
         $\widetilde{\mathcal{A}}^f(s',\psi) := \widetilde{\mathcal{A}}^f(s'\psi) \wedge \left(\widetilde{\mathcal{A}}^f(s',\varphi_1) \vee \widetilde{\mathcal{A}}^f(s,\psi) \vee \neg\Phi_{s',s} \right)$
         if $\widetilde{\mathcal{A}}(s',\psi)$ was changed and $s' \notin queue$ **then**
            add s' to $queue$

Algorithm 3. Compute symbolic assumptions for $\mathbf{A}(\varphi_1\,\mathbf{U}\,\varphi_2)$

Require: PKS fragment $\mathcal{K}$, CTL formula $\psi = \mathbf{A}(\varphi_1\,\mathbf{U}\,\varphi_2)$, initial assumptions $\widetilde{\mathcal{A}}_{in}$
Ensure: new symbolic assumptions $\widetilde{\mathcal{A}}$
   $\widetilde{\mathcal{A}} := \widetilde{\mathcal{A}}_{in}$
   for all non-border states s **do**
      $\widehat{\Phi}_s := \bigvee_{s \to s'} \Phi_{s,s'}$
      set $\widetilde{\mathcal{A}}^t(s,\psi) := \widetilde{\mathcal{A}}^t(s,\varphi_2)$
      set $\widetilde{\mathcal{A}}^f(s,\psi) := (\widetilde{\mathcal{A}}^f(s,\varphi_1) \vee \neg\widehat{\Phi}_s) \wedge \neg\widetilde{\mathcal{A}}^t(s,\varphi_2)$
   $T(s,s') := \Phi_{s,s'}$ for all $s \to s'$
   $queue := S$ (all states)
   while $queue$ not empty **do**
      select and remove s from $queue$
      for $(s',\Phi_{s',s})$ **in** $pred(s)$ **do**
         $T(s',s) := T(s',s) \wedge \neg\widetilde{\mathcal{A}}^t(s,\psi)$
         $\widetilde{\mathcal{A}}^t(s',\psi) := \widetilde{\mathcal{A}}^t(s',\psi) \vee \left(\widetilde{\mathcal{A}}^t(s',\varphi_1) \wedge \widehat{\Phi}_{s'} \wedge \bigwedge_{s' \to s} \neg T(s',s) \right)$
         $\widetilde{\mathcal{A}}^f(s',\psi) := \widetilde{\mathcal{A}}^f(s',\psi) \vee \left(\widetilde{\mathcal{A}}^f(s,\psi) \wedge \neg\widetilde{\mathcal{A}}^t(s',\psi) \wedge \Phi_{s',s} \right)$
         if $\widetilde{\mathcal{A}}(s',\psi)$ was changed and $s' \notin queue$ **then**
            add s' to $queue$

Algorithm 4. Solve cycles

Require: PKS fragment $\mathcal{K}$, CTL formula ψ, initial assumptions $\widetilde{\mathcal{A}}_{in}$
Ensure: new symbolic assumptions $\widetilde{\mathcal{A}}$
  $\mathcal{M}_s := \mathbf{tt}$ for all non-border states s
  for $\varphi \in tcl(\psi)$ {sorted from smallest} **do**
    for $s \in S$ **do**
      $\mathcal{U} := \mathcal{M}_s \wedge \neg\widetilde{\mathcal{A}}^t(s,\varphi) \wedge \neg\widetilde{\mathcal{A}}^f(s,\varphi)$
      $\widetilde{\mathcal{A}}^f(s,\varphi) := \widetilde{\mathcal{A}}^f(s,\varphi) \vee \mathcal{U}$
      $\mathcal{M}_s := \mathcal{M}_s \wedge \neg\mathcal{U}$

Algorithm 5. Main Idea of the Distributed Algorithm

Require: parameterised KS $\mathcal{K}$, CTL formula ψ, function f
Ensure: $\mathcal{F}$
  Partition $\mathcal{K}$ into $\mathcal{K}_1, \ldots, \mathcal{K}_n$
  for all $\mathcal{K}_i$ where $i \in \{1, \ldots, n\}$ **do in parallel**
    Take the initial assumption function
    repeat
      repeat
        Compute the new assumptions using the node algorithms (Alg. 1, 2, 3)
        Exchange relevant information with other nodes
      until all processes reach fixpoint
      Modify the assumption function to deal with cycles (Alg. 4)
    until everything is computed

Once the fixpoint is reached, there is additional computation to be made, as there still may be undefined assumptions left. This may happen in the case of the two *until* operators **EU**, **AU**; for more details see [13]. The minimal undefined assumptions are found and set to $\mathbf{ff}$, as described in Algorithm 4, and the computation is again restarted. These steps are repeated until a fixpoint is reached and no new assumptions are set in Algorithm 4.

It remains to explain the way of dealing with the initial parameter constraint Φ_I. The initial parameter constraint is orthogonal to the whole computation and we could, in principle, intersect the symbolic true assumptions with Φ_I after the distributed algorithm is finished. However, to prune the search space and speed up the computation somewhat, we intersect the symbolic assumption functions with Φ_I whenever we pass them to the SMT solver (i.e. whenever we need to know whether a symbolic assumption has changed).

Although the node algorithms have been (for clarity) formulated as recomputing everything in each iteration, this is of course unnecessary and we only recompute the part of assumption functions that have been computed as undefined ($\perp$) in the previous iteration. Formally, we restrict the computation of $\widetilde{\mathcal{A}}(s,\psi)$ to $\neg\widetilde{\mathcal{A}}^t_{in}(s,\psi) \wedge \neg\widetilde{\mathcal{A}}^f_{in}(s,\psi)$.

4 Application to Piecewise Multi-affine ODE Models

Let $\mathbb{P} \subseteq \mathbb{R}^m_{\geq 0}$ denote the *continuous parameter space* of dimension m. A parameterised piecewise multi-affine ODE model (PMA) is given by a system of ODEs of the form $\dot{x} = f(x, \mu)$ where $x = (x_1, \ldots, x_n) \in \mathbb{R}^n_{\geq 0}$ is a vector of variables, $\mu = (\mu_1, \ldots, \mu_m) \in \mathbb{P}$ is a vector of parameters, and $\bar{f} = (f_1, \ldots, f_n)$ is a vector of functions that satisfy the criterion that every f_i is piecewise multi-affine in x and affine in μ.

To approximate the PMA model with its finite quotient represented in terms of a discrete state-transition system, we employ the rectangular abstraction defined in [8] and further adapted in [3,12,26] (see [15] for overview).

We assume there is given a set of thresholds $\{\theta^i_1, \ldots, \theta^i_{n_i}\}$ for each variable x_i satisfying $\theta^i_1 < \theta^i_2 < \cdots < \theta^i_{n_i}$. Each f_i is assumed to be multi-affine on each n-dimensional interval $[\theta^1_{j_1}, \theta^1_{j_1+1}] \times \cdots \times [\theta^n_{j_n}, \theta^n_{j_n+1}]$. We call these intervals rectangles. Each rectangle is uniquely identified via an n-tuple of indices: $R(j_1, \ldots, j_n) = [\theta^1_{j_1}, \theta^1_{j_1+1}] \times \cdots \times [\theta^n_{j_n}, \theta^n_{j_n+1}]$, where the range of each j_i is $\{1, \ldots, n_i - 1\}$. We also define $VR(j_1, \ldots, j_n)$ to be the set of all vertices of $R(j_1, \ldots, j_n)$.

In order to establish a finite rectangular abstraction of the PMA model, special care has to be given to boundary rectangles. A boundary rectangle is any rectangle $R(j_1, \ldots, j_n)$ where for some i either $j_i = 1$ or $j_i = n_i - 1$. Any dimension i satisfying that condition is called a boundary dimension of $R(j_1, \ldots, j_n)$. We restrict ourselves to models where the dynamics is bounded in the range specified by lower and upper thresholds – trajectories cannot exit that range (note that this could occur only in boundary rectangles). Formally, all trajectories determined by the PMA model are required to keep $x_i \in [\theta^i_1, \theta^i_{n_i}]$. We restrict ourselves to parameter spaces where this requirement is satisfied for all parameter valuations. More precisely, for every boundary rectangle $R(j_1, \ldots, j_n)$ we assume that for all $\mu \in \mathbb{P}, i \in \{1, \ldots, n\}, x \in R(j_1, \ldots, j_n)$ it holds that $(j_i = 1 \wedge x_i = \theta^i_1) \Rightarrow f_i(x, \mu) > 0$ and $(j_i = n_i - 1 \wedge x_i = \theta^i_{n_i}) \Rightarrow f_i(x, \mu) < 0$.

In [15] it has been shown that rectangular abstraction is conservative with respect to almost all trajectories of the original (continuous) PMA model. In particular, almost every continuous trajectory in the PMA model is covered by a corresponding sequence of rectangles in its rectangular abstraction. However, there may exist a sequence of rectangles for which there is no corresponding continuous trajectory in the original PMA model.

The rectangular abstraction is encoded as a PKS $\mathcal{K} = (\mathbb{P}, S, I, \rightarrow, L)$ with $S = \{(j_1, \ldots, j_n) \mid \forall i : 1 \leq j_i \leq n_i\}$ where each $\alpha \in S$ represents the rectangle $R(\alpha)$. Let now $\alpha = (j_1, \ldots, j_n) \in S$, $1 \leq i \leq n$ and $d \in \{-1, +1\}$. We define $\alpha^{i,d} = (j_1, \ldots, j_i+d, \ldots, j_n)$ (if j_i+d is in the valid range). Thus $\alpha^{i,d}$ describe all the neighbouring rectangles of α. We further define $v^{i,+1}(\alpha) = VR(\alpha) \cap \{(\ldots, j_i + 1, \ldots)\}$ and $v^{i,-1}(\alpha) = VR(\alpha) \cap \{(\ldots, j_i, \ldots)\}$. To define the transition relation $\rightarrow$, every pair of states $\alpha, \alpha^{i,d} \in S$, $1 \leq i \leq n$, $d \in \{-1, 1\}$, is associated with a formula $\Phi_{\alpha, \alpha^{i,d}}$ symbolically encoding the set of parameter valuations $\mu \in \mathbb{P}$ for which the transition $\alpha \rightarrow \alpha^{i,d}$ is valid:

$$\Phi_{\alpha,\alpha^{i,d}} := \bigvee_{v \in v^{i,d}(\alpha)} d \cdot f_i(v,\mu) > 0 \tag{2}$$

Additionally, the rectangular abstraction approximates the potential existence of a fixed point in any rectangle $\alpha \in S$. This is achieved by means of introducing a self-transition $\alpha \rightarrow \alpha$ [8]. In particular, a self-transition is valid in a state $\alpha \in S$ for all parameter valuations $\mu \in \mathbb{P}$ satisfying $\mathbf{0} \in hull\{f(v,\mu) \mid v \in VR(\alpha)\}$ (the zero vector included in the convex hull of the rectangle vertices). This is symbolically encoded by the formula $\Phi_{\alpha,\alpha}$ defined in the following way:

$$\Phi_{\alpha,\alpha} := \exists c_1,\ldots,c_k : \left(\bigwedge_{i=1}^{k} c_i \geq 0 \right) \wedge \left(\sum_{i=1}^{k} c_i = 1 \right) \wedge \left(\sum_{i=1}^{k} c_i \cdot f(v_i,\mu) = 0 \right) \tag{3}$$

where $k = |VR(\alpha)|$ is the number of vertices of the rectangle α.

To express properties of rectangular abstraction dynamics, the atomic propositions are set to represent concentration inequalities, $AP = \{x_i \odot \theta_j^i \mid 1 \leq i \leq n, 1 \leq j \leq n_i\}, \odot \in \{\leq, \geq\}\}$. States of the PKS are labelled with the adequate constraints of AP. To partition the state space into PKS fragments, we utilise the regular structure of the state space as described in [27]. Note that the PKS constructed by the rectangular abstraction is always total.

5   Experimental Evaluation

We have implemented the distributed algorithm from Sect. 3 in a prototype tool written in Java using the MPJ Express implementation of MPI [2] and the Z3 SMT solver via its Java API [33]. In this section we report on experiments demonstrating scalability and practicability of our approach on case studies of two well-known biological systems.

In order to minimise computational overhead caused by calling Z3 on first-order SMT formulae with quantifiers constructed during the computation, we employ a simplification of abstraction of piecewise multi-affine systems that has been introduced in [3]. In particular, the non-trivial formula (3) representing the convex hull of vectors in rectangle vertices gives a minimal overapproximation of self-transitions by excluding a zero vector from linear combination of rectangle vertices vectors. This formula is replaced with a quantifier-free formula giving a coarser overapproximation:

$$\Phi_{\alpha,\alpha} := \neg \bigvee_{1 \leq i \leq n} \left((\Phi_{\alpha^{i,-1},\alpha} \wedge \Phi_{\alpha,\alpha^{i,+1}} \wedge \neg\Phi_{\alpha,\alpha^{i,-1}} \wedge \neg\Phi_{\alpha^{i,+1},\alpha}) \right.$$
$$\left. \vee \, (\neg\Phi_{\alpha^{i,-1},\alpha} \wedge \neg\Phi_{\alpha,\alpha^{i,+1}} \wedge \Phi_{\alpha,\alpha^{i,-1}} \wedge \Phi_{\alpha^{i,+1},\alpha}) \right)$$

In particular, we exclude self-transitions only in rectangles where there exists a dimension i in which the flow is guaranteed to be one-directional. More specifically, there is either the pair of transitions $\alpha^{i,-1} \rightarrow \alpha \rightarrow \alpha^{i,+1}$ or the pair of transitions $\alpha^{i,+1} \rightarrow \alpha \rightarrow \alpha^{i,-1}$ provided that the respective two transitions are the only transitions allowed in ith dimension through the rectangle α. This situation implies that the zero vector is not included in the convex hull of the rectangle vertices (its ith component must be non-zero). The condition is only necessary thus this simplification increases occurrence of spurious self-loops.

5.1   Case Study I: Repressilator

To demonstrate the scalability of the algorithm, we consider a PMA model of
the repressilator [12]. It is an approximation of the original model of a genetic
regulatory network representing a set of genes mutually inhibited in a closed
circle [22].

On this model, we evaluate the scalability of the algorithm from Sect. 3 on
a homogeneous cluster with 16 nodes each equipped with 16 GB of RAM and
a quad-core Intel Xeon 2 GHz processor. The analysis is provided according to the
number of states in combination with one independent and two interdependent
parameters, respectively. The considered property is $\mathbf{AG}\,\varphi$ where φ is an atomic
proposition specifying a particular subset of states.

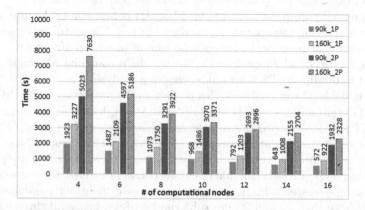

Fig. 1. Scalability achieved for two models approximating the repressilator system:
a rough model of the size $90 \cdot 10^3$ states and a refined model of the size $160 \cdot 10^3$ states.
Variants 1P represent analyses with a single uncertain parameter whereas variants 2P
reflect results achieved for two uncertain mutually dependent parameters. (Color figure
online)

5.2   Case Study II: Regulation of G_1/S Cell Cycle Transition

To demonstrate the applicability, we employ our approach on a non-linear ODE
model [37] describing a two-gene regulatory network of interactions between
the tumour suppressor protein pRB and the central transcription factor $E2F1$
(Fig. 2 (left)). For suitable parameter valuations, two distinct stable attractors
may exist (the so-called *bistability*). In [37], the authors have provided numerical
bifurcation analysis of $E2F1$ stable concentration depending on the degradation
parameter of pRB (ϕ_{pRB}). Note that traditional methods for bifurcation analysis
hardly scale to more than a single parameter.

We demonstrate that our algorithm can overcome some of the drawbacks of
numerical methods. In particular, we focus on synthesis of values of two interdependent model parameters with respect to satisfaction of the bistability property.

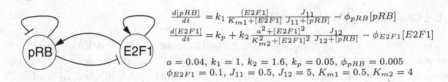

$$\frac{d[pRB]}{dt} = k_1 \frac{[E2F1]}{K_{m1}+[E2F1]} \frac{J_{11}}{J_{11}+[pRB]} - \phi_{pRB}[pRB]$$

$$\frac{d[E2F1]}{dt} = k_p + k_2 \frac{a^2+[E2F1]^2}{K_{m2}^2+[E2F1]^2} \frac{J_{12}}{J_{12}+[pRB]} - \phi_{E2F1}[E2F1]$$

$a = 0.04,\ k_1 = 1,\ k_2 = 1.6,\ k_p = 0.05,\ \phi_{pRB} = 0.005$
$\phi_{E2F1} = 0.1,\ J_{11} = 0.5,\ J_{12} = 5,\ K_{m1} = 0.5,\ K_{m2} = 4$

Fig. 2. G_1/S transition regulatory network (left) and its ODE model with default values according to [37] (right).

We deal with the degradation parameter ϕ_{pRB} and the production parameter of pRB (k_1). Additionally, we perform post-processing of achieved results by employing additional constraints on the parameter space (i.e., imposing a lower and upper bound on the production/degradation parameter ratio).

The original non-linear model (Fig. 2 (right)) is first converted into a PMA model by employing the approach introduced in [26]. This involves replacement of each non-linear function by an optimal sum of piecewise affine segments (40 segments for pRB and 20 for $E2F1$). Finally, the rectangular abstraction [8] is employed to obtain the PKS for model checking analysis.

The model has been analysed with respect to the properties $\varphi_1 = (\textbf{AG low})$, $\varphi_2 = (\textbf{AG high})$ and $\varphi_3 = (\textbf{EF AG low} \wedge \textbf{EF AG high})$ where $\texttt{low} = (E2F1 > 0.5 \wedge E2F1 < 2.5)$ (representing safe cell behaviour) and $\texttt{high} = (E2F1 > 4 \wedge E2F1 < 7.5)$ (representing excessive cell division). Both properties φ_1 (resp. φ_2) describe the presence and stability of low (resp. high) state and are guaranteed by the rectangular abstraction due to its conservativeness. More specifically, synthesised parameter valuations underapproximate the exact parameter valuation set. Note that φ_1 and φ_2 are subformulae of φ_3, hence all three formulae have been verified in a single run due to the principle of Algorithm 5.

The property φ_3 expresses the possibility of reaching both stable states from a given (initial) state. Such a state thus represents a decision point in the system dynamics. Due to the mixing of existential and universal quantifiers, the property is not preserved by the rectangular abstraction and can thus only be used for estimation (detailed numerical investigation needs to be employed further in the significantly restricted area of the parameter space).

The output of parameter synthesis follows Eq. (1), in particular, we obtain a table of all states satisfying a particular property provided that every state is accompanied with a synthesised constraint on the parameters. Technically, the constraints are given in the SMT-LIB format 2.5 [5]. Consequently, in order to compare and visualise satisfactory parameter valuations in a human-readable form the obtained results have to be further post-processed. The valid area of the parameter space can be visualised by solving the obtained constraints in sampled points. In Fig. 3 (up left), the parameter space with areas constrained by each of the three formulae is depicted (reachability of bistability is shown in *green*; $\texttt{low}$ and $\texttt{high}$ stable states are shown in *blue* and *red*, respectively).

Additionally, we can employ a static constraint $\Phi_I := \alpha < \frac{k_1}{\Phi_{pRB}} < \beta$ to restrict the resulting parameter space to a desired range of the

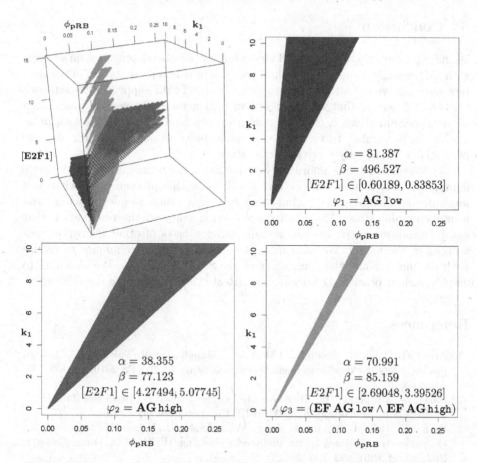

Fig. 3. Parameter space of G_1/S gene regulatory network. Each area meets the respective property: φ_1 (blue), φ_2 (red) and φ_3 (green). (Upper left) Valid parameter spaces sampled for arbitrary initial concentration of $E2F1$ (from 0 to 15 AU). (Other figures) Areas displaying valid ranges of the production/degradation ratio for respective formulae, computed by optimisation. Every figure displays the result for a distinct initial state of $E2F1$. Values of α and β were computed by optimisation. They represent the minimal (α) and maximal (β) ratio $\frac{k1}{\Phi_{pRB}}$ satisfying the particular property.

production/degradation parameters ratio. Moreover, we can use an SMT-based optimisation tool to solve a parametric optimisation problem to find a maximal bound α and a minimal bound β satisfying Φ_I. In our case we employ the tool Symba [29] to compute an over- (resp. under-) approximation of α (resp. β). The achieved ranges of parameters ratio that guarantee the respective formulae are shown in Fig. 3.

6   Conclusion

We have presented a novel parallel algorithm for parameter synthesis on systems with CTL specifications. The method uses a symbolic representation of parameters and employs the satisfiability modulo theories (SMT) approach to deal with first-order formulae that represent sets of parameters. The general description of the algorithm allows it to be used with various families of systems with parameters. In particular, to evaluate the applicability of our algorithm, we have presented a biologically motivated case study.

While evaluating our algorithm we have found the bottleneck to be the large number of calls to the SMT solver. To alleviate this problem somewhat, our implementation uses some optimisation techniques such as query caching and formula simplification. The main simplification relies on the observation that many transition constraints are actually strict subsets of other transition constraints in the model. We plan to explore more of these techniques to reduce both the number and the complexity of the SMT solver calls. We also plan to employ various other SMT solvers, e.g. dReal [23], and compare the efficiency.

References

1. Arney, D., Pajic, M., Goldman, J.M., Lee, I., Mangharam, R., Sokolsky, O.: Toward patient safety in closed-loop medical device systems. In: ICCPS 2010, pp. 139–148. ACM (2010)
2. Baker, M., Carpenter, B., Shafi, A.: MPJ express: towards thread safe Java HPC. In: IEEE Cluster Computing 2006. IEEE Computer Society (2006)
3. Barnat, J., Brim, L., Krejčí, A., Streck, A., Šafránek, D., Vejnár, M., Vejpustek, T.: On parameter synthesis by parallel model checking. IEEE/ACM Trans. Comput. Biol. Bioinf. **9**(3), 693–705 (2012)
4. Barnat, J., Brim, L., Šafránek, D.: High-performance analysis of biological systems dynamics with the divine model checker. Brief. Bioinf. **11**(3), 301–312 (2010)
5. Barrett, C., Fontaine, P., Tinelli, C.: The SMT-LIB standard: version 2.5. Technical report, Department of Computer Science, The University of Iowa (2015)
6. Basu, S., Pollack, R., Roy, M.F.: Algorithms in Real Algebraic Geometry (Algorithms and Computation in Mathematics). Springer-Verlag New York Inc, Secaucus (2006)
7. Batt, G., Page, M., Cantone, I., Gössler, G., Monteiro, P., de Jong, H.: Efficient parameter search for qualitative models of regulatory networks using symbolic model checking. Bioinformatics **26**(18), 603–610 (2010)
8. Batt, G., Yordanov, B., Weiss, R., Belta, C.: Robustness analysis and tuning of synthetic gene networks. Bioinformatics **23**(18), 2415–2422 (2007)
9. Bogomolov, S., Schilling, C., Bartocci, E., Batt, G., Kong, H., Grosu, R.: Abstraction-based parameter synthesis for multiaffine systems. In: Piterman, N., et al. (eds.) HVC 2015. LNCS, vol. 9434, pp. 19–35. Springer, Heidelberg (2015). doi:10.1007/978-3-319-26287-1_2
10. Brim, L., Dluhoš, P., Šafránek, D., Vejpustek, T.: STL*: extending signal temporal logic with signal-value freezing operator. Inf. Comput. **236**, 52–67 (2014). Special Issue on Hybrid Systems and Biology

11. Brim, L., Češka, M., Demko, M., Pastva, S., Šafránek, D.: Parameter synthesis by parallel coloured CTL model checking. In: Roux, O., Bourdon, J. (eds.) CMSB 2015. LNCS, vol. 9308, pp. 251–263. Springer, Heidelberg (2015)
12. Brim, L., Demko, M., Pastva, S., Šafránek, D.: High-performance discrete bifurcation analysis for piecewise-affine dynamical systems. In: Abate, A., et al. (eds.) HSB 2015. LNCS, vol. 9271, pp. 58–74. Springer, Heidelberg (2015). doi:10.1007/978-3-319-26916-0_4
13. Brim, L., Yorav, K., Žídková, J.: Assumption-based distribution of CTL model checking. STTT 7(1), 61–73 (2005)
14. Chiang, H.D., Wang, T.: On the number and types of unstable equilibria in nonlinear dynamical systems with uniformly-bounded stability regions. IEEE Trans. Autom. Control 61(2), 485–490 (2016)
15. Collins, P., Habets, L.C., van Schuppen, J.H., Černá, I., Fabriková, J., Šafránek, D.: Abstraction of biochemical reaction systems on polytopes. In: IFAC World Congress. pp. 14869–14875. IFAC (2011)
16. Dang, T., Donze, A., Maler, O., Shalev, N.: Sensitive state-space exploration. In: IEEE Conference on Decision and Control, pp. 4049–4054 (2008)
17. Donzé, A., Fanchon, E., Gattepaille, L.M., Maler, O., Tracqui, P.: Robustness analysis and behavior discrimination in enzymatic reaction networks. PLoS ONE 6(9), e24246 (2011)
18. Donzé, A., Krogh, B., Rajhans, A.: Parameter synthesis for hybrid systems with an application to simulink models. In: Majumdar, R., Tabuada, P. (eds.) HSCC 2009. LNCS, vol. 5469, pp. 165–179. Springer, Heidelberg (2009)
19. Donzé, A., Maler, O., Bartocci, E., Nickovic, D., Grosu, R., Smolka, S.: On temporal logic and signal processing. In: Chakraborty, S., Mukund, M. (eds.) ATVA 2012. LNCS, vol. 7561, pp. 92–106. Springer, Heidelberg (2012)
20. Dreossi, T., Dang, T.: Parameter synthesis for polynomial biological models. In: Proceedings of the 17th International Conference on Hybrid Systems: Computation and Control, HSCC 2014, pp. 233–242 (2014)
21. Dvorak, P., Chrast, L., Nikel, P.I., Fedr, R., Soucek, K., Sedlackova, M., Chaloupkova, R., Lorenzo, V., Prokop, Z., Damborsky, J.: Exacerbation of substrate toxicity by IPTG in Escherichia coli BL21(DE3) carrying a synthetic metabolic pathway. Microb. Cell Fact. 14(1), 1–15 (2015)
22. Elowitz, M.B., Leibler, S.: A synthetic oscillatory network of transcriptional regulators. Nature 403(6767), 335–338 (2000)
23. Gao, S., Kong, S., Clarke, E.M.: dReal: an SMT solver for nonlinear theories over the reals. In: Bonacina, M.P. (ed.) CADE 2013. LNCS, vol. 7898, pp. 208–214. Springer, Heidelberg (2013)
24. Gardner, T.S., Cantor, C.R., Collins, J.J.: Construction of a genetic toggle switch in Escherichia coli. Nature 403, 339–342 (1999)
25. Giacobbe, M., Guet, C.C., Gupta, A., Henzinger, T.A., Paixão, T., Petrov, T.: Model checking gene regulatory networks. In: Baier, C., Tinelli, C. (eds.) TACAS 2015. LNCS, vol. 9035, pp. 469–483. Springer, Heidelberg (2015)
26. Grosu, R., Batt, G., Fenton, F.H., Glimm, J., Le Guernic, C., Smolka, S.A., Bartocci, E.: From cardiac cells to genetic regulatory networks. In: Gopalakrishnan, G., Qadeer, S. (eds.) CAV 2011. LNCS, vol. 6806, pp. 396–411. Springer, Heidelberg (2011)
27. Jha, S., Shyamasundar, R.K.: Adapting biochemical kripke structures for distributed model checking. In: Priami, C., Ingólfsdóttir, A., Mishra, B., Riis Nielson, H. (eds.) Transactions on Computational Systems Biology VII. LNCS (LNBI), vol. 4230, pp. 107–122. Springer, Heidelberg (2006)

28. Li, W., Zhong, L., He, Y., Meng, J., Yao, F., Guo, Y., Xu, C.: Multiple steady-states analysis and unstable operating point stabilization in homogeneous azeotropic distillation with intermediate entrainer. Ind. Eng. Chem. Res. **54**(31), 7668–7686 (2015)

29. Li, Y., Albarghouthi, A., Kincaid, Z., Gurfinkel, A., Chechik, M.: Symbolic optimization with SMT solvers. In: POPL 2014, pp. 607–618. ACM (2014)

30. Madsen, C., Shmarov, F., Zuliani, P.: BioPSy: an SMT-based tool for guaranteed parameter set synthesis of biological models. In: Roux, O., Bourdon, J. (eds.) CMSB 2015. LNCS, vol. 9308, pp. 182–194. Springer, Heidelberg (2015)

31. Maler, O., Nickovic, D.: Monitoring temporal properties of continuous signals. In: Lakhnech, Y., Yovine, S. (eds.) FORMATS 2004 and FTRTFT 2004. LNCS, vol. 3253, pp. 152–166. Springer, Heidelberg (2004)

32. Milias-Argeitis, A., Engblom, S., Bauer, P., Khammash, M.: Stochastic focusing coupled with negative feedback enables robust regulation in biochemical reaction networks. J. R. Soc. Interface **12**(113), 20150831 (2015)

33. de Moura, L., Bjørner, N.S.: Z3: an efficient SMT solver. In: Ramakrishnan, C.R., Rehof, J. (eds.) TACAS 2008. LNCS, vol. 4963, pp. 337–340. Springer, Heidelberg (2008)

34. Raman, V., Donzé, A., Sadigh, D., Murray, R.M., Seshia, S.A.: Reactive synthesis from signal temporal logic specifications. In: HSCC 2015, pp. 239–248. ACM (2015)

35. Rizk, A., Batt, G., Fages, F., Soliman, S.: A general computational method for robustness analysis with applications to synthetic gene networks. Bioinformatics **25**(12), i169–i178 (2009)

36. Rosenfeld, N., Alon, U.: Response delays and the structure of transcription networks. J. Mol. Biol. **329**(4), 645–654 (2003)

37. Swat, M., Kel, A., Herzel, H.: Bifurcation analysis of the regulatory modules of the mammalian G1/S transition. Bioinformatics **20**(10), 1506–1511 (2004)

Complexity, Decidability

On Finite Domains in First-Order Linear Temporal Logic

Denis Kuperberg[1], Julien Brunel[2(✉)], and David Chemouil[2]

[1] TU Munich, Munich, Germany
[2] DTIM, Université fédérale de Toulouse, ONERA, Toulouse, France
julien.brunel@onera.fr

Abstract. We consider First-Order Linear Temporal Logic (FO-LTL) over linear time. Inspired by the success of formal approaches based upon finite-model finders, such as Alloy, we focus on finding models with finite first-order domains for FO-LTL formulas, while retaining an infinite time domain. More precisely, we investigate the complexity of the following problem: given a formula φ and an integer n, is there a model of φ with domain of cardinality at most n? We show that depending on the logic considered (FO or FO-LTL) and on the precise encoding of the problem, the problem is either NP-complete, NEXPTIME-complete, PSPACE-complete or EXPSPACE-complete. In a second part, we exhibit cases where the Finite Model Property can be lifted from fragments of FO to their FO-LTL extension.

Keywords: FO · LTL · Finite model property · Bounded satisfiability · Fragments

1 Introduction

1.1 Context

First-Order Logic (FO) has proven to be useful in numerous applications in computer science such as formal specification, databases, ontology languages, etc. It is particularly well-suited to reason about objects of a domain, their relations and the properties they satisfy. However, since "full" FO is undecidable, the formal *verification* of properties implies a relaxation of the problem *e.g.* considering less expressive fragments. Thus, one can restrict the specification language (*e.g.* Prolog) or impose some form of interaction for verification (*e.g.* theorem provers, proof assistants).

Another form of trade-off is to keep the whole logic and full automation but to rely on a sound but incomplete decision procedure. For instance, the Alloy Analyzer[1] for the Alloy [10] language (based upon relational first-order logic)

Research partly funded by ANR/DGA project Cx (ref. ANR-13-ASTR-0006) and by *fondation STAE* project BRIefcaSE.

[1] Available at http://alloy.mit.edu/alloy.

C. Artho et al. (Eds.): ATVA 2016, LNCS 9938, pp. 211–226, 2016.
DOI: 10.1007/978-3-319-46520-3_14

implements a *bounded-satisfiability* decision procedure. That is, the tool relies on a *finite-model finder*: it first bounds the number of objects in the domain and then runs a classical propositional SAT procedure [19]. Thanks to the performance of modern SAT engines, this approach has shown to be very efficient in practice to find counterexamples quickly when assessing specifications. This is one of the reasons for the success of Alloy, in the formal methods community [3,17,21].

However, in most software and systems specifications, one needs to represent the evolution of modeled entities along time. In Alloy, the common way to do so is to model time by adding a specific set of time instants [10], by giving axioms describing its structure (as traces for instance) and by adding an extra time parameter to every dynamic predicate. This is tedious and cumbersome, if not error-prone.

This shortcoming has long been identified and several propositions [7,16,20] have been made to extend Alloy with facilities for fancier modeling of *behavior*. Still, in all these approaches, the verification remains bounded (because the set of instants is, for instance). [6] makes a step further by implementing a bounded model-checking approach in Alloy allowing time loops. However, up to our knowledge, no Alloy extension leverages a temporal logic, such as LTL for instance, that enjoys a complete decision procedure. The idea of adding temporal logic to FO has been implemented in the tool TLA$^+$ [12], where the FO signature is that of ZFC, instead of the arbitrary signatures allowed in Alloy. These remarks led us to study the combination of FO and LTL, in particular to draw questions about the relation between the satisfiability of a FO-LTL formula and the fact that the first-order part of the model is finite. In the literature, the logic FO-LTL has drawn a lot of interest, for decidability questions as well as in database theory [2]. For instance [8,9] study decidable fragments, while [11,15] give incompleteness results.

1.2   Contributions

The first question we address here is that of the complexity of satisfiability for FO and FO-LTL when the FO part of the model is bounded (we call this problem BSAT(N) for a given bound N). We are interested in the cost in terms of algorithmic complexity of adding an LTL component to the FO specification language. In Sect. 3, we consider BSAT for FO and FO-LTL depending on whether the quantifier rank (*i.e.* the maximum number of nested quantifiers) of formulas is bounded and whether the bound on the domain is given in unary or binary encoding.

- For pure FO, BSAT(N) is NP-complete if the rank is bounded and if N is given in unary; NEXPTIME-complete otherwise. This case can admittedly be considered *folklore* but it seems it has not been published formally, so we detail it in the paper for the sake of completeness. We also provide detailed results, showing that formulas of rank 2 with unary predicates are sufficient for NEXPTIME-completeness.

– For FO-LTL, which has been less studied from the point of view of BSAT, we show that this division goes the same except that BSAT is PSPACE-complete in the first case and EXPSPACE-complete otherwise (recall that satisfiability for LTL alone is PSPACE-complete [14,18]). Again, rank 2 formulas with unary predicates are sufficient.

Secondly, since we are only interested in finite models of FO-LTL formulas, it is natural to study which fragments of FO-LTL enjoy the *finite model property* (FMP). Recall that a formula has the FMP if the existence of a model implies the existence of a *finite* one. Many fragments of FO have been shown to enjoy the FMP in the past decades [1,4].

– In Sect. 4.1, we show that any fragment of FO enjoying the FMP (as well as a mild assumption often met in practice) can be "lifted" as a fragment of FO-LTL using also **X** and **F** and still enjoying the FMP (provided the removal of the temporal operators leads back to the original FO fragment).
– We finally show in Sect. 4.2 that with temporal operators **U** or **G**, the FMP is lost, even with strong constraints on the way temporal operators interact with first-order quantifiers.

All these results provide a theoretical insight on the combination of LTL with bounded FO which may be useful in the context of decision procedures based upon SAT or SMT, or in formal methods such as extensions of Alloy or TLA$^+$. Another possible application may be in the analysis of *software product lines* [5] where various, related transition systems (which may be described using FO) represent a product family.

Due to space constraints, the detailed proofs for some results can be found in an extended version of this article available from the authors' homepages.

2   The Logic FO-LTL

In this section, we define precisely the logic FO-LTL and provide some elements on its expressiveness.

2.1   Syntax

Definition 1 (FO-LTL Syntax). *We define the syntax of FO-LTL in the standard way from the following elements (function symbols will also be considered in Sect. 4):*

– *a tuple of predicates $\mathcal{P} = (P_1, \ldots, P_k)$ (each of which is of any arity) which define relations, between elements of the system, that can vary in time,*
– *equality $=$ is considered as a particular binary predicate which is static, i.e., its value does not depend on time,*
– *an infinite countable set Var of variables,*
– *a finite set Const of constants, representing elements of the system,*
– *the Boolean connectives $\neg, \vee$,*

– *the existential quantifier* $\exists x$ *for each variable* $x \in Var$,
– *the temporal operators* $\mathbf{X}$ *(next) and* $\mathbf{U}$ *(until)*.

We also add the usual syntactic sugar: $\top, \bot, \wedge, \forall, \Rightarrow, \mathbf{G}, \mathbf{F}, \mathbf{R}$, *where*
$$F\varphi = \top \mathbf{U}\varphi, \qquad G\varphi = \neg(F(\neg\varphi)), \qquad \psi\,\mathbf{R}\,\varphi = \neg(\neg\varphi\mathbf{U}\neg\psi).$$

Example 1. Let us consider $\mathcal{P} = \{OK, fail\}$, where OK is a nullary predicate, *i.e.*, an atomic proposition, and *fail* is an unary predicate. We can define the following formula: $\mathbf{G}(\exists x.fail(x) \Rightarrow \mathbf{F}\,\mathbf{G}\,\neg OK)$. Intuitively, it expresses that a local bug endangers the whole system and no recovery is possible: if one element of the system fails at some point, then later the system must enter a state where it is not OK and remain in this state forever.

2.2 Semantics

Variables and constants (and more generally terms if we consider functions) are interpreted over a domain D. We consider that the domain and the interpretation of variables and constants do not vary in time. Only the interpretation of predicates can change. The time domain considered throughout the paper is $\mathbb{N}$.

Definition 2 (FO-LTL Structure). *An interpretation structure of FO-LTL is a tuple* $\mathcal{M} = (D, \sigma_{Const}, \rho)$ *where:*

– D *is the domain,*
– $\sigma_{Const} : Const \rightarrow D$ *is a valuation for constants,*
– $\rho = (P_1^i, \ldots, P_k^i)_{i \in \mathbb{N}}$ *gives the semantics of each predicate in* $\mathcal{P}$ *at each instant* $i \in \mathbb{N}$. *If* P_j *is a l-ary predicate, then* $P_j^i \subseteq D^l$ *for each instant* $i \in \mathbb{N}$.

We now define the satisfaction of a formula in a structure, in which case the latter is called a *model* of the former.

Definition 3 (Satisfaction Relation). *Given a structure* $\mathcal{M}$, *we inductively define the satisfaction relation* $\mathcal{M}, \sigma, i \models \varphi$, *where* σ *maps free variables of* φ *to elements in* D, *and* $i \in \mathbb{N}$ *is the current point in time.*

For ease of reading, x and y stand for both variables and constants in this definition. Moreover, we use $\overline{\sigma}$ *to denote the interpretation of both variables and constants:* $\overline{\sigma}(x) = \sigma(x)$ *if* $x \in Var$ *and* $\overline{\sigma}(x) = \sigma_{Const}(x)$ *if* $x \in Const$.

– $\mathcal{M}, \sigma, i \models x = y$ *if* $\overline{\sigma}(x) = \overline{\sigma}(y)$
– $\mathcal{M}, \sigma, i \models P_j(x_1, \ldots, x_n)$ *if* $(\overline{\sigma}(x_1), \ldots, \overline{\sigma}(x_n)) \in P_j^i$
– $\mathcal{M}, \sigma, i \models \neg\varphi$ *if* $\mathcal{M}, \sigma, i \not\models \varphi$
– $\mathcal{M}, \sigma, i \models \varphi \vee \psi$ *if* $\mathcal{M}, \sigma, i \models \varphi$ *or* $\mathcal{M}, \sigma, i \models \psi$
– $\mathcal{M}, \sigma, i \models \exists x.\varphi$ *if there exists* $a \in D$ *such that* $\mathcal{M}, \sigma[x \mapsto a], i \models \varphi$
– $\mathcal{M}, \sigma, i \models \mathbf{X}\varphi$ *if* $\mathcal{M}, \sigma, i+1 \models \varphi$
– $\mathcal{M}, \sigma, i \models \varphi\mathbf{U}\psi$ *if there exists* $j \geqslant i$ *such that* $\mathcal{M}, \sigma, j \models \psi$, *and for all p such that* $i \leqslant p < j$, *we have* $\mathcal{M}, \sigma, p \models \varphi$

A formula φ without free variables is satisfiable if and only if there exists a structure $\mathcal{M}$ such that $\mathcal{M}, \emptyset, 0 \models \varphi$, and in this case we just note $\mathcal{M} \models \varphi$. (The semantics with function symbols is defined in a similar straightforward way.)

Notice that FO-LTL can be viewed as a fragment of a first-order logic called 2FO, where quantifiers can range either over D or over time. It was shown in [11] that FO-LTL is strictly less expressive than 2FO, as opposed to the classical result that LTL and FO have the same expressive power over discrete time. Detailed definitions and examples regarding 2FO are provided in the extended version of this article.

3 Complexity of Bounded Satisfiability

We are interested in a problem occurring in practice, where a formula φ of FO or FO-LTL is given together with a bound N, and we want to check the existence of a model of φ with domain of size at most N. This problem is decidable, but its complexity is an interesting question that, as far as we know, has been overlooked (though the FO case can be considered unpublished folklore). We call this problem BSAT and we investigate its complexity for several variants. As explained earlier, this question is of practical interest given the success of formal methods based upon finite model-finding and considering possible temporal extensions of these.

To analyze the complexity of this problem in different settings, we first recall the usual notion of *(quantifier) rank* [13].

Definition 4 (Quantifier Rank). *The* (quantifier) *rank of a FO-LTL formula is defined by structural recursion as follows:*

- $\mathrm{rk}(x = y) = \mathrm{rk}(P(x_1, \ldots, x_k)) = 0$
- $\mathrm{rk}(\neg \varphi) = \mathrm{rk}(\mathbf{X}\,\varphi) = \mathrm{rk}(\varphi)$
- $\mathrm{rk}(\varphi \vee \psi) = \mathrm{rk}(\varphi \mathbf{U} \psi) = \max(\mathrm{rk}(\varphi), \mathrm{rk}(\psi))$
- $\mathrm{rk}(\exists x, \varphi) = 1 + \mathrm{rk}(\varphi)$.

We are interested in settings where the rank of formulas is bounded, or on the contrary any formula is allowed as input. Restricting rank to a certain bound is a natural assumption in practice, and allows a finer analysis of the parameterized complexity of the BSAT problem. As is standard practice, we write FO[k] (resp. FO-LTL[k]) for all FO (resp. FO-LTL) formulae of quantifier rank up to k.

This rank is not to be confused with the alternation depth, which increases only with alternations between $\forall$ and $\exists$ quantifiers (or in our case between $\exists$ and $\neg$). We chose here to use quantifier rank to reflect the limited number of variables specified in real-life examples by users, for instance using tools such as Alloy. Notice that bounding the quantifier rank does not trivialize the problem, because we allow arbitrary signatures (again, similarly to the Alloy syntax). We recall that most complexity results on logical formalisms in the literature are relative to fixed signatures.

The following theorem classifies the complexity of BSAT according to three parameters: FO alone versus FO-LTL, N given in unary or binary, and $\mathrm{rk}(\varphi)$ bounded or unbounded. Some of these results regarding FO may be part of folklore, but we reproduce them here for completeness.

Theorem 1. *We consider BSAT for three parameters: logic, encoding, bound on $\mathrm{rk}(\varphi)$ (ranked). The corresponding complexities are given in the following table (N is the bound on the model size, k the bound on $\mathrm{rk}(\varphi)$):*

	N unary	N binary
$FO[k]$	*NP-complete*	*NEXPTIME-complete*
FO	*NEXPTIME-complete* (even $N=2$)	*NEXPTIME-complete*
FO-$LTL[k]$	*PSPACE-complete*	*EXPSPACE-complete*
FO-LTL	*EXPSPACE-complete* (even $N=2$)	*EXPSPACE-complete*

Proofs are given in the remaining of this very Sect. 3.

3.1   First-Order Logic

Lemma 1. *The BSAT(N) problem for FO[k] with N in unary is NP-complete.*

Proof.

Membership in NP. We show membership in NP by polynomially reducing the problem to SAT. The reduction is informally described here, see   the extended version of this article   for the formal construction.

The input formula φ is turned into a quantifier-free formula φ' where quantifiers have been expanded: $\forall x$ (resp. $\exists x$) is replaced by $\bigwedge_{x \in [1,N]}$ (resp. $\bigvee_{x \in [1,N]}$). Constants are turned into integers in the same way, using an initial disjunction on their possible values.

We then turn φ' into a SAT instance φ'' by replacing every occurrence of predicate $R(\vec{a})$, where $\vec{a}$ is an integer vector, by a Boolean variable $x_{R,\vec{a}}$.

This reduction is polynomial because of the unary encoding of N and the bound on $\mathrm{rk}(\varphi)$, and preserves satisfiability.

NP-hardness. We now show that BSAT for unary FO[k] is NP-hard.

We perform a reduction from SAT: given a SAT instance with variables $x_1, \ldots x_n$, we build an instance of BSAT where $x_1, \ldots x_n$ are predicates of arity 0. We can then ask for the existence of a structure of size 0 (or 1), and this will answer the SAT problem. Since we do not need any quantifier to reduce to SAT, we obtain NP-hardness even if the bound on the rank is 0.   □

Lemma 2. *The BSAT(N) problem for FO[k] with N in binary is NEXPTIME-complete if $k \geqslant 2$, even restricted to unary predicates. It is NP-complete for $k = 1$.*

Proof. The proof is only sketched here, the detailed version can be found in the extended version of this article. The idea is to reduce directly from a non-deterministic Turing Machine running in exponential time.

Given such a machine M together with an input word u, we want to build a formula φ of FO[2] describing the run of M over u, such that φ has a model of size at most N if and only if M accepts u in at most N steps. Variables in φ will be used to describe positions of the tape of M as well as time instants in the computation of M. For this, we use unary predicates to encode the bits of the cell position $p(x)$ and time instant $t(x)$ described by an element x of the domain. We additionally use predicates $a(x)$ for a in the alphabet of the machine, and $q(x)$ for q in the state space of the machine to specify the content of the cell $p(x)$ at time $t(x)$. To avoid using formulas of rank 3, we also introduce a predicate $a'(x)$ to say that cell $p(x)$ is labelled a at time $t(x)+1$. We can express that this encoding is sound, and specify the existence of an accepting run of the machine using a formula φ of rank 2. Since N can be specified in binary, and since $|\varphi|$ is polynomial in the size of M, we can show that φ has a model of size N if and only if M has an accepting run of size exponential (2^{n^k}) in its input of size n.

The fact that the problem is in NEXPTIME is proven similarly as in Lemma 1, and is shown for a more general version of the problem in Lemma 4.

On the contrary, if $k = 1$, we show that any satisfiable formula φ of rank 1 has a model of size at most $|\varphi|$, therefore it is in NP to verify the existence of such a model. NP-hardness follows from Lemma 1.   □

Lemma 3. *The BSAT(N) problem for unranked FO with N in unary is NEXP-TIME-hard, even for $N = 2$.*

Proof. We show that this case is also NEXPTIME-hard.

As before, let M be a non-deterministic Turing machine running in exponential time 2^{n^k}.

This time, we will use predicates of unbounded arity, and encode positions in the tape using binary code. We will actually need only two elements in the structure, named 0 and 1.

To state that a position of binary encoding $\vec{x}$ is labelled by a letter a (resp. a state q), we will use a predicate $a(\vec{x})$ (resp. $q(\vec{x})$) of arity n^k, where each coordinate of $\vec{x}$ is given as a distinct argument.

To mimic the previous proof, we need to be able to compare 2 positions, using a predicate $\vec{x} < \vec{y}$ of arity $2n^k$. Once this order is axiomatized, the reduction can be done as in the previous case.

Therefore, we will only give the relevant new material here, *i.e.* the axioms for $\leqslant$ of arity $2n^k$ being a total order. These axioms must all be of polynomial length in n, in order to keep the overall reduction polynomial.

We use $\forall \vec{x}$ as a shorthand for $\forall x_1, \forall x_2, \ldots, \forall x_{n^k}$. In this way, it suffices to rewrite the axioms of total order using vectors instead of elements. This keeps the size of axioms polynomial, making it grow only by a factor n^k. Note that this does not guarantee that $\leqslant$ describes the lexicographic order on vectors, in particular the first position could be any vector, but this is not a problem.

Replacing all variables by vectors in the previous proof yields the required reduction.   □

The membership in NEXPTIME will be shown in the proof of Lemma 4.

Lemma 4. *The BSAT(N) problem for unranked FO with N in binary is in NEXPTIME.*

Proof. This result implies NEXPTIME-completeness for 3 variants of the First-Order BSAT problem.

Let $\varphi, \vec{e}$ be the input of the problem, where $\vec{e}$ is a binary encoding of N, so $N = O(2^{|\vec{e}|})$. Let $n = |\varphi| + |\vec{e}|$ be the size of the input, and $r = \text{rk}(\varphi)$. The algorithm from the proof of Lemma 1 can be adapted as follows:

- Guess a structure and write it on the tape: a predicate of arity k takes up to N^k cells, so the operation uses time (and space) $O(2^{nk})$.
- Unfold quantifiers of the formula and check predicates. This operation takes time $O(|\varphi|N^r) = O(2^{nr})$.

Overall, the time complexity is in $O(2^{n(k+r)}) = O(2^{n^2})$, since both k and r are bounded by n.

This ends the proof that the most "difficult" FO case of BSAT still has NEXPTIME complexity. Hardness (even for $N = 2$) follows from Lemma 2.   □

3.2 An Algorithm for the BSAT Problem for FO-LTL

We now turn to the BSAT problem for FO-LTL, and describe a generic algorithm that we will use for various settings of the problem.

Lemma 5. *The BSAT(N) problem for FO-LTL is in PSPACE if the rank is bounded and N is given in unary, and in EXPSPACE all three other cases.*

The algorithm consists in trying all sizes up to N, and for each of them expand the formula φ into a LTL formula, then use a PSPACE algorithm for LTL satisfiability.

Definition 5 (Expansion of an FO-LTL Formula). *Let us consider a finite domain D, a finite set of constants $Const$, a valuation $\sigma_{Const} : Const \rightarrow D$, a closed FO-LTL formula φ with constants in $Const$ and predicate symbols $P_1, \ldots, P_k$, of arities $\alpha_1, \ldots, \alpha_k$ respectively. We define the expansion $\exp(\varphi)$ of φ given the domain D as an LTL formula, using alphabet $A = \{A_i(\vec{a}) \mid 1 \leqslant i \leqslant k, \vec{a} \in D^{\alpha_i}\}$ by induction on φ. We assume that φ can use elements of D as constants, and σ_{Const} is extended to these new constants in the natural way.*

$$\exp(a = b) = \top \text{ if } \sigma_{Const}(a) = \sigma_{Const}(b) \text{ and } \bot \text{ otherwise}$$
$$\exp(P_i(a_1, \ldots, a_k)) = A_i(\sigma_{Const}(a_1), \ldots, \sigma_{Const}(a_k))$$

$\exp(\neg\varphi) = \neg\exp(\varphi)$ $\qquad\qquad$ $\exp(\varphi \vee \psi) = \exp(\varphi) \vee \exp(\psi)$

$\exp(\mathbf{X}\varphi) = \mathbf{X}\exp(\varphi)$ $\qquad\qquad$ $\exp(\varphi\mathbf{U}\psi) = \exp(\varphi)\mathbf{U}\exp(\psi)$

$\exp(\exists x, \varphi) = \bigvee_{a \in D} \exp(\varphi[x \leftarrow a])$

It is easy to show by induction that for any φ and D, we have

$$|\exp(\varphi)| = \Theta(|\varphi| \cdot |D|^{\mathrm{rk}(\varphi)}).$$

We can now adapt the algorithm from Lemma 1 to this new setting. In the case where the rank is bounded, we rewrite the formula to bound arity of predicates if the rank is bounded, and guess a structure of size D of size at most N together with σ_{Const}, using space polynomial in $|D|$ (so exponential in the input N is in binary). We then expand φ into $\exp(\varphi)$, of size $O(|\varphi| \cdot N^{\mathrm{rk}(\varphi)})$.

It remains to decide whether the LTL formula $\exp(\varphi)$ is satisfiable, which can be done using space polynomial in $|\exp(\varphi)|$ [18]. Therefore this algorithm uses space $O(|\varphi| \cdot N^{\mathrm{rk}(\varphi)})$. It is in PSPACE if the rank is bounded and N is in unary, and EXPSPACE in the other three cases.

3.3 Completeness Results for FO-LTL BSAT

We now show that this algorithm is optimal, by showing that BSAT for FO-LTL is either PSPACE-hard or EXPSPACE-hard depending on the setting.

Lemma 6. *The BSAT(N) problem for ranked and unranked FO-LTL with N in binary is EXPSPACE-complete, even for $N = 2$. In the ranked case, the bound must be at least 2. The BSAT(N) problem for FO-LTL$[k]$ with N in unary is PSPACE-complete.*

Proof. The main idea of the proof is to directly encode the run of a Turing machine using exponential space (polynomial space in the ranked case with N in unary), similarly as in the proof of Lemma 2. The main difference is that we now have additional LTL operators, that allow us to encode computation steps without any bound on the number of time instants. Therefore, the first-order domain D will only be used to encode positions of the tape via unary predicates specifying the bits of the position, and that is why we can now encode runs of machines using exponentially more time than space. The detailed reduction can be found in   the extended version of this article.   □

Finally, the last case is treated in the following lemma.

Lemma 7. *The BSAT(N) problem for unranked FO-LTL with N in unary is EXPSPACE-complete.*

Proof. We will show that this case is also EXPSPACE-hard, although we can no longer use an element of the structure for each cell of the Turing machine.

We can reuse ideas from Lemma 3, and encode positions using vectors of bits with predicates of unbounded arities. This time, only positions will be encoded this way, as time can be taken care of by LTL. Thus we can start from a machine where only space is exponentially bounded, and time can be doubly exponential.

The construction is then similar to the one from Lemma 3, and yields a reduction showing that this variant of BSAT is also EXPSPACE-complete, even for structures with only 2 elements.   □

Other examples of EXPSPACE-complete problems related to deciding small fragments of FO-LTL can be found in [8].

4   Finite Model Property

Since we are only interested in finite models of FO-LTL formulas, it is natural to study which fragments of FO-LTL enjoy the *finite model property* (FMP). We say that a formula has the FMP if the existence of a model implies the existence of a *finite* model (*i.e.*, with finite first-order domain but still infinite time structure). We also say that a fragment *Frag* of some logic has the FMP if all the formulas from *Frag* have the FMP. Many such fragments of FO were exhibited in the past decades.

Function Symbols. In this Section we will enrich the syntax of FO-LTL with function symbols. Each function has an arbitrary arity like a predicate, but yields a *term*, which will be interpreted as an element of the domain, as variables and constants. In this case, the parameters of the predicates (including equality) can be arbitrary terms, built by composing variables and constants with functions. For instance, if x and y are variables, a is a constant, f and g are functions, then $f(x, g(x), a) = g(y)$ is a formula.

Example 2 [1,4]. The following fragments of *FO*, named following the notation of [4], have the FMP:

- $[\exists^*\forall^*, all]_=$ (Ramsey 1930) the class of all sentences with quantifier prefix $\exists^*\forall^*$ over arbitrary relational vocabulary with equality.
- $[\exists^*\forall\exists^*, all]_=$ (Ackermann 1928) the class of all sentences with quantifier prefix $\exists^*\forall\exists^*$ over arbitrary relational vocabulary with equality.
- $[\exists^*\forall^2\exists^*, all]$ (Gödel 1932, Kalmár 1933, Schütte 1934) the class of all sentences with quantifier prefix $\exists^*\forall^2\exists^*$ over arbitrary relational vocabulary without equality.
- $[\exists^*, all, all]_=$ (Gurevich 1976) the class of all sentences with quantifier prefix $\exists^*$ over arbitrary vocabulary with equality.
- $[\exists^*\forall, all, (1)]_=$ (Grädel 1996) the class of all sentences with quantifier prefix $\exists^*\forall$ over vocabulary that contains one unary function and arbitrary predicate symbols with equality.
- $[all, (\omega), (\omega)]$ (Gurevich 1969, Löb 1967) the class of all sentences with arbitrary quantifier prefix over vocabulary that contains an arbitrary number of unary predicates and unary functions without equality
- FO_2 (Mortimer 1975) the class of all sentences of relational vocabulary that contains two variables and equality.

4.1   Lifting FMP from FO to FO-LTL

In this section, we first present general results that allow to lift the finite model property from FO fragments to their temporal extension with operators $\mathbf{X}$ and $\mathbf{F}$. Then, we focus on two particular fragments: the well known Ramsey fragment, for which the extension can be generalized to full LTL, and a fragment that does not fulfill the hypotheses of our general result, but for which the temporal extension with operators $\mathbf{X}$ and $\mathbf{F}$ still has the FMP.

Remark 1. In the following, we will only consider formulas in *negation normal form* (NNF), *i.e.* where negations have been pushed to the leaves. This means negations can only be applied to predicates. Notice that the syntactic sugar mentioned in Sect. 2.1, in particular the operator **R** (dual of **U**) now becomes necessary to retain full expressiveness.

Definition 6. *If Frag is a fragment of FO, and $OP \subseteq \{\mathbf{X}, \mathbf{F}, \mathbf{G}, \mathbf{U}, \mathbf{R}\}$ is a set of temporal operators, we define the fragment Frag + OP of FO-LTL as the formulas with temporal operators from OP, where the formula(s) obtained by removing unary temporal operators and replacing binary ones by $\vee$ or $\wedge$ (indifferently), is in Frag.*

A General Extension Result for Fragments with the FMP

Definition 7 ((Plus-)Replacement of a Formula). *If φ, ψ are FO-formulas, we say that ψ is a replacement of φ if ψ can be obtained from φ by replacing predicates and functions, i.e., by allowing different occurrences of the same predicate (resp. function) of φ to become distinct predicates (resp. functions) of same arity in ψ, but distinct predicates (resp. functions) in φ are always mapped to distinct predicates (resp. functions) in ψ.*

Additionally, we define the notion of plus-replacement *where the new predicates and functions can have increased arity.*

For instance $\forall x.\exists y.P(x) \vee Q(y)$ is a replacement of $\forall x.\exists y.P(x) \vee P(y)$. Likewise, the formula $\forall x.\exists y.P(x) \vee Q(y, x)$ is a plus-replacement of $\forall x.\exists y.P(x) \vee P(y)$.

Definition 8 (Stability Under (Plus-)Replacement). *We say that a fragment Frag of FO with FMP is* stable under replacement *(resp.* plus-replacement*) if for all $\varphi \in$ Frag and for all replacement (resp. plus-replacement) ψ of φ, we have that ψ has the FMP.*

In practice, many fragments with FMP considered in the literature are stable under (plus-)replacement. This is for example the case for most of the fragments from Example 2 (see Corollary 1).

Theorem 2 *(Frag + **X**). Let Frag be a fragment of FO with the FMP, stable under replacement. Then the fragment Frag + **X** of FO-LTL has the FMP.*

The proof of this theorem is presented in the extended version of this article. The following theorem, along the same lines, allows more temporal operators but has the stronger assumption of plus-replacement.

Theorem 3 *(Frag + $\{\mathbf{X}, \mathbf{F}\}$). Let Frag be a fragment of FO with FMP, stable under plus-replacement. Then Frag + $\{\mathbf{X}, \mathbf{F}\}$ also has the FMP.*

Proof. Let φ be a satisfiable formula of $Frag + \{\mathbf{X}, \mathbf{F}\}$. Let V be the set of variables used in φ and $\{\mathbf{F}_j, j \in J\}$ be the set of **F**-operators in φ, for some finite labeling set $J = \{1, 2, \ldots, |J|\}$ such that if $\mathbf{F}_j$ is under the scope of $\mathbf{F}_i$ then $i < j$.

For $\vec{x}$ a list of variables from V, $j \in J \cup \{0\}$, $k \in \mathbb{N}$, and θ a subformula of φ, we define $[\![\theta]\!]_{\vec{x}}^{j}$ inductively as follows:

$$[\![P(\vec{y})]\!]_{\vec{x}}^{j,k} = P_{j,k}(\vec{y}, \vec{x}) \qquad \text{variables can appear in both } \vec{y} \text{ and } \vec{x}$$
$$[\![f(\vec{y})]\!]_{\vec{x}}^{j,k} = f_{j,k}(\vec{y}, \vec{x}) \qquad \text{variables can appear in both } \vec{y} \text{ and } \vec{x}$$
$$[\![\exists z.\theta(\vec{y})]\!]_{\vec{x}}^{j,k} = \exists z [\![\theta(\vec{y})]\!]_{\vec{x}}^{j,k} \qquad\qquad [\![\forall z.\theta(\vec{y})]\!]_{\vec{x}}^{j,k} = \forall z [\![\theta(\vec{y})]\!]_{\vec{x},z}^{j,k}$$
$$[\![\theta(\vec{y}) \wedge \theta'(\vec{y}')]\!]_{\vec{x}}^{j,k} = [\![\theta(\vec{y})]\!]_{\vec{x}}^{j,k} \wedge [\![\theta'(\vec{y}')]\!]_{\vec{x}}^{j,k}$$
$$[\![\theta(\vec{y}) \vee \theta'(\vec{y}')]\!]_{\vec{x}}^{j,k} = [\![\theta(\vec{y})]\!]_{\vec{x}}^{j,k} \vee [\![\theta'(\vec{y}')]\!]_{\vec{x}}^{j,k}$$
$$[\![\mathbf{X}\,\theta(\vec{y})]\!]_{\vec{x}}^{j,k} = [\![\theta(\vec{y})]\!]_{\vec{x}}^{j,k+1} \qquad\qquad [\![\mathbf{F}_{j'}\,\theta(\vec{y})]\!]_{\vec{x}}^{j,k} = [\![\theta(\vec{y})]\!]_{\vec{x}}^{j',0}$$

To sum up, we index predicates and functions by the label j of the innermost occurrence of $\mathbf{F}$ that has it in its scope, as well as the number k of nested $\mathbf{X}$ since this occurrence. We also add all universally quantified variables as arguments. We additionally remove $\mathbf{F}$ and $\mathbf{X}$ operators in the process.

Let $\psi = [\![\varphi]\!]_{\emptyset}^{0,0}$. We show that ψ is satisfiable. Let $\mathcal{M} = (D, \rho)$ be a model of φ. This means that for each subformula $\mathbf{F}_j\,\theta(\vec{y})$ of φ under universally quantified variables $\vec{x}$, there is a function $t_j : D^{|\vec{x}|} \to \mathbb{N}$ such that $\theta(\vec{y})$ is true at time $t_j(\vec{x})$. We build a model of ψ by setting the value of $P_{j,k}(\vec{y}, \vec{x})$ to $P(\vec{y})$ at time $t_j(\vec{x}) + k$, where $\vec{x}$ is the list of new arguments of P_j (and same with functions). It is straightforward to verify that this is indeed a model of ψ.

Let φ' be φ where the $\mathbf{F}$'s and $\mathbf{X}$'s have been removed, by definition we have $\varphi' \in Frag$. Since ψ is a plus-replacement of φ' and $Frag$ is stable under plus-replacement, we have ψ has the FMP. Since ψ is satisfiable, there exists a finite model M_f of ψ. Finally, we build from M_f a finite model of φ. For this, we have to choose new values for the $t_j(\vec{x})$, so that no conflicts occur: if $(j, k, \vec{x}) \neq (j', k', \vec{x}')$, then $t_j(\vec{x}) + k \neq t_j(\vec{x}') + k'$. Let K be the maximal number of nested $\mathbf{X}$ (not interleaved with $\mathbf{F}$), and $(\vec{x}_i)_{0 \leqslant i \leqslant R}$ be an ordering of all possible vectors $\vec{x}$. We choose $t_j(\vec{x}) = (K+1) \times (R^j + i)$, in order to satisfy the injectivity condition: for all $j, j' \in [0, |J|]$, $k, k' \in [0, K]$, and $\vec{x}, \vec{x}' \in \{\vec{x}_i | 0 \leqslant i \leqslant R\}$, we have $t_j(\vec{x}) + k = t_{j'}(\vec{x}') + k'$ if and only if $(j, k, \vec{x}) = (j', k', \vec{x}')$. Notice moreover that we respect the condition that if $\mathbf{F}_j\,\varphi_j$ is a subformula of $\mathbf{F}_i\,\varphi_i$, then $j > i$ and thus for any value of $\vec{x}, \vec{y}$, we have $t_j(\vec{x}) > t_i(\vec{y})$.

Finally, we build a finite model of φ by setting the value of $P(\vec{y})$ (resp. $f(\vec{y})$) at time i to $P_{j,k}(\vec{y}, \vec{x})$ (resp. $f_{j,k}(\vec{y}, \vec{x})$) if $i = t_j(\vec{x}) + k$ for some $j, k, \vec{x}$, and choosing any values for other time instants.

So φ has a finite model and therefore $Frag + \{\mathbf{X}, \mathbf{F}\}$ has the FMP. $\qquad \square$

Remark 2. It is enough to consider plus-replacement where new arguments are only quantified universally, which is a weaker condition.

Corollary 1. *The following FO-LTL fragments, extending FO fragments mentioned in Example 2, have the FMP:*

$$[\exists^*\forall^*, all]_{=} + \{\mathbf{X}, \mathbf{F}\} \qquad\qquad [\exists^*\forall\exists^*, all]_{=} + \{\mathbf{X}, \mathbf{F}\}$$
$$[\exists^*\forall^2\exists^*, all] + \{\mathbf{X}, \mathbf{F}\} \qquad\qquad [\exists^*, all, all]_{=} + \{\mathbf{X}, \mathbf{F}\}$$
$$FO_2 + \{\mathbf{X}, \mathbf{F}\}$$

Specific Extensions for Two Fragments. In this section, we focus on two fragments of FO: a fragment for which our general result (Theorem 3) does not apply and a fragment for which our general result can be extended to full LTL.

The FMP of the following fragment, even if it is not stable under plus-replacement, can be lifted to its temporal extension with $\mathbf{X}$ and $\dot{\mathbf{F}}$.

Theorem 4. $[all, (\omega), (\omega)] + \{\mathbf{X}, \mathbf{F}\}$ *has the FMP.*

Proof. We show that any formula of this fragment has the FMP. We proceed by induction on the number of nested $\mathbf{F}$. The induction hypothesis is actually stronger than the FMP: we show by induction that for such a formula φ, if there is a model then there is a model M with finite domain D and a finite set of time instants T such that M only "looks at T", i.e. changing the values of predicates and functions outside of T does not change the truth value of φ.

We start with the base case where there is no $\mathbf{F}$. By Theorem 2 (and its proof), and since $[all, (\omega), (\omega)]$ is stable under replacement (even though it is not stable under plus-replacement), if φ has a model it has a finite one where only the values on a finite set of instants matter.

We now turn to the induction step, and consider a formula φ with $n + 1$ nested $\mathbf{F}$. By considering the outermost occurrences of $\mathbf{F}$, the formula φ can be written $\varphi'(\mathbf{F}\,\varphi_1, \mathbf{F}\,\varphi_2, \ldots, \mathbf{F}\,\varphi_k)$, where φ' contains no $\mathbf{F}$ but may contain quantifiers, and for every $i \in [1, k]$, φ_i has at most n nested $\mathbf{F}$ and may contain free variables.

We assume that φ has a model M, and without loss of generality we note j the index in $[1, k]$ such that $\mathbf{F}\,\varphi_i$ is true in M (for at least one valuation of its free variables) if and only if $i \leqslant j$. This means in particular that for all $i \leqslant j$, φ_i has a model. By the induction hypothesis, for all $i \leqslant j$, φ_i can be set to true in a model M_i with a finite domain D_i and that only looks at a finite set of instants T_i.

Moreover, $\varphi'' = \varphi'(\top, \ldots, \top, \bot, \ldots, \bot)$ (with j times $\top$) is satisfiable, and by the base case has a model M' with a finite domain D' that only looks at a finite set of instants T' (that will be used as the first instants of the model).

We now build a model M_f for φ with a finite domain D, that we define as a set of cardinality $\max(|D'|, |D_1|, |D_2|, \ldots, |D_j|)$.

We define a sequence of time instants $(t_i)_{1 \leqslant i \leqslant j}$ such that at time t_i the formula φ_i is true for a particular valuation of its free variables, and at $t_i + |T_i|$, it is true for another valuation of its free variables that are universally quantified, and so on, until we have considered all the possible values in D for these universally quantified variables. So we define the t_i inductively as follows: $t_1 = |T'|$ and $t_i = t_{i-1} + |T_{i-1}| \times |D|^r$, where r is the number of nested universal quantifiers in φ'.

We now describe the predicates and function values in M_f. At times $t \in [0, t_1 - 1]$, we mimic the model M'. This gives the value of predicates and functions for $|D'|$ elements of D. All the remaining elements can be set to behave as any element of D', for instance the first one. Since equality cannot be tested, and predicates and functions are monadic, the truth value of φ'' is preserved.

For all $i \in [1, j]$, we use M_i to fix the valuation of predicates and functions at times $[t_i, t_i + |T_i| - 1]$. Then, from $t_i + |T_i|$, we consider another possible assignment of universally quantified variables and define the valuation of predicates and functions accordingly. This way, we obtain a model of φ_i starting at time t_i, and therefore a model of $\mathbf{F} \varphi_i$ starting at time 0.

Since φ' is monotonous in its arguments (no $\mathbf{F}$ can be under a negation), and we preserved the value $\top$ for all $\mathbf{F} \varphi_i$ with $i \leqslant j$, the truth value of φ on M_f is that of φ', which is true thanks to the valuations on $[0, t_0]$.

We have therefore built a model M_f of φ with finite domain, and only looking at a finite number of time instants.   □

The result of Ramsey that the $\exists^* \forall^*$ fragment has the FMP is generalized in the following theorem. See the extended version of this article for a proof, omitted here due to space constraints.

Theorem 5. *We consider here FO-LTL without function symbols. Let* $\varphi = \exists x_1 \ldots \exists x_n . \psi(x_1, \ldots, x_n)$, *where* ψ *is a FO-LTL formula without any* $\exists$ *quantifiers. Then if* φ *is satisfiable, it has a model with domain of size at most* $n + c$, *where* c *is the number of constants in the vocabulary.*

4.2 Axioms of Infinity Using LTL

We now give examples showing that adding LTL to fragments of FO with the FMP allows to write axioms of infinity, therefore losing the FMP. This holds even when strong restrictions are enforced on the way LTL operators interact with first-order quantifiers.

Extending the Ramsey Fragment. First, let us remark that the constraint from Theorem 5 that existential quantifiers are not under the scope of temporal operators is necessary, as showed by the following formula which is only satisfiable by infinite models, using a unary predicate P:

$$\mathbf{G}(\exists x. P(x) \wedge \mathbf{X}\, \mathbf{G}\, \neg P(x)).$$

Indeed, it is straightforward to show that a different x_n is needed to satisfy the formula at each different time instant $n \in \mathbb{N}$, as the condition on the predicate P guarantees that the same x can never be used twice.

Separating Quantifiers and LTL. We now give examples where a fragment of FO loses the FMP when extended with LTL, even without nesting quantifiers under temporal operators.

The following FO-LTL formula is an axiom of infinity with a $\forall\exists$ quantifier prefix, and where no first-order quantifiers are under the scope of LTL operators. It uses one constant c and one unary predicate P:

$$\forall x \exists y. P(c) \wedge \mathbf{G}(P(x) \Rightarrow \mathbf{X}(P(y) \wedge \mathbf{G}\, \neg P(x))).$$

This sentence only has infinite models, as the predicate P must be true on a different element at each instant of time. However, as recalled in Example 2, in FO without LTL, if only one quantifier $\forall$ is used the FMP is guaranteed (or alternatively, formulas with two variables also have the FMP).

This example can actually be replaced using $\mathbf{U}$ instead of $\mathbf{G}$, showing that it suffices to be able to refer to an "unbounded" (as opposed to "infinite") number of time instants to force models to be infinite, as showed by the following example:

$$\forall x \exists y . P(c) \wedge ((P(x) \wedge P(y)) \mathbf{U}(\neg P(x) \wedge P(y))).$$

This time, we used values of the predicate P in the past instead of the future to guarantee that the same x cannot be used twice.

5 Conclusion

Motivated by the possible extension of formal methods based upon finite model finding (such as Alloy or various decision procedures based upon SAT or SMT techniques) with temporal reasoning, we have investigated FO-LTL with finite FO domains in two ways: (1) we studied the complexity of the satisfiability for FO-LTL (and FO alone) when the FO part of the model is bounded; (2) we studied cases where we can lift the FMP of FO fragments to their temporal extensions.

Several question are still open. On the complexity side, it remains to settle the case of FO-LTL[1] with N in binary. Related to the FMP, even if we showed in Sect. 4.1 that for a particular FO fragment that is not stable under plus-replacement, the FMP can still be lifted to its temporal extension with operators $\mathbf{X}$ and $\mathbf{F}$, it is not clear whether this assumption can be dropped in Theorem 3. Another open question is whether we can find a reasonable condition under which we can extend an FO fragment with temporal operators $\mathbf{G}$ or $\mathbf{U}$ without losing the FMP. Indeed, these operators bring an expressiveness that is very useful in practice but we showed in Sect. 4.2 that they behave badly with respect to the FMP.

References

1. Abadi, A., Rabinovich, A., Sagiv, M.: Decidable fragments of many-sorted logic. In: Dershowitz, N., Voronkov, A. (eds.) LPAR 2007. LNCS (LNAI), vol. 4790, pp. 17–31. Springer, Heidelberg (2007). doi:10.1007/978-3-540-75560-9_4
2. Abiteboul, S., Herr, L., den Bussche, J.V.: Temporal versus first-order logic to query temporal databases. In: Proceedings of the Fifteenth ACM SIGACT-SIGMOD-SIGART Symposium on Principles of Database Systems, 3–5 June 1996, Montreal, Canada, pp. 49–57 (1996)
3. Bagheri, H., Kang, E., Malek, S., Jackson, D.: Detection of design flaws in the android permission protocol through bounded verification. In: Bjørner, N., de Boer, F. (eds.) FM 2015. LNCS, vol. 9109, pp. 73–89. Springer, Heidelberg (2015). doi:10.1007/978-3-319-19249-9_6

4. Börger, E., Grädel, E., Gurevich, Y.: The Classical Decision Problem. Perspectives in Mathematical Logic. Springer, Heidelberg (1997)

5. Classen, A., Heymans, P., Schobbens, P., Legay, A., Raskin, J.: Model checking lots of systems: efficient verification of temporal properties in software product lines. In: ICSE 2010, pp. 335–344. ACM (2010)

6. Cunha, A.: Bounded model checking of temporal formulas with alloy. In: Ait Ameur, Y., Schewe, K.-D. (eds.) ABZ 2014. LNCS, vol. 8477, pp. 303–308. Springer, Heidelberg (2014)

7. Frias, M.F., Galeotti, J.P., Pombo, C.L., Aguirre, N.: DynAlloy: upgrading alloy with actions. In: ICSE, vol. 2005, pp. 442–451 (2005)

8. Hodkinson, I.M., Kontchakov, R., Kurucz, A., Wolter, F., Zakharyaschev, M.: On the computational complexity of decidable fragments of first-order linear temporal logics. In: TIME-ICTL, vol. 2003, pp. 91–98 (2003)

9. Hodkinson, I.M., Wolter, F., Zakharyaschev, M.: Decidable fragments of first-order temporal logics. Ann. Pure Appl. Logic **106**(1–3), 85–134 (2000)

10. Jackson, D.: Software Abstractions - Logic, Language, and Analysis. MIT Press, Cambridge (2006). http://mitpress.mit.edu/catalog/item/default.asp?ttype=2&tid=10928

11. Kamp, H.W.: Tense logic and the theory of linear order. Ph.D. thesis, University of Warsaw (1968)

12. Lamport, L.: Specifying Systems, the TLA+ Language and Tools for Hardware and Software Engineers. Addison-Wesley, Boston (2002)

13. Libkin, L.: Elements of Finite Model Theory. Texts in Theoretical Computer Science. An EATCS Series. Springer, Heidelberg (2004). http://dx.doi.org/10.1007/978-3-662-07003-1

14. Lichtenstein, O., Pnueli, A.: Checking that finite state concurrent programs satisfy their linear specification. In: Proceedings of the 12th ACM SIGACT-SIGPLAN Symposium on Principles of Programming Languages, pp. 97–107. ACM (1985)

15. Merz, S.: Decidability and incompleteness results for first-order temporal logics of linear time. J. Appl. Non-Class. Logics **2**(2), 139–156 (1992)

16. Near, J.P., Jackson, D.: An imperative extension to alloy. In: Frappier, M., Glässer, U., Khurshid, S., Laleau, R., Reeves, S. (eds.) ABZ 2010. LNCS, vol. 5977, pp. 118–131. Springer, Heidelberg (2010). doi:10.1007/978-3-642-11811-1_10

17. Newcombe, C., Rath, T., Zhang, F., Munteanu, B., Brooker, M., Deardeuff, M.: How Amazon web services uses formal methods. Commun. ACM **58**(4), 66–73 (2015). http://doi.acm.org/10.1145/2699417

18. Sistla, A.P., Clarke, E.M.: The complexity of propositional linear temporal logics. J. ACM **32**(3), 733–749 (1985)

19. Torlak, E., Jackson, D.: Kodkod: a relational model finder. In: Grumberg, O., Huth, M. (eds.) TACAS 2007. LNCS, vol. 4424, pp. 632–647. Springer, Heidelberg (2007). doi:10.1007/978-3-540-71209-1_49

20. Vakili, A., Day, N.A.: Temporal logic model checking in alloy. In: Derrick, J., Fitzgerald, J., Gnesi, S., Khurshid, S., Leuschel, M., Reeves, S., Riccobene, E. (eds.) ABZ 2012. LNCS, vol. 7316, pp. 150–163. Springer, Heidelberg (2012). doi:10.1007/978-3-642-30885-7_11

21. Zave, P.: Using lightweight modeling to understand Chord. SIGCOMM Comput. Commun. Rev. **42**(2), 49–57 (2012). http://doi.acm.org/10.1145/2185376.2185383

Decidability Results for Multi-objective Stochastic Games

Romain Brenguier and Vojtěch Forejt[(✉)]

Department of Computer Science, University of Oxford, Oxford, UK
vojfor@cs.ox.ac.uk

Abstract. We study stochastic two-player turn-based games in which the objective of one player is to ensure several infinite-horizon total reward objectives, while the other player attempts to spoil at least one of the objectives. The games have previously been shown not to be determined, and an approximation algorithm for computing a Pareto curve has been given. The major drawback of the existing algorithm is that it needs to compute Pareto curves for finite horizon objectives (for increasing length of the horizon), and the size of these Pareto curves can grow unboundedly, even when the infinite-horizon Pareto curve is small.

By adapting existing results, we first give an algorithm that computes the Pareto curve for determined games. Then, as the main result of the paper, we show that for the natural class of stopping games and when there are two reward objectives, the problem of deciding whether a player can ensure satisfaction of the objectives with given thresholds is decidable. The result relies on an intricate and novel proof which shows that the Pareto curves contain only finitely many points.

As a consequence, we get that the two-objective discounted-reward problem for unrestricted class of stochastic games is decidable.

1 Introduction

Formal verification is an area of computer science which deals with establishing properties of systems by mathematical means. Many of the systems that need to be modelled and verified contain controllable decisions, which can be influenced by a user, and behaviour which is out of the user's control. The latter can be further split into events whose presence can be quantified, such as failure rate of components, and events which are considered to be completely adversarial, such as acts of an attacker who wants to break into the system.

Stochastic turn-based games are used as a modelling formalism for such systems [6]. Formally, a stochastic game comprises three kinds of states, owned by one of three players: Player 1, Player 2, and the stochastic player. In each state, one or more transitions to successor states are available. At the beginning of a play, a token is placed on a distinguished initial state, and the player who controls it picks a transition and the token is moved to the corresponding successor state. This is repeated ad infinitum and a path, comprising an infinite sequence of states, is obtained. Player 1 and Player 2 have a free choice of transitions, and

© Springer International Publishing AG 2016
C. Artho et al. (Eds.): ATVA 2016, LNCS 9938, pp. 227–243, 2016.
DOI: 10.1007/978-3-319-46520-3_15

the recipe for picking them is called a strategy. The stochastic player is bound to pick each transition with a fixed probability that is associated with it.

The properties of systems are commonly expressed using rewards, where numbers corresponding to gains or losses are assigned to states of the system. The numbers along the infinite paths are then summed, giving the total reward of an infinite path, intuitively expressing the energy consumed or the profit made along a system's execution. Alternatively, the numbers can be summed with a discounting $\delta < 1$, giving discounted reward. It formalises the fact that immediate gains matter more than future gains, and it is particularly important in economics where money received early can be invested and yield interest.

Traditionally, the aim of one player is to make sure the expected (discounted) total reward exceeds a given bound, while the other player tries to ensure the opposite. We study the *multi-objective problem* in which each state is given a tuple of numbers, for example corresponding to both the profit made on visiting the state, and the energy spent. Subsequently, we give a bound on both profit and energy, and Player 1 attempts to ensure that the expected total profit and expected total energy exceed (or do not exceed) the given bound, while Player 2 tries to spoil this by making sure that at least one of the goals is not met.

The problem has been studied in [9], where it has been shown that Pareto optimal strategies might not exist, and the game might not be determined (for some bounds neither of the players have ε-optimal strategies). A value iteration algorithm has been given for approximating the Pareto curve of the game, i.e. the bounds Player 1 can ensure. The algorithm successively computes, for increasing n, the sets of bounds Player 1 can ensure if the length of the game is restricted to n steps. The approach has two major drawbacks. Firstly, the algorithm cannot decide, for given bounds, if Player 1 can achieve them. Secondly, it does not scale well since the representation of the sets can grow with increasing n, even if the ultimate Pareto curve is small.

The above limitations show that it is necessary to design alternative solution approaches. One of the promising directions is to characterise the shape of the set of achievable bounds, for computing it efficiently. The value iteration of [9] allows us to show that the sets are convex, but no further observations can be made, in particular it is not clear whether the sets are convex polyhedra, or if they can have infinitely many extremal points. The main result of our paper shows that for two-objective case and stopping games, the sets are indeed convex polyhedra, which directly leads to a decision algorithm. We believe that our proof technique is of interest on its own. It proceeds by assuming that there is an accumulation point on the Pareto curve, and then establishes that there must be an accumulation point in one of the successor states such that the *slope* of the Pareto curves in the accumulation points are equal. This allows us to obtain a cycle in the graph of the game in which we can "follow" the accumulation points and eventually revisit some of them infinitely many times. By further analysing slopes of points on the Pareto curves that are close to the accumulation point, we show that there are two points on the curve that are sufficiently far from each other yet have the same slope, which contradicts the assumption that they are near an accumulation point.

Our results also yield novel important contributions for non-stochastic games. Although there have recently been several works on non-stochastic games with multiple objectives, they a priori restrict to deterministic strategies, by which the associated problems become fundamentally different. It is easy to show that enabling randomisation of strategies extends the bounds Player 1 can achieve, and indeed, even in other areas of game-theory randomised strategies have been studied for decades: the fundamental theorem of game theory is that every finite game admits a *randomised* Nash equilibrium [15].

Related Work. Single-objective problems are well studied for stochastic games. For reachability objectives the games are determined and the problem of existence of an optimal strategy achieving a given value is in NP∩co-NP [10]; same holds for total reward objectives. In the multi-objective setting, [9] gives a value iteration algorithm for the multi-objective total reward problem. Although value iteration converges to the correct result, it does so only in infinite number of steps. It is further shown in [9] that when Player 1 is restricted to only use deterministic strategies, the problem becomes undecidable; the proof relies fundamentally on the strategies being deterministic and it is not clear how it can be extended to randomised strategies. The works of [1,2] extend the equations of [9] to expected energy objectives, and mainly concern a variant of multi-objective mean-payoff reward, where the objective is a "satisfaction objective" requiring that there is a set of runs of a given probability on which all mean payoff rewards exceed a given bound. [1] only studies existence of finite-memory strategies and the probability bound 1, and [2] in addition studies expectation objectives for multichain games, which is a very restricted class of games in which the expectation and probability-1 satisfaction objectives coincide. Very recently, [5] showed that quantitative satisfaction objective problem is coNP-complete.

In non-stochastic games, multi-objective optimisation has been studied for multiple mean-payoff objectives and energy games [18]. A comprehensive analysis of the complexity of synthesis of optimal strategies has been given in [7], and it has been shown that a variant of the problem is undecidable [17]. The work of [4] studies the complexity of problems related to exact computation of Pareto curves for multiple mean-payoff objectives. In [13], interval objectives are studied for total, mean-payoff and discounted reward payoff functions. The problems for interval objectives are a special kind of multi-objective problems that require the payoff to be within a given interval, as opposed to the standard single-objective setting where the goal is to exceed a given bound. As mentioned earlier, all the above works for non-stochastic games a priori restrict the players to use deterministic strategies, and hence the problems exhibit completely different properties than the problem we study.

Our Contribution. We give the following novel decidability results. Firstly, we show that the problem for *determined* stochastic games is decidable. Then, as the main result of the paper, we show that for non-determined games which also satisfy the stopping assumption and for two objectives, the set of achievable bounds forms a convex polyhedron. This immediately leads to an algorithm for computing Pareto curves, and we obtain the following novel results as corollaries.

– Two-objective discounted-reward problem for stochastic games is decidable.
– Two-objective total-reward problem for stochastic stopping games is decidable.

Although we phrase our results in terms of stochastic games, to our best knowledge, the above results also yield novel decidability results for multi-objective *non-stochastic games* when randomisation of strategies is allowed.

Outline of the Paper. In Sect. 3, we show a simple algorithm that works for determined games and show how to decide whether a stopping game is determined. In Sect. 4, we give decidability results for two-objective stopping games.

2 Preliminaries on Stochastic Games

We begin this section by introducing the notation used throughout the paper. Given a vector $v \in \mathbb{R}^n$, we use v_i to refer to its i-th component, where $1 \leq i \leq n$. The comparison operator $\leq$ on vectors is defined to be the componentwise ordering: $u \leq v \Leftrightarrow \forall i \in [1,n].\ u_i \leq v_i$. We write $u < v$ when $u \leq v$ and $u \neq v$. Given two vectors $u, v \in \mathbb{R}^n$, the *dot product* of u and v is defined by $u \cdot v = \sum_{i=1}^n u_i \cdot v_i$.

The sum of two sets of vectors $U, V \subseteq \mathbb{R}^n$ is defined by $U + V = \{u + v \mid u \in U, v \in V\}$. Given a set $V \in \mathbb{R}^n$, we define the *downward closure* of V as $\mathsf{dwc}(V) \stackrel{\text{def}}{=} \{u \mid \exists v \in V.\ u \leq v\}$, and we use $\mathsf{conv}(V)$ for the *convex closure* of V, i.e. the set of all v for which there are $v^1, \ldots v^n \in V$ and $w_1 \ldots w_n \in [0,1]$ such that $\sum_{i=1}^n w_i = 1$ and $v = \sum_{i=1}^n w_i \cdot v^i$. An *extremal point* of a set $X \subseteq \mathbb{R}^n$ is a vector $v \in X$ that is not a convex combination of other points in X, i.e. $v \notin \mathsf{conv}(X \setminus \{v\})$.

A function $f : \mathbb{R} \to \mathbb{R}$ is concave whenever for all $x, y \in \mathbb{R}$ and $t \in [0,1]$ we have $f(t \cdot x + (1-t) \cdot y) \geq t \cdot f(x) + (1-t) \cdot f(y)$. Given $x \in \mathbb{R}$, the *left slope* of f in x is defined by $\mathsf{lslope}(f, x) \stackrel{\text{def}}{=} \lim_{x' \to x^-} \frac{f(x) - f(x')}{x - x'}$. Similarly the *right slope* is defined by $\lim_{x' \to x^+} \frac{f(x) - f(x')}{x - x'}$. Note that if f is concave then both limits are well-defined, because by concavity $\frac{f(x) - f(x')}{x - x'}$ is monotonic in x'; nevertheless, the left and right slope might still not be equal.

A point $p \in \mathbb{R}^2$ is an *accumulation point* of f if $f(p_1) = p_2$ and for all $\varepsilon > 0$, there exists $x \neq p_1$ such that $(x, f(x))$ is an extremal point of f and $|p_1 - x| < \varepsilon$. Moreover, p is a *left (right) accumulation point* if in the above we in addition have $x < p_1$ (resp. $x > p_1$). We sometimes slightly abuse notation by saying that x is an extremal point when $(x, f(x))$ is an extremal point, and similarly for accumulation points.

A *discrete probability distribution* (or just *distribution*) over a (countable) set S is a function $\mu : S \to [0,1]$ such that $\sum_{s \in S} \mu(s) = 1$. We write $\mathcal{D}(S)$ for the set of all distributions over S, and use $\mathsf{supp}(\mu) = \{s \in S \mid \mu(s) > 0\}$ for the *support set* of $\mu \in \mathcal{D}(S)$.

We now define turn-based stochastic two-player games together with the concepts of strategies and paths of the game. We then present the objectives that are studied in this paper and the associated decision problems.

Stochastic Games. A *stochastic (two-player) game* is defined to· be a tuple $\mathcal{G} = \langle S, (S_\Box, S_\Diamond, S_\bigcirc), \Delta \rangle$ where S is a finite set of states partitioned into sets $S_\Box$, $S_\Diamond$, and $S_\bigcirc$; $\Delta : S \times S \to [0, 1]$ is a probabilistic transition function such that $\Delta(s, t) \in \{0, 1\}$ if $s \in S_\Box \cup S_\Diamond$ and $\sum_{t \in S} \Delta(s, t) = 1$ if $s \in S_\bigcirc$.

$S_\Box$ and $S_\Diamond$ represent the sets of states controlled by Player 1 and Player 2, respectively, while $S_\bigcirc$ is the set of stochastic states. For a state $s \in S$, the set of successor states is denoted by $\Delta(s) \stackrel{\text{def}}{=} \{t \in S \mid \Delta(s, t) > 0\}$. We assume that $\Delta(s) \neq \emptyset$ for all $s \in S$. A state from which no other states except for itself are reachable is called *terminal*, and the set of terminal states is denoted by $\text{Term} \stackrel{\text{def}}{=} \{s \in S \mid \Delta(s) = \{s\}\}$.

Paths. An *infinite path* λ of a stochastic game $\mathcal{G}$ is a sequence $(s_i)_{i \in \mathbb{N}}$ of states such that $s_{i+1} \in \Delta(s_i)$ for all $i \geq 0$. A *finite path* is a prefix of such a sequence. For a finite or infinite path λ we write $\text{len}(\lambda)$ for the number of states in the path. For $i < \text{len}(\lambda)$ we write λ_i to refer to the i-th state s_{i-1} of $\lambda = s_0 s_1 \dots$ and $\lambda_{\leq i}$ for the prefix of λ of length $i + 1$. For a finite path λ we write $\text{last}(\lambda)$ for the last state of the path. For a game $\mathcal{G}$ we write $\Omega\mathcal{G}^+$ for the set of all finite paths, and $\Omega\mathcal{G}$ for the set of all infinite paths, and $\Omega\mathcal{G}, s$ for the set of infinite paths starting in state s. We denote the set of paths that reach a state in $T \subseteq S$ by $\Diamond T \stackrel{\text{def}}{=} \{\lambda \in \Omega\mathcal{G} \mid \exists i . \lambda_i \in T\}$.

Strategies. We write $\Omega\mathcal{G}^\Box$ and $\Omega\mathcal{G}^\Diamond$ for the finite paths that end with a state of $S_\Box$ and $S_\Diamond$, respectively. A *strategy* of Player 1 is a function $\pi : \Omega\mathcal{G}^\Box \to \mathcal{D}(S)$ such that $s \in \text{supp}(\pi(\lambda))$ only if $\Delta(\text{last}(\lambda), s) = 1$. We say that π is *memoryless* if $\text{last}(\lambda) = \text{last}(\lambda')$ implies $\pi(\lambda) = \pi(\lambda')$, and *deterministic* if $\pi(\lambda)$ is Dirac for all $\lambda \in \Omega\mathcal{G}^+$, i.e. $\pi(\lambda)(s) = 1$ for some $s \in S$. A strategy σ for Player 2 is defined similarly replacing $\Omega\mathcal{G}^\Box$ with $\Omega\mathcal{G}^\Diamond$. We denote by Π and Σ the sets of all strategies for Player 1 and Player 2, respectively.

Probability Measures. A stochastic game $\mathcal{G}$, together with a strategy pair $(\pi, \sigma) \in \Pi \times \Sigma$ and an initial state s, induces an infinite Markov chain on the game (see e.g. [8]). We denote the probability measure of this Markov chain by $\mathbb{P}^{\pi, \sigma}_{\mathcal{G}, s}$. The expected value of a measurable function $g : S^\omega \to \mathbb{R}_{\pm\infty}$ is defined as $\mathbb{E}^{\pi, \sigma}_{\mathcal{G}, s}[g] \stackrel{\text{def}}{=} \int_{\Omega\mathcal{G}, s} g \, d\mathbb{P}^{\pi, \sigma}_{\mathcal{G}, s}$. We say that a game $\mathcal{G}$ is a *stopping game* if, for every strategy pair (π, σ), a terminal state is reached with probability 1, i.e. $\mathbb{P}^{\pi, \sigma}_{\mathcal{G}, s}(\Diamond \text{Term}) = 1$ for all s.

Total Reward. A reward function $\varrho \colon S \to \mathbb{Q}$ assigns a reward to each state of the game. We assume the rewards are 0 in all terminal states. The *total reward* of a path λ is $\varrho(\lambda) \stackrel{\text{def}}{=} \sum_{j \geq 0} \varrho(\lambda_j)$. Given a game $\mathcal{G}$, an initial state s, a vector of n rewards ϱ and a vector of n bounds $z \in \mathbb{R}^n$, we say that a pair of strategies (π, σ) *yields* an objective $\text{totrew}(\varrho, z)$ if $\mathbb{E}^{\pi, \sigma}_{\mathcal{G}, s}[\varrho_i] \geq z_i$ for all $1 \leq i \leq n$. A strategy $\pi \in \Pi$ *achieves* $\text{totrew}(\varrho, z)$ if for all σ we have that (π, σ) yields $\text{totrew}(\varrho, z)$; the vector z is then called *achievable*, and we use $\mathcal{A}_s$ for the set of all achievable vectors. A strategy $\sigma \in \Sigma$ *spoils* $\text{totrew}(\varrho, z)$ if for no $\pi \in \Pi$, the tuple (π, σ) yields $\text{totrew}(\varrho, z)$. Note that lower bounds (objectives $\mathbb{E}^{\pi, \sigma}_{\mathcal{G}, s}[\varrho_i] \leq z_i$) can be modelled by upper bounds after multiplying all rewards and bounds by -1.

A (lower) Pareto curve in s is the set of all maximal z such that for all $\varepsilon > 0$ there is $\pi \in \Pi$ that achieves the objective $\mathsf{totrew}(\varrho, z - \varepsilon)$. We use f_s for the Pareto curve, and for the two-objective case we treat it as a function, writing $f_s(x) = y$ when $(x, y) \in f_s$. We say that a game is *determined* if for all states, every bound can be spoiled or lies in the downward closure of the Pareto curve.[1] Note that the downward closure of the Pareto curve equals the closure of $\mathcal{A}_s$.

Discounted Reward. Discounted games play an important role in game theory. In these games, the rewards have a discount factor $\delta \in (0, 1)$ meaning that the reward received after j steps is multiplied by δ^j, and so a discounted reward of a path λ is then $\varrho(\lambda, \delta) = \sum_{j \geq 0} \varrho(\lambda_j) \cdot \delta^j$. We define the notions of achieving, spoiling and Pareto curves for discounted reward $\mathsf{disrew}(\varrho, \delta, z)$ in the same way as for total reward. Since the problems for discounted reward can easily be encoded using the total reward framework (by adding before each state a stochastic state from which with probability $(1 - \delta)$ we transition to a terminal state), from now on we will concentrate on total reward, unless specified otherwise.

The Problems. In this paper we study the following decision problems.

Definition 1 *(Total-reward problem). Given a stochastic game $\mathcal{G}$, an initial state s_0, and vectors of n reward functions ϱ and thresholds z, is $\mathsf{totrew}(\varrho, z)$ achievable from s_0?*

Definition 2 *(Discounted-reward problem). Given a stochastic game $\mathcal{G}$, an initial state s_0, vectors of n reward functions ϱ and thresholds z, and a discount factor $\delta \in (0, 1)$, is $\mathsf{disrew}(\varrho, \delta, z)$ achievable from s_0?*

In the particular case when n above is 2, we speak about *two-objective* problems.

Simplifying Assumption. In order to keep the presentation of the proofs simple, we will assume that each non-terminal state has exactly two successors and that only the states controlled by Player 2 have weights different from 0. Note that any stochastic game can be transformed into an equivalent game with this property in polynomial time, so we do not lose generality by this assumption.

Example 3 (Floor Heating Problem). As an example illustrating the definitions, as well as possible applications of our results, we consider a simplified version of the smart-house case study presented in [14] with a difference that we model both user comfort and energy consumption. Player 1, representing a controller, decides which rooms are heated, while the Player 2 represents the configuration of the house, for instance which door and windows are open, which cannot be influenced by the controller. The temperature in another room changes based on additional probabilistic factors. We illustrate this example in Fig. 1 and a simple model as a stochastic game is given in Fig. 2 (left). We have to control the floor heating of two rooms in a house, by opening at most one of the valves V_1 and V_2 at a time.

---

[1] The reader might notice that in some works, games are said to be determined when each vector can be either achieved by by one player, or spoiled by the other. This is not the case of our definition, where the notion of determinacy is *weaker* and only requires ability to spoil or achieve up to arbitrarily small ε.

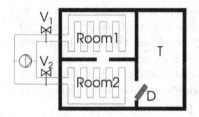

Fig. 1. A house with control-lable floor heating in two rooms.

The state of each room is either cold or hot, for instance in state H, C, the first room is warm while the second one is cold, and the third room has unknown temperature. Weights on the first dimension represent the energy consumption of the system while the second represent the comfort inside the house. Player 2 controls whether the door D between the second room and a third one is open or not. The temperature T in the other room of the house is controlled by stochastic transitions. For instance in the initial state (C, C), the controller can choose either to switch on the heating in room 1 or room 2. Then the second player chooses whether the door is opened or not and stochastic states determine the contribution of the other rooms: for instance from (H, C) if the second player chooses that the door is opened then depending on whether the temperature of the other room is low or high, room 2 can either stay cold or get heated through the door, and the next state in that case is (H, H) which is the terminal state. The objective is to optimise energy consumption and comfort until both rooms are warm. The Pareto curve for a few states of the game is depicted in Fig. 2 (right).

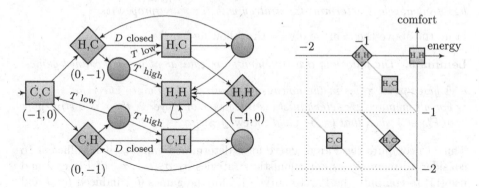

Fig. 2. A stochastic two-player game modelling the floor heating problem. Vectors under states denote a reward function when it is not $(0, 0)$. All probabilistic transitions have probability $\frac{1}{2}$. Pareto curves of a few states of the game are depicted on the right.

2.1 Equations for Lower Value

We recall the results of [1,9] showing that for stopping games the sets of achievable points $\mathcal{A}_s$ are the unique solution to the sets of equations defined as follows:

$$
X_s = \begin{cases}
\mathrm{dwc}(\{(0,\ldots,0)\}) & \text{if } s \in \mathsf{Term} \\
\mathrm{dwc}(\mathrm{conv}(\bigcup_{t \in \Delta(s)} X_t)) & \text{if } s \in S_\square \\
\varrho(s) + \mathrm{dwc}(\bigcap_{t \in \Delta(s)} X_t) & \text{if } s \in S_\lozenge \\
\mathrm{dwc}(\sum_{t \in \Delta(s)} \Delta(s, t) \cdot X_t) & \text{if } s \in S_\bigcirc
\end{cases}
$$

The equations can be used to design a value-iteration algorithm that itera-tively computes sets X_s^i for increasing i: As a base step we have $X_s^0 = \mathsf{dwc}(\boldsymbol{0})$ (where $\boldsymbol{0} = (0,\ldots,0)$); we then substitute X_s^i for X_s on the right-hand side of the equations, and obtain X_s^{i+1} as X_s on the left-hand side. The sets X_s^i so obtained converge to the least fixpoint of the equations above [1,9]. As we will show later, the sets X_s^i might be getting increasingly complex even though the actual solution X_s only comprises two extremal points.

3   Determined Games

In this section we present a simple algorithm which works under the assumption that the game is determined. For stopping games, we then give a procedure to decide whether a game is determined.

Theorem 3. *There is an algorithm working in exponential time, which given a determined stochastic two-player game, computes its Pareto-curve.*

For the proof of the theorem we will make use of the following:

Theorem 4 [9, Theorem. 7]. *Suppose Player 2 has a strategy σ such that for all π of Player 1 there is at least one $1 \leq i \leq n$ with $\mathbb{E}_{\mathcal{G},s}^{\pi,\sigma}(\boldsymbol{\varrho}_i) < z_i$. Then Player 2 has a memoryless deterministic strategy with the same properties.*

From the above theorem we obtain the following lemma.

Lemma 5. *The following two statements are equivalent for determined games:*

- *A given point z lies in the downward closure of the Pareto curve for s.*
- *For all memoryless deterministic strategies σ of Player 2, there is a strategy π of Player 1 such that (π, σ) yield $\mathsf{totrew}(\boldsymbol{\varrho}, \boldsymbol{z})$.*

Thus, to compute the Pareto curve for a determined game $\mathcal{G}$, it is sufficient to consider all memoryless deterministic strategies $\sigma_1, \sigma_2, \ldots, \sigma_m$ of Player 2 and use [11] to compute the Pareto curves $f_s^{\sigma_i}$ for the games $\mathcal{G}^{\sigma_i}$ induced by $\mathcal{G}$ and σ_i (i.e. $\mathcal{G}^{\sigma_i}$ is obtained from $\mathcal{G}$ by turning all $s \in S_\Diamond$ to stochastic vertices and stipulating $\Delta(s,t) = \sigma_i(s)$ for all successors t of s; in turn, $\mathcal{G}^{\sigma_i}$ is a Markov decision process), and obtain the Pareto curve for $\mathcal{G}$ as the pointwise minimum $V_s := \min_{1 \leq i \leq m} f_s^{\sigma_i}$.

To decide if a stopping game is determined, it is sufficient to take the downward closures of solutions V_s and check if they satisfy the equations from Sect. 2.1. Since in stopping games the solution of the equations is unique, if the sets are a solution they are also the Pareto curves and the game is determined. If any of the equations are not satisfied, then V_s are not the Pareto curves and the game is not determined. Note that for non-stopping games the above approach does not work: even if the sets do not change by applying one step of value iteration, it is still possible that the solution is not the least fixpoint, and so we cannot infer any conclusion.

4   Games with Two Objectives

We start this section by showing that the existing value iteration algorithm presented in Sect. 2.1 might iteratively compute sets X_s^i with increasing number of extremal points, although the actual resulting set X_s (and the associated Pareto curve f_s) is very simple. Consider the game from Fig. 3 (left). Applying the value-iteration algorithm given by the equations from Sect. 2.1 for n steps gives a Pareto curve in s_0 with $n - 1$ extremal points. Each extremal point corresponds to a strategy π_i that in s_0 chooses to go to s_2 when the number of visits of s_0 is less than i, and after that chooses to go to s_1. The upper bounds of the sets X_s^n for $n = 5$ and $n = 10$ are drawn in Fig. 3 (centre and right, respectively) using solid line, and their extremal points are marked with dots. The Pareto curve f_s is drawn with dashed blue line, and it consists of two extremal points, $(0, 1)$ and $(1, 0)$.

We now proceed with the main result of this section, the decidability of the two-objective strategy synthesis problem for stopping games. The result can be obtained from the following theorem.

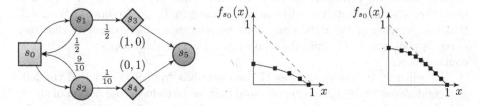

Fig. 3. An example showing that value iteration might produce Pareto curves with unboundedly many extremal points.

Theorem 6. *If $\mathcal{G}$ is a stopping stochastic two-player game with two objectives, and s a state of $\mathcal{G}$ then the Pareto curve f_s has only finitely many extremal points.*

The above theorem can be used to design the following algorithm. For a fixed number k, we create a formula φ_k over $(\mathbb{R}, +, \cdot, \leq)$ which is true if and only if for each $s \in S$ there are points $\boldsymbol{p}^{s,1}, \ldots, \boldsymbol{p}^{s,k}$ such that the sets $V_s \stackrel{\text{def}}{=}$ dwc(conv($\{\boldsymbol{p}^{s,1}, \ldots \boldsymbol{p}^{s,k}\}$)) satisfy the equations from Sect. 2.1. Using [16] we can then successively check validity of φ_k for increasing k, and Theorem 6 guarantees that we will eventually get a formula which is valid, and it immediately gives us the Pareto curve. We get the following result as a corollary.

Corollary 7. *Two-objective total reward problem is decidable in the case of stopping stochastic games, and two-objective discounted-reward problem is decidable in the case of stochastic games.*

Outline of the Proof of Theorem 6. The proof of Theorem 6 proceeds by assuming that there are infinitely many extremal points on the Pareto curve, and then deriving a contradiction. Firstly, because the game is stopping, an upper bound on the expected total reward that can be obtained with respect to a single total reward objective is $M := \sum_{i=0}^{\infty}(1 - p_{min}^{|S|})^i \cdot \varrho_{max}^{|S|}$ where $p_{min} = \min\{\Delta(s, s') \mid \Delta(s, s') > 0\}$ is the smallest transition probability, and $\varrho_{max} = \max_{i \in \{1,2\}} \max_{s \in S} \varrho_i(s)$ is the maximal reward assigned to a state. Thus, the Pareto curve is contained in a compact set, and this implies that there is an accumulation point on it. In Sect. 4.1, we show that we can follow one accumulation point p from one state to one of its successors, while preserving the same left slope. Moreover, in the neighbourhood of the accumulation point the rate at which the right slope decreases is quite similar to the decrease in the successors, in a way that is made precise in Lemmas 9, 10, and 11. This is with the exception of some stochastic states for which the decrease strictly slows down when going to the successors: we will exploit this fact to get a contradiction. We construct a transition system $T_{s_0,p}$, which keeps all the paths obtained by following the accumulation point p from s_0. We show that if $\mathcal{G}$ is a stopping game, then we can obtain a path in $T_{s_0,p}$ which visits stochastic states for which the decrease of the right slope strictly slows down. This relies on results for *inverse betting games*, which are presented in Sect. 4.2. Since this decrease can be repeated and there are only finitely many reachable states in $T_{s_0,p}$, we show in Sect. 4.3 that the decrease of the right slope must be zero somewhere, meaning that the curve is constant in the neighbourhood of an accumulation point, which is a contradiction.

We will rely on the properties of the equations from Sect. 2.1 and the left and right slopes of the Pareto curve. Note that we introduced the notion of slope only for two-dimensional sets, and so our proofs only work for two dimensions. Generalisations of the concept of slopes exist for higher dimensions, but simple generalisation of our lemmas would not be valid, as we will show later. Hence, in the remainder of this section, we focus on the two-objective case. For the simplicity of presentation, we will present all claims and proofs for *left* accumulation points. The case of right accumulation points is analogous.

4.1   Mapping Accumulation Points to Successor States

We start by enumerating some basic but useful properties of the Pareto curve and its slopes. First notice that it is a continuous concave function and we can prove the following:

Lemma 8. *Let f be a continuous concave function defined on $[a, b]$.*

1. *If $a < x < x' \leq b$ are two reals for which lslope(f) is defined, then lslope$(f, x) \geq$ rslope$(f, x) \geq$ lslope(f, x').*
2. *If (x, x') contains an extremal point of f then lslope$(f_s, x) \neq$ lslope(f_s, x').*
3. *If $x \in (a, b]$, then $\lim_{x' \to x^-}$ lslope$(f, x') = \lim_{x' \to x^-}$ rslope$(f, x') =$ lslope(f, x).*

To prove Theorem 6, we will use the equations from Sect. 2.1 to describe how accumulation points on a Pareto curve for s "map" to accumulation points on successors.

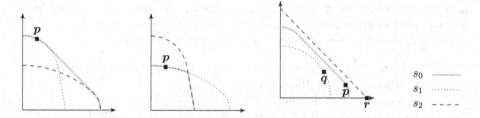

Fig. 4. An example of Pareto curve in a state s_0 with two successors s_1 and s_2, for the case of $s_0 \in S_\square$ (left), $s_0 \in S_\lozenge$ (centre), and $s_0 \in S_\bigcirc$ with uniform probabilities on transitions (right). In each case, the curve has infinitely many accumulation points.

Lemma 9. *Let s_0 be a Player 1 state with two successors s_1 and s_2, and let p be a left accumulation point of f_{s_0}. Then there is $\eta(s_0, p) > 0$ such that for all $\varepsilon \in (0, \eta(s_0, p))$, there is $s' \in \{s_1, s_2\}$ such that: 1. p is a left accumulation point in $f_{s'}$; 2. lslope$(f_{s_0}, p_1) =$ lslope$(f_{s'}, p_1)$; 3. $f_{s_0}(p_1 - \varepsilon) \geq f_{s'}(p_1 - \varepsilon)$ and rslope$(f_{s_0}, p_1 - \varepsilon) \geq$ rslope$(f_{s'}, p_1 - \varepsilon)$.*

Proof (Sketch). The point 1. follows from the fact that every extremal point in the Pareto curve for s_0 must be an extremal point in one of the successors. This is illustrated in Fig. 4 (left): p which is an extremal point for s_0 is also an extremal point for s_1. The point 2. follows because from a sequence of extremal points $(p^i)_{i \geq 0}$ on the Pareto curve of s_0 that converge to p, we can select a subsequence that gives extremal points on s' that converge to the left accumulation point p on s'. Finally, to prove 3. we use the fact that the right slope of f_{s_0} is always between those of f_{s_1} and of f_{s_2}. □

Lemma 10. *Let s_0 be a Player 2 state with two successors s_1 and s_2, and let p be a left accumulation point of f_{s_0}. There is $\eta(s_0, p) > 0$ such that for all $\varepsilon \in (0, \eta(s_0, p))$, there is $s' \in \{s_1, s_2\}$, such that: 1. $p - \varrho(s_0)$ is a left accumulation point in $f_{s'}$; 2. lslope$(s_0, p_1) =$ lslope$(s', p_1 - \varrho_1(s_0))$; 3. $f_{s_0}(p_1 - \varepsilon) = f_{s'}(p_1 - \varepsilon - \varrho_1(s_0))$ and rslope$(f_{s_0}, p_1 - \varepsilon) =$ rslope$(f_{s'}, p_1 - \varepsilon - \varrho_1(s_0))$.*

Proof (Sketch). A crucial observation here is that $f_{s_0}(p_1^i)$ is either $\varrho_2(s_0) + f_{s_1}(p_1^i - \varrho_1(s_0))$ or $\varrho_2(s_0) + f_{s_2}(p_1^i - \varrho_1(s_0))$. This is illustrated in Fig. 4 (center): $f_{s_0}(p_1) = \varrho_2(s_0) + f_{s_1}(p_1 - \varrho_1(s_0))$ (there $\varrho(s_0) = (0, 0)$). Hence when we take a sequence $(p_1^i)_{i \in \mathbb{N}}$, for some $\ell \in \{1, 2\}$ the value $f_{s_0}(p_1^i)$ equals $\varrho_2(s_0) + f_{s_\ell}(p_1^i - \varrho_1(s_0))$ infinitely many times. From this we get a converging sequence of points in s_ℓ, and obtain that the left slopes are equal in s_0 and s_ℓ. By further arguing that in any left neighbourhood of $p_1^i - \varrho_1(s_0)$ we can find infinitely many points with different left slopes, we obtain that there are also infinitely many extremal points in the neighbourhood and hence $p_1^i - \varrho_1(s_0)$ is a left accumulation point.

As for the last item, the important observation here is that if at some point p', f_{s_1} is strictly below f_{s_2} then the right slope of f_{s_0} corresponds to that of f_{s_1}, and if f_{s_1} equals f_{s_2} then the right slope of f_{s_0} corresponds to the minimum of the right slopes of f_{s_1} and f_{s_2} (it is also interesting to note that the left slope corresponds to the maximum of the two). □

Lemma 11. *Let s_0 be a stochastic state with two successors s_1 and s_2, and p a left accumulation point of f_{s_0}. There are points q and r on f_{s_1} and f_{s_2} respectively such that $p = \Delta(s_0, s_1) \cdot q + \Delta(s_0, s_2) \cdot r$. Moreover:*

1. *there is $(s', t) \in \{(s_1, q), (s_2, r)\}$ such that t is a left accumulation point of $f_{s'}$ and $\mathsf{lslope}(f_{s_0}, p_1) = \mathsf{lslope}(f_{s'}, t_1)$;*
2. *there is $\eta(s_0, p) > 0$ such that for all $\varepsilon \in (0, \eta(s_0, p))$:*
   - *there are $\varepsilon_1 \geq 0, \varepsilon_2 \geq 0$ such that $\mathsf{rslope}(f_{s_0}, p_1 - \varepsilon) \geq \mathsf{rslope}(f_{s_1}, q_1 - \varepsilon_1)$, $\mathsf{rslope}(f_{s_0}, p_1 - \varepsilon) \geq \mathsf{rslope}(f_{s_2}, r_1 - \varepsilon_2)$, and $\varepsilon = \Delta(s_0, s_1) \cdot \varepsilon_1 + \Delta(s_0, s_2) \cdot \varepsilon_2$;*
   - *if r is not a left accum. point in f_{s_2}, or $\mathsf{lslope}(f_{s_0}, p_1) \neq \mathsf{lslope}(f_{s_2}, r_1)$, then*

   $$f_{s_0}(p_1 - \varepsilon) = \Delta(s_0, s_1) \cdot f_{s_1}\left(\frac{p_1 - \varepsilon - \Delta(s_0, s_2) \cdot r_1}{\Delta(s_0, s_1)}\right) + \Delta(s_0, s_2) \cdot r_2;$$

   - *if q is not a left accum. point in f_{s_1}, or $\mathsf{lslope}(f_{s_0}, p_1) \neq \mathsf{lslope}(f_{s_1}, q_1)$, then*

   $$f_{s_0}(p_1 - \varepsilon) = \Delta(s_0, s_1) \cdot q_2 + \Delta(s_0, s_2) \cdot f_{s_1}\left(\frac{p_1 - \varepsilon - \Delta(s_0, s_1) \cdot q_1}{\Delta(s_0, s_2)}\right).$$

Proof (Sketch). We use the fact that for every extremal point p' there are unique extremal points q' and r' on f_{s_1} and f_{s_2}, respectively, such that $p' = \Delta(s_0, s_1) \cdot q' + \Delta(s_0, s_2) \cdot r'$.

To prove item 1, we show that for all extremal points p', $\mathsf{lslope}(s_0, p') = \min(\mathsf{lslope}(s_1, q'), \mathsf{lslope}(s_2, r'))$, which can be surprising at first glance since one could have expected a weighted sum of the left slopes. This fact is illustrated in Fig. 4 (right): $\mathsf{lslope}(s_0, p') = \mathsf{lslope}(s_1, q') \leq \mathsf{lslope}(s_2, r')$. The inequality $\mathsf{lslope}(s_0, p) \leq \mathsf{lslope}(s_1, q)$ (and similarly $\mathsf{lslope}(s_0, p) \leq \mathsf{lslope}(s_2, r)$), follows from concavity of f_{s_0}: because for all $\varepsilon > 0$ the inequality $f_{s_0}(p_1 - \varepsilon) \geq \Delta(s_0, s_1) \cdot f_{s_1}(q_1 - \frac{\varepsilon}{\Delta(s_0, s_1)}) + \Delta(s_0, s_2) \cdot f_{s_2}(r_1)$ holds true, from which we obtain $\lim_{\varepsilon \to 0+} \frac{f_{s_0}(p_1) - f_{s_0}(p_1 - \varepsilon)}{\varepsilon} \leq \lim_{\varepsilon \to 0+} \frac{f_{s_1}(q_1) - f_{s_1}(q_1 - \varepsilon)}{\varepsilon}$. Showing that the left slope is at least the minimum of the successors' slopes is significantly more demanding and technical, and we give the proof in the long version of this paper [3].

Proving the second point, is based on the observation that a point on the Pareto curve f_{s_0} is a combination of points of f_{s_1} and f_{s_2} that share a common tangent: in other words they maximize the dot product with a specific vector on their respective curves. From this observation it is possible to link the right slopes of these curves. The last two points hold because with the assumption, extremal points that converge to p from the left can be obtained as a combination from a fixed r and points on f_{s_2}.   □

Now we will prove that there are no left accumulation points on the Pareto curve. To do that, we will try to follow one in the game: if there is a left accumulation point in one state then at least one of its successors also has one, as the above lemmas show. By using the fact that the left slopes of left accumulation points are preserved we show that the number of reachable combinations (s, p), where $s \in S$ and p is a left accumulation point, is finite. We then look at points slightly to the left of the accumulation points, their distance to the accumulation point and right slopes are also mostly preserved except in stochastic states, where if only one successor has a left accumulation point, the decrease of the right slope accelerates (by Lemmas 11.2). By using the fact that in stopping games we can ensure visiting such stochastic states, we will show that for some states the right slope is constant on the left neighbourhood of the left accumulation point, which is a contradiction.

Assume we are given a state s_0 and a left accumulation point p^0 of f_{s_0}. We construct a transition system T_{s_0,p^0} where the initial state is (s_0, p^0), and the successors of a given configuration (s, p) are the states (s', p') such that s' is a successor of s, and p' is a left accumulation point of s with the same left slope on $f_{s'}$ as p on f_s. Lemmas 9, 10, and 11, ensure that all the reachable states have at least one successor.

Lemma 12. *For all reachable states (s, p) and (s', p') in the transition system T_{s_0,p^0}, if $s = s'$, then $p = p'$.*

Proof. Assume $s = s'$. By construction of T_{s_0,p^0}, the left slope in s of p and p' is the same: $\mathsf{lslope}(s, p_1) = \mathsf{lslope}(s_0, p_1^0) = \mathsf{lslope}(s_2, p'_1)$. Assume towards a contradiction that $p < p'$; the proof would work the same for $p' < p$. Since p' is a left accumulation point, there is an extremal point in (p_1, p'_1). Lemma 8.2 tells us that $\mathsf{lslope}(s_1, p_1) \neq \mathsf{lslope}(s_2, p'_1)$ which is a contradiction. Hence $p = p'$. $\square$

As a corollary of this lemma, the number of states that are reachable in T_{s_0,p^0} is finite and bounded by $|S|$.

4.2 Inverse Betting Game

To show a contradiction, we will follow a path with left accumulation points. We want this path to visit stochastic states which have only one successor in T_{s_0,p^0}. For that, we will prove a property of an intermediary game that we call an inverse betting game.

An *inverse betting game* is a two player game, given by $\langle V_\exists, V_\forall, E, (v_0, c_0), w \rangle$ where $V_\exists$ and $V_\forall$ are the set of vertices controlled by Eve and Adam, respectively, $\langle V_\exists \cup V_\forall, E \rangle$ is a graph whose each vertex has two successors, $(v_0, c_0) \in V \times \mathbb{R}$ is the initial configuration, and $w \colon E \to \mathbb{R}$ is a weight function such that for all $v \in V \colon \sum_{v'|(v,v')\in E} w(v, v') = 1$.

A configuration of the game is a pair $(v, c) \in V \times \mathbb{R}$ where v is a vertex and c a credit. The game starts in configuration (v_0, c_0) and is played by two players Eve and Adam. At each step, from a configuration (v, c) controlled by Eve, Adam suggests a valuation $d \colon E \to \mathbb{R}$ for the outgoing edges of v such that $\sum_{v'|(v,v')\in E} w(v, v') \cdot d(v, v') = c$. Eve then chooses a successor v' such that $(v, v') \in E$ and the game continues from configuration $(v', d(v, v'))$. From a configuration (v, c) controlled by Adam, Adam chooses a successor v' of v and keeps the same credit, hence the game continues from (v', c).

Intuitively, Adam has some credit, and at each step he has to distribute it by betting over the possible successors. Then Eve chooses the successor and Adam gets a credit equal to its bet divided by the probability of this transition. The game is *inverse* because Eve is trying to maximize the credit of Adam.

Theorem 13. *Let* $\langle V_\exists, V_\forall, E, (v_0, c_0), w\rangle$ *be an inverse betting game. Let* $T \subseteq V_\exists \cup V_\forall$ *be a target set and* $B \in \mathbb{R}$ *a bound. If from every vertex* $v \in V$, Eve *has a strategy to ensure visiting* T *then she has one to ensure visiting it with a credit* $c \geq 1$ *or to exceed the bound, that is, she can force a configuration in* $(T \times [c_0, +\infty)) \cup (V \times [B, +\infty))$.

Our next step is transforming the transition system T_{s_0, p^0} into such a game. Consider the inverse betting game $\mathcal{B}$ on the structure given by T_{s_0, p^0} where $V_\exists = S_\bigcirc$ are the states controlled by Eve, $V_\forall = S_\square \cup S_\diamond$ are controlled by Adam, $w((s, \boldsymbol{p}), (s', \boldsymbol{p}')) = \Delta(s, s')$ is a weight on edges and the initial configuration is $((s_0, \boldsymbol{p}^0), \varepsilon_0)$. Let U_{s_0, p^0} the set of terminal states and of stochastic states that have only one successor in T_{s_0, p^0}. We show that in the inverse betting game obtained from a stopping game $\mathcal{G}$, Eve can ensure visiting U_{s_0, p^0}.

Lemma 14. *If* $\mathcal{G}$ *is stopping, there is a strategy for* Eve *in* $\mathcal{B}$ *such that from every vertex* $v \in V$, *all outcomes visit* U_{s_0, p^0}.

Proof. Assume towards a contradiction that this is not the case, then by memoryless determinacy of turn-based reachability games (see e.g. [12]) there is a vertex v and a memoryless deterministic strategy σ_{Adam} of Adam, such that no outcomes of σ_{Adam} from v visit U_{s_0, p^0}. Let π and σ be the strategies of Player 1 and Player 2 respectively corresponding to σ_{Adam}. Formally, if $h \in \Omega_{\mathcal{G}}^{\square}$ then $\pi(h) = \sigma_{\mathsf{Adam}}(h)$ and if $h \in \Omega_{\mathcal{G}}^{\diamond}$ then $\sigma(h) = \sigma_{\mathsf{Adam}}(h)$.

We prove that all outcomes λ in $\mathcal{G}$ of π, σ from v are outcomes of σ_{Adam} in $\mathcal{B}$. This is by induction on the prefixes $\lambda_{\leq i}$ of the outcomes. It is clear when $\lambda_{\leq i}$ ends with states that are controlled by Player 1 and Player 2 by the way we defined π and σ, that $\lambda_{\leq i+1}$ is also compatible with σ_{Adam} in $\mathcal{B}$. For a finite path $\lambda_{\leq i}$ ending with stochastic state s in $\mathcal{G}$, two successors are possible. With the induction hypothesis that $\lambda_{\leq i}$ is compatible with σ_{Adam}, and by the assumption on σ_{Adam}, s does not belong to U_{s_0, p^0}. Therefore, both successors of s are also in T_{s_0, p^0}, and $\lambda_{\leq i+1}$ is compatible with σ_{Adam} in $\mathcal{B}$. This shows that outcomes in $\mathcal{G}$ of (π, σ) are also outcomes of σ_{Adam} in $\mathcal{B}$. Therefore, π and σ ensure that from v, we visit no state of U_{s_0, p^0} and thus no terminal state. This contradicts that the game is stopping. $\qquad\square$

Putting Theorem 13 and Lemma 14 together we can conclude the following:

Corollary 15. *If* $\mathcal{G}$ *is stopping then in* $\mathcal{B}$, *for any bound* B, Eve *has a strategy to ensure visiting* U_{s_0, p^0} *with a credit* $c \geq 1$ *or making* c *exceed* B.

4.3 Contradicting Sequence

We define $\theta(s_0, \boldsymbol{p}^0) = \min\{\eta(s, \boldsymbol{p}) \mid (s, \boldsymbol{p}) \text{ reachable in } T_{s_0, p^0}\}$, and consider a sequence of points that are $\theta(s_0, \boldsymbol{p}^0)$ close to $\boldsymbol{p}^0$ and with a right slope that is decreasing at least as fast as that of their predecessors.

Lemma 16. *For stopping games, given* $s_0 \in S$, $\boldsymbol{p}^0 \in \mathbb{R}^2$, *and* $\varepsilon_0 > 0$, *such that* $\varepsilon_0 < \theta(s_0, \boldsymbol{p}^0)$, *there is a finite sequence* $\pi(s_0, \boldsymbol{p}^0, \varepsilon_0) = (s_i, \boldsymbol{p}^i, \varepsilon_i)_{i \leq j}$ *such that:*

- $(s_i, \boldsymbol{p}^i)_{i \leq j}$ is a path in $T_{s_0, \boldsymbol{p}^0}$;
- for all $i \leq j$, $\mathsf{rslope}(f_{s_i}, \boldsymbol{p}_1^i - \varepsilon_i) \geq \mathsf{rslope}(f_{s_{i+1}}, \boldsymbol{p}_1^{i+1} - \varepsilon_{i+1})$.
- either $\varepsilon_j \geq \theta(s_0, \boldsymbol{p}^0)$ or $s_j \in U_{s_0, \boldsymbol{p}^0}$ and $\varepsilon_j \geq \varepsilon_0$.

The idea of the proof is that in $\mathcal{B}$, thanks to Lemmas 9, 10, and 11, Adam can always choose a successor such that $\mathsf{rslope}(f_{s_i}, \boldsymbol{p}_1^i - \varepsilon_i) \geq \mathsf{rslope}(f_{s_{i+1}}, \boldsymbol{p}_1^{i+1} - \varepsilon_{i+1})$. Then thanks to Corollary 15, there is a strategy for Eve to reach $(U_{s_0, \boldsymbol{p}^0} \times [c_0, +\infty)) \cup (V \times [B, +\infty))$. By combining the two strategies, we obtain an outcome that satisfies the desired properties.

We use the path obtained from this lemma to show that no matter how small ε_0 we choose, ε_i can grow to reach $\theta(s_0, \boldsymbol{p}^0)$.

Lemma 17. *For all states s with a left accumulation point $\boldsymbol{p}$ and for all $0 < \varepsilon < \theta(s, \boldsymbol{p})$, there is some $(s', \boldsymbol{p}')$ reachable in $T_{s,p}$ such that $\mathsf{rslope}(f_{s'}, \boldsymbol{p}_1' - \theta(s, \boldsymbol{p})) \leq \mathsf{rslope}(f_s, \boldsymbol{p}_1 - \varepsilon)$.*

Thanks to this lemma, we can now prove Theorem 6. Assume towards a contradiction that there is a left accumulation point $\boldsymbol{p}$ in the state s. Let $m = \min\{|\mathsf{slope}(f_{s'}, \boldsymbol{p}_1' - \theta(s, \boldsymbol{p})) \mid (s', \boldsymbol{p}')$ reachable in $T_{s,p}\}$ and $(s', \boldsymbol{p}')$ the configuration of $T_{s,p}$ for which this minimum is reached (it is reached because the number of reachable configurations is finite: this is a corollary of Lemma 12). Because of Lemma 17, $\mathsf{rslope}(f_s, \boldsymbol{p}_1 - \varepsilon)$ is greater than m. By Lemma 8.3, when ε goes towards 0, $\mathsf{rslope}(f_s, \boldsymbol{p}_1 - \varepsilon)$ converges to $\mathsf{lslope}(f_s, \boldsymbol{p}_1)$. This means that $\mathsf{lslope}(f_s, \boldsymbol{p}_1) \geq m$. Moreover, by construction of $T_{s,p}$, we also have that $\mathsf{lslope}(f_{s'}, \boldsymbol{p}_1') = \mathsf{lslope}(f_s, \boldsymbol{p}_1)$, so $\mathsf{lslope}(f_{s'}, \boldsymbol{p}_1') \geq m$. Because the slopes are decreasing (Lemma 8.2), $m = \mathsf{rslope}(f_{s'}, \boldsymbol{p}_1' - \theta(s, \boldsymbol{p})) \geq \mathsf{lslope}(f_{s'}, \boldsymbol{p}_1') \geq m$. Hence, the left and right slopes of $f_{s'}$ are constant on $[\boldsymbol{p}_1' - \theta(s, \boldsymbol{p}), \boldsymbol{p}_1']$, and Lemma 8.8 implies that there are no extremal point in $(\boldsymbol{p}_1' - \theta(s, \boldsymbol{p}), \boldsymbol{p}_1')$. This contradicts the fact that $\boldsymbol{p}'$ is a left accumulation point: there should be an extremal point in any neighbourhood on the left of $\boldsymbol{p}'$. Hence, f_s contains no accumulation point.

Remark 18. One might attempt to extend the proof of Theorem 6 to three or more objectives, but this does not seem to be easily doable. Although it is possible to use directional derivative (or pick a subgradient) instead of using left and right slope in such setting, an analogue of Lemma 8.2 cannot be proved because in multiple dimensions, two accumulation points can share the same directional derivative, for a fixed direction. It is also not easily possible to avoid this problem by following several directional derivatives instead of just one. This is because the slope in one direction may be inherited from one successor while the slope in another direction comes from another successor. We give more details and example of convex sets that would contradict generalisations of Lemma 8.2 and Lemma 10 in the long version of this paper [3].

5   Conclusions

We have studied stochastic games under multiple objectives, and have provided decidability results for determined games and for stopping games with two objectives. Our results provide an important milestone towards obtaining decidability for the general case, which is a major task which will require further novel insights into the problem. Another research direction concerns establishing an upper bound on the number of extremal points of a Pareto curve; such result would allow us to give upper complexity bounds for the problem.

Acknowledgements. The authors would like to thank Aistis Šimaitis and Clemens Wiltsche for useful discussions on the topic. The work was supported by EPSRC grant EP/M023656/1. Vojtěch Forejt is also affiliated with Masaryk University, Czech Republic.

References

1. Basset, N., Kwiatkowska, M., Topcu, U., Wiltsche, C.: Strategy synthesis for stochastic games with multiple long-run objectives. In: Baier, C., Tinelli, C. (eds.) TACAS 2015. LNCS, vol. 9035, pp. 256–271. Springer, Heidelberg (2015)
2. Basset, N., Kwiatkowska, M., Wiltsche, C.: Compositional strategy synthesis for stochastic games with multiple objectives. Technical report, Department of Computer Science, Oxford, UK (2016)
3. Brenguier, R., Forejt, V.: Decidability results for multi-objective stochastic games. arXiv preprint arXiv:1605.03811 (2016)
4. Brenguier, R., Raskin, J.: Pareto curves of multidimensional mean-payoff games. In: Kroening, D., Păsăreanu, C.S. (eds.) CAV 2015. LNCS, vol. 9207, pp. 251–267. Springer, Heidelberg (2015)
5. Chatterjee, K., Doyen, L.: Perfect-information stochastic games with generalized mean-payoff objectives. In: LICS (2016, to appear)
6. Chatterjee, K., Henzinger, T.A.: A survey of stochastic ω-regular games. J. Comput. Syst. Sci. **78**(2), 394–413 (2012)
7. Chatterjee, K., Randour, M., Raskin, J.: Strategy synthesis for multi-dimensional quantitative objectives. Acta Inf. **51**(3–4), 129–163 (2014)
8. Chen, T., Forejt, V., Kwiatkowska, M., Simaitis, A., Trivedi, A., Ummels, M.: Playing stochastic games precisely. In: Koutny, M., Ulidowski, I. (eds.) CONCUR 2012. LNCS, vol. 7454, pp. 348–363. Springer, Heidelberg (2012)
9. Chen, T., Forejt, V., Kwiatkowska, M., Simaitis, A., Wiltsche, C.: On stochastic games with multiple objectives. In: Chatterjee, K., Sgall, J. (eds.) MFCS 2013. LNCS, vol. 8087, pp. 266–277. Springer, Heidelberg (2013)
10. Condon, A.: The complexity of stochastic games. Inf. Comput. **96**(2), 203–224 (1992)
11. Etessami, K., Kwiatkowska, M., Vardi, M., Yannakakis, M.: Multi-objective model checking of Markov decision processes. LMCS **4**(4), 1–21 (2008)
12. Grädel, E., Thomas, W., Wilke, T. (eds.): Automata, Logics, and Infinite Games: A Guide to Current Research. LNCS. Springer, Heidelberg (2003)
13. Hunter, P., Raskin, J.: Quantitative games with interval objectives. In: FSTTCS (2014)
14. Larsen, K.G., Mikucionis, M., Muñiz, M., Srba, J., Taankvist, J.H.: Online and compositional learning of controllers with application to floor heating. In: TACAS (2016)
15. Nash Jr., J.F.: Equilibrium points in n-person games. Proc. Natl. Acad. Sci. USA **36**(1), 48–49 (1950)

16. Tarski, A.: A Decision Method for Elementary Algebra and Geometry. University of California Press, Berkeley (1951)
17. Velner, Y.: Robust multidimensional mean-payoff games are undecidable. In: Pitts, A. (ed.) FOSSACS 2015. LNCS, pp. 312–327. Springer, Heidelberg (2015)
18. Velner, Y., Chatterjee, K., Doyen, L., Henzinger, T.A., Rabinovich, A.M., Raskin, J.: The complexity of multi-mean-payoff and multi-energy games. Inf. Comput. **241**, 177–196 (2015)

A Decision Procedure for Separation Logic in SMT

Andrew Reynolds[1]([✉]), Radu Iosif[2], Cristina Serban[2], and Tim King[3]

[1] The University of Iowa, Iowa City, USA
andrew.j.reynolds@gmail.com
[2] Université de Grenoble Alpes, CNRS, VERIMAG, Grenoble, France
[3] Google Inc., Mountain View, USA

Abstract. This paper presents a complete decision procedure for the entire quantifier-free fragment of Separation Logic (SL) interpreted over heaplets with data elements ranging over a parametric multi-sorted (possibly infinite) domain. The algorithm uses a combination of theories and is used as a specialized solver inside a DPLL(T) architecture. A prototype was implemented within the CVC4 SMT solver. Preliminary evaluation suggests the possibility of using this procedure as a building block of a more elaborate theorem prover for SL with inductive predicates, or as back-end of a bounded model checker for programs with low-level pointer and data manipulations.

1 Introduction

Separation Logic (SL) [21] is a logical framework for describing dynamically allocated mutable data structures generated by programs that use pointers and low-level memory allocation primitives. The logics in this framework are used by a number of academic (SPACE INVADER [4]), and industrial (INFER [7]) tools for program verification. The main reason for choosing to work within the SL framework is its ability to provide compositional proofs of programs, based on the principle of *local reasoning*: analyzing different parts of the program (e.g. functions, threads), that work on *disjoint parts of the heap*, and combining the analysis results a posteriori.

The main ingredients of SL are: (i) the *separating conjunction* $\phi * \psi$, which asserts that ϕ and ψ hold for separate portions of the memory (heap), and (ii) the *magic wand* $\varphi \twoheadrightarrow \psi$, which asserts that any extension of the heap by a disjoint heap that satisfies φ must satisfy ψ. Consider, for instance, a memory configuration (heap), in which two cells are allocated, and pointed to by the program variables x and y, respectively, where the x cell has an outgoing selector field to the y cell, and vice versa. The heap can be split into two disjoint parts, each containing exactly one cell, and described by an atomic proposition x $\mapsto$ y

---

R. Iosif and C. Serban—Supported by the French National Research Agency project VECOLIB (ANR-14-CE28-0018).

C. Artho et al. (Eds.): ATVA 2016, LNCS 9938, pp. 244–261, 2016.
DOI: 10.1007/978-3-319-46520-3_16

and $y \mapsto x$, respectively. Then the entire heap is described by the formula $x \mapsto y * y \mapsto x$, which reads "x points to y and, separately, y points to x".

The expressive power of SL comes with the inherent difficulty of automatically reasoning about the satisfiability of its formulae, as required by push-button program analysis tools. Indeed, SL becomes undecidable in the presence of first-order quantification, even when the fragment uses only points-to predicates, without the separating conjunction or the magic wand [9]. Moreover, the quantifier-free fragment with no data constraints, using only points-to predicates $x \mapsto (y, z)$, where x, y and z are interpreted as memory addresses, is PSPACE-complete, due to the implicit quantification over memory partitions, induced by the semantics of the separation logic connectives [9].

This paper presents a decision procedure for quantifier-free SL which is entirely parameterized by a base theory T of heap locations and data, i.e. the sorts of memory addresses and their contents can be chosen from a large variety of available theories handled by Satisfiability Modulo Theories (SMT) solvers, such as linear integer (real) arithmetic, strings, sets, uninterpreted functions, etc. Given a base theory T, we call $SL(T)$ the set of separation logic formulae built on top of T, by considering points-to predicates and the separation logic connectives.

Contributions. First, we show that the satisfiability problem for the quantifier-free fragment of $SL(T)$ is PSPACE-complete, provided that the satisfiability of the quantifier-free fragment of the base theory T is in PSPACE. Our method is based on a semantics-preserving translation of $SL(T)$ into second-order T formulae with quantifiers over a domain of sets and uninterpreted functions, whose cardinality is polynomially bound by the size of the input formula. For the fragment of T formulae produced by the translation from $SL(T)$, we developed a lazy quantifier instantiation method, based on counterexample-driven refinement. We show that the quantifier instantiation algorithm is sound, complete and terminates on the fragment under consideration. We present our algorithm for the satisfiability of quantifier-free $SL(T)$ logics as a component of a $DPLL(T)$ architecture, which is widely used by modern SMT solvers. We have implemented the technique as a subsolver of the CVC4 SMT solver [2] and carried out experiments that handle non-trivial examples quite effectively. Applications of our procedure include:

1. Integration within theorem provers for SL with inductive predicates. Most inductive provers for SL use a high-level proof search strategy relying on a separate decision procedure for entailments in the non-inductive fragment, used to simplify the proof obligations, by discharging the non-inductive parts of both left- and right-hand sides, and attain an inductive hypothesis [6]. Due to the hard problem of proving entailments in the non-inductive fragment of SL, these predicates use very simple non-inductive formulae (a list of points-to propositions connected with separating conjunction), for which entailments are proved by syntactic substitutions and matching. Our work aims at extending the language of inductive SL solvers, by outsourcing entailments in a generic non-inductive fragment to a specialized procedure. To this

end, we conducted experiments on several entailments corresponding to finite unfoldings of inductive predicates used in practice (Sect. 6).

2. Use as back-end of a bounded model checker for programs with pointer and data manipulations, based on a complete weakest precondition calculus that involves the magic wand connective [15]. To corroborate this hypothesis, we tested our procedure on verification conditions automatically generated by applying the weakest precondition calculus described in [15] to several program fragments (Sect. 6).

Related Work. The study of the algorithmic properties of Separation Logic [21] has produced an extensive body of literature over time. We need to distinguish between SL with inductive predicates and restrictive non-inductive fragments, and SL without inductive predicates, which is the focus of this paper.

Regarding SL with fixed inductive predicates, Perez and Rybalchenko [16] define a theorem proving framework relying on a combination of SL inference rules dealing with singly-linked lists only, and a superposition calculus dealing with equalities and aliasing between variables. Concerning SL with generic user-provided inductive predicates, the theorem prover CYCLIST [6] builds entailment proofs using a sequent calculus. More recently, the tool SLIDE [14] reduces the entailment between inductive predicates to an inclusion between tree automata. The great majority of these inductive provers focus on applying induction strategies efficiently, and consider a very simple fragment of non-inductive SL formulae, typically conjunctions of equalities and disequalities between location variables and separated points-to predicates, without negations or the magic wand. On a more general note, the tool SPEN [10] considers also arithmetic constraints between the data elements in the memory cells, but fixes the shape of the user-defined predicates.

The idea of applying SMT techniques to decide satisfiability of SL formulae is not new. In their work, Piskac, Wies and Zufferey translate from SL with singly-linked list segments [17] and trees [18], respectively, into first-order logics (GRASS and GRIT) that are decidable in NP. The fragment handled in this paper is incomparable to the logics GRASS [17] and GRIT [18]. On one hand, we do not consider predicates defining recursive data structures, such as singly-linked lists. On the other hand, we deal with the entire quantifier-free fragment of SL, including arbitrary nesting of the magic wand, separating conjunction and classical boolean connectives. As a result, the decision problem we consider is PSPACE-complete, due to the possibility of arbitrary nesting of the boolean and SL connectives. To the best of our knowledge, our implementation is also the first to enable theory combination involving SL, in a fine-grained fashion, directly within the DPLL(T) loop.

The first theoretical results on decidability and complexity of SL without inductive predicates were given by Calcagno, Yang and O'Hearn [9]. They show that the quantifier-free fragment of SL without data constraints is PSPACE-complete by an argument that enumerates a finite (yet large) set of heap models. Their argument shows also the difficulty of the problem, however it cannot be directly turned into an effective decision procedure, because of the ineffectiveness of model enumeration. Building up on this small model property for the quantifier-free fragment of SL, a translation to first-order logic over uninterpreted sorts with empty signature is described in [8]. This translation is very similar to our translation to multi-sorted second-order logic, the main difference being using bounded tuples instead of sets of bounded cardinality. It also provides a decision procedure, though no implementation is available for comparison. A more elaborate tableau-based decision procedure is described by Méry and Galmiche [11]. This procedure generates verification conditions on-demand, but here no data constraints are considered, either.

Our procedure relies on a decision procedure for quantifier-free parametric theory of sets and on-demand techniques for quantifier instantiation. Decision procedures for the theory of sets in SMT are given in [1,23]. Techniques for model-driven quantifier instantiation were introduced in the context of SMT in [13], and have been developed recently in [5,19].

2 Preliminaries

We consider formulae in multi-sorted first-order logic, over a *signature* Σ consisting of a countable set of sort symbols and a set of function symbols. We assume that signatures always include a boolean sort Bool with constants $\top$ and $\bot$ denoting true and false respectively, and that each sort σ is implicitly equipped with an equality predicate $\approx$ over $\sigma \times \sigma$. Moreover, we may assume without loss of generality that equality is the only predicate belonging to Σ, since we can model other predicate symbols as function symbols with return sort Bool[1].

We consider a set Var of first-order variables, with associated sorts, and denote by $\varphi(\mathbf{x})$ the fact that the free variables of the formula φ belong to $\mathbf{x} \subseteq$ Var. Given a signature Σ, well-sorted terms, atoms, literals, and formulae are defined as usual, and referred to respectively as Σ-*terms*. We denote by $\phi[\varphi]$ the fact that φ is a subformula (subterm) of ϕ and by $\phi[\psi/\varphi]$ the result of replacing φ with ψ in ϕ. We write $\forall x.\varphi$ to denote universal quantification over variable x, where x occurs as a *free variable* in φ. If $\mathbf{x} = \langle x_1, \ldots, x_n \rangle$ is a tuple of variables, we write $\forall \mathbf{x}\, \varphi$ as an abbreviation of $\forall x_1 \cdots \forall x_n\, \varphi$. We say that a Σ-term is *ground* if it contains no free variables. We assume that Σ contains an if-then-else operator $\mathsf{ite}(b, \mathsf{t}, \mathsf{u})$, of sort Bool $\times \sigma \times \sigma \rightarrow \sigma$, for each sort σ, that evaluates to t if b is true, and to u, otherwise.

A Σ-*interpretation* $\mathcal{I}$ maps: (i) each set sort symbol $\sigma \in \Sigma$ to a non-empty set $\sigma^{\mathcal{I}}$, the *domain* of σ in $\mathcal{I}$, (ii) each function symbol $f \in \Sigma$ of sort $\sigma_1 \times \ldots \times \sigma_n \rightarrow \sigma$ to a total function $f^{\mathcal{I}}$ of sort $\sigma_1^{\mathcal{I}} \times \ldots \times \sigma_n^{\mathcal{I}} \rightarrow \sigma^{\mathcal{I}}$ if $n > 0$, and to an element of $\sigma^{\mathcal{I}}$ if $n = 0$, and (iii) each variable $x \in \mathbf{x}$ to an element of $\sigma_x^{\mathcal{I}}$, where σ_x is the sort symbol associated with x. We denote by $\mathsf{t}^{\mathcal{I}}$ the interpretation of a term t induced by the mapping $\mathcal{I}$. The satisfiability relation between Σ-interpretations

---

[1] For brevity, we may write $p(\mathbf{t})$ as shorthand for $p(\mathbf{t}) \approx \top$, where p is a function into Bool.

and Σ-formulae, written $\mathcal{I} \models \varphi$, is defined inductively, as usual. We say that $\mathcal{I}$ is *a model of* φ if $\mathcal{I} \models \varphi$.

A *first-order theory* is a pair $T = (\Sigma, \mathbf{I})$ where Σ is a signature and $\mathbf{I}$ is a non-empty set of Σ-interpretations, the *models* of T. For a formula φ, we denote by $[\![\varphi]\!]_T = \{\mathcal{I} \in \mathbf{I} \mid \mathcal{I} \models \varphi\}$ its set of T-models. A Σ-formula φ is T-*satisfiable* if $[\![\varphi]\!]_T \neq \emptyset$, and T-*unsatisfiable* otherwise. A Σ-formula φ is T-*valid* if $[\![\varphi]\!]_T = \mathbf{I}$, i.e. if $\neg\varphi$ is T-unsatisfiable. A formula φ T-*entails* a Σ-formula ψ, written $\varphi \models_T \psi$, if every model of T that satisfies φ also satisfies ψ. The formulae φ and ψ are T-*equivalent* if $\varphi \models_T \psi$ and $\psi \models_T \varphi$, and *equisatisfiable* (*in* T) if ψ is T-satisfiable if and only if φ is T-satisfiable. Furthermore, formulas φ and ψ are *equivalent* (*up to* $\mathbf{k}$) if they are satisfied by the same set of models (when restricted to the interpretation of variables $\mathbf{k}$). The T-satisfiability problem asks, given a Σ-formula φ, whether $[\![\varphi]\!]_T \neq \emptyset$, i.e. whether φ has a T-model.

2.1   Separation Logic

In the remainder of the paper we fix a theory $T = (\Sigma, \mathbf{I})$, such that the T-satisfiability for the language of quantifier-free boolean combinations of equalities and disequalties between Σ-terms is decidable. We fix two sorts Loc and Data from Σ, with no restriction other than the fact that Loc is always interpreted as a countably infinite set. We refer to *Separation Logic* for T, written SL (T), as the set of formulae generated by the syntax:

$$\phi := t \approx u \mid t \mapsto u \mid \mathsf{emp} \mid \phi_1 * \phi_2 \mid \phi_1 \mathbin{-\!\!*} \phi_2 \mid \phi_1 \wedge \phi_2 \mid \neg\phi_1$$

where t and u are well-sorted Σ-terms and that for any atomic proposition $t \mapsto u$, t is of sort Loc and u is of sort Data. Also, we consider that Σ has a constant nil of sort Loc, with the meaning that $t \mapsto u$ never holds when $t \approx \mathsf{nil}$. In the following, we write $\phi \vee \psi$ for $\neg(\neg\phi \wedge \neg\psi)$ and $\phi \Rightarrow \psi$ for $\neg\phi \vee \psi$.

Given an interpretation $\mathcal{I}$, a *heap* is a finite partial mapping $h : \mathsf{Loc}^{\mathcal{I}} \rightharpoonup_{\mathrm{fin}} \mathsf{Data}^{\mathcal{I}}$. For a heap h, we denote by $\mathrm{dom}(h)$ its domain. For two heaps h_1 and h_2, we write $h_1 \# h_2$ for $\mathrm{dom}(h_1) \cap \mathrm{dom}(h_2) = \emptyset$ and $h = h_1 \uplus h_2$ for $h_1 \# h_2$ and $h = h_1 \cup h_2$. For an interpretation $\mathcal{I}$, a heap $h : \mathsf{Loc}^{\mathcal{I}} \rightharpoonup_{\mathrm{fin}} \mathsf{Data}^{\mathcal{I}}$ and a SL(T) formula ϕ, we define the satisfaction relation $\mathcal{I}, h \models_{\mathsf{SL}} \phi$ inductively, as follows:

$$
\begin{array}{lcl}
\mathcal{I}, h \models_{\mathsf{SL}} \mathsf{emp} & \Longleftrightarrow & h = \emptyset \\
\mathcal{I}, h \models_{\mathsf{SL}} t \mapsto u & \Longleftrightarrow & h = \{(t^{\mathcal{I}}, u^{\mathcal{I}})\} \text{ and } t^{\mathcal{I}} \not\approx \mathsf{nil}^{\mathcal{I}} \\
\mathcal{I}, h \models_{\mathsf{SL}} \phi_1 * \phi_2 & \Longleftrightarrow & \exists h_1, h_2 \,.\, h = h_1 \uplus h_2 \text{ and } \mathcal{I}, h_i \models_{\mathsf{SL}} \phi_i, \text{ for all } i = 1, 2 \\
\mathcal{I}, h \models_{\mathsf{SL}} \phi_1 \mathbin{-\!\!*} \phi_2 & \Longleftrightarrow & \forall h' \text{ if } h' \# h \text{ and } \mathcal{I}, h' \models_{\mathsf{SL}} \phi_1 \text{ then } \mathcal{I}, h' \uplus h \models_{\mathsf{SL}} \phi_2
\end{array}
$$

The satisfaction relation for the equality atoms $t \approx u$ and the Boolean connectives $\wedge, \neg$ are the classical ones from first-order logic. In particular $t \approx t$ is always true, denoted by $\top$, for any given heap. The (SL, T)-*satisfiability* problem asks, given an SL formula φ, if there is a T-model $\mathcal{I}$ such that $(\mathcal{I}, h) \models_{\mathsf{SL}} \varphi$ for some heap h.

In this paper we tackle the (SL, T)-satisfiability problem, under the assumption that the quantifier-free data theory $T = (\Sigma, \mathbf{I})$ has a decidable satisfiability problem for constraints involving Σ-terms. It has been proved [9] that the satisfiability problem is PSPACE-complete for the fragment of separation logic in which Data is interpreted as the set of pairs of sort Loc. We generalize this result to any theory whose satisfiability problem, for the quantifier-free fragment, is in PSPACE. This is, in general, the case of most SMT theories, which are typically in NP, such as the linear arithmetic of integers and reals, possibly with sets and uninterpreted functions, etc.

3 Reducing SL (T) to Multisorted Second-Order Logic

It is well-known [21] that separation logic cannot be formalized as a classical (unsorted) first-order theory, for instance, due to the behavior of the $*$ connective, that does not comply with the standard rules of contraction $\phi \Rightarrow \phi * \phi$ and weakening $\phi * \varphi \Rightarrow \phi^2$. The basic reason is that $\phi * \varphi$ requires that ϕ and φ hold on *disjoint* heaps. Analogously, $\phi \twoheadrightarrow \varphi$ holds on a heap whose extensions, by disjoint heaps satisfying ϕ, must satisfy φ. In the following, we leverage from the expressivity of multi-sorted first-order theories and translate $\mathsf{SL}(T)$ formulae into quantified formulae in the language of T, assuming that T subsumes a theory of sets and uninterpreted functions.

The integration of separation logic within the DPLL(T) framework [12] requires the input logic to be presented as a multi-sorted logic. To this end, we assume, without loss of generality, the existence of a fixed theory $T = (\Sigma, \mathbf{I})$ that subsumes a theory of sets $\mathsf{Set}(\sigma)$ [1], for any sort σ of set elements, whose functions are the union $\cup$, intersection $\cap$ of sort $\mathsf{Set}(\sigma) \times \mathsf{Set}(\sigma) \to \mathsf{Set}(\sigma)$, singleton $\{.\}$ of sort $\sigma \to \mathsf{Set}(\sigma)$ and emptyset $\emptyset$ of sort $\mathsf{Set}(\sigma)$. We write $\ell \subseteq \ell'$ as a shorthand for $\ell \cup \ell' \approx \ell'$ and $\mathsf{t} \in \ell$ for $\{\mathsf{t}\} \subseteq \ell$, for any terms ℓ and ℓ' of sort $\mathsf{Set}(\sigma)$ and t of sort σ. The interpretation of the functions in the set theory is the classical (boolean) one.

Also, we assume that Σ contains infinitely many function symbols $\mathsf{pt}, \mathsf{pt}', \ldots \in \Sigma$ of sort $\mathsf{Loc} \to \mathsf{Data}$, where Loc and Data are two fixed sorts of T, such that for any interpretation $\mathcal{I} \in \mathbf{I}$, $\mathsf{Loc}^{\mathcal{I}}$ is an infinite countable set.

The main idea is to express the atoms and connectives of separation logic in multi-sorted second-order logic by means of a transformation, called *labeling*, which introduces (i) constraints over variables of sort $\mathsf{Set}(\mathsf{Loc})$ and (ii) terms over uninterpreted *points-to* functions of sort $\mathsf{Loc} \to \mathsf{Data}$. We describe the labeling transformation using judgements of the form $\phi \triangleleft [\overline{\ell}, \overline{\mathsf{pt}}]$, where ϕ is a $\mathsf{SL}(T)$ formula, $\overline{\ell} = \langle \ell_1, \ldots, \ell_n \rangle$ is a tuple of variables of sort $\mathsf{Set}(\mathsf{Loc})$ and $\overline{\mathsf{pt}} = \langle \mathsf{pt}_1, \ldots, \mathsf{pt}_n \rangle$ is a tuple of uninterpreted function symbols occurring under the scopes of universal quantifiers. To ease the notation, we write ℓ and pt instead of the singleton tuples $\langle \ell \rangle$ and $\langle \mathsf{pt} \rangle$. In the following, we also write $\bigcup \overline{\ell}$ for $\ell_1 \cup \ldots \cup \ell_n$, $\ell' \cap \overline{\ell}$ for $\langle \ell' \cap \ell_1, \ldots, \ell' \cap \ell_n \rangle$, $\ell' \cdot \overline{\ell}$ for $\langle \ell', \ell_1, \ldots, \ell_n \rangle$ and $\mathsf{ite}(\mathsf{t} \in \overline{\ell}, \overline{\mathsf{pt}}(\mathsf{t}) = \mathsf{u})$ for $\mathsf{ite}(\mathsf{t} \in \ell_1, \mathsf{pt}_1(\mathsf{t}) = \mathsf{u}, \mathsf{ite}(\mathsf{t} \in \ell_2, \mathsf{pt}_2(\mathsf{t}) = \mathsf{u}, \ldots, \mathsf{ite}(\mathsf{t} \in \ell_n, \mathsf{pt}_n(\mathsf{t}) = \mathsf{u}, \top) \ldots))$.

Intuitively, a labeled formula $\phi \triangleleft [\overline{\ell}, \overline{\mathsf{pt}}]$ says that it is possible to build, from any of its satisfying interpretations $\mathcal{I}$, a heap h such that $\mathcal{I}, h \models_{\mathsf{SL}} \phi$, where

---

² Take for instance ϕ as $x \mapsto 1$ and φ as $y \mapsto 2$.

$\mathrm{dom}(h) = \ell_1^{\mathcal{I}} \cup \ldots \cup \ell_n^{\mathcal{I}}$ and $h = \mathrm{pt}_1^{\mathcal{I}} \downarrow_{\ell_1^{\mathcal{I}}} \cup \ldots \cup \mathrm{pt}_n^{\mathcal{I}} \downarrow_{\ell_n^{\mathcal{I}}}{}^3$. More precisely, a variable ℓ_i defines a slice of the domain of the heap, whereas the restriction of pt_i to (the interpretation of) ℓ_i describes the heap relation on that slice. Observe that each interpretation of $\bar{\ell}$ and $\overline{\mathrm{pt}}$, such that $\ell_i^{\mathcal{I}} \cap \ell_j^{\mathcal{I}} = \emptyset$, for all $i \neq j$, defines a unique heap.

First, we translate an input $\mathsf{SL}(T)$ formula ϕ into a labeled second-order formula, with quantifiers over sets and uninterpreted functions, defined by the rewriting rules in Fig. 1. A labeling step $\phi[\varphi] \implies \phi[\psi/\varphi]$ applies if φ and ψ match the antecedent and consequent of one of the rules in Fig. 1, respectively. It is not hard to show that this rewriting system is confluent, and we denote by $\phi_{\Downarrow}$ the normal form of ϕ with respect to the application of labeling steps.

$$\frac{(\phi * \psi) \triangleleft [\bar{\ell}, \overline{\mathrm{pt}}]}{\neg \forall \ell_1 \forall \ell_2 \,.\, \neg(\ell_1 \cap \ell_2 \approx \emptyset \wedge \ell_1 \cup \ell_2 \approx \bigcup \bar{\ell} \wedge \phi \triangleleft [\ell_1 \cap \bar{\ell}, \overline{\mathrm{pt}}] \wedge \psi \triangleleft [\ell_2 \cap \bar{\ell}, \overline{\mathrm{pt}}])} \qquad \frac{(\phi \wedge \psi) \triangleleft [\bar{\ell}, \overline{\mathrm{pt}}]}{\phi \triangleleft [\bar{\ell}, \overline{\mathrm{pt}}] \wedge \psi \triangleleft [\bar{\ell}, \overline{\mathrm{pt}}]}$$

$$\frac{(\phi \mathrel{-\!\!*} \psi) \triangleleft [\bar{\ell}, \overline{\mathrm{pt}}]}{\forall \ell' \forall \mathrm{pt}' \,.\, (\ell' \cap (\bigcup \bar{\ell}) \approx \emptyset \wedge \phi \triangleleft [\ell', \mathrm{pt}']) \Rightarrow \psi \triangleleft [\ell' \cdot \bar{\ell}, \mathrm{pt}' \cdot \overline{\mathrm{pt}}]} \qquad \frac{(\neg \phi) \triangleleft [\bar{\ell}, \overline{\mathrm{pt}}]}{\neg(\phi \triangleleft [\bar{\ell}, \overline{\mathrm{pt}}])}$$

$$\frac{t \mapsto u \triangleleft [\bar{\ell}, \overline{\mathrm{pt}}]}{\bigcup \bar{\ell} \approx \{t\} \wedge \mathrm{ite}(t \in \bar{\ell}, \overline{\mathrm{pt}}(t) \approx u) \wedge t \not\approx \mathrm{nil}} \qquad \frac{\mathrm{emp} \triangleleft [\bar{\ell}, \overline{\mathrm{pt}}]}{\bigcup \bar{\ell} \approx \emptyset} \qquad \frac{\varphi \triangleleft [\bar{\ell}, \overline{\mathrm{pt}}]}{\varphi} \; \varphi \text{ is pure}$$

Fig. 1. Labeling rules

Example 1. Consider the $\mathsf{SL}(T)$ formula $(x \mapsto a \mathrel{-\!\!*} y \mapsto b) \wedge \mathrm{emp}$. The reduction to second-order logic is given below:

$((x \mapsto a \mathrel{-\!\!*} y \mapsto b) \wedge \mathrm{emp}) \triangleleft [\ell, \mathrm{pt}] \implies^*$
$\ell \approx \emptyset \wedge \forall \ell' \forall \mathrm{pt}' \,.\, \ell' \cap \ell \approx \emptyset \wedge \ell' \approx \{x\} \wedge \mathrm{ite}(x \in \ell', \mathrm{pt}'(x) \approx a, \top) \wedge x \not\approx \mathrm{nil} \Rightarrow$ $\blacksquare$
$\ell' \cup \ell \approx \{y\} \wedge \mathrm{ite}(y \in \ell', \mathrm{pt}'(y) \approx b, \mathrm{ite}(y \in \ell, \mathrm{pt}(y) \approx b, \top)) \wedge y \not\approx \mathrm{nil}$

The following lemma reduces the (SL, T)-satisfiability problem to the satisfiability of a quantified fragment of the multi-sorted second-order theory T, that contains sets and uninterpreted functions. For an interpretation $\mathcal{I}$, a variable x and a value $s \in \sigma_x^{\mathcal{I}}$, we denote by $\mathcal{I}[x \leftarrow s]$ the extension of $\mathcal{I}$ which maps x into s and behaves like $\mathcal{I}$ for all other symbols. We extend this notation to tuples $\bar{x} = \langle x_1, \ldots, x_n \rangle$ and $\bar{s} = \langle s_1, \ldots, s_n \rangle$ and write $\mathcal{I}[\bar{x} \leftarrow \bar{s}]$ for $\mathcal{I}[x_1 \leftarrow s_1] \ldots [x_n \leftarrow s_n]$. For a tuple of heaps $\bar{h} = \langle h_1, \ldots, h_n \rangle$ we write $\mathrm{dom}(\bar{h})$ for $\langle \mathrm{dom}(h_1), \ldots, \mathrm{dom}(h_n) \rangle$.

Lemma 1. *Given a $\mathsf{SL}(T)$ formula φ and tuples $\bar{\ell} = \langle \ell_1, \ldots, \ell_n \rangle$ and $\overline{\mathrm{pt}} = \langle \mathrm{pt}_1, \ldots, \mathrm{pt}_n \rangle$ for $n > 0$, for any interpretation $\mathcal{I}$ of T and any heap $h \colon \mathcal{I}, h \models_{\mathsf{SL}} \varphi$ if and only if*

---

^{3} We denote by $F \downarrow_D$ the restriction of the function F to the domain $D \subseteq \mathrm{dom}(F)$.

1. *for all heaps $\overline{h} = \langle h_1, \ldots, h_n \rangle$ such that $h = h_1 \uplus \ldots \uplus h_n$,*
2. *for all heaps $\overline{h}' = \langle h'_1, \ldots, h'_n \rangle$ such that $h_1 \subseteq h'_1, \ldots, h_n \subseteq h'_n$,*

we have $\mathcal{I}[\overline{\ell} \leftarrow \mathrm{dom}(\overline{h})][\overline{\mathsf{pt}} \leftarrow \overline{h}'] \models_T \varphi \triangleleft [\overline{\ell}, \overline{\mathsf{pt}}]\Downarrow .$

Although, in principle, satisfiability is undecidable in the presence of quantifiers and uninterpreted functions, the result of the next section strengthens this reduction, by adapting the labeling rules for $*$ and $-\!*$ (Fig. 1) to use bounded quantification over finite (set) domains.

4 A Reduction of SL (*T*) to Quantifiers Over Bounded Sets

In the previous section, we have reduced any instance of the (SL, T)-satisfiability problem to an instance of the T-satisfiability problem in the second-order multi-sorted theory T which subsumes the theory Set(Loc) and contains several quantified uninterpreted function symbols of sort Loc $\mapsto$ Data. A crucial point in the translation is that the only quantifiers occurring in T are of the forms $\forall \ell$ and $\forall \mathsf{pt}$, where ℓ is a variable of sort Set(Loc) and pt is a function symbol of sort Loc $\mapsto$ Data. Leveraging from a small model property for SL over the data domain Data $=$ Loc $\times$ Loc [9], we show that it is sufficient to consider only the case when the quantified variables range over a bounded domain of sets. In principle, this allows us to eliminate the universal quantifiers by replacing them with finite conjunctions and obtain a decidability result based on the fact that the quantifier-free theory T with sets and uninterpreted functions is decidable. Since the cost of a-priori quantifier elimination is, in general, prohibitive, in the next section we develop an efficient lazy quantifier instantiation procedure, based on counterexample-driven refinement.

For reasons of self-containment, we quote the following lemma [24] and stress the fact that its proof is oblivious of the assumption Data $=$ Loc $\times$ Loc on the range of heaps. Given a formula ϕ in the language SL(T), we first define the following measure:

$$|\phi * \psi| = |\phi| + |\psi| \quad |\phi -\!* \psi| = |\psi| \quad |\phi \wedge \psi| = \max(|\phi|, |\psi|) \quad |\neg\phi| = |\phi|$$
$$|\mathsf{t} \mapsto \mathsf{u}| = 1 \quad\quad |\mathsf{emp}| = 1 \quad\quad |\phi| = 0 \text{ if } \phi \text{ is a } \Sigma\text{-formula}$$

Intuitively, $|\phi|$ gives the maximum number of *invisible* locations in the domain of a heap h, that are not in the range of $\mathcal{I}$ and which can be distinguished by ϕ. For instance, if $\mathcal{I}, h \models_{\mathsf{SL}} \neg\mathsf{emp} * \neg\mathsf{emp}$ and the domain of h contains more than two locations, then it is possible to restrict $\mathrm{dom}(h)$ to $|\neg\mathsf{emp} * \neg\mathsf{emp}| = 2$ locations only, to satisfy this formula.

Let $\mathrm{Pt}(\phi)$ be the set of terms (of sort Loc $\cup$ Data) that occur on the left- or right-hand side of a points-to atomic proposition in ϕ. Formally, we have $\mathrm{Pt}(\mathsf{t} \mapsto \mathsf{u}) = \{\mathsf{t}, \mathsf{u}\}$, $\mathrm{Pt}(\phi * \psi) = \mathrm{Pt}(\phi -\!* \psi) = \mathrm{Pt}(\phi) \cup \mathrm{Pt}(\psi)$, $\mathrm{Pt}(\neg\phi) = \mathrm{Pt}(\phi)$ and $\mathrm{Pt}(\mathsf{emp}) = \mathrm{Pt}(\phi) = \emptyset$, for a Σ-formula ϕ. The small model property is given by the next lemma:

Lemma 2 *[24, Proposition 96]. Given a formula $\phi \in \mathsf{SL}(T)$, for any interpretation $\mathcal{I}$ of T, let $L \subseteq \mathsf{Loc}^{\mathcal{I}} \setminus \mathrm{Pt}(\phi)^{\mathcal{I}}$ be a set of locations, such that $\|L\| = |\phi|$ and $v \in \mathsf{Data}^{\mathcal{I}} \setminus \mathrm{Pt}(\phi)^{\mathcal{I}}$. Then, for any heap h, we have $\mathcal{I}, h \models_{\mathsf{SL}} \phi$ iff $\mathcal{I}, h' \models_{\mathsf{SL}} \phi$, for any heap h' such that:*

- *$\mathrm{dom}(h') \subseteq L \cup \mathrm{Pt}(\phi)^{\mathcal{I}}$,*
- *for all $\ell \in \mathrm{dom}(h')$, $h'(\ell) \in \mathrm{Pt}(\phi)^{\mathcal{I}} \cup \{v\}$*

Based on the fact that the proof of Lemma 2 [24] does not involve reasoning about data values, other than equality checking, we refine our reduction from the previous section, by bounding the quantifiers to finite sets of constants of known size. To this end, we assume the existence of a total order on the (countable) set of constants in Σ of sort Loc, disjoint from any Σ-terms that occur in a given formula ϕ, and define $\mathrm{Bnd}(\phi, C) = \{c_{m+1}, \ldots, c_{m+|\phi|}\}$, where $m = \max\{i \mid c_i \in C\}$, and $m = 0$ if $C = \emptyset$. Clearly, we have $\mathrm{Pt}(\phi) \cap \mathrm{Bnd}(\phi, C) = \emptyset$ and also $C \cap \mathrm{Bnd}(\phi, C) = \emptyset$, for any C and any ϕ.

We now consider labeling judgements of the form $\varphi \triangleleft [\overline{\ell}, \overline{\mathsf{pt}}, C]$, where C is a finite set of constants of sort Loc, and modify all the rules in Fig. 1, besides the ones with premises $(\phi * \psi) \triangleleft [\overline{\ell}, \overline{\mathsf{pt}}]$ and $(\phi \mathbin{-\!\!*} \psi) \triangleleft [\overline{\ell}, \overline{\mathsf{pt}}]$, by replacing any judgement $\varphi \triangleleft [\overline{\ell}, \overline{\mathsf{pt}}]$ with $\varphi \triangleleft [\overline{\ell}, \overline{\mathsf{pt}}, C]$. The two rules in Fig. 2 are the bounded-quantifier equivalents of the $(\phi * \psi) \triangleleft [\overline{\ell}, \overline{\mathsf{pt}}]$ and $(\phi \mathbin{-\!\!*} \psi) \triangleleft [\overline{\ell}, \overline{\mathsf{pt}}]$ rules in Fig. 1. As usual, we denote by $(\varphi \triangleleft [\overline{\ell}, \overline{\mathsf{pt}}, C]) {\Downarrow}$ the formula obtained by exhaustively applying the new labeling rules to $\varphi \triangleleft [\overline{\ell}, \overline{\mathsf{pt}}, C]$.

Observe that the result of the labeling process is a formula in which all quantifiers are of the form $\forall \ell_1 \ldots \forall \ell_n \forall \mathsf{pt}_1 \ldots \forall \mathsf{pt}_n . \bigwedge_{i=1}^{n} \ell_i \subseteq L_i \wedge \bigwedge_{i=1}^{n} \mathsf{pt}_i \subseteq L_i \times D_i \Rightarrow \psi(\overline{\ell}, \overline{\mathsf{pt}})$, where L_i's and D_i's are finite sets of terms, none of which involves quantified variables, and ψ is a formula in the theory T with sets and uninterpreted functions. Moreover, the labeling rule for $\phi \mathbin{-\!\!*} \psi \triangleleft [\overline{\ell}, \overline{\mathsf{pt}}, C]$ uses a fresh constant d that does not occur in ϕ or ψ.

Example 2 We revisit below the labeling of the formula $(x \mapsto a \mathbin{-\!\!*} y \mapsto b) \wedge \mathsf{emp}$:

$$((x \mapsto a \mathbin{-\!\!*} y \mapsto b) \wedge \mathsf{emp}) \triangleleft [\ell, \mathsf{pt}, C] \Longrightarrow^*$$
$$\ell \approx \emptyset \wedge \forall \ell' \subseteq \{x, y, a, b, c\} \, \forall \mathsf{pt}' \subseteq \{x, y, a, b, c\} \times \{x, y, a, b, d\}).$$
$$\ell' \cap \ell \approx \emptyset \wedge \ell' \approx \{x\} \wedge \mathsf{ite}(x \in \ell', \mathsf{pt}'(x) \approx a, \top) \wedge x \not\approx \mathsf{nil} \Rightarrow$$
$$\ell' \cup \ell \approx \{y\} \wedge \mathsf{ite}(y \in \ell', \mathsf{pt}'(y) \approx b, \mathsf{ite}(y \in \ell, \mathsf{pt}(y) \approx b, \top)) \wedge y \not\approx \mathsf{nil}.$$

where $\mathrm{Pt}((x \mapsto a \mathbin{-\!\!*} y \mapsto b) \wedge \mathsf{emp}) = \{x, y, a, b\}$. Observe that the constant c was introduced by the bounded quantifier labeling of the term $x \mapsto a \mathbin{-\!\!*} y \mapsto b$. ∎

The next lemma states the soundness of the translation of $\mathsf{SL}(T)$ formulae in a fragment of T that contains only bounded quantifiers, by means of the rules in Fig. 2.

Lemma 3 *Given a formula φ in the language $\mathsf{SL}(T)$, for any interpretation $\mathcal{I}$ of T, let $L \subseteq \mathsf{Loc}^{\mathcal{I}} \setminus \mathrm{Pt}(\varphi)^{\mathcal{I}}$ be a set of locations such that $\|L\| = |\varphi|$ and $v \in \mathsf{Data}^{\mathcal{I}} \setminus \mathrm{Pt}(\varphi)^{\mathcal{I}}$ be a data value. Then there exists a heap h such that $\mathcal{I}, h \models_{\mathsf{SL}} \varphi$ iff there exist heaps $\overline{h}' = \langle h'_1, \ldots, h'_n \rangle$ and $\overline{h}'' = \langle h''_1, \ldots, h''_n \rangle$ such that:*

$$\frac{\phi * \psi \triangleleft [\overline{\ell}, \overline{\mathsf{pt}}, C]}{\neg \forall \ell_1 \forall \ell_2 . \; \ell_1 \cup \ell_2 \subseteq C \cup \mathrm{Pt}(\phi * \psi) \Rightarrow \atop \neg(\ell_1 \cap \ell_2 \approx \emptyset \wedge \ell_1 \cup \ell_2 \approx \bigcup \overline{\ell} \wedge \phi \triangleleft [\ell_1 \cap \overline{\ell}, \overline{\mathsf{pt}}, C] \wedge \psi \triangleleft [\ell_2 \cap \overline{\ell}, \overline{\mathsf{pt}}, C])}$$

$$\frac{\phi \mathbin{-\!\!*} \psi \triangleleft [\overline{\ell}, \overline{\mathsf{pt}}, C]}{\begin{array}{l} \forall \ell' \forall \mathsf{pt}' . \; \ell' \subseteq C' \cup \mathrm{Pt}(\phi \mathbin{-\!\!*} \psi) \wedge \\ \mathsf{pt}' \subseteq (C' \cup \mathrm{Pt}(\phi \mathbin{-\!\!*} \psi)) \times (\mathrm{Pt}(\phi \mathbin{-\!\!*} \psi) \cup \{d\}) \Rightarrow \\ (\ell' \cap (\bigcup \overline{\ell}) \approx \emptyset \wedge \phi \triangleleft [\ell', \mathsf{pt}', C']) \Rightarrow \psi \triangleleft [\ell' \cdot \overline{\ell}, \mathsf{pt}' \cdot \overline{\mathsf{pt}}, C] \end{array}} \quad \begin{array}{l} C' = \mathrm{Bnd}(\phi \wedge \psi, C) \\ d \notin \mathrm{Pt}(\phi \mathbin{-\!\!*} \psi) \end{array}$$

Fig. 2. Bounded quantifier labeling rules

1. *for all* $1 \le i < j \le n$, *we have* $h'_i \# h'_j$,
2. *for all* $1 \le i \le n$, *we have* $h'_i \subseteq h''_i$ *and*
3. $\mathcal{I}[\overline{\ell} \leftarrow \mathrm{dom}(\overline{h}')][\overline{\mathsf{pt}} \leftarrow \overline{h}''][C \leftarrow L][d \leftarrow v] \models_T \varphi \triangleleft [\overline{\ell}, \overline{\mathsf{pt}}, C]\Downarrow$.

5 A Counterexample-Guided Approach for Solving SL (T) Inputs

This section presents a novel decision procedure for the (SL, T)-satisfiability of the set of quantifier-free SL (T) formulae φ. To this end, we present an efficient decision procedure for the T-satisfiability of $(\varphi \triangleleft [\ell, \mathsf{pt}, C])\Downarrow$, obtained as the result of the transformation described in Sect. 4. The main challenge in doing so is treating the universal quantification occurring in $(\varphi \triangleleft [\ell, \mathsf{pt}, C])\Downarrow$. As mentioned, the key to decidability is that all quantified formulae in $(\varphi \triangleleft [\ell, \mathsf{pt}, C])\Downarrow$ are equivalent to formulas of the form $\forall \mathbf{x}.(\bigwedge \mathbf{x} \subseteq \mathbf{s}) \Rightarrow \varphi$, where each term in the tuple $\mathbf{s}$ is a finite set (or product of sets) of ground Σ-terms. For brevity, we write $\forall \mathbf{x} \subseteq \mathbf{s}.\varphi$ to denote a quantified formula of this form. While such formulae are clearly equivalent to a finite conjunction of instances, the cost of constructing these instances is in practice prohibitively expensive. Following recent approaches for handling universal quantification [5,13,19,20], we use a counterexample-guided approach for choosing instances of quantified formulae that are relevant to the satisfiability of our input. The approach is based on an iterative procedure maintaining an evolving set of quantifier-free Σ-formulae Γ, which is initially a set of formulae obtained from φ by a purification step, described next.

We associate with each closed quantified formula a boolean variable A, called the *guard* of $\forall \mathbf{x}.\varphi$, and a (unique) set of Skolem symbols $\mathbf{k}$ of the same sort as $\mathbf{x}$. We write $(A, \mathbf{k}) \leftrightharpoons \forall \mathbf{x}.\varphi$ to denote that A and $\mathbf{k}$ are associated with $\forall \mathbf{x}.\varphi$. For a set of formulae Γ, we write $\mathrm{Q}(\Gamma)$ to denote the set of quantified formulae whose guard occurs within a formula in Γ. We write $\lfloor \psi \rfloor$ for the result of replacing in ψ all closed quantified formulae (not occurring beneath other quantifiers in ψ) with their corresponding guards. Conversely, we write $\lceil \Gamma \rceil$ to denote the result of replacing all guards in Γ by the quantified formulae they are associated with. Then $\lfloor \psi \rfloor^*$ denotes the smallest set of Σ-formulae:

$$\lfloor \psi \rfloor \in \lfloor \psi \rfloor^*$$
$$(\neg A \Rightarrow \lfloor \neg \varphi[\mathbf{k}/\mathbf{x}] \rfloor) \in \lfloor \psi \rfloor^* \quad \text{if } \forall \mathbf{x}.\varphi \in Q(\lfloor \psi \rfloor^*) \text{ where } (A, \mathbf{k}) \leftrightharpoons \forall \mathbf{x}.\varphi.$$

In other words, $\lfloor \psi \rfloor^*$ contains clauses that witness the negation of each universally quantified formula occurring in ψ. It is easy to see that if ψ is a Σ-formula possibly containing quantifiers, then $\lfloor \psi \rfloor^*$ is a set of quantifier-free Σ-formulae, and if all quantified formulas in ψ are of the form $\forall \mathbf{x} \subseteq \mathbf{s}.\varphi$ mentioned above, then all quantified formulas in $Q(\lfloor \psi \rfloor^*)$ are also of this form.

Example 3 If ψ is the formula $\forall x.(P(x) \Rightarrow \neg \forall y.R(x, y))$, then $\lfloor \psi \rfloor^*$ is the set:

$$\{A_1, \neg A_1 \Rightarrow \neg(P(k_1) \Rightarrow A_2), \neg A_2 \Rightarrow \neg R(k_1, k_2)\}$$

where $(A_1, k_1) \leftrightharpoons \forall x.(P(x) \Rightarrow \neg \forall y.R(x, y))$ and $(A_2, k_2) \leftrightharpoons \forall y.R(k_1, y)$. ∎

---

solve$_{\mathsf{SL}(T)}(\varphi)$:

> Let C be a set of fresh constants of sort Loc such that $|C| = |\varphi|$.
> Let ℓ and pt be a fresh symbols of sort Set(Loc) and Loc $\Rightarrow$ Data respectively.
> Return solve$_T(\lfloor (\varphi \triangleleft [\ell, \mathsf{pt}, C]) \Downarrow \rfloor^*)$.

solve$_T(\Gamma)$:

1. If Γ is T-unsatisfiable,
   > return "unsat",
   > else let $\mathcal{I}$ be a T-model of Γ.
2. If $\Gamma, A \models_T \lfloor \psi[\mathbf{k}/\mathbf{x}] \rfloor$ for all $\forall \mathbf{x}.\psi \in Q(\Gamma)$, where $(A, \mathbf{k}) \leftrightharpoons \forall \mathbf{x}.\psi$ and $A^{\mathcal{I}} = \top$,
   > return "sat",
   > else let $\mathcal{J}$ be a T-model of $\Gamma \cup \{A, \neg \lfloor \psi[\mathbf{k}/\mathbf{x}] \rfloor\}$ for some $\prec_{\Gamma,\mathcal{I}}$-minimal $\forall \mathbf{x} \subseteq \mathbf{s}.\psi$,
   > where $(A, \mathbf{k}) \leftrightharpoons \forall \mathbf{x} \subseteq \mathbf{s}.\psi$.
3. Let $\mathbf{t}$ be a vector of terms, such that $\mathbf{t} \subseteq \mathbf{s}$, and $\mathbf{t}^{\mathcal{J}} = \mathbf{k}^{\mathcal{J}}$.
   > Return solve$_T(\Gamma \cup \lfloor A \Rightarrow \psi[\mathbf{t}/\mathbf{x}] \rfloor^*)$.

Fig. 3. Procedure solve$_{\mathsf{SL}(T)}$ for deciding (SL, T)-satisfiability of SL(T) formula φ.

Our algorithm solve$_{\mathsf{SL}(T)}$ for determining the (SL, T)-satisfiability of input φ is given in Fig. 3. It first constructs the set C based on the value of $|\varphi|$, which it computes by traversing the structure of φ. It then invokes the subprocedure solve$_T$ on the set $\lfloor (\varphi \triangleleft [\ell, \mathsf{pt}, C]) \Downarrow \rfloor^*$ where ℓ and pt are fresh free symbols.

At a high level, the recursive procedure solve$_T$ takes as input a (quantifier-free) set of T-formulae Γ, where Γ is T-unsatisfiable if and only if $(\varphi \triangleleft [\ell, \mathsf{pt}, C]) \Downarrow$ is. On each invocation, solve$_T$ will either (i) terminate with "unsat", in which case φ is T-unsatisfiable, (ii) terminate with "sat", in which case φ is T-satisfiable, or (iii) add the set corresponding to the purification of the instance $\lfloor A \Rightarrow \psi[\mathbf{t}/\mathbf{x}] \rfloor^*$ to Γ and repeats.

In more detail, in Step 1 of the procedure, we determine the T-satisfiability of Γ using a combination of a satisfiability solver and a decision procedure for T^4. If Γ is T-unsatisfiable, since Γ is T-entailed by $\lceil\Gamma\rceil$, we may terminate with "unsat". Otherwise, there is a T-model $\mathcal{I}$ for Γ and T. In Step 2 of the procedure, for each A that is interpreted to be true by $\mathcal{I}$, we check whether $\Gamma \cup \{A\}$ T-entails $\lfloor\psi[\mathbf{k}/\mathbf{x}]\rfloor$ for fresh free constants $\mathbf{k}$, which can be accomplished by determining whether $\Gamma \cup \{A, \neg\lfloor\psi[\mathbf{k}/\mathbf{x}]\rfloor\}$ is T-unsatisfiable. If this check succeeds for a quantified formula $\forall\mathbf{x}.\psi$, the algorithm has established that $\forall\mathbf{x}.\psi$ is entailed by Γ. If this check succeeds for all such quantified formulae, then Γ is equivalent to $\lceil\Gamma\rceil$, and we may terminate with "sat". Otherwise, let $Q_{\mathcal{I}}^+(\Gamma)$ be the subset of $Q(\Gamma)$ for which this check did not succeed. We call this the set of *active quantified formulae* for $(\mathcal{I}, \Gamma)$. We consider an active quantified formula that is minimal with respect to the relation $\prec_{\Gamma,\mathcal{I}}$ over $Q(\Gamma)$, where:

$$\varphi \prec_{\Gamma,\mathcal{I}} \psi \quad \text{if and only if } \varphi \in Q(\lfloor\psi\rfloor^*) \cap Q_{\mathcal{I}}^+(\Gamma)$$

By this ordering, our approach considers innermost active quantified formulae first. Let $\forall\mathbf{x}.\psi$ be minimal with respect to $\prec_{\Gamma,\mathcal{I}}$, where $(A, \mathbf{k}) \leftrightharpoons \forall\mathbf{x}.\psi$. Since Γ, A does not T-entail $\lfloor\psi[\mathbf{k}/\mathbf{x}]\rfloor$, there must exist a model $\mathcal{J}$ for $\Gamma \cup \{\lfloor\neg\psi[\mathbf{k}/\mathbf{x}]\rfloor\}$ where $A^{\mathcal{J}} = \top$. In Step 3 of the procedure, we choose a tuple of terms $\mathbf{t} = (t_1, \ldots, t_n)$ based on the model $\mathcal{J}$, and add to Γ the set of formulae obtained by purifying $A \Rightarrow \psi[\mathbf{t}/\mathbf{x}]$, where A is the guard of $\forall\mathbf{x} \subseteq \mathbf{s}.\psi$. Assume that $\mathbf{s} = (s_1, \ldots, s_n)$ and recall that each s_i is a finite union of ground Σ-terms. We choose each $\mathbf{t}$ such that t_i is a subset of s_i for each $i = 1, \ldots n$, and $\mathbf{t}^{\mathcal{J}} = \mathbf{k}^{\mathcal{J}}$. These two criteria are the key to the termination of the algorithm: the former ensures that only a finite number of possible instances can ever be added to Γ, and the latter ensures that we never add the same instance more than once.

Theorem 1 *For all $SL(T)$ formulae φ, $\mathsf{solve}_{\mathsf{SL(T)}}(\varphi)$:*

1. *Answers "unsat" only if φ is (SL, T)-unsatisfiable.*
2. *Answers "sat" only if φ is (SL, T)-satisfiable.*
3. *Terminates.*

By Theorem 1, $\mathsf{solve}_{\mathsf{SL(T)}}$ is a decision procedure for the (SL, T)-satisfiability of the language of quantifier-free $\mathsf{SL}(T)$ formulae. The following corollary gives a tight complexity bound for the (SL, T)-satisfiability problem.

Corollary 1 *The (SL, T)-satisfiability problem is PSPACE-complete for any theory T whose satisfiability (for the quantifier-free fragment) is in PSPACE.*

---

[4] Non-constant Skolem symbols k introduced by the procedure may be treated as uninterpreted functions. Constraints of the form $k \subseteq S_1 \times S_2$ are translated to $\bigwedge_{c \in S_1} k(c) \in S_2$. Furthermore, the domain of k may be restricted to the set $\{c^{\mathcal{I}} \mid c \in S_1\}$ in models $\mathcal{I}$ found in Steps 1 and 2 of the procedure. This restriction comes with no loss of generality since, by construction of $(\varphi \triangleleft [\ell, \mathsf{pt}, C])\Downarrow$, k is applied only to terms occurring in S_1.

In addition to being sound and complete, in practice, the approach $\mathsf{solve}_{\mathsf{SL}(T)}$ terminates in much less time that its theoretical worst-case complexity, given by the above corollary. This fact is corroborated by our evaluation of our prototype implementation of the algorithm, described in Sect. 6, and in the following example.

Example 4 Consider the $\mathsf{SL}(T)$ formula $\varphi \equiv \mathsf{emp} \land (y \mapsto 0 \mathbin{-\!\!*} y \mapsto 1) \land y \not\approx \mathsf{nil}$. When running $\mathsf{solve}_{\mathsf{SL}(T)}(\varphi)$, we first compute the set $C = \{c\}$, and introduce fresh symbols ℓ and pt of sorts $\mathsf{Set}(\mathsf{Loc})$ and $\mathsf{Loc} \to \mathsf{Data}$ respectively. The formula $(\varphi \triangleleft [\ell, \mathsf{pt}, C]) \Downarrow$ is $\ell \approx \emptyset \land \forall \ell_4 \forall \mathsf{pt'}.\psi \land y \not\approx \mathsf{nil}$, where after simplification ψ is:

$$\psi_4 \equiv (\ell_4 \subseteq \{y, 0, 1, c\} \land \mathsf{pt'} \subseteq \{y, 0, 1, c\} \times \{y, 0, 1, d\}) \Rightarrow$$
$$(\ell_4 \cap \ell \approx \emptyset \land \ell_4 \approx \{y\} \land \mathsf{pt'}(y) \approx 0 \land y \not\approx \mathsf{nil}) \Rightarrow$$
$$(\ell_4 \cup \ell \approx \{y\} \land \mathsf{ite}(y \in \ell_4, \mathsf{pt'}(y) \approx 1, \mathsf{pt}(y) \approx 1) \land y \not\approx \mathsf{nil})$$

Let $(A_4, (k_1, k_2)) \leftrightharpoons \forall \ell_4 \forall \mathsf{pt'}.\psi_4$. We call the subprocedure solve_T on Γ_0, where:

$$\Gamma_0 \equiv \lfloor (\varphi \triangleleft [\ell, \mathsf{pt}, C]) \Downarrow \rfloor^* \equiv \{\ell \approx \emptyset \land A_4 \land y \not\approx \mathsf{nil}, \neg A_4 \Rightarrow \neg \psi_4[k_1, k_2/\ell_4, \mathsf{pt'}]\}.$$

The set Γ_0 is T-satisfiable with a model $\mathcal{I}_0$ where $A_4^{\mathcal{I}_0} = \top$. Step 2 of the procedure determines a model $\mathcal{J}$ for $\Gamma_0 \cup \{A_4, \neg \psi_4[k_1, k_2/\ell_4, \mathsf{pt'}]\}$.

Let t_1 be $\{y\}$, where we know $t_1^{\mathcal{J}} = k_1^{\mathcal{J}}$ since $\mathcal{J}$ must satisfy $k_1 \approx \{y\}$ as a consequence of $\neg \psi_4[k_1, k_2/\ell_4, \mathsf{pt'}]$. Let t_2 be a well-sorted subset of $\{y, 0, 1, c\} \times \{y, 0, 1, d\}$ such that $t_2^{\mathcal{J}} = k_2^{\mathcal{J}}$. Such a subset exists since $\mathcal{J}$ satisfies $k_2 \subseteq \{y, 0, 1, c\} \times \{y, 0, 1, d\}$. Notice that $t_2(y)^{\mathcal{J}} = 0^{\mathcal{J}}$ since $\mathcal{J}$ must satisfy $k_2(y) \approx 0$. Step 3 of the procedure recursively invokes solve_T on Γ_1, where:

$$\Gamma_1 \equiv \Gamma_0 \cup \lfloor A_4 \Rightarrow \psi_4[t_1, t_2/\ell_4, \mathsf{pt'}] \rfloor^*$$
$$\equiv \Gamma_0 \cup \{A_4 \Rightarrow y \not\approx \mathsf{nil} \Rightarrow (\{y\} \approx \{y\} \land \mathsf{ite}(y \in \{y\}, 0 \approx 1, \mathsf{pt}(y) \approx 1) \land y \not\approx \mathsf{nil})\}$$
$$\equiv \Gamma_0 \cup \{A_4 \Rightarrow y \not\approx \mathsf{nil} \Rightarrow \bot\}$$

The set Γ_1 is T-unsatisfiable, since the added constraint contradicts $A_4 \land y \not\approx \mathsf{nil}$. ∎

5.1   Integration in DPLL(T)

We have implemented the algorithm described in this section within the SMT solver CVC4 [2]. Our implementation accepts an extended syntax of SMT-LIB version 2 format [3] for specifying $\mathsf{SL}(T)$ formulae. In contrast to the presentation so far, our implementation does not explicitly introduce quantifiers, and instead treats SL atoms natively using an integrated subsolver that expands the semantics of these atoms in lazy fashion.

In more detail, given a $\mathsf{SL}(T)$ input φ, our implementation lazily computes the expansion of $(\varphi \triangleleft [\ell, \mathsf{pt}, C]) \Downarrow$ based on the translation rules in Figs. 1 and 2 and the counterexample-guided instantiation procedure in Fig. 3. This is accomplished by a module, which we refer to as the SL solver, that behaves analogously to a DPLL(T)-style *theory solver*, that is, a dedicated solver specialized for the T-satisfiability of a conjunction of T-constraints.

The DPLL(T) solving architecture [12] used by most modern SMT solvers, given as input a set of quantifier-free T-formulae Γ, incrementally constructs of set of literals over the atoms of Γ until either it finds a set M that entail Γ at the propositional level, or determines that such a set cannot be found. In the former case, we refer to M as a *satisfying assignment* for Γ. If T is a combination of theories $T_1 \cup \ldots \cup T_n$, then M is partitioned into $M_1 \cup \ldots \cup M_n$ where the atoms of M_i are either T_i-constraints or (dis)equalities shared over multiple theories. We use a theory solver (for T_i) to determine the T_i-satisfiability of the set M_i, interpreted as a conjunction. Given M_i, the solver will either add additional formulae to Γ, or otherwise report that M_i is T_i-satisfiable.

For SL (T) inputs, we extend our input syntax with a set of functions:

$$\mapsto: \mathsf{Loc} \times \mathsf{Data} \to \mathsf{Bool} \quad *^n : \mathsf{Bool}^n \to \mathsf{Bool} \qquad \mathsf{emp} : \mathsf{Bool}$$
$$-\!\!*: \mathsf{Bool} \times \mathsf{Bool} \to \mathsf{Bool} \quad \mathsf{lbl} : \mathsf{Bool} \times \mathsf{Set}(\mathsf{Loc}) \to \mathsf{Bool}$$

which we call *spatial functions*[5]. We refer to lbl as the *labeling predicate*, which can be understood as a placeholder for the $\lhd$ transformation in Figs. 1 and 2. We refer to $p(\mathbf{t})$ as an *unlabeled spatial atom* if p is one of $\{\mathsf{emp}, \mapsto, *^n, -\!\!*\}$ and $\mathbf{t}$ is a vector of terms not containing lbl. If a is an unlabeled spatial atom, We refer to $\mathsf{lbl}(a, \ell)$ as a *labeled spatial atom*, and extend these terminologies to literals. We assume that all occurrences of spatial functions in our input φ occur only in unlabeled spatial atoms. Moreover, during execution, our implementation transforms all spatial atoms into a *normal form*, by applying associativity to flatten nested applications of $*$, and distributing Σ-formulae over spatial connectives, e.g. $((\mathsf{x} \mapsto \mathsf{y} \wedge \mathsf{t} \approx \mathsf{u}) * \mathsf{z} \mapsto \mathsf{w}) \iff \mathsf{t} \approx \mathsf{u} \wedge (\mathsf{x} \mapsto \mathsf{y} * \mathsf{z} \mapsto \mathsf{w})$.

When constructing satisfying assignments for φ, we relegate the set of all spatial literals M_k to the SL solver. For all unlabeled spatial literals $(\neg)a$, we add to Γ the formula $(a \Leftrightarrow \mathsf{lbl}(a, \ell_0))$, where ℓ_0 is a distinguished free constant of sort $\mathsf{Set}(\mathsf{Loc})$. Henceforth, it suffices for the SL solver to only consider the labeled spatial literals in M_k. To do so, firstly, it adds to Γ formulae based on the following criteria, which model one step of the reduction from Fig. 1:

$$\mathsf{lbl}(\mathsf{emp}, \ell) \Leftrightarrow \ell \approx \emptyset \qquad\qquad \text{if } (\neg)\mathsf{lbl}(\mathsf{emp}, \ell) \in M_k$$
$$\mathsf{lbl}(t \mapsto u, \ell) \Leftrightarrow \ell \approx \{t\} \wedge \mathsf{pt}(t) \approx u \wedge t \not\approx \mathsf{nil} \qquad \text{if } (\neg)\mathsf{lbl}(t \mapsto u, \ell) \in M_k$$
$$\mathsf{lbl}((\varphi_1 * \ldots * \varphi_n), \ell) \Rightarrow (\varphi_1[\ell_1] \wedge \ldots \wedge \varphi_n[\ell_n]) \qquad \text{if } \mathsf{lbl}((\varphi_1 * \ldots * \varphi_n), \ell) \in M_k$$
$$\neg\mathsf{lbl}((\varphi_1 -\!\!* \varphi_2), \ell) \Rightarrow (\varphi_1[\ell_1] \wedge \neg\varphi_2[\ell_2]) \qquad \text{if } \neg\mathsf{lbl}((\varphi_1 -\!\!* \varphi_2), \ell) \in M_k$$

where each ℓ_i is a fresh free constant, and $\varphi_i[\ell_i]$ denotes the result of replacing each top-level spatial atom a in φ_i with $\mathsf{lbl}(a, \ell_i)$. These formulae are added eagerly when such literals are added to M_k. To handle negated $*$-atoms and positive $-\!\!*$-atoms, the SL solver adds to Γ formulae based on the criteria:

$$\neg\mathsf{lbl}((\varphi_1 * \ldots * \varphi_n), \ell) \Rightarrow (\neg\varphi_1[t_1] \vee \ldots \vee \neg\varphi_n[t_n]) \quad \text{if } \neg\mathsf{lbl}((\varphi_1 * \ldots * \varphi_n), \ell) \in M_k$$
$$\mathsf{lbl}((\varphi_1 -\!\!* \varphi_2), \ell) \Rightarrow (\neg\varphi_1[t_1, f_1] \vee \varphi_2[t_2, f_2]) \qquad \text{if } \mathsf{lbl}((\varphi_1 -\!\!* \varphi_2), \ell) \in M_k$$

---

[5] These functions are over the Bool sort. We refer to these functions as taking *formulae* as input, where formulae may be cast to terms of sort Bool through use of an if-then-else construct.

where each t_i and f_i is chosen based on the same criterion as described in Fig. 3. For wand, we write $\varphi_i[t_i, f_i]$ to denote $\varphi_i'[t_i]$, where φ_i' is the result of replacing all atoms of the form $t \mapsto u$ where $t \in t_1$ in φ_i by $f_i(t) \approx u$.

CVC4 uses a scheme for incrementally checking the T-entailments required by solve_T, as well as constructing models $\mathcal{J}$ satisfying the negated form of the literals in literals in M_k before choosing such terms [20]. The formula of the above form are added to Γ lazily, that is, after all other solvers (for theories T_i) have determined their corresponding sets of literals M_i are T_i-satisfiable.

Partial Support for Quantifiers. In many practical cases it is useful to check the validity of entailments between existentially quantified $\mathsf{SL}(T)$ formulae such as $\exists \mathbf{x} . \phi(\mathbf{x})$ and $\exists \mathbf{y} . \psi(\mathbf{y})$. Typically, this problem translates into a satisfiability query for an $\mathsf{SL}(T)$ formula $\exists \mathbf{x} \forall \mathbf{y} . \phi(\mathbf{x}) \wedge \neg\psi(\mathbf{y})$, with one quantifier alternation. A partial solution to this problem is to first check the satisfiability of ϕ. If ϕ is not satisfiable, the entailment holds trivially, so let us assume that ϕ has a model. Second, we check satisfiability of $\phi \wedge \psi$. Again, if this is unsatisfiable, then the entailment cannot hold, because there exists a model of ϕ which is not a model of ψ. Else, if $\phi \wedge \psi$ has a model, we add an equality $x = y$ for each pair of variables $(x, y) \in \mathbf{x} \times \mathbf{y}$ that are mapped to the same term in this model, the result being a conjunction $E(\mathbf{x}, \mathbf{y})$ of equalities. Finally, we check the satisfiability of the formula $\phi \wedge \neg\psi \wedge E$. If this formula is unsatisfiable, the entailment is valid, otherwise, the test is inconclusive. In Sect. 6, we applied this method manually, to test entailments between existentially quantified variables — general procedure for quantifier instantiation for $\mathsf{SL}(T)$ is envisaged in the near future.

6   Evaluation

We tested our implementation of the (SL, T)-satisfiability procedure in CVC4 (version 1.5 prerelease)[6] on two kinds of benchmarks: (i) finite unfoldings of inductive predicates with data constraints, mostly inspired by existing benchmarks, such as SL-COMP'14 [22], and (ii) verification conditions automatically generated by applying the weakest precondition calculus of [15] to the program loops in Fig. 4 several times. All experiments were run on a 2.80 GHz Intel(R) Core(TM) i7 CPU machine with with 8 MB of cache[7]. For a majority of benchmarks, the runtime of CVC4 is quite low, with the exception of the $n = 4, 8$ cases of the entailments between tree_1^n and tree_2^n formulae, which resulted in a timeout after 300 s. For benchmarks where CVC4 times out, the performance bottleneck resides in its ground decision procedure for finite sets, indicating efficient support for this theory is important for our approach to separation logic.

The first set of experiments is reported in Table 1. We have considered inductive predicates commonly used as verification benchmarks [22]. Here we check the

---

[6] Available at http://cvc4.cs.nyu.edu/web/.

[7] The CVC4 binary and examples used in these experiments are available at http://cvc4.cs.nyu.edu/papers/ATVA2016-seplog/.

```
1: while w ≠ nil do          1: while u ≠ nil do
2:   assert(w.data = 0)       2:   assert(u.data = 0)
3:   v := w;                  3:   w := u.next;
4:   w := w.next;             4:   u.next := v;
5:   dispose(v);              5:   v := u;
6: do                         6:   u := w;
                              7: do
```

(z)disp

$$ls^0(x) \triangleq emp \wedge x = nil$$
$$ls^n(x) \triangleq \exists y.\, x \mapsto y * ls^{n-1}(y)$$

(z)rev

$$zls^0(x) \triangleq emp \wedge x = nil$$
$$zls^n(x) \triangleq \exists y.\, x \mapsto (0,y) * zls^{n-1}(y)$$

Fig. 4. Program loops

validity of the entailment between lhs and rhs, where both predicates are unfolded $n = 1, 2, 3, 4, 8$ times. The second set of experiments, reported in Table 1, considers the verification conditions of the forms $\varphi \Rightarrow wp(l, \phi)$ and $\varphi \Rightarrow wp^n(l, \phi)$, where $wp(l, \phi)$ denotes the weakest precondition of the SL formula ϕ with respect to the sequence of statements l, and $wp^n(l, \phi) = wp(l, \ldots wp(l, wp(l, \phi)) \ldots)$

Table 1. Experimental results

lhs	rhs	$n=1$	$n=2$	$n=3$	$n=4$	$n=8$
Unfoldings of inductive predicates						
$lseg_1(x,y,a) \triangleq emp \wedge x=y \vee \exists z \exists b$. $x \mapsto (a,z)*lseg_1(z,y,b) \wedge b=a+10$	$lseg_2(x,y,a) \triangleq emp \wedge x=y \vee \exists z \exists b$. $x \mapsto (a,z)*lseg_2(z,y,b) \wedge a \leq b$	unsat <0.01 s	unsat <0.01 s	unsat <0.01 s	unsat 0.01 s	unsat 0.01 s
$tree_1(x,a) \triangleq emp \wedge x=nil \vee \exists y \exists z \exists b \exists c$. $x \mapsto (a,y,z)*tree_1(y,b)*tree_1(z,c) \wedge$ $b=a-10 \wedge c=a+10$	$tree_2(x,a) \triangleq emp \wedge x=nil \vee \exists y \exists z \exists b \exists c$. $x \mapsto (a,y,z)*tree_2(y,b)*tree_2(z,c) \wedge$ $b \leq a \wedge a \leq c$	unsat <0.01 s	unsat 0.06 s	unsat 1.89 s	timeout >300 s	timeout >300 s
$pos_1(x,a) \triangleq x \mapsto a \vee \exists y \exists b$. $x \mapsto a*pos_1(y,b)$	$neg_1(x,a) \triangleq \neg x \mapsto a \vee \exists y \exists b$. $x \mapsto a*neg_1(y,b)$	unsat 0.02 s	unsat 0.04 s	unsat 0.11 s	unsat 0.25 s	unsat 3.01 s
$pos_1(x,a) \triangleq x \mapsto a \vee \exists y \exists b$. $x \mapsto a*pos_1(y,b)$	$neg_2(x,a) \triangleq x \mapsto a \vee \exists y \exists b$. $\neg x \mapsto a*neg_2(y,b)$	unsat 0.01 s	unsat 0.05 s	unsat 0.11 s	unsat 0.23 s	unsat 2.10 s
$pos_1(x,a) \triangleq x \mapsto a \vee \exists y \exists b$. $x \mapsto a*pos_1(y,b)$	$neg_3(x,a) \triangleq x \mapsto a \vee \exists y \exists b$. $x \mapsto a*\neg neg_3(y,b)$	unsat 0.02 s	unsat 0.07 s	unsat 0.24 s	unsat 0.46 s	unsat 4.05 s
$pos_1(x,a) \triangleq x \mapsto a \vee \exists y \exists b$. $x \mapsto a*pos_1(y,b)$	$neg_4(x,a) \triangleq x \mapsto a \vee \exists y \exists b$. $\neg x \mapsto a*\neg neg_4(y,b)$	unsat 0.05 s	sat 0.24 s	unsat 0.33 s	sat 2.77 s	sat 24.72 s
$pos_2(x,a) \triangleq x \mapsto a \vee \exists y$. $x \mapsto a*pos_2(a,y)$	$neg_5(x,a) \triangleq \neg x \mapsto a \vee \exists y$. $x \mapsto a*neg_5(a,y)$	unsat 0.02 s	unsat 0.05 s	unsat 0.14 s	unsat 0.32 s	unsat 3.69 s
$pos_2(x,a) \triangleq x \mapsto a \vee \exists y$. $x \mapsto a*pos_2(a,y)$	$neg_6(x,a) \triangleq x \mapsto a \vee \exists y$. $\neg x \mapsto a*neg_6(a,y)$	sat 0.02 s	unsat 0.04 s	unsat 0.13 s	unsat 0.27 s	unsat 2.22 s
Verification conditions						
$ls^n(w)$	$wp(disp, ls^{n-1}(w))$	<0.01 s	0.02 s	0.05 s	0.12 s	1.97 s
$ls^n(w)$	$wp^n(disp, emp \wedge w=nil)$	<0.01 s	0.02 s	0.12 s	0.41 s	22.97 s
$zls^n(w)$	$wp(zdisp, zls^{n-1}(w))$	0.01 s	0.02 s	0.05 s	0.11 s	1.34 s
$zls^n(w)$	$wp^n(zdisp, emp \wedge w=nil)$	0.01 s	0.02 s	0.11 s	0.43 s	24.13 s
$ls^n(u)*ls^0(v)$	$wp(rev, ls^{n-1}(u)*ls^1(v))$	0.06 s	0.08 s	0.14 s	0.30 s	2.83 s
$ls^n(u)*ls^0(v)$	$wp^n(rev, u=nil \wedge ls^n(v))$	0.06 s	0.12 s	0.56 s	1.75 s	27.82 s
$zls^n(u)*zls^0(v)$	$wp(zrev, zls^{n-1}(u)*zls^1(v))$	0.22 s	0.04 s	0.12 s	0.25 s	2.16 s
$zls^n(u)*zls^0(v)$	$wp^n(zrev, u=nil \wedge zls^n(v))$	0.04 s	0.10 s	0.41 s	1.27 s	20.26 s

denotes the iterative application of the weakest precondition n times in a row. We consider the loops depicted in Fig. 4, where, for each loop l we consider the variant zl as well, which tests that the data values contained within the memory cells are 0, by the assertions on line 2. The postconditions are specified by finite unfoldings of the inductive predicates ls and zls (Fig. 4).

7   Conclusions

We have presented a decision procedure for quantifier-free $SL(T)$ formulas that relies on a efficient, counterexample-guided approach for establishing the T-satisfiability of formulas having quantification over bounded sets. We have described an implementation of the approach as an integrated subsolver in the $DPLL(T)$-based SMT solver CVC4, showing the potential of the procedure as a backend for tools reasoning about low-level pointer and data manipulations.

References

1. Bansal, K.: Decision procedures for finite sets with cardinality and local theory extensions. Ph.D. thesis, New York University (2016)
2. Barrett, C., Conway, C., Deters, M., Hadarean, L., Jovanovic, D., King, T., Reynolds, A., Tinelli, C.: CVC4. In: CAV 2011, pp. 171–177 (2011)
3. Barrett, C., Fontaine, P., Tinelli, C.: The SMT-LIB 2.5 standard. Technical report, The University of Iowa (2015). http://smt-lib.org/
4. Berdine, J., Calcagno, C., Cook, B., Distefano, D., O'Hearn, P.W., Wies, T., Yang, H.: Shape analysis for composite data structures. In: Damm, W., Hermanns, H. (eds.) CAV 2007. LNCS, vol. 4590, pp. 178–192. Springer, Heidelberg (2007)
5. Bjørner, N., Janota, M.: Playing with quantified satisfaction. In: LPAR 2015. EPIC, vol. 35, pp. 15–27 (2015)
6. Brotherston, J., Gorogiannis, N., Petersen, R.L.: A generic cyclic theorem prover. In: Jhala, R., Igarashi, A. (eds.) APLAS 2012. LNCS, vol. 7705, pp. 350–367. Springer, Heidelberg (2012)
7. Calcagno, C., Distefano, D.: Infer: an automatic program verifier for memory safety of C programs. In: Bobaru, M., Havelund, K., Holzmann, G.J., Joshi, R. (eds.) NFM 2011. LNCS, vol. 6617, pp. 459–465. Springer, Heidelberg (2011)
8. Calcagno, C., Gardner, P., Hague, M.: From separation logic to first-order logic. In: Sassone, V. (ed.) FOSSACS 2005. LNCS, vol. 3441, pp. 395–409. Springer, Heidelberg (2005)
9. Calcagno, C., Yang, H., O'Hearn, P.W.: Computability and complexity results for a spatial assertion language for data structures. In: Hariharan, R., Mukund, M., Vinay, V. (eds.) FSTTCS 2001. LNCS, vol. 2245, pp. 108–119. Springer, Heidelberg (2001)
10. Enea, C., Sighireanu, M., Wu, Z.: On automated lemma generation for separation logic with inductive definitions. In: Finkbeiner, B., et al. (eds.) ATVA 2015. LNCS, vol. 9364, pp. 80–96. Springer, Heidelberg (2015). doi:10.1007/978-3-319-24953-7_7
11. Galmiche, D., Méry, D.: Tableaux and resource graphs for separation logic. J. Logic Comput. 20(1), 189–231 (2010)

12. Ganzinger, H., Hagen, G., Nieuwenhuis, R., Oliveras, A., Tinelli, C.: DPLL(T): fast decision procedures. In: Alur, R., Peled, D.A. (eds.) CAV 2004. LNCS, vol. 3114, pp. 175–188. Springer, Heidelberg (2004)
13. Ge, Y., de Moura, L.: Complete instantiation for quantified formulas in satisfiabiliby modulo theories. In: Bouajjani, A., Maler, O. (eds.) CAV 2009. LNCS, vol. 5643, pp. 306–320. Springer, Heidelberg (2009)
14. Iosif, R., Rogalewicz, A., Vojnar, T.: Slide: Separation logic with inductive definitions. http://www.fit.vutbr.cz/research/groups/verifit/tools/slide/
15. Ishtiaq, S.S., O'Hearn, P.W.: BI as an assertion language for mutable data structures. ACM SIGPLAN Not. **36**, 14–26 (2001)
16. Navarro Pérez, J.A., Rybalchenko, A.: Separation logic + superposition calculus = heap theorem prover. ACM SIGPLAN Not. **46**(6), 556–566 (2011)
17. Piskac, R., Wies, T., Zufferey, D.: Automating separation logic using SMT. In: Sharygina, N., Veith, H. (eds.) CAV 2013. LNCS, vol. 8044, pp. 773–789. Springer, Heidelberg (2013)
18. Piskac, R., Wies, T., Zufferey, D., Piskac, R., Wies, T., Zufferey, D.: Automating separation logic with trees and data. In: Biere, A., Bloem, R. (eds.) CAV 2014. LNCS, vol. 8559, pp. 711–728. Springer, Heidelberg (2014)
19. Reynolds, A., Deters, M., Kuncak, V., Barrett, C.W., Tinelli, C.: Counterexample guided quantifier instantiation for synthesis in CVC4. In: CAV 2015, pp. 198–216 (2015)
20. Reynolds, A., King, T., Kuncak, V.: An instantiation-based approach for solving quantified linear arithmetic. CoRR abs/1510.02642 (2015)
21. Reynolds, J.C.: Separation logic: a logic for shared mutable data structures. In: Logic in Computer Science, LICS 2002, pp. 55–74 (2002)
22. Sighireanu, M., Cok, D.: Report on SL-COMP 2014. J. Satisf. Boolean Modeling Comput. **1**, 173–186 (2014)
23. Piskac, R., Kuncak, V., Suter, P., Steiger, R., Kuncak, V.: Sets with cardinality constraints in satisfiability modulo theories. In: Jhala, R., Schmidt, D. (eds.) VMCAI 2011. LNCS, vol. 6538, pp. 403–418. Springer, Heidelberg (2011)
24. Yang, H.: Local reasoning for stateful programs. Ph.D. thesis, University of Illinois at Urbana-Champaign (2001)

Solving Mean-Payoff Games on the GPU

Philipp J. Meyer[✉] and Michael Luttenberger

Institut für Informatik, Technische Universität München, Munich, Germany
meyerphi@in.tum.de, luttenbe@model.in.tum.de

Abstract. General purpose computation on graphics processing units (GPGPU) is a recent trend in areas which heavily depend on linear algebra, in particular solving large systems of linear equations. Many games, both qualitative (e.g. parity games) and quantitative (e.g. mean-payoff games) can be seen as systems of linear equations, too, albeit on more general algebraic structures. Building up on our GPU-based implementation of several solvers for parity games [8], we present in this paper a solver for mean-payoff games. Our implementation uses OpenCL which allows us to execute it without any changes on both the CPU and on the GPU allowing for direct comparison.

We evaluate our implementation on several benchmarks (obtained via reduction from parity games and optimization of controllers for hybrid systems [10]) where we obtain a speedup of up to 10 on the GPU in cases of MPGs with $20 \cdot 10^6$ nodes and $60 \cdot 10^6$ edges.

1 Introduction

In a mean-payoff game (MPG) [5] two players, $\mathsf{P}_{\max}$ und $\mathsf{P}_{\min}$, move a pebble through a directed graph (V, E), called the arena, where every node $v \in V$ is assigned an owner $o(v) \in \{\mathsf{P}_{\max}, \mathsf{P}_{\min}\}$ and every edge $(u, v) \in E$ is assigned a (w.l.o.g.) integer weight $w(u, v) \in \mathbb{Z}$. It is assumed that every node has at least one successor, therefore the players usually play forever, yielding an infinite path $(v_i)_{i \in \mathbb{N}}$ in (V, E) where it is assumed that the owner of v_i has chosen to move to v_{i+1}. $\mathsf{P}_{\max}$ has the goal to maximize the average of the weight accumulated in the limit, i.e. $\liminf_{T \to \infty} \frac{1}{1+T} \sum_{i=0}^{T} w(v_i, v_{i+1})$, and $\mathsf{P}_{\min}$ has the opposite goal.

It is well-known that for every MPGs there exist memoryless strategies $\sigma_{\max}$, $\sigma_{\min} \colon V \ni v \mapsto w \in vE$ and a valuation $\nu \colon V \to \mathbb{Q}$ s.t. when $\mathsf{P}_{\max}$ uses $\sigma_{\max}$ to determine where to move the pebble to — no matter how $\mathsf{P}_{\min}$ chooses to move — the resulting average reward will be at least $\nu(v)$ for v the node the pebble has been placed initially, and symmetrically for $\mathsf{P}_{\min}$ using $\sigma_{\min}$. Determining ν and optimal strategies for both players is known to be in NP∩coNP [13]. Computing optimal strategies and the optimal valuation ν can be reduced e.g. via binary search to the p-mean partition problem [3]: given $p \in \mathbb{Q}$, partition the set

This work was partially funded and supported by the Deutsche Forschungsgemeinschaft (DFG) through the project "Game-based Synthesis for Industrial Automation" and the TUM International Graduate School of Science and Engineering (IGSSE).

V into the subsets $V_{\leq p} = \{v \in V \mid \nu(v) \leq p\}$ and $V_{>p} = V \setminus V_{\leq p}$ (resp. $V_{\geq p}$ and $V_{<p}$).

Our interest in MPGs comes from optimizing permissive controllers which have been synthesized for hybrid systems [10]: the controller is obtained by discretizing the hybrid system into a game, thus its size directly grows with the resolution at which the system is discretized leading to controllers with several million states and transitions. The controller is only synthesized w.r.t. qualitative objectives like reachability or safety, but the controller is non-deterministic in the sense that it still might be allowed to choose from several actions. Essentially, the goal is to refine the controller such that it also minimizes the number of times at which it switches from one action to another action. One simple way to obtain such kind of a posteriori optimization is by formulating this problem as an MPG played essentially on the controller itself.[1] To this end, we require a solver that can handle also MPGs with several millions of states.

Motivated by the existing success in using graphic processing units (GPU) for formal verification [1,8] we present here our GPU-based implementation of a solver for MPGs. The main motivation for using GPUs is that in many cases they offer a higher computational power while consuming less energy at the same time than most CPUs. Because of this, GPUs have become a central component of super computers. Modern GPUs excel in particular in problems which can be solved by a large number of very homogeneously behaving threads e.g. like solving systems of linear equations. MPGs can be seen as a linear optimization problem, albeit w.r.t. the tropical semiring. The optimization problem associated with mean-payoff games can be solved using an approach called *strategy iteration* [3]: while strategy iteration is not known to yield a polynomial-time algorithm for solving MPGs, similar to the simplex method, worst-case behavior is observed very seldom. As no polynomial time algorithms for MPGs are known so far, strategy iteration is a reasonable approach for solving MPGs.

We benchmark our implementation on several problems coming from applications like the sketched optimization of a controller and from model checking and equivalence problems obtained via the reduction of parity games to MPGs. In order to assess the speedup that the GPU offers compared to standard CPUs, our implementation uses OpenCL, thus the same code can be run both on the CPU and the GPU. Our current implementation already achieves a speedup of approx. 8 to 10 on the GPU. We are currently optimizing the code further, and expect even higher speedups (see the section on future work for more details).

Closely related to MPGs are *parity games* which can be directly reduced to the 0-mean partition problem. The standard reduction works by encoding the node coloring explicitly as edge weights. Alternatively, the mapping of colors to edge weights can only be implicitly represented (similar to the path profiles of [12]) which requires only a slight change to our implementation but already leads to a significant speed-up for parity games.

---

[1] While mean-payoff parity games allow to directly combine qualitative and quantitative objects [4], our approach does not require any changes to synthesis of the controller, neither to synthesis itself nor to numerical aspects of the synthesis.

The current implementation, benchmarks and detailed results are available at www.model.in.tum.de/tools/gpumpg.

2   GPU-Specific Implementation

OpenCL is a framework for heterogeneous platforms consisting of several CPUs and GPUs. It is maintained by the Khronos Group. An OpenCL device consists of one or more *compute units (CU)* which themselves consist of one or more *processing units (PU)*. A *kernel* is a program which is to be executed in parallel: kernel instances are grouped into *work-groups* which are further subdivided into *work-items*. A work-group consists of instances of the same kernel, and the whole work-group is executed by a single CU. A work-item of a work-group executes one kernel instance using one or more PUs of the CU running its work-group. At any given point of time, all active work-items of a work-group execute the same instruction (or a NOP) which considerably influences the way algorithms have to be implemented on the GPU.

Due to the page limit, we can only give a very brief sketch of our implementation leaving aside all details on how to efficiently use the GPU: The edge relation of the arena is stored similar to the Yale format used for sparse matrices. The main problem consists of computing the least or greatest solution of min-max systems which are directly derived from the graph structure underlying the arena. To solve these systems, we implemented a variant of the Bellman-Ford algorithm directly for GPUs: roughly spoken, with every node v of the arena a work-item is associated which checks the successors of v for changes, and, if a change is found, accordingly updates the value for v.

The Bellman-Ford algorithm lies at the heart of the strategy iteration used for solving the p-mean partition problem. Given an initial memoryless strategy for P_{max}, the Bellman-Ford algorithm is used to compute an optimal counter strategy for P_{min}; this counter strategy is used in turn to improve P_{max}'s strategy by checking all nodes controlled by P_{max} if there are any successors which promise a higher limit-average than the successor currently proposed by the strategy — again this can be done in parallel by one work-item per node. As soon as P_{max}'s strategy cannot be improved anymore, we are guaranteed to have found an optimal strategy, and this solved the p-mean partition problem.

The p-mean partition problem is then used to recursively partition the MPG into smaller MPGs similar to a binary search: Initially, we solve the 0-mean partition problems yielding $V_{\leq 0}$ and $V_{\geq 0}$. The set of nodes $V_{=0} = V_{\leq 0} \cap V_{\geq 0}$ is obtained, and then the MPG is partitioned accordingly into smaller MPGs consisting of the nodes $V_{>0}$ resp. $V_{<0}$. Recursively and in parallel p-mean partition problems on these smaller MPGs are solved where for each of the smaller MPGs the new value for p is chosen by traversing the Stern-Brocot tree (see e.g. [7]) in combination with exponential search. This ensures that each value in the range of ν is reached within a logarithmic number of steps w.r.t. the size of the MPG. In this way, we compute ν and optimal strategies for P_{max} and P_{min}.

One requirement for the strategy iteration algorithm is that there are no nonpositive cycles controlled by P_{min}. To eliminate those cycles, we introduce additional implicit nodes on either all forward or all backward edges between nodes controlled by the same player. As an alternative, we also offer to directly remove nonpositive cycles before solving each p-mean partition problem.

3   Evaluation

All experiments were performed on a machine equipped with an Intel Core i7-6700K Processor at 4.0 GHz with 32 GB of RAM and an AMD Radeon R9 390 with 8 GB of RAM, running Windows 10 64 bit. We only present the time spent to solve the games while the time spent on disk I/O and set-up is excluded. Our benchmarks come from two sources: (1) optimization of synthesized controllers for hybrid system, (2) parity games related to model checking problems and equivalence testing of processes. The time limit was 12 h for the controller benchmark suite and 30 min for the parity games benchmark suite.

In case of the optimization of the hybrid controller, the controller is transformed into an MPG where switching from one action to another leads to a transition with zero payoff, while using the same action subsequently yields a transition with positive payoff. To this end, the states of the MPG are essentially the states of the controller extended by the action last used by the controller. The size of the synthesized controller depends on the resolution η used for discretizing the hybrid system. The results are summarized in Table 1. Note that larger games may have a simpler structure and smaller values, leading to a smaller solving time, e.g. when increasing η^{-1} from 1000 to 2000 or from 5000 to 6000.

We used the standard reduction of parity games to the 0-mean partition problem of MPGs to reformulate the model checking and equivalence problems coming from the benchmark suite[2] of [9] as MPGs. We selected only games with at least 500 000 nodes to give a useful comparison between GPU and CPU, as we could solve all smaller games in less than half a second. The game sizes range up to 40 million nodes and 167 million transitions. We also ran the tool PGSolver [6] on this suite with the solver `recursive`, which proved to be its most efficient solver. Table 2 and Fig. 1 give the obtained results.

We can solve all of the benchmarks, taking at most 2 h for the largest controller and 70 s for a single instance of the parity games. On the GPU, we achieve a speedup over the CPU ranging from 2 to 11, and on average about 5. PGSolver can only solve about half of the instances, as it runs out of memory in a lot of cases. We outperform PGSolver significantly on all but two benchmarks, where we are only half as fast. Even on the CPU we outperform PGSolver on all but eight benchmarks. This is even though PGSolver itself solves the original, smaller parity game and further uses several heuristics to recognize and solve trivial instances without actually using the selected solver.

For comparison, we also solved the parity games by implicitly mapping the colors to edge weights as color profiles. Solving the parity games directly this way gives a further speedup of 4 on average. Still, this shows our approach also works well directly on mean-payoff games, which are potentially harder to solve.

---

[2] Available at https://github.com/jkeiren/paritygame-generator.

Table 1. Timings in seconds for the controller synthesis benchmark suite, including speedup. The optimal value ν is the same for all nodes.

η^{-1}	$\frac{|V|}{10^6}$	$\frac{|E|}{10^6}$	ν	GPU	CPU	$\frac{CPU}{GPU}$
1000	0.4	1.2	$32/77$	54	288	5.3
2000	1.7	4.9	$5/12$	16	144	8.8
3000	4.0	11.1	$41/98$	339	3234	9.6
4000	7.1	19.8	$31/74$	407	3686	9.0
5000	11.2	30.9	$31/74$	484	4760	9.8
6000	16.0	44.5	$13/31$	404	4525	11.2
7000	21.9	60.6	$73/174$	1983	21700	10.9
8000	28.6	79.2	$199/474$	6313	>12 h	n/a

Table 2. Games in the parity games benchmark suites (#) and instances successfully solved on the GPU, on the CPU and by PGSolver (PG).

Suite	#	GPU	CPU	PG
Equiv	45	45	45	15
Model	58	58	58	44
Total	103	103	103	59

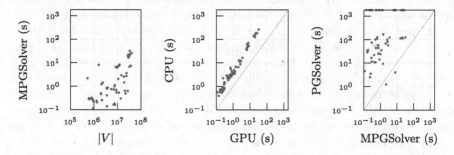

Fig. 1. Timings for the parity games benchmark suite, comparing GPU vs. CPU and our solver on the GPU vs. PGSolver. Negative results are set to 30 min.

In the experiments, the cycle elimination with implicit auxiliary nodes proved to be much more efficient than removing cycles directly, which often lead to timeouts on graphs with nonpositive cycles. Therefore we only used the implicit nodes, which caused minimal overhead even on graphs without cycles.

4   Conclusion and Future Work

Currently, the code is not optimized for the GPU, particularly the memory access pattern depends directly on the graph structure of the MPG. Still, the benchmarks indicate that GPUs offer a significant speedup of ten and more compared to CPUs. Also, we currently require an explicit representation of the system. However, as shown by the Divine model checker [2], explicit representation of the state space can be very successful in practice. To overcome possible memory limitations, a future goal is to incorporate the use of multiple GPUs in a single host system and the use of distributed system of PCs with multiple GPUs. This is also motivated by the fact that in recent years the price of GPUs dropped significantly faster than that of CPUs resp. the computational power available at a given price point increased much faster for GPUs. We thus believe that GPU-enabled solvers are relevant for model checking and synthesis in practice.

Further, we want to extend the solver by using symmetric strategy iteration [11], and we want to improve memory access by taking the graph structure of the MPG into account when arranging the nodes in memory.

Acknowledgments. We thank Majid Zamani and Matthias Rungger for kindly providing the example for the hybrid controller for our experimental evaluation.

References

1. Barnat, J., Bauch, P., Brim, L., Ceska, M.: Designing fast LTL model checking algorithms for many-core GPUs. J. Parallel Distrib. Comput. **72**(9), 1083–1097 (2012)
2. Barnat, J., et al.: DiVinE 3.0 - an explicit-state model checker for multithreaded C & C++ programs. In: Sharygina, N., Veith, H. (eds.) Computer Aided Verification. LNCS, vol. 8044, pp. 863–868. Springer, Heidelberg (2013)
3. Björklund, H., Sandberg, S., Vorobyov, S.: A combinatorial strongly subexponential strategy improvement algorithm for mean payoff games. In: Fiala, J., Koubek, V., Kratochvíl, J. (eds.) MFCS 2004. LNCS, vol. 3153, pp. 673–685. Springer, Heidelberg (2004). doi:10.1007/978-3-540-28629-5_52
4. Chatterjee, K., Majumdar, R.: Minimum attention controller synthesis for omega-regular objectives. In: Fahrenberg, U., Tripakis, S. (eds.) FORMATS 2011. LNCS, vol. 6919, pp. 145–159. Springer, Heidelberg (2011). doi:10.1007/978-3-642-24310-3_11
5. Ehrenfeucht, A., Mycielski, J.: Positional strategies for mean payoff games. Int. J. Game Theory **8**(2), 109–113 (1979)
6. Friedmann, O., Lange, M.: The PGSolver collection of parity game solvers. University of Munich (2009). http://www2.tcs.ifi.lmu.de/pgsolver/
7. Graham, R.L., Knuth, D.E., Patashnik, O.: Concrete Mathematics: A Foundation for Computer Science, 2nd edn. Addison-Wesley Longman Publishing Co., Inc., Boston (1994)
8. Hoffmann, P., Luttenberger, M.: Solving parity games on the GPU. In: Hung, D., Ogawa, M. (eds.) ATVA 2013. LNCS, vol. 8172, pp. 455–459. Springer, Heidelberg (2013). doi:10.1007/978-3-319-02444-8_34
9. Keiren, J.J.A.: Benchmarks for parity games. In: Dastani, M., Sirjani, M. (eds.) FSEN 2015. LNCS, vol. 9392, pp. 127–142. Springer, Heidelberg (2015). doi:10.1007/978-3-319-24644-4_9
10. Rungger, M., Zamani, M.: SCOTS: a tool for the synthesis of symbolic controllers. In: Proceedings of the 19th International Conference on Hybrid Systems: Computation and Control, HSCC 2016, pp. 99–104. ACM, New York (2016)
11. Schewe, S., Trivedi, A., Varghese, T.: Symmetric strategy improvement. In: Halldórsson, M.M., Iwama, K., Kobayashi, N., Speckmann, B. (eds.) ICALP 2015. LNCS, vol. 9135, pp. 388–400. Springer, Heidelberg (2015). doi:10.1007/978-3-662-47666-6_31
12. Vöge, J., Jurdziński, M.: A discrete strategy improvement algorithm for solving parity games. In: Emerson, E.A., Sistla, A.P. (eds.) CAV 2000. LNCS, vol. 1855, pp. 202–215. Springer, Heidelberg (2000). doi:10.1007/10722167_18
13. Zwick, U., Paterson, M.: The complexity of mean payoff games on graphs. Theor. Comput. Sci. **158**(1&2), 343–359 (1996)

Synthesis, Refinement

Synthesizing Skeletons for Reactive Systems

Bernd Finkbeiner and Hazem Torfah[✉]

Saarland University, Saarbrücken, Germany
torfah@react.uni-saarland.de

Abstract. We present an analysis technique for temporal specifications of reactive systems that identifies, on the level of individual system outputs over time, which parts of the implementation are determined by the specification, and which parts are still open. This information is represented in the form of a labeled transition system, which we call skeleton. Each state of the skeleton is labeled with a three-valued assignment to the output variables: each output can be true, false, or open, where true or false means that the value must be true or false, respectively, and open means that either value is still possible. We present algorithms for the verification of skeletons and for the learning-based synthesis of skeletons from specifications in linear-time temporal logic (LTL). The algorithm returns a skeleton that satisfies the given LTL specification in time polynomial in the size of the minimal skeleton. Our new analysis technique can be used to recognize and repair specifications that underspecify critical situations. The technique thus complements existing methods for the recognition and repair of overspecifications via the identification of unrealizable cores.

1 Introduction

The great advantage of synthesis is that it constructs an implementation automatically from a specification – no programming required. The great disadvantage of synthesis is that the synthesized implementation is only as good as its specification, and writing good specifications is extremely difficult.

Roughly speaking, there are two fundamental errors that can happen when writing a specification. The first type of error is to *overspecify* the system such that actually no implementation exists anymore. This type of error can be found by a synthesis algorithm (it fails!), and synthesis tools commonly assist in the repair of such errors by identifying an unrealizable core of the specification (cf. [1,11,12]). The second type of error is to *underspecify* the system such that not all implementations that satisfy the specification actually perform as intended. This type of error is much harder to detect. The synthesis succeeds, and even if we convince ourselves that the synthesis tool has actually chosen an implementation that performs as intended, there is no guarantee that this will again be the

---

This work was partially funded by the European Research Council (ERC) Grant OSARES (No. 683300) and by the Deutsche Telekom Foundation.

C. Artho et al. (Eds.): ATVA 2016, LNCS 9938, pp. 271–286, 2016.
DOI: 10.1007/978-3-319-46520-3_18

case when a new implementation is synthesized from the same or an extended specification.

The underlying problem is that synthesis algorithms have the freedom to resolve any underspecified behavior in the specification, and we have no way of knowing which parts of the behavior were fixed by the specification, and which parts were chosen by the synthesis algorithm.

In this paper, we introduce a new artifact that can be produced by synthesis algorithms and which provides exactly this information. We call this artifact the *skeleton* of the specification. We envision that synthesis algorithms would produce the skeleton along with the actual implementation, so that the user of the algorithm understands where the implementation is underspecified, and can, if so desired, strengthen the specification in critical areas.

A skeleton is a labeled transition system defined over three-valued sets of atomic propositions, where in each state of the skeleton an atomic proposition is either *true*, *false*, or *open*. For a given specification, the truth value of a proposition in some state of the skeleton is *open* if it can be replaced by *true* as well as by *false* without violating the specification. Consider for example the LTL formula $\bigcirc p$ for some atomic proposition p. Any transition system that satisfies the formula has truth value *true* for p in the second position of every path of the transition system. On the other hand, whether p is *true* or *false* in the initial state is not determined, either truth value would work. In this case, the skeleton would not fix a particular truth value, but rather leave the value of p in the initial state open. In a sense, the skeleton implements only those parts of the transition system that are determined by the specification.

Skeletons are useful to understand the meaning of partially written specifications. Consider, for example, an arbiter over two clients that share some resource. Each client can make a request to the source (via the inputs r_1 and r_2) and the arbiter can, accordingly, decide to give out grants via the outputs g_1 and g_2. A specification for the arbiter might begin with the property of mutual exclusion, i.e., the LTL formula $\square(\bar{g}_1 \vee \bar{g}_2)$ stating that only one of the clients should have access to the resource at a time. Figure 1 shows an implementation of this specification as a transition system and a skeleton. The transition system has a single state, and no grants are given at any time (see Fig. 1(a)). The skeleton shown in Fig. 1(b) reveals that all outputs are open, as indicated by the question mark. If we extend the specification with the property $\bar{g}_1 \wedge \bar{g}_2$, then the previous transition system does not need to change, because it already satsifies the extended specification. The skeleton, on the other hand, now indicates that the output in the initial state is determined. The output in subsequent states is still open (see Fig. 1(c)). Extending the specification further with the property $\square(r_1 \rightarrow \bigcirc g_1)$ results in a skeleton where the responses to requests from the first client are determined, and outputs in situations where there is no request from the first client are still open (see Fig. 1(e)). An implementation for this specification could be the transition system that never gives a grant to the second client (see Fig. 1(d)).

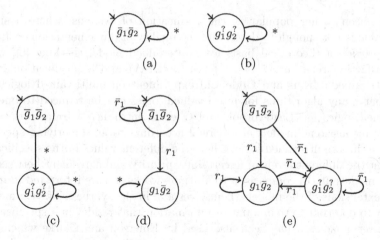

Fig. 1. Transition systems and skeletons for an arbiter specification. The symbol * denotes all possible input labels.

We study the *model checking* and *synthesis* problems for skeletons. For a given LTL formula φ and a skeleton S we say that S is a model of the LTL formula φ, if each trace in S satisfies following condition: If the truth value for some proposition p in some position of the trace is open, then φ must both have a model where p is *true* at this position, and a model where p is *false* at this position. Furthermore, if the trace has truth value *true* or *false* for p at some position, then *all* models of φ map p to the truth value *true* or *false*, respectively, at this position.

We show that given an LTL formula φ we can build a nondeterministic automaton that accepts a sequence over the three-valued semantics if it satisfies the satisfaction relation described above. The automaton is of doubly-exponential size in the length of the formula φ. With this automaton, the model checking problem can be solved in EXPSPACE.

To solve the synthesis problem, we could determinize the automaton and check whether there is a skeleton for the formula, along the lines of standard synthesis [16], but this construction would be very expensive. Instead, we introduce a synthesis algorithm for skeletons based on *learning*. We show that for each LTL formula, a skeleton that models the formula defines a safety language that can be learned using the learning algorithm L*. The algorithm can learn a skeleton for an LTL formula in time polynomial in the size of the minimal skeleton for the specification. The membership and equivalence queries of the L* algorithm are answered by the model checking algorithm introduced in this paper.

Related Work. There is a rich body of work on the synthesis of reactive systems from logical specifications [4,7,10,13,14]. Supplemented by many works that investigated the optimization of specification for synthesis and the identification of unrealizable specification [1,11,12]. Multi-valued extensions of logics have been rather popular in the verification of systems, where a simple truth value is not enough to determine the quality of implementations. Chechik et. al. provide a theoretical basis for multi-valued model checking [6], where the satisfaction relation $\mathcal{M} \models \varphi$ for a model $\mathcal{M}$ and a specification φ can be multi-valued. Bruns and Godefroid experiment on multi-valued logics and show that many algorithms for multi-valued logics can be reduced to ones for two-valued logics [5]. Easterbrook and Chechik introduce a framework where multiple inconsistent models are merged according to an underlying specification given in a multi-valued logic, where the different values in the specification represent the different levels of uncertainty, priority and agreement between the merged models [9]. In comparison to all these works, we are interested in multi-valued extensions of the models themselves and in the synthesis of such models, in order to determine the amount of information that resides in a specification.

The term skeleton has been also used by Emerson and Clarke which shall not be confused with the skeletons presented here. They presented a method for the synthesis of synchronization skeletons that abstract from details irrelevant to synchronization of concurrent systems [8]. In our skeletons, we stick to the structure of transition systems and leave place holders for the underspecified details, which may then be supplemented with further steps to a complete transition system.

2   Preliminaries

Alternating Automata. We define an *alternating Büchi automaton* as a tuple $\mathcal{A} = (\Sigma, Q, q_0, \delta, F)$, where Σ denotes a finite alphabet, Q denotes a finite set of states, $q_0 \in Q$ denotes a designated initial state, $\delta : Q \times \Sigma \rightarrow \mathbb{B}^+(Q)$ denotes a transition function, that maps a state and an input letter to a positive boolean combination of states, and finally the set $F \subseteq Q$ of accepting states.

We define infinite words over Σ as sequence $\sigma : \mathbb{N} \rightarrow \Sigma$. A Σ-tree is a pair $(\mathcal{T}, r)$ over a set of directions D, where $\mathcal{T}$ is a prefix-closed subset of D^* and $r : \mathcal{T} \rightarrow \Sigma$ is a labeling function. The empty sequence ϵ is called the *root*. The children of a node $n \in \mathcal{T}$ are nodes $C(n) = \{n \cdot d \in \mathcal{T} \mid d \in D\}$.

A *run* of an automaton $\mathcal{A} = (\Sigma, Q, q_0, \delta, F)$ on a sequence $\sigma : \mathbb{N} \rightarrow \Sigma$ is a Q-tree $(\mathcal{T}, r)$ with $r(\epsilon) = q_0$ and for all nodes $n \in \mathcal{T}$, if $r(n) = q$ then the set $\{r(n') \mid n' \in C(n)\}$ satisfies $\delta(q, \sigma(|n|))$.

A run $(\mathcal{T}, r)$ is *accepting* if for every infinite branch $n_0, n_1, \ldots$ the sequence $r(n_0)r(n_1) \ldots$ satisfies the *Büchi condition*, which requires that some state from F occures infinitely often in the sequence $r(n_0)r(n_1) \ldots$. The set of accepted words by the automaton $\mathcal{A}$ is the language of the automaton and is denoted by $L(\mathcal{A})$. An automaton is empty iff its language is the empty set.

A *nondeterministic* automaton is a special alternating automaton, where the image of δ consists only of such formulas that, when rewritten in disjunctive normal form, contain exactly one element of Q in every disjunct.

An alternating automaton is called *universal* if, for all states q and input letters α, $\delta(q, \alpha)$ is a conjunction. A universal and nondeterministic automaton is called *deterministic*.

A *Büchi* automaton is called a *safety* automaton if $Q = F$. Safety automata are denoted by a tuple (Σ, Q, q_0, δ). For safety automata, every run graph is accepting.

Safety Languages: A finite word $w = \{1, \ldots, i\} \to \Sigma$ over some finite alphabet Σ is called a bad-prefix for a language $L \subseteq \Sigma^\omega$, if every infinite word $\sigma \in (\mathbb{N} \to \Sigma)$ with prefix w is not in the language L. A language $L \subseteq (\mathbb{N} \to \Sigma)$ is called a safety language, if every $\sigma \notin L$ has a bad-prefix. We denote the set of bad-prefixes for a language L by $BP(L)$. For every safety language L we can define a finite word automaton $\mathcal{B} = (Q_\mathcal{B}, Q_{\mathcal{B},0}, F_\mathcal{B}, \delta_\mathcal{B})$ that accepts the language $BP(L)$. We call $\mathcal{B}$ the bad-prefix automaton of L.

Linear-Time Temporal Logic: We use Linear-time Temporal Logic (LTL) [15], with the usual temporal operators Next $\bigcirc$, Until $\mathcal{U}$ and the derived operators Eventually $\Diamond$ and Globally $\square$. LTL formulas are defined over a set of atomic propositions $AP = I \cup O$, which is partitioned into a set I of input propositions and a set O of output propositions. We denote the satisfaction of an LTL formula φ by an infinite sequence $\sigma \colon \mathbb{N} \to 2^{AP}$ of valuations of the atomic propositions by $\sigma \models \varphi$. For an LTL formula φ we define the language $L(\varphi)$ by the set $\{\sigma \in (\mathbb{N} \to 2^{AP}) \mid \sigma \models \varphi\}$.

Implementations: We represent implementations as *labeled transition systems*. For a given finite set Υ of directions and a finite set Σ of labels, a Σ-labeled Υ-transition system is a tuple $\mathcal{T} = (T, t_0, \tau, o)$, consisting of a finite set of states T, an initial state $t_0 \in T$, a transition function $\tau \colon T \times \Upsilon \to T$, and a labeling function $o \colon T \to \Sigma$. A *path* in $\mathcal{T}$ is a sequence $\pi \colon \mathbb{N} \to T \times \Upsilon$ of states and directions that follows the transition function, i.e., for all $i \in \mathbb{N}$ if $\pi(i) = (t_i, e_i)$ and $\pi(i+1) = (t_{i+1}, e_{i+1})$, then $t_{i+1} = \tau(t_i, e_i)$. We call a path initial if it starts with the initial state: $\pi(0) = (t_0, e)$ for some $e \in \Upsilon$. We denote the set of initial paths of $\mathcal{T}$ by $Path(T)$. For a path $\pi \in Path(T)$, we denote the sequence $\sigma_\pi \colon i \mapsto o(\pi(i))$, where $o(t, e) = (o(t) \cup e)$ by the *trace* of π. We call the set of traces of the paths of a transition system $\mathcal{T}$ the language of the $\mathcal{T}$, denoted by $L(\mathcal{T})$.

For a set of atomic propositions $AP = O \cup I$, we say that a 2^O-labeled 2^I-transition system $\mathcal{T}$ satisfies an LTL formula φ, if and only if $L(T) \subseteq L(\varphi)$, i.e., every trace of $\mathcal{T}$ satisfies φ. In this case we call $\mathcal{T}$ a model of φ.

Multi-valued Sets: A multi-valued set over an alphabet Σ and set of values Γ is a function $v \in (\Sigma \to \Gamma)$. The simplest type of multi-valued sets is the two-valued set which define the notion of sets as we know, where Σ is a set of symbols and $\Gamma = \{\bot, \top\}$, i.e., for a two-valued set v over Σ and Γ, a symbol $a \in \Sigma$ is in v if $v(a) = \top$, and not otherwise. The set of all multi-valued sets over an alphabet Σ and a set of values Γ is denoted by Γ^Σ, e.g., in the usual set notion this is the set $\{\bot, \top\}^\Sigma$ or as we know it 2^Σ for an alphabet Σ.

For a multi-valued set $v \in \Gamma^\Sigma$ and for $p \in \Sigma$ and $h \in \Gamma$ we define the multi-valued set $v' = v[p \mapsto h]$, where $v'(p) = h$ and for all $p' \in \Sigma \setminus \{p\}$, we have $v'(p') = v(p')$. For a multi-valued set $v \in \Gamma^{\Sigma}$ and for a set $\Sigma' \subseteq \Sigma$ the set $v_{\Sigma'} \in \Gamma^{\Sigma'}$ is the multi-valued set obtained by projection from Σ to Σ'.

3 Skeletons

An *open set* over an alphabet Σ is a three-valued set $v : \{\top, \bot, ?\}^{\Sigma}$, where each element $a \in \Sigma$ is either in v denoted by $v(a) = \top$, not in v denoted by $v(a) = \bot$, or it is open whether it is in the set or not, i.e., it could be one of both, denoted by $v(a) = ?$. In the remainder of the paper, we denote the set $\{\top, \bot, ?\}^{\Sigma}$ by 3^{Σ}. For two open sets $v, v' \in 3^{\Sigma}$ we define the partial order $\sqsubseteq$ such that $v \sqsubseteq v'$ if and only if for all symbols $a \in \Sigma$, $v(a) \preceq v'(a)$ with respect to the lattice $\preceq = \{(\bot, \bot), (\top, \top), (\bot, ?), (\top, ?), (?, ?)\}$.

We call a sequence σ an open sequence if it is a sequence over open sets, i.e., $\sigma \in (\mathbb{N} \to 3^{\Sigma})$. For two open sequences σ and σ' we define the partial order $\sqsubseteq$ such that $\sigma \sqsubseteq \sigma'$ if for all $i \in \mathbb{N}$, $\sigma(i) \sqsubseteq \sigma'(i)$. For a sequence $\sigma \in (\mathbb{N} \to 3^{\Sigma})$ and $\Sigma' \subseteq \Sigma$ the sequence $\sigma_{\Sigma'} \in (\mathbb{N} \to 3^{\Sigma'})$ is the sequence where for all i, $\sigma_{\Sigma'}(i) = \sigma(i)_{\Sigma'}$.

We define the satisfaction relation of LTL over open sequences as follows. Given an LTL formula φ over a set of atomic propositions $AP = O \cup I$, an open sequence σ satisfies φ, denoted by $\sigma \models \varphi$, if for each sequence $\sigma' \in L(\varphi)$ that is input equivalent to σ, i.e., $\sigma_I = \sigma'_I$, we have $\sigma' \sqsubseteq \sigma$. For a fixed sequence of inputs $\varsigma \in (\mathbb{N} \to 2^I)$, there is a unique open sequence σ with $\sigma_I = \varsigma$ that satisfies φ and that is minimial with respect to the partial order $\sqsubseteq$, i.e., for all sequences $\sigma' \in (\mathbb{N} \to 3^{AP})$ with $\sigma' \models \varphi$ and $\sigma'_I = \varsigma$, we have $\sigma \sqsubseteq \sigma'$. We call such sequence a *minimal satisfying sequence*. For an LTL formula φ, we denote the set of all minimal satisfying sequences by $\min(\varphi)$.

Building on the definitions of open sequences and transition systems we introduce the notion of *skeletons* of reactive systems, which are transition systems labeled with open sets from 3°.

Definition 1 (Skeleton). *For a set $AP = O \cup I$ of atomic propositions, a skeleton over AP is a 3°-labeled-2^I-transition system.*

The language of a skeleton $\mathcal{S}$ is the set of open sequences given by the set of its traces. Figure 2 shows four skeletons defined over the sets $I = \{r_1, r_2\}$ and $O = \{g_1, g_2\}$. Figures 2(a) and (b) both define the language $\{\sigma : \mathbb{N} \to 3^{AP} \mid \forall i. \sigma(i)(g_1) = \sigma(i)(g_2) = ?\}$, i.e., for all input sequences the values of the output propositions g_1 and g_2 are open in all positions. The language of the skeleton in Fig. 2(c) is the set $\{\sigma : \mathbb{N} \to 3^{AP} \mid \sigma(0)(g_1) = \sigma(0)(g_2) = \bot, \forall i > 0. \sigma(i)(g_1) = \top \wedge \sigma(i)(g_2) = ?\}$ where the values of g_1 are fixed in all positions and for g_2 only in the first position of the sequence.[1]

We say that a skeleton $\mathcal{S}$ is a *model* of an LTL formula φ denoted by $\mathcal{S} \models \varphi$, if $L(\mathcal{S}) = \min(\varphi)$. Intuitively, for an LTL formula φ, a skeleton gives an incomplete transition system where values of atomic propositions that are not

---

[1] Note that skeletons have no open values for input propositions.

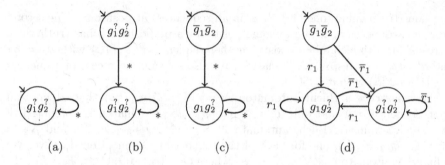

Fig. 2. Skeletons over the sets $I = \{r_1, r_2\}$ and $O = \{g_1, g_2\}$

deterministically fixed by φ, are left open, i.e., they are mapped to the value ? in the open set of a state. Consider the formula $\varphi = \bar{g}_1 \wedge \bar{g}_2 \wedge \Box(r_1 \rightarrow \bigcirc g_1)$. We notice that all transition systems that satisfy φ must have the label $\bar{g}_1 \bar{g}_2$ in the initial state. For the rest of the transition system, the formula forces only to label a state with g_1 in case the direction(input) leading to this state contains the proposition r_1, and leaves it open on how to label the states reached by other directions, or whether to label a state with g_2 if it is reached by an input where r_1 is true (Fig. 2(d)).

Building on the satisfaction relation between LTL and skeleton we investigate in the next sections the problems of model checking and synthesis of skeletons.

4   Model Checking Skeletons

We present an automata-based model checking algorithm for skeletons. Given an LTL formula φ we show that we can construct a nondeterministic Büchi automaton that recognizes the complement language $\overline{\min(\varphi)}$. Using the usual product construction, in this case, the product of the automaton and the skeleton, one can check whether the resulting automaton contains a path that simulates an accepting path in the nondeterministic automaton. If this is the case, then the language of the skeleton contains a sequence in $\overline{\min(\varphi)}$ and, thus, the skeleton is not a model for the formula φ. Using the construction of the product automaton we also show that checking whether a skeleton is a model of an LTL formula can be done in space exponential in the length of the formula.

Lemma 1. *Given an LTL formula φ we can build a nondeterministic Büchi automaton $\mathcal{N} = (3^{AP}, Q, q_0, F, \delta)$ such that $L(\mathcal{N}) = \overline{\min(\varphi)}$. The number of states of $\mathcal{N}$ is doubly-exponential in the length of φ.*

Construction. The language $\overline{\min(\varphi)}$ contains all sequences $\sigma : \mathbb{N} \rightarrow 3^{AP}$ that are not minimal satisfying open sequences for φ. These can be distinguished by two types of open sequences. The first type involves sequences σ where in some position i the truth value of a proposition $p \in AP$ is open (mapped to ?), although, in all sequences $\sigma' \in L(\varphi)$ with $\sigma_I = \sigma_I'$ the proposition p has the one same truth value (one of $\top$ or $\bot$ in all sequences) at position i. The second type are sequences σ, where in some position i a proposition p has truth value $\bot$(resp. $\top$), although, there exists another sequence $\sigma' \in L(\varphi)$ with $\sigma'_I = \sigma_I$ and $\sigma'(i)(p) = \top$(resp. $\bot$). The latter case also subsumes the case of sequences $\sigma \in (\mathbb{N} \to 2^{AP})$ with $\sigma \notin L(\varphi)$.

We construct a Büchi automaton $\mathcal{N} = (3^{AP}, Q, q_0, F, \delta)$ that accepts an open sequence σ if and only if $\sigma \notin \min(\varphi)$. The automaton is composed of two nondeterministic Büchi automata $\mathcal{N}_1 = (3^{AP}, Q_1, q_{0,1}, F_1, \delta_1)$ and $\mathcal{N}_2 = (3^{AP}, Q_2, q_{0,2}, F_2, \delta_2)$, one for each of the sequence types mentioned above. We define the automaton as $\mathcal{N} = \mathcal{N}_1 \vee \mathcal{N}_2$, where $Q = \{q_0\} \cup Q_1 \cup Q_2$, $F = F_1 \cup F_2$ and $\delta = \{(q_0, a, \delta_1(q_{0,1}, a) \vee \delta_2(q_{0,2}, a)) \mid a \in 3^{AP}\} \cup \delta_1 \cup \delta_2$.

Automaton $\mathcal{N}_1$ accepts a sequence $\sigma \in (\mathbb{N} \to 3^{AP})$ if σ has a position i where an atomic proposition $p \in AP$ is incorrectly marked as open. The automaton $\mathcal{N}_1$ can be constructed as follows:

Let $\mathcal{U}_1 = (2^{AP}, Q_1^{\mathcal{U}}, q_{0,1}^{\mathcal{U}}, F_1^{\mathcal{U}}, \delta_1^{\mathcal{U}})$ be a universal Büchi automaton for the formula $\neg\varphi$. We extend the automaton $\mathcal{U}_1$ to another universal Büchi automaton $\mathcal{U}_1^*$ over an extended alphabet $\{\top, \bot, ?, *_\top, *_\bot\}^{AP}$. We make use of the values $*_\top$ and $*_\bot$ to encode in the input sequence whether a mapping to $?$ is wrong, and whether it is wrong when replacing $?$ by $\top$ or by $\bot$. We define $\mathcal{U}_1^* = (\{\top, \bot, ?, *_\top, *_\bot\}^{AP}, Q_1^*, q_{0,1}^*, F_1^*, \delta_1^*)$ over two copies of the automaton $\mathcal{U}_1$(denoted by the numbers 1 and 2) where $Q_1^* = Q_1^{\mathcal{U}} \times \{1, 2\}$, $q_{0,1}^* = (q_{0,1}^{\mathcal{U}}, 1)$, $F_1^* = F_1^{\mathcal{U}} \times \{1, 2\}$. The transition function δ_1^* is given by the union of the following sets:

- $\{((q, h), v, \delta_1^{\mathcal{U}}(q, v)_{\{q' \in Q_1^{\mathcal{U}}/(q', h)\}}) \mid h \in \{1, 2\}, \forall p \in O.v(p) \in \{\top, \bot\}\}$
  where in both copies of the automaton $\mathcal{U}_1$, transitions over symbols v with no open values remain in the same copy and follow the structure of the transition relation $\delta_1^{\mathcal{U}}$ of $\mathcal{U}_1$. The operation $\{q' \in Q_1^{\mathcal{U}}/(q', h)\}$ substitutes every appearance of a state q' in $\delta_1^{\mathcal{U}}(q, v)$ by a state (q', h) from Q_1^*.
- $\{((q, h), v, (\delta_1^{\mathcal{U}}(q, v[p \mapsto \top]) \wedge \delta_1^{\mathcal{U}}(q, v[p \mapsto \bot]))_{\{q' \in Q_1^{\mathcal{U}}/(q', h)\}}) \mid$
  $h \in \{1, 2\}, p \in O, v(p) = ?\}$
  universal transitions for symbols where a proposition p has an open truth value imitating transitions for both truth values $\top$ and $\bot$ for p.
- $\{((q, 1), v, \delta_1^{\mathcal{U}}(q, v[p \mapsto \top])_{\{q' \in Q_1^{\mathcal{U}}/(q', 2)\}}) \mid p \in O, v(p) = *_\top\}$
  when we guess at some position i that an open truth value for a proposition p is wrong, and it is wrong when replacing it by $\top$ we follow the transition $\top$ to the second copy of $\mathcal{U}_1$ in which $?, *_\bot$ and $*_\top$ are treated equivalently. This helps to check, whether replacing $?$ by $\top$ results in accpeting run in $\mathcal{U}_1$, which means that at position i the truth value $\top$ violates the property φ, and thus it cannot be open at the that point.
- $\{((q, 1), v, \delta_1^{\mathcal{U}}(q, v[p \mapsto \bot])_{\{q' \in Q_1^{\mathcal{U}}/(q', 2)\}}) \mid p \in O, v(p) = *_\bot\}$
  which introduce transitions that involve the dual case of $*_\top$.
- $\{((q, 2), v, (\delta_1^{\mathcal{U}}(q, v[p \mapsto \top]) \wedge \delta_1^*(q, v[p \mapsto \bot]))_{\{q' \in Q_1^{\mathcal{U}}/(q', 2)\}}) \mid$
  $p \in O, v(p) \in \{*_\bot, *_\top\}\}$
  these transitions make sure that when moving to copy 2 of $\mathcal{U}_1$, values $*_\top$ and $*_\bot$ are treated equally to $?$, because after guessing that a $?$ is wrong it must be wrong for all continuations.

In order to obtain the desired automaton $\mathcal{N}_1$ over the alphabet 3^{AP} we first transform the automaton $\mathcal{U}_1^*$ to a nondeterministic automaton $\mathcal{N}_1^*$ with $L(\mathcal{U}_1^*) = L(\mathcal{N}_1^*)$ using a subset construction. This is necessary in order to merge all transitions $*_\perp$ at one level into one state. The same holds also for transitions $*_\top$. In this way, we can check whether at some position in a sequence a value ? is wrong by checking all possible branches of the automaton $\mathcal{U}_1^*$ at that level. The automaton $\mathcal{N}_1^*$ can be transformed now to the desired automaton $\mathcal{N}_1$ by projecting every transition label with values in $\{*_\top, *_\perp\}$ to a label $v' \in 3^{AP}$ such that for every $p \in O$, if $v(p) = *_\top$ or $v(p) = *_\perp$ then $v'(p) = ?$.

The size of the automaton $\mathcal{U}_1$ is exponential in the length of φ using the transformation of LTL formulas into alternating Büchi automata [17], and then using a subset construction. The transformation to $\mathcal{U}_1^*$ from $\mathcal{U}_1$, and to $\mathcal{N}_1$ from $\mathcal{N}_1^*$ are both polynomial, and exponential from $\mathcal{U}_1^*$ to $\mathcal{N}_1^*$. Thus, the size of $\mathcal{N}_1$ is doubly-exponential in the length of φ.

In a similar way, we can construct the automaton $\mathcal{N}_2$. Automaton $\mathcal{N}_2$ accepts a sequence $\sigma \in (\mathbb{N} \to 3^{AP})$ if a proposition $p \in AP$ is incorrectly mapped to $\top$ or $\perp$. Starting with the alternating Büchi automaton for the formula φ, we extend the alphabet with symbols $*_\top$ and $*_\perp$ and build an automaton $\mathcal{U}_2^* = (\{\top, \perp, ?, *_\top, *_\perp\}^{AP}, Q_2^*, q_{0,2}^*, F_2^*, \delta_2^*)$. Whenever we read a symbol v where some $p \in O$ is mapped to $*_\top(*_\perp)$, the automaton follows the transition for $v(p) = \perp(\top)$. After turning $\mathcal{U}_2^*$ to a nondeterministic automaton and projecting, a label v is replaced by a label v' such that for every $p \in O$, if $v(p) = *_\top$ or $v(p) = *_\perp$ then $v'(p) = \top$ or $v'(p) = \perp$, respectively. The automaton $\mathcal{N}_2$ is doubly-exponential in the length of φ.

Proof. Let $\sigma \in (\mathbb{N} \to 3^{AP})$. We distinguish three cases:

- $\sigma \in \overline{\min(\varphi)}$ and for some i and some $p \in O$, the mapping $\sigma(i)(p) = ?$ is wrong. We assume, w.l.o.g., that for all $\sigma' \in L(\varphi)$ with $\sigma_I = \sigma'_I$, that $\sigma'(i)(p) = \top$, and that i is the first position for which $\sigma(i)(p) = ?$ is wrong. A run of the automaton $\mathcal{N}_1$ over σ is a sequence $r \in (\mathbb{N} \to 2^{Q_1^*})$. Let $r = X_0 X_1 \ldots$ be the run of the automaton $\mathcal{N}$ on σ, where $X_0 = \{q_{0,1}^*\}$, and up to the position i the run follows for each mapping to ? the transitions in $\mathcal{N}_1$ that were transitions for mappings to ? in the automaton $\mathcal{N}_1^*$ before the projection, i.e., all sets X_j with $j \leq i$ contain only states $(q, 1)$ from Q_1^*, where $q \in Q_1^{\mathcal{U}}$. In the position i, where the mapping to ? is incorrect, the run follows the transition with ? in state X_i of $\mathcal{N}_1$ that can be mapped to a transition $*_\perp$ in the automaton $\mathcal{N}_1^*$ which moves to a set X_{i+1} with only states $(q, 2)$ from Q_1^*, i.e., the transition that checks whether replacing ? at i with $\perp$ always leads to rejecting states for possible instantiations of upcoming ?s. As $\mathcal{U}_1^*$ is built from copies of the automaton $\mathcal{U}_1$ for the formula $\neg\varphi$, following the transition for $*_\perp$ means replacing at position i the value ? with $\perp$, which can only lead to rejecting runs, because the automaton $\mathcal{U}_1$ accepts no sequence where p is mapped to value $\perp$ at position i.
- $\sigma \in \overline{\min(\varphi)}$ and for some i and some $p \in O$, $\sigma(i)(p)$ is incorrectly mapped to $\top$ or to $\perp$. With the same argumentation of the last case over the structure of the automaton $\mathcal{N}_2$ the claim can be proven.

– $\sigma \in \min(\varphi)$. In this case, for each position i, for each proposition $p \in O$ such that $\sigma(i)(p) = ?$, and for each instantiation of $?$ for p in position i, there are instantiations for all other $?$ values in σ and for all propositions such that the resulting sequence $\sigma' \in (\mathbb{N} \to 2^{AP})$ is in $L(\varphi)$. Let $r = X_0 X_1 ...$ be a run of $\mathcal{N}_1$ on σ. If r follows all transitions for a mapping to $?$ that correspond to a transition for the value $?$ in $\mathcal{N}_1^*$, then all sets X_j for $j \geq 0$ have states $(q, 1)$ of $\mathcal{U}_1^*$ where $q \in Q_1^{\mathcal{U}}$ and the run is not accepting, because the run simulates a universal run tree in $\mathcal{U}_1^*$ with at least one non-accepting branch, because there is an instantiation for σ that is a model of φ. If at any point, the run r takes a transition for some mapping to $?$ that corresponds to a transition $*_\perp$ or $*_\top$ in the automaton $\mathcal{N}_1^*$, then the run cannot be accepting, otherwise there is a mapping to $?$ for some proposition $p \in O$ in some position in σ for which all other $?$ in σ cannot be instantiated appropriately in order to get a model in σ.

In a similar way we can also prove that $\mathcal{N}_2$ has no accepting run for σ.

$\square$

To check whether a skeleton $\mathcal{S}$ is a model for a given LTL formula φ we compute the product $\mathcal{P} = \mathcal{S} \times \mathcal{N}$ where $\mathcal{N}$ is nondeterministic Büchi automaton with $L(\mathcal{N}) = \overline{\min(\varphi)}$ constructed in Lemma 1. If $\mathcal{P}$ contains a path that simulates an accepting path in $\mathcal{N}$, then $\mathcal{S}$ has a path that violates the property φ, i.e., there is a sequence in the language $L(\mathcal{S})$ that is not in $\min(\varphi)$.

Instead of constructing the product automaton $\mathcal{P}$ one can also guess a run in $\mathcal{P}$ and check whether it is accepting[2]. Based on this idea, the complexity of model checking skeleton is given by the following theorem.

Theorem 1. *Checking whether a skeleton $\mathcal{S}$ is a model for an LTL formula φ is in* EXPSPACE.

5   Synthesis of Skeletons

For a set of atomic propositions $AP = I \cup O$, to check whether there is 2^O-labeled 2^I-transition system $\mathcal{T}$ that satisfies a given LTL formula φ, one would construct a deterministic ω-automaton $\mathcal{D}$ (for example a parity automaton) with $L(\mathcal{D}) = L(\varphi)$, interpret the automaton as a tree automaton over trees with labels from 3° and directions from 2^I and check its emptiness. In case, the language of the automaton is not empty the procedure returns a transition system $\mathcal{T}$ that models the formula φ. In the same fashion, we can construct a deterministic ω-automaton for the language $\min(\varphi)$ (for example by determinizing the automaton from Lemma 1) and check whether there is a skeleton that is a model for φ by performing an emptiness check over tree automaton interpretation of the deterministic automaton.

---

[2] This follows the idea of the PSPACE model checking algorithm for LTL over transition systems [3].

The deterministic automaton is very expensive to construct (triple exponential in the formula φ). Instead, we show that we can avoid this construction of the large deterministic automaton using learning. In comparison to transition systems, given an LTL formula, we show that it has a unique minimal skeleton that models the formula. The language of the skeleton is a safety language, and thus, can be characterized by a bad-prefix automaton, which is a finite word automaton. We use the learning algorithm L* to learn the deterministic bad-prefix automaton [2], which can be easily transformed to a skeleton that models the formula. The learning algorithm learns the skeleton in time polynomial in the size of the minimal skeleton.

5.1 Learning Skeletons

In the following we present an algorithm for learning skeletons of LTL formulas. Our algorithm is based on the L* algorithm for learning deterministic finite automata introduced by Dana Angluin [2]. The setting of the L* algorithm involves two key actors, the *learner* and the *teacher*. The learner tries to learn a language known to the teacher by learning a minimal deterministic finite word automaton for the language. The interaction between the learner and the teacher is driven by two types of queries: *membership queries*, where the learner asks whether a particular word is in the language, and *equivalence queries*, to check whether a learned deterministic finite automaton indeed defines the language to be learned. Here, the teacher responds either with a "yes" or with a counterexample, which is a word in the symmetric difference of the language of the learned automaton and the actual language. A teacher is called *minimally adequate*, if she can answer membership and equivalence queries.

Theorem 2 [2]. *Given a minimally adequate Teacher for an unknown regular language L, we can construct a minimal finite word automaton that accepts L, in time polynomial in the number of states of the automaton and the length of the largest counterexample returned by the teacher.*

For an LTL formula φ we show that the language of a skeleton that satisfies φ is a safety language. This can be characterized by a language over finite words, namely the language of bad-prefixes. The L* algorithm can learn a finite automaton for the language of bad-prefixes, which in turn can then be transformed to a skeleton for the property φ.

Lemma 2. *For an LTL formula φ, the language $\min(\varphi)$ is a safety language.*

Proof. We show that every $\sigma \in \overline{\min(\varphi)}$ has a bad-prefix. We distinguish two cases for σ:

- There is a point i in σ and a proposition p such that $\sigma(i)(p) = \top$(or $\bot$) and there is a sequence $\sigma' \in L(\varphi)$ with $\sigma_I = \sigma'_I$ and $\sigma'(i)(p) = \bot$(or$\top$). Thus, any finite sequence $v_0 \ldots v_i \in (3^{AP})^*$ with $(v_0 \ldots v_i)_I = (\sigma(0) \ldots \sigma(i))_I$ and $v_i(p) \neq ?$ is a bad-prefix for $\min(\varphi)$.

– There is a point i in σ and a proposition p such that $\sigma(i)(p) =?$ and for all $\sigma' \in L(\varphi)$ with $\sigma_I = \sigma'_I$ we have $\sigma'(i)(p)$ is solely $\top$ or solely $\bot$. In this case, every finite sequence $v_0 \ldots v_i \in (3^{AP})^*$ with $(v_0 \ldots v_i)_I = (\sigma(0) \ldots \sigma(i))_I$ and $v_i(p) =?$ is a bad-prefix for $\min(\varphi)$.   □

From the last lemma we deduce, that a skeleton $\mathcal{S}$ for an LTL formula φ can be seen as a safety automaton that accepts the language of minimal satisfying open sequences for φ. In particular, there is a bad-prefix automaton $\mathcal{B}$ that accepts the language of bad-prefixes of the language $\min(\varphi)$.

We use the L* algorithm to learn a deterministic bad-prefix automaton for the language $\min(\varphi)$. Figure 3 shows a high level flow graph of the learning algorithm[3]. The learner poses a series of membership questions before making a conjecture about the bad-prefix automaton. With a membership query the learner asks whether a finite word $w \in (3^{AP})^*$ is a bad-prefix for $\min(\varphi)$. If w is a bad-prefix then the teacher returns *yes*, and *no* otherwise. The equivalence queries allow the learner to check whether a skeleton $\mathcal{S}$ is correct, i.e., $L(\mathcal{S}) = \min(\varphi)$. The teacher either confirms the automaton or returns a counterexample to the learner. The latter is either a bad-prefix that is not rejected by $\mathcal{B}$ or word $w \in (3^{AP})^*$ that is not a bad-prefix for $\min(\varphi)$ yet is in the language of $\mathcal{B}$. The black box shown in Fig. 3 between the bad-prefix automaton and a skeleton, is a check whether the safety language characterized by the bad-prefix automaton can be represented by a skeleton. We will refer to this check as the *output consistency check* and will explain it later in more detail.

The skeleton returned by the learning procedure is minimal and it is unique.

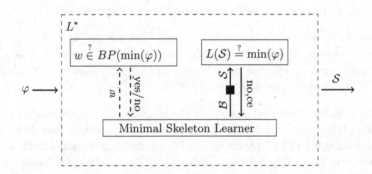

Fig. 3. A modified L* for learning minimal skeletons of LTL formulas

Lemma 3. *For each LTL formula φ there is a unique (up to isomorphism) minimal skeleton $\mathcal{S}$ such that $\mathcal{S} \models \varphi$.*

---

[3] For more details on the L* algorithm we refer the reader to [2].

Proof. Let $\mathcal{S} = (S, s_0, \tau, o)$ and $\mathcal{S}' = (S', s'_0, \tau', o')$ be two minimal skeletons for φ, i.e., $|S| = |S'| = c$ and there is no skeleton $\mathcal{S}'' = (S'', s''_0, \tau'', o'')$ for φ with $|S''| < c$. We show that $\mathcal{S}$ and $\mathcal{S}'$ define the same skeleton up to isomorphism. Let $\beta = \{(s, s') \in S \times S' \mid \forall \sigma_I \in (2^I)^*. \; \tau^*(s0, \sigma_I) = s \leftrightarrow \tau'^*(s'_0, \sigma_I) = s'\}$. The relation β is bijective because τ^* and τ'^* are both functional and complete. Thus, there is a one-to-one mapping between the states of $\mathcal{S}$ and those of $\mathcal{S}'$, and for each $(s_1, i, s_2) \in \tau$ we have $(\beta(s_1), i, \beta(s_2)) \in \tau'$. For each $(s, s') \in \beta$ it is also the case that $o(s) = o'(s')$, otherwise, there is an input sequence that distinguishes a trace in $\mathcal{S}$ from the corresponding one in $\mathcal{S}'$, which contradicts the assumption that $L(\mathcal{S}) = L(\mathcal{S}')$. This implies that $\mathcal{S}$ is isomorphic to $\mathcal{S}'$.   □

In the next sections we show how membership and equivalence queries can be solved algorithmically.

5.2   Membership Queries

In this section we show that using the ideas of the automaton presented in Lemma 1 we can check whether a word is a bad-prefix in space exponential in the length of φ.

Theorem 3. *Given an LTL formula φ and a finite word $w \in (3^{AP})^*$, checking whether w is a bad-prefix for $\min(\varphi)$ is in* EXPSPACE.

Proof. A finite word $w \in (3^{AP})^*$ is a bad-prefix for $\min(\varphi)$ if $w = w_0 \ldots w_n$ has a prefix and there is a sequence of input values ς and no sequence $\sigma : \mathbb{N} \to 3^{AP}$ with $\sigma_I = \varsigma$ can extend w to a sequence in $w \cdot \sigma \in \min(\varphi)$. Let $\mathcal{U} = (\Sigma, Q, q_0, \delta, F)$ be a universal Büchi automaton such that $L(\mathcal{U}) = L(\neg\varphi)$. The idea is to iteratively construct a run of the automaton $\mathcal{U}$ and check if the run is accepting (remember that a run of $\mathcal{U}$ is Q-tree). Given the input word w, we first guess which position i of w contains a wrong mapping and compute the set of states of the run tree over $w_0 \ldots w_i$ reached at this position. Then, we compute the set of states reached via choosing the transition for which the guessed position i is wrong. Form here on, we guess the next input and branch universally for all valuations of the output propositions, and compute the next set of reached states. This is repeated $2^{|Q|}$ times (At latest at position $2^{|Q|}$ we reach a set of states, that was seen before and enter a loop in the run). If during the procedure a valid accepting configuration of the universal automaton was guessed, then we have found a sequence of inputs ς for which no σ with $\sigma_I = \varsigma$ extends the prefix of $w_0 \ldots w_i$ to a sequence in $\min(\varphi)$. Thus, w is a bad-prefix for $\min(\varphi)$. In each step we only need to remember the currently reached set of states of $\mathcal{U}$, and whether we have seen an accepting configuration of $\mathcal{U}$. Furthermore, the number of iteration can be encoded in binary and is polynomial in the size of $\mathcal{U}$, which in turn is exponential in the length of φ.   □

5.3   Equivalence Queries

We move now to equivalence queries. To check whether a skeleton is a model for a formula φ we apply the model checking algorithm presented in Sect. 4.

The learning algorithm first constructs a bad-prefix automaton for the language $\min(\varphi)$. We show that this automaton can be turned into a safety automaton for $\min(\varphi)$ on which we can simulate a skeleton for φ. In case we cannot simulate the skeleton on top of the safety automaton, then there is no skeleton that models the formula φ.

Lemma 4. *Given a deterministic bad-prefix automaton $\mathcal{B}$ for a safety property φ, we can construct a deterministic safety automaton $\mathcal{S}$ for φ in time linear in the size of $\mathcal{B}$.*

Construction. Let $\mathcal{B} = (\Sigma, Q, q_0, F, \delta)$ be a bad-prefix automaton for some property φ and we assume it is complete. We construct a safety automaton $\mathcal{S} = (\Sigma, Q', q_0', \delta')$ for φ by first removing all states in F and then by iteratively removing all resulting sink states in the automaton.

Remark 1. Note that if $\mathcal{B}$ is minimal, so is $\mathcal{S}$.

Before we move on to the construction we consider following fact about skeletons and the language $\min(\varphi)$ for some formula φ. Let $AP = O \cup I$ be the set of atomic propositions. Let $\mathcal{S} = (S, s_0, \tau, o)$ be a skeleton that models the formula φ. Let $\pi_1 = (s_0, i_1)(s_1, i_1)\ldots$ and $\pi_2 = (s_0, i_1)(s_1, i_2)\ldots$ be paths in $\mathcal{S}$ where $s_0, s_1 \in S$ and $i_1, i_2 \in I$. Then, both sequences $\sigma_{\pi_1} = (o(s_0) \cup i_1)(o(s_1) \cup i_1)\ldots$ and $\sigma_{\pi_2} = (o(s_0) \cup i_1)(o(s_1) \cup i_2)\ldots$, must be in the set $\min(\varphi)$, otherwise $\mathcal{S}$ is not a model of φ. This means, if the language $\min(\varphi)$ contains sequences $(o_1 \cup i_1)(o_2 \cup i_1)\ldots$ and $(o_1 \cup i_1)(o_2' \cup i_2)\ldots$ with $o_2 \neq o_2'$ then there is no skeleton that models φ, because $\min(\varphi) = L(\mathcal{S})$ and both traces cannot be trace of the skeleton at the same time.

Definition 2 (Output Consistent). *For a set of atomic propositions $AP = O \cup I$, a safety automaton $\mathcal{A} = (3^{AP}, Q, q_0, \delta)$ is output consistent, if for each state $q \in Q$ there is a unique mapping $v \in \{\bot, \top, ?\}^O$ and for all transitions $(q, v', q') \in \delta$, $v'(p) = v(p)$ for all propositions $p \in O$.*

Lemma 5. *Given an LTL formula φ, if there is an output consistent safety automaton $\mathcal{A}$ for the language $\min(\varphi)$, we can transform $\mathcal{A}$ to a skeleton $\mathcal{S}$ that models φ. The size of $\mathcal{S}$ is equal to the size of $\mathcal{A}$.*

Construction. Let φ be an LTL formula and let $\mathcal{A} = (3^{AP}, Q, q_0, \delta)$ be an output consistent safety automaton for the language $\min(\varphi)$ constructed from a deterministic bad-prefix automaton as in Lemma 4. Let $Q = \{q_0, q_1 \ldots q_n\}$. We can construct a skeleton $\mathcal{S} = (S, s_0, \tau, o)$, where $S = \{s_0, \ldots, s_n\}$ and $o(s_i) = X \cap O$ for $(q_i, X, q') \in \delta$ for some $q' \in Q$, and $(s_i, Y, s_j) \in \tau$ for $Y \subseteq I$ when $(q_i, o(s_i) \cup Y, q_j) \in \delta$. The skeleton $\mathcal{S}$ models φ, because it simulates the language of $\mathcal{A}$.

Lemma 6. *Given a formula φ, if an output consistent safety automaton $\mathcal{A}$ with $L(\mathcal{A}) = \min(\varphi)$ is minimal then the skeleton $\mathcal{S}$ extracted form $\mathcal{A}$ is also minimal.*

Proof. This follows from the fact that we can use the reverse of the construction presented in Lemma 5 to construct the safety automaton from the skeleton. Assume S was not minimal, then there is a skeleton S' with less number of states. This one, however, can be transformed backwards to a output consistent automaton of same size, which contradicts the assumption.   □

Once we obtain a candidate skeleton, we check whether the skeleton is a model of the formula using the model checking algorithm presented in Sect. 4. If the skeleton is not a model, the algorithm returns a counterexample, which is a lasso-shaped trace in the candidate skeleton. As this trace must contain a bad-prefix, we can iteratively check all prefixes of the trace using membership queries until we reach the (shortest) bad-prefix.

Using the results presented in Theorem 1 (Equivalence query checking is in EXPSPACE), Theorem 2 (L^* learns a minimal bad-prefix automaton in polynomial time in the size of the minimal automaton), Theorem 3 (Membership checking is in EXPSPACE), Lemma 2 (The language $\min(\varphi)$ can be characterized by a finite automaton), Lemma 3 (The minimal skeleton is unique), Lemma 5 (The safety automaton is a skeleton), and Lemma 6, we can conclude now with following theorem.

Theorem 4. *Given an LTL formula φ, we can construct a skeleton S that models φ in time polynomial in the size of the minimal skeleton of φ.*

6   Conclusion

We have presented an analysis technique for temporal specifications of reactive systems that identifies, on the level of individual system outputs over time, which parts of the implementation are determined by the specification, and which parts are still open. Based on the algorithms developed in this paper, a synthesis tool can represent this information in the form of a skeleton for the reactive system. Skeletons are more informative than conventional transition systems in identifying critical situations that are still underspecified.

Our automaton-based model checking algorithm for skeletons also serves as the teaching oracle in the learning-based synthesis algorithm. The learning algorithm L^* can be used to synthesize minimal skeletons because skeletons define safety languages, which can be characterized by a unique minimal bad-prefix automaton. Once the automaton is learned, it can directly be transformed into a skeleton for the specification. The skeleton is minimal and can be constructed in time polynomial in the number of states of the skeleton.

In the development of a reactive system, skeletons can be seen as an intermediate step between the specification of the system and its implementation. In future work, we plan to investigate this aspect further, by exploring an incremental development process, where the refinement of the specification is guided by the identification of underspecified situations through the skeletons synthesized from the intermediate specifications.

References

1. Alur, R., Moarref, S., Topcu, U.: Counter-strategy guided refinement of GR(1) temporal logic specifications. In: Formal Methods in Computer-Aided Design, FMCAD 2013, pp. 26–33. IEEE (2013)
2. Angluin, D.: Learning regular sets from queries and counterexamples. Inf. Comput. **75**(2), 87–106 (1987)
3. Baier, C., Katoen, J.-P.: Principles of Model Checking (Representation and Mind Series). MIT Press, Cambridge (2008)
4. Bloem, R., Jobstmann, B., Piterman, N., Pnueli, A., Saar, Y.: Synthesis of reactive(1) designs. J. Comput. Syst. Sci. **78**(3), 911–938 (2012)
5. Bruns, G., Godefroid, P.: Model checking with multi-valued logics. In: Díaz, J., Karhumäki, J., Lepistö, A., Sannella, D. (eds.) ICALP 2004. LNCS, vol. 3142, pp. 281–293. Springer, Heidelberg (2004). doi:10.1007/978-3-540-27836-8_26
6. Chechik, M., Devereux, B., Easterbrook, S., Gurfinkel, A.: Multi-valued symbolic model-checking. ACM Trans. Softw. Eng. Methodol. **12**(4), 371–408 (2003)
7. Church, A.: Logic, arithmetic, and automata. In: Proceedings of International Congress Mathematicians (Stockholm, 1962), pp. 23–35. Inst. Mittag-Leffler, Djursholm (1963)
8. Clarke, E.M., Allen Emerson, E.: Design and synthesis of synchronization skeletons using branching-time temporal logic. In: Kozen, D. (ed.) Logic of Programs. LNCS, pp. 52–71. Springer, Heidelberg (1982)
9. Easterbrook, S., Chechik, M.: A framework for multi-valued reasoning over inconsistent viewpoints. In: Proceedings of the 23rd International Conference on Software Engineering, ICSE 2001, pp. 411–420. IEEE Computer Society (2001)
10. Finkbeiner, B., Schewe, S.: Bounded synthesis. Int. J. Softw. Tools Technol. Transf. **15**(5–6), 519–539 (2013)
11. Könighofer, R., Hofferek, G., Bloem, R.: Debugging unrealizable specifications with model-based diagnosis. In: Barner, S., Harris, I., Kroening, D., Raz, O. (eds.) HVC 2010. LNCS, vol. 6504, pp. 29–45. Springer, Heidelberg (2011). doi:10.1007/978-3-642-19583-9_8
12. Li, W., Dworkin, L., Seshia, S.A.: Mining assumptions for synthesis. In: Singh, S., Jobstmann, B., Kishinevsky, M., Brandt, J. (eds.) 9th IEEE/ACM International Conference on Formal Methods and Models for Codesign, MEMOCODE 2011, Cambridge, UK, 11–13 July 2011, pp. 43–50. IEEE (2011)
13. Manna, Z., Wolper, P.: Synthesis of communicating processes from temporal logic specifications. ACM Trans. Program. Lang. Syst. **6**(1), 68–93 (1984)
14. Pnueli, A., Rosner, R.: On the synthesis of a reactive module. In: Proceedings of the 16th ACM SIGPLAN-SIGACT Symposium on Principles of Programming Languages, POPL 1989, pp. 179–190. ACM, New York (1989)
15. Pnueli, A.: The temporal logic of programs. In: Proceedings of the 18th Annual Symposium on Foundations of Computer Science, SFCS 1977, pp. 46–57. IEEE Computer Society (1977)
16. Rosner, R.: Modular synthesis of reactive systems. Ph.D. thesis, Weizmann Institute of Sceince, Rehovot, Israel (1992)
17. Vardi, M.Y.: Alternating automata and program verification. In: Leeuwen, J. (ed.) Computer Science Today. LNCS, vol. 1000, pp. 471–485. Springer, Heidelberg (1995). doi:10.1007/BFb0015261

Observational Refinement and Merge
for Disjunctive MTSs

Shoham Ben-David[1](✉), Marsha Chechik[2], and Sebastian Uchitel[3]

[1] University of Waterloo, Waterloo, Canada
shohambd@gmail.com
[2] University of Toronto, Toronto, Canada
[3] University of Buenos Aires, Buenos Aires, Argentina

Abstract. Modal Transition System (MTS) is a well studied formalism for partial model specification. It allows a modeller to distinguish between required, prohibited and possible transitions. Disjunctive MTS (DMTS) is an extension of MTS that has been getting attention in recent years. A key concept for (D)MTS is *refinement*, supporting a development process where abstract specifications are gradually refined into more concrete ones. Refinement comes in different flavours: *strong*, *observational* (where τ-labelled transitions are taken into account), and *alphabet* (allowing the comparison of models defined on different alphabets). Another important operation on (D)MTS is that of *merge*: given two models M and N, their merge is a model P which refines both M and N, and which is the least refined one.

In this paper, we fill several missing parts in the theory of DMTS refinement and merge. First and foremost, we define observational refinement for DMTS. While an elementary concept, such a definition is missing from the literature to the best of our knowledge. We prove that our definition is sound and that it complies with all relevant definitions from the literature. Based on the new observational refinement for DMTS, we examine the question of DMTS merge, which was defined so far for strong refinement only. We show that observational merge can be achieved as a natural extension of the existing algorithm for strong merge of DMTS. For alphabet merge however, the situation is different. we prove that DMTSs do not have a merge under alphabet refinement.

1 Introduction

Labelled Transition Systems (LTSs) [15] are a formalism for modelling and reasoning about system behaviour. Modal Transition Systems (MTSs) [17] are an extension of LTSs that distinguishes between *required*, *prohibited* and *possible* transitions, allowing a model to be only partially specified. MTSs come equipped with the notion of *refinement*, supporting a development process where abstract model specifications can be gradually refined into more concrete ones, until a fully defined model – an LTS – is obtained. An MTS thus serves as a specification for a set of LTSs – its *implementations*.

© Springer International Publishing AG 2016
C. Artho et al. (Eds.): ATVA 2016, LNCS 9938, pp. 287–303, 2016.
DOI: 10.1007/978-3-319-46520-3_19

Refinement of MTSs was investigated along two different dimensions. The first examines *modal vs. thorough* refinements [1,2,16]. Given MTSs M and N, we say that N *modally* refines M if there exists a relation R between the states of M and N such that required transitions in M are simulated by N, and possible transitions from N are simulated by M. In contrast, N *thoroughly* refines M if its set of implementations (denoted by $[\![N]\!]$) is a subset of $[\![M]\!]$. Modal refinement is sound but not complete with respect to implementations. That is, if N modally refines M then $[\![N]\!] \subseteq [\![M]\!]$, but the opposite does not always hold [16]. Thorough refinement however, is much more complex to determine (EXPTIME-complete for thorough refinement vs. PTIME-complete for modal refinement [6]), making modal refinement more attractive for practical applications.

The second dimension of MTS refinement is that of refinement *flavour*. Three different flavours have been defined for refinement of MTSs: *strong* [17], where required transitions in the original model must exist in the refined model; *observational* [11,14], where unobservable (τ-labelled) transitions are taken into account; and *alphabet* refinement [12], where MTSs defined on different sets of labels can be compared. In an alphabet refinement, labels in one MTS that are not known to the other MTS are being *hidden*, by replacing them with τ transitions. An observational refinement is then used for the comparison.

The first part of this paper deals with the refinement definition of an extension of MTSs, known as Disjunctive MTSs (DMTSs) [18]. In a DMTS, a disjunction of required transitions can be defined, increasing the expressiveness of model specifications. DMTSs have been attracting growing attention in recent years. Their conjunction as well as model checking were considered in [4], and structural refinement was defined for them in [7]. Different variants of DMTSs have been defined and analyzed [8,9,19], and DMTSs are treated as first-class citizens in the family of transition systems [1,5,16].

Yet, to the best of our knowledge, modal observational refinement of DMTSs was never fully defined. While strong refinement was already given in [18], where DMTSs were first introduced, we found only two places in the literature where observational refinement of DMTSs was considered. In [19] the authors proposed a modal observational refinement definition for a subset of DMTS called dMTS, where all transitions of a single disjunct must have the same label. τ-labels were allowed on "possible" transitions only. In [3], we proposed an observational *implementation* definition. Using that definition, a model L was said to be a refinement of a DMTS M only if L was an LTS (making it a *thorough* refinement definition). τ-transitions were allowed to exist only in L and not in M. Modal observational refinement for full DMTSs is thus still missing from the literature.

Such a definition is the first contribution of our paper. We provide the definition, which is subtle and non-trivial, and prove that it agrees with the relevant definitions from the literature. Specifically, we prove that it agrees with [3] when implementations are concerned; with strong refinement of DMTS [18] when the compared models have no τ-transitions; and with observational refinement of MTSs [14] when models compared are MTSs. Most importantly, we prove that our definition is sound with respect to implementations.

The second part of the paper deals with the operation of conjunction, or *merge* of modal transition systems. Given two models, it is often desirable to compute a new model that captures all of their common implementations. Such an operation supports independent development of different aspects of an intended behaviour, followed by the composition of them into a single model that accurately captures all aspects. The merge of two (D)MTSs M and N is a (D)MTS that is a common refinement of both, and is the *least* refined one. Thus it is sometimes called the least common refinement or the *LCR*.

Merge has been investigated in the literature for MTSs as well as for DMTSs, for strong, observational and alphabet refinements [3,4,10,12,13,19,20]. It was shown that MTSs are not closed for merge under strong refinement [10,13] (which implies that they are not closed under observational and alphabet merges as well, since observational merge must agree with strong merge when no τ-transitions are involved). For DMTSs, a strong merge algorithm was given in [4]. Observational merge however, was only considered for the restricted subset of dMTS where τ-labels are allowed on possible transitions only [19].

Our second contribution is thus an observational merge algorithm for DMTS. Using our new observational refinement definition, we show that the strong merge algorithm of [4] can be naturally extended to support observational merge as well.

Our third contribution deals with *minimal common refinements* (MCRs) [20] under alphabet refinement. An MCR of two models M and N is a common refinement P of them such that no other common refinement is less refined than it. Other common refinements may exist though, that are *incomparable* with P. For cases where a least common refinement (LCR) does not exist, it was suggested that the merge of two models could be represented by a (possibly infinite) set of MCRs. Algorithms for finding MCRs in special cases were proposed in [10,12,20], for strong as well as for alphabet merge. It was assumed that, unlike LCR, an MCR of two models always existed (given that the models are *consistent*, i.e., they have at least one implementation in common). We prove this assumption to be wrong: we give an example of two DMTSs that, although consistent, do not have an MCR under alphabet refinement.

Table 1 summarizes the known results for refinement and merge of MTSs and DMTSs. We use '(?)' to indicate the parts that were missing before this paper, and mark our results in blue.

Table 1. Known results for MTS and DMTS. Our contributions are indicated by (?).

| | REFINEMENT | | MERGE | | | | | |
	Strong	Observational	Strong LCR	Strong MCR	Observational LCR	Observational MCR	Alphabet LCR	Alphabet MCR
MTS	✓ [17]	✓ [11,14]	✗ [13]	✗ [10]	✗	✗	✗	✗
DMTS	✓ [18]	✓ (?)	✓ [4]	✓	✓ (?)	✓ (?)	✗ [3]	✗ (?)

The rest of the paper is organized as follows. In Sect. 2 we give preliminary definitions. We present observational refinement of DMTSs in Sect. 3, and then answer positively the question of merge for DMTSs under observational refinement (Sect. 4). Section 5 answers negatively the question of the existence of an MCR under alphabet refinement. We conclude the paper in Sect. 6. Proofs of most theorems are omitted due to lack of space.

2 Preliminaries

2.1 LTSs and MTSs

All models considered in this paper are finite-state, where the set of states, the set of labels and the set of transitions are all finite.

We start with the concept of *Labelled Transition Systems* (LTSs) [15] which are commonly used for modeling concurrent systems.

Definition 1 (LTS [15]). *A Labeled Transition System (LTS) is a structure (S, L, δ, s^0), where S is a set of states, L is a set of labels, $\delta \subseteq (S \times L \times S)$ is the transition relation, and $s^0 \in S$ is the initial state.*

Modal Transition Systems (MTSs) [17] are used to specify sets of LTSs. An MTS distinguishes between two types of transitions – *possible* and *required*. Transitions that do not appear at all are considered to be prohibited.

Definition 2 (MTS [17]). *A Modal Transition System (MTS) M is a structure $(S, L, \delta^p, \delta^r, s^0)$, where S is a set of states, L is a set of labels, $s_0 \in S$ is the initial state, $\delta^p \subseteq (S \times L \times S)$ is the* possible *transition relation, $\delta^r \subseteq (S \times L \times S)$ is the* required *transition relation. In addition, it is required that $\delta^r \subseteq \delta^p$.*

Note that in an MTS, every 'required' transition is also 'possible'. When the required and possible transitions coincide, the MTS is actually an LTS.

We use the notation $m \xrightarrow{\ell}_p m'$ to denote a possible transition $(m, \ell, m') \in \delta^p$, and $m \xrightarrow{\ell}_r m'$ to denote a required transition $(m, \ell, m') \in \delta^r$. In figures, we use $m \xrightarrow{\ell?} m'$ for a possible transition and $m \xrightarrow{\ell} m'$ for a required transition. If the model is an LTS, all transitions are simply $i \xrightarrow{\ell} i'$.

Strong refinement for MTSs has been defined by Larsen and Thomsen [17].

Definition 3 (Strong Modal Refinement of MTS [17]). *Let $M = (S_M, L, \delta^p_M, \delta^r_M, m^0)$ and $N = (S_N, L, \delta^p_N, \delta^r_N, n^0)$ be MTSs. We say that N is a strong refinement of M (denoted $M \preceq_s N$) if there exists a strong refinement relation $R_s \subseteq S_M \times S_N$, such that $(m^0, n^0) \in R_s$ and if $(m, n) \in R_s$ then*

1. *for every transition $(n \xrightarrow{\ell}_p n')$ in N, there exists a transition $(m \xrightarrow{\ell}_p m')$ in M such that $(m', n') \in R_s$; and*
2. *for every transition $(m \xrightarrow{\ell}_r m')$ in M, there exists $(n \xrightarrow{\ell}_r n')$ in N such that $(m', n') \in R_s$.*

Since every LTS is also an MTS, we can compare MTSs and LTSs using modal refinement. Let M be an MTS and I be an LTS. We say that I is an *implementation* of M if $M \preceq_s I$. The set of all implementations of a model M is denoted by $[\![M]\!]$. An MTS N is said to *thoroughly* refine a model M if $[\![N]\!] \subseteq [\![M]\!]$. As mentioned above, modal refinement is sound with respect to implementations: $M \preceq_s N$ implies $[\![N]\!] \subseteq [\![M]\!]$, but it is not complete [16].

Adding Unobservable Actions. MTSs have also been considered in a situation where some of the actions are internal (labeled τ), and are *unobservable* to the outside viewer. When τ-transitions are present, we use a relaxed, *observational*, version of refinement, allowing a finite sequence of τ-transitions to exist between observable ones. Huttel and Larsen [14] were the first to suggest an observational refinement for MTSs. Fischbein et al. [10,11] demonstrated some unintuitive phenomena allowed by the definition of [14], and proposed a different, more intuitive observational refinement, which we adopt here.

We use L_τ to denote the set of labels $L \cup \{\tau\}$. We use $m \xrightarrow{\hat{\ell}}_r m'$ (or $m \xrightarrow{\hat{\ell}}_p m'$) to mean that either $\ell \neq \tau$ and $m \xrightarrow{\ell}_r m'$ ($m \xrightarrow{\ell}_p m'$) holds, or $\ell = \tau$ and $m = m'$. If $\ell = \tau$, no transition (and therefore no label) exists at all. Note that $\hat{\ell}$ can never be τ.

Definition 4 (Observational Modal Refinement of MTSs [10]). *Let* $M = (S_M, L_\tau, \delta^p_M, \delta^r_M, m^0)$ *and* $N = (S_N, L_\tau, \delta^p_N, \delta^r_N, n^0)$ *be MTSs. We say that* N *is an observational refinement of* M, *denoted* $M \preceq_o N$, *if there exists a relation* $R_o \subseteq S_M \times S_N$ *such that* $(m^0, n^0) \in R_o$, *and whenever* $(m, n) \in R_o$, *we have:*

1. *for every* $(n \xrightarrow{\ell}_p n')$ *in* N, *there exists a sequence of transitions in* M:
   $m_0 \xrightarrow{\tau}_p m_1 \xrightarrow{\tau}_p \cdots \xrightarrow{\tau}_p m_j \xrightarrow{\hat{\ell}}_p m'$, *such that* $m = m_0$, $(m_k, n) \in R_o$ *for* $0 \leq k \leq j$, *and* $(m', n') \in R_o$; *and*
2. *for every* $(m \xrightarrow{\ell}_r m')$ *in* M, *there exist a sequence of transitions in* N:
   $n_0 \xrightarrow{\tau}_r n_1 \xrightarrow{\tau}_r \cdots \xrightarrow{\tau}_r n_j \xrightarrow{\hat{\ell}}_r n'$, *such that* $n = n_0$, $(m, n_k) \in R_o$ *for* $0 \leq k \leq j$, *and* $(m', n') \in R_o$.

Note that by Definition 4, a refining τ-sequence can be of length 0. If $\ell = \tau$, then no refining transition is required to exist at all. Like in the strong refinement case, if I is an LTS and $M \preceq_o N$, we say that I is an *observational implementation* of M. The set of observational implementations of M is denoted by $[\![M]\!]_o$. N is a *thorough observational refinement* of M iff $[\![N]\!]_o \subseteq [\![M]\!]_o$.

2.2   DMTSs

Disjunctive Modal Transition Systems (DMTSs) [18] extend MTS by allowing required transitions to be disjunctive.

Definition 5 (DMTS [18]). *A Disjunctive Modal Transition System (DMTS)* M *is a structure* $(S, L, \delta^p, \Delta^r, s^0)$, *where* S *is a set of states,* L *is a set of labels,* $\delta^p \subseteq (S \times L \times S)$ *is the* possible *transition relation,* $\Delta^r \subseteq (S \times 2^{L \times S})$ *is the* disjunctive required *transition relation, and* $s^0 \in S$ *is the initial state.*

We denote a disjunctive required transition in Δ^r by $\langle s, V \rangle$, where V is a set of pairs $V = \{(l_1, s_1), \ldots, (l_n, s_n)\}$ with $l_1, \ldots, l_n \in L$ and $s_1, \ldots, s_n \in S$. A disjunct $(l_i, s_i) \in V$ is sometimes called a *leg*, and the entire disjunctive transition – a *DT*. In figures, a disjunction between transitions is shown using a bullet. For example, $\overset{a}{\underset{b}{\longrightarrow}}\!\!\!\bullet$ is a DT with two legs, on a and b. For example, Fig. 1 shows a DMTS A. It has two DTs emanating from state 0: one with two legs, on labels c and τ, and the other with 3 legs, on labels b, τ and c.

We follow [4] to require also that (1) if $\langle s, V \rangle \in \Delta^r$ then V is not empty, and (2) for all $\langle s, V \rangle \in \Delta^r$ and $(\ell, s') \in V$, we have that $(s, \ell, s') \in \delta^p$. That is, every leg in every DT is *possible* in the model.

A DMTS N strongly refines a DMTS M, if, roughly speaking, every possible transition in N is also possible in M (like in the MTS case), and if for every DT in M, there exists a DT in N with at least one leg from the original DT.

Definition 6 (Strong Modal Refinement of DMTS [18]). *Let $M = (S_M, L, \delta^p_M, \Delta^r_M, m^0)$ and $N = (S_N, L, \delta^p_N, \Delta^r_N, n^0)$ be DMTSs. We say that N is a strong refinement of M, denoted $M \preceq_S N$, if there exists a strong refinement relation $R_S \subseteq S_M \times S_N$, such that $(m^0, n^0) \in R_S$, and if $(m, n) \in R_S$ then*

1. *for every possible transition $(n \overset{\ell}{\longrightarrow}_p n')$ in N, there exists a transition $(m \overset{\ell}{\longrightarrow}_p m')$ in M such that $(m', n') \in R_S$; and*
2. *for every DT $\langle m, V \rangle \in \Delta^r_M$, there exists a DT $\langle n, U \rangle \in \Delta^r_N$, such that for every leg $(\ell, n') \in U$ there exists a leg $(\ell, m') \in V$ with $(m', n') \in R_S$.*

Like in the MTS case, we now consider models with τ-transitions. A DT $\langle m, V \rangle$ can thus include legs $(\tau, m') \in V$. To the best of our knowledge, modal observational refinement for DMTSs has not been defined and we do so in Sect. 3.

[3] defined observational implementation for DMTSs, thereby handling the case where the refining model is an LTS:

Definition 7 (Observational Implementation of DMTSs [3]). *Let $M = (S_M, L_\tau, \delta^p_M, \Delta^r_M, m^0)$ be a DMTS and $I = (S_I, L_\tau, \delta_I, i^0)$ be an LTS. We say that I is an observational implementation of M if there exists an observational implementation relation $R_{OI} \subseteq S_M \times S_I$, such that $(m^0, i^0) \in R_{OI}$, and for all $(m, i) \in R_{OI}$ the following hold:*

1. *for every transition $i \overset{\ell}{\longrightarrow} i'$ in I, there exists a sequence of possible transitions in M, $m_0 \overset{\tau}{\longrightarrow}_p m_1 \overset{\tau}{\longrightarrow}_p \ldots \overset{\tau}{\longrightarrow}_p m_j \overset{\hat{\ell}}{\longrightarrow}_p m'$, such that $m = m_0$, $(m_k, i) \in R_{OI}$ for $0 \leq k \leq j$, and $(m', i') \in R_{OI}$; and*
2. *for every DT $\langle m, V \rangle \in \Delta^r_M$, there exists a sequence of transitions in I, $i_0 \overset{\tau}{\longrightarrow} i_1 \overset{\tau}{\longrightarrow} \ldots \overset{\tau}{\longrightarrow} i_j \overset{\hat{\ell}}{\longrightarrow} i'$, such that $i = i_0$, $(m, i_k) \in R_{OI}$ for $0 \leq k \leq j$, and there exists a leg $(\ell, m') \in V$ such that $(m', i') \in R_{OI}$.*

Both strong and observational refinements compare models that are defined on the same set of labels (alphabet). Yet it is often useful to consider models that share only a subset of their alphabets [20]. We do that via *alphabet* refinement:

we first *hide* labels of N that are unknown to M, by replacing them with τ's, and then use observational refinement to compare them.

Definition 8 (Hiding). *Let $M = (S_M, \alpha M, \delta^p, \Delta^r, m^0)$ be a DMTS and X be a set of labels. M with the labels of X hidden, denoted $M \backslash X$, is a DMTS $(S_M, (\alpha M \backslash X) \cup \{\tau\}, \delta_1^p, \Delta_1^r, m^0)$, where Δ_1^r is derived from Δ^r by replacing every leg $(\ell, m') \in V$ in a DT $\langle m, V \rangle \in \Delta^r$, with a leg (τ, m') if and only if $\ell \in X$. The set δ_1^p is derived from δ^p in the same way, replacing possible transitions $m \xrightarrow{\ell}_p m'$ by $m \xrightarrow{\tau}_p m'$ if and only if $\ell \in X$. For a set of labels Y, we use $M @ Y$ to denote $M \backslash (\alpha M \setminus Y)$.*

Definition 9 (Alphabet Refinement [20]). *A (D)MTS $N = (S_N, L_N, \delta_N^p, \Delta_N^r, n^0)$ is an* alphabet refinement *of a DMTS $M = (S_M, L_{M'}, \delta_M^p, \Delta_M^r, m^0)$, denoted $M \preceq_A N$, if $L_M \subseteq L_N$ and $N @ L_M$ is an observational refinement of M.*

2.3   Merge

A *merge* of two models M and N is a common refinement of M and N that is the *least* refined. The merge of two models is therefore also called their *least common refinement* (LCR). For thorough refinement, the merge is a model P such that $[\![P]\!] = [\![M]\!] \cap [\![N]\!]$. For modal refinement, we look for P such that $M \preceq P$ and $N \preceq P$, and for every other common refinement Q, we have that $P \preceq Q$ (where $\preceq$ can be a strong, observational or alphabet refinement relation). In practice, there are many cases where an LCR does not exist. To relax the requirement of an LCR, the concept of a *minimal common refinement* (MCR) [20] was introduced. P is an MCR of M and N if there does not exist a common refinement that is less refined than P. There could, however, exist common refinements that are incomparable to P.

MTSs are not closed for merge (no LCR and no MCR) for strong refinement [10,13]. This implies that they are not closed for observational and alphabet refinements as well, since if an observational merge algorithm were to exist for MTSs, it would also have to apply to the case with no τ-transitions. Note that the other direction does not hold: if a merge over a strong refinement exists, it does not imply the existence of its counterpart for observational or alphabet refinement.

DMTSs were shown to be closed for strong merge [4]. Note that the existence of an LCR implies the existence of an MCR, but the other direction does not hold. It was shown that DMTSs are not closed for alphabet merge (no LCR exists) [3].

3   Observational Refinement of DMTS

In this section, we define modal observational refinement for DMTSs, a notion that we found missing from the literature. In Sect. 3.1, we define observational refinement for DMTS, and in Sect. 3.2, we provide "sanity checks" showing that our observational refinement is a reasonable extension of existing definitions.

3.1   Observational Refinement Definition

In the MTS world, the difference between strong and observational refinements is that a finite path of τ-transitions is allowed to occur before a transition labelled ℓ (see Definition 4). In the DMTS world, for strong refinement, a disjunctive transition replaces MTS's required transition. For the observational case for DMTSs, we introduce a new construction which we call a *disjunctive cone*.

We start with defining a *must path*.

Definition 10 (Must Path). *Let $M = (S, L_\tau, \delta^p, \Delta^r, s)$ be a DMTS, and let $x_0, x' \in S$ be states. A* must path *of length i from x_0 to x' in M is a sequence of 'legs' $x_0 \xrightarrow{l_1} x_1 \xrightarrow{l_2} \cdots \xrightarrow{l_{i-1}} x_{i-1} \xrightarrow{l_i} x'$ such that there exist $V_0, V_1, ..., V_{i-1} \in 2^{L_\tau \times S}$ with $\langle x_0, V_0 \rangle \in \Delta^r$, $(l_1, x_1) \in V_0$, $\langle x_1, V_1 \rangle \in \Delta^r$, $(l_2, x_2) \in V_1$, $\cdots$, $\langle x_{i-1}, V_{i-1} \rangle \in \Delta^r$ and $(l_i, x') \in V_{i-1}$.*

A must path $\pi = x_0 \xrightarrow{l_1} x_1 \xrightarrow{l_2} \cdots \xrightarrow{l_{i-1}} x_{i-1} \xrightarrow{l_i} x'$ is *maximal* in M if either $x' = x_i$ for some x_i on π (that is, π has a loop), or if from x' there is no outgoing required transition in M.

Definition 11 (Disjunctive Cone). *Let $M = (S, L_\tau, \delta^p, \Delta^r, s^0)$ be a DMTS, and $x \in S$ be a state. A* disjunctive cone *with a root x in M is a DMTS $C_x = (S_c, L_\tau, \delta_c^p, \Delta_c^r, x)$ such that $S_c \subseteq S$, $\delta_c^p \subseteq \delta^p$, $\Delta_c^r \subseteq \Delta^r$, and for every $s \in S_c$ (1) there exists a must path from x to s, and (2) there exists at most one DT $\langle s, V \rangle \in \Delta_c^r$.*

A disjunctive cone $C \subseteq M$ is a connected sub-model of M, where each state has a single (or none) outgoing DT. Note that each DT in M is either entirely in C or not at all (that is, all legs of the DT should be taken). A disjunctive cone is a natural extension of a path in MTS to the disjunctive setting of DMTS.

Since every DT may have τ-legs, a disjunctive cone may have must paths that consist of only τ-transitions. For a given disjunctive cone C_x with a root x, we denote the set of all maximal must paths in C_x that start at x and include only τ-transitions by T_{C_x}.

Example 1 (Disjunctive Cone). *Consider a DMTS B in Fig. 1. State 6 of B has two outgoing DTs: $\langle 6, \{(c, 7)\} \rangle$ and $\langle 6, \{(b, 8), (\tau, 9)\} \rangle$. The sub-DMTSs $C_6^1 \subset B$ and $C_6^2 \subset B$ are two of B's disjunctive cones with root 6, each containing a single DT from 6.*

Let $\langle m, V \rangle$ be a DT in a DMTS M. When dealing with modal refinement, we have to compare it to a DT $\langle n, U \rangle$ in a refining model N. As in the case of MTS, we use $(\hat{\ell}, n') \in U$ to mean that either $\ell \neq \tau$, or $\ell = \tau$ and $n' = n$. Here as well, $\hat{\ell}$ itself can never be τ. Note, however, that if $(\hat{\ell}, n') \in U$ is the single leg in U and if $\ell = \tau$, then the leg $(\hat{\ell}, n')$ does not actually exist, which makes U *empty*. This contradicts our requirement that a DT should never be empty. We thus use the notation DT* for a DT $\langle n, U \rangle$ where U is potentially empty. Note that if a DT* $\langle n, \emptyset \rangle$ observationally refines a DT $\langle m, V \rangle$ via some observational refinement R_O, it means that there exists a leg (τ, m') in V such that $(m', n) \in R_O$.

We now introduce the main definition of the paper.

Definition 12 (Observational Refinement of DMTS). *Let $M = (S_M, L_\tau, \delta_M^p,$ $\Delta_M^r, m^0)$ and $N = (S_N, L_\tau, \delta_N^p, \Delta_N^r, n^0)$ be DMTSs. We say that N observationally refines M ($M \preceq_O N$) if there exists an observational refinement relation $R_O \subseteq S_M \times S_N$, such that $(m^0, n^0) \in R_O$, and if $(m, n) \in R_O$ then the following hold:*

1. *for every transition $(n \xrightarrow{\ell}_p n')$ in N, there exists a possible path in M:*
   $m_0 \xrightarrow{\tau}_p m_1 \xrightarrow{\tau}_p m_2 \xrightarrow{\tau}_p \cdots \xrightarrow{\tau}_p m_j \xrightarrow{\hat{\ell}}_p m'$ *such that $m_0 = m$ and $(m_i, n) \in R_O$ for $0 \leq i \leq j$ and $(m', n') \in R_O$; and*
2. *for every DT $\langle m, V \rangle \in \Delta_M^r$, there exists a disjunctive cone $C_n \subseteq N$ with root n and set of τ-paths T_{C_n}, such that all paths in T_{C_n} are finite, and for every $\pi = n_0 \xrightarrow{\tau}_r n_1 \xrightarrow{\tau}_r n_2 \xrightarrow{\tau}_r \cdots \xrightarrow{\tau}_r n_j$ in T_{C_n}, for every n_i on π where $0 \leq i \leq j$,*
   (a) *$(m, n_i) \in R_O$, and*
   (b) *there exists a DT* $\langle n_i, U_i \rangle \in \Delta_c^r$, *such that for every leg $(\hat{\ell}, n_i') \in U_i$ there is a leg $(\ell, m') \in V$ with $(m', n_i') \in R_O$.*

The refining disjunctive cone in N for a DT $\langle m, V \rangle$ consists of DTs that may have both τ-labelled and ℓ-labelled legs, with $\ell \neq \tau$. All the ℓ-labelled legs must have a corresponding leg in V. τ-legs do not correspond to legs in V. Thus, if a DT includes only τ-labelled legs, then it satisfies Condition 2(b) of Definition 12 *vacuously*, although the DT is not empty. This is because Condition 2(b) talks only about legs that are not labelled with τ. Note also that the DT $\langle n_i, U_i \rangle$ must include the leg (τ, n_{i+1}) (for $i < j$), since n_i has at most one outgoing DT in C_n. Paths with τ-transitions are finite, guaranteeing that a DT with no τ-legs is reached eventually on every τ-path.

Example 2 (Observational Refinement). *The DMTS B in Fig. 1 is an observational refinement of the DMTS A from the same figure, with the observational refinement relation $R_O = \{(0,6), (5,7), (2,8), (0,9), (3,10), (0,11), (3,12)\}$. The disjunctive cone C_6^1 refines the DT $\langle 0, V \rangle \in$ A, where $V = \{(b, 2), (\tau, 1), (c, 3)\}$.*

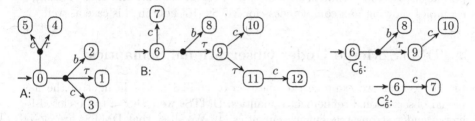

Fig. 1. Example DMTSs. DMTS B is an observational refinement of DMTS A. Sub-DMTSs $C_6^1 \subset$ B and $C_6^2 \subset$ B are examples of disjunctive cones.

The set of τ-paths of C_6^1 consists of the transition $6 \xrightarrow{\tau} 9$. Both $(0,6)$ and $(0,9)$ belong to R_O as required by Condition 2.(a) of Definition 12. Condition 2.(b) of Definition 12 also holds: from state 6 there exists a DT with leg $(b,8)$ refining V, and from state 9 the leg $(c,10)$ refines V as well.

3.2   Compatibility with Existing Definitions

We verify the validity of Definition 12 by proving a few theorems that ensure its compatibility with the relevant definitions from Sect. 2. The proofs of all theorems are given in the Appendix.

Theorem 1 ensures our definition agrees with observational implementation refinement for DMTSs.

Theorem 1 (Compatibility with Observational Implementations). *Let M be a DMTS and I be an LTS. I is an observational implementation of M (Definition 7) if and only if it is an observational refinement of M (Definition 12).*

For DMTSs with no τ-transitions, Theorem 2 indicates that our definition agrees with strong refinement of DMTSs (Definition 6).

Theorem 2 (Compatibility with Strong Refinement). *Let M and N be two τ-free DMTSs. Then $M \preceq_S N$ if and only if $M \preceq_O N$.*

Next, since DMTSs extend MTSs, we need to make sure that observational refinement for DMTSs agrees with the one for MTSs.

Theorem 3 (Compatibility with the MTS Refinement). *Let M and N be MTSs. Then $M \preceq_O N$ (Definition 4) if and only if $M \preceq_O N$ (Definition 12).*

Finally, Theorem 4 is the main result of this section, stating that our definition is in fact *sound*, that is, if N refines M according to Definition 12, then the set of implementations of N is included in the set of implementations of M.

Theorem 4 (Soundness). *If $M \preceq_O N$ then $[\![N]\!] \subseteq [\![M]\!]$.*

Note that an observational refinement relation for DMTS cannot be *complete* with respect to implementations. This is because the definition must be compatible with strong refinement and with MTS refinement, and thus the simple examples showing non-completeness for MTSs [16] hold in this case as well.

4   DMTS Merge Under Observational Semantics

In this section, we examine the question of DMTS merge in light of the new modal observational refinement semantics. DMTSs were shown to be closed for merge under strong refinement semantics [4]. We show that DMTSs are closed under observational merge as well.

In order for two DMTSs to be merged, the models must be *consistent*, that is, they must have at least one common observational implementation. The algorithm for merging two DMTSs is based on a *consistency relation* between the states of the models to be merged. States m and n are in a consistency relation if for each DT $\langle m, V \rangle$, at least one leg in V has a corresponding possible transition from n (possibly after a finite sequence of possible τ-transitions) and vice versa:

Definition 13 (Observational DMTSs Consistency Relation (based on [4])). *An observational consistency relation between DMTSs $M = (S_M, L_\tau, \delta_M^p, \Delta_M^r, m^0)$ and $N = (S_N, L_\tau, \delta_N^p, \Delta_N^r, n^0)$ is a relation $\mathcal{C} \subseteq S_M \times S_N$ s.t. $(m^0, n^0) \in \mathcal{C}$ and $\forall (m, n) \in \mathcal{C}$, the following holds:*

1. $\forall \langle m, V \rangle \in \Delta_M^r$, $\exists (l, m') \in V$ *and a sequence of possible transitions* $n_0 \overset{\tau}{\longrightarrow}_p$ $n_1 \overset{\tau}{\longrightarrow}_p \cdots \overset{\tau}{\longrightarrow}_p n_j \overset{\hat{\ell}}{\longrightarrow}_p n'$ *in* N *such that* $(m, n_i) \in \mathcal{C}$ *for* $0 \leq i \leq j$, *and* $(m', n') \in \mathcal{C}$; *and*

2. $\forall \langle n, U \rangle \in \Delta_N^r$, $\exists (\ell, n') \in U$ *and* $m_0 \overset{\tau}{\longrightarrow}_p m_1 \overset{\tau}{\longrightarrow}_p \cdots \overset{\tau}{\longrightarrow}_p m_j \overset{\hat{\ell}}{\longrightarrow}_p m'$ *in* M *such that* $(m_i, n) \in \mathcal{C}$ *for* $0 \leq i \leq j$ *and* $(m', n') \in \mathcal{C}$.

Based on a consistency relation $\mathcal{C}$ between M and N, we can now merge them into a single DMTS that represents models that are common to both. The composition is done by constructing, for each DT $\langle m, V \rangle$ in M (or N), a corresponding DT $\langle p, W \rangle$ in the merged model P, where a leg (ℓ, p') exists in W whenever (i) (ℓ, m') exists in V, (ii) a sequence of transitions $n_0 \overset{\tau}{\longrightarrow}_p n_1 \overset{\tau}{\longrightarrow}_p \cdots \overset{\tau}{\longrightarrow}_p n_j \overset{\hat{\ell}}{\longrightarrow}_p n'$ is possible in N, such that $(m, n_i) \in \mathcal{C}$ for $0 \leq i \leq j$, and (iii) $(m', n') \in \mathcal{C}$.

Definition 14 (Merge (based on [4])). *Let M and N be DMTSs with the same vocabulary L, and let $\mathcal{C}$ be a consistency relation between them. The $+$ operator between M and N is defined as $[M + N]_\mathcal{C} = (\mathcal{C}, L_\tau, \delta_{M+N}^p, \Delta_{M+N}^r, (m^0, n^0))$. δ_{M+N}^p and Δ_{M+N}^r are defined to be the smallest relations that satisfy the following rules:*

(RP) $\dfrac{\langle m, V \rangle}{\langle (m,n), W \rangle}, where\, W = \{(l, (m', n')) \mid (l, m') \in {} \wedge$

$\qquad n \overset{\tau}{\longrightarrow}_p n_1 \overset{\tau}{\longrightarrow}_p \cdots \overset{\tau}{\longrightarrow}_p n_j \overset{\hat{\ell}}{\longrightarrow}_p n'\, in\, N, \wedge(m, n_j) \in \mathcal{C} \wedge (m', n') \in \mathcal{C}\}$

(PR) $\dfrac{\langle n, U \rangle}{\langle (m,n), W \rangle}, where\, W = \{(l, (m', n')) \mid (l, n') \in U \wedge$

$\qquad m \overset{\tau}{\longrightarrow}_p m_1 \overset{\tau}{\longrightarrow}_p \cdots \overset{\tau}{\longrightarrow}_p m_k \overset{\hat{\ell}}{\longrightarrow}_p m'\, in\, M, \wedge(m_j, n) \in \mathcal{C} \wedge (m', n') \in \mathcal{C}\}$

$(PP1)$ $\dfrac{m \overset{\ell}{\longrightarrow}_p m',\ n \overset{\tau}{\longrightarrow}_p n_1 \overset{\tau}{\longrightarrow}_p \cdots \overset{\tau}{\longrightarrow}_p n_j \overset{\hat{\ell}}{\longrightarrow}_p n' \wedge (m_j, n) \in \mathcal{C} \wedge (m', n') \in \mathcal{C}}{(m, n) \overset{\ell}{\longrightarrow}_p (m', n')}$

$(PP2)$ $\dfrac{n \overset{\ell}{\longrightarrow}_p n',\ m \overset{\tau}{\longrightarrow}_p m_1 \overset{\tau}{\longrightarrow}_p \cdots \overset{\tau}{\longrightarrow}_p m_k \overset{\hat{\ell}}{\longrightarrow}_p m' \wedge (m, n_j) \in \mathcal{C} \wedge (m', n') \in \mathcal{C}}{(m, n) \overset{\ell}{\longrightarrow}_p (m', n')}$

The difference between the above definition and the one in [4] is in the treatment of the τ-transitions (just like the difference between the strong and the observational refinement). When constructing a DT $\langle (m, n), W \rangle \in [M + N]_\mathcal{C}$

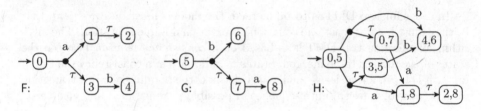

Fig. 2. H is an observational merge of F and G. The nodes of H are labelled with pairs of the consistency relation between F and G.

that corresponds to a DT $\langle m, V \rangle \in M$ (rule RP), we skip τ-transitions in N that lead to an appropriate transition corresponding to a leg in V. The skipped τ-transitions are instead considered by rule PR when a DT in $[M + N]_{\mathcal{C}}$ is introduced for N.

Example 3. *Consider DMTSs F and G from Fig. 2. The two models are consistent, with the maximal consistency relation* $\mathcal{C} = \{(0,5), (3,5), (4,6), (0,7), (1,8), (2,8)\}$. *DMTS H is their merge. It includes two DTs, one corresponding to the single DT of F (constructed by the RP rule), and the other – corresponding to the DT of G (constructed by the PR rule).*

When $\mathcal{C}$ is the largest consistency relation between M and N, the composition $[M + N]_{\mathcal{C}}$ becomes the *merge* of M and N. We state that formally below.

Theorem 5 (Correctness of Observational DMTS Merge). *Let M and N be DMTSs with the same vocabulary. If $\mathcal{C}$ is the largest consistency relation between the states of M and N, then $[M + N]_{\mathcal{C}}$ is the LCR of M and N.*

5 No MCR Under Alphabet Refinement

We now look at the merge of two models that are defined over different alphabets. In such a case, we deal with the *alphabet* merge, that is, we use the alphabet refinement (Definition 9) to determine if a model P is a common refinement of models M and N. In [3], we showed that DMTSs are not closed for merge under *thorough* alphabet refinement. Since modal refinement is sound with respect to implementations, this implies non-closure of merge w.r.t. *modal* alphabet refinement as well. Thus the question of the existence of an LCR is answered negatively. What about an MCR? Recall that the existence of an LCR implies the existence of an MCR, but the opposite direction does not hold. Can the merge of two DMTSs be represented as a set of minimal common refinements $P_1, P_2, \cdots$ such that no other common refinement is strictly less refined than them? In this section, we answer the MCR question negatively as well.

What makes alphabet merge different from strong and observational ones is the fact that different types of refinements are mixed together. Let M and N be DMTSs over the alphabets L_M and L_N, respectively, with no τ-transitions. A common refinement P of M and N is defined over the alphabet $L_M \cup L_N$. We then use hiding and observational refinement to compare P to M and N. Let Q be another common refinement of M and N. Note that P and Q are now defined over the same alphabet, and if no τ-transitions exist, we use strong refinement to compare them. Thus, transitions in P that were considered unobservable when a relation was defined between P and M, are treated as observable in a refinement relation between P and Q. While the number of τ-transitions for the observational refinement does not matter, as long as the sequence is finite, this number does matter for strong refinement. This difference makes it impossible to find a minimal common alphabet refinement, as we show in this section.

In Sect. 5.1, we introduce two lemmas proven in the Appendix. We use them to prove the main theorem in Sect. 5.2.

5.1 Facts About Strong Refinement

We examine a strong refinement relation between two DMTSs, and show that a sequence of possible transitions is preserved under such a relation, and so does a sequence of required transitions.

Definition 15 (Maybe Path). *Let $M = (S_M, L_\tau, \delta^p, \Delta^r, s_m)$ be a DMTS and $y, y' \in S_M$ be states. A sequence of possible transitions $y \xrightarrow{l_1}_p y_1 \xrightarrow{l_2}_p \ldots \xrightarrow{l_{i-1}}_p y_{i-1} \xrightarrow{l_i}_p y'$ in M is called a* maybe path *of length i from y to y'.*

Lemma 1. *Let $M = (S_M, L_\tau, \delta^p, \Delta^r, s_m)$ and $N = (S_N, L_\tau, \delta^p, \Delta^r, s_n)$ be DMTSs such that $M \preceq_S N$, with a strong refinement relation R_S. Let $(m, n) \in R_S$. Let $y_1 \in S_N$ be a state in N. If there exists a maybe path from n to y_1 of length i in N, then there must exist a state $x_1 \in S_M$ and a maybe path of length i from m to x_1 such that $(x_1, y_1) \in R_S$.*

Let C_x be a disjunctive cone. States with no outgoing DTs in C_x are called *front states*. We denote the set of front states of C_x by F_{C_x}. The *depth* of a disjunctive cone is the length of the longest maximal must path in C_x (see Definition 10). Note that if C_x is of depth $i < \infty$, then all maximal must paths in C_x are finite, and each of them ends in a front state of C_x.

Example 4. *Consider the disjunctive cone C_6^1 in Fig. 1 (Sect. 3.1). Its depth is 2, and its set of front states is $F_{C_6^1} = \{8, 10\}$.*

Lemma 2. *Let $M = (S_M, L, \delta^p, \Delta^r, s_m)$ and $N = (S_N, L, \delta^p, \Delta^r, s_n)$ be DMTSs such that $M \preceq_S N$ with the strong refinement relation R_S. Let $(m, n) \in R_S$. Let C_m be a disjunctive cone from m of depth $i < \infty$, and let F_{C_m} be the set of front states in C_m. Then there exists a must path π from n to a state $y \in S_N$ and there exists a state $x \in F_{C_m}$, such that $(x, y) \in R_S$ and $|\pi| \le i$.*

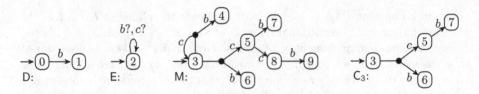

Fig. 3. Two DMTSs D and E that do not have an MCR. M is an example of an alphabet common refinement of D and E, and $C_3 \subset M$ is a disjunctive cone.

5.2   No MCR

We now prove the main result of the section, stated in the theorem below.

Theorem 6. *Consistent DMTSs do not always have a minimal common alphabet refinement.*

In order to prove this theorem we introduce two very simple DMTSs, D and E, shown in Fig. 3. They are consistent with each other and have many common alphabet refinements, yet they do not have an MCR, as we prove below.

Let us first study the nature of a common alphabet refinement M of D and E. Since $D \preceq_A M$, all states in M correspond, in the observational alphabet relation, to either D_0 or D_1. We call them 0-states and 1-states, respectively. 0-states in M are those that appear *before* a transition labeled b on a path from the initial state. 1-states in M appear *after* a transition labeled b. 0-states and 1-states cannot be related via the observation alphabet relation since from a 0-state we eventually reach a b-labelled transition, while from a 1-state such a transition cannot be reached. We thus have the following observation.

Observation 1. *Let M and N be common refinements of D and E such that* $M \preceq_S N$ *with the refinement relation* R_S. *For every* $(x, y) \in R_S$, *either both x and y are 0-states, or they are both 1-states.*

From every 0-state x, a 1-state is guaranteed to be reached. Otherwise, x cannot correspond to D_0 since there is a required transition on b from D_0. An observational refinement allows a finite number of τ-transitions to exist, after which a required transition on b must be present. Thus, from every 0-state x, there must exist a DT such that all of its legs lead, without loops, to a 1-state.

Observation 2. *Let M be a common refinement of D and E. From every 0-state in M there must exist a DT such that none of its legs form a loop on c-labelled transitions.*

Otherwise, there is a refinement of x that does not reach a 1-state. More formally, we have the following claim.

Claim 1. *From every 0-state x in M, there exists a disjunctive cone C_x with finite maximal must paths such that all of its front states are 1-states.*

Proof. Assume by way of contradiction that there exists a 0-state x such that for all disjunctive cones starting from x, at least one front state is a 0-state. Let us examine a maximal such disjunctive cone C_x, in the sense that no DT can be added from any front state s (either because a DT does not exist from s or because adding any DT will form a directed loop). Then s contradicts Observation 2.   □

Example 5. *DMTS M in Fig. 3 is a common alphabet refinement of* D *and* E. *Its 0-states are 3,5,8 and its 1-states are 4,6,7,9. DMTS* C_3 *is a disjunctive cone for which all of its front states are 1-states. By Claim 1, such a disjunctive cone must exist in every common alphabet refinement of* D *and* E.

Based on the above observations and Claim 1, we can now prove Theorem 6. The idea of the proof is to construct, for any given common refinement M of D and E, a common refinement M′ that is strictly less refined than M (M′ $\preceq_S$ M and M $\npreceq_S$ M′). This would show that no common refinement can be minimal.

Proof of Theorem 6. Let $M = (S_M, L, \delta^p, \Delta^r, s^m)$ be a common alphabet refinement of D and E. We construct a less refined common alphabet refinement M′. We first examine disjunctive cones C in M, from 0-states, with front states that are 1-states. By Claim 1, such a disjunctive cone exists from every 0-state. Let $\mathcal{DC}$ be the set of all such disjunctive cones in M:

$$\mathcal{DC} = \{C_x \mid x \text{ is a 0-state, } C_x \text{ is a disjunctive cone where } F_{C_x} \text{ has only 1-states}\}$$

Consider the depth $|C_x|$ of disjunctive cones in $\mathcal{DC}$. Let $k_1 = max\{|C_x| \mid C_x \in \mathcal{DC}\}$. Let $k = 2k_1$. We now construct $M′ = (S′_M, L, \delta'^p, \Delta'^r, s'_m)$ as follows:

- we define $s'_m = s_m$;
- we add k states: $S'_M = S_M \cup \{y_1, \cdots, y_k\}$;
- we add k possible transitions to δ^p: $\delta'^p = \delta^p \cup \{s'_m \xrightarrow{c}_p y_1 \xrightarrow{c}_p y_2 \xrightarrow{c}_p \cdots \xrightarrow{c}_p y_k\}$;
- and we add k required transitions to Δ^r: $\Delta'^r = \Delta^r \cup \{y_k \xrightarrow{c}_r y_{k-1} \xrightarrow{c}_r \cdots \xrightarrow{c}_r y_1 \xrightarrow{c}_r s'_m\}$.

Clearly, M′ is a common alphabet refinement of D and E: all new states are 0-states. Also, M refines M′ by removing the transition $s_m \xrightarrow{c}_p y_1$. Thus, M′ $\preceq_S$ M.

It remains to be shown that M $\npreceq_S$ M′. Assume by way of contradiction that M $\preceq_S$ M′. Thus, there exists a refinement relation R_S between M and M′ such that $(s_m, s'_m) \in R_S$. In M′, there is a maybe path from s'_m to y_k (by construction). By Lemma 1, there exists a maybe path in M from s_m to a state x, and $(x, y_k) \in R_S$. Since y_k is a 0-state, and x is related to y_k, we have by Observation 1 that x is also a 0-state. By Claim 1, there exists a disjunctive cone C_x in M from x, such that all its front states are 1-states. Let i be the depth of C_x. We know that $i \leq k_1$ (by the definition of k_1). Since $(x, y_k) \in R_S$, by Lemma 2, there exists a must path π from y_k to a 1-state in M′ with $|\pi| \leq i$. However, by our construction, the shortest must path in M′ from y_k to a 1-state is of length $k + 1$ (k transitions to get back from y_k to s'_m and at least another b-labelled transition to get to a 1-state). Recall that $k = 2k_1$. We get that $|\pi| \leq i \leq k_1$ but also $|\pi| > 2k_1$ – a contradiction.   □

6   Conclusion

In this paper, we revisited DMTSs and added a few pieces to the puzzle of their analysis. We defined DMTS modal observational refinement, a definition that was missing in the literature. We then used this definition to show that DMTSs are closed under observational merge, but that for the alphabet merge, even a minimal common refinement cannot be found.

In [3], we introduced a new formalism, rDMTS, and characterized the class of rDMTSs that are closed for alphabet merge. Since no *modal* observational refinement existed at that time, we defined merge using thorough refinement. We plan to extend the theory of rDMTSs to support modal alphabet refinement as well. This will provide the first practical solution for merging of models defined over different alphabets, since the complexity of modal refinement is much lower than that of thorough (PTIME-complete vs. EXPTIME-complete [6]).

References

1. Antonik, A., Huth, M., Larsen, K.G., Nyman, U., Wasowski, A.: Complexity of decision problems for mixed and modal specifications. In: FoSSaCS, pp. 112–126 (2008)
2. Antonik, A., Michael, H., Larsen, K.G., Nyman, U., Wasowski, A.: Exptime-complete decision problems for modal and mixed specifications. Electr. Notes Theor. Comput. Sci. **242**(1), 19–33 (2009)
3. Ben-David, S., Chechik, M., Uchitel, S.: Merging partial behaviour models with different vocabularies. In: D'Argenio, P.R., Melgratti, H. (eds.) CONCUR 2013 – Concurrency Theory. LNCS, vol. 8052, pp. 91–105. Springer, Heidelberg (2013)
4. Beneš, N., Černá, I., Křetínský, J.: Modal transition systems: composition and LTL model checking. In: Bultan, T., Hsiung, P.-A. (eds.) ATVA 2011. LNCS, vol. 6996, pp. 228–242. Springer, Heidelberg (2011)
5. Beneš, N., Křetínský, J., Larsen, K.G., Møller, M.H., Srba, J.: Parametric modal transition systems. In: Bultan, T., Hsiung, P.-A. (eds.) ATVA 2011. LNCS, vol. 6996, pp. 275–289. Springer, Heidelberg (2011)
6. Beneš, N., Křetínský, J., Larsen, K.G., Srba, J.: Checking thorough refinement on modal transition systems is EXPTIME-complete. In: Leucker, M., Morgan, C. (eds.) ICTAC 2009. LNCS, vol. 5684, pp. 112–126. Springer, Heidelberg (2009)
7. Fahrenberg, U., Legay, A., Traonouez, L.-M.: Structural refinement for the modal nu-calculus. In: Ciobanu, G., Méry, D. (eds.) ICTAC 2014. LNCS, vol. 8687, pp. 169–187. Springer, Heidelberg (2014)
8. Fantechi, A., Gnesi, S.: Formal modeling for product families engineering. In: SPLC, pp. 193–202 (2008)
9. Fecher, H., Schmidt, H.: Comparing disjunctive modal transition systems with a one-selecting variant. J. Logic Algebraic Program. **77**(1–2), 20–39 (2008)
10. Fischbein, D.: Foundations for behavioural model elaboration using modal transition systems. Ph.D. thesis, Imperial College London (2012)
11. Fischbein, D., Braberman, V., Uchitel, S.: A sound observational semantics for modal transition systems. In: Leucker, M., Morgan, C. (eds.) ICTAC 2009. LNCS, vol. 5684, pp. 215–230. Springer, Heidelberg (2009)

12. Fischbein, D., D'Ippolito, N., Brunet, G., Chechik, M., Uchitel, S.: Weak alphabet merging of partial behavior models. ACM Trans. Softw. Eng. Methodol. (TOSEM) **21**(2), 9 (2012)
13. Fischbein, D., Uchitel, S.: On correct and complete strong merging of partial behaviour models. In: SIGSOFT FSE, pp. 297–307 (2008)
14. Hüttel, H., Larsen, K.G.: The use of static constructs in a modal process logic. In: Proceedings of Logic at Botik, Symposium on Logical Foundations of Computer Science, Pereslav-Zalessky, USSR, pp. 163–180 (1989)
15. Keller, R.M.: Formal verification of parallel programs. Commun. ACM **19**(7), 371–384 (1976)
16. Larsen, K.G., Nyman, U., Wąsowski, A.: On modal refinement and consistency. In: Caires, L., Vasconcelos, V.T. (eds.) CONCUR 2007. LNCS, vol. 4703, pp. 105–119. Springer, Heidelberg (2007)
17. Larsen, K.G., Thomsen, B.: A modal process logic. In: LICS, pp. 203–210 (1988)
18. Larsen, K.G., Xinxin, L.: Equation solving using modal transition systems. In: LICS, pp. 108–117 (1990)
19. Lüttgen, G., Vogler, W.: Modal interface automata. Logical Methods Comput. Sci. **9**(3) (2013)
20. Uchitel, S., Chechik, M.: Merging partial behavioural models. In: SIGSOFT FSE, pp. 43–52 (2004)

Equivalence-Based Abstraction Refinement for μHORS Model Checking

Xin Li[✉] and Naoki Kobayashi[✉]

The University of Tokyo, Tokyo, Japan
{li-xin,koba}@kb.is.s.u-tokyo.ac.jp

Abstract. Kobayashi and Igarashi proposed model checking of μHORS (recursively-typed higher-order recursion schemes), by which a wide range of programs such as object-oriented programs and multi-threaded programs can be precisely modeled and verified. In this work, we present a procedure for μHORS model checking that improves the procedure based on automata-based abstraction refinement proposed by Kobayashi and Li. The new procedure optimizes each step of the abstract-check-refine paradigm of the previous procedure. Specially, it combines the strengths of automata-based and type-based abstraction refinement as equivalence-based abstraction refinement. We have implemented the new procedure, and confirmed that it always outperformed the original automata-based procedure on runtime efficiency, and successfully verified all benchmarks which were previously impossible.

1 Introduction

The model checking of higher-order recursion schemes (HORS) can be considered as a generalization of finite-state and pushdown model checking, and has been recently applied to automated verification of higher-order programs [6,10,13]. A HORS [5,12] is a simply-typed higher-order grammar that generates a possibly infinite tree called a value tree. The model checking problem for HORS is to check whether the value tree generated by HORS satisfies a given tree property. The problem is decidable [12] and a few efficient algorithms had been developed for it [3,14], despite its extremely high worst-case complexity. Since HORS can be considered as a simply-typed higher-order functional program with recursion and tree constructors, the verification of functional programs (after predicate abstraction if necessary) can be naturally reduced to HORS model checking.

Although HORS can serve as a precise model for simply-typed higher-order functional programs, it could not be used for describing more expressive programs, such as functional programs with recursive types, object-oriented programs, and multi-threaded programs. To improve the expressiveness of HORS, Kobayashi and Igarashi introduced μHORS, an extension of HORS with recursive types, and studied a model checking problem for it [7]. Using μHORS, object-oriented programs and multi-threaded programs can be precisely modeled. They showed that μHORS model checking is undecidable, and developed a sound procedure for it based on the inference of recursive intersection types

© Springer International Publishing AG 2016
C. Artho et al. (Eds.): ATVA 2016, LNCS 9938, pp. 304–320, 2016.
DOI: 10.1007/978-3-319-46520-3_20

that certify the safety of the grammar. The procedure is also relatively complete with respect to recursive intersection types: the grammar is eventually proved to be safe, if it is typable under some recursive intersection type system.

Kobayashi and Li later proposed an automata-based abstraction refinement procedure for μHORS model checking [8]. Following the *abstract-check-refine* paradigm, their procedure abstracts the configuration graph (that is the product reduction) of the grammar and the property automaton [6] as a finite graph, called *abstract configuration graph* (ACG), such that each term is abstracted as a state of a given finite tree automaton during the reduction, and the tree automaton is gradually refined for abstraction by counterexamples. Their procedure is sound and relatively complete with respect to a regular set of term trees: the grammar is eventually proved to be safe if there exists a regular set of term trees that is a safety inductive invariants for the grammar. Although their procedure is more efficient than the one proposed by Kobayashi and Igarashi, it is still not scalable enough as exhibited by their experiments.

To boost the scalability of μHORS model checking, we present a procedure that improves each step in the abstract-check-refine paradigm of the previous automata-based procedure as follows:

(1) It combines the strengths of automata-based and type-based abstraction refinement as equivalence-based abstraction refinement: terms are identified to be equivalent during the reduction if and only if they are abstracted as the same state of the tree automaton and inhabit the same (non-recursive) intersection type; and such an equivalence relation is gradually refined by counterexamples.

(2) The ACG construction is optimized so that the abstraction is more precise (i.e., the resulting ACG is in smaller size) than that of the original procedure, and therefore, our procedure is expected to scale better as confirmed by experiments.

(3) An ACG is constructed by expanding different kinds of nodes in a specific order and by classifying the edges as two kinds of abstract and concrete reduction, respectively, so that the feasibility checking step (as to whether a counterexample is spurious or not) can be replaced by a simple and lightweight traversal of the error trace.

We have implemented the new procedure, and our empirical study showed that, it always outperformed the original procedure on runtime efficiency, and successfully verified all benchmarks from [8] which were previously impossible.

On the technical side, our new procedure also preserves the properties of the automata-based procedure, i.e., it is sound and relatively complete with respect to safety invariants in terms of a regular tree language. Note that, we are concerned with μHORS model checking in this work, but our techniques are applicable to the type-based abstraction refinement procedure for simply-typed HORS model checking [14].

The rest of the paper is organized as follows: Sect. 2 reviews μHORS model checking. Section 3 describes an improved procedure for μHORS model checking and its properties. Section 4 reports the implementation and experimental results. Section 5 discusses related work and Sect. 6 concludes the paper. The proofs of the theorems can be found in a full version of the paper [11].

2   Preliminaries

Let N_+ be the set of positive integers, and let E be a (finite) set. A tree D is a prefix-closed subset of N_+^* such that $\pi j \in D$ implies $\{\pi, \pi 1, \ldots, \pi(j-1)\} \subseteq D$, and an *E-labeled tree* is a map from a tree to E. We write $dom(f)$ for the domain of a map f. A *ranked alphabet* Σ is a map from a finite set of symbols to non-negative integers, such that $\Sigma(a)$ denotes the arity of each symbol $a \in dom(\Sigma)$. A *Σ-labeled ranked tree* T is a Σ-labeled tree satisfying that $T(\pi) = a$ implies $\{i \mid \pi i \in dom(T)\} = \{1, \ldots, \Sigma(a)\}$ for any $\pi \in dom(T)$. Here, an element $a \in dom(\Sigma)$ is used as a tree constructor.

The set of *recursive types*, ranged over by κ, is defined by:

$$\kappa \text{ (recursive types)} ::= \alpha \mid \kappa_1 \to \cdots \to \kappa_m \to \mathsf{o} \mid \mu\alpha.\kappa$$

where $m \geq 0$, α is a type variable, and $\mu\alpha.\kappa$ is an equi-recursive type with α bound by μ within the scope κ [2]. Here, $\to$ binds tighter than the binding operator μ. Intuitively, the type o represents (term) trees, and $\mu\alpha.\kappa$ represents a solution (that is a finite or infinite regular tree) to the type equation $\alpha = \kappa$, and therefore $\mu\alpha.\kappa = [\mu\alpha.\kappa/\alpha]\kappa$, e.g., $\mu\alpha.\alpha \to \mathsf{o}$ and $(\mu\alpha.\alpha \to \mathsf{o}) \to \mathsf{o}$ are identical. The type $\kappa_1 \to \cdots \to \kappa_m \to \mathsf{o}$ describes a function value that takes as arguments of type $\kappa_1, \ldots, \kappa_m$ and returns a tree. As usual, we call a type κ *closed* if all the type variables in κ are bound. We only consider closed types in the sequel.

Given a set of variables $\mathcal{V}$, a set of function symbols $\mathcal{F}$ that is disjoint with $\mathcal{V}$, and a ranked alphabet Σ, the set of *applicative terms* (or shortly *terms*), ranged over by t, is defined by: t (terms)$::= x \mid a \mid t_1 t_2$, where x ranges over $\mathcal{V} \cup \mathcal{F}$, and a ranges over $dom(\Sigma)$. A ground term is a term that contains no variables in $\mathcal{V}$.

A *type environment* $\mathcal{K}$ for recursive types is a map from $\mathcal{V} \cup \mathcal{F} \cup dom(\Sigma)$ to recursive types. The type judgement relation $\mathcal{K} \vdash t : \kappa$ is the least relation closed under the following rules:

$$\overline{\mathcal{K}, x : \kappa \vdash x : \kappa} \qquad \overline{\mathcal{K} \vdash a : \underbrace{\mathsf{o} \to \cdots \to \mathsf{o}}_{\Sigma(a)} \to \mathsf{o}} \qquad \frac{\mathcal{K} \vdash t_0 : \kappa_1 \to \kappa_2 \qquad \mathcal{K} \vdash t_1 : \kappa_1}{\mathcal{K} \vdash t_0 t_1 : \kappa_2}$$

Definition 1. *A $\mu\textbf{HORS}$ $\mathcal{G}$ is a tuple $(\mathcal{N}, \Sigma, \mathcal{R}, S)$, where*

- *$\mathcal{N}$ is a map from a set of non-terminal symbols to their recursive types.*
- *Σ is a ranked alphabet, and $dom(\Sigma)$ is called a set of terminal symbols.*
- *$\mathcal{R}$ is a set of rewriting rules in the form $F\,x_1 \cdots x_m \to t$ where F is a non-terminal symbol and $\mathcal{N}(F) = \kappa_1 \to \cdots \to \kappa_m \to \mathsf{o}$, and t is an applicative term such that $\mathcal{N}, x_1:\kappa_1, \ldots, x_m:\kappa_m \vdash t : \mathsf{o}$. There exists exactly one rewriting rule for each non-terminal symbol F in $dom(\mathcal{N})$.*
- *$S \in dom(\mathcal{N})$ is called start symbol with $\mathcal{N}(S) = \mathsf{o}$.*

A μHORS [7] is a HORS [12] extended with recursive types, and can be considered a higher-order, call-by name, and recursively-typed functional program that generates a (possibly infinite) term tree.

Given a μHORS $\mathcal{G}$, the rewrite relation $\longrightarrow_{\mathcal{G}}$ on terms is defined by:

$$\frac{F\,\tilde{x} \to t \in \mathcal{R}}{F\,\tilde{s} \longrightarrow_{\mathcal{G}} [\tilde{s}/\tilde{x}]t} \qquad \frac{t_i \longrightarrow_{\mathcal{G}} t_i' \qquad i \in [1..\Sigma(a)]}{a\,t_1\cdots t_i\cdots t_{\Sigma(a)} \longrightarrow_{\mathcal{G}} a\,t_1\cdots t_i'\cdots t_{\Sigma(a)}}$$

where $\tilde{x}$ and $\tilde{s}$ denote sequences of variables and terms, respectively.

Let $\bot \notin dom(\Sigma)$ be a fresh symbol. Let $\Sigma^{\bot}$ be the ranked alphabet that extends Σ with $\bot$ such that $\Sigma^{\bot}(\bot) = 0$. For a ground term t of type o, we define the $\Sigma^{\bot}$-labeled ranked tree $t^{\bot}$ inductively as follows:

$$(a\,t_1\cdots t_{\Sigma(a)})^{\bot} = a\,(t_1{}^{\bot})\cdots(t_{\Sigma(a)}{}^{\bot}) \qquad (F\,\tilde{s})^{\bot} = \bot$$

We define a partial order $\sqsubseteq$ on $\Sigma^{\bot}$-labeled ranked trees such that $C[\bot] \sqsubseteq C[t]$ for any tree t and tree context C. Let $\bigsqcup$ be the least upper-bound of trees with respect to $\sqsubseteq$. The *value tree* $\mathbf{Tree}(\mathcal{G})$ of $\mathcal{G}$ is a $\Sigma^{\bot}$-labeled tree $\bigsqcup\{t^{\bot} \mid S \longrightarrow_{\mathcal{G}}^{*} t\}$.

Example 1. Let $\mathcal{G}_1 = (\Sigma, \mathcal{N}, \mathcal{R}, S)$ where $\Sigma = \{\mathsf{a} \mapsto 3, \mathsf{b} \mapsto 1, \mathsf{c} \mapsto 0\}$, $\mathcal{N} = \{S \mapsto \mathsf{o}, F \mapsto \mu\alpha.(\alpha \to (\mathsf{o} \to \mathsf{o}) \to (\mathsf{o} \to \mathsf{o}) \to \mathsf{o}), B \mapsto (\mathsf{o} \to \mathsf{o}) \to \mathsf{o} \to \mathsf{o}\}$, $\mathcal{R} = \{S \to F\,F\,\mathsf{b}\,\mathsf{b}, B\,h\,x \to \mathsf{b}(h\,x)$
$\quad F\,f\,k\,g \to \mathsf{a}\,(k\mathsf{c})\,(g(g\mathsf{c}))\,(f\,f\,(Bk)\,(Bg))\}$

S is reduced as follows:

$S \to F\,F\,\mathsf{b}\,\mathsf{b} \to \mathsf{a}\,(\mathsf{b}\,\mathsf{c})\,(\mathsf{b}^2\,\mathsf{c})\,(F\,F\,(B\,\mathsf{b})\,(B\,\mathsf{b})) \to \cdots$

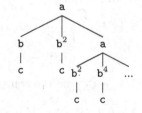

$\mathbf{Tree}(\mathcal{G}_1)$ is shown to the right.

Definition 2. *A **trivial tree automaton** (TTA) $\mathcal{A}$ is a tuple (Σ, Q, δ, Q_0), where Σ is a ranked alphabet, Q is a set of states, $\delta \subseteq Q \times dom(\Sigma) \times Q^*$ satisfying that $m = \Sigma(a)$ if $(q, a, q_1\cdots q_m) \in \delta$, and $Q_0 \subseteq Q$. Given a Σ-labeled ranked tree T. A run tree of $\mathcal{A}$ over T is a Q-labeled ranked tree R such that (i) $dom(R) = dom(T)$, (ii) $R(\epsilon) \in Q_0$, and (iii) $(R(\pi), T(\pi), R(\pi 1)\cdots R(\pi\Sigma(a))) \in \delta$ for any $\pi \in dom(R)$. $\mathcal{A}$ accepts T if there is a run tree of $\mathcal{A}$ over T. We denote by $\mathcal{L}(\mathcal{A})$ the set of trees accepted by $\mathcal{A}$, and by $\mathcal{L}(\mathcal{A}, q)$ the set of trees accepted by the automaton $(\Sigma, Q, \delta, \{q\})$. $\mathcal{A}$ is top-down deterministic if (i) $|Q_0| = 1$ and (ii) $(q, a, q_1\cdots q_m), (q, a, q_1'\cdots q_m') \in \delta$ implies $q_i = q_i'$ for each $i \in [1..m]$; and is moreover total if there exists $(q, a, q_1\cdots q_{\Sigma(a)}) \in \delta$ for any $q \in Q$ and $a \in dom(\Sigma)$. We often write $\delta(q, a) = q_1\cdots q_m$ for $(q, a, q_1\cdots q_m) \in \delta$ when $\mathcal{A}$ is top-down deterministic. Dually, $\mathcal{A}$ is bottom-up deterministic if $(q, a, q_1\cdots q_m), (q', a, q_1\cdots q_m) \in \delta$ implies $q = q'$, and is total if there exists $(q, a, q_1\cdots q_{\Sigma(a)}) \in \delta$ for any $q_1, \ldots, q_{\Sigma(a)} \in Q$ and $a \in dom(\Sigma)$.*

Trivial automata are originally considered by Aehlig [1] as non-deterministic Büchi tree automata where all the states are accepting. Note that, for finite trees, a topdown (resp bottom-up) deterministic TTA is just an ordinary topdown (resp bottom-up) deterministic finite tree automaton [4]. In this paper, we only consider topdown deterministic TTA.

We fix a μHORS $\mathcal{G} = (\mathcal{N}, \Sigma, \mathcal{R}, S)$ and a topdown deterministic TTA $\mathcal{A} = (\Sigma, Q, \delta, q_0)$ for the rest of paper. Let $\mathcal{A}^{\perp}$ denote the automaton $(\Sigma^{\perp}, Q, \delta \cup \{(q, \perp, \epsilon) \mid q \in Q\}, \delta, q_0)$. A μHORS *model checking problem* is to decide whether $\mathbf{Tree}(\mathcal{G}) \in \mathcal{L}(\mathcal{A}^{\perp})$. The μHORS model checking problem is undecidable [7], and we are concerned with sound and incomplete procedures for it.

Example 2. Let $\mathcal{A}_1$ be $(\Sigma, \{q_0, q_1, q_2, q_3\}, \delta, \{q_3\})$ where Σ is as given in Example 1, and δ is given as follows:

$$\{(q_3, \mathsf{a}, q_2 q_0 q_3), (q_0, \mathsf{b}, q_1), (q_1, \mathsf{b}, q_0), (q_2, b, q_2), (q_2, \mathsf{c}, \epsilon), (q_0, \mathsf{c}, \epsilon)\}.$$

$\mathcal{A}_1$ accepts the trees every path from the root to a leaf are labeled with an even number of b's by taking the second branch of a. In particular, $\mathcal{A}_1$ accepts the $\mathbf{Tree}(\mathcal{G}_1)$ in Example 1.

At the heart of practical procedures for higher-order model checking (e.g., [6,8,14]) is an algorithm for expanding a *configuration graph* of $\mathcal{G}$ and $\mathcal{A}$, starting with the root (S, q_0). A node in the graph is a pair (t, q) where t is a term and $q \in Q$ is a state of $\mathcal{A}$, and the edges obey the relation $\longrightarrow_{\mathcal{G}, \mathcal{A}}$ defined by the following rules:

- $(F t_1 \cdots t_m, q) \longrightarrow_{\mathcal{G}, \mathcal{A}} ([t_1/x_1, \ldots, t_m/x_m]s, q)$ if $F x_1 \cdots x_m \to s \in \mathcal{R}$.
- $(a t_1 \cdots t_m, q) \longrightarrow_{\mathcal{G}, \mathcal{A}} (t_i, q_i)$ if $(q, a, q_1 \cdots q_m) \in \delta$ for $i \in [1..m]$.
- $(a t_1 \cdots t_m, q) \longrightarrow_{\mathcal{G}, \mathcal{A}} \mathtt{fail}$ if $\delta(q, a)$ is undefined in $\mathcal{A}$.

Let $\longrightarrow_{\mathcal{G}, \mathcal{A}}^*$ be the transitive and reflexive closure of $\longrightarrow_{\mathcal{G}, \mathcal{A}}$.

Fact 3 $(S, q_0) \longrightarrow_{\mathcal{G}, \mathcal{A}}^* \mathtt{fail}$ *if and only if* $\mathbf{Tree}(\mathcal{G}) \notin \mathcal{L}(\mathcal{A}^{\perp})$.

We consider the counterexample-guided abstraction refinement paradigm for model checking, and explore the following two finite means of guiding the abstraction refinement procedure: term automata and intersection types.

Term Automata [8]. A term automaton $\mathcal{B} = (\Sigma_{\mathcal{B}}, Q_{\mathcal{B}}, \delta_{\mathcal{B}}, q_{\mathcal{B}, 0})$ is a bottom-up deterministic and total finite tree automaton that accepts a regular set of *well-typed* ground term trees (with respect to the types of $\mathcal{G}$ on terminal and non-terminal symbols, and the type judgement relation $\mathcal{K} \vdash t : \kappa$ defined above).

We define an equivalence relation $\sim_{\mathcal{B}}$ on terms over $\Sigma_{\mathcal{B}}$ by, for any t and t', $t \sim_{\mathcal{B}} t'$ if and only if $\forall q \in Q_{\mathcal{B}}. t \in \mathcal{L}(\mathcal{B}, q) \Leftrightarrow t' \in \mathcal{L}(\mathcal{B}, q)$. That is, t and t' are equivalent if and only if they are accepted and rejected by the same states of $\mathcal{B}$.

Intersection Types. The higher-order model checking problem can be characterized as an intersection type inference problem [6,7,9]. Here, we limit our focus to non-recursive intersection types for rejection of the grammar by the complement of $\mathcal{A}$, and refer it shortly as intersection types or rejection types. The set of intersection types for $\mathcal{A}$ is given as follows:

$$\tau \text{ (strict types)} ::= q \mid \sigma \to \tau \qquad \sigma \text{ (intersection types)} ::= \bigwedge \{\tau_1, \dots, \tau_k\}$$

where $q \in Q$ and $k \geq 0$. We write $\top$ for the empty intersection $\bigwedge \emptyset$. Note that, non-recursive intersection types are finitely many because the set of base types, i.e., the states of $\mathcal{A}$, is finite.

A type environment Γ is a set of type bindings in the form $h : \tau$, where $h \in dom(\mathcal{N}) \cup dom(\Sigma) \cup \mathcal{V}$. Note that, a type environment may have multiple type bindings for h. The type judgement $\Gamma \vdash_{\mathcal{A}} t : \tau$ is defined below following [3]. Note that, since we are concerned with a top-down deterministic TTA as the property automaton, the rejection types used in our setting has a specific form.

$$\frac{}{\Gamma, x : \tau \vdash_{\mathcal{A}} x : \tau} \qquad \frac{\delta(q, a) = (q_1 \cdots q_m) \quad \forall i. i \in [1..m]}{\Gamma \vdash_{\mathcal{A}} a : \underbrace{\top \to \dots \to \top}_{i-1} \to q_i \to \underbrace{\top \to \dots \to \top}_{m-i} \to q}$$

$$\frac{\delta(q, a) \text{ is undefined}}{\Gamma \vdash_{\mathcal{A}} a : \underbrace{\top \to \dots \to \top}_{\Sigma(a)} \to q} \qquad \frac{\Gamma \vdash_{\mathcal{A}} t_1 : \bigwedge \{\tau_1, \dots, \tau_n\} \to \tau \quad \Gamma \vdash_{\mathcal{A}} t_2 : \tau_i \ (\forall i. \ i \in [1..n])}{\Gamma \vdash_{\mathcal{A}} t_1 t_2 : \tau}$$

For any term t, we define $\mathcal{T}_{[\Gamma]}(t) = \bigwedge \{\tau \mid \Gamma \vdash_{\mathcal{A}} t : \tau\}$.

We define an equivalence relation on terms by, for any terms t and t', $t \sim_{\Gamma} t'$ if and only if $\forall \tau. \Gamma \vdash_{\mathcal{A}} t : \tau \Leftrightarrow \Gamma \vdash_{\mathcal{A}} t' : \tau$. That is, t and t' are equivalent if they inhabit the same intersection types in Γ.

Example 3. Consider $\mathcal{A}_1$ in Example 2. We have $\mathcal{T}_{[\Gamma]}(a) = \bigwedge \{\tau_1, \tau_2, \tau_3\}$. where $\tau_1 = q_1 \to \top \to \top \to q_3$, $\tau_2 = \top \to q_0 \to \top \to q_3$, and $\tau_3 = \top \to \top \to q_3 \to q_3$. $\mathcal{T}_{[\Gamma]}(b) = \bigwedge \{q_1 \to q_0, q_0 \to q_1, q_2 \to q_2\}$. $\mathcal{T}_{[\Gamma]}(c) = \bigwedge \{q_1, q_3\}$.

Definition 4. *An inductive invariant I for $\mathcal{G}$ is a set I of ground terms satisfying that, (i) $S \in I$; (ii) if $t \in I$ and $t \longrightarrow_{\mathcal{G}} t'$, then $t' \in I$. An inductive invariant I is regular if it is accepted by a finite tree automaton. A **safety invariant** for $\mathcal{G}$ (with respect to $\mathcal{A}$) is a regular inductive invariant I such that $t \in I$ implies $t^{\perp} \in \mathcal{L}(\mathcal{A}^{\perp})$, i.e., I contains no invalid term trees [8].*

Fact 5 *If there exists a safety invariant for $\mathcal{G}$ wrt $\mathcal{A}$, then $\mathbf{Tree}(\mathcal{G}) \in \mathcal{L}(\mathcal{A}^{\perp})$.*

A procedure for μHORS model checking is *sound* in the sense that, the grammar is safe if the procedure reports so, and *relatively complete* if the procedure eventually terminates and reports that the grammar is safe if there exists a safety invariant for $\mathcal{G}$ with respect to $\mathcal{A}$. The procedure may not terminate.

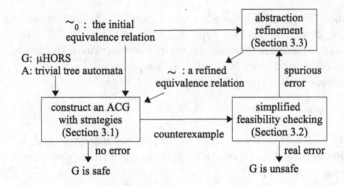

Fig. 1. Overview of the model checking procedure $MC_\sim(\mathcal{G}, \mathcal{A})$ for μHORS

3   The Model Checking Procedure

We give an overview of the new procedure $MC_\sim(\mathcal{G}, \mathcal{A})$ in Fig. 1 which depicts the high-level abstract-check-refine diagram explored in the procedure. The procedure takes as inputs a μHORS $\mathcal{G}$, a TTA $\mathcal{A}$, and an equivalence relation $\sim$ of a *finite* index on terms (i.e., $\sim$ induces a finite number of equivalence classes) which is used for directing the abstraction and refinement. Here, we combine the automata-based abstraction refinement [8] with the type-based approach [14], by taking $\sim = \sim_\mathcal{B} \cap \sim_\Gamma$.

Initially, $\sim_0 = \sim_{\mathcal{B}_0} \cap \sim_{\Gamma_0}$ provided with an initial term automata $\mathcal{B}_0{}^1$ and $\Gamma_0 = \emptyset$. Starting with $\sim = \sim_0$, the procedure works as follows: The abstraction step constructs a finite *abstract configuration graph* (ACG) as an abstraction of the configuration graph for $\mathcal{G}$ and $\mathcal{A}$, with *various strategies* (Sect. 3.1) and with the following twist that unifies [8,14]: any two nodes (t, q) and (t', q') are identified as equivalent and collapsed if and only if $t \sim t'$ and $q = q'$. Since $\sim$ has a finite index, there can be finitely many distinguished nodes in an ACG. If a closed ACG is constructed without containing any `fail` node, we conclude that the grammar is safe. Otherwise, a counterexample $\overset{\rightarrow}{CE}$ is raised during the ACG construction, and checked as to whether it is spurious or not (i.e., whether CE corresponds to a concrete reduction sequence that leads to `fail`). Thanks to the strategies applied to the ACG construction, this step is done by a simple and lightweight traversal of CE, called *simplified feasibility checking* (Sect. 3.2). If CE is a real error, we conclude that the grammar is unsafe. Otherwise, we refine the abstraction $\sim$ by refining $\sim_\mathcal{B}$ [8] and $\sim_\Gamma$ (Sect. 3.3), independently, so that the same CE would not occur in the future iterations. The loop is iterated until the grammar is proved or disproved. The procedure may not terminate since the model checking problem is undecidable in general.

---

[1] Note that, the choice of $\mathcal{B}_0$ would not affect relative completeness but practical efficiency of the procedure. An interested reader may wish to consult [8] for some approaches to constructing $\mathcal{B}_0$.

3.1   Constructing Abstract Configuration Graph with Strategies

Overview of the Original ACG Construction. At the heart of model checking procedures in [8,14] is an algorithm for constructing an ACG. Below we review the automata-based algorithm (i.e., take $\sim\,=\sim_{\mathcal{B}}$). Let $\mathcal{L}$ be a set of labels. A node in an ACG is either `fail` or a pair (t,q) of a state q in $\mathcal{A}$ and an *abstract applicative term* t given by: $t::=a \mid F \mid x^{\ell} \mid t_1 t_2$, where $a \in dom(\Sigma)$, $F \in dom(\mathcal{N})$, and x^{ℓ} is an *abstract variable* annotated with a label $\ell \in \mathcal{L}$. Besides the graph, a map ρ is constructed from abstract variables to terms they are bound with. A map l_{α} from edges to reduction labels is also maintained.

Starting with the root (S, q_0), the algorithm *non-deterministically* and *fairly* takes a node N in the graph and expands it as follows (Here, by fairness, we mean any node to be expanded would be eventually chosen, so that if the grammar is unsafe, an error trace would be eventually detected. It can be achieved for instance using an FIFO queue):

- Call $Expand_{\mathcal{N}}(N)$ for $N = (F\,s_1 \cdots s_m, q)$: given $F\,x_1 \cdots x_m \to t \in \mathcal{R}$, for each $i \in [1..m]$, an abstract variable $x_i^{\ell_i}$ is generated for representing the real argument s_i, where $\ell_i \in \mathcal{L}$ is fresh, and $\rho(x_i^{\ell_i}) = s_i$. A node $N' = ([x_1^{\ell_1}/x_1, \ldots, x_m^{\ell_m}/x_m]t, q)$ is generated and $l_{\alpha}(N, N') = F$.
- Call $Expand_{\Sigma}(N)$ for $N = (a\,s_1 \cdots s_m, q)$: if there exists $(q, a, q_1, \cdots, q_m)$ in δ, a node $N' = (s_i, q_i)$ is generated for each $i \in [1..m]$ and $l_{\alpha}(N, N') = (a, i)$; Otherwise, a `fail` node is generated.
- For each $x^{\ell'} \in dom(\rho)$, call $Expand_{\mathcal{V}}(N, (l, l'))$ for $N = (x^{\ell} s_1 \cdots s_m, q)$: a node $N' = (t\,s_1 \cdots s_m, q)$ is generated by replacing x^{ℓ} with the term $t = \rho(x^{\ell'})$ and $l_{\alpha}(N, N') = \varepsilon$. Besides, the edge (N, N') is labelled by (ℓ, ℓ').

For each abstract variable x^{ℓ} such that $\rho(x^{\ell}) = s$ for some s, we define a term $\rho^+(x^{\ell}) = [\rho^+(x_1^{\ell_1})/x_1^{\ell_1}, \ldots, \rho^+(x_n^{\ell_n})/x_n^{\ell_n}]s$, where $x_1^{\ell_1}, \ldots, x_n^{\ell_n}$ are variables occurring in s. Note that, a fresh label ℓ is always used in the construction. So the above equation cannot be circular and $\rho^+(x^{\ell})$ is well defined. We extend the definition to any term t by $\rho^+(t) = [\rho^+(x_1^{\ell_1})/x_1^{\ell_1}, \ldots, \rho^+(x_n^{\ell_n})/x_n^{\ell_n}]t$, where $x_1^{\ell_1}, \ldots, x_n^{\ell_n}$ are variables in t.

Any two nodes $N = (C[x_1^{\ell_1}, \ldots, x_n^{\ell_n}], q)$ and $N' = (C[x_1^{\ell_1'}, \ldots, x_n^{\ell_n'}], q)$ are equivalent, denoted by $N \equiv N'$, if and only if $\rho^+(x_i^{\ell_i}) \sim \rho^+(x_i^{\ell_i'})$ for each $i \in [1..n]$. During the expansion, all $\equiv$-equivalent nodes are merged in the graph, by which an abstraction is applied to the reduction. The effect of the abstraction is reflected when expanding the variable-headed nodes. We call an ACG *closed* if no more nodes or edges can be added above. A closed ACG always exists and is finite, given that $\sim$ has a finite index.

Constructing an ACG with Strategies. Based on the original ACG construction above, Algorithm 1 constructs an ACG with various strategies for giving directions to the graph expansion:

(1) A set $\mathcal{E}$ of *expandable label pairs* is constructed (line 35, 37), and it maintains the label pairs that can be used for expanding variable-headed nodes (line

Algorithm 1. Constructing an ACG with Strategies

```
 1  proc Update(N, N′, tag)
 2  begin
 3      if not tag then
 4          ⟶_{c,0} := ⟶_{c,0} ∪ {(N, N′)};
 5          add N′ to ws_0
 6      else
 7          ⟶_{c,1} := ⟶_{c,1} ∪ {(N, N′)};
 8          add N′ to ws_1
 9  end

10  proc NewExpand(ℰ_{new})
11  begin
12      foreach (ℓ, ℓ′) ∈ ℰ_{new} do
13          foreach N = (x^ℓ s̃, q) ∈ 𝒞 do
14              N′ := Expand_v(N, (l, l′));
15              Update(N, N′, 1)
16  end

17  proc TakeNode(ws_0, ws_1)
18  begin
19      if ws_0 ≠ ∅ then
20          take N′ from ws_0
21      else
22          if ws_1 ≠ ∅ then
23              take N′ from ws_1
24          else raise an exception
25      return N′
26  end

27  ⟶_{c,0} := ∅;  ⟶_{c,1} := ∅;
28  ws_0 := ∅; ws_1 := ∅; ℰ := ∅;
29  add (S, q_0) to ws_0;
30  while ws_0 ≠ ∅ and ws_1 ≠ ∅ do
31      N := TakeNode(ws_0, ws_1);
32      InferType(𝒞, N);
33      if N ≡ N′ for some N′ ≠ N ∈ 𝒞 then
34          merge N with N′;
35          ℰ_{new} := EqLabels(N′, N) \ ℰ;
36          NewExpand(ℰ_{new});
37          ℰ := ℰ ∪ ℰ_{new};
38      else
39          if t = F s̃ then
40              N′ := Expand_𝒩(N);
41              Update(N, N′, 0)
42          if t = a s̃ then
43              Succs := Expand_Σ(N);
44              foreach N′ ∈ Succs do
45                  Update(N, N′, 0);
46                  if N′ = fail then
47                      return a counterexample
48          if t = x^ℓ s̃ then
49              foreach (ℓ, ℓ′) ∈ ℰ^† do
50                  N′ := Expand_v(N, (l, l′));
51                  if ℓ = ℓ′ then Update(N, N′, 0)
52                  else Update(N, N′, 1)
53  return the grammar is safe;
```

12, 49), where $\mathcal{E}^†$ denotes the disjoint union of $\mathcal{E}$ and $\{(\ell, \ell) \mid \ell \in \mathcal{L}\}$. Those labels pairs in $\mathcal{E}$ result from merging the node $N = (C[x_1^{\ell_1}, \ldots, x_n^{\ell_n}], q)$ with $N' = (C[x_1^{\ell'_1}, \ldots, x_n^{\ell'_n}], q)$ (line 34–35), defined by

$$EqLabels(N', N) = \{(\ell'_i, \ell_i) \mid \forall i \in [1..n].\ \ell_i \neq \ell'_i\}$$

When new expandable pairs are found, those related variable-headed nodes are expanded with more successors (line 10–15).

(2) A specific order of expanding the graph is enforced using two worksets ws_0 and ws_1 for managing the nodes to be expanded. When taking a node from worksets (line 17–26), it always first takes a node from ws_0 if it is non-empty, and it takes a node from ws_1, otherwise. We classify edges $\longrightarrow_{\mathcal{C}}$ of the graph into two disjoint sets such that $\longrightarrow_{\mathcal{C}} = \longrightarrow_{c,1} \cup \longrightarrow_{c,0}$ (line 1–9).

For nodes expanded from variable-headed nodes such that the head variable x^ℓ is replaced with the term $\rho(x^{\ell'})$ with $\ell \neq \ell'$, they are added to ws_1, and the resulting edges belong to $\longrightarrow_{c,1}$ (line 15, 52). For other nodes, they are added to ws_0 and the resulting edges belong to $\longrightarrow_{c,0}$ (line 41, 45, 51).

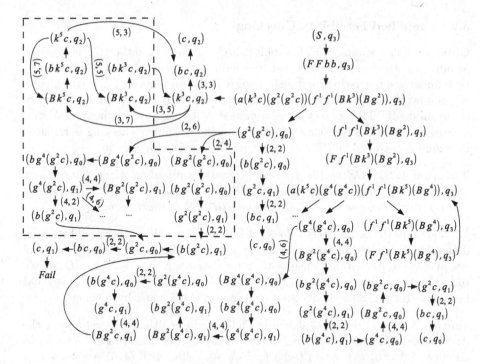

Fig. 2. A snapshot of an abstract configuration graph $\mathcal{C}$

Enforcing expandable label pairs in $\mathcal{E}$ reduces redundant reduction sequences in an ACG that do not have any corresponding concrete reduction sequences. Thus, the abstraction becomes more precise. The advantage of (2) will be seen in Sect. 3.2 for simplifying the feasibility checking step.

Example 4. Recall $\mathcal{G}_1$ in Example 1 and $\mathcal{A}_1$ in Example 2. Assume Bb $\not\sim$ b, BBb $\sim$ Bb, and Bbc $\not\sim$ c (e.g., $\sim=\sim_{\Gamma_0}$). Figure 2 shows a snapshot of part of an ACG for $\mathcal{G}_1$ and $\mathcal{A}_1$ without optimization, where for simplicity, we omit generating abstract variables for representing arguments of function calls to $B\,h\,x \rightarrow \mathsf{b}(h\,x)^2$. The binding relations are given as follows:

$$\rho(f^1) = F \qquad \rho(g^2) = \rho(k^3) = \mathsf{b} \qquad \rho(g^4) = B\,g^2$$
$$\rho(k^5) = B\,k^3 \qquad \rho(g^6) = B\,g^4 \qquad \rho(k^7) = B\,k^5$$

The node $(Ff_1(Bk^5)(Bg^4), q_3)$ has a child $(\mathsf{a}(k^7\mathsf{c})(g^6(g^6\mathsf{c}))(f^1f^1(Bk^7)(Bg^6))$, $q_3)$, which is merged with the node $(\mathsf{a}(k^5\mathsf{c})(g^4(g^4\mathsf{c}))(f^1f^1(Bk^5)(Bg^4)), q_3)$. If the graph is constructed by Algorithm 1, we have $\mathcal{E} = \{(5,7),(4,6)\}$ by merging the two nodes above, so that the entire subgraph circled by the dashed lines is not generated. Indeed, none of them has a corresponding concrete reduction.

---

[2] It does not change the graph structure by doing so, because the arguments of B occurring in the reduction could never be merged according to the assumption on $\sim$.

3.2   Simplified Feasibility Checking

Given a counterexample CE, feasibility checking checks whether CE is spurious or not, i.e., whether there is a concrete reduction sequence that leads to `fail` by taking the same reduction labels along CE. When a cyclic CE is considered, it examines those (finite) abstract reduction sequences by unfolding CE up to a certain depth. Thanks to the order-guided ACG construction in Algorithm 1, we can conclude the following theorem, and the feasibility checking is replaced by a simple traversal of CE as to whether there exists an edge in $\longrightarrow_{C,1}$.

Theorem 1. *Let CE be the first counterexample raised by Algorithm 1. Then, (i) if there does not exist any edge on CE that belongs to $\longrightarrow_{C,1}$, then CE is a real error and the grammar is unsafe; and (ii) CE is spurious otherwise.*

The claim (ii) in Theorem 1 does not hold in general if CE is raised by a non-deterministic algorithm for constructing an ACG. The key is that, the usage of ws_0 and ws_1 in Algorithm 1 ensures that, for the edge $N \longrightarrow_{C,1} N'$ in CE nearest to `fail`, the complete subgraph rooted with N only having edges in $\longrightarrow_{C,0}$ has been constructed. Since it does not contain `fail`, CE must be spurious.

Example 5. Recall the ACG shown in Fig. 2, excluding the part enclosed by the dashed line. There is a counterexample CE leading to `fail`. Since CE contains an edge $((g^4(g^4c), q_0) \longrightarrow_{C,1} ((B\, g^4(g^4c), q_0)$ labelled with $(4,6)$, we know it is spurious by Theorem 1.

3.3   Abstraction Refinement of $\sim\ =\ \sim_B \cap \sim_\Gamma$

Figure 3 gives a sub-procedure *InferType*(C, N) that infers rejection types from a counterexample CE, when type-based abstraction refinement is combined with automata-based procedure as called at line 32 in Algorithm 1. The procedure takes as inputs an open ACG C and the current node $N \in C$ to be expanded in the graph. Similar to the notion defined in [14], we say (t, q) is Γ-*rejected* if

```
 1: if N is Γ-rejected then {
 2:     take CE = e₀...eₙ from C
        that leads from (S, q₀) to N;
 3: if {e₀,...,eₙ} ⊆ ⟶_{C,0} then
 4:     return the grammar is unsafe;
 5: else {
 6:     take a rejecting trail σ from CE;
 7:     infer a type environment Γ' from σ;
 8:     refine B to be B' by CE [8];
 9:     call MC∼(G, A) with ∼ = ∼_{B'} ∩ ∼_{Γ'};
10: }}
```

Fig. 3. *InferType*(C, N): a sub-procedure for rejection type inference where C is an open ACG, and $N = (t, q)$ is a node in C to be expanded.

$\Gamma \vdash_A t : q$. If N is Γ-rejected, the procedure takes a counterexample CE from $\mathcal{C}$ (line 2). If CE does not contain any edge in $\longrightarrow_{C,1}$, then $(S, q_0) \longrightarrow^*_{\mathcal{C},0}$ fail and it is a real error (line 3–4). Otherwise, a rejecting trail is taken from CE (line 6) from which a type environment Γ' is computed (line 7). By separately refining $\sim_B$ as in [8] (line 8), $\sim$ is refined and another round of model checking is triggered (line 9).

Our choice of rejecting trail is similar to the rejecting region defined in [14] (that is a subgraph of an ACG in which each node reaches to a Γ-rejected leaf), except that we are concerned with an open graph whereas a closed ACG is required by [14] for their abstraction and refinement.

Definition 6. *A trail is an alternating sequence of vertices and edges of a graph that starts and ends with vertices. Given $CE = e_0 \ldots e_n$ where $N_0 = (S, q_0)$, $N_{n+1} = N$ and $e_i = (N_i, N_{i+1}) \in \longrightarrow_{\mathcal{C}}$ for each $i \in [0..n]$. A rejecting trail $\sigma = N_k e_k N_{k+1} e_{k+1} \ldots N_{n+1}$ ($k \in [0..n+1]$) for CE is the longest trail, satisfying,*
  (a) $\{e_k, \ldots, e_n\} \cap \longrightarrow_{C,1} = \emptyset$; and
  (b) For any $j \in [k..n]$, $(N_j, N') \notin \longrightarrow_{C,1}$ for any N' if $N_j = (x^\ell \, \tilde{s}, q)$.

The first condition says that σ only contains edges in $\longrightarrow_{C,0}$, and the second condition requires that, for any variable-headed node N_j in σ, N_j does not have any open successor to be reduced in the graph since $\mathcal{C}$ is an open graph. Note that, σ is unique for a given CE and could be just the Γ-rejected node N.

Given the rejecting trail $\sigma = N_k e_k N_{k+1} e_{k+1} \ldots N_{n+1}$, rejection types are inferred from σ similar to [9,14]. Starting with the Γ-rejected node N_n, types are extracted backwards along the trail as follows: for each node $N_i = (h s_1 \ldots s_m, q)$ in σ where $i \in [0..n-k]$ and $h \in \Sigma \cup dom(\mathcal{N}) \cup \mathcal{V}$, if $h \in dom(\mathcal{N}) \cup \mathcal{V}$ (i.e., if h is headed by a non-terminal or a variable), we have

$$\Gamma^{(j)}(h) = \Gamma^{(j+1)}(h) \wedge \tau_j \text{ with } \tau_j = \bigwedge \mathcal{T}_{[\Gamma^{(j+1)}]}(s_1) \to \cdots \to \bigwedge \mathcal{T}_{[\Gamma^{(j+1)}]}(s_m) \to q$$

and otherwise, $\Gamma^{(j)}(h) = \Gamma^{(j+1)}(h)$ when h is a terminal symbol, where $j = n-i$ and $\Gamma^{(n+1)} = \Gamma$. For any variable or non-terminal h that do not appear in head positions of nodes in σ, their types keep unchanged, i.e., $\Gamma^{(j)}(h) = \Gamma^{(j+1)}(h)$.

Theorem 2. *Given Γ is computed by the procedure in Fig. 3. For any node $N = (t, q)$ in the ACG, N is Γ-rejected implies that $(\rho^+(t), q) \longrightarrow^*_{\mathcal{G},\mathcal{A}}$ fail.*

By Theorem 2, we can safely raise a counterexample once a Γ-*rejected* node N is found, with no need for expanding it.

Example 6. Recall the previous error path CE in Fig. 2. Let $\Gamma = \emptyset$. The rejecting node is (c, q_1), and the rejecting trail σ is the sequence from the node $(Bg^4(g^4 c), q_0)$ to the node (c, q_1). By type inference, we have Γ': $\{g^2 : q_1 \to q_0, g^4 : q_1 \to q_1, B : (q_1 \to q_0) \to q_1 \to q_1, B : (q_1 \to q_1) \to q_1 \to q_0\}$ which ensures that $B\,b \not\sim_\Gamma B\,B\,b$, so that the grammar can be proved safe in the next iteration of model checking.

3.4 Properties of the Procedure

Given a closed ACG $\mathcal{C}$ constructed by Algorithm 1, and let $\mathbb{C}$ be the configuration graph (CG) for $\mathcal{G}$ and $\mathcal{A}$. We show that there exists a weak simulation relation between $\mathbb{C}$ and $\mathcal{C}$.

Let $\mathcal{C} = (Node_{\mathcal{C}}, \longrightarrow_{\mathcal{C}})$, where $Node_{\mathcal{C}}$ is a finite set of nodes and $\longrightarrow_{\mathcal{C}} = \longrightarrow_{\mathcal{C},0} \cup \longrightarrow_{\mathcal{C},1}$ is a set of edges. Let $GNode_{\mathcal{C}} \subseteq Node_{\mathcal{C}}$ be the set of nodes where for any (t, q) in $GNode_{\mathcal{C}}$, t is headed by a terminal or a non-terminal symbol, and let $VNode_{\mathcal{C}} = Node_{\mathcal{C}} \setminus GNode_{\mathcal{C}}$ be the set of variable-headed nodes. Let $\rightarrow_\tau = \longrightarrow_{\mathcal{C}} \cap (VNode_{\mathcal{C}} \times Node_{\mathcal{C}})$, and the reflexive and transitive closure of $\rightarrow_\tau$ is denoted by $\rightarrow_\tau^*$. Let $\rightarrow_\alpha = \longrightarrow_{\mathcal{C}} \cap (GNode_{\mathcal{C}} \times Node_{\mathcal{C}})$. Let $\Rightarrow_{\mathcal{C}} \subseteq \rightarrow_\alpha \rightarrow_\tau^* \cap (GNode_{\mathcal{C}} \times GNode_{\mathcal{C}})$. Recall that $l_\alpha(N, N') = \epsilon$ for any $(N, N') \in \rightarrow_\tau$. We extend l_α to $\Rightarrow_{\mathcal{C}}$ by, for any $(N, N') \in \Rightarrow_{\mathcal{C}}$ where $N \rightarrow_\alpha N'' \rightarrow_\tau^* N'$, $l_\alpha(N, N') = l_\alpha(N, N'')$.

Let $\mathbb{C} = (Node_{\mathbb{C}}, \rightarrow_\gamma)$ for $\mathcal{G}$ and $\mathcal{A}$, where $Node_{\mathbb{C}}$ is the (possibly infinite) set of nodes, and $\rightarrow_\gamma \subseteq Node_{\mathbb{C}} \times Node_{\mathbb{C}}$ is the set of edges, respectively. Let l_γ be a map from edges in $\mathbb{C}$ to reduction labels as usual. We also write $M \xrightarrow{a}_\gamma M'$ if $M \rightarrow_\gamma M'$ and $a = l_\gamma(M, M')$.

Definition 7. *For any abstract term t, we define $h(t)$ as the least set of ground terms satisfying: (a) $h(x^\ell) \supseteq h(x^{\ell'})$ if $(\ell, \ell') \in \mathcal{E}$; (b) $h(x^\ell) \supseteq h(\rho(x^\ell))$; (c) $h(t_1 t_2) \supseteq \{t_1' t_2' \mid t_1' \in h(t_1), t_2' \in h(t_2)\}$; and (d) $h(a) \supseteq \{a\}$ for any $a \in dom(\Sigma) \cup dom(\mathcal{N})$. A binary relation $\preceq \subseteq Node_{\mathbb{C}} \times GNode_{\mathcal{C}}$ is defined by, for any node $M = (s, q)$ in $Node_{\mathbb{C}}$ and any node $N = (t, q')$ in $GNode_{\mathcal{C}}$,*

$$M \preceq N \text{ if and only if } s \in h(t) \text{ and } q = q'.$$

Definition 8. *A relation $R \subseteq Node_{\mathbb{C}} \times Node_{\mathcal{C}}$ is a weak simulation if for every $(M, N) \in R$, (i) $M \preceq N$, and (ii) for any node M' and for any a such that $M \xrightarrow{a}_\gamma M'$, there exists a node N' such that $N \Rightarrow_{\mathcal{C}} N'$, $(M', N') \in R$, and $l_\alpha(N, N') = l_\gamma(M, M')$. Let M_0 and N_0 be the unique entry nodes of a CG and an ACG, respectively. We say that the ACG weakly simulates the CG if there exists a weak simulation R such that $(M_0, N_0) \in R$.*

Theorem 3 (Soundness). $\preceq$ *is a weak simulation.*

It immediately follows Theorem 3 that, if a closed ACG does not contain any `fail` nodes, then the grammar is safe.

Theorem 4 (Relative Completeness). $MC_\sim(\mathcal{G}, \mathcal{A})$ *terminates and verifies that the grammar is safe, if there exists a safety invariant for $\mathcal{G}$ wrt $\mathcal{A}$.*

4   Experiments

We have implemented a prototype of the optimized procedure based on the model checker MUHORSAR [8], and the tool is written in OCaml. We use Z3 4.3.3 (http://z3.codeplex.com/) as the backend constraint solver for automata-based abstraction refinement. We have evaluated the tools on examples from two categories of applications, including verification problems of FJ (Featherweight Java) programs and that of multi-threaded boolean programs with recursion. We are concerned with checking safety properties of the target programs. For multi-threaded programs, we studied properties of mutual exclusion (e.g., the Peterson's algorithm), deadlock-freedom (e.g., for various solutions to the dining philosopher problem), and checking of assertion violation (e.g., for simplified variants of Bluetooth drivers). Most of examples are taken from [7,8] with a few examples newly-added as negative instances. Due to space, we only show those examples that couldn't be verified efficiently by the original procedure. An interested reader may wish to consult [7,8] for details of those examples and safety properties that have been checked against them. All experiments were conducted on a machine having a Mac OS X v.10.9.2, 1.7 GHz Intel Core i7 processor and 8 GB RAM.

The preliminary experimental results for comparing the verification time taken by MuHorSar with and without optimizations are summarized in Table 1 for verifying FJ programs and in Table 2 for verifying multi-threaded programs, respectively. The column "scheme" shows the names of the examples. The columns "$\#\mathcal{G}$" and "$\#\mathcal{A}$" show the number of rules of the schemes and the size of the property automaton for each example, respectively. The column "R" gives the answer whether the property is satisfied (Y) or violated (N). The column "MuHorSar" gives the runtime taken by the original procedure. The column "MuHorSar$^+$" gives the runtime with optimizing the abstraction refinement in MuHorSar, like enforcing $\mathcal{E}$, etc. The column "MuHorSar$^+_{\sim}$" shows the runtime by further combining the procedure with type-based abstraction refinement. The runtime is given in seconds, or "—" for timeout which is set to be 3 min. The number enclosed by parentheses shows the number of required abstraction refinement iterations, and we omit to show it in the table when it is zero, i.e., no abstraction refinement is needed.

As shown in both tables, the new procedure effectively improves the runtime of the original procedure. In particular, it successfully verified all of the bench-

Table 1. Results for verifying FJ programs

Scheme	$\#\mathcal{G}$	$\#\mathcal{A}$	R	MuHorSar		MuHorSar$^+$		MuHorSar$^+_{\sim}$	
L-filter	122	1	Y	1.391	(6)	0.867		0.919	
L-risers	122	1	Y	1.402	(6)	0.877		0.916	
Stack-br	39	1	Y	0.309	(13)	0.071	(1)	0.060	(1)
		3		0.391	(13)	0.063	(1)	0.066	(1)
		5		0.408	(13)	0.065	(1)	0.063	(1)
Queue-br	61	1	Y	0.253	(2)	0.194		0.203	
		3		0.251	(2)	0.213		0.206	
		5		0.261	(2)	0.196		0.200	
Nat	35	1	Y	17.723	(147)	0.110		0.122	

Table 2. Results for verifying multi-threaded boolean programs with recursion

Scheme	#$\mathcal{G}$	#$\mathcal{A}$	R	MuHorSar		MuHorSar$^+$		MuHorSar$^+_\sim$	
Locks-e	103	5	N	0.168	(1)	0.155		0.139	
Dining-e	135	5	N	2.948	(28)	0.541		0.406	
Dining-sp-e	193	5	N	11.685	(97)	0.884		0.833	
Bluetooth	129	1	N	2.484	(26)	2.722	(14)	0.947	(5)
Bluetooth-v1	158	1	N	—		68.819	(141)	3.658	(9)
Bluetooth-v2	166	1	N	—		13.820	(54)	1.869	(9)
Plotter-e	90	4	N	0.278	(3)	0.221		0.181	
Dining-tan-e	303	5	N	—		5.923	(7)	5.824	(5)
Peterson-e	74	2	N	0.589	(4)	0.257		0.270	
Locks	95	5	Y	0.742		0.222		0.238	
Plotter	88	4	Y	0.204		0.226		0.314	
Peterson	74	2	Y	3.548	(2)	0.477		0.662	
Peterson-d	80	9	Y	—		1.514		2.138	
Dekker	94	2	Y	—		0.447		0.657	
Pc-monitor	71	5	Y	0.331		0.222		0.354	
Pc-sp	111	5	Y	2.238		0.219		0.370	
Dining-tan	303	5	Y	—		18.229		23.007	

marks that were previously impossible. We found that enforcing expandable label pairs by $\mathcal{E}$ is very effective in scaling-up the model checking procedure, expected by reducing a large portion of redundant reduction sequences in an ACG.

5   Related Work

This work is an optimization and improvement of the automata-based procedure for μHORS model checking proposed by Kobayashi and Li [8]. Their abstraction-refinement approach explores a finite tree automaton for abstracting and identifying term trees (as states of the automaton) for constructing the abstract configuration graph, and often outperforms the first procedure for μHORS model checking proposed in [7]. Their idea is inspired by the type-directed abstraction refinement approach in [14], but is different in achieving (relative) completeness. In fact, the type-based approach applied to simply-typed HORS model checking in [14] would not ensure the same relative completeness as that is achieved by the automata-based procedure in [8], if applied to μHORS model checking.

This work makes an attempt to further improve the line of work. We combine automata-based and type-based abstraction refinement as an equivalence-based abstraction refinement, to take strengths of both approaches. We also proposed various optimizations to improve each step of the abstract-check-refine paradigm. Our improvements target on μHORS model checking but the ideas are applicable to improve the state-of-the-art model checker PREFACE for simply-typed HORS as well [14]. PREFACE is the model checker for HORS that first reported to scale to recursion schemes of several thousand rules. We expect that our approaches, such as enforcing expandable label pairs to reduce the size of an ACG, distinguishing abstract and concrete reductions in an ACG and working with an open configuration graph, etc., would be useful for further improving its scalability.

6 Conclusion

We have proposed systematic approaches to improve the runtime efficiency of the automata-based abstraction refinement procedure for μHORS model checking. First, our approach combines the existing work on automata-based and type-based abstraction refinement techniques for higher-order model checking [7,8,14]. Next, we propose techniques for improving each step of the abstract-check-refine paradigm explored by the procedure. The new model checking procedure preserves the soundness and relative completeness properties of the original automata-based procedure [8]. We have implemented the new procedure, and confirmed by empirical study on examples of μHORS that, it always outperforms the original μHORS model checker MUHORSAR, and successfully verified all benchmarks that were previously impossible. We are concerned with μHORS model checking but our approaches are applicable to the state-of-the-art model checker PREFACE for simply-typed HORS [14], and we expect our approaches would be useful for improving its scalability as well.

Acknowledgment. We would like to thank anonymous referees for useful comments. This work was supported by JSPS Kakenhi 15H05706.

References

1. Aehlig, K.: A finite semantics of simply-typed lambda terms for infinite runs of automata. Logical Methods Comput. Sci. **3**(3), 1–23 (2007)
2. Amadio, R.M., Cardelli, L.: Subtyping recursive types. ACM Trans. Program. Lang. Syst. **15**(4), 575–631 (1993)
3. Broadbent, C.H., Kobayashi, N.: Saturation-based model checking of higher-order recursion schemes. In: Rocca, S.R.D. (ed.) CSL 2013. LIPIcs, vol. 23, pp. 129–148. Schloss Dagstuhl - Leibniz-Zentrum fuer Informatik (2013)
4. Comon, H., Dauchet, M., Gilleron, R., Löding, C., Jacquemard, F., Lugiez, D., Tison, S., Tommasi, M.: Tree automata techniques and applications (2007). http://www.grappa.univ-lille3.fr/tata. Accessed 12 Oct 2007
5. Knapik, T., Niwiński, D., Urzyczyn, P.: Higher-order pushdown trees are easy. In: Nielsen, M., Engberg, U. (eds.) FOSSACS 2002. LNCS, vol. 2303, pp. 205–222. Springer, Heidelberg (2002)
6. Kobayashi, N.: Model checking higher-order programs. J. ACM **60**(3), 20 (2013)
7. Kobayashi, N., Igarashi, A.: Model-checking higher-order programs with recursive types. In: Felleisen, M., Gardner, P. (eds.) ESOP 2013. LNCS, vol. 7792, pp. 431–450. Springer, Heidelberg (2013)

8. Kobayashi, N., Li, X.: Automata-based abstraction refinement for μHORS model checking. In: Proceedings of LICS 2015, pp. 713–724. IEEE Computer Society (2015)
9. Kobayashi, N., Ong, C.H.L.: A type system equivalent to the modal mu-calculus model checking of higher-order recursion schemes. In: Proceedings of LICS 2009, pp. 179–188. IEEE Computer Society Press (2009)
10. Kobayashi, N., Sato, R., Unno, H.: Predicate abstraction and CEGAR for higher-order model checking. In: Hall, M.W., Padua, D.A. (eds.) PLDI 2011, pp. 222–233. ACM (2011)
11. Li, X., Kobayashi, N.: Equivalence-based abstraction refinement for μHORS model checking. Full version, available from the first author's web page (2016)
12. Ong, C.H.L.: On model-checking trees generated by higher-order recursion schemes. In: Proceedings of LICS 2006, pp. 81–90. IEEE Computer Society Press (2006)
13. Ong, C.H.L., Ramsay, S.: Verifying higher-order programs with pattern-matching algebraic data types. In: Ball, T., Sagiv, M. (eds.) POPL 2011, pp. 587–598. ACM Press (2011)
14. Ramsay, S., Neatherway, R., Ong, C.H.L.: An abstraction refinement approach to higher-order model checking. In: Jagannathan, S., Sewell, P. (eds.) POPL 2014. ACM (2014)

Optimization, Heuristics, Partial-Order Reductions

Greener Bits:
Formal Analysis of Demand Response

Christel Baier[1]($\boxtimes$), Sascha Klüppelholz[1]($\boxtimes$), Hermann de Meer[2]($\boxtimes$),
Florian Niedermeier[2]($\boxtimes$), and Sascha Wunderlich[1]($\boxtimes$)

[1] Technische Universität Dresden, Dresden, Germany
{baier,klueppel,wunder}@tcs.inf.tu-dresden.de
[2] University of Passau, Passau, Germany
{hermann.demeer,florian.niedermeier}@uni-passau.de

Abstract. Demand response is a promising approach to deal with the emerging power generation fluctuations introduced by the increasing amount of renewable energy sources fed into the grid. Consumers need to be able to adapt their energy consumption with respect to the given demand pattern and at the same time ensure that their adaptation (i.e., response) does not interfere with their various operational objectives. Finding, evaluating and verifying adaptation strategies which aim to be optimal w.r.t. multiple criteria is a challenging task and is currently mainly addressed by hand, heuristics or guided simulation. In this paper we carry out a case study of a demand response system with an energy adaptive data center on the consumer side for which we propose a formal model and perform a quantitative system analysis using probabilistic model checking. Our first contribution is a fine-grained formal model and the identification of significant properties and quantitative measures (e.g., expected energy consumption, average workload or total penalties for violating adaptation contracts) that are relevant for the data center as an adaptive consumer. The formal model can serve as a starting point for the application of different formal analysis methods. The second contribution is an evaluation of our approach using the prominent model checker PRISM. We report on the experimental results computing various functional properties and quantitative measures that yield important insights into the viability of given adaptation strategies and how to find close-to-optimal strategies.

1 Introduction

In modern society, a permanent and reliable availability of electrical power has become an indispensable good for many aspects of life. However, the continuously

The authors are supported by the DFG through the Collaborative Research Center SFB 912 – HAEC, the Excellence Initiative by the German Federal and State Governments (cluster of excellence cfAED and Institutional Strategy), the Research Training Groups QuantLA (GRK 1763) and RoSI (GRK 1907), and by the EU through the European Union's Seventh Framework Programme FP7 in the context of the DC4Cities project (grant agreement No. 609304).

© Springer International Publishing AG 2016
C. Artho et al. (Eds.): ATVA 2016, LNCS 9938, pp. 323–339, 2016.
DOI: 10.1007/978-3-319-46520-3_21

increasing demand for electrical energy comes at a price: guaranteeing stability under almost any load condition requires a constant adaptation of power generation to keep production and volatile demand in equilibrium. However, power plants capable of quickly adapting their power output to balance the grid are usually driven by fossil fuels and therefore carbon-intensive. From an environmental perspective, this is highly undesirable and an increased feed-in of renewable energy is encouraged. Energy sources like wind or solar are exhibiting volatile availability patterns and can therefore not provide the same balancing capabilities as fossil fuel based power plants. A promising approach to cope with these shortcomings is demand response (DR) exerting control over power demand on the consumer side. DR is widely recognized as a promising approach to reduce the costs for mitigating operational instability of power grids when incorporating renewable energy sources, but standardization is still underway [5]. Many recent works focus on the design of DR-programs that define the communication protocol between power producers and power consumers. Current DR-programs can be classified into three categories: price-based, incentive-/event-based and demand reduction bids (see, e.g., [29]).

For participants in a DR-system to be a valuable asset to a distribution system operator, the adaptation to a DR-request needs to be enacted reliably. At the same time, the respective participant needs to ensure the power adaptation does not interfere with operational objectives. The quantitative impact of a DR-interaction on power demand and operational performance on the consumer side needs to be foreseeable and is well suited for analysis via formal methods, as it may impact critical processes on both power grid and consumer side. Data centers are particularly well-suited for participation in DR as they consume large amounts of energy and provide many opportunities in dynamically adapting to external demands by applying advanced resource and workload management strategies. Data center DR-systems have been considered from several perspectives, e.g., pricing [22,31], implementation [10], communication [6], and contract design [7]. Working prototypes of DR-systems for data centers were implemented in EU FP7 projects ALL4Green [6] and DC4Cities [20,25], where the latter focuses on the possibility of continuously adapting to a given power plan.

Despite wide recognition of the potential of DR, data centers are currently hardly participating in DR, mainly due to the fact that the design of efficient adaptation strategies is a non-trivial task. The goal of this paper is to show that formal methods can contribute to this task, e.g., by providing guarantees on cost/utility requirements in worst-case scenarios and by evaluating existing resource management strategies to gain insights for the design of efficient scheduling strategies.

Contribution. In this paper we provide a detailed formal model for DR-systems with data centers on the consumer side. The model is compositional and uses Markov decision processes (MDPs) equipped with reward functions to capture various quantitative measures. The choices in the MDP stand for the possible workload scheduling. The base model consists of components for the data center, a request generator, the service load, and a component for green energy forecast. For the sake of simplicity we assume a simple incentive-based DR-program and present possible extensions that allow for addressing alternative and more complex DR-scenarios by refining the components of the base model. For the analysis we use probabilistic model checking (PMC) to compute minimal and maximal probabilities and expectations that provide guarantees in worst-case scenarios as well as insights for the design of efficient scheduling strategies maximizing or minimizing various performance and costs objectives. The class of considered measures subsumes conventional cost-/utility indices important for DR-systems (e.g., *Power Usage Efficiency* (PUE) [28], and *Energy-Response Time Product* (ERP) [15]). We illustrate the feasibility of the modeling and analysis approach in experimental studies on the base model and report here on the scalability and insights gained in the process. The experiments were carried out using extensions of the prominent probabilistic model checker PRISM [21].

Related Work. We are not aware of any work describing a quantitative analysis of DR-systems using PMC. Currently, load adjustment in data centers under DR-programs is usually not formally modeled or analyzed. Planning and verification in power grids is often performed via special simulators (e.g., PowerWorld Simulator [18]). However, these are mostly used for strategic decisions on power grid development in the long term or to find solutions to the question which electrical loads to shed in an emergency (see, e.g., [9,16,23]). The latter problem is closely related to demand response, however loads are assigned priorities and decisions on power generation side are made only in case of emergencies. Other existing work focuses on coordination between different energy sources (e.g., [30]) with the goal to optimize a performance index such as PUE or ERP. Solutions are found by solving equality constrained optimization problems or mixed integer linear programs and then evaluated using simulation of large real-world workload traces and current energy prices (e.g., [11,30,31]). Other formal approaches in the context of DR address, e.g., the stability of a given Markov model [8] or provide uncertainty models in which Markov chains are combined with additional random transition matrices [24]. Model checking and in particular PMC has been applied to related problems, e.g., for energy-aware task scheduling [17] and dynamic power management [26], but also for controller synthesis (e.g., [13]).

2   Scenario

Especially in future smart grid scenarios, in which high amounts of renewable power generation are to be expected, both events of energy surplus and scarcity have to be considered as the controllability of many renewable sources is very limited. Therefore, demand response requests (DR-requests) are considered as a mechanism to trigger increasing or decreasing power demands. In this work, we visit a demand response scenario, in which an energy management authority is creating DR-requests for power adaptation in order to influence the power demand on consumer side. In the following, we will assume a demand response request to contain (1) the start and the end of the adaptation time-interval and (2) a target power demand range during this time period.

A DR-request may arrive at the consumer side at any point in time (typically probabilities are non-uniformly distributed). Failing to adhere to the power bounds during the demand response interval will cause a penalty. Figure 1 shows the high level interaction diagram in the assumed DR-system.

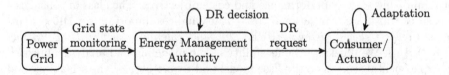

Fig. 1. High level DR-system overview.

Consumer Side. On the consumer side, we assume that parts of the load can be shifted for a certain time. For simplicity we assume that processing workload causes a proportional increase in the power demand. In general, one needs to be aware of the correlation between workload and the corresponding power demand, which is in turn directly influenced by the (re)scheduling of workload. To reliably reach the power demand requested in the DR-request workload has to be rescheduled in such a way as to reach target power demand, while at the same time ensuring, e.g., that all work is scheduled until a given deadline. Here, we assume that all workload has to be processed until the end of a day. Failing to schedule workload until the deadline will result in a (load-specific) penalty. Apart from work which can be rescheduled (batch load), we assume that certain work (service load) has to be immediately processed. The fraction of workload to be processed immediately is assumed to be varying in time, however always less than the total load capacity. This type of workload can neither be rescheduled nor canceled. Figure 2 shows an example of the rescheduling process.

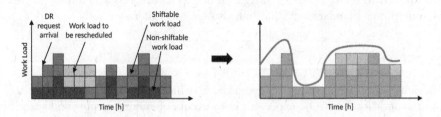

Fig. 2. Example adaptation of a flexible load.

Additionally, we assume that - in line with our future smart grid setting - the consumer side is equipped with local renewable energy generation capabilities (e.g., small wind turbine or solar panels). The power generated at different points in time can be forecasted by utilizing weather data and/or information on historical generation. However, due to possible fluctuation (e.g., solar radiation on cloudy days), forecasting errors are common and will cause deviations of actual generation from the forecast values.

Objectives. Generally, objectives may fall into one of the following categories. One can either optimize cost or utility measures (1) on the consumer side, (2) on the energy management authority side, or (3) on both sides given certain additional constraints. In this paper we focus on the consumer side, but the methods are also applicable for optimization on the energy management authority side and mixtures thereof.

Data Centers. A specific use case of demand response are data centers. Participation of data centers within demand response systems is highly attractive, as they have automation frameworks already in place, making automated processing of demand response requests possible. Additionally, data centers consume large amounts of electrical energy and therefore are well suited to create a significant impact when adapting their power demand. We assume data centers to process two basic types of load: interactive and batch. Interactive load is characterized by service level agreements which require strict bounds on response time for users to have a high quality of experience. Therefore interactive load cannot be rescheduled and has to be processed immediately. Typical examples include web servers, stock traders and virtualized desktop environments. In contrast, batch load may be processed at any time while completing before its deadline. Batch jobs may therefore be arranged in a way as to adapt data center power demand according to demand response requests.

3   Theoretical Foundations

Throughout the paper, we assume the reader is familiar with Markovian models. A brief summary of the relevant concepts for Markov decision processes is provided below. For more details, we refer to, e.g., [27].

Markov Decision Processes. An MDP is a tuple $\mathcal{M} = (S, \mathrm{Act}, P, \mathrm{AP}, \mathsf{L})$, with a finite set of states S, a finite set of actions Act, transition probabilities $P : S \times \mathrm{Act} \times S \to [0, 1]$, a finite set of atomic propositions AP and a labeling function $\mathsf{L} : S \to 2^{\mathrm{AP}}$. We require that the values $P(s, \alpha, s')$ are rational and $\sum_{s' \in S} P(s, \alpha, s') \in \{0, 1\}$ for all states $s \in S$ and actions $\alpha \in \mathrm{Act}$. The triples (s, α, s') with $P(s, \alpha, s') > 0$ are called *transitions*. Action α is said to be *enabled* in state s if $P(s, \alpha, s') > 0$ for some state s'. Act(s) denotes the set of actions that are enabled in $s \in S$. To avoid terminal behaviors, we require that Act$(s) \neq \varnothing$ for all states s. Paths in an MDP $\mathcal{M}$ can be seen as sample runs. Formally, they are finite or infinite sequences where states and actions alternate, i.e., $\pi = s_0 \alpha_0 s_1 \alpha_1 \ldots \in (S \times \mathrm{Act})^* S \cup (S \times \mathrm{Act})^\omega$ with $\alpha_i \in \mathrm{Act}(s_i)$ and $P(s_i, \alpha_i, s_{i+1}) > 0$ for all i. In the following, we assume that an initial state s is given. For a path property ϕ, we write $\mathrm{Pr}_{\mathcal{M}}^{\sigma}(\phi)$ for the probability of ϕ in $\mathcal{M}$ under scheduler σ. Additionally, we write $\mathrm{Pr}_{\mathcal{M}}^{\min}(\phi)$ and $\mathrm{Pr}_{\mathcal{M}}^{\max}(\phi)$ for the minimal and maximal probabilities for ϕ among all schedulers σ. In case the action set Act is a singleton it can be omitted, since the behavior is then completely deterministic and the MDP degenerates to a Markov chain (MC).

Reward Functions. A reward function rew : $S \times$ Act $\rightarrow \mathbb{N}$, annotates state-action pairs with a natural number. Each reward function can be lifted to assign to each finite path its accumulated value $\text{rew}(s_0 \alpha_0 s_1 \alpha_1 \dots s_n \alpha_n) = \sum_{i=0}^{n-1} \text{rew}(s_i, \alpha_i)$. For a set of states G and a scheduler σ such that $\text{Pr}_{\mathcal{M}}^{\sigma}(\Diamond G) = 1$ we can then introduce the expected reward until reaching G. To define the expected reward, we let P_G^r be the set of paths $\pi = s_0 \alpha_0 s_1 \dots$ such that there exists an $n \in \mathbb{N}$ with $s_n \in G$, $s_i \notin G$ for all $i < n$ and $\text{rew}(s_0 \dots s_n) = r$. Then $\text{Ex}_{\mathcal{M}}^{\sigma}[\text{rew}](\Diamond G) = \sum_{r=0}^{\infty} r \cdot \text{Pr}_{\mathcal{M}}^{\sigma}(P_G^r)$. As before we define the extremal expectations $\text{Ex}_{\mathcal{M}}^{\min}$ and $\text{Ex}_{\mathcal{M}}^{\max}$ for minimizing and maximizing schedulers.

4 Formal Model

In this section we present an MDP-based compositional model for demand response formalized for the use case of a data center. As described in Sect. 2 the scenario consists of the data center on the consumer side and an energy authority sending DR-requests. The data center needs to schedule batch work and interactive work, it reacts to DR-requests and can have additional green energy sources available. In our model those influences are formalized using stochastic distributions and the nondeterministic choices within the data center constitute an MDP model that yields the basis for further formal analysis. Based on this setting, the goal is to find appropriate adaptation strategies (i.e., resolving the nondeterminism in the MDP) that optimize for various cost/utility objectives, as introduced later in this section.

In our model we fix the number of batch work jobs $J_0 \in \mathbb{N}$ that the data center can schedule over one day, as well as a number $T \in \mathbb{N}$ of discrete time steps into which the day is divided, which can be seen as the resolution of the time domain. At every time point the data center can decide which batch work should be scheduled next. The maximal number of simultaneous jobs is fixed as capacity $\in \mathbb{N}$. The data center's scheduling decision is influenced by the amount of interactive work (service load), the available energy and the received DR-requests from the energy authority, which can arrive at any time. In the base model it is assumed that requests can not be refused. Furthermore, all jobs and services are already in the shape of an independent *least schedulable unit (LSU)*, i.e., work packages which cannot be interrupted, have no dependencies and require one energy unit over its lifetime.

The model is equipped with simple reward functions to capture the amount of green energy that was produced, the amount of brown energy that had to be bought, the number of time steps, and penalties for violating DR-requests. For the latter, rather simple functions are used, but in general one could use arbitrary complex functions to capture penalties.

4.1   Component Model

The base model consists of the following four components, each represented as individual Markov chains or MDPs: stochastic service load and DR-request generators $\mathcal{M}_{serv}$ and $\mathcal{M}_{req}$, a green-energy forecast $\mathcal{M}_{fc}$ and the data center itself $\mathcal{M}_{dc}$. From those components one large MDP is then composed for the composite model, i.e., $\mathcal{M} = \mathcal{M}_{serv} \otimes \mathcal{M}_{fc} \otimes \mathcal{M}_{req} \otimes \mathcal{M}_{dc}$.

The compositional modeling approach allows to easily generate variants, e.g., with less, more or other participants and hence it facilitates the maintainability of the model. In Sect. 4.2 we will discuss some possible refinements and extensions of our base model. We now consider the details of the four base components.

$\mathcal{M}_{serv}$ - **Service Load Generator.** The service load of a data center is assumed to be stochastically distributed. For any point in time $t \in \{ 0, 1, \ldots, T \}$ a random variable $\mathsf{service}(t) \in \{ 0, 1, \ldots, \mathsf{capacity} \}$ is given, signifying the number of interactive jobs to be executed at time t. From this, a Markov chain $\mathcal{M}_{serv}$ can be derived, with states of the form (t, c) for $c = \mathsf{service}(t)$. The probability of a transition $(t, c) \to (t + 1, c')$ in $\mathcal{M}_{serv}$ is the probability of $\mathsf{service}(t + 1)(c')$.

$\mathcal{M}_{fc}$ - **Green-Energy Forecast.** To reflect the probabilistic green-energy production, another random variable $\mathsf{produce}(t) \in \{ 0, 1, \ldots, \mathsf{prodmax} \}$ is introduced for each point in time $t \in \{ 0, 1, \ldots, T \}$. Intuitively, this variable represents the possible energy production values at time t, which may depend on the weather, season or time of day. Similar to the service load, a Markov chain $\mathcal{M}_{fc}$ with states (t, e) for $e = \mathsf{produce}(t)$ can be derived. The probability for $(t, e) \to (t + 1, e')$ is the probability of $\mathsf{produce}(t + 1)(e')$.

$\mathcal{M}_{req}$ - **Request Generator.** We are given statistical information on the arrival of DR-requests and their format. A DR-request arriving at some time point t with rate $r \in [0, 1]$ is represented by a triple (I, l, u) with a discrete time interval $I \subseteq [t, T]$ and lower and upper resource bounds $l, u \in \mathbb{N}$ such that $0 \leq l \leq u \leq \mathsf{capacity}$. Intuitively, a DR-request (I, l, u) signifies that at each time point $t \in I$ the resource requirements should be between l and u. Hence, the number of jobs executed at time t should be in that interval. A single DR-request $R_i = ([t_1, t_2], l, u)$ can be modeled as a degenerated Markov chain (i.e., all probabilities are 1) $\mathcal{A}_i$ as follows:

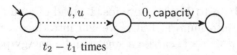

The request generator then has an initial state with outgoing transitions to each DR-request R_i with probability r_i and a self-loop with probability $1 - \sum_{i=0}^{n} r_i$.

$\mathcal{M}_{dc}$ - **Data Center.** The data center keeps track of the current time step value $t \in \{ 0, 1, \ldots, T \}$ and the number J of jobs that are still to be processed. Initially at time point $t = 0$, $J = J_0$ and J will decrease until either $J = 0$ or the day is over, i.e., $t = T$. At each point in time, the data center can choose to schedule a number $j \leq \min\{\, J, \mathsf{capacity}\,\}$ of jobs. These choices are modeled nondeterministically. Whether or not the action of choosing j jobs at time point t will be enabled depends on the produced service load $\mathsf{service}(t)$. Hence, the enabled actions in the composite model $\mathcal{M}$ will be the following. Let $s = (t, c, e, l, u, J)$ be a state of $\mathcal{M}$. Then, the action of choosing $j \in \mathbb{N}$ jobs should be enabled in $\mathcal{M}$ iff $c + j \leq \min\{\, J, \mathsf{capacity}\,\}$, i.e., iff the interactive load plus the number of scheduled jobs is not larger than the capacity and enough jobs are still available.

Penalties and Other Reward Functions. For modeling the costs of violating a DR-request at time t we introduce a reward function $\mathsf{penalty}$. The penalty to be paid in state $s = (t, c, e, l, u, J)$ of $\mathcal{M}$ when scheduling $j \in \mathbb{N}$ jobs is defined as

$$\mathsf{penalty}(s, j) = \mathsf{lpenalty}(s, j) + \mathsf{upenalty}(s, j)$$

i.e., the sum of a penalty for violating the lower or upper bound given as two separate reward functions defined as follows:

$$\mathsf{lpenalty}(s, j) = \max\{\, c + j - l, 0\,\} \qquad \mathsf{upenalty}(s, j) = \max\{\, u - c - j, 0\,\}$$

for state is $s = (t, c, e, l, u, J)$ in $\mathcal{M}$. In general, the penalty function (and other cost/utility functions) can be nearly any complex arithmetic expression over variables in the model. In particular, the reward functions do not affect the state space of $\mathcal{M}$ and hence do not contribute to the complexity of the model.

Besides the reward function for penalties we introduce reward functions that can then be used inside formulas for various objectives as detailed in Sect. 4.3. Specifically, we use #steps, #jobs and #requests for the number of time steps, finished jobs and accepted DR requests. The latter is only relevant in the model variants where the data center can refuse incoming DR-requests. Furthermore, green signifies the produced green energy and brown the bought grid energy.

4.2 Model Variants

In the following we introduce several variants which allow modifying the scenario to be considered by replacing components of the compositional model. More variants can be found in the extended version [4].

Heterogenous Jobs and Dependencies. Instead of assuming that every job can be decomposed into uniform LSUs, we can introduce a more general case. There, each job $j \in J \subseteq \mathbb{N} \times \mathbb{N}$ carries a length and a energy-per-time-unit value. The data center component is then more complicated. Intuitively, each state in $\mathcal{M}_{\mathsf{dc}}$ now carries two pieces of information: a set W of jobs currently worked on and a set O of jobs which are still pending. The energy consumed in a state is the sum of the energy-per-time-unit values of the jobs in its working set W. Outgoing transitions of a state s in $\mathcal{M}_{\mathsf{dc}}$ are then labeled by a subset $A \subseteq O$ of open jobs and lead to a state s', in which A becomes the set of jobs currently worked on and $O \setminus A$ becomes the new set of open jobs. To allow dependencies among jobs, they are partially ordered in a set $(J, \leq)$ where $j_1 \leq j_2$ if j_1 has to be completed before j_2 can be scheduled. This variant introduces a combinatorial blowup in the data center component and hence the composed model.

Hard Limits. It is possible to represent hard limits on the DR-requests, i.e., for a request (I, l, u) to disallow using less energy than l or more energy than u while the request is active. This can be modeled by modifying the enabled actions of $\mathcal{M}$ as follows. In a state $s = (t, c, l, u, J)$, the action j is enabled iff $c + j \leq \min\{ J, \mathsf{capacity} \}$ as before and additionally $l \leq c + j \leq u$ must hold.

Accepting and Refusing DR-Requests. Instead of forcing DR-request, we may equip the data center with additional non-deterministic choices for accepting or refusing DR-requests. Adaptation strategies for the data center may then refuse a DR-request by not scheduling the corresponding action. In this setting additional reward functions are of interest, e.g., a reward function for tracking the bounties for accepted DR-requests.

Adding an Adaptation Strategy. Another important variant allows for analyzing specific adaptation strategies. This way, a consumer can formally evaluate currently implemented strategies with respect to various objectives. This amounts to adding a (possibly randomized) scheduler that resolves the non-deterministic choices in $\mathcal{M}_{\mathsf{dc}}$, resulting in a Markov chain $\mathcal{M}'$. One can then compare the results for $\mathcal{M}'$ with theoretically optimal strategies in $\mathcal{M}$ w.r.t. a given objective.

Multiple Data Centers and Different DR-Protocols. It is possible to introduce copies and variants of $\mathcal{M}_{\mathsf{dc}}$ to model multiple data centers. DR-protocols which do not require interaction between the energy authority and the data center like incentive-based and price-based ones can be modeled by modifying the enabled actions or by introducing further reward functions.

4.3 Objectives

In this section we introduce different kinds of evaluation criteria that are important in the given setting, in particular for optimizing various cost and performance measures. We illustrate their relevance for demand response with example objectives formulated for the data center scenario. For the formulas, we use the usual temporal operators $\Diamond$ (eventually) and $\Box$ (always).

The first class of objectives is concerned with the confidence in our model. Model checking of such purely functional properties can be applied in addition to, e.g., simulation of the model. Typically, one is concerned with whether the minimal or maximal probability of certain temporal events is either zero or one, or with probabilities and expected values for costs/utility being within reasonable bounds. We present here a few examples that can be computed using standard PMC-methods. E.g., to search for unintended deadlocks, one can check whether the minimal probability of reaching the end of the day (eod) is one, as then no scheduler can avoid reaching the end of the day.

$$\mathrm{Pr}_{\mathcal{M}}^{\min}(\Diamond \, \mathsf{eod}) = 1 \tag{1}$$

The above formula can be enriched, e.g., with a step bound, to ensure that the end of the day will be reached within the desired number of steps.

$$\mathrm{Pr}_{\mathcal{M}}^{\min}(\Diamond^{\#\mathrm{steps}=T}\ \mathsf{eod}) = 1 \tag{2}$$

It is also of interest to compute the probability to finish all jobs using an optimal scheduler and to check whether the result is within reasonable boundaries.

$$\mathrm{Pr}_{\mathcal{M}}^{\max}(\Diamond\,(J = 0)) \tag{3}$$

Furthermore, the maximal probability for surviving the day without using brown energy (and to complete all jobs) is significant, although in general very low.

$$\mathrm{Pr}_{\mathcal{M}}^{\max}(\Box\ \mathsf{green\_only}) \tag{4}$$
$$\mathrm{Pr}_{\mathcal{M}}^{\max}(\Box\ \mathsf{green\_only} \wedge \Diamond\,(J = 0)) \tag{5}$$

The atomic proposition green_only signifies that no brown energy was used.

The second important class of objectives concerns the optimization of a single quantitative measure addressing either cost or utility, both either from the consumer perspective or the energy authority perspective. Within this class of properties we cannot address trade-offs. As utility measures one could, for example, compute the probability for finishing at least $n \in \mathbb{N}$ jobs by the end of the day, or the expected numbers of jobs that could be finished by the end of the day assuming optimal schedulers.

$$\mathrm{Pr}_{\mathcal{M}}^{\max}(\Diamond^{\#\mathrm{jobs}\geq n}\ \mathsf{eod}) \tag{6}$$

$$\mathrm{Ex}_{\mathcal{M}}^{\max}[\#\mathsf{jobs}](\Diamond\,\mathsf{eod}) \tag{7}$$

On the cost side there is, e.g., the probability of surviving the day when the amount of brown energy used is bounded by $n \in \mathbb{N}$, or the minimal and maximal expected penalty when a DR-request was not fulfilled either until the end of the day or until all jobs are done.

$$\mathrm{Pr}_{\mathcal{M}}^{\max}(\Diamond^{\mathrm{brown}\leq n}\ \mathsf{eod}) \tag{8}$$
$$\mathrm{Ex}_{\mathcal{M}}^{\max}[\mathsf{penalty}]\,(\Diamond\,\mathsf{eod}) \tag{9}$$
$$\mathrm{Ex}_{\mathcal{M}}^{\min}[\mathsf{penalty}]\,(\Diamond\,\mathsf{eod}) \tag{10}$$
$$\mathrm{Ex}_{\mathcal{M}}^{\max}[\mathsf{penalty}]\,(\Diamond\,(J = 0)) \tag{11}$$
$$\mathrm{Ex}_{\mathcal{M}}^{\min}[\mathsf{penalty}]\,(\Diamond\,(J = 0)) \tag{12}$$

Another important cost measure is the minimal and maximal expected time (number of steps) until all jobs are done or the end of the day has been reached.

$$\mathrm{Ex}_{\mathcal{M}}^{\min}[\#\mathsf{steps}]\,(\Diamond((J = 0) \vee \mathsf{eod})) \tag{13}$$
$$\mathrm{Ex}_{\mathcal{M}}^{\max}[\#\mathsf{steps}]\,(\Diamond((J = 0) \vee \mathsf{eod})) \tag{14}$$

Considering utility and cost measures, one is typically interested in their trade-off, ideally (although impossible) for maximizing the utility and minimizing the cost at the same time. In the following we will consider quantiles and conditional probabilities as important instances of this class and illustrate their relevance in the demand response setting again with a few examples.

Quantile queries ask for the maximal or minimal value of a variable such that the probability threshold for a property is still within a defined range. They can be computed by the techniques in [1]. Interesting quantiles are, e.g., the maximum number of jobs that can be finished within one day with probability at least $p \in (0, 1)$ or the maximum number of DR-requests that can be accepted such that the probability of finishing all jobs by the end of the day is sufficiently high. An analogous quantile can be formulated considering the minimal penalty rather than the maximum number of DR-requests.

$$\max\{\, j \in \mathbb{N} : \mathrm{Pr}_{\mathcal{M}}^{\max}(\lozenge^{\#\mathsf{jobs} \geq j} \; \mathsf{eod}) \geq p \,\} \tag{15}$$

$$\max\{\, r \in \mathbb{N} : \mathrm{Pr}_{\mathcal{M}}^{\max}(\lozenge^{\#\mathsf{requests} < r} \; (J = 0)) > p \,\} \tag{16}$$

$$\min\{\, y \in \mathbb{N} : \mathrm{Pr}_{\mathcal{M}}^{\max}(\lozenge^{\mathsf{penalty} \leq y} \; (J = 0)) > p \,\} \tag{17}$$

An alternative way of combining multiple simple measures are conditional probabilities in which one measure serves as condition and another serves as the objective of interest. They can be solved using the techniques in [2].

$$\mathrm{Pr}_{\mathcal{M}}^{\max}(\square \, \mathsf{green\_only} \mid \lozenge \, (J = 0)) \tag{18}$$

$$\mathrm{Pr}_{\mathcal{M}}^{\max}(\lozenge \, (J = 0) \mid \square \, \mathsf{green\_only}) \tag{19}$$

This formula queries the maximum probability for consuming green energy only given the condition that all jobs will be finished eventually. In Formula (19) the roles of the objective of interest and the condition are swapped. The following are formulas conditional versions of Formulas (8) and (6).

$$\mathrm{Pr}_{\mathcal{M}}^{\max}(\lozenge^{\mathsf{brown} \leq n} \; \mathsf{eod} \mid \square \, (J > 0)) \qquad \mathrm{Pr}_{\mathcal{M}}^{\max}(\lozenge^{\#\mathsf{jobs} \geq n} \; \mathsf{eod} \mid \square \, \mathsf{green\_only})$$

Additional Objectives. While the above values can be computed with standard PMC-techniques, the following objectives require special PMC-algorithms.

A simple objective is to finish all queued jobs with minimal expected accumulated penalty. Formally, one wants to find a scheduler σ for $\mathcal{M}$ such that $\mathrm{Pr}_{\mathcal{M}}^{\sigma}(\lozenge \, (J = 0)) = 1$ and the expected accumulated penalty is minimal among all schedulers τ with $\mathrm{Pr}_{\mathcal{M}}^{\tau}(\lozenge \, (J = 0)) = 1$. This task can be solved by the techniques in [14]. Another example objective for which no PMC-methods are available so far is to find the minimal q and a scheduler σ such that $\mathrm{Pr}_{\mathcal{M}}^{\sigma}(\lozenge \, (J = 0)) = 1$ and the penalty is at most q in each step, i.e., $\mathrm{Pr}_{\mathcal{M}}^{\sigma}(\square(\mathsf{penalty} \leq q) \wedge \lozenge \, (J = 0))$. To solve this, we first assign the minimal value $q_0(s)$ to each state such that there is a path originating in s which has at most $q_0(s)$ penalty in each step and reaches $(J = 0)$, i.e., $s \models \exists(\mathsf{penalty} \leq q_0(s) \, \mathrm{U} \, (J = 0))$, which can be calculated by a modified version of Dijkstra's algorithm in polynomial time. The series $(q_i(s))_{i \in \mathbb{N}}$ with $q_{i+1} = \min_{\alpha \in \mathrm{Act}(s)}\{\, \mathsf{penalty}(s, \alpha) + \max_{s', P(s, \alpha, s') > 0} q_i(s') \,\}$ then converges to a value $q(s)$ which is the minimal value q in question. Note that in an acyclic MDP as given here, there is actually no iteration necessary and the value q can be calculated directly via back-propagation from the terminal states, i.e., the states with $(J = 0)$.

Further objectives based on the accumulation techniques in [3] can be found in [4]. Among others, the common index Power Usage Efficiency (PUE) can be expressed by them.

5   Experiments

We used the tool ProFeat [12] for specifying a parameterized version of the base model as described in Sect. 4. ProFeat is then used for creating the relevant instances for fixed parameter sets. Throughout this section we will report on three instances as shown in Table 1a.

Table 1. Considered instances of models, formulas and requests.

(a) Model and formula instances

	time T	jobs J_0	n in Form.(6)	n in Form.(8)
$\mathcal{M}_{24}$	24	60	40	6
$\mathcal{M}_{48}$	48	120	80	12
$\mathcal{M}_{96}$	96	240	160	24

(b) Requests

	shape	probability
R_0	no request	0.7
R_1	$([t, t+2], 0, 2)$	0.12
R_2	$([t, t+2], 2, 4)$	0.18

With its parameters, $\mathcal{M}_{24}$ can be thought of as having a time resolution of one hour steps over one day. Similarly, $\mathcal{M}_{96}$ has a time resolution of 15 min. The capacity and the maximal production of green energy are fixed to 4 for all instances. We considered here two possible DR-requests with time-independent distribution as shown in Table 1b. The probability distributions for the service load are modeled in a time-independent fashion and are given by binomial distributions with a trail success probability of 0.4. The probability distributions for the load are time-dependent and pre-generated with random values. Table 2 shows the number of reachable states in the MDP for the three instances.

The model instances generated by ProFeat are in the input format of the prominent probabilistic model checker PRISM [21]. We used PRISM's symbolic engine, which uses multi-terminal binary decision diagrams (MTBDDs) for representing MDPs. As the size of MTBDDs crucially depends on the order in which variables occur in the MTBDD, we applied the reordering techniques described in [19] to end up with more compact model representations. This step was very effective, as the number of MTBDD nodes and hence the memory consumption could be reduced by up to 95 %. This is reflected in Table 2 where the number of MTBDD nodes before and after reordering and the time for reordering is depicted. For the analysis we used the development version of PRISM 4.3 with

additional implementations of the algorithms for computing conditional probabilities and quantiles. For the entire result section we used $\varepsilon = 10^{-4}$ (absolute
values) for the convergence check of the numerical methods. Our experiments
were run on a machine with an Intel Xeon E5-2680 CPU with 16 physical cores
clocked at 2.7 GHz. The symbolic engine never exceeded the 1 GB memory limit.
The models together with the tools are available with the extended version [4]
under https://wwwtcs.inf.tu-dresden.de/ALGI/PUB/ATVA16/.

5.1   Results

Table 2 shows the sizes of the generated models and the time for composing the
model. It can be seen that our model scales well with increasing time resolution.
A general overview of the model checking results is given in Table 3. It shows the
result for each numbered non-quantile query in Sect. 4.3 and the time it took to
process it. Again, we can see that the model checking times scale well with the
time resolution of the model. Even for 96 time steps the model checking times
are acceptable. Formulas 1–5 show that the basic confidence in our model is
high. There are no deadlock states as can be seen in Formulas 1 and 2, i.e., the
time always progresses to its final value. The probability to globally use green
energy only is very low (Formula 4) and even lower when we are trying to finish
all jobs (Formula 5), which is to be expected in this scenario. Similarly, the
maximal probability for finishing all jobs in time (Formula 3) is smaller than 1
but positive which is expected under the given parameters. The value decreases
with increasing model size due to the fixed capacity of 4 in each model instance
even though the proportion between time and jobs stays the same.

Table 2. Model sizes and build times.

	Reachable states	Transitions	BDD nodes	Reordered	Reorder time	Build time
$\mathcal{M}_{24}$	931401	18947025	327320	31609	3.472 s	0.23 s
$\mathcal{M}_{48}$	3841426	81269400	551716	39203	6.863 s	0.27 s
$\mathcal{M}_{96}$	15546726	338279825	1014437	59686	15.000 s	0.95 s

The results for the Formulas 6–14 describe optimal values for single measures
in the system. The probability for finishing two thirds of the total job pool (see
Table 1a) is very high as can be seen in Formula 6. Accordingly, the expected
number of finished jobs at the end of the day as seen in Formula 7 is close to
the maximum. Formula 8 gives the probability to survive using at most 1/4
brown energy units on average per time step, which is almost impossible in
the given setting. The expected total penalty until the end of the day is given
in the Formulas 9 (maximal) and 10 (minimal). While the minimal penalty
is low but non-zero, the maximal penalty is almost 1/2 units on average per
two time step. The minimal penalty can be achieved by never scheduling any
jobs. The expected total penalties until finishing all jobs is however infinite (see

Table 3. PMC-results (see Sect. 5.1).

Formula	24 steps/60 jobs		48 steps/120 jobs		96 steps/240 jobs	
	Result	Time	Result	Time	Result	Time
(1)	true	0.1 s	true	0.0 s	true	0.1 s
(2)	true	0.4 s	true	0.2 s	true	0.7 s
(3)	0.543	31.5 s	0.392	104.2 s	0.244	748.4 s
(4)	$1*10^{-4}$	1.7 s	$7*10^{-5}$	2.4 s	$5*10^{-5}$	6.8 s
(5)	0	3.8 s	0	0.9 s	0	2.3 s
(6)	0.999	25.9 s	0.999	128.9 s	0.999	1062.8 s
(7)	56.66	52.5 s	114.252	68.2 s	229.610	569.8 s
(8)	0.059	5.4 s	0.012	25.0 s	6.10^{-4}	244.5 s
(9)	12.737	26.0 s	25.617	27.7 s	51.380	239.3 s
(10)	0.897	1.3 s	1.805	31.8 s	3.620	275.5 s
(11)	∞	0.0 s	∞	0.0 s	∞	0.0 s
(12)	∞	0.6 s	∞	1.3 s	∞	9.3 s
(13)	23.376	3.5 s	47.431	19.9 s	95.559	421.8 s
(14)	23.999	0.4 s	48.000	0.7 s	95.999	4.1 s
(18)	1.0	51.7 s	1.0	111.0 s	1.0	317.5 s
(19)	1.0	81.9 s	1.0	121.6 s	1.0	292.9 s

Formulas 11 and 12) since it is not guaranteed that all jobs will be finished (see Formula 3). Formulas 13 and 14 give the expected number of time steps until all jobs are finished or time runs out. The reason for these numbers being so close to the maximal number of time steps is that the job pool size is very close to the expected number of jobs to be finished (see Formula 7). Figure 3 shows quantile values for a variant of $\mathcal{M}_{24}$ with 120 initial jobs. Figure 3b shows the maximal probabilities for finishing a certain number of jobs until the end of the day. As expected, the probability is decreasing with higher job requirements and drops around the expected number of jobs calculated in Formula 7. The maximal probabilites for finishing all jobs with a given penalty bound is shown in Fig. 3a. Probabilities of at least 0.6 cannot be reached, independent of the penalty bound. This is immediately obvious from the results of Formula 3. The calculated quantile values are also useful for protocol design, since they give optimal parameters for jobs and penalties while retaining guarantees on the system reliability. A detailed overview of the quantile values for Formulas 15 and 17 can be found in [4]. The conditional probabilities for Formulas 18 and 19 are always 1. Intuitively, a maximizing scheduler for Formula 18 can try to work as many jobs as possible with green energy and can choose not to schedule any jobs anymore as soon as brown energy needs to be used. On the other hand, a scheduler for Formula 19 can start using brown energy as soon as the jobs cannot be finished anymore.

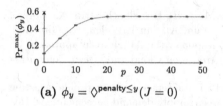

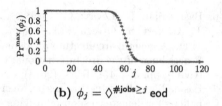

(a) $\phi_y = \Diamond^{\mathsf{penalty} \leq y}(J = 0)$

(b) $\phi_j = \Diamond^{\#\mathsf{jobs} \geq j} \mathsf{eod}$

Fig. 3. Probability values for ϕ_y and ϕ_j.

6   Conclusion

The purpose of the paper was to show the general feasibility of probabilistic model checking techniques for the analysis of demand-response systems. We provided a compositional model with components for the service load, the green-energy forecast, a request generator and an abstract model for the data center. Each components can easily be adapted and refined. We identified a series of important functional properties and performance measures that can serve as evaluation criteria for different strategies for scheduling jobs and provide useful insights for the design and refinement of the energy-aware workload management in data centers. The report on the experimental studies carried out with the model checker PRISM shows that several performance measures relevant to real systems are computable in reasonable time frames, up to a time resolution of 15 min. At the same time, this scenario can be seen as a stress test for the calculation of quantile values, in which the reordering techniques of [19] were crucial. Future work will include the consideration of variants of the model as discussed in Sect. 4 for different DR protocols with distributions that are derived from a real-world data center.

References

1. Baier, C., Daum, M., Dubslaff, C., Klein, J., Klüppelholz, S.: Energy-utility quantiles. In: Badger, J.M., Rozier, K.Y. (eds.) NFM 2014. LNCS, vol. 8430, pp. 285–299. Springer, Heidelberg (2014)
2. Baier, C., Klein, J., Klüppelholz, S., Märcker, S.: Computing conditional probabilities in Markovian models efficiently. In: Ábrahám, E., Havelund, K. (eds.) TACAS 2014 (ETAPS). LNCS, vol. 8413, pp. 515–530. Springer, Heidelberg (2014)
3. Baier, C., Klein, J., Klüppelholz, S., Wunderlich, S.: Weight monitoring with linear temporal logic: complexity and decidability. In: Proceedings of the Joint Meeting of the Twenty-Third EACSL Annual Conference on Computer Science Logic (CSL) and the Twenty-Ninth Annual ACM/IEEE Symposium on Logic in Computer Science (LICS), pp. 11:1–11:10. ACM (2014)
4. Baier, C., Klüppelholz, S., de Meer, H., Niedermeier, F., Wunderlich, S.: Greener bits: formal analysis of demand response. Technical report, TU Dresden (2016). http://www.tcs.inf.tu-dresden.de/ALGI/PUB/ATVA16/
5. Balijepalli, V., Pradhan, V., Khaparde, S., Shereef, R.: Review of demand response under smart grid paradigm. In: 2011 IEEE PES on Innovative Smart Grid Technologies-India (ISGT India), pp. 236–243. IEEE (2011)

6. Basmadjian, R., Lovasz, G., Beck, M., de Meer, H., Hesselbach-Serra, X., Botero, J., Klingert, S., Ortega, M.P., Lopez, J., Stam, A., van Krevelen, R., Girolamo, M.D.: A generic architecture for demand response: the ALL4Green approach. In: Proceedings of the 3rd International Conference on Cloud and Green Computing (CGC), pp. 464–471. IEEE (2013)
7. Basmadjian, R., Mueller, L., de Meer, H.: Data centres' power profile selecting policies for demand response: insights of green supply demand agreement. Ad Hoc Netw. **25**, 581–594 (2015)
8. Boudec, J.L., Tomozei, D.-C.: Stability of a stochastic model for demand-response. Stoch. Syst. **3**(1), 11–37 (2013)
9. Chan, S., Schweppe, F.: A generation reallocation and load shedding algorithm. IEEE Trans. Power Appar. Syst. **1**(PAS–98), 26–34 (1979)
10. Chen, H., Coskun, A.K., Caramanis, M.C.: Real-time power control of data centers for providing regulation service. In: Proceedings of the 52nd IEEE Conference on Decision and Control, pp. 4314–4321 (2013)
11. Chen, N., Ren, X., Ren, S., Wierman, A.: Greening multi-tenant data center demand response. SIGMETRICS Perform. Eval. Rev. **43**(2), 36–38 (2015)
12. Chrszon, P., Dubslaff, C., Klüppelholz, S., Baier, C.: Family-based modeling and analysis for probabilistic systems – featuring PROFEAT. In: Stevens, P., Wąsowski, A. (eds.) FASE 2016. LNCS, vol. 9633, pp. 287–304. Springer, Heidelberg (2016). doi:10.1007/978-3-662-49665-7_17
13. David, A., Grunnet, J.D., Jessen, J.J., Larsen, K.G., Rasmussen, J.I.: Application of model-checking technology to controller synthesis. In: Aichernig, B.K., de Boer, F.S., Bonsangue, M.M. (eds.) Formal Methods for Components and Objects. LNCS, vol. 6957, pp. 336–351. Springer, Heidelberg (2011)
14. Forejt, V., Kwiatkowska, M., Norman, G., Parker, D.: Automated verification techniques for probabilistic systems. In: Bernardo, M., Issarny, V. (eds.) SFM 2011. LNCS, vol. 6659, pp. 53–113. Springer, Heidelberg (2011)
15. Gandhi, A., Gupta, V., Harchol-Balter, M., Kozuch, M.: Optimality analysis of energy-performance trade-off for server farm management. Perform. Eval. **67**(11), 1155–1171 (2010)
16. Huang, G.M., Nair, N.: An OPF based algorithm to evaluate load curtailment incorporating voltage stability margin criterion. In: Proceedings of NAPS Conference (2001)
17. Katoen, J.-P.: Model checking: one can do much more than you think!. In: Arbab, F., Sirjani, M. (eds.) FSEN 2011. LNCS, vol. 7141, pp. 1–14. Springer, Heidelberg (2012)
18. Kaur, H., Brar, Y.S., Randhawa, J.S.: Optimal power flow using power world simulator. In: Proceedings of the 2010 IEEE Electric Power and Energy Conference (EPEC), pp. 1–6 (2010)
19. Klein, J., Baier, C., Chrszon, P., Daum, M., Dubslaff, C., Klüppelholz, S., Märcker, S., Müller, D.: Advances in symbolic probabilistic model checking with PRISM. In: Chechik, M., Raskin, J.-F. (eds.) TACAS 2016. LNCS, vol. 9636, pp. 349–366. Springer, Heidelberg (2016). doi:10.1007/978-3-662-49674-9_20
20. Klingert, S., Niedermeier, F., Dupont, C., Giuliani, G., Schulze, T., de Meer, H.: Renewable energy-aware data centre operations for smart cities the DC4Cities approach. In: Proceedings of the International Conference on Smart Cities and Green ICT Systems (SMARTGREENS), pp. 1–9 (2015)
21. Kwiatkowska, M., Norman, G., Parker, D.: PRISM 4.0: verification of probabilistic real-time systems. In: Gopalakrishnan, G., Qadeer, S. (eds.) CAV 2011. LNCS, vol. 6806, pp. 585–591. Springer, Heidelberg (2011)

22. Liu, Z., Liu, I., Low, S., Wierman, A.: Pricing data center demand response. In: Proceedings of the 2014 ACM International Conference on Measurement and Modeling of Computer Systems (SIGMETRICS), pp. 111–123 (2014)
23. Medicherla, T., Billinton, R., Sachdev, M.: Generation rescheduling and load shedding to alleviate line overloads-analysis. IEEE Trans. Power Appar. Syst. **PAS–98**(6), 1876–1884 (1979)
24. Meidani, H., Ghanem, R.: Multiscale Markov models with random transitions for energy demand management. Energy Build. **61**, 267–274 (2013)
25. Niedermeier, F., Duschl, W., Möller, T., de Meer, H.: Increasing data centre renewable power share via intelligent smart city power control. In: Proceedings of the 2015 ACM International Conference on Future Energy Systems, pp. 241–246 (2015)
26. Norman, G., Parker, D., Kwiatkowska, M., Shukla, S., Gupta, R.: Using probabilistic model checking for dynamic power management. Formal Aspects Comput. **17**(2), 160–176 (2005)
27. Puterman, M.: Markov Decision Processes: Discrete Stochastic Dynamic Programming. Wiley, New York (1994)
28. Qureshi, A.: Power-demand routing in massive geo-distributed systems. Ph.D. thesis, Massachusetts Institute of Technology (2010)
29. Siano, P.: Demand response and smart grids—a survey. Renew. Sustain. Energy Rev. **30**, 461–478 (2014)
30. Zhou, Z., Liu, F., Li, B., Li, B., Jin, H., Zou, R., Liu, Z.: Fuel cell generation in geo-distributed cloud services: a quantitative study. In: Proceedings of the 34th International Conference on Distributed Computing Systems (ICDCS), pp. 52–61 (2014)
31. Zhou, Z., Liu, F., Li, Z.: Pricing bilateral electricity trade between smart grids and hybrid green datacenters. In: Proceedings of the 2015 ACM International Conference on Measurement and Modeling of Computer Systems (SIGMETRICS), pp. 443–444. ACM (2015)

Heuristics for Checking Liveness Properties with Partial Order Reductions

Alexandre Duret-Lutz[1], Fabrice Kordon[2,3], Denis Poitrenaud[3,4], and Etienne Renault[1(✉)]

[1] LRDE, EPITA, Kremlin-Bicêtre, France
Etienne.Renault@lrde.epita.fr
[2] Sorbonne Universités, UPMC University, Paris 06, France
[3] CNRS UMR 7606, LIP6, 75005 Paris, France
[4] USPC, Université Paris Descartes, Paris, France

Abstract. Checking liveness properties with partial-order reductions requires a cycle proviso to ensure that an action cannot be postponed forever. The proviso forces each cycle to contain at least one fully expanded state. We present new heuristics to select which state to expand, hoping to reduce the size of the resulting graph. The choice of the state to expand is done when encountering a "dangerous edge". Almost all existing provisos expand the source of this edge, while this paper also explores the expansion of the destination and the use of SCC-based information.

1 Introduction

The automata-theoretic approach to explicit LTL model checking explores a Labeled Transition System (LTS). Among the various techniques that have been suggested to tackle the well known state explosion problem, partial-order reductions (POR) reduce the size of the LTS by exploiting the interleaving semantics of concurrent systems. Under interleaved execution semantics, n independent actions (or events) lead to $n!$ possible interleavings. Numerous executions may only correspond to the permutation of independent actions: POR considers only some representative executions, ignoring all other ones [3,9,12].

The selection of the representative executions is performed on-the-fly while exploring the LTS: for each state, the exploration algorithm only considers a nonempty *reduced* subset of all *enabled* actions, such that all omitted actions are independent from those in the *reduced* set. The execution of omitted actions is then postponed to a future state. However if the same actions are consistently ignored along a cycle, they may never be executed. To avoid this *ignoring problem*, an extra condition called *proviso* is required. When checking liveness properties, the *proviso* forces every cycle of the LTS to contain at least one *expanded* state where all actions are considered.

This paper proposes several heuristics that can be combined to build new original provisos. Since POR reductions aim to reduce the number of states and transitions, we evaluate each proviso using these two criteria. This analysis reveals new provisos that outperform the state of the art [1,9]. After the preliminaries of Sect. 2, we deconstruct a state-of-the-art proviso [1] in Sect. 3. In

© Springer International Publishing AG 2016
C. Artho et al. (Eds.): ATVA 2016, LNCS 9938, pp. 340–356, 2016.
DOI: 10.1007/978-3-319-46520-3_22

Sect. 4, we explore a new way to choose the state to be expanded among the cycle. Finally Sect. 5 presents improvements based on SCC information.

2   Preliminaries

A Labeled Transition System (LTS) is a tuple $L = \langle S, s^0, Act, \delta \rangle$ where S is a finite set of states, $s^0 \in S$ is a designated initial state, Act is a set of actions and $\delta \subseteq S \times Act \times S$ is a (deterministic) transition relation where each transition is labeled by an action. If $(s, \alpha, d) \in \delta$, we note $s \to d$ and say that d is a *successor* of s. We denote by $post(s)$ the set of all successors of s.

A *path* between two states $s, s' \in S$ is a finite and non-empty sequence of adjacent transitions $\rho = (s_1, \alpha_1, s_2)(s_2, \alpha_2, s_3) \ldots (s_n, \alpha_n, s_{n+1}) \in \delta^+$ with $s_1 = s$ and $s_{n+1} = s'$. When $s = s'$ the path is a *cycle*.

A non-empty set $C \subseteq S$ is a Strongly Connected Component (SCC) iff any two different states $s, s' \in C$ are connected by a path, and C is maximal w.r.t. inclusion. If C is not maximal we call it a *partial* SCC.

For the purpose of partial-order reductions, an LTS is equipped with a function $reduced : S \to 2^S$ that returns a subset of successors reachable via a reduced set of actions. For any state $s \in S$, we have $reduced(s) \subseteq post(s)$ and $reduced(s) = \emptyset \implies post(s) = \emptyset$. The $reduced$ function must satisfy other conditions depending on whether we use *ample set*, *stubborn set* or *persistent set* [3, for a survey see]. The algorithms we present do not depend on the actual technique used.

In this paper, we consider a DFS-based exploration of the LTS using a given $reduced$ function. We survey different provisos that modify the exploration to ensure that at least one state of each cycle is expanded. We will first present simple provisos that capture cycles by detecting *back-edges* of the DFS (i.e., an edge reaching a state on the DFS stack), and always expanding one of its extremities. Then more complex provisos can be presented: to avoid some expansion around each back-edge, they also have to detect any edge that reachs a state that has been explored but is no longer on the stack, as this edge *may* be part of a cycle.

3   Provisos Inspired from Existing Work

This section presents two well known provisos solving the *ignoring problem* for liveness properties: the proviso introduced by Peled [9] and implemented in Spin [2], and the one of Evangelista and Pajault [1]. The latter proviso augments the former with several mechanisms to reduce the number of expansions. To show how each mechanism is implemented and its effect on the number of expansions, we introduce each mechanism incrementally as a new proviso.

Source Expansion. Algorithm 1, that we call SOURCE, corresponds to the proviso of Peled [9]. The global variable v stores the set of visited states. Each state on v has a Boolean flag to distinguish states that are on the DFS stack (IN) from those that left it (OUT).

Algorithm 1. The SOURCE proviso, adapted from Peled [9].	**Algorithm 2.** Conditional source expansion.
1 **Procedure** SOURCE($s \in S$) 2 $todo \leftarrow reduced(s)$ 3 $v.add(s)$ 4 $v.setColor(s, \text{IN})$ 5 $e \leftarrow |todo| \neq |post(s)|$ 6 **while** ($\neg todo.empty()$) **do** 7 $s' \leftarrow todo.pick()$ 8 **if** ($\neg v.contains(s')$) **then** 9 SOURCE(s') 10 **else if** ($e \wedge v.color(s') = \text{IN}$) **then** 11 $todo.add(post(s) \setminus reduced(s))$ 12 $e \leftarrow \text{FALSE}$ 13 $v.setColor(s, \text{OUT})$	1 **Procedure** CONDSOURCE($s \in S$) 2 $todo \leftarrow reduced(s)$ 3 $v.add(s)$ 4 $v.setColor(s, (|todo| \neq |post(s)|$? 5 $\text{IN} : \text{OUT}))$ 6 **while** ($\neg todo.empty()$) **do** 7 $s' \leftarrow todo.pick()$ 8 **if** ($\neg v.contains(s')$) **then** 9 CONDSOURCE(s') 10 **else if** ($v.color(s) = \text{IN} \wedge$ 11 $v.color(s') = \text{IN}$) **then** 12 $todo.add(post(s) \setminus reduced(s))$ 13 $v.setColor(s, \text{OUT})$ 14 $v.setColor(s, \text{OUT})$

This proviso expands any state s (the *source*) that has a successor s' (the *destination*) on the stack. This amounts to augmenting $todo$ (line 11) with all the successors in $post(s)$ that were skipped by $reduced(s)$. The Boolean e prevents states from being expanded multiple times. Overall, this proviso can be implemented with two extra bits per state (one for e, and one for IN/OUT).

This proviso relies on the fact that each cycle contains a back-edge, and therefore expanding the source of each back-edge will satisfy the constraint of having at least one expanded state per cycle.

Conditional Source Expansion. Some expansions performed by SOURCE could be avoided: the expansion of the source s of a back-edge need only to be performed when its destination s' is not already expanded.

Algorithm 2 shows that this conditional expansion can be achieved by simply changing the semantic of IN and OUT. The IN status now means that a state is on the DFS stack and is not expanded. When a state s is discovered, its color is set to OUT instead of IN (line 5) whenever $reduced(s)$ did not produce a set smaller than $post(s)$. Doing so allows getting rid of the e variable.

Prioritizing Already Known Successors. In SOURCE and CONDSOURCE, the decision to expand a state s occurs only when a back-edge has been discovered. However this discovery may occur after having visited several other successors of s, and the recursive calls on these successors are unaware that s will eventually be expanded. This may cause superfluous expansions as shown in Fig. 1.

Algorithm 3 shows how this could be fixed. Among the successors of s, the known states are processed first, making sure that s is expanded (if it has to) before processing its other successors. CONDSOURCEKNOWN forces that ordering by using a set *postponed* to delay the visit of unknown successors; another implementation would be to reorder $todo$ to keep known states first. This latter implementation

Fig. 1. If edges 1, 2, 3, are explored in that order, CONDSOURCE will expand both states. Prioritizing back-edges(i.e., 3, 1, 2) only expands s.

does not require additional memory (the set *postponed*) but it doubles the number of tests of the form $v.contains(s')$.

Algorithm 3. Prioritizing known successors

```
1  Procedure CONDSOURCEKNOWN(s ∈ S)
2  |  todo ← reduced(s)
3  |  v.add(s)
4  |  v.setColor(s, (|todo| ≠ |post(s)| ? IN : OUT))
5  |  postponed ← ∅
6  |  while (¬todo.empty()) do
7  |  |  s' ← todo.pick()
8  |  |  if (¬v.contains(s')) then
9  |  |  |  postponed.add(s')
10 |  |  else if (v.color(s) = IN ∧ v.color(s') = IN) then
11 |  |  |  todo.add(post(s) \ reduced(s))
12 |  |  |  v.setColor(s, OUT)
13 |  while (¬postponed.empty()) do
14 |  |  s' ← postponed.pick()
15 |  |  if (¬v.contains(s')) then
16 |  |  |  CONDSOURCEKNOWN(s')
17 |  v.setColor(s, OUT)
```

Algorithm 4. Detecting expanded states on the DFS using weights

```
1  Procedure WEIGHTEDSOURCE(s ∈ S)
2  |  todo ← reduced(s)
3  |  v.add(s)
4  |  v.setColor(s, ORANGE)
5  |  v.setWeight(s, w)
6  |  if (|todo| = |post(s)|) then
7  |  |  todo ← EXPAND(s, todo)
8  |  while (¬todo.empty()) do
9  |  |  s' ← todo.pick()
10 |  |  if (¬v.contains(s')) then
11 |  |  |  WEIGHTEDSOURCE(s')
12 |  |  |  if (v.color(s) = ORANGE ∧ v.color(s') = RED) then
13 |  |  |  |  v.setColor(s, PURPLE)
14 |  |  else if (v.color(s) ∈ {ORANGE, PURPLE}) then
15 |  |  |  if (v.color(s') = RED) then
16 |  |  |  |  todo ← EXPAND(s, todo)
17 |  |  |  else if (v.color(s') ∈ {ORANGE, PURPLE}) then
18 |  |  |  |  if (v.weight(s') = w) then
19 |  |  |  |  |  todo ← EXPAND(s, todo)
20 |  |  |  |  else
21 |  |  |  |  |  v.setColor(s, PURPLE)
22 |  switch (v.color(s)) do
23 |  |  case GREEN : w ← w − 1
24 |  |  case ORANGE : v.setColor(s, GREEN)
25 |  |  case PURPLE : v.setColor(s, RED)
26 Function EXPAND (s ∈ S, succ ⊆ S)
27 |  succ.add(post(s) \ reduced(s))
28 |  v.setColor(s, GREEN)              /* scan stack here in WEIGHTEDSOURCESCAN */
29 |  w ← w + 1
30 |  return succ
```

Detecting Expanded States on the DFS. When a back-edge $s \rightarrow s'$ is detected, the DFS stack contains the states forming a path between s' and s. Some of these states could already be fully expanded. A generalization of the optimization implemented in CONDSOURCE would therefore be to expand s only if there is no expanded state between s' and s. A consequence is that we might have back-edges in which neither the source nor the destination have been expanded. If we decide not to expand s, there might exist another path between s' and s (but not on the current DFS) that will later form a cycle without expanded state [1, cf. Fig. 6]. Therefore a different way of ensuring that each cycle contains an expanded state is required. [1] fixed this problem by marking such states as dangerous so that they can trigger an expansion when encountered on another cycle without expanded state.

Detecting the presence of expanded states along the cycle is done by assigning each state s of the DFS a weight that represents the number of expanded states seen since the initial state (s excluded). WEIGHTEDSOURCE (Algorithm 4) maintains this count in the global variable w.

The dangerousness of each state is indicated with four colors:

- GREEN means that any cycle through this state already contains an expanded state, so reaching this state does not require any more extension. A state can be marked as GREEN if it is expanded or if all its successors are GREEN.
- ORANGE and PURPLE states are unexpanded states on the DFS stack (their successors have not all been visited). The PURPLE states are those for which a non-GREEN successor has been seen.
- RED states are considered dangerous and should trigger an expansion when reached. A PURPLE state becomes RED once its successors have been all visited.

In Algorithm 4, two situations trigger an expansion. A source s is expanded when processing an edge $s \rightarrow s'$ where s' is marked RED (line 16), or when $s \rightarrow s'$ is a back-edge and there is no expanded state between s' and s (line 18).

While Algorithm 4 stores the weights in v it is only needed for the states on the DFS. The states on the stack need two bits to store one of the four colors, but states outside the DFS require only one bit as they are either RED or GREEN.

Combining Prioritization and Detection of Expanded States on DFS. The proviso $C2_c^L$ presented by [1] (renamed WEIGHTEDSOURCEKNOWN, see Algorithm 5) corresponds to the combination of the last two ideas. The main difference is that the second loop (line 21) working on successors ignored by the first loop also performs an expansion (line 28) whenever it discovers a RED successor. This was not the case in Algorithm 3 because in CONDSOURCEKNOWN the only dangerous successors are those on the DFS stack.

Early Propagation of Green in the DFS Stack. Evangelista and Pajault [1] also introduce a variant of WEIGHTEDSOURCEKNOWN in which the GREEN color of a state can be propagated to its predecessors in the DFS stack before the actual backtrack. This propagation could prevent other states from being colored in red [1, cf. Fig. 8]. As soon as a state is expanded (i.e., in the EXPAND function), the DFS stack is scanned backward and all ORANGE states that are ready to be popped (i.e., they do not have any pending successors left to be processed) can be marked as GREEN. This backward scan stops on the first state that is either GREEN or PURPLE, or that has some unprocessed successors. This idea can be applied to all WEIGHTED algorithms.

Algorithm 5. Combining WEIGHTEDSOURCE and CONDSOURCEKNOWN [1]

```
 1  Procedure WEIGHTEDSOURCEKNOWN(s ∈ S)
 2  │  todo ← reduced(s) v.add(s) v.setColor(s, ORANGE) v.setWeight(s, w) if
    │  (|todo| = |post(s)|) then
 3  │  └  todo ← EXPAND(s, todo)                    /* defined in Algorithm [4] */
 4  │  postponed ← ∅ while (¬todo.empty()) do
 5  │  │  s' ← todo.pick() if (¬v.contains(s')) then
 6  │  │  │  postponed.add(s')
 7  │  │  else if (v.color(s) ∈ {ORANGE, PURPLE}) then
 8  │  │  │  if (v.color(s') = RED) then
 9  │  │  │  │  todo ← EXPAND(s, todo)
10  │  │  │  else if (v.color(s') ∈ {ORANGE, PURPLE}) then
11  │  │  │  │  if (v.weight(s') = w) then
12  │  │  │  │  │  todo ← EXPAND(s, todo)
13  │  │  │  │  else
14  │  │  │  │  └  v.setColor(s, PURPLE)
15  │  while (¬postponed.empty()) do
16  │  │  s' ← postponed.pick() if (¬v.contains(s')) then
17  │  │  │  WEIGHTEDSOURCEKNOWN(s') if
    │  │  │  (v.color(s) = ORANGE ∧ v.color(s') = RED) then
18  │  │  │  └  v.setColor(s, PURPLE)
19  │  │  else if (v.color(s) ∈ {ORANGE, PURPLE} ∧ v.color(s') = RED) then
20  │  │  └  postponed ← EXPAND(s, postponed)
21  │  switch (v.color(s)) do
22  │  │  case GREEN : w ← w − 1
23  │  │  case ORANGE : v.setColor(s, GREEN)
24  │  └  case PURPLE : v.setColor(s, RED)
```

---

eBecause it has to scan the stack, this algorithm may not be presented as a recursive procedure like we did so far. However if WEIGHTEDSOURCE or WEIGHTEDSOURCEKNOWN were implemented as non-recursive procedures, the place to perform the stack scanning would be in function EXPAND, as defined on page 4. The modification also requires keeping track of whether a state is GREEN because it has been expanded, or because it has been marked during such a stack scanning: an additional bit is needed for this.

We call these two variants WEIGHTEDSOURCESCAN and WEIGHTED-SOURCEKNOWN. The latter one corresponds to the proviso $C2_{C*}^L$ presented by Evangelista and Pajault [1].

Evaluation. We evaluate the above 7 provisos (as well as more provisos we shall introduce in the next sections) on state-spaces generated from 38 models from the BEEM benchmark [7]. We selected models[1] such that every category of Pelánek's classification [8] is represented.

We compiled each model using a version of DiVinE 2.4 patched by the LTSminteam[2]. This tool produces a shared library that allows on-the-fly exploration of the state-space, as well as all the information required to implement a *reduced* function. This library is then loaded by Spot[3], in which we implemented all the provisos described here. Our *reduced(s)* method implements the stubborn-set method from Valmari [12] as described by Pater [5, p. 21] in a deterministic way: for any state s, *reduced(s)* always returns the same set.

Because provisos can be sensitive to the exploration order (Fig. 1 is one such example), we ran each model 100 times with different transition orders. Table 1 sums these runs for all models, and shows:

- the size of the full (non-reduced) state-space (FULL),
- the size of the reduced state-space using each of the above proviso,
- the size of the reduced state-space, applying just *reduced* without any proviso (NONE). Even if this graph that cannot be used for verification in practice (it ignores too many runs), NONE was used as a lower bound by Evangelista and Pajault [1].

Table 1. Comparison of the provisos of Sect. 3. Columns present the number of states and transitions (by million) summed over all runs, their ratio compared to the non-reduced graphs, and the number of states investigated per milliseconds. Provisos with a reference correspond to state-of-the-art algorithms.

	states (10^6)		transitions (10^6)		st/ms
FULL	784.45	100.00%	2,677.73	100.00%	17.90
SOURCE [9]	303.21	38.65%	679.16	25.36%	12.33
WEIGHTEDSOURCE	263.43	33.58%	537.56	20.08%	11.68
WEIGHTEDSOURCEKNOWN [1]	262.63	33.48%	534.35	19.96%	11.77
CONDSOURCE	252.83	32.23%	518.80	19.37%	11.85
CONDSOURCEKNOWN	251.05	32.00%	510.91	19.08%	11.89
WEIGHTEDSOURCESCAN	250.49	31.93%	505.98	18.90%	11.67
WEIGHTEDSOURCEKNOWNSCAN [1]	248.11	31.63%	498.68	18.62%	11.70
NONE	57.58	7.34%	97.65	3.65%	22.65

---

[1] The full benchmark can be found at: https://www.lrde.epita.fr/~renault/benchs/ATVA-2016/results.html.

[2] http://fmt.cs.utwente.nl/tools/ltsmin/#divine.

[3] https://spot.lrde.epita.fr.

In addition to showing the contribution of each individual idea presented in the above section, Table 1 confirms state-of-the-art results [1]. However, since these values are sums, they are biased towards the largest models. Section 5 will present the most relevant provisos after normalizing the results model by model, in order to be less sensitive to their size.

We observe that WEIGHTEDSOURCEKNOWNSCAN outperforms (18 % fewer states) SOURCE as measured by Evangelista and Pajault [1]. We note that SOURCE processes more states per millisecond, because it maintains less information than WEIGHTEDSOURCEKNOWN.

Surprisingly, CONDSOURCE, despite its simplicity, is more efficient than WEIGHTEDSOURCEKNOWN. This might be due to RED states introduced in WEIGHTEDSOURCEKNOWN, as they can generate additional expansions. WEIGHTEDSOURCEKNOWN can only be competitive with other provisos when combined with the scan of the DFS stack as integrated in WEIGHTEDSOURCE-KNOWN. The additional implementation complexity required to update the weights and to scan the stack only provides a very small benefit in term of size; however it can be seen in the last column that the runtime overhead is negligible: all provisos process the same number of states per millisecond.

4   New Provisos Based on Destination Expansion

The SOURCE proviso relies on the fact that each cycle contains a back-edge, so expanding the source of this edge guarantees that each cycle will have an expanded state. This guarantee would hold even if the *destination* of each back-edge was expanded instead. This idea, already proposed by Nalumasu and Gopalakrishnan [4] in a narrower context, brought promising results. This section investigates this idea more systematically yielding many new proviso variants.

Destination Expansion. The simplest variant, called DEST (Algorithm 6) is a modification of SOURCE that expands the destination of back-edges instead of the source. This requires a new Boolean per state to mark (line 10) whether a state on the stack should be expanded (line 12) during backtrack.

As previously, it is possible to perform a conditional expansion (not marking the destination if the source is already expanded) and to prioritize the visit of some successors. Contrary to SOURCE, where it is preferable to consider known states first, it is better to visit unknown successors (or self-loops) first with DEST, since those successors might ultimately mark the current state for expansion, therefore avoiding the need to expand the destinations of this state's back-edges.

In DEST, the recursive visit of unknown successors could mark the current state for later expansion: in this case, successors that are on the DFS stack have been marked uselessly. The next algorithm avoids these pointless expansions.

Algorithm 7, called CONDDESTUNKNOWN implements the prioritization of successors (lines 8–13) as well as the conditional expansion (line 12). The main loop investigates new successors first (through recursive calls), handles self-loops, and postpones the processing of dangerous states. Then, either the current state is marked and must be expanded, or all the dangerous direct successors of the current state are marked to be expanded later (when backtracking these states, after returning from the recursive calls, line 14).

Mixing Destination Expansion and Dangerousness. Previous provisos can still perform useless expansions. When an edge $s \to d$ returning to the DFS is detected, the destination d is marked to be expanded. However during the backtrack of the DFS stack, we might encounter another marked state q that is expanded because it belongs to another cycle. Thus d and q are both expanded, but since q belongs to the two cycles, the expansion of d was superfluous.

Algorithm 6. Expanding destination instead of source

```
 1  Procedure Dest(s ∈ S)
 2      todo ← reduced(s)
 3      v.add(s)
 4      v.setMark(s, FALSE)
 5      while (¬todo.empty()) do
 6          s' ← todo.pick()
 7          if (¬v.contains(s')) then
 8              Dest(s')
 9          else
10              v.setMark(s', TRUE)

11      if (v.mark(s)) then
12          todo ←
13              post(s) \ reduced(s)
14          while (¬todo.empty())
            do
15              s' ← todo.pick()
16              if (¬v.contains(s'))
                then
17                  Dest(s')
```

Algorithm 7. Prioritizing unknown successors with conditional expansion of destination

```
 1  Procedure CondDestUnknown(s ∈ S)
 2      todo ← reduced(s)
 3      v.add(s)
 4      v.setMark(s, |todo| = |post(s)|)
 5      postponed ← ∅
 6      while (¬todo.empty()) do
 7          s' ← todo.pick()
 8          if (¬v.contains(s')) then
 9              CondDestUnknown(s')
10          else if (s = s') then
11              v.setMark(s, TRUE)
12          else if (¬v.mark(s) ∧ ¬v.mark(s')) then
13              postponed.add(s')
14      if (v.mark(s)) then
15          todo ← post(s) \ reduced(s)
16          while (¬todo.empty()) do
17              s' ← todo.pick()
18              if (¬v.contains(s')) then
19                  CondDestUnknown(s')
20      else
21          while (¬postponed.empty()) do
22              s' ← postponed.pick()
23              v.setMark(s', TRUE)
24      v.setMark(s, TRUE)
```

ColoredDest (Algorithm 8) proposes a solution to this problem. It reuses the color mechanism introduced in WeightedSource (all Weighted algorithms use colors), but without the weights. Here, useless expansions are also tracked by propagating GREEN (line17); the difference is that only the PURPLE states that are marked will be expanded (lines19–25), not the ORANGE ones.

As done previously, we can prioritize unknown states, resulting in a new variant: ColoredDestUnknown. This avoids useless markings (line14). However, mixing this variant with the stack scanning technique is not interesting. Indeed, propagating the GREEN color as early as possible is pointless since the expansion is done when backtracking (i.e., as late as possible): the color will be naturally propagated anyway when it has to be used.

Algorithm 8. Mixing destination expansion and dangerousness.

```
 1  Procedure COLOREDDEST(s ∈ S)
 2      todo ← reduced(s)
 3      v.add(s)
 4      v.setColor(s, (|todo| ≠ |post(s)| ? ORANGE : GREEN))
 5      v.setMark(s, FALSE)
 6      while (¬todo.empty()) do
 7          s' ← todo.pick()
 8          if (¬v.contains(s')) then
 9              COLOREDDEST(s') if (v.color(s) = ORANGE) ∧ (v.color(s') = RED) then
10                  v.setColor(s, PURPLE)
11          else if (v.color(s) ∈ {ORANGE, PURPLE}) ∧ (v.color(s') ≠ GREEN) then
12              v.setColor(s, PURPLE)
13              v.setMark(s', TRUE)
14      switch (v.color(s)) do
15          case ORANGE :
16              v.setColor(s, GREEN)
17          case PURPLE :
18              if (v.mark(s)) then
19                  v.setColor(s, GREEN)
20                  todo ← post(s) \ reduced(s)
21                  while (¬todo.empty()) do
22                      s' ← todo.pick()
23                      if (¬v.contains(s')) then
24                          COLOREDDEST(s')
25              else
26                  v.setColor(s, RED)
```

Of course, weights can also be used in addition to colors. In WEIGHTEDDEST (Algorithm 9), we use a slightly different implementation of weights than in WEIGHTEDSOURCE: instead of storing the number of expanded states seen above any state of the DFS stack, we store the depth of each state, and maintain a stack of the depths of all expanded states on the DFS stack. This alternate representation of weights is not necessary in WEIGHTEDDEST, but will be useful for the next extension we present.

In WEIGHTEDDEST, when a back-edge $s \to s'$ discovers a dangerous state s' on the DFS stack (lines19–21), the algorithm can use the additional stack e to decide whether s' actually needs to be marked for expansion: if the depth of s' is less than the depth of the last expanded state, then a state has been expanded between s' and s, and the marking can be avoided. However, and as in WEIGHTEDSOURCE, when an edge $s \to s'$ reaches a RED state s', the source has to be expanded immediately (lines23–25) since there is no way to know whether this edge could be part of a cycle without expanded state.

The reason we introduced the depth-based representation of weights is for another heuristic we call DEEPESTDEST. If a state s has several back-edges $s \to s_1, s \to s_2, \ldots, s \to s_n$ to different states $s_1, s_2, \ldots, s_n$ on the DFS stack, then all these back-edges close cycles that all pass through the deepest of these states, which is the only one needing to be marked for (possible) expansion. Note that in this situation (one source, with n back-edges), SOURCE would immediately expand one state (the source), COLOREDDEST and WEIGHTEDDEST would mark n states for (possible) expansion, while DEEPESTDEST would mark only one.

DEEPESTDEST, which we do not present to save space, can be implemented by modifying Algorithm 9 as follows: instead of marking a destination for

---

Algorithm 9. Adapting weights to the expansion of destination states.

```
1  Procedure WEIGHTEDDEST(s ∈ S)
2      todo ← reduced(s)
3      v.add(s)
4      v.setColor(s, ORANGE)
5      v.setMark(s, FALSE)
6      d ← d + 1
7      v.setDepth(s, d)
8      if (|todo| = |post(s)|) then
9          v.setColor(s, GREEN)
10         e.push(d)
11     while (¬todo.empty()) do
12         s' ← todo.pick()
13         if (¬v.contains(s')) then
14             WEIGHTEDDEST(s')
15             if (v.color(s) = ORANGE) ∧ (v.color(s') = RED) then
16                 v.setColor(s, PURPLE)
17         else if (v.color(s) ∈ {ORANGE, PURPLE}) ∧ (v.color(s') ≠ GREEN) then
18             v.setColor(s, PURPLE)
19             if (v.color(s') ∈ {ORANGE, PURPLE}) then
20                 if (e.empty() ∨ v.depth(s') > e.top()) then
21                     v.setMark(s', TRUE)
22             else if (v.color(s') = RED) then
23                 v.setColor(s, GREEN)
24                 e.push(d)
25                 todo ← todo ∪ (post(s) \ reduced(s))
26     switch (v.color(s)) do
27         case GREEN :
28             e.pop()
29         case ORANGE :
30             v.setColor(s, GREEN)
31         case PURPLE :
32             if (v.mark(s)) then
33                 v.setColor(s, GREEN)
34                 e.push(d)
35                 todo ← post(s) \ reduced(s)
36                 while (¬todo.empty()) do
37                     s' ← todo.pick()
38                     if (¬v.contains(s')) then
39                         WEIGHTEDDEST(s')
40                 e.pop()
41             else
42                 v.setColor(s, RED)
43     d ← d - 1
```

expansion at line 21, simply collect the deepest destination, and mark that single destination in the same block as line 42.

Evaluation. Table 2 presents the performance of the provisos presented in this section. Some provisos measured here, such as CONDDEST, WEIGHTEDDESTUNKNOWN, and DEEPESTDESTUNKNOWN have not been explicitly presented, but the techniques they combine should be obvious from their name. All WEIGHTEDDEST and DEEPESTDEST variants could also be combined with the SCAN technique however these combinations did not achieve interesting performances.

Table 2. Comparison of the provisos of Sect. 4. For reference, we highlight the performance of WEIGHTEDSOURCEKNOWN, the best proviso of Sect. 3.

	states (10^6)		transitions (10^6)		st/ms
DEEPESTDESTUNKNOWN	276.51	35.25%	570.52	21.31%	11.81
DEEPESTDEST	275.31	35.10%	566.63	21.16%	11.87
WEIGHTEDDESTUNKNOWN	273.94	34.92%	563.61	21.05%	11.83
DEST	272.79	34.77%	508.17	18.98%	14.48
WEIGHTEDDEST	272.68	34.76%	559.73	20.90%	11.80
WEIGHTEDSOURCEKNOWNSCAN [1]	248.11	31.63%	498.68	18.62%	11.70
CONDDEST	213.98	27.28%	413.15	15.43%	12.57
CONDDESTUNKNOWN	213.92	27.27%	412.75	15.41%	12.52
COLOREDDEST	213.92	27.27%	412.93	15.42%	12.54
COLOREDDESTUNKNOWN	213.83	27.26%	412.27	15.40%	12.46

As for the SOURCE family of provisos, using a conditional expansion brings the most benefits. The UNKNOWN variants generally show a very small effect (slightly positive or slightly negative) on a proviso, so this does not seem to be an interesting heuristic. The WEIGHTED and DEEPEST variants are disappointing. We believe this is due to mixing destination expansions (for back-edges) and source expansions (for RED states). However, next section will show that, when combined with others techniques, they bring promising results.

The better provisos of this table are therefore CONDDEST and COLOREDDEST (with or without UNKNOWN) with very close results. Note that both provisos are easy to implement, and have a small memory footprint: CONDDEST requires one additional bit per state, while COLOREDDEST needs three bits. This is smaller than what WEIGHTEDSOURCEKNOWN requires.

5   Improving Provisos with SCCs

To test the emptiness of the product between a state-space and a specification, an explicit model checker can use two kinds of emptiness checks: those based on

Nested Depth First Search (NDFS) [11], and those based on enumerating the
Strongly Connected Components (SCC) [10].

All provisos presented so far apply to both NDFS or SCC-based setups. In
this section, we present two ideas that are only relevant to model checkers using
SCC-based emptiness checks, since they exploit the available information about
(partial) SCCs.

In all SCC-based emptiness checks, states may be partitioned in three sets:
live states, dead states, and unknown states. Unknown states are states that
have not yet been discovered. Dead states are states that belong to SCCs that
have been entirely visited. The remaining states are live, and their SCCs might
be only partially known.

Using Dead SCCs. The first idea is rather trivial. In the COLORED or
WEIGHTED provisos presented so far, RED states are always considered dangerous. When we discover an edge $s \to s'$ to a RED state s', we either expand
the source s (all WEIGHTED provisos), or propagate the RED color to s (for
COLOREDDEST). But these actions are superfluous when the state s' is known
to belong to a dead SCC: in that case s and s' are in different SCCs so they
cannot appear on the same cycle, and the edge may be simply ignored.

Using Live SCCs Through Highlinks. In WEIGHTED provisos, we can derive
additional insights about cycles in live SCCs. When we discover an edge $s \to s'$
to a RED state s' that is also live, then s' necessarily belongs to the same SCC as
s. This means that $s \to s'$ closes at least one cycle, even if s' is not on the DFS
stack: therefore one state on the cycles including s' and s has to be marked for
expansion, and only states from the DFS can be marked as such. The default
solution used by WEIGHTED provisos would be to expand the source s, but we
have also seen previously that expanding states that are that are higher (i.e.,
less deep) in the DFS stack improves results.

In order to expand higher states, we
equip each live state x with a pointer called
$highlink(x)$ that gives a DFS state (preferably the highest) that is common to all known
cycles passing through x. Figure 2 shows
a snapshot of an algorithm computing the
SCC, where a partial SCC is highlighted. In
this configuration, $highlink(s') = q_3$. When
an edge $s \to s'$ reaches a state s' that is
live and RED, we therefore have to ensure
that some state between $highlink(s')$ and s
is expanded: since these two states are on
the stack, and s is deeper than $highlink(s')$,
we prefer to expand the latter. Furthermore,
using the same weight implementation as

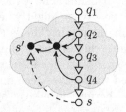

Fig. 2. White states and edges with
white arrows denote the DFS stack.
Black states have been fully visited.
The cloud represents the only (partial, non trivial) SCC that has been
discovered so far. Dashed-edge has
not yet been visited.

Algorithm 9, we can easily check whether there exists an expanded state between $highlink(s')$ and s to avoid additional work.

In the example of Fig. 2, once s, q_4, and q_3 are popped from the DFS stack $highlink(s')$ should be updated to value of $highlink(q_3)$ which is q_2. In our implementation, these updates are performed lazily in a way that is similar to the path-compression technique used in the union-find data structure [6]: when we query the highlink of a state and find that it points to a state q that is not on the DFS stack, we update it to $highlink(q)$.

Because it would require introducing an SCC-based algorithm, and because we consider that the fine details of how to update $highlink(x)$ efficiently in this context is not necessary to reach our conclusion, we have decided to not present this algorithm formally. Our implementation is however publicly available (see footnote 1).

Evaluation. Table 3 presents the performances of the provisos presented in this section. We prefix by DEAD and HIGHLINK the provisos of previous sections when combined with the two SCC-based heuristics. Note that dead states are also ignored in HIGHLINK variants.

We observe that the DEAD variants only improve the original non-DEAD variants by 3 %. On the contrary, the HIGHLINK variants bring an important benefit. For instance the addition of HIGHLINK to DEADWEIGHTEDDEST reduces the number of states by 25 % and the number transitions by 30 %. The improvements are similar when using HIGHLINK on top of the state-of-the-art WEIGHTEDSOURCEKNOWN variants. These results confirm that the case where an edge leading to a (non-dead) RED state is well handled by this HIGHLINK.

Table 3. Comparison of the provisos of Sect. 5. For reference, we recall the performances of DEEPESTDEST, WEIGHTEDDEST that are the support of heuristics presented in this section, and those of COLOREDDEST, the best proviso so far.

	states (10^6)		transitions (10^6)		st/ms
DEEPESTDEST	275.31	35.10%	566.63	21.16%	11.87
DEADDEEPESTDEST	269.10	34.30%	543.64	20.30%	11.92
WEIGHTEDDEST	272.68	34.76%	559.73	20.90%	11.80
DEADWEIGHTEDDEST	270.62	34.50%	554.91	20.72%	11.88
DEADWEIGHTEDSOURCEKNOWNSCAN	247.68	31.57%	497.79	18.59%	11.67
COLOREDDEST	213.92	27.27%	412.93	15.42%	12.54
DEADCOLOREDDEST	213.87	27.26%	412.80	15.42%	12.53
HIGHLINKWEIGHTEDDEST	207.41	26.44%	393.22	14.68%	12.44
HIGHLINKWEIGHTEDDESTSCAN	206.23	26.29%	391.05	14.60%	12.41
HIGHLINKWEIGHTEDSOURCEKNOWN	203.20	25.90%	386.84	14.45%	12.20
HIGHLINKWEIGHTEDSOURCEKNOWNSCAN	203.08	25.89%	386.60	14.44%	12.12
HIGHLINKDEEPESTDEST	192.84	24.58%	349.89	13.07%	13.20
HIGHLINKDEEPESTDESTSCAN	191.78	24.45%	347.95	12.99%	13.21

Note that while DEEPESTDEST combinations did not achieve interesting performances so far, it outperforms all provisos presented in this paper when combined with HIGHLINK and SCAN techniques.

Among the 46 provisos we implemented and benched (see footnote 1), we selected the 16 most relevant: all the SOURCE-based strategies (to see the contribution of each optimization), the bests DEST-based ones (i.e., without weights), and finally the best of each SCC-based strategy.

Figure 3 shows box plots of standard score computed for selected provisos and all models. The standardization is performed as follows. For each model M, we take the set of 1600 runs generated (100 runs per proviso), and compute a mean number of states μ_M and a standard deviation σ_M. The standard score of a run r is $\frac{states(r)-\mu_M}{\sigma_M}$. Therefore a score of 2 signifies that the run is two standard deviations away from the mean (of selected provisos) for the given model. Figure 3 shows the distribution of these scores as box plots. Each line shows a box that spans between the first and third quartiles, and is split by the median. The whiskers show the ranges of values below the first and above the third quartile that are not further away from the quartiles than 1.5 times the interquartile range. Other values are shown as outliers using circles.

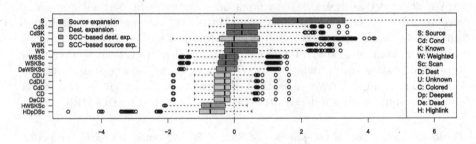

Fig. 3. Distributions of standard scores for a selection of provisos.

The ranking of provisos in Fig. 3 differs from previous tables that were biased toward large models. However, if we omit some permutations between provisos that have close median standard score, the order stays globally the same.

If we look at provisos that do not exploit SCCs, the best provisos appear to be all the CONDDEST variants, but they are very close to the state-of-the-art WEIGHTEDSOURCEKNOWNSCAN [1]. Introducing SCC-based provisos clearly brings another level of improvements, where, on the contrary to previous provisos, expanding the source or the destination does not make a serious difference.

6 Conclusion

Starting from an overview of state-of-the-art provisos for checking liveness properties, we have proposed new provisos based on the expansion of the destination instead of the source. These new provisos have been successfully combined with existing heuristics (SCAN, (UN)KNOWN, WEIGHTED) and new ones (COLORED, DEEPEST, DEAD, and HIGHLINK).

For source expansion, our results confirm and extend those of Evangelista and Pajault [1] who have shown that WEIGHTEDSOURCEKNOWN and WEIGHTEDSOURCEKNOWN were better than SOURCE. However when deconstructing these provisos to evaluate each optimization independently, we discovered that most of the gain can be obtained by implementing a very simple proviso, CONDSOURCE, that does not require maintaining weights or scanning the stack.

Expanding the destination of edges, even in very simple implementations like CONDDEST, appears to be competitive with state-of-the-art provisos using source-based expansions. When using an NDFS-based emptiness check, we recommend to use CONDDEST since it remains very simple to implement, requires small memory footprint and achieves good results.

We have also shown how to exploit SCC-based information to limit the number of expansions: the use of HIGHLINK brings a solid improvement to all provisos. When using an SCC-based emptiness check, our preference goes to HIGHLINKWEIGHTEDSOURCEKNOWN that does not require scanning the stack.

From this extensive analysis, we also observe: (1) the WEIGHTED-variants ruins the benefits of DEST-based provisos without HIGHLINKS, while they increase performances of SOURCE-based ones, (2) the (UN)KNOWN variants only bring a modest improvements while they double the number of visited transitions, (3) the SCAN heuristic is not of interest when combined with HIGHLINKS but is efficient otherwise. A scatter plot (see footnote 1) comparing the best of SOURCE-based provisos with the best of DEST-based ones, shows that they are complementary.

Most of the heuristics presented in this paper are derived from state-of-the-art provisos which have been proven correct [1,9]. Since reproducing the proof schemes for all the 46 provisos we presented in this paper would be laborious, and considering they were implemented, we opted for an extensive test campaign checking that, for randomly generated LTS, all provisos produce reduced graphs containing at least one expanded state per cycle.

Finally, note that SOURCE is for instance implemented in Spin. However, the *reduced* function implemented in Spin is different than ours: it returns either a single transition, or all transitions. With such a *reduced* function, some of the variants we presented make no sense (KNOWN, UNKNOWN, DEEPEST), and the results might be completely different. We leave the evaluation of the effect of different *reduced* functions on the provisos as a future work.

References

1. Evangelista, S., Pajault, C.: Solving the ignoring problem for partial order reduction. STTT **12**(2), 155–170 (2010)
2. Holzmann, G.J.: The model checker Spin. IEEE Trans. Softw. Eng. **23**(5), 279–295 (1997)

3. Laarman, A., Pater, E., Pol, J., Hansen, H.: Guard-based partial-order reduction. In: STTT, pp. 1–22 (2014)
4. Nalumasu, R., Gopalakrishnan, G.: An efficient partial order reduction algorithm with an alternative proviso implementation. FMSD **20**(1), 231–247 (2002)
5. Pater, E.: Partial order reduction for PINS. Technical report, University of Twente, March 2011
6. Patwary, M.M.A., Blair, J., Manne, F.: Experiments on union-find algorithms for the disjoint-set data structure. In: Festa, P. (ed.) SEA 2010. LNCS, vol. 6049, pp. 411–423. Springer, Heidelberg (2010)
7. Pelánek, R.: BEEM: benchmarks for explicit model checkers. In: Bošnački, D., Edelkamp, S. (eds.) SPIN 2007. LNCS, vol. 4595, pp. 263–267. Springer, Heidelberg (2007)
8. Pelánek, R.: Properties of state spaces and their applications. STTT **10**, 443–454 (2008)
9. Peled, D.: Combining partial order reductions with on-the-fly model-checking. In: Dill, D.L. (ed.) CAV 1994. LNCS, vol. 818, pp. 377–390. Springer, Heidelberg (1994)
10. Renault, E., Duret-Lutz, A., Kordon, F., Poitrenaud, D.: Three SCC-based emptiness checks for generalized Büchi automata. In: McMillan, K., Middeldorp, A., Voronkov, A. (eds.) LPAR-19 2013. LNCS, vol. 8312, pp. 668–682. Springer, Heidelberg (2013)
11. Schwoon, S., Esparza, J.: A note on on-the-fly verification algorithms. In: Halbwachs, N., Zuck, L.D. (eds.) TACAS 2005. LNCS, vol. 3440, pp. 174–190. Springer, Heidelberg (2005)
12. Valmari, A.: Stubborn sets for reduced state space generation. In: Rozenberg, G. (ed.) Advances in Petri Nets 1990. LNCS, vol. 483, pp. 491–515. Springer, Heidelberg (1991)

Partial-Order Reduction for GPU Model Checking

Thomas Neele[1,2]([✉]), Anton Wijs[2], Dragan Bošnački[2], and Jaco van de Pol[1]

[1] University of Twente, Enschede, The Netherlands
[2] Eindhoven University of Technology, Eindhoven, The Netherlands
t.s.neele@tue.nl

Abstract. Model checking using GPUs has seen increased popularity over the last years. Because GPUs have a limited amount of memory, only small to medium-sized systems can be verified. For on-the-fly explicit-state model checking, we improve memory efficiency by applying partial-order reduction. We propose novel parallel algorithms for three practical approaches to partial-order reduction. Correctness of the algorithms is proved using a new, weaker version of the cycle proviso. Benchmarks show that our implementation achieves a reduction similar to or better than the state-of-the-art techniques for CPUs, while the amount of runtime overhead is acceptable.

1 Introduction

The practical applicability of model checking [1,10] has often been limited by state-space explosion. Successful solutions to this problem have either depended on efficient algorithms for state space reduction, or on leveraging new hardware improvements. To capitalize on new highly parallel processor technology, multi-core [14] and GPU model checking [7] have been introduced. In recent years, this approach has gained popularity and multiple mainstream model checkers already have multi-threaded implementations [3,9,11,14,16]. In general, designing multi-threaded algorithms for modern parallel architectures brings forward new challenges typical for concurrent programming. For model checking, developing concurrent versions of existing state space algorithms is an important task.

The massive number of threads that run in parallel makes GPUs attractive for the computationally intensive task of state space exploration. Their parallel power can speed-up model checking by up to two orders of magnitude [2,12,26,28]. Although the amount of memory available on GPUs has increased significantly over the last years, it is still a limiting factor.

In this work we aim to improve the memory efficiency of GPU-based model checking. Therefore, we focus on reconciling *partial-order reduction* (POR) techniques [13,21,23] with a GPU-based model checking algorithm [27]. POR exploits

We gratefully acknowledge the support of NVIDIA Corporation with the donation of the GeForce Titan X used for this research.

C. Artho et al. (Eds.): ATVA 2016, LNCS 9938, pp. 357–374, 2016.
DOI: 10.1007/978-3-319-46520-3_23

the fact that the state space may contain several paths that are similar, in the sense that their differences are not relevant for the property under consideration. By pruning certain transitions, the size of the state space can be reduced. Hence, POR has the potential to increase the practical applicability of GPUs in model checking.

Contributions. We extend GPUEXPLORE [27], one of the first tools that runs a complete model checking algorithm on the GPU, with POR. We propose GPU algorithms for three practical approaches to POR, based on ample [15], cample [6] and stubborn sets [23]. We improve the cample-set approach by computing clusters on-the-fly. Although our algorithms contain little synchronization, we prove that they satisfy the action ignoring proviso by introducing a new version of the so called cycle proviso, which is weaker than previous versions [8, 21], possibly leading to better reductions. Our implementation is evaluated by running benchmarks with models from several other tools. We compare the performance of each of the approaches with LTSMIN [16], which implements state-of-the-art algorithms for explicit-state multi-core POR.

The rest of the paper is organized as follows: Sect. 2 gives an overview of related work and Sect. 3 introduces the theoretic background of partial-order reduction and the GPU architecture. The design of our algorithms is described in Sect. 4 and a formal correctness proof is given in Sect. 5. Finally, Sect. 6 presents the results obtained from executing our implementation on several models and Sect. 7 provides a conclusion and suggestions for future work.

2 Related Work

Partial-Order Reduction. Bošnački et al. have defined cycle provisos for general state expanding algorithms [8] (GSEA, a generalization of *depth-first search* (DFS) and *breadth-first search* (BFS)). Although the proposed algorithms are not multi-core, the theory is relevant for our design, since our GPU model checker uses a BFS-like exploration algorithm.

POR has been implemented in several multi-core tools: Holzmann and Bošnački [14] implemented a multi-core version of SPIN that supports POR. They use a slightly adapted cycle proviso that uses information on the local DFS stack.

Barnat et al. [4] have defined a parallel cycle proviso that is based on a topological sorting of the state space. A state space cannot be topologically sorted if it contains cycles. This information is used to determine which states need to be fully expanded. Their implementation provides competitive reductions. However, it is not clear from the paper whether it is slower or faster than a standard DFS-based implementation.

Laarman and Wijs [19] designed a multi-core version of POR that yields better reductions than SPIN's implementation, but has higher runtimes. The scalability of the algorithm is good up to at least 64 cores.

GPU Model Checking. General purpose GPU (GPGPU) techniques have already been applied in model checking by several people, all with a different approach: Edelkamp and Sulewski [12] perform successor generation on the GPU and apply delayed duplicate detection to store the generated states in main memory. Their implementation performs better than DIVINE, it is faster and consumes less memory per state. The performance is worse than multi-core SPIN, however.

Barnat et al. [2] perform state-space generation on the CPU, but offload the detection of cycles to the GPU. The GPU then applies the *Maximal Accepting Predecessors* (MAP) or *One Way Catch Them Young* (OWCTY) algorithm to find these cycles. This results in a speed-up over both multi-core DIVINE and multi-core LTSMIN.

GPUEXPLORE by Wijs and Bošnački [26,27] performs state-space exploration completely on the GPU. The tool can check for absence of deadlocks and can also check safety properties. The performance of GPUEXPLORE is similar to LTSMIN running on about 10 threads.

Bartocci et al. [5] have extended SPIN with a CUDA implementation. Their implementation has a significant overhead for smaller models, but performs reasonably well for medium-sized state spaces.

Wu et al. [28] also implemented a complete model checker in CUDA. They adopted several techniques from GPUEXPLORE, and added dynamic parallelism and global variables. The speed up gained from dynamic parallelism proved to be minimal. A comparison with a sequential CPU implementation shows a good speed-up, but it is not clear from the paper how the performance compares with other parallel tools.

GPUs have also been applied in probabilistic model checking: Bošnački et al. [7,25] speed up value-iteration for probabilistic properties by solving linear equation systems on the GPU. Češka et al. [9] implemented parameter synthesis for parametrized continuous time Markov chains.

3   Background

Before we introduce the theory of POR, we first establish the basic definitions of labelled transitions systems and concurrent processes.

Definition 1. *A labelled transition system (LTS) is a tuple* $\mathcal{T} = (S, A, \tau, \hat{s})$, *where:*

- *S is a finite set of states.*
- *A is a finite set of actions.*
- *$\tau : S \times A \times S$ is the relation that defines transitions between states. Each transition is labelled with an action $\alpha \in A$.*
- *$\hat{s} \in S$ is the initial state.*

Let $enabled(s) = \{\alpha | (s, \alpha, t) \in \tau\}$ be the set of actions that is enabled in state s and $succ(s, \alpha) = \{t | (s, \alpha, t) \in \tau\}$ the set of successors reachable through some action α. Additionally, we lift these definitions to take a set of states or actions as argument. The second argument of $succ$ is omitted when all actions are considered: $succ(s) = succ(s, A)$. If $(s, \alpha, t) \in \tau$, then we write $s \xrightarrow{\alpha} t$. We call a sequence of actions and states $s_0 \xrightarrow{\alpha_1} s_1 \xrightarrow{\alpha_2} \ldots \xrightarrow{\alpha_n} s_n$ an *execution*. We call the sequence of states visited in an execution a *path*: $\pi = s_0 \ldots s_n$. If there exists a path $s_0 \ldots s_n$, then we say that s_n is *reachable* from s_0.

To specify concurrent systems consisting of a finite number of finite-state processes, we define a *network* of LTSs [20]. In this context we also refer to the participating LTSs as *concurrent processes*.

Definition 2. *A network of LTSs is a tuple $\mathcal{N} = (\Pi, V)$, where:*

- *Π is a list of n processes $\Pi[1], \ldots, \Pi[n]$ that are modelled as LTSs.*
- *V is a set of synchronization rules $(\boldsymbol{t}, a)$, where a is an action and $\boldsymbol{t} \in \{0, 1\}^n$ is a synchronization vector that denotes which processes synchronize on a.*

For every network, we can define an LTS that represents its state space.

Definition 3. *Let $\mathcal{N} = (\Pi, V)$ be a network of processes. $\mathcal{T}_\mathcal{N} = (S, A, \tau, \hat{s})$ is the LTS induced by this network, where:*

- *$S = S[1] \times \cdots \times S[n]$ is the cross-product of all the state spaces.*
- *$A = A[1] \cup \cdots \cup A[n]$ is the union of all actions sets.*
- *$\tau = \{(\langle s_1, \ldots, s_n \rangle, a, \langle t_1, \ldots, t_n \rangle) \mid \exists (\boldsymbol{t}, a) \in V : \forall i \in \{1..n\} : \boldsymbol{t}(i) = 1 \Rightarrow (s_i, a, t_i) \in \tau[i] \wedge \boldsymbol{t}(i) = 0 \Rightarrow s_i = t_i\}$ is the transition relation that follows from each of the processes and the synchronization rules.*
- *$\hat{s} = \langle \hat{s}[0], \ldots, \hat{s}[n] \rangle$ is the combination of the initial states of the processes.*

We distinguish two types of actions: (1) *local actions* that do not synchronize with other processes, i.e. all rules for those actions have exactly one element set to 1, and (2) *synchronizing actions* that do synchronize with other processes. In the rest of this paper we assume that local actions are never blocked, i.e. if there is a local action $\alpha \in A[i]$ then there is a rule $(\boldsymbol{t}, \alpha) \in V$ such that element i of $\boldsymbol{t}$ is 1 and the other elements are 0. Note that although processes can only synchronize on actions with the same name, this does not limit the expressiveness. Any network can be transformed into a network that follows our definition by proper action renaming.

During state-space exploration, we exhaustively generate all reachable states in $\mathcal{T}_\mathcal{N}$, starting from the initial state. When all successors of s have been identified, we say that s has been *explored*, and once a state s has been generated, we say that it is *visited*.

3.1 Partial-Order Reduction

We first introduce the general concept of a reduction function and a reduced state space.

Definition 4. *A reduced LTS can be defined according to some reduction function* $r : S \to 2^A$. *The reduction of* T *w.r.t.* r *is denoted by* $T_r = (S_r, A, \tau_r, \hat{s})$, *such that:*

- *$(s, \alpha, t) \in \tau_r$ if and only if $(s, \alpha, t) \in \tau$ and $\alpha \in r(s)$.*
- *S_r is the set of states reachable from $\hat{s}$ under τ_r.*

POR is a form of state-space reduction for which the reduction function is usually computed while exploring the original state space (*on-the-fly*). That way, we avoid having to construct the entire state space and we are less likely to encounter memory limitations. However, a drawback is that we never obtain an overview of the state space and the reduction function might be larger than necessary.

The main idea behind POR is that not all interleavings of actions of parallel processes are relevant to the property under consideration. It suffices to check only one representative execution from each equivalence class of executions. To reason about this, we define when actions are *independent*.

Definition 5. *Two actions* α, β *are independent in state* s *if and only if* $\alpha, \beta \in enabled(s)$ *implies:*

- $\alpha \in enabled(succ(s, \beta))$
- $\beta \in enabled(succ(s, \alpha))$
- $succ(succ(s, \alpha), \beta) = succ(succ(s, \beta), \alpha)$

Actions are globally independent if they are independent in every state $s \in S$.

Based on the theory of independent actions, the following restrictions on the reduction function have been developed [10]:

C0a $r(s) \subseteq enabled(s)$.
C0b $r(s) = \emptyset \Leftrightarrow enabled(s) = \emptyset$.
C1   For all $s \in S$ and executions $s \xrightarrow{\alpha_1} s_1 \xrightarrow{\alpha_2} \ldots \xrightarrow{\alpha_{n-1}} s_{n-1} \xrightarrow{\alpha_n} s_n$ such that $\alpha_1, \ldots, \alpha_n \notin r(s)$, α_n is independent in s_{n-1} with all actions in $r(s)$.

C0b makes sure that the reduction does not introduce new deadlocks. C1 implies that all $\alpha \in r(s)$ are independent of $enabled(s) \setminus r(s)$. Informally, this means that only the execution of independent actions can be postponed to a later state. A set of actions that satisfies these criteria is called a *persistent set*. It is hard to compute the smallest persistent set, therefore several practical approaches have been proposed, which will be introduced in Sect. 4.

If r is a persistent set, then all deadlocks in an LTS T are preserved in T_r. Therefore, persistent sets can be used to speed up checking for deadlocks. However, safety properties are generally not preserved due to the *action-ignoring problem*. This occurs whenever some action in the original system is ignored indefinitely, i.e. it is never selected for the reduction function. Since we are dealing with finite state spaces and condition C0b is satisfied, this can only occur on a cycle. To prevent action-ignoring, another condition, called the *action-ignoring proviso*, is applied to the reduction function.

C2ai For every state $s \in S_r$ and every action $\alpha \in enabled(s)$, there exists an execution $s \xrightarrow{\alpha_1} s_1 \xrightarrow{\alpha_2} \ldots \xrightarrow{\alpha_n} s_n$ in the reduced state space, such that $\alpha \in r(s_n)$.

Applying this proviso directly by means of Valmari's SCC approach [22] introduces quite some runtime overhead. For this reason, several stronger versions of the action-ignoring proviso have been defined, generally called *cycle provisos*. Since GPUEXPLORE does not follow a strict BFS order, we will use the *closed-set proviso* [8] (*Closed* is the set of states that have been visited and for which exploration has at least started):

C2c There is at least one action $\alpha \in r(s)$ and state t such that $s \xrightarrow{\alpha} t$ and $t \notin Closed$. Otherwise, $r(s) = enabled(s)$.

3.2 GPU Architecture

CUDA[1] is a programming interface developed by NVIDIA to enable general purpose programming on a GPU. It provides a unified view of the GPU ('device'), simplifying the process of developing for multiple devices. Code to be run on the device ('kernel') can be programmed using a subset of C++.

On the hardware level, a GPU is divided up into several *streaming multiprocessors* (SM) that contain hundreds of cores. On the side of the programmer, threads are grouped into *blocks*. The GPU schedules thread blocks on the SMs. One SM can run multiple blocks at the same time, but one block cannot execute on more than one SM. Internally, blocks are executed as one or more *warps*. A warp is a group of 32 threads that move in lock-step through the program instructions.

Another important aspect of the GPU architecture is the memory hierarchy. Firstly, each block is allocated *shared memory* that is shared between its threads. The shared memory is placed on-chip, therefore it has a low latency. Secondly, there is the global memory that can be accessed by all the threads. It has a high bandwidth, but also a high latency. The amount of global memory is typically multiple gigabytes. There are three caches in between: the L1, L2 and the texture cache. Data in the global memory that is marked as read-only (a 'texture') may be placed in the texture cache. The global memory can be accessed by the CPU ('host'), thus it also serves as an interface between the host and the device. Figure 1 gives a schematic overview of the architecture.

The bandwidth between the SMs and the global memory is used optimally when a continuous block of 32 integers is fetched by a warp. In that case, the memory transaction is performed in parallel. This is called *coalesced* access.

---

[1] https://developer.nvidia.com/cuda-zone.

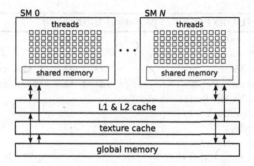

Fig. 1. Schematic overview of the GPU hardware architecture

4   Design and Implementation

4.1   Existing Design

GPUEXPLORE [27] is an explicit-state model checker that can check for deadlocks and safety properties. GPUEXPLORE executes all the computations on the GPU and does not rely on any processing by the CPU.

The global memory of the GPU is occupied by a large hash table that uses open addressing with rehashing. The hash table stores all the visited states, distinguishing the states that still need to be explored (*Open* set) from those that do not require this (*Closed*). It supports a *findOrPut* operation that inserts states if they are not already present. The implementation of findOrPut is thread-safe and lockless. It uses the *compareAndSwap* (CAS) operation to perform atomic inserts.

The threads are organized as follows: each thread is primarily part of a block. As detailed in Sect. 3.2, the hardware enforces that threads are grouped in warps of size 32. We also created logical groups, called *vector groups*. The number of threads in a vector group is equal to the number of processes in the network (cf. Sect. 3). When computing successors, threads cooperate within their vector group. Each thread has a vector group thread id (*vgtid*) and is responsible for generating the successors of process $\Pi[vgtid]$. Successors following from synchronizing actions are generated in cooperation. Threads with vgtid 0 are *group leaders*. When accessing global memory, threads cooperate within their warp and read continuous blocks of 32 integers for coalesced access. Note that the algorithms presented here specify the behaviour of one thread, but are run on multiple threads and on multiple blocks. Most of the synchronization is hidden in the functions that access shared or global memory.

A high-level view on the algorithm of GPUEXPLORE is presented in Algorithm 1. This kernel is executed repetitively until all reachable states have been explored. Several iterations may be performed during each launch of the kernel (NUMITERATIONS is fixed by the user). Each iteration starts with *work gathering*: blocks search for unexplored states in global memory and copy those states to the work tile in shared memory (line 4). Once the work tile is full,

Algorithm 1. GPUEXPLORE exploration framework

Data: __global__ table[ ]
Data: __shared__ workTile[ ], cache[ ]

```
1  vgid ← tid / numProc;                    /* index of the vector group */
2  vgtid ← tid mod numProc;                 /* id of the thread in the group */
3  foreach i ∈ 0 . . . NUMITERATIONS do
4  │   workTile ← gatherWork();
5  │   __syncthreads();
6  │   s ← workTile[vgid];
7  │   foreach t ∈ succ_vgtid(s) do
8  │   │   storeInCache(t);
9  │   __syncthreads();
10 │   foreach t ∈ cache do
11 │   │   if isNew(t) then
12 │   │   │   findOrPutWarp(t);
13 │   │   │   markOld(t);
```

the __syncthreads function from the CUDA API synchronizes all threads in the block and guarantees that writes to the work tile are visible to other threads (line 5). Then, each vector group takes a state from the work tile (line 6) and generates its successors (line 7). To prevent non-coalesced accesses to global memory, these states are first placed in a cache in shared memory (line 8). When all the vector groups in a block are done with successor generation, each warp scans the cache for new states and copies them to global memory (line 12). The states are then marked old in the cache (line 13), so they are still available for local duplicate detection later on. For details on successor computation and the hash table, we refer to [27].

In the following sections, we will show how the generation of successors on lines 7 and 8 can be adjusted to apply POR.

4.2 Ample-Set Approach

The ample-set approach is based on the idea of *safe* actions [15]: an action is safe if it is independent of all actions of all other processes. While exploring a state s, if there is a process $\Pi[i]$ that has only safe actions enabled in s, then $r(s) = enabled_i(s)$ is a valid ample set, where $enabled_i(s)$ is the set of actions of process $\Pi[i]$ enabled in s. Otherwise, $r(s) = enabled(s)$. In our context of an LTS network, only local actions are safe, so reduction can only be applied if we find a process with only local actions enabled.

An outline of the GPU ample-set algorithm can be found in Algorithm 2. First, the successors of processes that have only local actions enabled are generated. These states are stored in the cache (line 4) by some thread i, and their location in the cache is stored in a buffer that has been allocated in shared memory for each thread (line 5). Then, line 8 finds the location of the states in global

Algorithm 2. Successor generation under the ample-set approach

---

    Data: __global__ table[ ]
    Data: __shared__ cache[ ], buf[ ][ ], reduceProc[ ]

1 $bufCount \leftarrow 0$, $reduceProc[vgid] \leftarrow numProcs$;
2 **if** $processHasOnlyLocalTrans(s, vgtid)$ **then**
3   **foreach** $t \in succ_{vgtid}(s)$ **do**
4        $location \leftarrow$ `storeInCache(`t`)`;
5        $buf[tid][bufCount] \leftarrow location$;
6        $bufCount \leftarrow bufCount + 1$;
7 **foreach** $i \in [0..bufCount - 1]$ **do**
8     $j \leftarrow$ `findGlobal(`$cache[buf[tid][i]]$`)`;
9   **if** $j =$ NotFound $\vee$ `isNew(`$table[j]$`)` **then**
10   **atomicMinimum**($\&reduceProc[vgid], vgtid$);
11 __syncthreads();
12 **if** $reduceProc[vgid] < numProcs \wedge reduceProc[vgid] \neq vgtid$ **then**
13   **foreach** $i \in [0..bufCount - 1]$ **do**
14   `markOld(`$cache[buf[tid][i]]$`)`;
15 __syncthreads();
16 **if** $reduceProc[vgid] = vgtid$ **then**
17   **foreach** $i \in [0..bufCount - 1]$ **do**
18   `markNew(`$cache[buf[tid][i]]$`)`;
19 **if** $reduceProc[vgid] \geq numProcs$ **then**
20   `/* generate the remaining successors                    */`

---

memory. This step is performed by threads cooperating in warps to ensure coalesced memory accesses. If the state is not explored yet (line 9), then the cycle proviso has been satisfied and thread i reports it can apply reduction through the *reduceProc* shared variable (line 10). In case the process of some thread has been elected for reduction ($reduceProc[vgid] < numProcs$), the other threads apply the reduction by marking successors in their buffer as old in the cache, so they will not be copied to global memory later. Finally, threads corresponding to elected processes get a chance to mark their states as new if they have been marked as old by a thread from another vector group (line 18). In case no thread can apply reduction, the algorithm continues as normal (line 19).

4.3 Clustered Ample-Set Approach

In our definition of a network of LTSs, local actions represent internal process behaviour. Since most practical models frequently perform communication, they have only few local actions and consist mainly of synchronizing actions. The ample-set approach relies on local actions to achieve reduction, so it often fails to reduce the state space. To solve this issue, we implemented *cluster-based* POR [6]. Contrary to the ample-set approach, all actions of a particular set of processes (the *cluster*) are selected. The notion of safe actions is still key. However, the definition is now based on clusters. An action is safe with respect to a cluster $\mathcal{C} \subseteq \{1, \ldots, n\}$ (n is the number of processes in the network), if it is part of a process of that cluster and it is independent of all actions of processes outside the cluster. Now, for any cluster $\mathcal{C}$ that has only actions enabled that are safe with respect to $\mathcal{C}$, $r(s) = \bigcup_{i \in \mathcal{C}} enabled_i(s)$ is a valid cluster-based ample (*cample*) set. Note that the cluster containing all processes always yields a valid cample set.

Whereas Basten and Bošnački [6] determine a tree-shaped cluster hierarchy a priori and by hand, our implementation computes the cluster on-the-fly. This should lead to better reductions, since the fixed hierarchy only works for parallel processes that are structured as a tree. Dynamic clustering works for any structure, for example ring or star structured LTS networks. In [6], it is argued that computing the cluster on-the-fly is an expensive operation, so it should be avoided. Our approach is, when we are exploring a state s, to compute the smallest cluster $\mathcal{C}$, such that $\forall i \in \mathcal{C} : C[i] \subseteq \mathcal{C}$, where $C[i]$ is the set of processes that process i synchronizes with in the state s. This can be done by running a simple fixed-point algorithm, with complexity $O(n)$, once for every $C[i]$ and finding the smallest from those fixed points. This gives a total complexity of $O(n^2)$. However, in our implementation, n parallel threads each compute a fixed point for some $C[i]$. Therefore, we are able to compute the smallest cluster in linear time with respect to the amount of processes. Dynamic clusters do not influence the correctness of the algorithm, the reasoning of [6] still applies.

The algorithm for computing cample-sets suffers from the fact that it is not possible to determine a good upper bound on the maximum amount of successors that can follow from a single state. Therefore, it is not possible to statically allocate a buffer, as was done for Algorithm 2. Dynamic allocation in shared memory is not supported by CUDA. The only alternative is to alternate between successor generation and checking whether the last state is marked as *new* in global memory. During this process, each thread tracks whether the generated successors satisfy the cycle proviso and with which other processes it synchronizes, based on the synchronization rules. The next step is to share this information via shared memory. Then, each thread computes a fixed-point as detailed above. The group leader selects the smallest of those fixed-points as cluster. All actions of processes in that closure will form the cample set. Finally, states are marked as *old* or *new* depending on whether they follow from an action in the cample set.

4.4 Stubborn-Set Approach

The stubborn-set approach was originally introduced by Valmari [23] and can yield better reductions than the ample-set approach. This technique is more complicated and can lead to overhead, since it reasons about all actions, even those that are disabled. The algorithm starts by selecting one enabled action and builds a stubborn set by iteratively adding actions as follows: for enabled actions α, all actions that are dependent on α are added. For disabled actions β, all actions that can enable β are added. When a closure has been reached, all enabled actions in the stubborn set together form a persistent set.

Our implementation uses bitvectors to store the stubborn set in shared memory. One bitvector can be used to represent a subset of the synchronization rules and the local actions. In case we apply the cycle proviso, we need four such bitvectors: to store the stubborn set, the set of enabled actions, the set of actions that satisfy the cycle proviso and a work set to track which actions still need to be processed. This design may have an impact on the practical applicability of the algorithm, since the amount of shared memory required is relatively high. However, this is the only approach that results in an acceptable computational overhead.

To reduce the size of the computed stubborn set, we use the *necessary disabling sets* and the heuristic function from Laarman et al. [17]. Contrary to their implementation, we do not compute a stubborn set for all possible choices of initial action. Our implementation deterministically picks an action, giving preference to local actions. Effectively, we sacrifice some reduction potential in order to minimize the overhead of computing a stubborn set.

In GPUEXPLORE, it is not possible to determine in constant time whether a certain action is enabled. Therefore, we chose to generate the set of enabled actions before computing the stubborn set. This also allows us to check which actions satisfy the cycle proviso. With this information saved in shared memory, a stubborn set can be computed efficiently. In case the set of actions satisfying the cycle proviso is empty, the set of all actions is returned. Otherwise, the group leader selects one initial action that satisfies the cycle proviso for the work set. Then, all threads in the group execute the closure algorithm in parallel. After computation of the stubborn set has finished, all successors following from actions in the set are generated and stored in the cache.

5   Proof of Correctness

The correctness of applying Bošnački et al.'s [8] closed-set proviso C2c in a multi-threaded environment is not immediately clear. The original correctness proof is based on the fact that for every execution, states are removed from *Open* (the set of unexplored states) in a certain sequence. In a multi-threaded algorithm, however, two states may be removed from *Open* at the same time. To prove that the algorithms introduced in the previous section satisfy the action ignoring proviso, we introduce a new version of the cycle proviso:

Lemma 1 (Closed-Set Cycle Proviso). *If a reduction algorithm satisfies conditions C0a, C0b and C1 and selects for every cycle $s_0 \xrightarrow{\alpha_0} s_1 \xrightarrow{\alpha_1} \ldots \xrightarrow{\alpha_{n-1}} s_n \xrightarrow{\alpha_n} s_0$ in the reduced state space with $\beta \in enabled(s_0)$ and $\beta \neq \alpha_i$ for all $0 \leq i \leq n$, (i) at least one transition labelled with β or (ii) at least one transition that, during the generation of the reduced state space, led to a state outside the cycle that has not been explored yet (i.e. $\exists i \exists (s_i, \gamma, t) \in \tau : \gamma \in r(s_i) \land t \notin$ Closed); then condition C2ai is satisfied.*

Proof. Suppose that action $\beta \in enabled(s_0)$ is always ignored, i.e. condition C2ai is not satisfied. This means there is no execution $s_0 \xrightarrow{\alpha_0} s_1 \xrightarrow{\alpha_1} \ldots \xrightarrow{\alpha_{n-1}} s_n \xrightarrow{\beta} t$

where $\alpha_i \in r(s_i)$ for all $0 \leq i < n$. Because we are dealing with finite state spaces, every execution that infinitely ignores β has to end in a cycle. These executions have a 'lasso' shape, they consist of an initial phase and a cycle. Let $s_0 \xrightarrow{\alpha_0} s_1 \xrightarrow{\alpha_1} \ldots \xrightarrow{\alpha_{i-1}} s_i \xrightarrow{\alpha_i} \ldots \xrightarrow{\alpha_{n-1}} s_n \xrightarrow{\alpha_n} s_i$ be the execution with the longest initial phase, i.e. with the highest value i (see Fig. 2). Since condition C1 is satisfied, β is independent of any α_k and thus enabled on any s_k with $0 \leq k \leq n$. It is assumed that for at least one of the states $s_i \ldots s_n$ an action exiting the cycle is selected. Let s_j be such a state. Since β is ignored, $\beta \notin r(s_j)$. According to the assumption, one of the successors found through $r(s_j)$ has not been in *Closed*. Let this state be t. Any finite path starting with $s_0 \ldots s_j t$ cannot end in a deadlock without taking action β at some point (condition C0b). Any infinite path starting with $s_0 \ldots s_j t$ has a longer initial phase (after all $j + 1 > i$) than the execution we assumed had the longest initial phase. Thus, our assumption is contradicted.   □

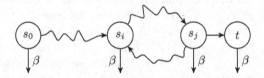

Fig. 2. 'Lasso' shaped path from the proof of Lemma 1

Before we prove that our algorithms satisfy the action ignoring proviso, it is important to note three things. Firstly, that the work gathering function on line 4 of Algorithm 1 moves the gathered states from *Open* to *Closed*. Secondly, the ample/stubborn set generated by our algorithms satisfies conditions C0a, C0b and C1, also when executed by multiple vector groups (the proof for this is omitted from this paper). And lastly, in this theorem the ample-set approach is used as an example, but the reasoning applies to all three algorithms.

Theorem 1. *Algorithm 2 produces a persistent set that satisfies our action-ignoring proviso, even when executed on multiple blocks.*

Proof. Let $s_0 \xrightarrow{\alpha_0} s_1 \xrightarrow{\alpha_1} \ldots \xrightarrow{\alpha_{n-2}} s_{n-1} \xrightarrow{\alpha_{n-1}} s_0$ be a cycle in the reduced state space. In case α_0 is dependent on all other enabled actions in s_0, there is no action to be ignored and C2ai is satisfied.

In case there is an action in s_0 that is independent of α_0, this action is prone to being ignored. Let us call this action β. Because condition C1 is satisfied, β is also enabled in the other states of the cycle: $\beta \in enabled(s_i)$ for all $0 \leq i < n$.

We now consider the order in which states on the cycle can be explored by multiple blocks. Let s_i be one of the states of this cycle that is gathered from *Open* first (line 4, Algorithm 1). There are two possibilities regarding the processing of state s_{i-1}:

- s_{i-1} is gathered from *Open* at exactly the same time as s_i. When the processing for s_{i-1} arrives at line 9 of Algorithm 2, s_i will be in *Closed*.
- s_{i-1} is gathered later than s_i. Again, s_i will be in *Closed*.

Since s_i is in *Closed* in both cases, at least one other action will be selected for $r(s_{i-1})$. If all successors of s_{i-1} are in *Closed*, then β has to be selected. Otherwise, at least one transition to a state that is not in *Closed* will be selected. Now we can apply the closed-set cycle proviso (Lemma 1).   □

6   Experiments

We want to determine the potential of applying POR in GPU model checking and how it compares to POR on a multi-core platform. Additionally, we want to determine which POR approach is best suited to GPUs. We will focus on measuring the reduction and overhead of each implementation.

We implemented the proposed algorithms in GPUEXPLORE[2]. Since GPUEX-PLORE only accepts EXP models as input, we added an EXP language front-end to LTSMIN [16] to make a comparison with a state-of-the-art multi-core model checker possible. We remark that it is out of the scope of this paper to make an absolute speed comparison between a CPU and a GPU, since it is hard to compare completely different hardware and tools. Moreover, speed comparisons have already been done before [5,27,28].

GPUEXPLORE was benchmarked on an NVIDIA Titan X, which has 24 SMs and 12 GB of global memory. We allocated 5 GB for the hash table. Our code was run on 3120 blocks of 512 threads and performed 10 iterations per kernel launch (cf. Sect. 4.1), since these numbers give the best performance [27].

LTSMIN was benchmarked on a machine with 24 GB of memory and two Intel Xeon E5520 processors, giving a total of 16 threads. We used BFS as search order. The stubborn sets were generated by the closure algorithm described by Laarman et al. [17].

The models that were used as benchmarks have different origins. Cache, sieve, odp, transit and asyn3 are all EXP models from the examples included in the CADP toolkit[3]. 1394, acs and wafer stepper are originally mCRL2[4] models and have been translated to EXP. The leader_election, lamport, lann, peterson and szymanski models come from the BEEM database and have been translated from DVE to EXP. The models with a .1-suffix are enlarged versions of the original models [27]. The details of the models can be found in Table 1. 'stub. set size' indicates the maximum size of the stubborn set, which is equal to the amount of synchronization rules plus the total amount of local actions.

For the first set of experiments, we disabled the cycle proviso, which is not needed when checking for deadlocks. For each model and for each POR approach, we executed the exploration algorithm ten times. The average size of the reduced

[2] Sources are available at https://github.com/ThomasNeele/GPUexplore.

[3] http://cadp.inria.fr.

[4] http://mcrl2.org.

Table 1. Overview of the models used in the benchmarks

model	#states	#transitions	stub. set size	model	#states	#transitions	stub. set size
cache	616	4,631	222	odp.1	7,699,456	31,091,554	556
leader_election1	4,261	12,653	4,712	1394.1	10,138,812	96,553,318	300
acs	4,764	14,760	134	asyn3	15,688,570	86,458,183	1,315
sieve	23,627	84,707	941	lamport8	62,669,317	304,202,665	305
odp	91,394	641,226	464	szymanski5	79,518,740	922,428,824	481
1394	198,692	355,338	301	peterson7	142,471,098	626,952,200	2,880
acs.1	200,317	895,004	139	lann6	144,151,629	648,779,852	48
transit	3,763,192	39,925,524	73	lann7	160,025,986	944,322,648	48
wafer_stepper.1	3,772,753	19,028,708	880				

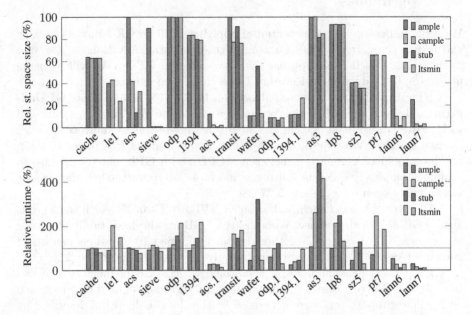

Fig. 3. State space and runtime of POR (no cycle proviso) relative to full exploration.

state space relative to the full state space is plotted in the first chart of Fig. 3 (the full state space has a size of 100 % for each model). The error margins are not depicted because they are very small (less than one percent point).

The first thing to note is that the state spaces of the `leader_election1` and `peterson7` models cannot be computed under the stubborn-set approach. The reason is that the amount of synchronization rules is very high, so the amount of shared memory required to compute a stubborn set exceeds the amount of shared memory available.

On average, the stubborn-set approach offers the best reduction, followed by the cample-set approach. Only for the `wafer_stepper.1` model, the stubborn-set approach offers a significantly worse reduction. As expected, the cample-set approach always offers roughly similar or better reduction than the ample-set approach, since it is a generalization of the ample-set approach. Overall, the reduction achieved by GPUEXPLORE and LTSMIN is comparable. Note that for GPUEXPLORE, any reduction directly translates into memory saving. For LTSMIN, this may not be the case, since its database applies *tree compression* [18].

Additionally, we measured the time it took to generate the full and the reduced state space. To get a good overview of the overhead resulting from POR, the relative performance is plotted in the second chart of Fig. 3. For each platform, the runtime of full state-space exploration is set to 100 % and is indicated by a red line. Again, the error margins are very small, so we do not depict them. These results show that the ample-set approach induces no significant overhead. For models where good reduction is achieved, it can speed-up the exploration process by up to 3.6 times for the acs.1 model. On the other hand, both the cample and stubborn-set approach suffer from significant overhead. When no or little reduction is possible, this slows down the exploration process by 2.6 times and 4.8 times respectively for the asyn3 model. This model has the largest amount of synchronization rules after the leader_election1 and peterson7 models.

For the smaller models, the speed-up that can be gained by the parallel power of thousands of threads is limited. If a *frontier* (search layer) of states is smaller than the amount of states that can be processed in parallel, then not all threads are occupied and the efficiency drops. This problem can only get worse under POR. For the largest models, the overhead for LTSMIN is two times lower than for GPUEXPLORE's stubborn-set approach. This shows that our implementation

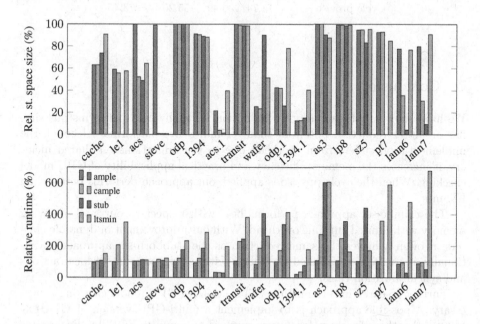

Fig. 4. State space and runtime of POR with cycle proviso relative to full exploration.

not only has overhead from generating all successors twice, but also from the stubborn-set computation.

In the second set of experiments, we used POR with cycle proviso. Figure 4 shows the size of the state space and the runtime. As expected, less reduction is achieved. The checking of the cycle proviso induces only a little extra overhead (not more than 5 %) for the ample-set and the cample-set approach. The extra overhead for the stubborn-set approach can be significant, however: up to 36 % for the lamport8 model (comparing the amount of states visited per second). Here, the reduction achieved by LTSMIN is significantly worse. This is due to the fact that LTSMIN checks the cycle proviso after generating the smallest stubborn set. If that set does not satisfy the proviso, then the set of all actions is returned. Our approach, where the set consisting of only the initial action already satisfies the cycle proviso, often finds a smaller stubborn set. Therefore, GPUEXPLORE achieves a higher amount of reduction when applying the cycle proviso.

Table 2 shows the average size of the reduced state space for each implementation. Since GPUEXPLORE's stubborn-set implementation cannot compute $\mathcal{T}_r$ for leader_election1 and peterson7, those models have been excluded.

Table 2. Average relative size of reduced state spaces

Average size $\mathcal{T}_r$ (%)	ample	cample	stubborn	ltsmin
No proviso	58.97	43.08	42.30	41.80
Cycle proviso	73.74	56.49	55.26	73.45

7   Conclusion

We have shown that partial-order reduction for many-core platforms has similar or better reduction potential than for multi-core platforms. Although the implementation suffers from overhead due to the limitations on shared memory, it increases the memory efficiency and practical applicability of GPU model checking. When the cycle proviso is applied, our approach performs better than LTSmin.

The cample-set approach performs best with respect to our goal of saving memory with limited runtime overhead. With our improvement of dynamic clusters, it often achieves the same reduction as the stubborn-set approach. Additionally, it can also be applied to models with a large amount of local actions and synchronization rules.

Further research into the memory limitations of GPU model checking is necessary. A possible approach is to implement a multi-GPU version of GPUEXPLORE. Another direction for future work is to support POR for linear-time properties, as recently, GPUEXPLORE was extended to check such properties on-the-fly [24].

Acknowledgements. The authors would like to thank Alfons Laarman for his suggestions on how to improve this work.

References

1. Baier, C., Katoen, J.P.: Principles of Model Checking. MIT Press, Cambridge (2008)
2. Barnat, J., Bauch, P., Brim, L., Češka, M.: Designing fast LTL model checking algorithms for many-core GPUs. J. Parallel Distrib. Comput. **72**(9), 1083–1097 (2012)
3. Barnat, J., Brim, L., Ročkai, P.: DiVinE multi-core – a parallel LTL model-checker. In: Cha, S.S., Choi, J.-Y., Kim, M., Lee, I., Viswanathan, M. (eds.) ATVA 2008. LNCS, vol. 5311, pp. 234–239. Springer, Heidelberg (2008)
4. Barnat, J., Brim, L., Ročkai, P.: Parallel partial order reduction with topological sort proviso. In: Proceedings of the 8th IEEE International Conference on Software Engineering and Formal Methods, pp. 222–231. IEEE (2010)
5. Bartocci, E., Defrancisco, R., Smolka, S.A.: Towards a GPGPU-parallel SPIN model checker. In: Proceedings of SPIN 2014, pp. 87–96. ACM, San Jose (2014)
6. Basten, T., Bošnački, D., Geilen, M.: Cluster-based partial-order reduction. Proc. ASE **11**(4), 365–402 (2004)
7. Bošnački, D., Edelkamp, S., Sulewski, D., Wijs, A.: Parallel probabilistic model checking on general purpose graphics processors. STTT **13**(1), 21–35 (2010)
8. Bošnački, D., Leue, S., Lluch-Lafuente, A.: Partial-order reduction for general state exploring algorithms. STTT **11**(1), 39–51 (2009)
9. Češka, M., Pilař, P., Paoletti, N., Brim, L., Kwiatkowska, M.: PRISM-PSY: precise GPU-accelerated parameter synthesis for stochastic systems. In: Chechik, M., Raskin, J.-F. (eds.) TACAS 2016. LNCS, vol. 9636, pp. 367–384. Springer, Heidelberg (2016)
10. Clarke, E.M., Grumberg, O., Peled, D.: Model Checking. MIT Press, Cambridge (2001)
11. Dalsgaard, A.E., Laarman, A., Larsen, K.G., Olesen, M.C., van de Pol, J.: Multi-core reachability for timed automata. In: Jurdziński, M., Ničković, D. (eds.) FORMATS 2012. LNCS, vol. 7595, pp. 91–106. Springer, Heidelberg (2012)
12. Edelkamp, S., Sulewski, D.: Efficient explicit-state model checking on general purpose graphics processors. In: van de Pol, J., Weber, M. (eds.) Model Checking Software. LNCS, vol. 6349, pp. 106–123. Springer, Heidelberg (2010)
13. Godefroid, P., Wolper, P.: A partial approach to model checking. Inf. Comput. **110**(2), 305–326 (1994)
14. Holzmann, G.J., Bošnački, D.: The design of a multicore extension of the SPIN model checker. IEEE Trans. Softw. Eng. **33**(10), 659–674 (2007)
15. Holzmann, G.J., Peled, D.: An improvement in formal verification. In: Hogrefe, D., Leue, S. (eds.) Formal Description Techniques VII. FIP Advances in Information and Communication Technology, pp. 197–211. Springer, New York (1995)
16. Kant, G., Laarman, A., Meijer, J., van de Pol, J., Blom, S., van Dijk, T.: LTSmin: high-performance language-independent model checking. In: Baier, C., Tinelli, C. (eds.) TACAS 2015. LNCS, vol. 9035, pp. 692–707. Springer, Heidelberg (2015)
17. Laarman, A., Pater, E., van de Pol, J., Weber, M.: Guard-based partial-order reduction. In: Bartocci, E., Ramakrishnan, C.R. (eds.) SPIN 2013. LNCS, vol. 7976, pp. 227–245. Springer, Heidelberg (2013)

18. Laarman, A., van de Pol, J., Weber, M.: Parallel recursive state compression for free. In: Groce, A., Musuvathi, M. (eds.) SPIN 2011. LNCS, vol. 6823, pp. 38–56. Springer, Heidelberg (2011)
19. Laarman, A., Wijs, A.: Partial-order reduction for multi-core LTL model checking. In: Yahav, E. (ed.) HVC 2014. LNCS, vol. 8855, pp. 267–283. Springer, Heidelberg (2014)
20. Lang, F.: Exp.Open 2.0: a flexible tool integrating partial order, compositional, and on-the-fly verification methods. In: Romijn, J.M.T., Smith, G.P., van de Pol, J. (eds.) IFM 2005. LNCS, vol. 3771, pp. 70–88. Springer, Heidelberg (2005)
21. Peled, D.: All from one, one for all: on model checking using representatives. In: Courcoubetis, C. (ed.) CAV 1993. LNCS, vol. 697, pp. 409–423. Springer, Heidelberg (1993)
22. Valmari, A.: A stubborn attack on state explosion. In: Clarke, E.M., Kurshan, R.P. (eds.) Computer-Aided Verification. LNCS, vol. 531, pp. 156–165. Springer, Heidelberg (1991)
23. Valmari, A.: Stubborn sets for reduced state space generation. In: Rozenberg, G. (ed.) Advances in Petri Nets 1990. LNCS, vol. 483, pp. 491–515. Springer, Heidelberg (1991)
24. Wijs, A.: BFS-based model checking of linear-time properties with an application on GPUs. In: Chaudhuri, S., Farzan, A. (eds.) CAV 2016. LNCS, vol. 9780, pp. 472–493. Springer, Heidelberg (2016)
25. Wijs, A.J., Bošnački, D.: Improving GPU sparse matrix-vector multiplication for probabilistic model checking. In: Donaldson, A., Parker, D. (eds.) SPIN 2012. LNCS, vol. 7385, pp. 98–116. Springer, Heidelberg (2012)
26. Wijs, A., Bošnački, D.: GPUexplore: many-core on-the-fly state space exploration using GPUs. In: Ábrahám, E., Havelund, K. (eds.) TACAS 2014. LNCS, vol. 8413, pp. 233–247. Springer, Heidelberg (2014)
27. Wijs, A., Bošnački, D.: Many-core on-the-fly model checking of safety properties using GPUs. STTT 18(2), 1–17 (2015)
28. Wu, Z., Liu, Y., Sun, J., Shi, J., Qin, S.: GPU accelerated on-the-fly reachability checking. In: Proceedings of the 20th International Conference on Engineering of Complex Computer Systems, pp. 100–109. IEEE (2015)

Efficient Verification of Program Fragments: *Eager POR*

Patrick Metzler[⊠], Habib Saissi, Péter Bokor, Robin Hesse, and Neeraj Suri

Technische Univeristät Darmstadt, Darmstadt, Germany
{metzler,saissi,pbokor,hesse,suri}@deeds.informatik.tu-darmstadt.de

Abstract. Software verification of concurrent programs is hampered by an exponentially growing state space due to non-deterministic process scheduling. Partial order reduction (POR)-based verification has proven to be a powerful technique to handle large state spaces.

In this paper, we propose a novel dynamic POR algorithm, called *Eager POR* (EPOR), that requires considerably less overhead during state space exploration than existing algorithms. EPOR is based on a formal characterization of program fragments for which exploration can be scheduled in advance and dependency checks can be avoided. We show the correctness of this characterization and evaluate the performance of EPOR in comparison to existing state-of-the-art dynamic POR algorithms. Our evaluation shows substantial improvement in the runtime performance by up to 91 %.

Keywords: Model checking · Partial order reduction · Concurrent programs

1 Introduction

Automated verification of concurrent programs is known to be a hard problem [13]. The non-determinism of scheduling results in an exponential number of possible interleavings that need to be systematically explored by a program verifier. By constraining the considered class of properties, for instance to deadlock and local state reachability, POR techniques [10] attempt to tackle this problem by reducing the number of interleavings to be explored. A dependency relation between transitions gives raise to equivalence classes of executions, referred to as *Mazurkiewicz traces* [8], such that it is sufficient for a program verifier to explore only one representative per Mazurkiewicz trace.

The effectiveness of POR approaches relies on the precision of the dependency relation. In the original POR approaches, dependencies are calculated statically leading to an inaccurate over-approximation. Dynamic partial order

Péter Bokor is also affiliated with IncQuery Labs Ltd., Budapest, Hungary.

© Springer International Publishing AG 2016
C. Artho et al. (Eds.): ATVA 2016, LNCS 9938, pp. 375–391, 2016.
DOI: 10.1007/978-3-319-46520-3_24

reduction approaches [1, 3, 6] tighten the precision of the dependency relation by considering only dependencies occurring at runtime, leading to a less redundant exploration.

While exploring the state space of a program, dynamic POR algorithms identify pairs of dependent transitions which additionally need to be explored in reversed order so that all Mazurkiewicz traces are covered. Such pairs of transitions constitute a *reversible race* [1]. In order to detect all reversible races of a system, a dynamic POR algorithm checks for each transition whether it constitutes a race with any previous transition in the current path. During each such race check, the algorithm needs (often multiple times) to check whether two transitions are dependent. Therefore, dependency checks constitute a large part of any dynamic POR algorithm's runtime overhead.

In this paper, we propose *Eager POR* (EPOR), an optimization of dynamic POR algorithms such as SDPOR [1] that significantly reduces the number of dependency checks. EPOR *eagerly* creates schedules to bundle dependency checks for sequences of transitions instead of checking dependencies in every visited state. These sequences, called *sections*, correspond to program fragments of one or more statements of each process. By checking races in a section only once, many additional race checks and dependency checks can be avoided. A new constraint system-based representation of Mazurkiewicz traces ensures that all reversible races inside a section are explored in both orderings. As a result, EPOR requires significantly fewer dependency checks compared to other DPOR algorithms where dependencies are checked after the execution of every transition.

Contributions. Our contributions are threefold. (1) We introduce a general optimization of POR algorithms that explores program fragments, called sections. We formally model section-based exploration by a constraint system representation of Mazurkiewicz traces and proof its correctness. (2) We present a dynamic POR algorithm called EPOR that enables efficient verification of concurrent programs against local state properties and deadlocks. EPOR shows how to extend existing POR algorithms with section-based exploration. Finally, (3) we implement and evaluate EPOR using well established benchmarks written in a simplified C-like programming language.

2   Motivating Example

As a motivating example, consider the Readers-Writers benchmark in Fig. 1 (also used in [1,3]). Process 1 writes to the shared variable x (t_1), Processes 2 and 3 read from x (t_2 and t_3). The dynamic dependencies for all states are

Process 1:	Process 2:	Process 3:
t_1: write x	t_2: read x	t_3: read x

Fig. 1. Readers-writers benchmark with one writer and two readers.

$D = \{(t_1, t_2), (t_2, t_1), (t_1, t_3), (t_3, t_1)\}$; the operations t_2 and t_3 are commutative (do not constitute a race), while both t_1, t_2 and t_1, t_3 are non-commutative, (constitute a race).

Our approach is based on the observation that the set of all Mazurkiewicz traces of program fragments as in the Readers-writers example can be calculated without exploring any program states and checking for races between operations only once. The program of Fig. 1 has 4 (Mazurkiewicz) traces and the dynamic POR algorithm SDPOR [1] explores one execution per trace. Each execution consists of 3 events, hence SDPOR performs 3 race checks per execution (each time an operation is appended to the current partial execution, a check is performed whether the current operation constitutes a race with any previous operation of the current partial execution). Each race check consists of several dependency checks (in order to decide whether e_1 and e_2 constitute a race, pairwise dependencies need to be determined for all events that occur between e_1 and e_2). In total, SDPOR performs 12 race checks and 25 dependency checks.

By exploiting the fact that all executions consist of the same operations and contain the same races, it is possible to reduce the number of race checks to 3 and the number of dependency checks to 8: after exploring an arbitrary execution of the program, we know that each execution consists of t_1, t_2, and t_3 and contains the races $(t_1, t_2), (t_1, t_3)$ (either in this or in reversed order), which can be determined using 3 race checks. We construct four partial orders $\{(t_1, t_2), (t_1, t_3)\}$, $\{(t_2, t_1), (t_1, t_3)\}$, $\{(t_1, t_2), (t_3, t_1)\}$, and $\{(t_2, t_1), (t_3, t_1)\}$, which correspond to the four traces of the program. By computing a linear extension of each partial order, we obtain an execution of each trace. In Sect. 3.2, we explain how to generalize this idea to systems with dynamic dependencies.

3   Constraint System-Based POR

3.1   System Model

This section introduces basic notions about the system model and notations used throughout the rest of this paper.

We write $u = a_1 \ldots a_n$ for the sequence consisting of the elements $a_1, \ldots, a_n$ and define $range(u) := \{1, \ldots, n\}$. The empty sequence is denoted by ε. Concatenation of a sequence u and a sequence v or an element t is written as $u \cdot v$ or $u \cdot t$, respectively. For $i \in range(u)$, we define $u[i] := a_i$, $l[\ldots i] := a_1 \ldots a_i$, and $l[i \ldots] := a_i \ldots a_n$. We model concurrent programs as *transition systems* $TS = (PID, S, s_0, T)$, where PID is a finite set of process identifiers, S is a finite set of states, $s_0 \in S$ is the initial state of the system, and T is a finite set of transitions such that

- each transition $t \in T$ is mapped to a unique process identifier $pidt \in PID$
- for all $t \in T$, $t : S \rightharpoonup S$ (transitions are partial functions from S to S), where we write $t \in enabled(s)$ if t is defined at s
- for all $s_1, \ldots, s_{n+1} \in S$ and any finite sequence $t_1 \ldots t_n \in T$ such that $t_i(s_i) = s_{i+1}$, $s_1 \neq s_{n+1}$ (the state graph is acyclic)

- transitions do not disable other transitions:

$$\forall t, t' \in T. \forall s, s' \in S. s \xrightarrow{t} s' \wedge t' \in enabled(s) \wedge t' \notin enabled(s') \Rightarrow t = t'$$

- transitions do enable only transitions from the same process: $\forall t, t' \in T. \forall s, s' \in S. s \xrightarrow{t} s' \wedge t' \notin enabled(s) \wedge t' \in enabled(s') \Rightarrow pidt = pidt'$
- at most one transition per process is enabled at a given state: $\forall s \in S. \forall t, t' \in T. pidt = pidt' \wedge t, t' \in enabled(s) \Rightarrow t = t'$

To require that transitions do not disable other transitions simplifies the presentation but is not a general limitation as distinguishing between the termination and temporary blocking of a process would obviate the need for this restriction. A similar restriction is used in [1]. Acyclicity restricts our method to terminating programs in favor of a stateless exploration.

For the rest of this paper, we assume that there is an arbitrary transition system $TS = (PID, S, s_0, T)$ which models a concurrent program under analysis. Where not otherwise mentioned, we refer to this transition system.

Paths in the state graph of TS correspond to (partial) executions of the program modeled by TS. We represent such paths as transition sequences $t_1 \ldots t_n$ for some $t_1, \ldots, t_n \in T$. We write $s_1 \xrightarrow{t_1 \ldots t_n} s_{n+1}$ if there exist states $s_2, \ldots, s_{n+1} \in S$ such that $s_i \xrightarrow{t_i} s_{i+1}$ for all $1 \leq i \leq n$, i.e., $t_1 \ldots t_n$ corresponds to a path in the state graph of TS. Furthermore, if $s_1 \xrightarrow{u} s_2$ for some states s_1, s_2 and a transition sequence u, we write $u(s_1)$ to denote the state s_2 and call u a feasible sequence at s_1, written $u \in feasible(s_1)$.

A particular occurrence of a transition in a transition sequence is called an *event*. In a transition sequence $u = t_1 \ldots t_n$ feasible at s_0, we represent an event t_i by its index i in u.

We distinguish between data dependencies and dependencies caused by the program control flow of a process. The latter is modeled by a *program order* for TS, which is a partial order $PO \subseteq T \times T$ such that $\forall (t_1, t_2) \in PO. pidt_1 = pidt_2$ (PO only relates transitions of the same process) and $\forall t, t' \in T. \forall s, s' \in S. s \xrightarrow{t} s' \wedge t' \notin enabled(s) \wedge t' \in enabled(s') \Rightarrow (t, t') \in PO$ (transitions enable only transitions which are successors w.r.t. the program order) and $\forall (t, t') \in PO. \exists s, s' \in S. s \xrightarrow{t} s' \wedge t' \notin enabled(s) \wedge t' \in enabled(s')$ (two transitions are in relation w.r.t. the program order only if the first transitions enables the second transition). We write $t_1 <_{PO} t_2$ for $(t_1, t_2) \in PO$.

Dynamic data dependencies are modeled by a relation $D \subseteq T \times T \times S$ such that $\forall t_1, t_2 \in T. \forall s \in S. (t_1, t_2, s) \notin D \Rightarrow (t_1 \in enabled(s) \wedge t_2 \in enabled(s) \Rightarrow \exists s'. s \xrightarrow{t_1 t_2} s' \wedge s \xrightarrow{t_2 t_1} s')$. Furthermore, $\forall t_1, t_2 \in T. \forall s \in S. (t_1, t_2, s) \in D \Rightarrow (t_1, t_2) \notin PO$ (transitions in program order are not data dependent).

The combination of program order and data dependency gives rise to partial orders that characterize the Mazurkiewicz traces of TS. For transition sequences $v = t_1 \ldots t_n$ and v' feasible at some state $s = u(s_0)$, we represent the ordering induced by dynamic data dependencies as the sequence $dep(u, v)$, defined as the sequence that consists of the elements of $\{(i, j) : (t_i, t_j, t_1 \ldots t_{i-1}(s)) \in D \wedge i < j\}$

ordered with respect to $(i,j) < (i',j')$ if $i < i'$, or $i = i'$ and $j < j'$. We define Mazurkiewicz equivalence as $v \simeq v'$ if $dep(u,v) = dep(u,v')$.

For a given transition t and a state s, we write $dependencies(t,s) := \{t' : (t,t',s) \in D\}$ for the set of transitions that are dependent with t.

As we use SDPOR as a basis to present EPOR, we adapt the corresponding definition of reversible races [1]. Two data dependent transitions t_i, t_j in some transition sequence $u = t_1 \ldots t_n$ feasible at s_0 constitute a reversible race, written $i \precsim_u j$, if there exists an equivalent sequence in which t_i and t_j are adjacent and dependent; formally, we define $i \precsim_u j \Leftrightarrow (i,j) \in dep(\varepsilon, u) \wedge \forall i < k < j . (i,k) \notin dep(\varepsilon, u) \vee (k,j) \notin dep(\varepsilon, u) \wedge t_j \in enabled(t_1 \ldots t_{i-1} t_{k_1} \ldots t_{k_m}(s_0))$, where $t_{k_1} \ldots t_{k_m}$ is the sequence $t_{i+1} \ldots t_{j-1}$ with all transitions removed that are neither data dependent nor in program order with t_j.

3.2 Exploring Programs in Sections

Requirements for Sections. As described in our motivating example (Sect. 2), EPOR requires only 3 instead of 12 race detections and only 8 instead of 25 dependency checks when exploring the Readers-Writers program. This reduction is possible because two conditions are met: every maximal transition sequence feasible at the initial state of Readers-Writers contains the same transitions and dependencies do not depend on states (it is possible to precisely calculate all dependencies statically).

In order to generalize our approach to arbitrary programs, we identify program fragments called *sections* where a generalization of these two conditions hold: (A) every execution of the section contains the same set of events and (B) dependencies inside the section do not change during any execution of the section (it is possible to precisely calculate all dependencies of the section with the information given at the first state of the section). Once all traces for a section are explored, EPOR performs the same race checks as SDPOR in order to find races between events before and inside the current section.

Throughout this section, we use the program of Fig. 2 as an example to explain conditions (A) and (B). Here, three processes work on the shared variables x, y, and z, where x is array of length two. The statements labeled t_{00}, t_{01}, and t_{10} constitute a section. Including t_{11} in the same section would violate condition (A) and including t_{20} would violate condition (B), as detailed below.

In order to meet condition (A), we have to ensure that no transition is enabled in one trace of a section while it is disabled in another trace of the section. For this, we define *branching transitions* as transitions which enable different program order successors depending on the state it is executed in:

Process 0:	Process 1:	Process 2:
t_{00}: y := 0	t_{10}: **if** x[0] = 0	t_{20}: y := 1
t_{01}: x[y] := 1	t_{11}: **then** z := 1	

Fig. 2. A program with branchings.

$$branching(t) :\Leftrightarrow \exists s, s' \in S. t \in enabled(s) \wedge t \in enabled(s') \wedge$$
$$(enabled(t(s)) \setminus enabled(s)) \neq (enabled(t(s')) \setminus enabled(s')).$$

For the example of Fig. 2, the statement t_{11} cannot be part of the same section as t_{10} because t_{10} is a branching transition and t_{11} is a program order successor of t_{10}.

As long as sections do not contain any branching transition together with one of its program order successors, condition (A) is satisfied. To see this, assume that there exists a transition sequence u in a section such that u becomes unfeasible when transformed to u' by swapping only transitions that are not in program order relation. Let t_1 be the first transition in u that is not enabled at the corresponding state in u'. Since transitions cannot disable other transitions by definition, there exists some transition t_2 that occurs before t_1 in u and enables t_1 in u but does not enable t_1 in u'. We have $t_2 <_{PO} t_1$, hence t_2 occurs before t_1 in u' as well. Transition t_2 is enabled in both u and u' because t_1 is the first transition not enabled in u'. Since t_2 enables different transitions depending on the state it is executed in, it is a branching transition, contradiction.

A section satisfies condition (B) if all of its traces contain the same set of dependencies or, equivalently, if the dependencies inside the section can be determined at the first state of the section. This condition holds if swapping two dependent transitions inside a section does not influence whether following transitions are dependent. We characterize such a pair of dependent transitions that influences following dependencies as *hiding dependency* so that the absence of hiding dependencies implies (B):

$$t_1 \xrightarrow{*}_s t_2 :\Leftrightarrow \exists s_1, s_1', s_2, s_2' \in S. s \xrightarrow{t_1} s_1 \xrightarrow{t_2} s_1' \wedge s \xrightarrow{t_2} s_2 \xrightarrow{t_1} s_2'$$
$$\wedge dependencies(t_2, s_1') \neq dependencies(t_2, s_2').$$

In the example of Fig. 2, the statement t_{20} cannot be in the same section as statement t_{00} because they constitute a hiding dependency: the order in which t_{00} and t_{20} are executed influences the fact whether t_{01} and t_{10} are dependent and constitute a race.

A section which contains no hiding dependency trivially satisfies condition (B). Although dependencies inside of sections have to be independent of states inside the section, dynamic information about dependencies that is known at the beginning of a section can be accounted for. Therefore, EPOR makes use of all dynamic dependency information just as SDPOR.

Implementing Section Construction. In order to implement an algorithm that relies on sections, it is desirable to determine where the next section ends with only small overhead. Therefore, we present two static checks which detect branching transitions (in order to ensure condition (A)) and hiding dependencies (in order to ensure condition (B)).

When translating a program into a transition system, we statically classify all transitions that model a branching statement as a branching transition, where a branching statement is a statement with multiple program order successors, e.g., a conditional jump, an if-then-else construct, or a loop. This over-approximates the set of all branching transitions (for example, a conditional jump with an unsatisfiable condition would still be classified as a branching transition).

We prepare the check whether two transitions form a hiding dependency by a static dependency analysis. For each transition t, we calculate the set of program variables that can influence the address which is accessed by t. For each such variable, all transitions writing to the variable are marked as potentially influencing the address of t's memory access. Two transitions with disjoint sets of address-influencing transitions do not constitute a hiding dependency.

Constructing Mazurkiewicz Traces. Once transitions and the races of a section are known (e.g., by executing an arbitrary interleaving until the end of the current section), it is possible to calculate all Mazurkiewicz traces without calculating any further program states as follows. A Mazurkiewicz trace can be calculated by constructing a directed graph with statements as nodes and an edge between two statements t and t' whenever t should occur before t' in all representatives of the Mazurkiewicz trace. If the resulting graph is acyclic, it induces a partial order that directly corresponds to a Mazurkiewicz trace and any of its linear extensions is a representative of the Mazurkiewicz trace. Otherwise, the graph contains a cycle and there exists no execution that obeys the ordering of the graph.

For the example of Fig. 2, we start by calculating a Mazurkiewicz trace of the section containing t_{00}, t_{01}, and t_{10}. We calculate the Mazurkiewicz trace where t_{01} occurs before t_{10} by defining the following graph:

$$t_{00} \xrightarrow{\text{po}} t_{01} \xrightarrow{\text{dep}} t_{10}$$

The edge (t_{00}, t_{01}) represents the program order of Process 1 and the edge (t_{01}, t_{10}) represents the (only) race of the section. Because the graph is acyclic, there exists a linear extension of the induced partial order, $t_{00}t_{01}t_{10}$, and we found a Mazurkiewicz trace of the program. By swapping the direction of the edge (t_{01}, t_{10}), we obtain a graph for another Mazurkiewicz trace where the race $t_{01} \precsim_{t_{00}t_{01}t_{10}} t_{10}$ is reversed. We do not swap the edge (t_{00}, t_{01}) because it represents the program order, which is obeyed by all executions.

A linear extension of the induced partial order can be constructed in linear time w.r.t. the number of nodes by iteratively removing a minimal node (a node with no incoming edge) and all its outgoing edges [11]. If no minimal node is found, the graph is cyclic.

By calculating Mazurkiewicz traces as described, it is possible to construct representatives of all Mazurkiewicz traces "in advance", i.e., without performing any (typically expensive) program state computations.

3.3   Formal Foundations of Trace Construction

This section formalizes the notions introduced in Sect. 3.2 and details how EPOR constructs Mazurkiewicz traces from a given transition sequence.

Section 3.2 describes sections as program fragments and specifies two conditions (A) and (B) they have to satisfy in order to support our POR algorithm. At the transition system level, we model a section as the set of transition sequences that correspond to an execution of the program fragment of the section. We write $section(u)$, where u is feasible at s_0, for the set of transition sequences that are feasible at $u(s_0)$ and include exactly those transitions that model the statements of a section. Formally, $section(u)$ includes all transition sequences $v = t_1 \ldots t_k$ that are feasible at $u(s_0)$ and satisfy (where conditions (A) and (B) have been introduced informally in Sect. 3.2):

(A): for each branching transition t in v, no transition in program order with t follows t in v: $\forall 1 \le i \le k.\ branching(t_i) \Rightarrow \forall i < j \le k.\ \neg t_i <_{PO} t_j$.

(B): v contains no hiding dependency: $\forall 1 \le i \le k.\ \forall i < j \le k.\ \neg t_i \xrightarrow{*}_s t_j$, where $s = t_1 \cdot \ldots \cdot t_{i-1}(s_0)$.

- maximality: There is no transition t such that $v \cdot t$ satisfies the above requirements.

For some $section(u)$, a POR algorithm ideally explores only a subset $section\text{-}rep(u) \subseteq section(u)$ that contains exactly one representative of each Mazurkiewicz trace of the transition sequences in $section(u)$. In order to formalize the generation of $section\text{-}rep(u)$, we introduce *trace constraint systems*. Each satisfiable trace constraint system corresponds to the fragment of a Mazurkiewicz trace. The constraints of a trace constraint system in conjunction with the program order specify the fragment's partial order of events. By swapping those constraints, it is possible to reverse races and thereby generate all transition sequences of $section\text{-}rep(u)$ for some u.

Formally, a trace constraint system is a tuple $c = (A, C, l)$ where

- $A = \{1, \ldots, k\}$ for some k (the variables of c).
- C is a list of pairs $(i, j) \in A \times A$ (the constraints of c).
- $l : A \to T$ is a function which labels the elements of A with transitions.

If for a given transition sequence $v = t_1 \ldots t_n$ feasible at some $s = u(s_0)$ we have $k = n$, $l(i) = t_i$ for all $1 \le i \le n$, and $C = dep(u, v)$, we call c the trace constraint system of u at s and write $c = CS(u, v)$.

Given a state $u(s_0)$ for some transition sequence u, one can construct a transition sequence v from $section(u)$ by starting with $v = \varepsilon$ and iteratively adding transitions enabled at $u \cdot v(s_0)$ until adding another transition would violate one of the conditions (A) and (B). All remaining transition sequences of $section\text{-}rep(u)$ can subsequently be constructed by the use of trace constraint systems as follows. First, the trace constraint system $CS(u, v)$ that corresponds to the trace of v is constructed. Subsequently, all trace constraint systems which are equal to $CS(u, v)$ except for one or more swapped constraints are constructed. The set of these constraint systems is called $traces(u)$ and defined as

$$traces(u):=\{(range(v), C, l) : \forall i \in range(v). \, l(i) = v[i]$$
$$\wedge range(C) = range(dep(u, v))$$
$$\wedge \forall i \in range(C). \, (C[i] = dep(u, v)[i]$$
$$\vee \exists \alpha_1, \alpha_2 \in range(v). \, (C[i] = (\alpha_2, \alpha_1) \wedge dep(u, v)[i] = (\alpha_1, \alpha_2)))\}$$
$$\text{for some } v \in section(u).$$

A solution v of a trace constraint system $c = (A, C, l)$, written $v \in solutions(c)$, is a transition sequence that (1) contains exactly the transitions that occur in the image of l and (2) obeys the constraints in C and (3) respects the program order for the transitions they contain. Formally, we require for v that the following holds.

- There exists an injective (1-to-1) function $\sigma : A \to A$ such that $\forall(\alpha_1, \alpha_2) \in A. \, (\sigma(\alpha_1), \sigma(\alpha_2)) \in C \Rightarrow \alpha_1 \geq \alpha_2$ (σ respects the constraints C) and $\forall \alpha_1, \alpha_2 \in A. \, (l(\sigma(\alpha_1)) <_{PO} l(\sigma(\alpha_2))) \Rightarrow \alpha_1 \geq \alpha_2$ (σ respects the program order PO).
- $v = l(\sigma(1)) \cdots l(\sigma(n))$

We call c *satisfiable* if a solution of c exists. A solution of a satisfiable c can be constructed in linear time w.r.t. the number of transitions that are contained in c. For example, create a linear extension of the partial order induced by the union of the constraints of c and the program order for the transitions occurring in c. If this union contains cycles, c is not satisfiable, which is easily detected by a linear extension algorithm.

Using the notion of $traces(u)$, one can construct $section\text{-}rep(u)$ as a set that contains exactly one solution of each satisfiable trace constraint system in $traces(u)$. As each trace constraint system in $traces(u)$ is unique, only one representative of each trace of $section(u)$ is constructed, enabling an optimal POR exploration. Correctness of section-based exploration is provided by the following theorem; given two transition sequences v_1, v_2 in $section(u)$, there exists a constraint system c in $traces(u)$ whose solutions are equivalent to v_2.

Theorem 1 (Correctness of Section-Based Exploration). $\forall u \in feasible(s_0). \, \forall v \in section(u). \, \exists c \in traces(u). \, \forall w \in solutions(c). \, w \simeq v$

Proof. Let $u \in feasible(s_0), v_1, v_2 \in section(u)$. Because of condition (A) in the definition of $section()$, v_1 and v_2 contain the same events (1). Because of condition (B) in the definition of $section()$, the same data dependencies appear in v_1 and v_2 ($D|_{dom(v_1)} = D|_{dom(v_2)}$) (2). Let $traces(u)$ be calculated on the basis of $CS(v_1)$; by definition, all constraint systems in $traces(u)$ contain exactly the transitions of $dom(v_1)$ and contain exactly one constraint for each data dependency in $D|_{dom(v_1)}$. Additionally, there exists a constraint system in $traces(u)$ for every ordering of races in $dom(v_1)$. Hence, and because of (1) and (2), there exists some $c \in traces(u)$ whose constraints correspond to the ordering of races in v_2. By the definition of $solutions()$, all transition sequences $w \in solutions(c)$

are linear extensions of the partial order induced by the constraints of c and the program order for $dom(v_1)$. Hence, $w \simeq v_2$.

3.4   The Algorithm: *Eager POR*

This section presents our algorithm EPOR. It is an extension of the SDPOR algorithm [1]. Instead of exploring single transitions at each recursive call, EPOR creates schedules for sections of the transition system under analysis. If no schedule is currently present, EPOR creates new schedules for all transition sequences in the section starting at the current state. If a schedule is present, it is used to guide the exploration. Checks for races inside a section are only performed once when schedules are created; checks for races between an event before the current section and an event inside the current section are still performed at every recursive call in order to ensure correctness.

As EPOR is based on SDPOR, we repeat basic definitions from SDPOR's pseudo code [1]. Let u be a transition sequence feasible at the initial state s_0. The next transition of a process p at some state $u(s_0)$ is denoted by $next_u(p)$ and $u \cdot p$ denotes $u \cdot next_u(p)$. For two processes p_1, p_2 with $t_1 = next_u(p_1), t_2 = next_u(p_2)$, we write $u \vDash p_1 \lozenge p_2$ to denote that t_1 and t_2 are independent, i.e., $(t_1, t_2, u(s_0)) \notin D$ and $(t_1, t_2) \notin PO$. Overloading the notation $enabled()$, we define $enabled(u) = \{p : \exists t \in enabled(u(s_0)). pidt = p\}$. For $v \in feasible(u(s_0))$, define $p \in I_u(v) \Leftrightarrow \exists v'. u \cdot v \simeq u \cdot p \cdot v'$. For event e in u, $pre(u, e)$ denotes the prefix of u up to but not including e and $notdep(u, e)$ denotes the subsequence of u that contains all events that occur after e in u but are not dependent with e in u.

The main routine `Explore`(u, *sec-start*) takes as arguments a transition sequence u that identifies the current state of the transition system and an integer *sec-start* that identifies the index in u at which the last section of u starts. The initial call is `Explore`(ε, 0) so that the exploration starts at the initial state. EPOR uses three global variables *sleep*, *backtrack*, and *schedule*, which map a transition sequence to a set of processes. For some transition sequence u feasible at the initial state, $sleep(u)$ corresponds to the sleep set at state $u(s_0)$; $backtrack(u)$ holds processes whose transitions need to be explored at state $u(s_0)$ in order to reverse races between two events of different sections; $schedule(u)$ holds processes which are scheduled at state $u(s_0)$ in order to explore a section.

At some call `Explore`(u, *sec-start*), EPOR first checks whether a deadlock is reached or u is sleep set-blocked (line 4). Subsequently, if no schedule for the current state is present, the subroutine `Fill_schedule` calculates *section-rep*(u) (as described in Sect. 3.3) and corresponding schedules (lines 6–8).

The loop in lines 10–15 explores any transitions of processes that are scheduled for the current state in order to explore a section. The subroutine `race_detection` checks whether there are reversible races between an event before the start of the current section (as specified in variable *sec-start*) and an event inside the current section. This avoids race checks between two events that are both inside the current section. For every reversible race that is found, the reversed race is scheduled for later exploration just as in the SDPOR algorithm.

Finally, the loop in lines 16–21 explores any transitions of processes that have been scheduled for the current state in order to reverse a race. Before the race check, the marker for the start of the current section is updated so that all reversible races in the current transition sequence are found.

Correctness. EPOR is correct in the sense that it explores a representative of every Mazurkiewicz trace that starts at s_0 and ends at a deadlock, which is expressed by the following theorem.

Theorem 2 (Correctness of EPOR). $\forall u \in feasible(s_0). \forall w \in feasible(u(s_0))$ $. \exists v. v \simeq w \wedge$ Explore$(u, length(u))$ *calls* Explore$(v, \cdot)$, *i.e., v is explored.*

Proof. By ind. on the ordering $\propto$ where $u_1 \propto u_2$ if Explore$(u_1, \cdot)$ returned before Explore$(u_2, \cdot)$ (as in [1]). Base case: trivial, as $feasible(u(s_0)) = \varnothing$. Inductive step: By [1], it is sufficient to prove that $sleep(u)$ is a source set for $feasible(u)$. Indirectly assume that $\exists w \in feasible(u(s_0)). \forall p \in sleep(u). \forall v, w'. u \cdot w \cdot v \not\simeq u \cdot p \cdot w'$. Then there exists a race $i \precsim_{u \cdot p \cdot w'} j$ that distinguishes $u \cdot w \cdot v$ and $u \cdot p \cdot w'$. Case (1): i and j belong to different sections. EPOR in lines 11 and 18 performs the same backtracking as SDPOR, hence $\exists q \in sleep(u). q \in I_u(notdep(u \cdot p \cdot w', p))$. By the induction hypothesis, $\exists v_1, v_2. u \cdot w \cdot v_1 \simeq u \cdot q \cdot v_2.$. Case (2): i and j belong to the same section $section(u')$ f.s. u'. By the definition of fill_schedule, $section$-$rep(u')$ is explored. By Theorem 1, $section$-$rep(u')$ contains a representative of every trace in $section(u')$. Hence, $\exists q \in sleep(u). q \in I_u(u \cdot w)$.

```
1  initially: Explore(ε, 0)
2  global variables:
        sleep, backtrack, schedule = λu.∅
3  Explore(u, sec-start):
4  if (enabled(u) \ sleep(u)) = ∅ then
5     return
6  if schedule(u) = ∅ then
7     sec-start := length(u)
8     Fill_Schedule(u)
9  Done := ∅
10 while ∃p ∈ (schedule(u) \ Done) do
11    Race_Detection(u, sec-start, p)
12    sleep(u) := {p' ∈ sleep(u) : u ⊨ p◊p'}
13    Explore(u · p, sec-start)
14    add p to Done
15    add p to sleep(u)
16 while ∃p ∈ (backtrack(u) \ sleep(u)) do
17    sec-start := length(u)
18    Race_Detection(u, sec-start, p)
```

```
19    sleep(u) := {p' ∈ sleep(u) : u ⊨ p◊p'}
20    Explore(u · p, sec-start)
21    add p to sleep(u)
22
23 Fill_Schedule(u):
24 foreach v ∈ section-rep(u) do
25    foreach prefix v' = e₁...eₙ of v do
26       add pid(eₙ) to schedule(u · v')
27       sleep(u · v') := {p' ∈ sleep(u · v') : u ⊨
              p◊p'}
28
29 Race_Detection(u, sec-start, p):
30 foreach e ∈ u[...sec-start] with
              e ≾_{u·p} nextᵤ(p) do
31    u' := pre(u, e)
32    v := notdep(u, e) · p
33    if I_{u'}(v) ∩ backtrack(u') = ∅ then
34       add some p' ∈ I_{u'}(v) to backtrack(u')
```

Fig. 3. The EPOR algorithm.

4   Implementation and Evaluation

We implemented EPOR and SDPOR in the Python programming language and ran it on multiple benchmark programs that are written in a simple imperative programming language where processes communicate over shared memory. We used sequential consistency as a memory model, which corresponds to total program orders. Two events are data dependent if one of the events writes to a memory location the other event either reads from or writes to. All experiments were run on 8 Intel i7-4790 CPUs at 3.60 GHz with 16 GB main memory.

We use the runtime and the number of dependency checks as main metrics for the comparison of EPOR and SDPOR. A dependency check determines whether two events are in the dynamic dependency relation of the current transition system and is often performed several times in order to determine whether two events constitute a reversible race. The complete results can be found in an extended version of this paper [9]. A missing runtime indicates that the corresponding algorithm did not terminate for the given benchmark configuration within 35000 s ($\sim$ 9.7 h) or required more than 16 GB of memory.

In Table 1, we present results for four benchmarks which have previously been used to evaluate dynamic POR algorithms. The Readers-Writers, Indexer, and Last Zero benchmarks are used in [1] to evaluate SDPOR; the Shared Pointer benchmark is borrowed from [6]. The Readers-Writers (N) benchmark contains a single writer and $N - 1$ readers. The Indexer (N) benchmark consists of N

Table 1. Comparison of EPOR and SDPOR on four well-known benchmarks.

Benchmark	Algorithm	Time (s)	Traces	Dep. Checks	Speedup(%)
Readers-Writers (9)	SDPOR	0.668	256	60885	—
Readers-Writers (9)	EPOR	0.400	256	3204	40.1
Readers-Writers (20)	SDPOR	6874.472	524288	1570045995	—
Readers-Writers (20)	EPOR	2728.742	524288	17827145	60.3
Indexer (12)	SDPOR	0.413	8	27072	—
Indexer (12)	EPOR	0.284	8	19325	31.2
Indexer (16)	SDPOR	13060.033	32768	1345407904	—
Indexer (16)	EPOR	7998.984	32805	466384458	38.8
Last Zero (6)	SDPOR	0.911	96	66384	—
Last Zero (6)	EPOR	0.724	96	29570	20.5
Last Zero (16)	SDPOR	*Not terminating*			
Last Zero (16)	EPOR	18408.671	262144	7232899654	—
Shared Pointer (50)	SDPOR	32.529	101	14074966	—
Shared Pointer (50)	EPOR	17.398	101	11459539	46.5
Shared Pointer (100)	SDPOR	238.968	201	192707828	—
Shared Pointer (100)	EPOR	170.762	201	154590222	28.5

processes that write to a shared hash table. It is the only benchmark presented here that contains hiding dependencies. The scheduling of an execution influences the control flow behaviour. The parameter of the Indexer benchmark specifies the number of processes. The Last Zero (N) benchmark consists of $N - 1$ processes that update a shared array and an additional process that reads the same array. Again, the scheduling of an execution influences the control flow behaviour. The Shared Pointer (N) benchmark consists of two equal processes which execute a loop N times, followed by an update of the respective other's process pointer.

In all four benchmarks, EPOR shows a speed-up over SDPOR for the highest parameter. The number of dependency checks is always lower for EPOR than for SDPOR (except for Indexer (11), where no races occur), while the number of explored maximal transition sequences is equal between EPOR and SDPOR for all configurations.

In order to investigate the performance of EPOR in special cases, we have designed two artificial benchmarks Ring and Branching, which are depicted in Fig. 4b and a. They loosely resemble the communication of processes which communicate in a ring, for example as in a ring election protocol. Every line is executed atomically. The Branching benchmark consists of two branching statements and two assignments; whether the assignments are executed depends on the scheduling of a particular execution. In the Ring benchmark, each process likewise communicates with its next process, but without control flow branchings. The Ring benchmark is similar to the Readers-Writers benchmark, but shows a higher number of dependencies, as each process is both reading and writing. Selected results for these two benchmarks are depicted in Table 2.

Process PID:
x[(PID+1)%l] := x[PID]

(a) Ring

Process PID:
if x[PID] == 0 then
    x[(PID+1)%l] := 1
if x[PID] == 0 then
    x[(PID+1)%l] := 1

(b) Branching

Process PID:
x[(PID+1)%l] := x[PID]
x[(PID+1)%l] := x[PID]

(c) Ring Extended

Fig. 4. Three artificial benchmarks (x is a global array of length l, a is a local variable. Each program statement is executed atomically.)

For the Ring and Branching benchmarks, EPOR requires considerably less dependency checks than SDPOR for all configurations. The number of explored traces is equal for EPOR and SDPOR except for the Branching benchmark with 9 to 11 processes. The speed-up of EPOR over SDPOR is very prominent for the Ring benchmark; SDPOR does not terminate for 19 processes. Equally significantly, EPOR requires several orders of magnitude less dependency checks than SDPOR. For the Branching benchmark, EPOR still shows a considerable speed-up over SDPOR, however, the saving in terms of dependency checks is lower than for the Ring benchmark.

Table 2. Comparison of EPOR and SDPOR on two simple benchmarks.

Benchmark	Algorithm	Time (s)	Traces	Dep. Checks	Speedup(%)
Ring (17)	SDPOR	5984.174	131070	734642101	—
Ring (17)	EPOR	538.031	131070	2096753	91.0
Ring (19)	SDPOR	*Not terminating*			
Ring (19)	EPOR	2884.695	524286	8653144	—
Branching (5)	SDPOR	1.180	311	145186	—
Branching (5)	EPOR	1.045	311	114640	11.4
Branching (11)	SDPOR	19068.490	318363	2200202598	—
Branching (11)	EPOR	8220.448	318978	1343673801	56.9

Less Unsatisfiable Trace Constraint Systems. Interestingly, EPOR shows a much higher runtime overhead than SDPOR for a slightly changed Ring benchmark as depicted in Fig. 4c (Ring Extended). Here, each process repeats its assignment so that the program order is not empty as opposed to the Ring benchmark.

As will be detailed later, EPOR (in its original form) does not scale as well for this benchmark as for the benchmarks previously presented. We explain this by the fact that EPOR generates at most 2 unsatisfiable trace constraint systems for the previous benchmarks while the number of unsatisfiable trace constraint systems for the Ring Extended benchmark increases with the number of processes. These additional unsatisfiable constraint systems occur due to the dependency structure of the Ring Extended benchmark. Each process consists of two transitions, which model its two assignments. Each of these transitions depends on both transitions of the previous process and additionally on both transitions of the next process. Consequently, when combining the constraints of a trace constraint system for the Ring Extended benchmark with the program order between the two transitions of each process, a cycle occurs with considerably higher probability than it is the case for the Ring benchmark.

For program fragments with dense dependencies as in the Ring Extended benchmark, we propose an alternative definition of sections in order to reduce the generation of unsatisfiable trace constraint systems. Specifically, sections are shortened so that no trace constraint systems are generated whose constraints show cycles due to a combination with the program order. We call these adapted sections *short sections*. Cycles due to the program order can be avoided by permitting only one dependent transition per process inside a single short section. Formally, we define short sections by adding the following constraint to the definition of sections given in Sect. 3.3) such that all transition sequences $v = t_1 \ldots t_k \in section(u)$ additionally satisfy $\forall 1 \leq i, j, m, n \leq k . (i, j) \in dep(u, v) \wedge (m, n) \in dep(u, v) \wedge pidt_i = pidt_m \Rightarrow i = m$.

We have implemented the EPOR algorithm with short sections instead of sections, denoted by EPOR-SH, and compare it with EPOR and SDPOR on the

Table 3. Comparison of EPOR, EPOR-SH (short sections), and SDPOR on the Ring Extended benchmark.

Benchmark	Algorithm	Timec(s)	Traces	Dep. Checks	Unsat. TCS	Speedup(%)
Ring Extended (6)	SDPOR	70.729	38466	7537485	0	—
Ring Extended (6)	EPOR	3412.561	38466	144095	16738750	−4724.8
Ring Extended (6)	EPOR-SH	72.869	38466	6747840	126	−3.0
Ring Extended (8)	SDPOR	6552.194	1548546	806537903	0	—
Ring Extended (8)	EPOR	*Not terminating*				
Ring Extended (8)	EPOR-SH	5061.882	1548546	720212287	510	22.7

Ring Extended benchmark. The observed numbers are shown in Table 3. For 6 processes, EPOR-SH still shows a considerable number of unsatisfiable constraint systems but reduces this number by more than 99 % in comparison to EPOR with original sections. While EPOR is more than 47 times slower than SDPOR for 6 processes and does not terminate for 8 processes, EPOR-SH is only slightly slower than SDPOR for 6 processes and more than 22 % faster than SDPOR for 8 processes. Hence, the overhead of generating the remaining unsatisfiable trace constraint systems is still small enough so that EPOR-SH outperforms SDPOR. The performance of EPOR-SH on our remaining benchmarks is included in an extended version of this paper [9].

In order to increase the robustness of EPOR, it is perceivable to dynamically adapt the section length to the dependency structure of the program. Additionally, we expect that the number of generated unsatisfiable trace constraint systems can be reduced by exploiting information about the infeasibility of a constraint system to prevent the generation of further trace constraint systems that contain the same cycle (with or without program order). Such optimizations would further improve the performance of EPOR and EPOR-SH.

5   Related Work

Static POR techniques use a static approximation of dependencies [2,5,10,12]. While both static and dynamic POR algorithms can be augmented with section-based exploration as in EPOR, we focus on dynamic dependency calculation, which drastically increases the state space reduction for, e.g., Indexer benchmark.

Dynamic POR has been introduced by Flanagan and Godefroid [3]. Their algorithm DPOR computes a *persistent set* of transitions to explore in every visited state. Like many POR algorithms, DPOR has been combined with the *sleep set* technique [4]. For every visited state, the corresponding sleep set contains transitions whose exploration would be redundant and is avoided.

Abdulla, Aronis, Jonsson, and Sagonas have proposed two model checking algorithms based on DPOR [1], named SDPOR and ODPOR, replacing persistent sets with *source sets*. In some cases, the source set of a state is smaller than the smallest persistent set of this state, which improves the state graph reduction.

EPOR uses source sets in order to reverse races between sections but avoids redundant race checks and source set calculations inside of sections.

The ODPOR algorithm is an extension of SDPOR that can increase the amount of state space reduction for certain benchmarks, however adding runtime overhead that is not always compensated by a higher state space reduction: for many benchmarks, SDPOR is faster than ODPOR due to less runtime overhead [1]. Consequently, we compare our algorithm EPOR to SDPOR instead of ODPOR in order to investigate whether even the lower runtime overhead of SDPOR can be reduced.

CDPOR by Gueta et al. [6] handles sequences of transitions, similar to EPOR and unlike DPOR, SDPOR, and ODPOR. However, CDPOR explores only transitions of a single process at once, while EPOR handles transition sequences of all processes and of varying length.

POR approaches for relaxed memory models have been proposed, e.g., [15]. Our system model handles systems with relaxed memory models by using partial program orders. Symbolic model checking (both bounded and unbounded) using POR has been addressed, e.g., in [7,14]. We present EPOR as an improvement of dependency calculation in concrete-state dynamic POR algorithms but do not see any fundamental difficulty in using it for symbolic POR.

6 Conclusion

We present section-based exploration, a dynamic POR approach that eagerly creates schedules for program fragments. In comparison to known dynamic POR algorithms, it avoids redundant race and dependency checks. We introduce trace constraint systems as a formalization of section-based exploration and prove its correctness. While our approach does not depend on a particular POR algorithm, we implement section-based exploration in EPOR and compare it to SDPOR. Our results show that EPOR is able to reduce the runtime overhead by up to 91 % and increase the tractable program size.

References

1. Abdulla, P.A., Aronis, S., Jonsson, B., Sagonas, K.F.: Optimal dynamic partial order reduction. In: POPL (2014)
2. Bokor, P., Kinder, J., Serafini, M., Suri, N.: Supporting domain-specific state space reductions through local partial-order reduction. In: ASE (2011)
3. Flanagan, C., Godefroid, P.: Dynamic partial-order reduction for model checking software. In: POPL (2005)
4. Godefroid, P.: Using partial orders to improve automatic verification methods. In: Clarke, E.M., Kurshan, R.P. (eds.) CAV 1990. LNCS, vol. 531, pp. 176–185. Springer, Heidelberg (1990)
5. Godefroid, P., Pirottin, S.: Refining dependencies improves partial-order verification methods (extended abstract). In: Courcoubetis, C. (ed.) CAV 1993. LNCS, vol. 697, pp. 438–449. Springer, Heidelberg (1993)
6. Gueta, G., Flanagan, C., Yahav, E., Sagiv, M.: Cartesian partial-order reduction. In: Bošnački, D., Edelkamp, S. (eds.) SPIN 2007. LNCS, vol. 4595, pp. 95–112. Springer, Heidelberg (2007)

7. Kahlon, V., Wang, C., Gupta, A.: Monotonic partial order reduction: an optimal symbolic partial order reduction technique. In: Bouajjani, A., Maler, O. (eds.) CAV 2009. LNCS, vol. 5643, pp. 398–413. Springer, Heidelberg (2009)
8. Mazurkiewicz, A.W.: Trace theory. In: Advances in Petri Nets (1986)
9. Metzler, P., Saissi, H., Bokor, P., Hesse, R., Suri, N.: Efficient verification of program fragments: Eager POR (extended). In: Nelson, S.P., Meyer, V. (eds.) ATVA 2016. LNCS, vol. 9938, pp. 375–391. Springer, Heidelberg (2016). http://www1.deeds. informatik.tu-darmstadt.de/External/PublicationData/1/atva2016-epor.pdf
10. Peled, D.: All from one, one for all: on model checking using representatives. In: Courcoubetis, C. (ed.) CAV 1993. LNCS, vol. 697, pp. 409–423. Springer, Berlin (1993)
11. Pruesse, G., Ruskey, F.: Generating linear extensions fast. SIAM J. Comput **23**, 373–386 (1994)
12. Valmari, A.: Stubborn sets for reduced state space generation. In: Applications and Theory of Petri Nets (1989)
13. Valmari, A.: The state explosion problem. In: Lectures on Petri Nets I (1996)
14. Wachter, B., Kroening, D., Ouaknine, J.: Verifying multi-threaded software with impact. In: FMCAD (2013)
15. Zhang, N., Kusano, M., Wang, C.: Dynamic partial order reduction for relaxed memory models. In: PLDI (2015)

Solving Procedures, Model Checking

Skolem Functions for DQBF

Karina Wimmer[1]([⊠]), Ralf Wimmer[1,2], Christoph Scholl[1], and Bernd Becker[1]

[1] Albert-Ludwigs-Universität Freiburg, Freiburg im Breisgau, Germany
{wimmerka,wimmer,scholl,becker}@informatik.uni-freiburg.de
[2] Dependable Systems and Software, Saarland University, Saarbrücken, Germany

Abstract. We consider the problem of computing Skolem functions for
satisfied dependency quantified Boolean formulas (DQBFs). We show
how Skolem functions can be obtained from an elimination-based DQBF
solver and how to take preprocessing steps into account. The size of the
Skolem functions is optimized by don't-care minimization using Craig
interpolants and rewriting techniques. Experiments with our DQBF
solver HQS show that we are able to effectively compute Skolem functions with very little overhead compared to the mere solution of the
formula.

1 Introduction

Solver-based techniques have proven successful in many areas, ranging from formal verification of hard- and software systems [1,6] over automatic test pattern
generation [12,14] to planning [36]. While research on solving quantifier-free
Boolean formulas (the famous SAT-problem [10]) has reached a certain level of
maturity, designing and improving algorithms for quantified Boolean formulas
(QBFs) is in the focus of active research. However, there are applications like the
verification of partial circuits [18,37], the synthesis of safe controllers [7], and
the analysis of games with incomplete information [32] for which QBF is not
expressive enough to provide a compact and natural formulation. The reason is
that QBF requires linearly ordered dependencies of the existential variables on
the universal ones: Each existential variable implicitly depends on all universal
variables in whose scope it is. Relaxing this condition yields so-called *dependency
quantified Boolean formulas (DQBFs)*. DQBFs are strictly more expressive than
QBFs in the sense that an equivalent QBF formulation can be exponentially
larger than a DQBF formulation. This comes at the price of a higher complexity
of the decision problem: DQBF is NEXPTIME-complete [32], compared to QBF,
which is "only" PSPACE-complete. Encouraged by the success of SAT and QBF
solvers and driven by the mentioned applications, research on solving DQBFs has

This work was partly supported by the German Research Council (DFG) as part of
the project "Solving Dependency Quantified Boolean Formulas" and by the Sino-
German Center for Research Promotion as part of the project CAP (GZ 1023).

C. Artho et al. (Eds.): ATVA 2016, LNCS 9938, pp. 395–411, 2016.
DOI: 10.1007/978-3-319-46520-3_25

started during the last few years [16,17,19,41], yielding first prototypic solvers like IDQ [17] and HQS [19].

All currently available DQBF solvers are restricted to a pure yes/no answer regarding the satisfiability of the formula, allowing to decide whether an incomplete circuit is realizable, whether a controller with certain properties can be synthesized, and whether a player has a winning strategy in a game. But typically a pure yes/no answer is not satisfactory: In case a circuit is realizable, one wants to have an implementation; if a controller is synthesizable, one wants to get a realization of it; and in a game, where a player has a winning strategy, one wants to know such a winning strategy. These implementations, realizations, and strategies all correspond to so-called *Skolem functions* for the existential variables in a DQBF. While for different paradigms to solve QBFs, Skolem functions can be computed (see below for an overview of related work), we are not aware of any paper that considers the computation of Skolem functions for DQBF.

So, this is the first paper that shows how Skolem functions can be obtained from elimination-based QBF or DQBF solvers like AIGsolve [33,34] or HQS [19]. We do not only take into account the core operations for eliminating variables [19], but also the preprocessing steps [41], which are essential for an efficient solution of the formula. We propose to apply don't-care minimization to reduce the representation size of the computed Skolem functions. We have implemented the described techniques in our DQBF solver HQS; preliminary experiments show not only that we have found a feasible approach to Skolem function computation, but also that the overhead during the solution of the formulas is small.

Due to space restrictions we are only able to give short proof sketches for the main theorems. Detailed proofs are available in a technical report [40].

Related Work. Computing Skolem functions has not been studied for DQBF so far. Therefore we concentrate on related work in QBF solving.

sKIzzo [5] and SQUOLEM [25] are QBF solvers which are based on Skolemization: The existential variables are replaced by an encoding of the Skolem functions' unknown truth tables. In case of sKIzzo, the entries of the truth tables are variables, resulting in an (exponentially larger) SAT problem. This SAT problem is represented compactly using OBDDs [39] and solved by an adapted SAT solver. A satisfying assignment corresponds to Skolem functions for the QBF. SQUOLEM is based on eliminating variables v in the QBF prefix from right to left by considering clauses containing v which describe the function table of v's Skolem function.

Balabanov and Jiang [3] and Goultiaeva et al. [20] laid the foundations for extracting Skolem functions from SAT/UNSAT proofs for QBFs in form of term/clause resolution trees. Such proofs can be obtained from search-based QBF solvers like DEPQBF [29,31]. However, this approach is not applicable to DQBF: resolution is – in contrast to QBF – not a complete decision procedure for DQBF [2]; in general it is not possible to decide a DQBF using resolution.

Heule et al. [23] consider the extraction of Skolem functions when preprocessing is applied before the actual solving process. They represent the different preprocessing steps in a unified framework, called QRAT. Such QRAT logs can be used to derive Skolem functions for the original formula.

CAQE [38] is a very recent QBF solver, which is based on decomposing the QBF into a sequence of simpler propositional formulas. CAQE also supports the computation of Skolem functions.

Structure of this Paper. In the next section, we introduce the necessary foundations on DQBFs, Skolem functions, and don't-care minimization of Boolean functions. In Sect. 3 we consider the main elimination operations, which are used in the solver core of HQS. The following section shows how preprocessing steps can be taken into account. We present experimental results in Sect. 5 and conclude the paper in Sect. 6.

2   Foundations

The Boolean values are denoted by $\mathbb{B} = \{0, 1\}$. For a set V of Boolean variables, the set of all variable assignments of V is $\mathbf{A}(V) = \{\nu : V \to \mathbb{B}\}$. We extend variable assignments $\nu \in \mathbf{A}(V)$ to quantifier-free Boolean formulas ϕ: $\nu(\phi)$ is the value obtained by replacing all variables v occurring in ϕ with their value $\nu(v)$ and applying the usual rules of Boolean algebra.

A literal ℓ is either a Boolean variable $v \in V$ or its negation $\neg v$. The sign of a literal is given by $\text{sign}(v) = 1$ and $\text{sign}(\neg v) = 0$ for $v \in V$. A clause is a disjunction of literals, and a formula is in conjunctive normal form (CNF) if it is a conjunction of (non-tautological) clauses. We often identify a clause with its set of literals, and a CNF with its set of clauses. For quantifier-free Boolean formulas ϕ and ψ over variables V and a variable $v \in V$, the notation $\phi[\psi/v]$ denotes the formula which results from replacing all occurrences of v in ϕ simultaneously by ψ. $\text{var}(\phi)$ is the set of variables occurring in ϕ. We treat $\text{var}(\phi)$ as a variable if it is a singleton. We sometimes identify ϕ with its represented function f_ϕ: for $\nu \in \mathbf{A}(V)$, we set $f_\phi(\nu) := \nu(\phi)$. A formula ϕ is a representation of a Boolean function g iff $g = f_\phi$. Each Boolean function can be represented as a formula. By ITE we denote the if-then-else function, i. e., $\text{ITE}(a, b, c) = (a \wedge b) \vee (\neg a \wedge c)$.

2.1   Dependency Quantified Boolean Formulas

Dependency quantified Boolean formulas are obtained by prefixing quantifier-free Boolean formulas with so-called Henkin quantifiers [21].

Definition 1 (Syntax of DQBF). *Let $V = \{x_1, \ldots, x_n, y_1, \ldots, y_m\}$ be a finite set of Boolean variables. A dependency quantified Boolean formula (DQBF) Ψ over V has the form $\Psi := \forall x_1 \ldots \forall x_n \exists y_1(D_{y_1}) \ldots \exists y_m(D_{y_m}) : \phi$, where $D_{y_i} \subseteq \{x_1, \ldots, x_n\}$ is the dependency set of y_i for $i = 1, \ldots, m$, and ϕ is a quantifier-free Boolean formula over V, called the matrix of Ψ.*

$U_\Psi = \{x_1, \ldots, x_n\}$ is the set of universal and $E_\Psi = \{y_1, \ldots, y_m\}$ the set of existential variables. A literal ℓ is existential (universal, resp.) iff $\operatorname{var}(\ell) \in E_\Psi$ ($\operatorname{var}(\ell) \in U_\Psi$). Sometimes we assume that ϕ is given in CNF.

A QBF (in prenex normal form) is a DQBF such that $D_y \subseteq D_{y'}$ or $D_{y'} \subseteq D_y$ holds for any two existential variables $y, y' \in E_\Psi$.

To simplify notation, we define a dependency function $\operatorname{dep}_\Psi : V \to 2^{U_\Psi}$ as follows: $\operatorname{dep}_\Psi(v) = \{v\}$ if v is universal and $\operatorname{dep}_\Psi(v) = D_v$ if v is existential.

The semantics of a DQBF is typically defined by so-called Skolem functions.

Definition 2 (Semantics of DQBF). *Let Ψ be a DQBF as above. It is satisfiable if there are functions $s_y : \mathbf{A}(D_y) \to \mathbb{B}$ for $y \in E_\Psi$ such that replacing each $y \in E_\Psi$ by (a Boolean expression representing) s_y turns ϕ into a tautology. Such functions $(s_y)_{y \in E_\Psi}$ are called Skolem functions for Ψ.*

Deciding whether a given DQBF is satisfiable is NEXPTIME-complete [32].

Definition 3 (Equisatisfiability, Equivalence of DQBFs). *Let $\Psi_i = Q_i : \phi_i$ for $i = 1, 2$ be two DQBFs over variables V. Ψ_1 and Ψ_2 are equisatisfiable ($\Psi_1 \triangleq \Psi_2$), if Ψ_1 is satisfiable iff Ψ_2 is. Ψ_1 and Ψ_2 are logically equivalent ($\Psi_1 \equiv \Psi_2$) if $Q_1 = Q_2$ and $\nu(\phi_1) = \nu(\phi_2)$ for all $\nu \in \mathbf{A}(V)$.*

Logically equivalent formulas that are satisfiable have the same Skolem functions.

The main operations used by elimination-based solvers like HQS [19] to solve DQBFs are variants of variable elimination. For standard Boolean logic, elimination of variables can be performed in different ways, resulting in logically equivalent formulas of typically different sizes and structures:

Lemma 1 ([24]). *Let ϕ be a Boolean formula and x a variable of ϕ. We have:*

$$\exists x : \phi \quad \triangleq \phi[0/x] \vee \phi[1/x] \quad \equiv \phi\Big[\phi[1/x]/x\Big] \quad \equiv \phi\Big[\neg\phi[0/x]/x\Big] .$$

This lemma will be used later to obtain formulas for the Skolem functions of existential variables in DQBFs. As we will see later, don't-care minimization can be applied to these Skolem functions to obtain some with a small representation.

2.2 Don't-Care Minimization of Boolean Functions

Definition 4 (Incompletely Specified Boolean Function). *Let V be a set of Boolean variables. An incompletely specified Boolean function f is given by a don't-care set $\operatorname{DC}(f) \subseteq \mathbf{A}(V)$ and an on-set $\operatorname{ON}(f) \subseteq \mathbf{A}(V)$ such that $\operatorname{DC}(f) \cap \operatorname{ON}(f) = \emptyset$. We additionally define the off-set $\operatorname{OFF}(f) := \mathbf{A}(V) \setminus (\operatorname{DC}(f) \cup \operatorname{ON}(f))$.*

Of course it suffices to specify any two sets of $\operatorname{ON}(f)$, $\operatorname{OFF}(f)$, and $\operatorname{DC}(f)$.

Definition 5 (Complete Extension). *Let f be an incompletely specified Boolean function. A function $f^* : \mathbf{A}(V) \to \mathbb{B}$ is a complete extension of f iff $f^*(\nu) = 1$ for all $\nu \in \operatorname{ON}(f)$ and $f^*(\nu) = 0$ for all $\nu \in \operatorname{OFF}(f)$.*

The goal of don't-care minimization is: Given an incompletely specified Boolean function f, find a complete extension f^* of f with a small representation by a circuit or an and-inverter graph (AIG) [27]. This can be done, e.g., by using Craig interpolants.

Definition 6 (Craig Interpolant, [11]). Let $\phi = \phi_A \wedge \phi_B$ be a (quantifier-free) Boolean formula that is unsatisfiable. A *Craig interpolant* for (ϕ_A, ϕ_B) is a Boolean formula ϕ_I such that: (a) ϕ_I contains only variables which appear in both ϕ_A and ϕ_B, (b) $\phi_A \Rightarrow \phi_I$ is a tautology, and (c) $\phi_I \wedge \phi_B$ is unsatisfiable.

Lemma 2. *Let f be an incompletely specified function over V and $\varphi_{\mathrm{ON}(f)}$, $\varphi_{\mathrm{OFF}(f)}$ be Boolean formulas for $\mathrm{ON}(f)$ and $\mathrm{OFF}(f)$, respectively, i.e., for every assignment $\nu \in \mathbf{A}(V)$, we have $\nu(\varphi_{\mathrm{OFF}(f)}) = 1$ iff $\nu \in \mathrm{OFF}(F)$ and $\nu(\varphi_{\mathrm{ON}(f)}) = 1$ iff $\nu \in \mathrm{ON}(f)$.*

Then every Craig interpolant for $(\varphi_{\mathrm{ON}(f)}, \varphi_{\mathrm{OFF}(f)})$ represents a complete extension of f.

This lemma will be exploited for don't-care minimization when eliminating existential variables.

Lemma 3 ([24]). *Let ϕ be a Boolean formula and x a variable in ϕ. Then each Craig interpolant ϕ_I w.r.t. $\phi_A := \neg\phi[0/x] \wedge \phi[1/x]$ and $\phi_B := \neg\phi[1/x] \wedge \phi[0/x]$ satisfies. $\exists x : \phi \triangleq \phi[\phi_I/x]$.*

Craig interpolants can be derived from a resolution tree which shows the unsatisfiability of the formula [35]. They find numerous applications in system design, see e.g., [30].

3 Undoing Elimination Steps

In the following we assume that a DQBF of the form:

$$\Psi^0 = \forall x_1 \ldots \forall x_n \exists y_1(D_{y_1}^0) \ldots \exists y_m(D_{y_m}^0) : \phi^0$$

is given with dependency sets $D_{y_i}^0 \subseteq \{x_1, \ldots, x_n\}$ for $i = 1, \ldots, m$. We abbreviate the quantifier prefix by Q^0 and write $\Psi^0 = Q^0 : \phi^0$.

DQBF preprocessors and elimination-based DQBF solvers execute a sequence of transformation steps on the formula until a pure SAT problem is obtained. Thereby we obtain a sequence of equisatisfiable formulas $\Psi^i = Q^i : \phi^i$ for $i = 1, \ldots, k^*$ such that Ψ^i results from Ψ^{i-1} by applying one transformation step and Ψ^{k^*} is an existential formula that can be solved using a SAT solver.

For Ψ^{k^*}, Skolem functions are simply given by a satisfying assignment. The main idea of the paper is to show how Skolem functions for Ψ^{i-1} can be derived from Skolem functions for Ψ^i, finally resulting in Skolem functions for the original formula Ψ^0.

In the following, we consider the quantifier prefix as a set of tuples formed by quantifiers, variables, and – for existential variables – their dependency sets.

The set of universal variables in Ψ^i is denoted by U^i and the set of existential variables by E^i. For a variable $y \in E^i$, D_y^i is its dependency set in Ψ^i, i.e.,

$$Q^i = \{\forall x \mid x \in U^i\} \cup \{\exists y(D_y^i) \mid y \in E^i\}.$$

3.1   Universal Expansion

Universal expansion [9,18] eliminates a universal variable x^* from a DQBF. If any existential variables depend upon x^*, they have to be copied to allow them taking different values for $x^* = 0$ and $x^* = 1$.

Lemma 4 (Universal Expansion). *Let $(s_y^k)_{y \in E^k}$ be Skolem functions for the existential variables in Ψ^k and assume that Ψ^k was obtained from Ψ^{k-1} by expanding the universal variable $x^* \in U^{k-1}$ such that, for $y \in E^{k-1}$ with $x^* \in D_y^{k-1}$, y' is the copy of y appearing in the 1-cofactor w. r. t. x. In detail:*

$$Q^k : \phi^k = \left(Q^{k-1} \setminus \left(\{\forall x^*\} \cup \{\exists y(D_y^{k-1}) \mid y \in E^{k-1} \wedge x^* \in D_y^{k-1}\} \right) \right)$$
$$\cup \left\{ \exists y(D_y^{k-1} \setminus \{x^*\}), \exists y'(D_y^{k-1} \setminus \{x^*\}) \mid y \in E^{k-1} \wedge x^* \in D_y^{k-1} \right\} :$$
$$\left(\phi^{k-1}[0/x^*] \wedge \phi^{k-1}[1/x^*][y'/y \text{ for all } y \in E^{k-1} \text{ with } x^* \in D_y^{k-1}] \right).$$

Then $(s_y^{k-1})_{y \in E^{k-1}}$ with $s_y^{k-1} = s_y^k$ if $x^* \notin D_y^{k-1}$, and $s_y^{k-1} = \text{ITE}(x^*, s_{y'}^k, s_y^k)$ if $x^* \in D_y^{k-1}$ are Skolem functions for the existential variables in Ψ^{k-1}.

Proof Sketch. We replace the existential variables with their Skolem functions and show that the resulting formula, which only contains universal variables, is a tautology for both $x^* = 0$ and $x^* = 1$. To do so, one can exploit the fact that $(s_y^k)_{y \in E^k}$ are Skolem functions for the formula after elimination. For a detailed proof see [40].   □

3.2   Elimination of Existential Variables

Elimination of existential variables is done like in QBF. It is applicable for variables which depend upon all universal variables [19].

Lemma 5. *Let $(s_y^k)_{y \in E^k}$ be Skolem functions for the existential variables in Ψ^k and assume that Ψ^k was obtained from Ψ^{k-1} by eliminating the existential variable $y^* \in E^{k-1}$ (which requires $D_{y^*}^{k-1} = U^{k-1}$). In detail:*

$$Q^k : \phi^k = Q^{k-1} \setminus \{\exists y^*(D_{y^*}^{k-1})\} : \left(\phi^{k-1}[0/y^*] \vee \phi^{k-1}[1/y^*] \right)$$

Then $(s_y^{k-1})_{y \in E^{k-1}}$ with $s_y^{k-1} = s_y^k$ if $y \neq y^*$, and $s_{y^*}^{k-1} = \phi^{k-1}[1/y^*]$ $[s_z^k/z \text{ for } z \in E^k]$ are Skolem functions for the existential variables in Ψ^{k-1}.

Proof Sketch. We replace the existential variables by their Skolem functions and show that the resulting formula, which contains only universal variables, is a tautology. For this we assume an arbitrary assignment ν of the universal variables and distinguish the cases where $\nu(s_{y^*}^{k-1}) = 0$ and where $\nu(s_{y^*}^{k-1}) = 1$. In both cases simple equivalence transformations show that ν satisfies the formula.   □

Remark 1 (Blockwise Elimination). For improving efficiency of variable elimination, typically sets of variables are eliminated en bloc without creating intermediate results. For existential variable sets, these intermediate results, however, are required for Skolem function computation. A possible way to deal with this is to redo the quantification variable by variable if in the end the formula is satisfied and Skolem functions are to be computed.

Remark 2 (Alternative Skolem Function). As a Skolem function for y^*, we could also use $s_{y^*}^{k-1} := \neg\phi^{k-1}[0/y^*][s_y^k/y \text{ for } y \in E^k]$. The proof is analogous to the proof of Lemma 5.

Remark 3 (Don't-Care Minimization of Skolem Functions). Any complete extension of the following incompletely specified Boolean function can be used as a Skolem function for y^* in Lemma 5:

$$\mathrm{ON}(s_{y^*}^{k-1}) = \left(\phi^{k-1}[1/y^*] \wedge \neg\phi^{k-1}[0/y^*]\right)[s_y^k/y \text{ for } y \in E^k],$$

$$\mathrm{OFF}(s_{y^*}^{k-1}) = \left(\neg\phi^{k-1}[1/y^*] \wedge \phi^{k-1}[0/y^*]\right)[s_y^k/y \text{ for } y \in E^k],$$

$$\mathrm{DC}(s_{y^*}^{k-1}) = \left(\phi^{k-1}[1/y^*] \wedge \phi^{k-1}[0/y^*]\right)[s_y^k/y \text{ for } y \in E^k].$$

The don't-care set $\mathrm{DC}(s_{y^*}^{k-1})$ can be exploited to minimize the size of $s_{y^*}^{k-1}$'s representation, e.g., by using Craig interpolation, cf. Lemma 3.

Remark 4 (Skolem Functions for SAT Problems). If the result of the elimination process is a pure SAT problem with only existential quantifiers, we can solve it using a SAT solver. In case the formula is satisfiable, any satisfying assignment corresponds to (constant) Skolem functions for the existential variables.

Example 1. Consider the DQBF $\Psi^0 = \forall x_1 \forall x_2 \exists y_1(x_1) \exists y_2(x_2) : \phi^0(x_1, x_2, y_1, y_2)$. Elimination yields the following sequence of matrices:

$$\phi^0(x_1, x_2, y_1, y_2) \xrightarrow{\forall x_1} \phi^1(x_2, y_1, y_1', y_2) \xrightarrow{\exists y_2} \phi^2(x_2, y_1, y_1') \xrightarrow{\forall x_2} \phi^3(y_1, y_1').$$

$\phi^3(y_1, y_1')$ is a SAT-Problem. Assume that the SAT-solver returns $y_1 = a$ and $y_1' = b$ as a satisfying assignment. We need to compute Skolem functions for y_1 and y_2 in ϕ^0. The following table shows the Skolem functions for the individual formulas:

	Skolem function for		
Formula	y_1	y_1'	y_2
Ψ^3	a	b	n/a
Ψ^2	a	b	n/a
Ψ^1	a	b	$\phi^1(x_2, a, b, 1)$
Ψ^0	$(\neg x_1 \wedge a) \vee (x_1 \wedge b)$	n/a	$\phi^1(x_2, a, b, 1)$

4 Handling Pre- and Inprocessing Steps

Typically preprocessing is used to simplify the formula before the actual solution process starts. It is well known that preprocessing can reduce the computation times for solving the formula by orders of magnitude [41]. Thereby the set of variables occurring in the formula as well as its set of clauses change. For details about the preprocessing steps for DQBF, we refer the reader to [41].

The procedure for taking preprocessing steps into account is the same as for the elimination steps: We assume that Skolem functions $(s_y^k)_{y \in U^k}$ for Ψ^k are given and show how to obtain Skolem functions $(s_y^{k-1})_{y \in U^{k-1}}$ for the formula Ψ^{k-1} before applying a preprocessing operation.

4.1 Equivalence Transformations and Universal Reduction

All operations which replace the formula Ψ^{k-1} by a logically equivalent formula Ψ^k (see Definition 3) preserve Skolem functions and can essentially be ignored for the computation of Skolem functions. This applies (among others) to the following preprocessing techniques: addition of resolvents, deletion of subsumed clauses, and hidden literal addition [22, 41].

Universal reduction removes a variable $x^* \in U^{k-1}$ from a clause $C \in \phi^{k-1}$ if C does not contain an existential variable which depends on x^*. In general, the resulting matrix ϕ^k is not logically equivalent to ϕ^{k-1}. However, universal reduction changes neither the set of existential variables nor their Skolem functions. Therefore universal reduction steps can be ignored when computing Skolem functions.

4.2 Replacing Variables by Constants

Different techniques identify variables in the formula which must or may be replaced by constants: unit and failed literals, contradicting implication chains, backbones (variables which have the same value in all satisfying assignments of the matrix) [26], pure literals, or more generally, monotonic literals. For these techniques, Skolem functions can be derived using the following lemma.

Lemma 6 (Replacement by Constants). *Assume that Ψ^k is created from Ψ^{k-1} by replacing an existential variable $y^* \in E^{k-1}$ by a constant value $c \in \mathbb{B}$, i. e., $Q^k : \phi^k = Q^{k-1} \setminus \{\exists y^*(D_{y^*}^{k-1})\} : \phi^{k-1}[c/y^*]$.*

If $(s_y^k)_{y \in E^k}$ are Skolem functions for Ψ^k, then $(s_y^{k-1})_{y \in E^{k-1}}$ are Skolem functions for Ψ^{k-1}, where $s_y^{k-1} = s_y^k$ for $y \neq y^*$, and $s_{y^*}^{k-1} = c$.

While for backbones, the constant Skolem function is the only possibility, for monotonic variables other Skolem functions might be available. However, a constant function has a representation of minimum size and is therefore preferred.

4.3 Equivalent Variables

If the preprocessor detects that the existential variable $y^* \in E^{k-1}$ is equivalent to the literal ℓ, then either the whole formula is unsatisfied if ℓ is universal and y^* does not depend on ℓ. Otherwise all occurrences of y^* can be replaced by ℓ. For the Skolem function of y^* the following lemma holds:

Lemma 7 (Equivalent Literals). *Let Ψ^k result from Ψ^{k-1} by replacing the existential variable $y^* \in E^{k-1}$ by the literal ℓ, i. e.,*

$$Q^k : \phi^k = Q^{k-1} \setminus \{\exists y^* (D_{y^*}^{k-1})\} : \phi^{k-1}[\ell/y^*].$$

If $(s_y^k)_{y \in E^k}$ are Skolem functions for Ψ^k, then $(s_y^{k-1})_{y \in E^{k-1}}$ are Skolem functions for Ψ^{k-1}, where

$$s_y^{k-1} := \begin{cases} s_y^k, & \text{if } y \neq y^*, \\ \ell, & \text{if } y = y^* \text{ and } \mathrm{var}(\ell) \in U^{k-1}, \\ s_{\mathrm{var}(\ell)}^k, & \text{if } y = y^* \text{ and } \mathrm{var}(\ell) \in E^{k-1} \text{ and } \mathrm{sign}(\ell) = 1, \\ \neg s_{\mathrm{var}(\ell)}^k, & \text{if } y = y^* \text{ and } \mathrm{var}(\ell) \in E^{k-1} \text{ and } \mathrm{sign}(\ell) = 0. \end{cases}$$

4.4 Structure Extraction

For solvers which do not rely on a CNF-representation of the formula, the reconstruction of the Boolean expression from which the CNF was generated is often beneficial. This is particularly the case if Tseitin transformation was applied to a circuit. Thereby clauses are detected which represent the equivalence $y^* \equiv \eta$ where η is the function computed by a logical gate and y^* the existential variable introduced by Tseitin transformation for the output of the gate. In the resulting representation y^* is replaced by η. Accordingly, a Skolem function for y^* can be obtained from the Skolem functions of the existential variables $\mathrm{var}(\eta)$:

Lemma 8 (Structure Extraction). *Let Ψ^k result from Ψ^{k-1} by replacing $y^* \in E^{k-1}$ by the expression η such that $y^* \notin \mathrm{var}(\eta)$ and*

$$\bigcup_{y \in \mathrm{var}(\eta) \cap E^{k-1}} D_y^{k-1} \subseteq D_{y^*}^{k-1}.$$

That means $Q^k : \phi^k = Q^{k-1} \setminus \{\exists y^* (D_{y^*}^{k-1})\} : \phi^{k-1}[\eta/y^*]$. If $(s_y^k)_{y \in E^k}$ are Skolem functions for Ψ^k, then $(s_y^{k-1})_{y \in E^{k-1}}$ are Skolem functions for Ψ^{k-1} where $s_y^{k-1} = s_y^k$ if $y \neq y^*$, and $s_{y^*}^{k-1} = \eta[s_z^k/z$, for $z \in \mathrm{var}(\eta) \cap E^k]$.

4.5 Variable Elimination by Resolution

In QBF, an existential variable y^* can be eliminated by resolution if it belongs to the inner-most quantifier block[1]. Thereby all clauses containing y^* or $\neg y^*$

---

[1] If the inner-most quantifier block is universal, it can be removed by universal reduction.

are replaced by all possible resolvents w. r. t. y^*. Having a closer look at how a Skolem function can be obtained for y^*, we can see that the condition of y^* being in the inner-most quantifier block can be strengthend such that it is also applicable to DQBF, where there is in general no linear order on the variables.

Let $y^* \in E^{k-1}$ be an existential variable. We partition the set ϕ^{k-1} of clauses into $\phi_{y^*}^{k-1} = \{C \in \phi^{k-1} \mid y^* \in C\}$, $\phi_{\neg y^*}^{k-1} = \{C \in \phi^{k-1} \mid \neg y^* \in C\}$, and $\phi_{\emptyset}^{k-1} = \phi^{k-1} \setminus (\phi_{y^*}^{k-1} \cup \phi_{\neg y^*}^{k-1})$.

Lemma 9 (Resolution). *Assume that Ψ^k results from Ψ^{k-1} by eliminating variable y^* using resolution, i. e.,*

$$Q^k : \phi^k = Q^{k-1} \setminus \{\exists y^*(D_{y^*}^{k-1})\} : \phi_{\emptyset}^{k-1} \cup \{C \otimes_{y^*} C' \mid C \in \phi_{y^*}^{k-1} \wedge C' \in \phi_{\neg y^*}^{k-1}\},$$

where $C \otimes_{y^*} C'$ denotes the resolvent of C and C' w. r. t. y^*. This can be done if one of the following conditions holds:

- *Case 1:* $\mathrm{dep}_{\Psi^{k-1}}(y^*) \supseteq \bigcup_{C \in \phi_{y^*}^{k-1}} \bigcup_{\ell \in C \setminus \{y^*\}} \mathrm{dep}_{\Psi^{k-1}}(\ell),$
- *Case 2:* $\mathrm{dep}_{\Psi^{k-1}}(y^*) \supseteq \bigcup_{C' \in \phi_{\neg y^*}^{k-1}} \bigcup_{\ell \in C' \setminus \{\neg y^*\}} \mathrm{dep}_{\Psi^{k-1}}(\ell).$

If $(s_y^k)_{y \in E^k}$ are Skolem functions for Ψ^k, then $(s_y^{k-1})_{y \in E^{k-1}}$ are Skolem functions for Ψ^{k-1} where, for the two cases, s_y^{k-1} is defined as follows:

$$s_y^{k-1} = \begin{cases} s_y^k, & \text{if } y \neq y^*, \\ \neg \phi_{y^*}^{k-1}[0/y^*][s_z^k/z \text{ for } z \in E^k], & \text{if } y = y^* \text{ and Case 1 applies}, \\ \neg \phi_{\neg y^*}^{k-1}[1/y^*][s_z^k/z \text{ for } z \in E^k], & \text{if } y = y^* \text{ and Case 2 applies}. \end{cases}$$

For a proof see [41]. If both cases apply, we can use don't-care minimization to reduce the AIG size of the Skolem function $s_{y^*}^{k-1}$ for the eliminated variable y^*.

Variable elimination by resolution is sound for DQBF also in a third case when an existential variable $y^* \in E^{k-1}$ fulfills the conditions for structure extraction [41]. (Depending on the solver back-end, one might prefer elimination by resolution instead of structure extraction in order to preserve the CNF structure of the matrix.) It is easy to see that in this case the Skolem function $s_{y^*}^{k-1}$ can simply computed from $(s_y^k)_{y \in E^k}$ as in Sect. 4.4.

4.6 Blocked Clause Elimination (BCE)

BCE [22] allows to delete certain clauses C from a formula without changing its truth value. This is the case if all resolvents of C w. r. t. one of its existential literals $\ell \in C$ are tautologies and if the dependency set of the variable that makes the resolvent a tautology is a subset of var(ℓ)'s dependency set [41].

Definition 7 (Outer Clause, Outer Formula). *Let $\psi = Q : \phi$ be a DQBF, $C \in \phi$ a clause, and $\ell \in C$ a literal of C. The outer clause of C on ℓ is given by*

$$\mathcal{OC}(\psi, C, \ell) = \{\kappa \in C \mid \kappa \neq \ell \wedge \mathrm{dep}_\psi(\kappa) \subseteq \mathrm{dep}_\psi(\ell)\}.$$

Let ℓ be a literal in a DQBF ψ. The outer formula of ψ on ℓ is given by

$$\mathcal{OF}(\psi, \ell) = \{\mathcal{OC}(\psi, D, \neg \ell) \mid D \in \phi \wedge \neg \ell \in D\}.$$

Now we can define blocked clauses for DQBF [41]:

Definition 8 (Blocked Clause). *Let* $\psi = Q : \phi$ *be a DQBF,* $C \in \phi$ *a clause. The clause* C *is* blocked *if there is an existential literal* $\ell \in C$ *such that* $\mathcal{OC}(\psi, C, \ell) \cup \mathcal{OC}(\psi, D, \neg\ell)$ *is a tautology for all* $D \in \phi$ *with* $\neg\ell \in D$.

It is known that blocked clauses can be deleted from a DQBF without changing its truth value [41].

Similar to the QBF case, which is described in [23], we can derive Skolem functions in case of blocked clause elimination using the following lemma:

Lemma 10 (Blocked Clause Elimination). *Let* Ψ^k *be created from* Ψ^{k-1} *by deleting the clause* C, *which is blocked in* Ψ^{k-1} *w. r. t. the existential literal* $\ell \in C$, *i. e.,* $Q^k : \phi^k = Q^{k-1} : \phi^{k-1} \setminus \{C\}$. *If* $(s_y^k)_{y \in E^k}$ *are Skolem functions for* Ψ^k, *then* $(s_y^{k-1})_{y \in E^{k-1}}$ *are Skolem functions for* Ψ^{k-1} *where*

$$
s_y^{k-1} = \begin{cases} s_y^k, & \text{if } y \neq \mathrm{var}(\ell), \\ ITE(\mathcal{OF}(\Psi^{k-1}, \ell)[s_z^k/z \text{ for } z \in E^k], \text{ sign}(\ell), \ s_y^k), & \text{if } y = \mathrm{var}(\ell). \end{cases}
$$

Proof Sketch. Let $y^* := \mathrm{var}(\ell)$. First, $s_{y^*}^{k-1}$ depends only on variables in $D_{y^*}^{k-1}$ because $\mathcal{OF}(\Psi^{k-1}, \ell)$ contains only variables v with $\mathrm{dep}_{\Psi^{k-1}}(v) \subseteq \mathrm{dep}_{\Psi^{k-1}}(y^*)$.

Second, we have to show that $\phi^{k-1}[s_z^{k-1}/z \text{ for } z \in E^{k-1}]$ is a tautology. We show $\nu\big(\phi^{k-1}[s_z^{k-1}/z \text{ for } z \in E^{k-1}]\big) = 1$ for every assignment $\nu \in \mathbf{A}(U^{k-1})$. We partition the clauses into those which contain ℓ, those which contain $\neg\ell$, and the remaining ones. We distinguish the cases where $\nu\big(\mathcal{OF}(\Psi^{k-1}, \ell)\big)$ is 0 and where it is 1, and prove that in both cases all clauses are satisfied. Details can be found in [40]. □

The effectiveness of blocked clause elimination is often increased by adding hidden and covered literals before testing whether a clause is blocked. Adding hidden literals yields an equivalent DQBF (see Sect. 4.1), but the addition of covered literals has to be taken into account when computing Skolem functions.

For detailed information how to handle covered literal addition, we refer the reader to the extended version [40] of this paper.

5 Experimental Results

We extended our DQBF solver HQS [19][2]. by the possibility to compute Skolem functions for satisfied DQBFs. The computation of Skolem functions works in two phases: During the solution process we collect the necessary data and store it on a stack. When the satisfiability of the formula has been determined, we free the other data structures of the solver and extract the Skolem functions from the collected data. During the extraction phase, HQS supports optimizing the

---

[2] A recent binary of HQS, all DQBF benchmarks we used as well as our proof checker are available at https://projects.informatik.uni-freiburg.de/projects/dqbf.

Skolem functions of eliminated existential variables according to Remarks 2 and 3. If don't-care optimization using Craig interpolation is enabled, we choose a Skolem function for the eliminated existential variable $y^* \in E^{k-1}$ among $\phi^{k-1}[1/y^*]$, $\neg\phi^{k-1}[0/y^*]$, and the computed interpolant, taking one with minimal AIG size. If interpolation is disabled, we only choose among the first two options.

Additionally, in a post-processing step, we can use the tool ABC [8] to further optimize the Skolem function representations. It supports AIG rewriting based on so-called *internal* don't cares. In contrast to the *external* don't cares that we proposed in Remark 3, they encompass values which cannot appear at internal signals of the AIG.

HQS is accompanied by a proof checker, which verifies that the Skolem functions depend only on the allowed variables and that replacing the existential variables in the formula by their Skolem function indeed yields a tautology. Checking whether the Skolem functions depend only on the allowed variables is performed just by traversing the AIGs and computing the *structural* support, since, by construction, the AIGs of the Skolem functions do not structurally depend on more than the allowed variables.[3] Logic optimizations done by ABC could increase the structural support in principle, but since logic optimization does not change the represented Boolean functions semantically, additional variables in the structural support which are introduced by ABC can be removed by replacing them by arbitrary constants.[4] The second and more important part of the check is done by replacing the existential variables by their Skolem functions and by calling a SAT-solver to verify that the resulting formula is a tautology. As a SAT-solver, we have used Minisat 2.2 [13]. We have applied this proof checker to all computed Skolem functions and confirmed their correctness.

All experiments were run on one Intel Xeon E5-2650v2 CPU core at 2.60 GHz clock frequency and 64 GB of main memory under Linux (kernel version 3.13) as operating system, running in 64 bit mode. We aborted all experiments which either took more than 3600 s CPU time or more than 8 GB ($= 2^{30}$ bytes) of main memory. As benchmarks we used 4811 DQBF instances from different sources: DQBFs resulting from equivalence checking of incomplete circuits [15,17,18], controller synthesis problems [7], and instances obtained from converting SAT instances into DQBFs that depend only on a logarithmic number of variables [4].

First we compare the number of instances which could be solved and for which Skolem functions could be computed in different solver configurations. Table 1 shows the results. Out of the 4811 instances, on aver-

Table 1. Solved instances

Variant	Solved	Unsat	Sat	Skolem
w/o Skolem functions	4008	3286	722	n/a
w/o optimizations	4010	3289	721	721
+ interpolation	4010	3289	721	721
+ ABC	4009	3287	722	722
+ interpolation + ABC	4008	3287	721	721

age 4010 could be solved; of those instances, 3288 were UNSAT, 722 SAT. Skolem functions were obtained for all of the solved SAT instances, i. e., we could not

---

[3] Of course, the semantical support could also be checked by a series of SAT calls.

[4] However, this case never occurred in our experiments.

only decide realizability, but even determine implementations of controllers or the unknown circuit parts. These numbers are independent of whether interpolation and/or ABC were used to optimize the size of the Skolem functions. The small deviations seem to be due to random effects from scheduling and influences from other processes. The numbers change by one or two when we re-run the solver in the same configuration.

This is consistent with Fig. 1, which shows the influence of *data collection* on the computation time (left) until the truth value of the formula has been determined and on the peak memory consumption (right) until the computation of Skolem functions has been finished. The memory consumption of ABC is not taken into account, because it runs when HQS has terminated and needed less memory than HQS in all cases. A mark below the diagonal means that the variant on the vertical axis performs better for that instance than the variant on the horizontal axis. The figures show that the solution time only changes by a small amount due to data collection. The memory consumption increases only slightly in most cases. In a few exceptions, the memory consumption even decreases. The reason is that the Skolem functions share AIG nodes with the formula in the solver core. This changes the way how the AIG manager can optimize the AIG representation, which can actually lead to lower memory consumption.

The final extraction phase takes a few seconds at most, even if the optimizations are enabled. Since the internal data structures of the solver have already been freed at that point, the peak memory consumption does not occur during Skolem function computation, but during the solution process.

In Fig. 2, we compare the effectiveness of optimizing the Skolem functions by don't-care minimization and rewriting. We ran HQS on the satisfiable instances with five different configurations: (1) without any optimization of the Skolem functions (besides taking the smaller one of $\phi^{k-1}[1/y^*]$ and $\neg\phi^{k-1}[0/y^*]$ for eliminated existential variables, cf. Remark 2); (2) applying ABC to the obtained Skolem functions; (3) using interpolation according to Lemma 2; and (4) using

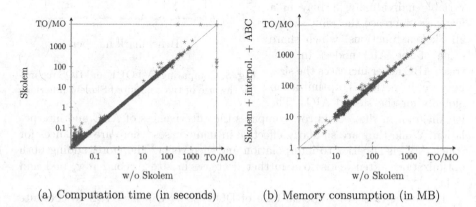

(a) Computation time (in seconds)   (b) Memory consumption (in MB)

Fig. 1. Influence of data collection on the computation time (left) and memory consumption with and without computation of Skolem functions (right)

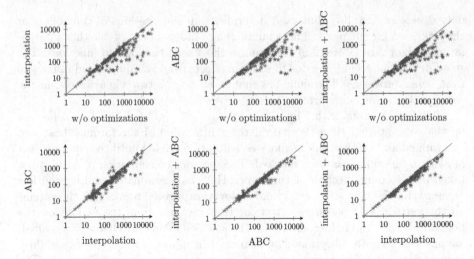

Fig. 2. The sizes (number of AND nodes) in the Skolem functions' AIG representations with different optimizations enabled. Note that the axes are logarithmically scaled.

both interpolation and ABC. The diagrams show the values for all (roughly) 722 instances for which we were able to compute Skolem functions.

We can observe that both interpolation (first row, left) and ABC (first row, mid) in isolation have, on average, a positive effect on the sizes of the Skolem functions. Nevertheless, since we perform don't-care optimization using interpolation for each eliminated existential variable individually, it may in a few cases increase the joint size of all Skolem functions, which share some of the AIG nodes. In contrast, ABC never increases the size, because it performs optimization globally for the shared AIGs. The

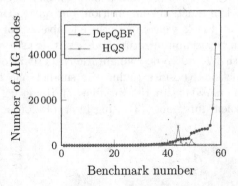

Fig. 3. Comparing DEPQBF and HQS regarding the size of the computed Skolem functions

left diagram in the second row compares the effectiveness of ABC and interpolation. While they are similarly effective in many cases, there are instances for which ABC is superior to interpolation and vice versa. Therefore, adding both optimizations often leads to a further decrease in size (second row, mid and right).

Because QBFs are a special case of DQBFs, we can use HQS to compute Skolem functions for satisfied QBFs. In Fig. 3, we compare the sizes of the Skolem functions generated by HQS with those generated by the state-of-the-art QBF solver DEPQBF 5.0 [28,29] for a set of satisfiable QBF instances from the QBF

Gallery 2013[5] and from partial equivalence checking [37] (with a single black box). Since HQS (and in particular its preprocessor) is not optimized for solving QBF instances, we abstain from a detailed comparison of the running times of HQS and DEPQBF. DEPQBF is often (but not always) faster than HQS. In a few cases, the generation of Skolem functions with DEPQBF failed because the necessary resolution proof became too large (we aborted DEPQBF when the size of the dumped resolution proof exceeded 20 GB).

Figure 3 shows the sizes of the Skolem functions computed by DEPQBF and by HQS (with interpolation and ABC). To enable a fair comparison, we also applied ABC with the same commands to the Skolem functions generated using DEPQBF. We can observe that HQS' Skolem functions are in most cases smaller (often significantly) than those obtained from DEPQBF.

In summary, we can conclude that the proposed method allows the computation of Skolem function for satisfied DQBFs with very little overhead regarding computation time and memory consumption. Applying interpolation and ABC to decrease the size of the Skolem functions has in general a positive effect. Regarding the sizes of the computed Skolem functions, HQS is at least comparable to the QBF solver DEPQBF on small to medium size QBF instances.

6   Conclusion

We have shown how Skolem functions can be computed for satisfiable DQBFs. They play a crucial role in many applications from implementations of missing circuit parts or controllers to winning strategies in games. We have shown how don't-care minimization can help reduce the size of the Skolem functions. In a series of experiments we demonstrated that the computation of Skolem functions is not only possible in theory but also feasible in practice: both the overhead during the solution process and the time for extracting the functions from the collected data are small.

An open problem is the certification of unsatisfiability. For QBFs this can be done by negating the formula and then computing Skolem functions (which are here called Herbrand functions). This is not possible for DQBFs [2] because DQBFs are not closed under negation.[6] Finding ways to certify the unsatisfiability of a DQBF is an important task for future work.

References

1. Ashar, P., Ganai, M.K., Gupta, A., Ivancic, F., Yang, Z.: Efficient SAT-based bounded model checking for software verification. In: Proceedings of ISoLA. Technical report, vol. TR-2004-6, pp. 157–164. University of Cyprus (2004)
2. Balabanov, V., Chiang, H.K., Jiang, J.R.: Henkin quantifiers and Boolean formulae: a certification perspective of DQBF. Theor. Comput. Sci. **523**, 86–100 (2014)

---

[5] See http://www.kr.tuwien.ac.at/events/qbfgallery2013/.

[6] The DQBF-variant we consider is called S-form DQBF in [2]. Its negation yields a so-called H-form DQBF, which does not support the computation of Skolem functions.

3. Balabanov, V., Jiang, J.R.: Unified QBF certification and its applications. Formal Methods Syst. Des. **41**(1), 45–65 (2012)
4. Balabanov, V., Jiang, J.H.R.: Reducing satisfiability and reachability to DQBF (2015). Talk at the International Workshop on Quantified Boolean Formulas (QBF)
5. Benedetti, M.: Evaluating QBFs via symbolic Skolemization. In: Baader, F., Voronkov, A. (eds.) LPAR 2004. LNCS (LNAI), vol. 3452, pp. 285–300. Springer, Heidelberg (2005)
6. Biere, A., Cimatti, A., Clarke, E.M., Strichman, O., Zhu, Y.: Bounded model checking. Adv. Comput. **58**, 117–148 (2003)
7. Bloem, R., Könighofer, R., Seidl, M.: SAT-based synthesis methods for safety specs. In: McMillan, K.L., Rival, X. (eds.) VMCAI 2014. LNCS, vol. 8318, pp. 1–20. Springer, Heidelberg (2014)
8. Brayton, R., Mishchenko, A.: ABC: an academic industrial-strength verification tool. In: Touili, T., Cook, B., Jackson, P. (eds.) CAV 2010. LNCS, vol. 6174, pp. 24–40. Springer, Heidelberg (2010)
9. Bubeck, U., Kleine Büning, H.: Dependency quantified horn formulas: models and complexity. In: Biere, A., Gomes, C.P. (eds.) SAT 2006. LNCS, vol. 4121, pp. 198–211. Springer, Heidelberg (2006)
10. Cook, S.A.: The complexity of theorem-proving procedures. In: Proceedings of STOC, pp. 151–158. ACM Press (1971)
11. Craig, W.: Linear reasoning. a new form of the Herbrand-Gentzen theorem. J. Symbolic Logic **22**(3), 250–268 (1957)
12. Czutro, A., Polian, I., Lewis, M.D.T., Engelke, P., Reddy, S.M., Becker, B.: Thread-parallel integrated test pattern generator utilizing satisfiability analysis. Int. J. Parallel Programm. **38**(3–4), 185–202 (2010)
13. Eén, N., Sörensson, N.: An extensible SAT-solver. In: Giunchiglia, E., Tacchella, A. (eds.) SAT 2003. LNCS, vol. 2919, pp. 502–518. Springer, Heidelberg (2004)
14. Eggersglüß, S., Drechsler, R.: A highly fault-efficient SAT-based ATPG flow. IEEE Des. Test Comput. **29**(4), 63–70 (2012)
15. Finkbeiner, B., Tentrup, L.: Fast DQBF refutation. In: Sinz, C., Egly, U. (eds.) SAT 2014. LNCS, vol. 8561, pp. 243–251. Springer, Heidelberg (2014)
16. Fröhlich, A., Kovásznai, G., Biere, A.: A DPLL algorithm for solving DQBF. In: International Workshop on Pragmatics of SAT (POS) (2012)
17. Fröhlich, A., Kovásznai, G., Biere, A., Veith, H.: iDQ: instantiation-based DQBF solving. In: International Workshop on Pragmatics of SAT (POS). EPiC Series, vol. 27, pp. 103–116. EasyChair (2014)
18. Gitina, K., Reimer, S., Sauer, M., Wimmer, R., Scholl, C., Becker, B.: Equivalence checking of partial designs using dependency quantified Boolean formulae. In: Proceedings of ICCD, pp. 396–403. IEEE CS (2013)
19. Gitina, K., Wimmer, R., Reimer, S., Sauer, M., Scholl, C., Becker, B.: Solving DQBF through quantifier elimination. In: Proceedings of DATE. IEEE (2015)
20. Goultiaeva, A., Van Gelder, A., Bacchus, F.: A uniform approach for generating proofs and strategies for both true and false QBF formulas. In: Proceedings of IJCAI, pp. 546–553. IJCAI/AAAI (2011)
21. Henkin, L.: Some remarks on infinitely long formulas. In: Infinitistic Methods: Proceedings of the 1959 Symposium on Foundations of Mathematics, pp. 167–183. Pergamon Press, Warsaw (1961)
22. Heule, M., Järvisalo, M., Lonsing, F., Seidl, M., Biere, A.: Clause elimination for SAT and QSAT. J. Artif. Intell. Res. **53**, 127–168 (2015)
23. Heule, M., Seidl, M., Biere, A.: Efficient extraction of Skolem functions from QRAT proofs. In: Proceedings of FMCAD, pp. 107–114. IEEE (2014)

24. Jiang, J.-H.R.: Quantifier elimination via functional composition. In: Bouajjani, A., Maler, O. (eds.) CAV 2009. LNCS, vol. 5643, pp. 383–397. Springer, Heidelberg (2009)

25. Jussila, T., Biere, A., Sinz, C., Kroning, D., Wintersteiger, C.M.: A first step towards a unified proof checker for QBF. In: Marques-Silva, J., Sakallah, K.A. (eds.) SAT 2007. LNCS, vol. 4501, pp. 201–214. Springer, Heidelberg (2007)

26. Kilby, P., Slaney, J.K., Thiébaux, S., Walsh, T.: Backbones and backdoors in satisfiability. In: Proceedings of NAI/IAAI, pp. 1368–1373. AAAI Press/The MIT Press (2005)

27. Kuehlmann, A., Paruthi, V., Krohm, F., Ganai, M.K.: Robust Boolean reasoning for equivalence checking and functional property verification. IEEE Trans. CAD Integr. Circ. Syst. **21**(12), 1377–1394 (2002)

28. Lonsing, F., Bacchus, F., Biere, A., Egly, U., Seidl, M.: Enhancing search-basedQBF solving by dynamic blocked clause elimination. In: Davis, M., Fehnker, A., McIver, A., Voronkov, A. (eds.) LPAR-20 2015. LNCS, vol. 9450, pp. 418–433. Springer, Heidelberg (2015)

29. Lonsing, F., Biere, A.: DepQBF: a dependency-aware QBF solver. J. Satisfiability Boolean Modell. Comput. **7**(2–3), 71–76 (2010)

30. McMillan, K.L.: Applications of Craig interpolants in model checking. In: Halbwachs, N., Zuck, L.D. (eds.) TACAS 2005. LNCS, vol. 3440, pp. 1–12. Springer, Heidelberg (2005)

31. Niemetz, A., Preiner, M., Lonsing, F., Seidl, M., Biere, A.: Resolution-based certificate extraction for QBF. In: Cimatti, A., Sebastiani, R. (eds.) SAT 2012. LNCS, vol. 7317, pp. 430–435. Springer, Heidelberg (2012)

32. Peterson, G., Reif, J., Azhar, S.: Lower bounds for multiplayer non-cooperative games of incomplete information. Comput. Math. Appl. **41**(7–8), 957–992 (2001)

33. Pigorsch, F., Scholl, C.: Exploiting structure in an AIG based QBF solver. In: Proceedings of DATE, pp. 1596–1601. IEEE (2009)

34. Pigorsch, F., Scholl, C.: An AIG-based QBF-solver using SAT for preprocessing. In: Proceedings of DAC, pp. 170–175. ACM Press (2010)

35. Pudlák, P.: Lower bounds for resolution and cutting planes proofs and monotone computations. J. Symbolic Logic **62**(3), 981–998 (1997)

36. Rintanen, J., Heljanko, K., Niemelä, I.: Planning as satisfiability: parallel plans and algorithms for plan search. Artif. Intell. **170**(12–13), 1031–1080 (2006)

37. Scholl, C., Becker, B.: Checking equivalence for partial implementations. In: Proceedings of DAC, pp. 238–243. ACM Press (2001)

38. Tentrup, L., Rabe, M.N.: CAQE: a certifying QBF solver. In: Proceedings of FMCAD, pp. 136–143. IEEE (2015)

39. Wegener, I.: Branching Programs and Binary Decision Diagrams. Discrete Mathematics and Applications. SIAM, SIAM Monographs on Philadelphia (2000)

40. Wimmer, K., Wimmer, R., Scholl, C., Becker, B.: Skolem functions for DQBF (extended version). Technical report, FreiDok plus, Universitätsbibliothek Freiburg, Freiburg im Breisgau, Germany, June 2016. https://www.freidok.uni-freiburg.de

41. Wimmer, R., Gitina, K., Nist, J., Scholl, C., Becker, B.: Preprocessing for DQBF. In: Heule, M., et al. (eds.) SAT 2015. LNCS, vol. 9340, pp. 173–190. Springer, Heidelberg (2015). doi:10.1007/978-3-319-24318-4_13

STL Model Checking of Continuous and Hybrid Systems

Hendrik Roehm[1]([⊠]), Jens Oehlerking[1], Thomas Heinz[1], and Matthias Althoff[2]

[1] Robert Bosch GmbH, Corporate Research, Renningen, Germany
{hendrik.roehm,jens.oehlerking,thomas.heinz2}@de.bosch.com
[2] Department of Informatics, Technische Universität München, Munich, Germany
althoff@in.tum.de

Abstract. Signal Temporal Logic (STL) is a formalism for reasoning about temporal properties of continuous-time traces of hybrid systems. Previous work on this subject mostly focuses on robust satisfaction of an STL formula for a particular trace. In contrast, we present a method solving the problem of formally verifying an STL formula for continuous and hybrid system models, which exhibit uncountably many traces. We consider an abstraction of a model as an evolution of reachable sets. Through leveraging the representation of the abstraction, the continuous-time verification problem is reduced to a discrete-time problem. For the given abstraction, the reduction to discrete-time and our decision procedure are sound and complete for finitely represented reach sequences and sampled time STL formulas. Our method does not rely on a special representation of reachable sets and thus any reachability analysis tool can be used to generate the reachable sets. The benefit of the method is illustrated on an example from the context of automated driving.

Keywords: Model checking · Reachability analysis · Hybrid systems · Temporal logic · Continuous time

1 Introduction

In recent years, the functionality and complexity of products, production processes, and software has been increasing. Furthermore, the interaction between the physical parts of a system (mechanics, thermodynamics, sensors, actuators, and others) and its computational elements is becoming tighter and is organized over large networks, which has resulted in so-called *cyber-physical systems* [14,21]. Due to their advanced capabilities, newly developed cyber-physical systems often fulfill safety-critical tasks that were previously only entrusted to humans; see, e.g., automated road vehicles, surgical robots, automatic operation of smart grids, and collaborative human-robot manufacturing [18,22]. The aforementioned trends drastically increase the demand for formal verification methods of hybrid (mixed discrete/continuous) systems.

Hybrid systems contain the interplay of discrete and continuous dynamics and therefore are inherently difficult to verify formally [18,23]. As a result, most hybrid system researchers have focused on solving reach-problems and reach-avoid-problems: for all possible initial states and all possible disturbances, the

© Springer International Publishing AG 2016
C. Artho et al. (Eds.): ATVA 2016, LNCS 9938, pp. 412–427, 2016.
DOI: 10.1007/978-3-319-46520-3_26

system has to avoid forbidden regions while reaching a goal set [6,13]. There are
several tools for reach-avoid problems, which compute sets of reachable states
over time and check for intersection of these sets with forbidden regions [2,12].
More complicated formal specifications based on temporal logics, such as computation tree logic (CTL), linear temporal logic (LTL), or μ-calculus, have mostly
been applied to the verification of purely discrete systems or timed automata
[4,7,9]. For hybrid systems, a continuous-time and real-valued version of such
temporal logics, called Signal Temporal Logic (STL), has been proposed as a
formal specification language [16]. However, STL has mainly not been used for
verification of hybrid systems, but for checking single traces only, e. g., for runtime monitoring and for test generation [1,15,17,26,27]. Therefore, there is a
demand for formal verification techniques which are able to verify a temporal
(STL) property for all (infinitely many) possible traces of a hybrid system.

In this work, we propose a new idea to verify specifications in STL for a
hybrid system. Given a hybrid system S and an STL property φ, we propose
the following steps to formally verify φ on S, as shown in Fig. 1:

1. A new *reachset temporal logic (RTL)* is defined (Sect. 3). The semantics of
   RTL is directly defined on the reach sequence, which corresponds to an infinite
   set of traces. A *reach sequence* is a function mapping time to the set of
   states reachable from a set of initial states and uncertain inputs. Therefore,
   with RTL, we are able to reason about infinitely many traces with a finite
   representation, in contrast to STL, which cannot be used to directly verify
   an infinite set of traces by simply evaluating the STL formula.
2. A *transformation* from sampled time STL to RTL is defined (Sect. 4). We
   prove that this transformation is sound and complete with respect to finitely
   represented reach sequences and give a sound transformation from general
   STL to sampled time STL. Therefore, we are able to translate the STL verification problem on traces to an RTL verification problem on reach sequences.
3. A *model checking* algorithm is introduced to formally verify an STL property
   on a reach sequence using the transformation from STL to RTL and the
   semantics of RTL (Sect. 5).

Our theory does not rely on a special representation of reach sequences. Since
there exist many reachability analysis tools, such as Cora [2], SpaceEx [12],
and C2E2 [10], which can compute reach sequences, our approach is broadly
applicable. We show the benefits of our model checking method on an example
from the domain of automated driving (Sect. 6).

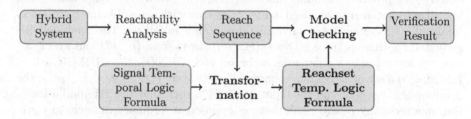

Fig. 1. Structure of the proposed model checking method. Bold parts are novel.

Note that we are working with overapproximations of exact reach sequences, because reachability analysis for hybrid systems is undecidable in general [20]. There are already some model checking techniques for temporal properties related to LTL: in order to be able to verify an uncountable set of possible traces, one can translate a temporal logic called Hybrid LTL (HyLTL) to a (Büchi) monitor automaton [8]. After parallel composition of the monitor automaton with the hybrid system to be verified, the verification problem reduces to finding a loop in the reach sequence. A problem of the HyLTL model checking approach is that to the best of our knowledge, there is no proof for the soundness of the verification result for the proposed method using overapproximative methods and bounded time horizons, which are common for reachability analysis tools due to undecidability. Another drawback of the HyLTL approach is that parallel composition drastically complicates the hybrid automaton and the reachability analysis so that the composition typically becomes so large that it is infeasible to analyze. With our method, temporal properties can be verified without changing the hybrid automaton, see the example in Sect. 6.

There are several works that also present approaches for model checking of hybrid systems that restrict to discrete time traces [11,24]. However, these works typically give no formal guarantees for the satisfaction on the continuous time traces, either because they sample the time, or one has to make additional assumptions about the behavior between the sampling points. In contrast, we formally reason about the continuous time traces.

2   Preliminaries

Linked to our model checking method are hybrid systems and Signal Temporal Logic, which are shortly introduced in the following.

2.1   Hybrid Systems

Our methods are defined on a sequence of reachable sets of states and thus are invariant to the modeling formalism that describes the evolution of a hybrid system. However, in order to describe how hybrid traces and reach sequences are generated, without loss of generality we use *hybrid automata* as a well-established modeling formalism [19]. In the following, we introduce hybrid automata in a non-formal way. Because the dynamics of real systems are typically not known exactly, we propose including non-deterministic behavior. Components of a hybrid automaton are visualized in Fig. 2 together with a possible reach sequence. Informally, the semantics of a hybrid automaton is as follows: The combined discrete and continuous trace $\xi(t) = (v(t), x(t))$ starts from (v^0, x^0) and $x(t) \in \mathbb{R}^n$ changes according to a differential inclusion $\dot{x}(t) \in \mathcal{H}(v(t), x(t), u(t))$ [25], where $\mathcal{H}(v, x, u)$ is a set of values based on the discrete state $v(t) \in \{v_1, v_2, \ldots, v_p\}$, the continuous state $x(t)$, and the input $u(t) \in \mathbb{R}^m$, such that the differential inclusion models many possible solutions as opposed to ordinary differential equations. If the continuous state is within a *guard set*, the corresponding transition

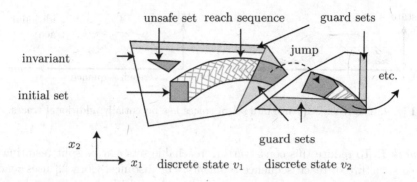

Fig. 2. Illustration of the evolution of a reachable set of a hybrid automaton.

to a new discrete state can be taken. It has to be taken if the state would leave an *invariant*, which is the region in which the differential inclusion of the current discrete state is defined. After the discrete transition is taken (in zero time), the continuous state is updated according to a *jump function*, which models possible instantaneous changes of the continuous state. For ease of presentation, we assume that a hybrid automaton is non-Zeno and non-blocking.

A *trace* $\xi : \mathbb{R}_{\geq 0} \to \mathbb{R}^n$ of the hybrid automaton S is of the form

$$\xi(t) = \begin{cases} \xi_0(t), \text{ for } t \in [0, t_1) \\ \xi_1(t), \text{ for } t \in [t_1, t_2) \\ \dots \end{cases}$$

where $\xi_i : [t_i, t_{i+1}) \to \mathbb{R}^n$ are the evolutions between discrete transitions. The set of all traces of a system S is denoted by *Traces*(S). In contrast to discrete systems, one cannot generate a tree of possible traces for a system with continuous state variables, since its number of traces is uncountably large. Thus, algorithms for computing reach sequences of systems involving continuous states do not preserve traces anymore, but only store the set of values for points in time and time intervals. A function $\mathbf{R} : \mathbb{R}_{\geq 0} \to \mathcal{P}(\mathbb{R}^n)$ mapping to the power set $\mathcal{P}(\mathbb{R}^n)$ is called a *reach sequence* of S, iff

$$\forall t \in \mathbb{R}_{\geq 0} : \{\xi(t) \mid \xi \in \mathit{Traces}(S)\} \subseteq \mathbf{R}(t) \tag{1}$$

holds. The reach sequence is called exact, iff (1) holds with '$\subseteq$' replaced by '$=$'. An evaluation $\mathbf{R}(t)$ for one point in time t is called a *reachable set*. Typically, other papers use the terminology reachable set only. However, in our work the distinction between reach sequence and reachable set is important for rigorous formulation and understandability. Due to undecidability, exact reachable sets typically cannot be obtained for hybrid systems. The set of traces corresponding to $\mathbf{R}$ is defined as

$$\mathcal{C}(\mathbf{R}) = \{\xi \mid \forall t \geq 0 : \xi(t) \in \mathbf{R}(t)\}$$

and contains the set of traces *Traces*(S) and potentially additional traces (even if $\mathbf{R}$ is exact), as visualized in Fig. 3.

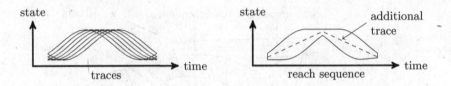

Fig. 3. The reach sequence of a set of traces has potentially additional traces.

Remark 1. To reduce this conservatism, reachable sets can be split resulting in a tree structure of reach sequence segments. For instance, Cora [2] uses reachable set splitting for accuracy reasons resulting in multiple branches with reach sequences that progress independently. Every path of the tree from the root to a leaf represents one reach sequence. While we focus on one reach sequence in this paper, the results can also be applied to the more general case by considering all reach sequences that can be generated from the tree.

Reachability analysis tools such as Cora can compute (overapproximative) reachable sets R_i for points at time t_i and reachable sets $\overline{R}_i$ for time intervals $[t_i, t_{i+1}]$. We call reachable sequences of the form

$$\mathbf{R} = (t_0, R_0)\,((t_0, t_1), \overline{R}_0)\,(t_1, R_1)\,((t_1, t_2), \overline{R}_1)\,\ldots\,((t_m, t_{m+1}), \overline{R}_m), \qquad (2)$$

finitely represented reach sequences, where R_i and $\overline{R}_i$ are sets of states, $t_0 = 0$, $t_{m+1} = \infty$, and define

$$\mathbf{R}(t) = R_i, \text{ iff } t = t_i \quad \text{and} \quad \mathbf{R}(t) = \overline{R}_i, \text{ iff } t \in (t_i, t_{i+1}). \qquad (3)$$

The considered time structure with alternating points and open intervals is similar to the one for timed automata, see [5].

2.2 Signal Temporal Logic (STL)

Values of traces are real numbers that vary over time. Hence, STL is a temporal logic to describe properties of continuous-timed and real-valued traces. We briefly introduce STL following Maler et al. [16]. An STL formula consists of atomic predicates (such as $x > 3$), which are composed using logical and temporal operators. The syntax of an STL formula over a finite set of atomic predicates $p \in AP$ is

$$\varphi := p \mid \neg\varphi \mid \varphi_1 \vee \varphi_2 \mid \varphi_1\,\mathcal{U}_{[a,b]}\varphi_2.$$

The trace satisfaction semantics of an STL formula φ for a trace ξ is defined recursively on φ:

$$
\begin{aligned}
\xi \models_T p &\iff \pi_p(\xi(0)) = true \\
\xi \models_T \neg\varphi &\iff \neg(\xi \models_T \varphi) \\
\xi \models_T \varphi_1 \vee \varphi_2 &\iff (\xi \models_T \varphi_1) \vee (\xi \models_T \varphi_2) \\
\xi \models_T \varphi_1\,\mathcal{U}_{[a,b]}\varphi_2 &\iff \exists t \in [a,b] : \langle\xi\rangle_t \models_T \varphi_2 \text{ and } \forall t' \in [0,t) : \langle\xi\rangle_{t'} \models_T \varphi_1
\end{aligned}
$$

using a predicate evaluation function π_p and the suffix notation $\langle\xi\rangle_a(t) = \xi(t+a)$, which shifts the trace in time. For instance, the *until*-operator $p\ \mathcal{U}_{[a,b]}q$ states that p has to hold for all times until q holds for one point in time. Other common temporal operators can be derived from these operators, such as the *finally*-operator $\mathcal{F}_{[a,b]}\varphi := true\ \mathcal{U}_{[a,b]}\varphi$ and the *globally*-operator $\mathcal{G}_{[a,b]}\varphi := \neg\mathcal{F}_{[a,b]}\neg\varphi$. For brevity of notation, we also introduce the continuous *next*-operator

$$\xi \models_T \mathcal{X}_a\varphi \quad \Leftrightarrow \quad \langle\xi\rangle_a \models_T \varphi \quad \Leftrightarrow \quad \xi \models_T true\ \mathcal{U}_{[a,a]}\varphi.$$

An STL formula in which no temporal operators are present is called a non-temporal formula in the following. Inspired by LTL, we define the statisfaction of an STL formula on a set of traces M as

$$M \models_T \varphi \quad \Leftrightarrow \quad \forall\xi \in M : \xi \models_T \varphi.$$

Formally, the STL verification task for a hybrid system S is to check whether $Traces(S) \models_T \varphi$ holds. Since a verification method has to reason about uncountably many traces, the problem is often replaced by falsification in practice, searching for a trace ξ with $\xi \not\models_T \varphi$. However, falsification cannot prove that φ holds. Note that $Traces(S) \not\models_T \varphi$ does not imply $Traces(S) \models_T \neg\varphi$, because of the $\forall$-quantifier over the traces.

3   Reachset Temporal Logic (RTL)

Evaluation of an STL formula cannot be directly done for an infinite set of traces. Therefore, we introduce a new temporal logic that is defined on reach sequences instead of traces (such as STL), which we refer to as *Reachset Temporal Logic* (RTL). By transforming an STL formula into an RTL formula, we can leverage RTL for model checking the STL formula on a hybrid system, as visualized in Fig. 1. The syntax and semantics of RTL are defined so that STL formulas can be transferred and expressed on reach sequences and have therefore some commonalities with STL, but also important differences.

Definition 1 (RTL Syntax). *An RTL formula has the syntax*

$$\psi := \mathcal{A}\varrho \mid \psi_1 \wedge \psi_2 \mid \psi_1 \vee \psi_2 \mid \mathcal{X}_a\psi \mid \psi_1\ \mathcal{U}_{[a,b]}\ \psi_2 \mid \psi_1\ \mathcal{R}_{[a,b]}\ \psi_2$$

where ϱ is a propositional formula $\varrho := p \mid \varrho_1 \vee \varrho_2 \mid \neg\varrho$ over a finite set AP of predicates $p \in AP$.

Note that since we want to work with overapproximations of exact reachable sets, we have the negation operator only for non-temporal formulas, which is the reason for the syntactic split into ψ and ϱ.

Definition 2 (RTL Semantics). *For a propositional formula ϱ and a state r the semantics is*

$$
\begin{aligned}
r &\models_P p & &\Leftrightarrow & &\pi_p(r) \\
r &\models_P \neg\varrho & &\Leftrightarrow & &r \not\models_P \varrho \\
r &\models_P \varrho_1 \vee \varrho_2 & &\Leftrightarrow & &(r \models_P \varrho_1) \vee (r \models_P \varrho_2).
\end{aligned}
$$

For a reach sequence $\mathbf{R}$ *and a formula* ψ, *the semantics is defined as*

$$\mathbf{R} \models_R \mathcal{A}\varrho \qquad\qquad \Leftrightarrow \forall r \in \mathbf{R}(0) : r \models_P \varrho \tag{4}$$

$$\mathbf{R} \models_R \psi_1 \wedge \psi_2 \qquad \Leftrightarrow (\mathbf{R} \models_R \psi_1) \wedge (\mathbf{R} \models_R \psi_2) \tag{5}$$

$$\mathbf{R} \models_R \psi_1 \vee \psi_2 \qquad \Leftrightarrow (\mathbf{R} \models_R \psi_1) \vee (\mathbf{R} \models_R \psi_2) \tag{6}$$

$$\mathbf{R} \models_R \mathcal{X}_a \psi \qquad\qquad \Leftrightarrow \langle \mathbf{R} \rangle_a \models_R \psi \tag{7}$$

$$\mathbf{R} \models_R \psi_1 \mathcal{U}_{[a,b]} \psi_2 \quad \Leftrightarrow \exists t \in [a,b] : (\langle \mathbf{R} \rangle_t \models_R \psi_2) \wedge (\forall i \in [0,t) : \langle \mathbf{R} \rangle_i \models_R \psi_1) \tag{8}$$

$$\mathbf{R} \models_R \psi_1 \mathcal{R}_{[a,b]} \psi_2 \quad \Leftrightarrow \forall t \in [a,b] : (\langle \mathbf{R} \rangle_t \models_R \psi_2) \vee (\exists i \in [0,t) : \langle \mathbf{R} \rangle_i \models_R \psi_1) \tag{9}$$

where $\langle \mathbf{R} \rangle_a(t) := \mathbf{R}(t+a)$ *is the shift operator and* $a \in \mathbb{R}_{\geq 0}, b \in \mathbb{R}_{\geq 0}$ *with* $a \leq b$.

Two RTL formulas ψ_1, ψ_2 are equivalent, denoted as $\psi_1 \equiv \psi_2$, iff the satisfaction is the same for all possible reach sequences. The operators $\mathcal{F}$ and $\mathcal{G}$ are defined similarly to STL:

$$\mathcal{F}_{[a,b]}\psi := true\, \mathcal{U}_{[a,b]}\psi \ (\text{finally}) \quad \text{and} \quad \mathcal{G}_{[a,b]}\psi := false\, \mathcal{R}_{[a,b]}\psi \ (\text{globally})$$

To give an example, we consider the formula $\mathcal{F}_{[0,1]}\mathcal{A}\varrho$. A reach sequence $\mathbf{R}$ has to satisfy that ϱ holds for all states in one $\mathbf{R}(t)$ between time 0 and 1. Expressed on the set of traces $\mathcal{C}(\mathbf{R})$ corresponding to $\mathbf{R}$, this implies that all traces satisfy ϱ for one common point in time, compared to the requirement $\mathcal{F}_{[0,1]}\varrho$ for all traces:

$$\mathbf{R} \models_R \mathcal{F}_{[0,1]}\mathcal{A}\varrho \quad \Leftrightarrow \quad \exists t \in [0,1] : \mathcal{C}(\mathbf{R}) \models_T \mathcal{F}_{[t,t]}\varrho \quad \Rightarrow \quad \mathcal{C}(\mathbf{R}) \models_T \mathcal{F}_{[0,1]}\varrho.$$

Since a set of traces satisfies an STL formula if each trace satisfies the formula, the traces are "checked" independently of each other, i.e. it is not possible to reason about a variable point $t \in [a,b]$ in time at which something holds for all traces in a set. Therefore, this cannot be expressed by STL. In contrast, RTL is able to express common satisfaction of predicates.

4   Transformation from STL to RTL

Differences of STL and RTL described in the previous section have some important implications for the transformation between these temporal logics. In this section we present a transformation Υ mapping an STL formula to an RTL formula. We first give some properties of a sound and complete transformation and then present a transformation for sampled time formulas and finitely represented reach sequences (Sect. 4.1). We further show that the results can be extended by transforming general STL formulas to sampled time formulas (Sect. 4.2). The methods will be used later to model check STL formulas, as shown in Fig. 1.

With a mapping Υ from STL to RTL we are able to transfer the verification task on the traces of a reach sequence $\mathcal{C}(\mathbf{R}) \models_T \varphi$ into a reach sequence verification task $\mathbf{R} \models_R \Upsilon(\varphi)$. Since we do not want to lose expressiveness, we demand from the transformation Υ that

$$\mathbf{R} \models_R \Upsilon(\varphi) \;\Rightarrow\; \mathcal{C}(\mathbf{R}) \models_T \varphi \quad \text{and} \quad \mathcal{C}(\mathbf{R}) \models_T \varphi \;\Rightarrow\; \mathbf{R} \models_{\dot{R}} \Upsilon(\varphi)$$

holds, which we call soundness and completeness, respectively, for the reach sequence abstraction. If soundness and completeness is given for Υ, the semantical domain can be changed without changing the verification result. The following lemma gives some properties of a sound and complete Υ.

Lemma 1. *Let the STL formulas φ_i and the non-temporal formula ϱ be given. A sound and complete transformation Υ has the following properties:*

$$\Upsilon(\varrho) \;\equiv\; \mathcal{A}\varrho \qquad\qquad\qquad \text{non-temporal transformation} \qquad (10)$$
$$\Upsilon(\varphi_1 \wedge \varphi_2) \;\equiv\; \Upsilon(\varphi_1) \wedge \Upsilon(\varphi_2) \qquad\qquad \wedge - distributivity. \qquad (11)$$

Furthermore, the $\vee$-distributivity

$$\Upsilon(\varphi_1 \vee \varphi_2) \;\equiv\; \Upsilon(\varphi_1) \vee \Upsilon(\varphi_2) \qquad\qquad \vee - distributivity \qquad (12)$$

does also hold, if $tsupp(\varphi_1) \cap tsupp(\varphi_2) = \emptyset$ for

$$tsupp(\varphi) := \{t \mid \exists \xi, \xi' : \mathbb{R} \to \mathbb{R}^n, (\xi \models_T \varphi) \wedge (\xi' \not\models_T \varphi) \wedge (\forall t' \neq t : \xi(t') = \xi'(t'))\},$$

which are the points in time where a change in the trace can affect whether φ is true or not.

Proof. For non-temporal properties ϱ, (10) follows from

$$\mathcal{C}(\mathbf{R}) \models_T \varrho \;\Leftrightarrow\; \forall \xi \in \mathcal{C}(\mathbf{R}) : \xi \models_T \varrho \;\Leftrightarrow\; \forall r \in \mathbf{R}(0) : r \models_P \varrho \;\Leftrightarrow\; \mathbf{R} \models_R \mathcal{A}\varrho.$$

From soundness and completeness of Υ and the RTL semantics follows

$$\mathbf{R} \models_R \Upsilon(\varphi_1 \wedge \varphi_2) \Leftrightarrow \mathcal{C}(\mathbf{R}) \models_T \varphi_1 \wedge \varphi_2 \qquad\qquad\qquad (13)$$
$$\mathcal{C}(\mathbf{R}) \models_T \varphi_1 \wedge \varphi_2 \Leftrightarrow \forall \xi \in \mathcal{C}(\mathbf{R}) : \xi \models_T \varphi_1 \wedge \varphi_2 \qquad\qquad (14)$$
$$\Leftrightarrow \forall \xi \in \mathcal{C}(\mathbf{R}) : \xi \models_T \varphi_1 \wedge \forall \xi \in \mathcal{C}(\mathbf{R}) : \xi \models_T \varphi_2$$
$$\mathcal{C}(\mathbf{R}) \models_T \varphi_1 \wedge \mathcal{C}(\mathbf{R}) \models_T \varphi_2 \Leftrightarrow \mathbf{R} \models_R \Upsilon(\varphi_1) \wedge \mathbf{R} \models_R \Upsilon(\varphi_2) \qquad (15)$$
$$\Leftrightarrow \mathbf{R} \models_R \Upsilon(\varphi_1) \wedge \Upsilon(\varphi_2)$$

which proves (11). The equivalences (13) and (15) hold also for $\vee$. Let us assume $\mathcal{C}(\mathbf{R}) : \xi \models_T \varphi_1 \vee \varphi_2$ holds, but not $\mathcal{C}(\mathbf{R}) : \xi \models_T \varphi_1 \vee \mathcal{C}(\mathbf{R}) : \xi \models_T \varphi_2$. Then, there exist ξ_1, ξ_2 with $\xi_1 \not\models_T \varphi_1$ and $\xi_2 \not\models_T \varphi_2$. Because of the empty time support intersection and the special structure of $\mathcal{C}(\mathbf{R})$, we can construct ξ with $\xi(t) = \xi_1(t)$ for $t \in tsupp(\varphi_1)$ and $\xi(t) = \xi_2(t)$ otherwise. Since $\xi \in \mathcal{C}(\mathbf{R})$ and $\xi \not\models_T \varphi_1$, $\xi \not\models_T \varphi_2$, this is a contradiction and therefore (12) holds, because the other direction can also be easily shown. □

Based on the properties from Lemma 1, one can see the subtle differences between a well-defined complete and a non-complete transformation. Let us consider the STL formula $\varphi := (\varrho_0 \wedge \mathcal{X}_1 \varrho_1) \vee \mathcal{X}_1 \varrho_0$, which could be transformed to $\psi := (\mathcal{A}\varrho_0 \wedge \mathcal{X}_1 \mathcal{A}\varrho_1) \vee \mathcal{X}_1 \mathcal{A}\varrho_0$ by simply adding the $\mathcal{A}$-operator to the non-temporal subformulas of the STL formula φ. However, if we first rewrite φ to the equivalent formula $(\varrho_0 \vee \mathcal{X}_1 \varrho_0) \wedge \mathcal{X}_1(\varrho_0 \vee \varrho_1)$ and transform it, we get $\psi' := (\mathcal{A}\varrho_0 \vee \mathcal{X}_1 \mathcal{A}\varrho_0) \wedge \mathcal{X}_1 \mathcal{A}(\varrho_0 \vee \varrho_1) \equiv (\mathcal{A}\varrho_0 \wedge \mathcal{X}_1 \mathcal{A}(\varrho_0 \vee \varrho_1)) \vee \mathcal{X}_1 \mathcal{A}\varrho_0$. The formula ψ' does not force all the traces to satisfy ϱ_1 at time 1, if one trace does not satisfy ϱ_0 at time 1. Since ψ' also implies φ, it is a sound transformation of φ which is less restrictive than ψ. As one can see from this example, a sound and complete transformation cannot simply be constructed by structural induction over the parts of an STL formula, even if no nested temporal operators are used. Different parts of a formula are able to interact with each other if they are composed with the $\vee$-operator. In the following, we build upon Lemma 1 and give a sound and complete transformation function for sampled time formulas.

4.1   Sound and Complete Transformation for Sampled Time Formulas

Operators can appear arbitrarily nested in STL formulas. Given a fixed $c > 0$, we call the subclass of STL which restricts formulas to

$$\varphi := \varrho \mid \neg\varphi \mid \varphi_1 \vee \varphi_2 \mid \mathcal{X}_c\varphi \mid \mathcal{F}_{(0,c)}\varrho \mid \mathcal{G}_{(0,c)}\varrho, \quad \varrho := p \mid \neg\varrho \mid \varrho_1 \vee \varrho_2$$

sampled time STL with timestep c. For example $p \vee \mathcal{F}_{(0,c)}p \vee \mathcal{X}_c\left(p \vee \mathcal{F}_{(0,c)}p \vee \mathcal{X}_c p\right)$ can be seen as a sampled time version of the STL formula $\mathcal{F}_{[0,2c]}p$. Since standard equivalences hold on STL formulas, such as $\neg\mathcal{X}_c\varphi \equiv \mathcal{X}_c\neg\varphi$, $\neg\mathcal{F}_{(0,c)}\varphi \equiv \mathcal{G}_{(0,c)}\neg\varphi$, and $\mathcal{X}_c(\varphi_1 \vee \varphi_2) \equiv \mathcal{X}_c\varphi_1 \vee \mathcal{X}_c\varphi_2$, each sampled time formula has an equivalent sampled time formula in conjunctive normal form $\bigwedge_i \bigvee_j \mathcal{X}_c^j(\varphi_{ij} \vee \varrho_{ij})$ with φ_{ij} of the form $\bigvee_k \mathcal{F}_{(0,c)}\varrho_k \vee \bigvee_l \mathcal{G}_{(0,c)}\varrho_l$, non-temporal formulas ϱ_{ij}, and the $\mathcal{X}$-operator in series $\mathcal{X}_c^j := \mathcal{X}_{j \cdot c}$. Based on the conjunctive normal form, we are able to introduce a sound and complete transformation Υ considering finitely represented reach sequences and given that c divides all time intervals of the reach sequence. Since finitely represented reach sequences can be produced by Cora [2] and SpaceEx [12] for instance, this is of practical relevance.

Lemma 2. *Let a sampled time formula be given in conjunctive normal form. Then, the transformation Υ from STL to RTL defined via*

$$\Upsilon\left(\bigwedge_i \bigvee_j \mathcal{X}_c^j(\varphi_{ij} \vee \varrho_{ij})\right) := \bigwedge_i \bigvee_j \mathcal{X}_c^j(\Upsilon(\varphi_{ij}) \vee \mathcal{A}\varrho_{ij}) \tag{16}$$

$$\Upsilon\left(\bigvee_{k \in K} \mathcal{F}_{(0,c)}\varrho_k \vee \bigvee_{l \in L} \mathcal{G}_{(0,c)}\varrho_l\right) := \mathcal{X}_{\frac{c}{2}}\left(\mathcal{A}\varrho' \vee \bigvee_{l \in L} \mathcal{A}(\varrho_l \vee \varrho')\right), \tag{17}$$

$$\text{with } \varrho' := \bigvee_{k \in K} \varrho_k$$

is sound and complete for finitely represented reach sequences $\mathbf{R} = (t_0, R_0)$ $((t_0, t_1), \overline{R}_0)$ (t_1, R_1) ... $((t_m, t_{m+1}), \overline{R}_m)$, *which are c-divisible, where c-divisibility holds if and only if* $t_i \in \mathbb{N}c := \{0, c, 2c, \ldots\}$ *holds for all* i.

Proof. Soundness and completeness can be proven by structural induction. Since we define the transformation such that $\Upsilon(\varphi_1 \wedge \varphi_2) \equiv \Upsilon(\varphi_1) \wedge \Upsilon(\varphi)$ holds, it can be shown similarly as in Lemma 1 that it is sufficient to show soundness and completeness for $\bigvee_j \mathcal{X}_c^j(\varphi_{ij} \vee \varrho_{ij})$, which works similarly, because different time branches have different time supports $tsupp(\mathcal{X}_c^j(\varphi_{ij} \vee \varrho_{ij})) \subseteq [j, j+1)$. Therefore it is sufficient to show soundness and completeness for (17). For brevity reasons, we do not give the proof for general formulas, but prove that the two terms

$$\mathcal{C}(\mathbf{R}) \models_T \mathcal{G}_{(0,c)}\varrho_1 \vee \mathcal{G}_{(0,c)}\varrho_2 \vee \mathcal{F}_{(0,c)}\varrho_3 \tag{18}$$

$$\mathbf{R} \models_R \mathcal{X}_{\frac{c}{2}}\mathcal{A}(\varrho_1 \vee \varrho_3) \vee \mathcal{X}_{\frac{c}{2}}\mathcal{A}(\varrho_2 \vee \varrho_3) \tag{19}$$

are equivalent. Let us assume that (19) holds and therefore without loss of generality $\mathbf{R} \models_R \mathcal{X}_{\frac{c}{2}}\mathcal{A}(\varrho_1 \vee \varrho_3)$ holds. Since $\mathbf{R}$ is a finitely represented reach sequence which changes values only at points in time divisible by c, also $R \models_R \mathcal{G}_{(0,c)}\mathcal{A}(\varrho_1 \vee \varrho_3)$ and therefore $\mathcal{C}(\mathbf{R}) \models_T \mathcal{G}_{(0,c)}(\varrho_1 \vee \varrho_3)$ holds, which implies (18). On the other hand, let us assume (19) does not hold. Therefore

$$\mathbf{R} \not\models_R \mathcal{X}_{\frac{c}{2}}\mathcal{A}(\varrho_1 \vee \varrho_3) \wedge \mathbf{R} \not\models_R \mathcal{X}_{\frac{c}{2}}\mathcal{A}(\varrho_2 \vee \varrho_3)$$

$$\Rightarrow \exists r_1 \in \mathbf{R}\left(\frac{c}{2}\right) : r_1 \models_p \neg\varrho_1 \wedge \neg\varrho_3 \quad \wedge \quad \exists r_2 \in \mathbf{R}\left(\frac{c}{2}\right) : r_2 \models_p \neg\varrho_2 \wedge \neg\varrho_3$$

holds. Hence, Eq. (18) does not hold, because the trace

$$\xi(t) := \begin{cases} r_1, & t \in \left(0, \frac{c}{2}\right) \\ r_2, & t \in \left[\frac{c}{2}, c\right) \\ \text{any } r \in R(t), & \text{otherwise} \end{cases}$$

is contained in $\mathcal{C}(\mathbf{R})$ but does not satisfy the formula in (18).   □

Lemma 2 proves that the RTL formula $\psi := (\mathcal{A}\varrho_0 \wedge \mathcal{X}_1\mathcal{A}(\varrho_0 \vee \varrho_1)) \vee \mathcal{X}_1\mathcal{A}\varrho_0$ is a sound and complete transformation of the formula $(\varrho_0 \wedge \mathcal{X}_1\varrho_1) \vee \mathcal{X}_1\varrho_0$ considered in the previous section. As we have seen above, the formula $\mathcal{F}_{[0,2c]}p$ has an equivalent sampled time notation. Therefore, it can be transformed to $\psi' := \mathcal{A}p \vee \mathcal{X}_{\frac{c}{2}}\mathcal{A}p \vee \mathcal{X}_{\frac{c}{2}}^2\mathcal{A}p \vee \mathcal{X}_{\frac{c}{2}}^3\mathcal{A}p \vee \mathcal{X}_{\frac{c}{2}}^4\mathcal{A}p$ using Lemma 2. Since we do not have any temporal operators but the shift operator in ψ and ψ', the formulas can easily be checked on a reach sequence. This is the basis for our model checking approach in Sect. 5. Note that $\frac{c}{2}$ can be seen as a compatible sample time that jumps from one point in time kc to the next open interval $(kc, (k+1)c)$ or from an open interval $(kc, (k+1)c)$ to the next point in time $(k+1)c$ respectively, as shown in Fig. 4.

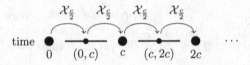

Fig. 4. The next operator $\mathcal{X}_{\frac{c}{2}}$ points to the next interval or point.

4.2   Transformation of General STL to Sampled Time STL

Rewriting a general STL formula as an sampled time formula enables us to use the results of the previous section for general STL formulas. The rewriting is sound and therefore, we are able to reason about the satisfaction of an STL formula on reach sequences. The main idea is to leverage the finite representation of a given STL formula φ for rewriting and use rules of the form $\xi \models_T \varphi \Leftarrow \xi \models_T \varphi'$ to rewrite φ to a sampled time version φ' in a sound manner. If we have such rules, they can also be applied to $\mathcal{C}(\mathbf{R})$.

Lemma 3. *Let φ be an STL formula which can be written as $f(\varphi_1, \ldots, \varphi_n)$, where f is a function composing φ_i by $\wedge$, $\vee$, and $\mathcal{X}_c$. Let $\xi \models_T \varphi_i \Leftarrow \xi \models_T \varphi'_i$ for all i and ξ. Then*

$$\mathcal{C}(\mathbf{R}) \models_T \varphi \Leftarrow \mathcal{C}(\mathbf{R}) \models_T \varphi'$$

holds with $\varphi' = f(\varphi'_1, \ldots, \varphi'_n)$.

Proof. Let us assume $\xi \models_T \varphi'_1 \wedge \varphi'_2$, which is equivalent to $\xi \models_T \varphi'_1 \wedge \xi \models_T \varphi'_2$, holds for all ξ. From the rewriting rules it follows that $\xi \models_T \varphi_1 \wedge \xi \models_T \varphi_2$ and therefore $\xi \models_T \varphi_1 \wedge \varphi_2$ holds also. The proof follows from

$$\mathcal{C}(\mathbf{R}) \models_T \varphi_1 \wedge \varphi_2 \quad\Leftrightarrow\quad \forall \xi \in \mathcal{C}(\mathbf{R}) : \xi \models_T \varphi_1 \wedge \varphi_2$$
$$\Leftarrow \quad \forall \xi \in \mathcal{C}(\mathbf{R}) : \xi \models_T \varphi'_1 \wedge \varphi'_2 \quad\Leftrightarrow\quad \mathcal{C}(\mathbf{R}) \models_T \varphi'_1 \wedge \varphi'_2$$

by structural induction over $\wedge$, $\vee$, and $\mathcal{X}_c$. $\square$

Finally, we need a set of rewriting rules that are sufficient to rewrite general STL formulas as sampled time ones.

Lemma 4. *Let an STL formula φ be given, which is c-divisible, where c-divisibility holds if c divides all bounds of temporal operators of φ. Without loss of generality, we assume that φ is in negation normal form. Hence, φ can be written as $f(\varphi_1, \ldots, \varphi_n)$, where f is a function composing φ_i by $\wedge$, $\vee$, and $\mathcal{X}_c$ and the outmost operator of each φ_i is a temporal operator or φ_i is non-temporal. Then, for any temporal φ_i there is a rewriting in Table 1 or one of the following equivalences using subformulas $\widehat{\varphi}_i$*

$$\widehat{\varphi}_1 \, \mathcal{U}_{[0,0]} \widehat{\varphi}_2 \equiv \widehat{\varphi}_2, \quad \widehat{\varphi}_1 \, \mathcal{R}_{[0,0]} \widehat{\varphi}_2 \equiv \widehat{\varphi}_2, \quad \mathcal{F}_I \mathcal{X}_1 \widehat{\varphi}_1 \equiv \mathcal{X}_1 \mathcal{F}_I \widehat{\varphi}_1, \quad \mathcal{G}_I \mathcal{X}_1 \widehat{\varphi}_1 \equiv \mathcal{X}_1 \mathcal{G}_I \widehat{\varphi}_1$$

such that φ can be rewritten to $rw(\varphi) = f(\varphi'_1, \ldots, \varphi'_n)$ in a sound manner. The formula φ can be rewritten to a sampled time version with timestep c by iteratively using the rewriting $\varphi \mapsto rw(\varphi) \mapsto rw^2(\varphi) \mapsto \ldots$ until no rewriting rule matches anymore.

Table 1. For all ξ the formula $\xi \models_T \varphi_i \Leftarrow \xi \models_T \varphi_i'$ holds for each pair φ_i, φ_i' in the table. For readability reasons, we use $I = (0, c)$ and assume $c = 1$.

φ_i	φ_i'
$\varphi_1\,\mathcal{U}_{[i,j]}\varphi_2$	$\varphi_1 \wedge \mathcal{G}_I\varphi_1 \wedge \mathcal{X}_1\left(\varphi_1\,\mathcal{U}_{[i-1,j-1]}\varphi_2\right)$
$\varphi_1\,\mathcal{U}_{[0,j]}\varphi_2$	$\varphi_2 \vee \left(\varphi_1 \wedge \mathcal{G}_I\varphi_1 \wedge \left(\mathcal{F}_I\varphi_2 \vee \mathcal{X}_1\left(\varphi_1\,\mathcal{U}_{[0,j-1]}\varphi_2\right)\right)\right)$
$\varphi_1\,\mathcal{R}_{[i,j]}\varphi_2$	$\varphi_1 \vee \mathcal{F}_I\varphi_1 \vee \mathcal{X}_1\left(\varphi_1\,\mathcal{R}_{[i-1,j-1]}\varphi_2\right)$
$\varphi_1\,\mathcal{R}_{[0,j]}\varphi_2$	$\varphi_2 \wedge \left(\varphi_1 \vee \left(\mathcal{G}_I\varphi_2 \wedge \left(\mathcal{F}_I\varphi_1 \vee \mathcal{X}_1\left(\varphi_1\,\mathcal{R}_{[0,j-1]}\varphi_2\right)\right)\right)\right)$
$\mathcal{G}_I(\varphi_1 \wedge \varphi_2)$	$\mathcal{G}_I\varphi_1 \wedge \mathcal{G}_I\varphi_2$
$\mathcal{G}_I(\varphi_1 \vee \varphi_2)$	$\mathcal{G}_I\varphi_1 \vee \mathcal{G}_I\varphi_2$
$\mathcal{F}_I(\varphi_1 \wedge \varphi_2)$	$(\mathcal{G}_I\varphi_1 \wedge \mathcal{F}_I\varphi_2) \vee (\mathcal{F}_I\varphi_1 \wedge \mathcal{G}_I\varphi_2)$
$\mathcal{F}_I(\varphi_1 \vee \varphi_2)$	$\mathcal{F}_I\varphi_1 \vee \mathcal{F}_I\varphi_2$
$\mathcal{F}_I(\varphi_1\,\mathcal{U}_{[i,j]}\varphi_2)$	$\mathcal{G}_I\varphi_1 \wedge \mathcal{X}_1\left(\varphi_1 \wedge \mathcal{G}_I\varphi_1 \wedge \mathcal{F}_I(\varphi_1\,\mathcal{U}_{[i-1,j-1]}\varphi_2)\right)$
$\mathcal{F}_I(\varphi_1\,\mathcal{U}_{[0,j]}\varphi_2)$	$\mathcal{F}_I\varphi_2 \vee \left(\mathcal{G}_I\varphi_1 \wedge \mathcal{X}_1\left(\varphi_2 \vee \left(\varphi_1 \wedge \mathcal{G}_I\varphi_1 \wedge \mathcal{F}_I(\varphi_1\,\mathcal{U}_{[0,j-1]}\varphi_2)\right)\right)\right)$
$\mathcal{G}_I(\varphi_1\,\mathcal{U}_{[i,j]}\varphi_2)$	$\mathcal{G}_I\varphi_1 \wedge \mathcal{X}_1\left(\varphi_1 \wedge \mathcal{G}_I\varphi_1 \wedge \mathcal{G}_I(\varphi_1\,\mathcal{U}_{[i-1,j-1]}\varphi_2)\right)$
$\mathcal{G}_I(\varphi_1\,\mathcal{U}_{[0,j]}\varphi_2)$	$\mathcal{G}_I\varphi_2 \vee \left(\mathcal{G}_I\varphi_1 \wedge \mathcal{X}_1\left(\varphi_2 \vee \left(\varphi_1 \wedge \mathcal{G}_I\varphi_1 \wedge \mathcal{G}_I(\varphi_1\,\mathcal{U}_{[0,j-1]}\varphi_2)\right)\right)\right)$
$\mathcal{F}_I(\varphi_1\,\mathcal{R}_{[i,j]}\varphi_2)$	$\mathcal{F}_I\varphi_1 \vee \mathcal{X}_1\left(\varphi_1 \vee \mathcal{F}_I\varphi_1 \vee \mathcal{F}_I(\varphi_1\,\mathcal{R}_{[i-1,j-1]}\varphi_2)\right)$
$\mathcal{F}_I(\varphi_1\,\mathcal{R}_{[0,j]}\varphi_2)$	$\mathcal{F}_I(\varphi_1 \wedge \varphi_2) \vee \left(\mathcal{G}_I\varphi_2 \wedge \mathcal{X}_1\left(\varphi_2 \wedge \left(\varphi_1 \vee \left(\mathcal{G}_I\varphi_2 \wedge \mathcal{F}_I\,\varphi_1\,\mathcal{R}_{[0,j-1]}\varphi_2\right)\right)\right)\right)$
$\mathcal{G}_I(\varphi_1\,\mathcal{R}_{[i,j]}\varphi_2)$	$\mathcal{G}_I\varphi_1 \vee \mathcal{X}_1\left(\varphi_1 \vee \mathcal{G}_I(\varphi_1\,\mathcal{R}_{[i-1,j-1]}\varphi_2)\right)$
$\mathcal{G}_I(\varphi_1\,\mathcal{R}_{[0,j]}\varphi_2)$	$\mathcal{G}_I(\varphi_2) \wedge \left(\mathcal{G}_I\varphi_1 \vee \mathcal{X}_1\left(\varphi_2 \wedge \left(\varphi_1 \vee \left(\mathcal{G}_I\varphi_2 \wedge \mathcal{G}_I(\varphi_1\,\mathcal{R}_{[0,j-1]}\varphi_2)\right)\right)\right)\right)$

Proof. Since we assume c-divisibility and negation normal form, each temporal operator of the subformula is a $\mathcal{U}$-operator or an $\mathcal{R}$-operator and one of the first 4 rewriting rules of Table 1 can be applied. After the first rewriting step, there are potentially formulas nested in $\mathcal{G}_I$ or $\mathcal{F}_I$. For every possible operator there is exactly one rewriting rule. With Lemma 3, it is sufficient to prove the soundness of the rewriting rules in Table 1. Let us consider $c = 1$ and the formula $\varphi_1\,\mathcal{U}_{[0,j]}\varphi_2$, which is true if φ_2 holds, $\exists t \in (0,1) : \mathcal{G}_{[0,t)}\varphi_1 \wedge \mathcal{X}_t\varphi_2$ holds, or $\mathcal{G}_{[0,1)}\varphi_1 \wedge \mathcal{X}_1(\varphi_1\,\mathcal{U}_{[0,j-1]}\varphi_2)$ holds. By overapproximating $\exists t \in (0,1) : \mathcal{G}_{[0,t)}\varphi_1 \wedge \mathcal{X}_t\varphi_2$ with $\mathcal{G}_{[0,1)}\varphi_1 \wedge \mathcal{F}_{(0,1)}\varphi_2$ we obtain the rewritten formula. The other formulas can be proven similarly. □

If needed, temporal formula such as $p\,\mathcal{U}_{[0,0.9]}q$ can als be rewritten to $p\,\mathcal{U}_{[0,1]}q$ in a sound manner, if $c = 1$ should be enforced. However, this is typically not needed since one can choose alternatives such as $c = 0.9$ or $c = 0.1$ which also depends on the reach sequence. As an example, the formula $\varphi := p\,\mathcal{U}_{[0,2]}q$ with atomic propositions p and q can be rewritten as follows:

$$\varphi \rightarrow \varphi_2 \vee \left(\varphi_1 \wedge \mathcal{G}_I\varphi_1 \wedge \left(\mathcal{F}_I\varphi_2 \vee \mathcal{X}_1\left(\varphi_1\,\mathcal{U}_{[0,1]}\varphi_2\right)\right)\right)$$
$$\rightarrow \varphi_2 \vee \left(\varphi_1 \wedge \mathcal{G}_I\varphi_1 \wedge \left(\mathcal{F}_I\varphi_2 \vee \mathcal{X}_1\left(\varphi_2 \vee \left(\varphi_1 \wedge \mathcal{G}_I\varphi_1 \wedge \left(\mathcal{F}_I\varphi_2 \vee \mathcal{X}_1\varphi_2\right)\right)\right)\right)\right).$$

Now that we have solved the problem of transforming an STL formula to an RTL formula defined on the reach sequence, we present a model checking algorithm in the next section.

5 STL Model Checking

Our model checking approach for STL formulas is presented in the following. The foundation of the approach follows from Lemmas 2 to 4 and is summarized in the following theorem.

Theorem 1. *Let φ be an STL formula, $\mathbf{R}$ be a reach sequence of a hybrid automaton S, and $\mathbf{R}$ and φ be c-divisible. The formula φ can be transformed to an RTL formula $\psi = \bigwedge_i \bigvee_j \mathcal{X}_{\frac{c}{2}}^j \bigvee_k \mathcal{A}\varrho_{ijk}$ with non-temporal properties ϱ_{ijk}, where*

$$\mathcal{C}(\mathbf{R}) \models_T \varphi \quad \Leftarrow \quad \mathbf{R} \models_R \bigwedge_i \bigvee_j \mathcal{X}_{\frac{c}{2}}^j \bigvee_k \mathcal{A}\varrho_{ijk}$$

holds and therefore, the transformation is sound. If φ is equivalent to a sampled time STL formula, the transformation is complete. Hence, $\mathbf{R} \models_R \psi$ implies $Traces(S) \models_T \varphi$, which proves φ for the hybrid automaton S.

It remains to show how $\bigwedge_i \bigvee_j \mathcal{X}_{\frac{c}{2}}^j \bigvee_k \mathcal{A}\varrho_{ijk}$ can be evaluated on a reach sequence $\mathbf{R}$. This can be reduced to the problem $\mathbf{R} \models_R \mathcal{X}_{\frac{c}{2}}^j \mathcal{A}\varrho_{ijk}$. The satisfaction result is obtained by evaluating all such subformulas and then computing the Boolean value of the remaining logical formula.

Our RTL syntax and semantics, as well as the transformation from STL to RTL, are independent of the representation of the reachable sets $\mathbf{R}(t)$ and the predicates used. However, to implement a model checking algorithm, we have to define a representation and a set of predicates we rely on. Therefore, we assume that the reachable sets are represented by (sets of) polytopes as in SpaceEx [12] and Cora [2]. Given a set of vectors $c_1, \ldots, c_k$ and values $d_1, \ldots, d_k$, a *polytope* is defined as the set $poly(c_1, \ldots, c_k, d_1, \ldots, d_k) = \bigcap_{i=1}^k \{x \in \mathbb{R}^n \mid c_i^T x \leq d_i\}$, which is the intersection of halfspaces. We consider the set AP of atomic predicates of the form $a^T x \sim b$, where $a \in \mathbb{R}^n$, $b \in \mathbb{R}$, and $\sim \in \{<, \leq, >, \geq\}$, which are also halfspace restrictions. For instance, the evaluation of $\mathcal{A}(x \leq 5)$ for a reach sequence is visualized in Fig. 5. Note that the formula is only satisfied if all states x satisfy $x \leq 5$.

Given a formula of the type $\mathcal{A}\varrho$, the logical part ϱ can be transformed into disjunctive normal form $\varrho = \bigvee_i \bigwedge_j (a_{ij}^T x \sim b_{ij})$ with $\sim \in \{<, \leq\}$. Because $\bigwedge_j (a_{ij}^T x \sim b_{ij})$ corresponds to the polytope region $poly_i = poly(a_{i1}, \ldots, b_{i1}, \ldots)$, the check $\mathbf{R} \models_R \mathcal{X}_t \mathcal{A}\varrho$ can be performed by the polytope inclusion check $\mathbf{R}(t) \subseteq \bigcup poly_i$, which can be implemented using standard polytope libraries.

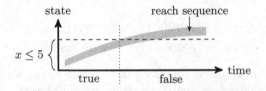

Fig. 5. Predicate evaluation for several points in time t: $\mathbf{R} \models_R \mathcal{X}_t \mathcal{A}(x \leq 5)$.

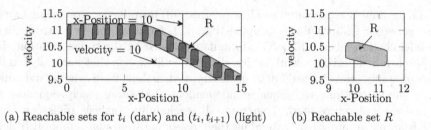

(a) Reachable sets for t_i (dark) and (t_i, t_{i+1}) (light)   (b) Reachable set R

Fig. 6. Automated driving example for a reach sequence.

6 Example

In the following, we provide an example for our model checking method from the domain of automated driving. For automated driving, it is important to verify safety properties such as the absence of collisions. While driving, this can be done by periodically checking that a collision is not possible for a bounded time of the planned trajectory using the reach sequence [3]. However, there are also other safety relevant *temporal* properties which should be verified. Based on the results in this paper, the verification of these properties can be easily integrated in the existing verification scheme.

For example, when a vehicle is traversing a crossing, it should not block the crossing and should maintain a certain velocity until it reaches the other side. This can be expressed on the traces as an STL property similar to $\varphi :=$ $v \geq 10 \, \mathcal{U}_{[0,2]} x \geq 10$, where v is the velocity and x is the distance covered. We use Cora [2] and the vehicle model of Althoff and Dolan [3] to compute the reachable sequence of the vehicle as visualized in Fig. 6. To verify φ with the reach sequence, we transform φ to a sampled time RTL formula. An exemplary transformation result for φ is

$$\mathcal{A}q \vee (\mathcal{A}(p \vee q) \wedge \mathcal{X}_{\frac{c}{2}} \mathcal{A}p \wedge (\mathcal{X}_{\frac{c}{2}} \mathcal{A}q \vee \mathcal{X}_{\frac{c}{2}}^2 \mathcal{A}q \vee (\mathcal{X}_{\frac{c}{2}}^2 \mathcal{A}(p \vee q) \wedge \mathcal{X}_{\frac{c}{2}}^3 \mathcal{A}p \wedge (\mathcal{X}_{\frac{c}{2}}^3 \mathcal{A}q \vee \mathcal{X}_{\frac{c}{2}}^4 \mathcal{A}q))))$$

for $c = 1$, $p = v \geq 10$, and $q = x \geq 10$. In this example, reachability analysis, which is the basis for verification of both safety and temporal properties, takes 3.8 s. Checking that the resulting reach sequence satisfies the RTL formula takes only 0.15 additional seconds. With Theorem 1 we can conclude that the STL formula φ holds for all possible evolutions of the system.

7 Conclusion

We introduce a model checking technique for STL formulas, which leverages reachable sets computed by reachability analysis tools. This is done by: (i) Defining the Reachset Temporal Logic (RTL), whose semantics is defined on reachable sets instead of traces, on which previous temporal logics are defined (e.g. STL); (ii) introducing a sound and complete transformation from sampled time STL to

RTL for finitely represented reach sequences; (iii) introducing a rewriting scheme for general STL formula to sampled time STL formula; and (iv) introducing a model checking method for RTL formulas obtained by the transformation. The approach is especially useful for non-deterministic models that naturally exhibit uncountably many traces due to necessary abstractions from original dynamics. Our model checking technique is independent of the way reach sequences are obtained and represented. Therefore, all reachability analysis tools can benefit from our approach by extending their reasoning from non-temporal (safety) properties to temporal properties. This is demonstrated by an example from automated driving, where the online verification of the absence of collisions is extended to online verification of temporal properties.

Future work could intensify the interconnection of the reachability analysis and the verification part to develop the method further. Additionally, the semantics of RTL can be extended in the sense of robust semantics as used by Metric Temporal Logic [11].

Acknowledgment. The authors gratefully acknowledge financial support by the European Commission project UnCoVerCPS under grant number 643921.

References

1. Ahmadyan, S.N., Kumar, J.A., Vasudevan, S.: Runtime verification of nonlinear analog circuits using incremental time-augmented RRT algorithm. In: Proceedings of Design, Test & Automation in Europe (2013)
2. Althoff, M.: An introduction to CORA . In: Proceedings of the Workshop on Applied Verification for Continuous and Hybrid Systems, pp. 120–151 (2015)
3. Althoff, M., Dolan, J.M.: Reachability computation of low-order models for the safety verification of high-order road vehicle models. In: American Control Conference, pp. 3559–3566. IEEE (2012)
4. Alur, R., Courcoubetis, C., Dill, D.L.: Model-checking for real-time systems. In: Proceedings of 5th Symposium on Logic in Computer Science, pp. 414–425 (1990)
5. Alur, R., Feder, T., Henzinger, T.A.: The benefits of relaxing punctuality. J. ACM **43**(1), 116–146 (1996)
6. Asarin, E., et al.: Recent progress in continuous and hybrid reachability analysis. In: Conference on Computer Aided Control Systems Design, pp. 1582–1587 (2006)
7. Baier, C., Katoen, J.-P.: Principles of Model Checking. MIT Press, Cambridge (2008)
8. Bresolin, D.: HyLTL: a temporal logic for model checking hybrid systems. In: Proceedings Third International Workshop on Hybrid Autonomous Systems, pp. 73–84. HAS (2013)
9. Clarke, E.M., Grumberg, O., Peled, D.A.: Model Checking. MIT Press, Cambridge (2000)
10. Duggirala, P.S., Mitra, S., Viswanathan, M., Potok, M.: C2E2: a verification tool for stateflow models. In: Baier, C., Tinelli, C. (eds.) TACAS 2015. LNCS, vol. 9035, pp. 68–82. Springer, Heidelberg (2015)
11. Fainekos, G.E., Pappas, G.J.: Robustness of temporal logic specifications for continuous-time signals. Theor. Comput. Sci. **410**(42), 4262–4291 (2009)

12. Frehse, G., et al.: SpaceEx: scalable verification of hybrid systems. In: Computer Aided Verification, pp. 379–395 (2011)
13. Guéguen, H., Lefebvre, M., Zaytoon, J., Nasri, O.: Safety verification and reachability analysis for hybrid systems. Ann. Rev. Control **33**(1), 25–36 (2009)
14. Lee, E.A.: CPS foundations. In: Design Automation Conference, pp. 737–742 (2010)
15. Lee, I., Kannan, S., Kim, M., Sokolsky, O., Viswanathan, M.: Runtime assurance based on formal specifications. In: Proceedings of the International Conference on Parallel and Distributed Processing Techniques and Applications (1999)
16. Maler, O., Nickovic, D., Pnueli, A.: Checking temporal properties of discrete, timed and continuous behaviors. In: Avron, A., Dershowitz, N., Rabinovich, A. (eds.) Pillars of Computer Science. LNCS, vol. 4800, pp. 475–505. Springer, Heidelberg (2008)
17. Maler, O., Ničković, D.: Monitoring properties of analog and mixed-signal circuits. J. Softw. Tools Technol. Transfer **15**, 247–268 (2013)
18. Mitra, S., Wongpiromsarn, T., Murray, R.M.: Verifying cyber-physical interactions in safety-critical systems. IEEE Secur. Priv. **11**(4), 28–37 (2013)
19. Pinto, A., Sangiovanni-Vincentelli, A.L., Carloni, L.P., Passerone, R.: Interchange formats for hybrid systems: review and proposal. In: Morari, M., Thiele, L. (eds.) HSCC 2005. LNCS, vol. 3414, pp. 526–541. Springer, Heidelberg (2005)
20. Platzer, A., Clarke, E.M.: The image computation problem in hybrid systems model checking. In: Bemporad, A., Bicchi, A., Buttazzo, G. (eds.) HSCC 2007. LNCS, vol. 4416, pp. 473–486. Springer, Heidelberg (2007)
21. Poovendran, R.: Cyberphysical systems: close encounters between two parallel worlds. Proc. IEEE **98**(8), 1363–1366 (2010)
22. Rajkumar, R., Lee, I., Sha, L., Stankovic, J.: Cyber-physical systems: the next computing revolution. In: Design Automation Conference, pp. 731–736 (2010)
23. Sanwal, M.U., Hasan, O.: Formal verification of cyber-physical systems: coping with continuous elements. In: Proceedings of the 16th International Conference on Computational Science and its Applications, pp. 358–371 (2013)
24. Sauter, G., Dierks, H., Fränzle, M., Hansen, M.R.: Lightweight hybrid model checking facilitating online prediction of temporal properties. In: Proceedings of the 21st Nordic Workshop on Programming Theory, NWPT09, pp. 20–22 (2009)
25. Smirnov, G.V.: Introduction to the Theory of Differential Inclusions. American Mathematical Society, Providence (2002)
26. Tan, L., Kim, J., Sokolsky, O., Lee, I.: Model-based testing and monitoring for hybrid embedded systems. In: Model-Based Testing and Monitoring for Hybrid Embedded Systems, pp. 487–492 (2004)
27. Wang, Z., Zaki, M.H., Tahar, S.: Statistical runtime verification of analog and mixed signal designs. In: Conference on Signals, Circuits and Systems (2009)

Clause Sharing and Partitioning
for Cloud-Based SMT Solving

Matteo Marescotti[(✉)], Antti E.J. Hyvärinen, and Natasha Sharygina

Università della Svizzera italiana, Lugano, Switzerland
matteo.marescotti@usi.ch

Abstract. Satisfiability modulo theories (SMT) allows the modeling and solving of constraint problems arising from practical domains by combining well-engineered and powerful solvers for propositional satisfiability with expressive, domain-specific background theories in a natural way. The increasing popularity of SMT as a modelling approach means that the SMT solvers need to handle increasingly complex problem instances. This paper studies how SMT solvers can use cloud computing to scale to challenging problems through sharing of learned information in the form of clauses with approaches based on both divide-and-conquer and algorithm portfolios. Our initial experiments, executed on the OpenSMT2 solver, show that parallelization with clause sharing speeds up the solving of instances, on average, by a factor of four or five depending on the problem domain.

1 Introduction

The *Satisfiability Modulo Theories* (SMT) [5] approach to constraint solving consists of determining whether a logical formula is satisfiable, given that some of the Boolean variables have an interpretation in *background theories*. The expressiveness of SMT makes it suitable for a vast range of application domains, including software and hardware model checking [4,9], bioinformatics [26], and optimization [24], and has recently attained significant interest from a wide range of users. The computational cost of solving SMT instances can be very high, given that already propositional satisfiability is an NP-complete problem and the introduction of background theories can only make the problem harder. The SMT solvers tackle complexity with a tightly integrated loop where the SAT solver attempts to find a satisfying solution and queries the validity of a candidate solution from the theory solvers. In case the candidate solution is shown to be invalid the theory solvers and the SAT solver work together to extract new expressive constraints in the form of learned clauses, by combining theory specific information and resolution.

This work studies how employing parallelism and in particular cloud computing can be used in helping SMT solvers to scale to increasingly hard problems. We study two different approaches: a portfolio where several copies of a randomized SMT solver is run on a single instance; and an approach where the

SMT instance is divided into several partitions that are guaranteed by construction not to share models, and each partition is solved by an SMT solver. We combine these two approaches in a natural way by having several SMT solvers work on each partition. The emphasis of the work is in how the different ways of organizing the search can co-operate to speed up the solving. We implement the co-operation by having SMT solvers working on the same partition share the clauses they learn during the execution.

To study the effects of parallelism and clause sharing we implement the approach using the SMT solver OpenSMT2 [13] and experiment with two particularly central background theories, the quantifier-free theories of uninterpreted functions and equalities [5] (QF_UF) and linear real arithmetics [7] (QF_LRA). The experimental results suggest that both the portfolio and the partitioning based approach can greatly benefit from clause sharing. Interestingly, a comparison between portfolio and partitioning reveals that the portfolio approach performs better even if the partitioning is combined with portfolio. We give an analysis in the form of a case study to understand the reason for this and confirm the effect in a more controlled experiment. Finally we discuss to what extent the results obtained with OpenSMT2 can be generalized to other SMT solvers. In particular clause sharing with partitioning is tedious to implement in a solver and therefore we make the comparison in an indirect way, studying the run-time distribution of the Yices2 solver [6] in comparison to OpenSMT2.

Related Work. The portfolio approach combined with clause sharing has been implemented using the SMT solver Z3 [25]. The implementation provides an efficient clause sharing strategy within the same computer using lockless queues that hold references to the lemmas that a solver core wants to export. The experimental evaluations show that clause sharing leads to a substantial speedup on benchmarks from the QF_IDL logic. In contrast to this work, we support two SMT theories (QF_UF and QF_LRA), and exploit the advantages of combining portfolio with search-space partitioning. Moreover our implementation is designed to run in a cluster or a cloud in addition to a single machine. Similarly to Z3, the SMT solver CVC4 [3] supports a portfolio-style parallel solving. Unlike our approach, the approach used in CVC4 is designed to run in a single computer and does not implement clause sharing.

In [14] we introduced the parallelization tree formalism for combining portfolio and search-space partitioning. The work also describes and reports results on the QF_UF logic on some instantiation of the framework. Our work extends this tool based on the OpenSMT2 SMT solver by introducing clause sharing and the logic QF_LRA.

A divide-and-conquer approach for the quantifier-free bit-vector logic has been implemented on top of the SMT solver Boolector [23]. A portfolio parallelization approach for the logic of quantifier-free bit-vectors and bit-vector arrays is presented in [21]. Compared to these, our work differs in the supported theories and in that we support cloud computing and are not limited to pure divide-and-conquer or portfolio approach.

In this work we use techniques similar to those used in parallel SAT solving. The more elaborate problem descriptions of SMT constitute a significant theoretical and engineering challenge for parallelization. In addition the use of SMT allows extending these techniques to a different domain. While the results are to some extent preliminary it seems already that there are substantial differences in how the techniques perform in the two domains. Given the close relation of the topics there is a significant amount of relevant research on parallel SAT solving, overviewed for instance in [17]. In particular we point out the portfolio approach combined with clause sharing implemented in ManySAT [8] and HordeSAT [2]. A promising future direction for SMT is the combination of search-space partitioning and clause sharing [1].

Recently there has been a renewed interest in parallel model checking. In [22], the authors give a method for parallel concolic execution, while [10] introduces a method for using massive parallelism to obtain a high coverage in an explicit-state model-checking approach in a stochastic way. These differ from our work in that they do not provide solutions directly for SMT solving.

In this paper we first introduce the basic concepts required for interpreting our results in Sect. 2, and then describe implementation details in Sect. 3. The experimental results obtained with the implementation are presented in Sect. 4, and conclusions are drawn in Sect. 5.

2   Background

This section gives an overview of how SMT solvers work concentrating on the mechanisms that are relevant for interpreting the framework, implementation, and experimental results we present in the following sections. In describing the preliminaries we use the set notation.

A literal is a Boolean variable x or its negation $\neg x$. A clause is a set of literals and a propositional formula in conjunctive normal form (CNF) is a set of clauses. Throughout the text we use both a set of literals and disjunction, and a set of clauses and a conjunction, interchangeably. An assignment σ is a set of literals such that for no variable x, both $x \in \sigma$ and $\neg x \in \sigma$. A variable x is *assigned* if either $x \in \sigma$ or $\neg x \in \sigma$. An assignment σ satisfies a clause c if $\sigma \cap c \neq \emptyset$ and a formula F if it satisfies all its clauses.

Most SMT solvers are based on the DPLL(T) framework [20] which takes as input a problem instance presented as a propositional formula where some of the Boolean variables have an interpretation as Boolean relations, such as equalities, disequalities, and inequalities, in a theory T. A DPLL(T) solver consists of a solver for the propositional satisfiability problem (SAT) and one or more theory solvers that are capable of reasoning on a conjunction of Boolean relations over the theory T. In the pre-processing phase the input formula is converted into an equisatisfiable propositional formula F in CNF while preserving the special T-interpretations of the Boolean variables.

The SMT solving process is driven by a SAT solver maintaining a set of clauses which initially consists of the formula F. During the search the SAT solver builds an assignment σ and alternates between two phases.

- In the *propagation* phase the solver identifies clauses $c = l_1 \vee \ldots \vee l_n$ such that (i) there is a single unassigned literal $l_i \in c$, and (ii) σ falsifies the literals $l_j, 1 \leq j \leq n, j \neq i$. Any such literal l_i is added to σ until no new clauses satisfying (i) and (ii) can be found.
- In the *decision* phase the solver chooses a literal l_i unassigned in σ and adds it to σ.

A *conflict* occurs if during the propagation phase the SAT solver detects a clause with all literals falsified. The decisions and propagations are stored in the *implication graph* [16], a directed graph having as nodes the literals of the assignment σ and as edges the arches $\{(\neg l_j, l_i) \mid 1 \leq j \leq n, j \neq i\}$ obtained in the propagation phase.[1]

A SAT solver *learns* a clause c by performing essentially resolution steps directed by the implication graph when it finds a conflict. The learned clauses are by construction guaranteed to be logical consequences of F, and are both used in guiding the search and added temporarily to the clause database to reduce the number of assignments the solver needs to cover during the search. Finally the solver makes with a decreasing frequency a *restart* where the assignment σ is cleared and the search is continued without otherwise changing the state of the solver.

The SAT solver queries periodically whether the conjunction of the theory atoms in σ is consistent with the theory. In case a theory solver determines an inconsistency it identifies a subset $\sigma' \subseteq \sigma$ that causes the inconsistency and returns the clause $c_T := \{\neg l \mid l \in \sigma'\}$ to the SAT solver. Minimizing σ' is critical for the good performance of the SMT solvers (see, e.g., [7,19]). The clause c_T is used together with the implication graph to learn a clause c in the way described above for clause learning. The solving process terminates when either the clause database becomes unsatisfiable or a satisfying assignment consistent with the theory T is found.

Parallel Algorithm Portfolios. An algorithm portfolio [11] is a set of algorithms that compete in finding a solution for a given problem. The decision phase employs an heuristic for choosing l_i and introduces in a natural way nondeterminism into the solver. Small changes to the heuristic can cause big changes in the run time of the solver. For example, Fig. 5 shows the effect of allowing the SAT solver to make random choices against the heuristic in small number of cases to a single instance. The lines labeled OpenSMT2 and Yices2 illustrate the probability of solving an instance from the QF_LRA category of the SMT-LIB benchmark collection in a given time or number of decisions for the SMT solvers OpenSMT2 and Yices2 [6], respectively. A natural algorithm portfolio can be obtained by seeding differently the pseudo-random-number generator of the SMT solver and running several solvers in parallel.

Clause Sharing. In clause sharing the clauses learned by an SMT solver while solving a formula F are distributed among the solvers in the parallel portfolio.

---

[1] We equate x and $\neg\neg x$.

Since clause learning plays an important part of the SMT solving process this sharing can speed up the parallel solving process. For example the shared clauses make it easier to produce the required clauses in case of unsatisfiability, and reduce the number of assignments the solver covers before finding a satisfying assignment.

Search Space Partitioning. The SMT solver bases its search on the SAT solver, and therefore a natural way of dividing the work and avoiding overlap for the solvers is to constrain the SMT formula F into partitions $F_1, \ldots, F_n$ such that the original formula is satisfiable if and only if one of $F_1, \ldots, F_n$ is satisfiable. This can be done through adding additional constraints C_i to the formula F, resulting in the partition $F_i := F \wedge C_i$. In principle conjoining a single literal $\{l\}$ to the formula F halves the search space, but this happens rarely in practice. Often the resulting partitions F_i will have overlap in their search due to the heuristics of the solver and therefore the observed speedup will be less dramatic. The situation is made worse by the unpredictability of the SMT solver run time in case the instance is unsatisfiable. Assuming the shape of the run-time distribution is the same for both the instance F and the partition F_i, it can be shown that independent of the number of partitions there are distributions for which the expected run time increases when partitioning is done as described above [15]. To lessen this effect several more complex parallelization algorithms combining elements from search-space partitioning and algorithm portfolios have been suggested [14]. For example running a parallel portfolio for each partition makes it less likely that one of the partitions will require excessive time for being solved.

Constructing Partitions. We use in this work an approach for constructing partitions called *scattering*, initially introduced in [12]. Given a formula F, a number of partitions to be created n, and a sequence of positive $d_1, \ldots, d_{n-1}$ the partitions are obtained following the iteration

$$
\begin{aligned}
F_1 &:= F \wedge l_1^1 \wedge \ldots \wedge l_{d_1}^1 \\
F_k &:= F \wedge (\neg l_1^1 \vee \ldots \vee \neg l_{d_1}^1) \wedge \ldots \wedge (\neg l_1^{k-1} \vee \ldots \vee \neg l_{d_{k-1}}^{k-1}) \wedge l_1^k \wedge \ldots \wedge l_{d_k}^k \\
F_n &:= F \wedge (\neg l_1^1 \vee \ldots \vee \neg l_{d_1}^1) \wedge \ldots \wedge (\neg l_1^{n-1} \vee \ldots \vee \neg l_{d_{n-1}}^{n-1})
\end{aligned}
$$

The goal of using the sequence d_i is to make the search space of each F_i as close as possible to $1/n$ of the search space of the instance F. We obtain the sequence d_i by assuming that conjoining a disjunction of k literals with a formula F reduces the size of the search space by factor of $(1 - 1/2^k)$. For example for $n = 2$ partitions this gives $d_1 = 1$, while for $n = 8$ we get the sequence $d_1 = 3, d_2 = 3, d_3 = 3, d_4 = 3, d_5 = 2, d_6 = 2$, and $d_7 = 1$. Note that the number of constructed partitions in this method does not have to be a power of 2. Finally, the literals l_i^j are chosen using the same heuristic the SMT solver uses during the search.

3   The Parallelization Framework

In this section we present the framework uses in the experiments of the paper for studying the effect of parallelization approaches and clause sharing. We give an overview of the framework in Fig. 1. The framework is designed to run on a cluster of computers or a cloud, even though it is also possible to run the system on a single computer. The design follows a client-server approach in which the server, acting as a front-end to the user, receives input instances in the SMTLIB2 format[2], and at the same time handles the connection with the clients, managing client failures and asynchronous new client connections gracefully. The clients are implemented as SMT solvers wrapped by a network layer that handles the connection with the server.

The server works in two modes: depending on the configuration it either splits the instance into several partitions using the scattering approach described in Sect. 2, or runs in a pure portfolio mode without splitting. In the beginning of the solving the server distributes either the partitions or the original formula to the solvers in all the available clients.

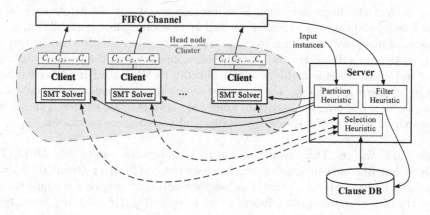

Fig. 1. Parallel SMT solver framework with clause sharing

During the solving phase, each client contacts the server both to publish newly learned clauses and to request new interesting clauses published by the clients. To avoid problems with the high throughput we use a *FIFO Channel* that allows multiple clients to push clauses to the server without turnaround delays. Once a batch of clauses is received, the server uses the *filter heuristic* to choose potential clauses for merging them with the previously received clauses into the clause database (*Clause DB* in Fig. 1). Hence, at any given time, that database will contain all the learned clauses sent by the clients and that have passed the filter heuristic of the server. Inside the clause database the clauses

---

[2] http://smtlib.cs.uiowa.edu.

are divided by partitions and each client has only access to the clauses published by the solvers working on the same partition.

Upon a restart each client will ask for clauses from the server. However, the request cannot be replied by sending the entire clause set of the partition that is being solved, because it usually consists of prohibitively many clauses. A high number of clauses slows down the client solver since the overhead related to the growth of the internal data structure is higher than the speedup obtained from the clauses. To address the problem, the framework allows the use of the *selection heuristic* which attempts to choose clauses that are particularly promising for the problem at hand. The current version implements naïve heuristics for both filtering and selection. The filtering heuristic is based on the number of literals inside each clause: clauses with more than a fixed number of literals will be discarded. The selection heuristic works by randomly selecting a fixed number of clauses from the database, and each new set will replace the old one inside the solver.

3.1 Implementation

The goal of the implementation is to provide scalability, fault-tolerance, and low latencies during data transfer, as well as ease of use and portability from a cluster of machines to a single machine with many cores or CPUs. In the rest of this section we will present the central choices made during the implementation. The implementation is highly modular in order to allow studying the effects of its components in isolation. For example the system can handle several different policies for scheduling the partitions among the solvers in the cluster. This allows research on how to best combine portfolio and search-space partitioning.

The SMT Solver. The abstract framework allows the use of any DPLL(T) solver, but our current implementation uses the SMT solver OpenSMT2 [13]. OpenSMT2 is a light-weight SMT solver that currently supports the quantifier-free theories of uninterpreted functions with equalities (QF_UF) and linear real arithmetics (QF_LRA). The solver is written in C++ and has been developed in Università della Svizzera italiana since 2008. The code is easily approachable because of its limited size of roughly 50,000 lines of code and the object-oriented architecture. In addition it is released under the MIT license[3]. Most recently the solver competed in the SMT competitions in 2014 and 2015, performing in the mid-range in the competition. The implementation is efficient featuring low-level memory management and a cache-friendly design for many of the central algorithms. These reasons make it our choice over other, maybe more optimised tools.

Networking. The server and the clients communicate using our custom-built message passing protocol through TCP/IP sockets, making the solution light-weight, easy to implement and modify as well as portable by being compatible

---

[3] http://opensource.org/licenses/MIT.

with clusters, cloud computing and single computers. The network components of the implementation are shown in Fig. 1. Almost all the connections consist of *push* message passing which achieves the goal to be as fast as possible by avoiding the turnaround time. The connection between solvers and the selection heuristic is the only one that does not use the push mechanism, but instead needs a pull request. This choice has been made since the schedule at which the clients can receive clauses is unpredictable, making push impractical. To indicate the pull request, the interaction is drawn with dashed lines.

A Binary Format for SMT. In order to use clause sharing we must ensure that the internal clausal representation of each instance is the same in every client solver. This property cannot be guaranteed by the SMTLIB2 language since small changes in the input formula might result in subtle optimizations that will dramatically change the CNF structure seen by the SAT solver embedded in the SMT solver. For that reason we designed a binary format for SMT, representing the internal state of OpenSMT2. This format is used for data transfers between each client and the server but also results in us being forced to limit ourselves to a specific SMT solver.

FIFO Channel and Clause DB. For these challenges we use REDIS[4], an open source in-memory data structure store, used as database, cache, and message broker. In order to get a scalable, fast, and fault-tolerant push connection from multiple sources we use the *Publisher/Subscriber messaging paradigm* of REDIS. The clauses are stored using the REDIS *SET* feature that automatically handles cases where a clause would be added to clause database that is syntactically equal to an already present clause. The SET feature is used by both the filter and the selection heuristics.

4   Experiments

This section describes the experiments we performed on the implementation described in the paper. The implementation is available at http://verify.inf.usi.ch/opensmt. The experiments concentrate on four topics: Sect. 4.1 demonstrates how the clause sharing works on the (i) pure portfolio and (ii) the approach where we split the instance into partitions and use a portfolio for solving each partition; Sect. 4.2 studies the difference between the approaches (i) and (ii) above; Sect. 4.3 reports how the filtering heuristic affects the performance of the algorithm; and Sect. 4.4 compares the cloud-based implementation against a sequential version of OpenSMT2 and a widely used reference solver Z3 [18].

Our hardware configuration is kept the same in all experiments we run. The experiments were run in a cluster where we used eight compute nodes for the clients and the head node for the server. Each compute node is equipped with two CPU Quad-Core AMD Opteron 2384 and 16GB of RAM. During the experiments each cluster node had eight client processes implementing the SMT solver

---

[4] http://redis.io.

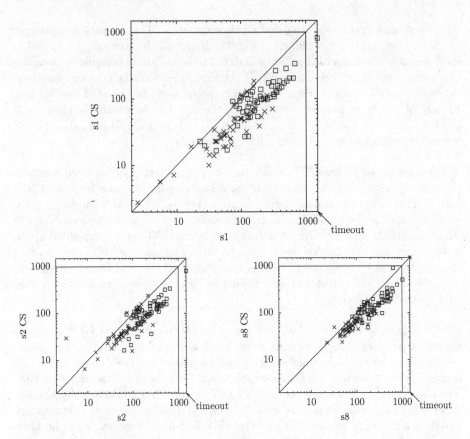

Fig. 2. Using clause sharing against not using clause sharing with 1, 2, and 8 partitions. Framework run with 64 solvers on the QF_LRA benchmark set

OpenSMT2, resulting in total of 64 solvers in the entire cluster. We did not explicitly limit the memory available to the solvers. The timeout is fixed everywhere to 1000 s. The search-space partitioning heuristic, when used, is the scattering approach [12].

We used a fixed benchmark set obtained from the SMTLIB2 benchmarks repository[5] and the QF_LRA and QF_UF theories. The set from the QF_LRA theory was created by selecting the instances with an average sequential execution time between 100 and 1000 s (including those in timeout) using OpenSMT2; the set consists of 106 instances in total. The benchmark set for the QF_UF theory consists of 254 instances. This set includes all instances that could be solved with the sequential OpenSMT2 between 100 and 1000 s; 11 instances which are known to be difficult for OpenSMT2 and time out in 1000 s; and 200 randomly chosen instances of which half are guaranteed to be satisfiable and the other half unsatisfiable.

---

[5] http://smtlib.cs.uiowa.edu/benchmarks.shtml.

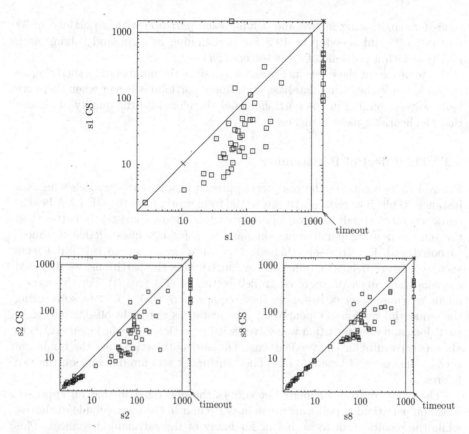

Fig. 3. Using clause sharing against not using clause sharing with 1, 2, and 8 partitions. Framework run with 64 solver on the QF_UF benchmark set

In the figures we use the labels *S1*, *S2* and *S8* to indicate the number of partitions created from the input instance. Therefore the label *S1* indicates the pure portfolio approach. The label *CS* indicates that clause sharing is used. Throughout the plots we denote satisfiable instances with the symbol × and unsatisfiable instances with the symbol □.

4.1 The Effect of Clause Sharing

Our first experiments show how sharing clauses affects the solving time using different partitioning methods for QF_LRA (Fig. 2) and QF_UF (Fig. 3). For both figures the graph on the top shows how the parallelization algorithm based on pure portfolio benefits most from clause sharing: with both theories it gives a 2.05 times speedup, as well as one more QF_LRA instance and nine more QF_UF instances solved within the timeout compared to not using clause sharing.

With both theories the combination of portfolio and search-space partitioning performs worse than pure portfolio: the speedup due to clause sharing is 1.97

times for partitioning in two and solving each partition with a portfolio of 32 solvers (*S2*), and speedup of 1.67 for partitioning in eight and solving each partition with a portfolio of eight solvers (*S8*).

To some extent these results are expected, since the number of learned clauses available inside the clause database for a single portfolio is bigger when there are more solvers running in the portfolios, and therefore also the quality of clauses that the heuristic picks is higher.

4.2   The Effect of Partitioning

Figure 4 (*left*) compares the portfolio approach against the approach where an instance is split into eight partitions in the framework, from the QF_LRA benchmark set. Interestingly the portfolio approach is almost consistently better than the approach using partitioning, in particular for the unsatisfiable instances (denoted with □). To study this effect in more detail and to rule out effects such as network delays or time used in constructing the partitions, we designed a second experiment in more controlled setting (Fig. 4 (*right*)). For this experiment we chose a set of instances that require more than 1000 s to solve using the sequential version of OpenSMT2. The instances were split off-line into eight partitions and each partition was solved with a portfolio of eight OpenSMT2s to obtain the results for the vertical axis. The horizontal axis shows the minimum solving time over 64 OpenSMT2s. The benchmark sets are different on the two figures.

The more controlled experiment verifies the phenomenon that an approach based on partitioning performs worse in particular in the unsatisfiable instances, while the results seem to be better for many of the satisfiable instances. This behavior is often observed when the shape of the distribution of an unsatisfiable instance has most of the probability mass at relatively low run times but still a significant mass at significantly higher run time [15]. In such cases the effect

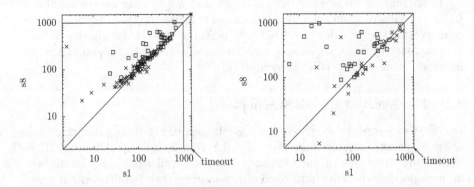

Fig. 4. Comparing *S1* against *S8* on the QF_LRA benchmark set. The graph on the left shows the results using the framework of Sect. 3, the graph on the right shows a controlled experiment where network delays are removed.

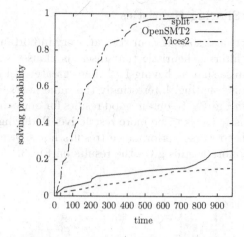

Fig. 5. Run time distribution for solving an example instance with a single solver compared to the distribution of one of the splits. For reference the figure also shows the decision distribution for the Yices2 SMT solver on the original problem (the scale is not shown).

of partitioning that tends to make instances easier to solve is not enough to compensate the benefit from a pure portfolio approach. To further study this phenomenon we chose one of the instances where this effect was particularly pronounced, and constructed the run time distribution for OpenSMT2 for this instance and a partition that was empirically difficult. The results for this experiment are reported in Fig. 5. First, the run time distribution shows that there is only a 25 % probability that OpenSMT2 solves this instance within the timeout of 1000 s, even though the fastest run time for this instance is only slightly above 10 s. This explains the good behavior of the portfolio approach. Second, based on the experiment it is possible that the partition run time is in fact higher than that of the original instance run time. The difference is not big and therefore this could be an effect caused by low amount of samples (64 in total). Finally, to understand to what extent this phenomenon is generalizable to other SMT solvers we ran the original instance 64 times using a randomized version of the SMT solver Yices2. Instead of reporting the run-time distribution, we show the number of decisions Yices2 did on this problem, since the run times were too low to get meaningful results. We can see that also for Yices2 the amount of decisions needed varies greatly but the shape of the distribution seems to be different. The observation that the run time with another SMT solver is much faster suggests that this instance can be solved by using an optimization that is not implemented on OpenSMT2 and that in such cases it is not safe to draw the conclusion that the partitioning approach would not work well if this optimization were implemented in the underlying solver.

4.3   The Clause Sharing Heuristics

Figure 6 shows that clause sharing heuristics are very important: the experiment performed using a filtering heuristic that discards clauses with more that 30 literals results in clause sharing having 1.12 times greater run time compared to the run without clause sharing. Interestingly the same heuristic is working well for QF_LRA (used in Fig. 2). To obtain good results for our benchmark instances in QF_UF the heuristic needs to be more restrictive. Reducing the threshold to 10 literals still leads to worse performance (results not shown), and discarding clauses with five or more literals gives the results on Fig. 3.

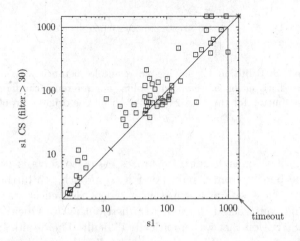

Fig. 6. Using clause sharing with a loose filtering heuristic against not using clause sharing. Framework run with 64 solvers on the QF_UF benchmark set.

4.4   Comparison to Other Solvers

Figure 7 compares the best known configuration of the framework against the solvers OpenSMT2 and Z3 for QF_LRA (*top*) and for QF_UF (*bottom*). The results are very promising when compared to OpenSMT2. For instances with sequential run time higher than one second and for which neither the sequential or the parallel solver timed out the average case speed-up is 4.78 for QF_LRA and 4.01 for QF_UF. Our implementation is not yet competitive against Z3 in the majority of instances. This is due to the lack of optimizations in the underlying solver. Based on the experimental evidence presented in this section it seems reasonable that if either the optimizations available in Z3 were implemented in OpenSMT2 or the approach presented in this work were implemented in Z3 the results would be similarly promising in comparison to Z3.

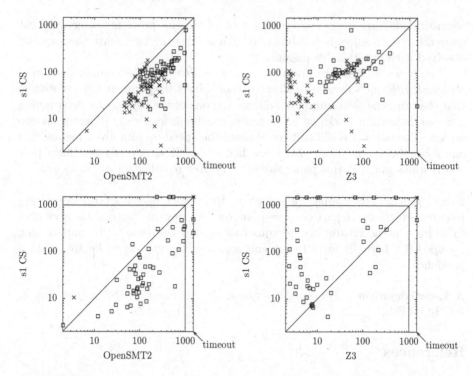

Fig. 7. Our best configuration against OpenSMT2 and Z3 for QF_LRA (*top*) and QF_UF(*bottom*)

5 Conclusions

SMT solving in cloud environments so far has received relatively little attention from the community developing and researching SMT solvers. This paper addresses the challenges related to integrating one of the key components of a modern SMT solver, the sharing of learned clauses, to parallel SMT solving algorithms. We provide a generic framework for clause sharing in a cloud computing environment and implement a system that supports clause sharing with parallelization algorithms based on both a portfolio and splitting the input formula into partitions.

The framework and the parallelization algorithms are agnostic to the underlying theories used by the SMT solver. We provide results on two fundamental theories: the quantifier-free theories of uninterpreted functions and equality (QF_UF), and linear real arithmetics (QF_LRA). The results show that both theories can benefit significantly from clause sharing, but especially QF_UF is sensitive to the heuristic used for selecting clauses to be shared. In the experiments we also observe that the partitioning approach, while working relatively well for QF_UF, performs somewhat worse for QF_LRA in the benchmark set we study on this paper. We conjecture that this results from the partitioning heuristic behaving in an unexpected way where the problems sometimes get more difficult to solve, in combination with a run-time increasing phenomenon observed with unsatisfiable instances.

Finally we address the question of how well the parallel computing results obtained with one solver generalize to other solvers. Experimentally we observe that the run-time distribution of an instance, one of the key factors determining how parallelization works on an instance, can be dramatically different on two solvers. Therefore it is difficult to estimate the speed-up of a given instance on one solver based on results from another solver. It is nevertheless likely that observations made in this paper would carry over to other solvers in general.

Future Work. The framework we set in this paper opens several interesting research directions. In particular we point out two central open questions we plan to address in the future: how to construct a good heuristic for (i) partitioning for QF_LRA and (ii) for filtering and selecting the clauses to be shared in a portfolio.

Acknowledgements. This work was financially supported by SNF project number 200021_153402.

References

1. Audemard, G., Hoessen, B., Jabbour, S., Piette, C.: Dolius: A distributed parallel SAT solving framework. In: Berre, D.L. (ed.) POS-14. EPiC Series, vol. 27, pp. 1–11. EasyChair (2014)
2. Balyo, T., Sanders, P., Sinz, C.: HordeSat: a massively parallel portfolio SAT solver. In: Heule, M., et al. (eds.) SAT 2015. LNCS, vol. 9340, pp. 156–172. Springer, Heidelberg (2015). doi:10.1007/978-3-319-24318-4_12
3. Barrett, C., Conway, C.L., Deters, M., Hadarean, L., Jovanović, D., King, T., Reynolds, A., Tinelli, C.: CVC4. In: Gopalakrishnan, G., Qadeer, S. (eds.) CAV 2011. LNCS, vol. 6806, pp. 171–177. Springer, Heidelberg (2011)
4. Biere, A., Cimatti, A., Clarke, E., Zhu, Y.: Symbolic model checking without BDDs. In: Cleaveland, W.R. (ed.) TACAS 1999. LNCS, vol. 1579, pp. 193–207. Springer, Heidelberg (1999)
5. Detlefs, D., Nelson, G., Saxe, J.B.: Simplify: a theorem prover for program checking. J. ACM **52**(3), 365–473 (2005)
6. Dutertre, B.: Yices 2.2. In: Biere, A., Bloem, R. (eds.) CAV 2014. LNCS, vol. 8559, pp. 737–744. Springer, Heidelberg (2014)
7. Dutertre, B., de Moura, L.: A fast linear-arithmetic solver for DPLL(T). In: Ball, T., Jones, R.B. (eds.) CAV 2006. LNCS, vol. 4144, pp. 81–94. Springer, Heidelberg (2006)
8. Hamadi, Y., Jabbour, S., Sais, L.: ManySAT: a parallel SAT solver. J. Satisfiability Boolean Model. Comput. **6**(4), 245–262 (2009)
9. Henzinger, T.A., Jhala, R., Majumdar, R., Sutre, G.: Software verification with BLAST. In: Ball, T., Rajamani, S.K. (eds.) SPIN 2003. LNCS, vol. 2648, pp. 235–239. Springer, Heidelberg (2003)

10. Holzmann, G.J.: Cloud-based verification of concurrent software. In: Jobstmann, B., et al. (eds.) VMCAI 2016. LNCS, vol. 9583, pp. 311–327. Springer, Heidelberg (2016). doi:10.1007/978-3-662-49122-5_15
11. Huberman, B.A., Lukose, R.M., Hogg, T.: An economics approach to hard computational problems. Science 275(5296), 51–54 (1997)
12. Hyvärinen, A.E.J., Junttila, T.A., Niemelä, I.: A distribution method for solving SAT in grids. In: Biere, A., Gomes, C.P. (eds.) SAT 2006. LNCS, vol. 4121, pp. 430–435. Springer, Heidelberg (2006)
13. Hyvärinen, A.E.J., Marescotti, M., Alt, L., Sharygina, N.: OpenSMT2: an SMT solver for multi-core and cloud computing. In: Creignou, N., Le Berre, D., Le Berre, D., Le Berre, D., Le Berre, D., Le Berre, D. (eds.) SAT 2016. LNCS, vol. 9710, pp. 547–553. Springer, Heidelberg (2016). doi:10.1007/978-3-319-40970-2_35
14. Hyvärinen, A.E.J., Marescotti, M., Sharygina, N.: Search-space partitioning for parallelizing SMT solvers. In: Heule, M., et al. (eds.) SAT 2015. LNCS, vol. 9340, pp. 369–386. Springer, Heidelberg (2015). doi:10.1007/978-3-319-24318-4_27
15. Hyvärinen, A.E.J., Junttila, T.A., Niemelä, I.: Partitioning search spaces of a randomized search. Fundamenta Informaticae 107(2–3), 289–311 (2011)
16. Marques-Silva, J.P., Sakallah, K.A.: GRASP: a search algorithm for propositional satisfiability. IEEE Trans. Comput. 48(5), 506–521 (1999)
17. Martins, R., Manquinho, V.M., Lynce, I.: An overview of parallel SAT solving. Constraints 17(3), 304–347 (2012)
18. de Moura, L., Bjørner, N.S.: Z3: an efficient SMT solver. In: Ramakrishnan, C.R., Rehof, J. (eds.) TACAS 2008. LNCS, vol. 4963, pp. 337–340. Springer, Heidelberg (2008)
19. Nieuwenhuis, R., Oliveras, A.: Proof-producing congruence closure. In: Giesl, J. (ed.) RTA 2005. LNCS, vol. 3467, pp. 453–468. Springer, Heidelberg (2005)
20. Nieuwenhuis, R., Oliveras, A., Tinelli, C.: Solving SAT and SAT modulo theories: from an abstract Davis-Putnam-Logemann-Loveland procedure to DPLL(T). J. ACM 53(6), 937–977 (2006)
21. Palikareva, H., Cadar, C.: Multi-solver support in symbolic execution. In: Sharygina, N., Veith, H. (eds.) CAV 2013. LNCS, vol. 8044, pp. 53–68. Springer, Heidelberg (2013)
22. Rakadjiev, E., Shimosawa, T., Mine, H., Oshima, S.: Parallel SMT solving and concurrent symbolic execution. In: 2015 IEEE TrustCom/BigDataSE/ISPA, Helsinki, Finland, August 20–22, 2015, vol. 3, pp. 17–26 (2015). http://dx.doi.org/10.1109/Trustcom.2015.608
23. Reisenberger, C.: PBoolector: a parallel SMT solver for QF_BV by combining bit-blasting with look-ahead. Master's thesis, Johannes Kepler Univesität Linz, Linz, Austria (2014)
24. Sebastiani, R., Tomasi, S.: Optimization modulo theories with linear rational costs. ACM Trans. Comput. Logic 16(2), 12:1–12:3 (2015)
25. Wintersteiger, C.M., Hamadi, Y., de Moura, L.: A concurrent portfolio approach to SMT solving. In: Bouajjani, A., Maler, O. (eds.) CAV 2009. LNCS, vol. 5643, pp. 715–720. Springer, Heidelberg (2009)
26. Yordanov, B., Wintersteiger, C.M., Hamadi, Y., Kugler, H.: SMT-based analysis of biological computation. In: Brat, G., Rungta, N., Venet, A. (eds.) NFM 2013. LNCS, vol. 7871, pp. 78–92. Springer, Heidelberg (2013)

Symbolic Model Checking for Factored Probabilistic Models

David Deininger, Rayna Dimitrova[✉], and Rupak Majumdar

MPI-SWS, Kaiserslautern and Saarbrücken, Germany
{david.deininger,rayna,rupak}@mpi-sws.org

Abstract. The long line of research in probabilistic model checking has resulted in efficient symbolic verification engines. Nevertheless, scalability is still a key concern. In this paper we ask two questions. First, can we lift, to the probabilistic world, successful hardware verification techniques that exploit local variable dependencies in the analyzed model? And second, will those techniques lead to significant performance improvement on models with such structure, such as dynamic Bayesian networks?

To the first question we give a positive answer by proposing a probabilistic model checking approach based on factored symbolic representation of the transition probability matrix of the analyzed model. Our experimental evaluation on several benchmarks designed to favour this approach answers the second question negatively. Intuitively, the reason is that the effect of techniques for reducing the size of BDD-based symbolic representations do not carry over to quantitative symbolic data structures. More precisely, the size of MTBDDs depends not only on the number of variables but also on the number of different terminals they have (which influences sharing), and which is not reduced by these techniques.

1 Introduction

Probabilistic model checking is a formal technique for analyzing finite-state models of systems that exhibit randomized behaviour against (quantitative) temporal specifications. Model checking tools, such as PRISM [13], have been successfully applied to a variety of systems, such as randomized distributed protocols, biological processes, and randomized algorithms for leader election.

State-of-the-art probabilistic model checkers such as PRISM implement symbolic model checking algorithms on top of data structures such as BDDs and MTBDDs [16]. It is well known that these data structures allow efficient sharing of state within the model checker and offer significant benefits in time and space requirements for model checking large probabilistic systems.

However, the scalability of automatic probabilistic verification remains to be a concern. A natural question is whether the structure of the probabilistic model can be exploited to provide further optimizations in state storage during model checking. For example, consider probabilistic models that exhibit local dependencies, where variables depend on a small number of "neighboring" variables.

© Springer International Publishing AG 2016
C. Artho et al. (Eds.): ATVA 2016, LNCS 9938, pp. 444–460, 2016.
DOI: 10.1007/978-3-319-46520-3_28

Such local structure is common and natural in distributed algorithms and networks, in which a process communicates only with its immediate neighbours. In this setting the model can be described in a factored representation such as a Bayesian network that captures these local dependencies. Current approaches to probabilistic model checking do not benefit from the structure of the analyzed models, as this is typically lost during the translation into the verifier's internal representation as a monolithic BDD or MTBDD. Exploiting structure is identified as one of the rules of thumb in symbolic probabilistic verification [12], but most implementations only consider simple variable ordering heuristics.

In hardware model checking, one way to exploit structure is to retain the transition relation of a circuit in *partitioned* fashion [6]. Instead of computing a monolithic transition relation as a conjunction of BDDs representing modules executing in parallel, partitioned representations maintain a list of BDDs for each module. During successor computation, partitioned BDDs are manipulated one at a time using early quantification, which keeps the size of intermediate BDDs small. Partitioned approaches have been used with great success to reduce state space explosion in symbolic model checking, often by orders of magnitude [7]. It is thus natural to ask if these techniques can be successfully extended and applied to improve the efficiency of the verification of factored probabilistic models.

This is the question which we study in this paper. We have implemented a model checker for PCTL for factored probabilistic models. It accepts factored probabilistic models, in the form of dynamic Bayesian networks. These models admit a natural straightforward factored symbolic representation of their transition matrices. Our model checker uses a partitioned representation of the transition matrices as sets of MTBDDs. We extend matrix-vector multiplication based on MTBDDs to use partitioned representations of the transition probability matrix. Furthermore, we show that this procedure can be seamlessly integrated in the power method for iteratively solving systems of linear equations, which lies at the core of quantitative PCTL model checking [2,3].

We experimentally compare the performance of PCTL model checking using partitioned versus monolithic representations on a set of scalable benchmarks that exhibit local structure. We compare our implementation against an equivalent implementation that uses a global, non-partitioned transition relation (to ensure we only capture the effect of monolithic vs. partitioned representations and do not confound our results with orthogonal heuristics). We also compare against the PRISM model checker to ensure our global representation-based implementation is comparable to the state-of-the-art.

Unfortunately, our results in the quantitative setting are negative. While *qualitative* PCTL model checking inherits the benefits of partitioned non-probabilistic model checking, we show that even on factored models, *quantitative* model checking does not significantly benefit from partitioned representations. On all but the simplest examples and properties, computing the matrix vector product on the factored representation using early variable elimination (the quantitative analogue of early quantification) does not help: while the number of variables in the MTBDD does decrease, the intermediate products have a large number of constant terms as terminal nodes. This decreases the amount of sharing, consequently not reducing the size of the MTBDD. Overall, for quantitative specifications, partitioned representations and early variable elimination does not significantly improve run times or memory requirements over global representations. (Although, some improvement is seen on the simplest examples).

Our negative observations carry over to different structures of the dependency graph: linear, tree, and grid topologies. The tree and grid topologies specifically were chosen to be difficult for the classical methods as there is no natural variable ordering facilitating MTBDD reasoning. With the exception of particularly easy properties that only refer to a small part of the model, these examples turned out to be hard even for the approach using the partitioned transition relation.

While our experimental results are negative, we consider them an important contribution to the research landscape in probabilistic verification. Partitioning is an intuitive heuristic, and works well in non-probabilistic settings. Our objective was to evaluate if it can be easily and naturally applied to improve the performance of probabilistic reasoning. It was surprising to us that it does not improve quantitative model checking, but to the best of our knowledge, no prior experimental comparison pointed this out. We hope that our results, showing which avenues have turned out unsuccessful, will be valuable to others aiming to improve the efficiency of probabilistic verification.

Related Work. Several lines of work have investigated connections between model checking of temporal properties and inference in dynamic Bayesian networks. In [14] model checking techniques are used to perform inference in dynamic Bayesian networks for queries specified in probabilistic CTL. There, a dynamic Bayesian network is converted to probabilistic reactive modules, which are in turn encoded as an MTBDD by the PRISM model checker. Their approach does not modify the internal data structures and algorithms of the probabilistic model checker to make use of the model's structure. In [15], inference techniques are used to perform approximate model checking of dynamic Bayesian networks against finite-horizon probabilistic linear temporal properties.

2   Probabilistic Model Checking

2.1   Probabilistic Models and Temporal Logics

A *discrete-time Markov chain (DTMC)* is a tuple $M = (S, P, AP, L)$, where S is a finite set of states, $P \colon S \times S \to [0, 1]$ is a transition probability function, such that $\sum_{s' \in S} P(s, s') = 1$ for every state $s \in S$, AP is a finite set of atomic propositions, and $L \colon S \to 2^{AP}$ is a labelling function mapping each state to the set of propositions that hold true in it. The transition probability function P can be interpreted as a $|S| \times |S|$ real matrix, where $|S|$ is the number of states.

A *path* in M is a finite or infinite sequence $s_0, s_1, \ldots$ of states in S such that for each i it holds that $P(s_i, s_{i+1}) > 0$. Given a state $s \in S$, we denote with $\mathsf{Paths}(M, s)$ the set of paths in M originating in the state s.

We now recall the syntax of Probabilistic Computation Tree Logic (PCTL). We fix a set AP of *atomic propositions*. The set of PCTL formulas over AP consists of two types of formulas: *state formulas* and *path formulas*. State formulas are formed according to the grammar $\Phi ::= \text{tt} \mid a \mid \Phi_1 \wedge \Phi_2 \mid \neg\Psi \mid \mathbb{P}_J(\varphi)$, where $a \in AP$, Φ_1, Φ_2 and Ψ are state formulas, $J \subseteq [0,1]$ is a real interval, and φ is a path formula. Path formulas are defined by the grammar $\varphi ::= \bigcirc\Phi \mid \Phi_1\mathcal{U}\Phi_2 \mid \Phi_1\mathcal{U}^{\leq k}\Phi_2$, where Φ, Φ_1 and Φ_2 are state formulas, and $k \in \mathbb{N}$. As usual, we define the derived operators $\Diamond\varphi = \text{tt}\,\mathcal{U}\,\varphi$ and $\Box\varphi = \neg\Diamond\neg\varphi$. The *qualitative* fragment of PCTL restricts the interval J in the probability operator $\mathbb{P}_J$ to the cases $\mathbb{P}_{=1} = \mathbb{P}_{[1,1]}$ and $\mathbb{P}_{=0} = \mathbb{P}_{[0,0]}$.

The semantics of PCTL with respect to Markov chains is defined as follows. Let $M = (S, P, AP, L)$ be a DTMC. Then, PCTL state formulas are interpreted over states of M, while path formulas are interpreted over paths. The satisfaction relations $\models$ are defined as usual for assertions, Boolean and temporal operators [3]. Formulas containing the probability operator $\mathbb{P}$ are interpreted using a probability measure over sets of paths. More specifically, the satisfaction of $\mathbb{P}_J(\varphi)$ in a state s is determined by the probability measure of the set of paths $\Pi_\varphi = \{\pi \in \mathsf{Paths}(M,s) \mid M, \pi \models \varphi\}$, for which it is known that it is measurable. More precisely, with each DTMC M and state s in M we can associate a probability measure Pr_s^M such that for every path formula φ the set of paths Π_φ is measurable [3]. Then, we define $M, s \models \mathbb{P}_J(\varphi)$ iff $Pr_s^M(\Pi_\varphi) \in J$.

It is well known that for the satisfaction of qualitative PCTL formulas in a finite-state DTMC $M = (S, P, AP, L)$ the precise values of the probabilities assigned by P do not play a role. We thus define the transition relation function $T : S \times S \rightarrow \{0,1\}$ such that for $s, s' \in S$ we have $T(s, s') = 1$ iff $P(s, s') > 0$. This defines the graph $G_M = (S, E)$ corresponding to M, with vertices the states of M, and set of edges $E \subseteq S \times S$ such that $(s, s') \in E$ iff $T(s, s') = 1$.

2.2 Probabilistic Model Checking

Given a DTMC $M = (S, P, AP, L)$ and a PCTL state formula Φ, the *model checking problem* asks to determine whether $M, s \models \Phi$ holds for every $s \in S$.

The model checking problem for PCTL can be solved by computing the set $\mathsf{Sat}_M(\Phi) = \{s \in S \mid M, s \models \Phi\}$ of states in M that satisfy Φ, and then checking if $\mathsf{Sat}_M(\Phi) = S$. The set $\mathsf{Sat}_M(\Phi)$ can be computed recursively in a bottom-up manner, following the syntax tree of the formula Φ. The key step is computing the set $\mathsf{Sat}_M(\Phi)$ for a formula of the form $\Phi = \mathbb{P}_J(\varphi)$, where φ is a path formula for which we have already computed $\mathsf{Sat}_M(\Psi)$ for every state subformula Ψ.

If $\Phi = \mathbb{P}_J(\bigcirc\Psi)$, we check if $\left(\sum_{s' \in \mathsf{Sat}_M(\Psi)} P(s, s')\right) \in J$. The probabilities can be computed by multiplying the probability matrix P with the characteristic vector of $\mathsf{Sat}_M(\Psi)$, i.e. a vector $(b_{s'})_{s' \in S}$ with $b_{s'} = 1$ iff $s' \in \mathsf{Sat}_M(\Psi)$.

For an until formula $\varphi = \Phi_1\mathcal{U}\Phi_2$ or $\varphi = \Phi_1\mathcal{U}^{\leq k}\Phi_2$ we first compute sets $\widehat{S}_{=1} \subseteq \{s \in S \mid Pr(M, s \models \varphi) = 1\}$ and $\widehat{S}_{=0} \subseteq \{s \in S \mid Pr(M, s \models \varphi) = 0\}$ such that in the states in $\widehat{S}_{=1}$ the formula φ is satisfied with probability 1 and in the states in $\widehat{S}_{=0}$ it holds with probability 0. Furthermore we require that $\mathsf{Sat}_M(\Phi_2) \subseteq \widehat{S}_{=1}$ and that $S \setminus (\mathsf{Sat}_M(\Phi_1) \cup \mathsf{Sat}_M(\Phi_2)) \subseteq \widehat{S}_{=0}$. The remaining states $S_? = S \setminus (\widehat{S}_{=1} \cup \widehat{S}_{=0})$ are the ones for which the probability has to still be computed. To this end, we define the matrix $A = (P(s, s'))_{s,s' \in S_?}$, which restricts P to states in $S_?$, and the vector $(b_s)_{s \in S_?}$, with $b_s = P(s, \widehat{S}_{=1})$.

The vector $(Pr(s \models \Phi_1 \mathcal{U} \Phi_2))_{s \in S_?}$ is the least fixed point of the operator $\Upsilon \colon [0,1]^{S_?} \to [0,1]^{S_?}$, with $\Upsilon(c) = A \cdot c + b$. This formulation can be rewritten into a system of linear equations $(I - A) \cdot c = b$, where I is the identity matrix of dimension $|S_?| \times |S_?|$. Choosing $\widehat{S}_{=0}$ to be exactly the set $\{s \in S \mid Pr(M, s \models \varphi) = 0\}$ guarantees that this system of equations has a unique solution [3].

For bounded until formulas $\varphi = \Phi_1 \mathcal{U}^{\leq k} \Phi_2$ we have to take $\widehat{S}_{=1} = \mathsf{Sat}_M(\Phi_2)$, that is, the set of states that reach Φ_2 in zero steps, and can compute the vector of probabilities $(Pr(s \models \Phi_1 \mathcal{U}^{\leq k} \Phi_2))_{s \in S_?}$ as the vector $c^{(n)}$, where $c^{(0)} = (0)_{s \in S_?}$ and $c^{(i+1)} = \Upsilon(c^{(i)})$ for $i \geq 0$. Finally, $\mathsf{Sat}_M(\Phi) = \{s \in S \mid Pr(M, s \models \varphi) \in J\}$.

Thus, computing the set $\mathsf{Sat}_M(\Phi)$ for a quantitative formula $\Phi = \mathbb{P}_J(\varphi)$ is reduced to computing the sets $\mathsf{Sat}_M(\mathbb{P}_{=1}(\varphi)) = \{s \in S \mid Pr(M, s \models \varphi) = 1\}$ and $\mathsf{Sat}_M(\mathbb{P}_{=0}(\varphi)) = \{s \in S \mid Pr(M, s \models \varphi) = 0\}$ for the respective qualitative formulas and then solving a system of linear equations.

The sets $\mathsf{Sat}_M(\mathbb{P}_{=1}(\varphi))$ and $\mathsf{Sat}_M(\mathbb{P}_{=0}(\varphi))$ do not depend on the exact values in P and can be computed based on the graph $G_M = (S, E)$ associated with M.

The set $\mathsf{Sat}_M(\mathbb{P}_{=0}(\Phi_1 \mathcal{U} \Phi_2))$ can be computed by first computing the set of states $\mathsf{Sat}_M(\mathbb{P}_{>0}(\Phi_1 \mathcal{U} \Phi_2))$ backward reachable from $\mathsf{Sat}_M(\Phi_2)$ by visiting only states in $\mathsf{Sat}_M(\Phi_1)$, and then taking $\mathsf{Sat}_M(\mathbb{P}_{=0}(\Phi_1 \mathcal{U} \Phi_2)) = S \setminus \mathsf{Sat}_M(\mathbb{P}_{>0}(\Phi_1 \mathcal{U} \Phi_2))$. The bounded until case is analogous.

The set $\mathsf{Sat}_M(\mathbb{P}_{=1}(\Phi_1 \mathcal{U} \Phi_2))$ can also be computed by backward reachability in a graph modified as follows. Let $G'_M = (S, E')$ be obtained from G_M by making all states in the set $D = \mathsf{Sat}_M(\Phi_2) \cup (S \setminus (\mathsf{Sat}_M(\Phi_1) \cup \mathsf{Sat}_M(\Phi_2)))$ absorbing. That is, $(s, s') \in E'$ iff $s \notin D$ and $(s, s') \in E$, or $s \in D$ and $s = s'$. Then, as shown in [3], it holds that $\mathsf{Sat}_M(\mathbb{P}_{=1}(\Phi_1 \mathcal{U} \Phi_2)) = S \setminus \mathsf{Pre}^*_{G'_M}(S \setminus (\mathsf{Pre}^*_{G'_M}(\mathsf{Sat}_M(\Phi_2))))$, where, $\mathsf{Pre}^*_{G'_M}(U)$ are the states backward reachable from the set U in G'_M.

2.3   Symbolic Model Checking

Let $M = (S, P, AP, L)$ be a DTMC and suppose that X is a set of Boolean variables such that $S = \{0,1\}^X$, i.e., X is a Boolean encoding of S, and the set AP consists of atomic propositions, one for each variable in X. Let $n = |X|$, and as usual, let $X' = \{x' \mid x \in X\}$ be the set of "next state" variables for X.

The transition probability function P can be encoded as a real valued function of Boolean vectors $\rho \colon \mathbb{B}^n \times \mathbb{B}^n \to \mathbb{R}$, and the transition relation function T can be described by a function $\delta \colon \mathbb{B}^n \times \mathbb{B}^n \to \mathbb{B}$. Similarly, sets of states and probability vectors are represented as functions from $\mathbb{B}^n$ to $\mathbb{B}$ and $\mathbb{R}$, respectively.

In symbolic verification, Boolean functions are often succinctly represented as reduced ordered binary decision diagrams (BDDs) [5]. Given a fixed total ordering of the variables in $X \cup X'$, BDDs represent the Boolean functions on $\mathbb{B}^n \times \mathbb{B}^n$ in a one-to-one manner. There exist efficient methods for computing existential abstraction, application of Boolean operators and variable renaming using BDDs. The size of the BDD representing a given function is heavily influenced by the ordering of the variables, and it is well known that finding an optimal ordering is a hard problem. A commonly used heuristic, which performs quite well in practice, is to interleave non-primed and primed variables $x < x' < y < y' < \ldots$.

In quantitative verification, a generalization of BDDs, called multi-terminal BDDs (MTBDDs) [8] are used to succinctly represent real-valued functions. The matrix and vector arithmetic operations used in PCTL model checking can be efficiently performed on their MTBDD-based representation [1, 10].

Given a fixed variable ordering, the size of the BDD representation of a Boolean function is influenced by the number of variables on which this function actually depends. The same holds for MTBDDs, where, in addition, the number of values in the co-domain of the functions has an impact on the size of the corresponding MTBDD. In the following subsection we describe a class of probabilistic models, whose structure allows for a factored symbolic representation of its transition relation and transition probability functions. Such a factored representation is a collection of BDDs, or respectively MTBDDs, that capture local dependencies between the variables describing the model, and are, often significantly smaller than those describing the transitions between global states.

2.4 Dynamic Bayesian Networks

Intuitively, a *Bayesian network* is a graph-like representation of dependence conditions on a set of random variables, coupled with some representation of the distributions associated with these random variables. More formally, a Bayesian network over a set of variables V is tuple $B = (G, \Theta)$, where $G = (V, D)$ is a directed acyclic graph with vertices the variables in V and set of edges $D \subseteq V \times V$ describing the dependencies between these variables, and Θ is a set of conditional probability distributions (CPDs), one for each variable in V, as we now explain.

For a set of variables $Y \subseteq V$, let $Val(Y)$ be the set of valuations of the variables Y, that is, the functions that map each variable $y \in Y$ to a value in its domain $Val(y)$. With $Pa_B(v) = \{u \in V \mid (u, v) \in D\}$ we denote the set of parent nodes of v in G. These are the variables on whose value the probability distribution of v directly depends. More precisely, for each variable $v \in V$ the set Θ contains a CPD $\Theta_{v|Pa_B(v)} = Pr(v \mid Pa_B(v))$. When $Val(V)$ is finite, the CPD of each variable v is usually represented by a *conditional probability table* that maps every valuation in $Val(Pa_B(v))$ to a probability distribution over $Val(v)$.

Dynamic Bayesian networks (DBN) describe systems evolving over time. A DBN over a set of variables V is a two-slice Bayesian network $B = (G, \Theta)$ over $V \cup V'$, where $Pa_B(v) = \emptyset$ for each $v \in V$. That is, the CPDs of the variables V in B depend on none of the other variables, while the CPDs of the variables in V' can depend on variables in both V and V'. More precisely, since the dependency graph G is acyclic, the CPD of a next-state variable v' can depend on the current values of V as well as on the next-state values of variables different from v.

A DBN $B = (G, \Theta)$ over a set of variables V can be seen as a factored representation of a Markov chain. The DTMC $M_B = (S, P, AP, L)$ induced by

B has set of states $S = Val(V)$. The transition probability function $P(s, s') = Pr_B(X' = s' \mid X = s)$ is defined according to the probability distribution described by B. We choose $AP = S$ and define $L(s) = \{s\}$.

The *model checking problem for dynamic Bayesian networks* asks, given a DBN $B = (G, \Theta)$, whose induced DTMC is $M_B = (S, P, AP, L)$, and a PCTL state formula Φ over AP, to determine whether $M_B, s \models \Phi$ for every $s \in S$.

3   Model Checking Qualitative PCTL

3.1   Factored BDD Representation

Let $B = (G, \Theta)$ be a DBN over a set of finite-state variables V. Suppose w.l.o.g. that for each $v \in V$ it holds that $|Val(v)|$ is a power of 2. Then, with each $v \in V$ we associate a set of Boolean variables X_v such that X_v is a Boolean encoding of $Val(v)$. With X'_v we denote the set of next-state Boolean variables.

Let $X = \bigcup_{v \in V} X_v$ and $X' = \bigcup_{v \in V} X'_v$. Then, $Val(X)$ are the states of the DTMC $M_B = (S, P, AP, L)$ induced by B, and the transition relation function of M_B can be represented by a BDD $\delta(X, X')$ over the variables $X \cup X'$.

Since each $v' \in V'$ depends directly only on $Pa_B(v')$, the variables in X'_v depend directly only on $\widehat{X}_{v'} = (\bigcup_{u \in Pa_B(v') \cap V} X_u) \cup (\bigcup_{u \in Pa_B(v') \cap V'} X'_u)$. We represent each $\Theta_{v' \mid Pa_B(v')}$ by a BDD $\delta_v(X, X')$, whose support is $X'_v \cup \widehat{X}'_v$.

If $Pa_B(v') = \{u_1, \ldots, u_k\}$, we use $(\mathbf{v}, \mathbf{u}_1, \ldots, \mathbf{u}_k, p) \in \Theta_{v' \mid Pa_B(v')}$ to denote the elements of the conditional probability table $\Theta_{v' \mid Pa_B(v')}$ for v', i.e., the fact that $Pr_B(v' = \mathbf{v} \mid u_1 = \mathbf{u}_1, u_2 = \mathbf{u}_2, \ldots, u_k = \mathbf{u}_k) = p$.

For each $v \in V$ and $\mathbf{v} \in Val(v)$, we denote with $\beta_{v, \mathbf{v}}(X)$ the BDD for the Boolean formula over X equivalent to the atomic predicate $v = \mathbf{v}$. Similarly for $v' \in V'$ we have $\beta_{v', \mathbf{v}}(X')$. Now, for each $v \in V$, we define the BDD $\delta_v(X, X') =$

$$\bigvee_{\mathbf{v} \in Val(v')} \left(\beta_{v', \mathbf{v}}(X') \wedge \bigvee_{\substack{(\mathbf{v}, \mathbf{u}_1, \ldots, \mathbf{u}_k, p) \in \Theta_{v \mid Pa_B(v)} \\ p > 0}} (\beta_{u_1, \mathbf{u}_1}(X) \wedge \ldots \beta_{u_k, \mathbf{u}_k}(X)) \right).$$

Proposition 1. *For a DBN $B = (G, \Theta)$ over variables V with induced DTMC $M_B = (S, P, AP, L)$ whose transition relation is δ it holds that $\delta = \bigwedge_{v \in V} \delta_v$.*

3.2   Image Computation with Factored BDDs

Consider a Boolean formula $\Psi(X)$ that describes a set of states in the DTMC $M_B = (S, P, AP, L)$. The formula $\mathsf{Pre}(\Psi)(X) = \exists X'. \delta(X, X') \wedge \Psi(X')$ describes the set of states that have a successor in M_B which is a Ψ-state. The BDD describing $\mathsf{Pre}(\Psi)$ can be computed by applying the standard conjunction and existential abstraction operations to the BDDs for $\delta(X, X')$ and $\Psi(X')$.

When $\delta(X, X')$ is given in the factored form $\delta_{v_1}(X, X'), \ldots, \delta_{v_n}(X, X')$, where $V = \{v_1, \ldots, v_n\}$, we can avoid constructing the BDD for the global transition relation δ, and instead use the partitioned form in the computation of $\mathsf{Pre}(\Psi)$. Depending on the functions $\delta_{v_1}(X, X'), \ldots, \delta_{v_n}(X, X')$ and the number of variables on which each of them depends, their individual size can be much smaller than the size of δ. Furthermore, since each δ_v depends only on a subset of X', it is possible that applying *early quantification* [6] can lead to avoiding a blow-up of intermediate results during the computation of $\mathsf{Pre}(\Psi)$. Such conjunctive partitioning of the transition relation has been successfully used for efficient forward-image computation in the verification of hardware models [6].

Here we describe the application of this approach to the Pre-image computation for the DBN $B = (G, \theta)$. Let $\pi : \{1, \ldots, n\} \to V$ be an ordering of the variables in V. We will explain later how to choose a potentially good ordering based on the dependency graph G of the DBN. For each $v \in V$, let $Y_v \subseteq X'$ be the set of variables in X' on which δ_v depends, that is $y \in Y_v$ iff $y \in X'$ and $\delta_v[0/y] \neq \delta_v[1/y]$, where $\delta_v[0/y]$ is the formula obtained from δ_v by substituting 0 for the variable y. Also, let $Z_v = Y_v \setminus \left(\bigcup_{i=\pi^{-1}(v)+1}^{n} Y_{\pi(i)} \right)$ be the set of variables in X' on which δ_v depends, but none of δ_u with $\pi^{-1}(u) > \pi^{-1}(v)$ depends on them. Note that the sets Z_v are pairwise disjoint. Then, $\mathsf{Pre}(\Psi)$ is computed by:

$$\Psi_1(X, X') = \exists Z_{\pi(1)} \left(\delta_{\pi(1)}(X, X') \wedge \Psi(X') \right)$$
$$\Psi_2(X, X') = \exists Z_{\pi(2)} \left(\delta_{\pi(2)}(X, X') \wedge \Psi_1(X, X') \right)$$
$$\cdots$$
$$\Psi_n(X, X') = \exists Z_{\pi(n)} \left(\delta_{\pi(n)}(X, X') \wedge \Psi_{n-1}(X, X') \right)$$
$$\mathsf{Pre}(\Psi)(X) = \exists (X' \setminus (\bigcup_{v \in V} Z_v)) \Psi_n(X, X').$$

The ordering π of the variables in X' is important, as it determines how many variables are existentially abstracted at each intermediate step, which can in turn influence the size of the intermediate BDDs. We now describe a heuristic that uses the dependency graph G to find a good ordering. Let G' be the restriction of G to the nodes V'. By traversing the graph G' in post-order we can compute π such that for every $i, j \in \{1, \ldots, n\}$, if $\pi(i) = v$, $\pi(j) = u$ and there is an edge in G' from u to v, then $i < j$. This allows for eliminating the variables X'_u at step j of the computation of $\mathsf{Pre}(\Psi)$, as none of the transition relations $\delta_{\pi(k)}$ considered at the subsequent steps $k > i$ depends on X'_u. Additionally, if variables $u \in V'$ and $v \in V'$ are mutually unreachable in G' but $|Y_u| < |Y_v|$, then δ_v will appear earlier in the ordering, leading to the elimination of more variables.

3.3 Reachability Computation

As we recalled in Sect. 2, the sets $\mathsf{Sat}(\mathbb{P}_{=0}(\Phi_1 \mathcal{U} \Phi_2))$ and $\mathsf{Sat}(\mathbb{P}_{=1}(\Phi_1 \mathcal{U} \Phi_2))$ can be computed by backward graph reachability starting from $\mathsf{Sat}(\Phi_2)$ in the (possibly modified) graph G_{M_B}. Here we show how to do that using the factored symbolic representation of the edge relation in G_{M_B}, constructed as above.

As usual, $\mathsf{Sat}(\mathbb{P}_{>0}(\Phi_1 \mathcal{U} \Phi_2))$ is computed as the least fixpoint $\mu U.\mathsf{Sat}(\Phi_2) \vee (\mathsf{Pre}(U) \wedge \mathsf{Sat}(\Phi_1))$, which corresponds to computing the states backward reachable from $\mathsf{Sat}(\Phi_2)$ that are in $\mathsf{Sat}(\Phi_1)$. For the computation of $\mathsf{Sat}(\mathbb{P}_{=1}(\Phi_1 \mathcal{U} \Phi_2))$, instead of restricting the transition relations δ_v to the set $(S \setminus (\mathsf{Sat}(\Phi_1) \cup \mathsf{Sat}(\Phi_2))$

in order to represent the transition relation of the modified graph, we use the following fixpoint expressions with the unmodified partitioned transition relation:

$$\Psi(X) = \neg\mu U.\mathsf{Sat}(\Phi_2) \vee (\mathsf{Pre}(U) \wedge \mathsf{Sat}(\Phi_1) \wedge \neg\mathsf{Sat}(\Phi_2)),$$
$$\mathsf{Sat}(\mathbb{P}_{=1}(\Phi_1 \,\mathcal{U}\, \Phi_2)) = \neg\mu U.\Psi \vee (\mathsf{Pre}(U) \wedge \mathsf{Sat}(\Phi_1) \wedge \neg\mathsf{Sat}(\Phi_2)).$$

Next and bounded until formulas are handled in a similar way using the preimage computation based on the factored transition relation.

4 Model Checking Quantitative PCTL

4.1 Factored MTBDD Representation

Let $B = (G, \Theta)$ be a DBN over a set of finite-state variables V, and let the sets of variables $X = \bigcup_{v \in V} X_v$ and $X' = \bigcup_{v \in V} X'_v$ be as in the previous section. The transition probability matrix P of the induced DTMC $M_B = (S, P, AP, L)$ can be represented as an MTBDD ρ over the variables $X \cup X'$. Here we use again the structure of the DBN and the local dependencies implied by it to give a factored representation of ρ as the element-wise product of matrices ρ_v for $v \in V$.

As before, if $Pa_B(v') = \{u_1, \ldots, u_k\}$, we use $(\mathbf{v}, \mathbf{u}_1, \ldots, \mathbf{u}_k, p) \in \Theta_{v' \mid Pa_B(v')}$ to denote the elements of the conditional probability table $\Theta_{v' \mid Pa_B(v')}$ for v'.

For each $v \in V$ and $\mathbf{v} \in Val(v)$ (respectively $v' \in V'$ and $\mathbf{v} \in Val(v')$), we denote with $\mu_{v,\mathbf{v}}(X)$ (respectively $\mu_{v',\mathbf{v}}(X')$) the MTBDD for the Boolean formula equivalent to the atomic predicate $v = \mathbf{v}$ (respectively $v' = \mathbf{v}$). For $p \in \mathbb{R}$, we denote with μ_p the MTBDD that maps each assignment to $X \cup X'$ to the constant p. For each $v \in V$, we define the MTBDD $\rho_v(X, X') = \sum_{\mathbf{v} \in Val(v')} (\mu_{v',\mathbf{v}}(X') * \psi_{v,\mathbf{v}})$, where $\psi_{v,\mathbf{v}} = \sum_{\substack{(\mathbf{v}, \mathbf{u}_1, \ldots, \mathbf{u}_k, p) \in \Theta_{v \mid Pa_B(v)} \\ p > 0}} (\mu_p * \mu_{u_1, \mathbf{u}_1}(X) * \ldots * \mu_{u_k, \mathbf{u}_k}(X))$, and where $+$ and $*$ denote respectively sum and multiplication of real-valued functions represented as MTBDDs. Each ρ_v represents a real matrix whose rows are indexed by $Val(X)$, and whose columns are indexed by $Val(X')$. The matrix ρ_v describes the local dependency of the variables X'_v on the remaining variables. The transition probability matrix of M_B is obtained by taking the element-wise product of the transition probability matrices for the individual variables.

Proposition 2. *For a DBN $B = (G, \Theta)$ over variables $V = \{v_1, \ldots, v_n\}$ with induced DTMC $M_B = (S, P, AP, L)$ whose transition probability function is ρ it holds that $\rho = \rho_{v_1} * \ldots * \rho_{v_n}$.*

4.2 Matrix-Vector Multiplication with Factored MTBDDs

Let $A(X, X')$ be an MTBDD representing a square real matrix such that $Val(X)$ are the row indices and $Val(X')$ are the column indices. Let $b(X)$ be an MTBDD representing a real vector with indices $Val(X')$. The matrix-vector product

$c = Ab$ can be computed symbolically [1] as $c(X) = \exists X'.A(X,X') * b(X')$, where $*$ is the multiplication operation for real-valued functions (MTBDDs) and $\exists$ is the sum-abstraction. In our case, the transition probability matrix is given in factored form $\rho = \rho_{v_1} * \ldots * \rho_{v_n}$. Since the element-wise multiplication $*$ is associative and commutative, we can perform matrix-vector multiplication without computing ρ upfront as $\exists X'.\rho_{v_1}(X,X') * \ldots * \rho_{v_n}(X,X') * b(X')$.

Furthermore, as in the previous section we can employ early quantification whenever possible, trying to reduce the size of intermediate MTBDDs.

As we will see in our experimental results in Sect. 5, however, in the majority of the cases early quantification does not reduce the size of the intermediate MTBDDs. Although it might reduce the number of variables the function depends on, existential abstraction may increase the number of terminal nodes, thus affecting the amount of sharing between subgraphs of the MTBDD.

4.3 Solving Linear Equations

As we recalled in Sect. 2, model checking quantitative PCTL reduces to computing the satisfaction sets for qualitative formulas and solving systems of linear equations with real coefficients. Usually, symbolic methods based on MTBDDs for solving such systems employ iterative methods [16], since those do not require modifying the matrix during the computation, which is important for the compactness of the MTBDD representation. In order to seamlessly use the factored representation of the matrix, we use the power method, which only requires matrix-vector multiplication operations with the transition probability matrix.

As in the qualitative case, for until and bounded until formulas, instead of restricting each of the factors to the set $S_?$, which can introduce dependency on additional variables, we apply the restriction to the candidate solution vector at each step. We let $c^{(0)}(s) = 1$ for $s \in S_{=1}$ and $c^{(0)}(s) = 0$ for $s \in S_{=0} \cup S_?$, and then iteratively compute $c^{(i+1)} = Ac^{(i)} + b$, where at each step we modify $c^{(i)}$ according to S_1 and S_0. The power method receives as an input parameter a real value ε, and the iteration terminates when $||c^{(i+1)} - c^{(i)}||_\infty < \varepsilon$. As the power method is guaranteed to converge [3], we can compute an approximation to the solution vector up to a theoretically arbitrary precision. Using the power method based on partitioned transition probability matrix we compute $\mathsf{Sat}(\mathbb{P}_J(\Phi_1 \, \mathcal{U} \, \Phi_2))$. The method applies the matrix-vector multiplication procedure we described, using the ordering π to determine the order of applications of existential abstraction. Next properties are handled directly using the matrix-vector multiplication procedure for factored MTBDDs, and bounded until formulas are handled analogously to unbounded until formulas as described in Sect. 2.

5 Experimental Evaluation

We evaluate our approach on a set of several benchmarks. We have implemented a prototype PCTL model checker based on factored symbolic representations. Our tool is implemented in C++ using version 2.5.0 of the CUDD library [18]. In order to compare the performance of our technique to classical symbolic PCTL model checking we also implemented all procedures using monolithic symbolic representation.[1] We also compare to the state-of-the-art symbolic probabilistic model checker PRISM [13], version 4.3.

For the comparison with PRISM, we use options -m -cuddmaxmem 2g, that is, the symbolic engine with memory limit for CUDD increased to 2 GB. Each experiment was run on a 3 GHz Intel Xeon processor with a timeout of 10 h.

We consider several probabilistic systems that can be naturally modelled as DBNs, and which exhibit different structure of their underlying dependency graphs. In our first example this graph has a simple linear structure, and thus, there exists a natural variable ordering, in which variables that directly depend on each other are close. The canonical Herman's protocol benchmark [11], which we consider next, also falls into this category. As an instance with a more complex dependency structure we then consider a network model where nodes are organized in a full binary tree. Such dependency structure arises commonly in fault tree analysis [17]. We also consider an instance with a grid structure, as an abstraction of device networks such as sensor and communication grids [9].

Now we describe the benchmarks and give a summary of our experimental results. Then, in Subsect. 5.1 we interpret and discuss these results.

Network with a Linear Topology. As our first benchmark we consider a network of N computers organized in a simple linear topology: for each $i \in \{1, \ldots, N-1\}$ there is an unidirectional connection from machine i to machine $i + 1$. Each machine is associated with a Boolean variable up_i, which indicates whether at the current step the machine is up or down. A machine which is up can fail with probability p in the next step. A machine $i > 1$ which is down, can be rebooted with probability q, only if machine $i - 1$ is up in the current step. This defines conditional probability distributions $Pr(up'_i \mid up_i, up_{i-1})$ for $i = 2, \ldots, N$.

We used values $p = q = 0.4$ and considered the following verification tasks:

(1) The property $\mathbb{P}_{=1}(\lozenge$ "all machines are down") holds in every state.
(2) Compute the probability of $\lozenge^{\leq 10}$ "machine N is down", for the initial state in which all machines are up.
(3) Compute the probability of $\lozenge^{\leq 10}$ "exactly one machine is up", for the initial state in which all machines are up.

The sizes of the MTBDDs for the partitioned and the global transition relations for $N \in \{10, 20, 30\}$ are shown in Table 1. There we also show the peak BDD size reached during the verification of the qualitative property (1). The table also contains these results for selected instances of the other benchmarks.

Figure 1 shows a comparison of the peak MTBDD size reached during verification task (2) executed for $N = 10, \ldots, 23$. For this specific quantitative property the peak size when using the factored representation remains constant, and when using the monolithic transition relation grows. This is not the case for verification task (3), as it can be seen from Fig. 2, which shows that for the

---

[1] The code is available at http://www.mpi-sws.org/~rayna/atva16-experiments/.

Table 1. Model (MTBDD) size and peak BDD size for the verification of the respective qualitative property for several instances of each of the considered models.

	Model MTBDD size			Peak BDD size	
	Partitioned	Global	PRISM	Partitioned	Global
Linear $N = 10$	7 (for $i = 1$); 10 (for $i > 1$)	1111	1111	11	29
Linear $N = 20$	7 (for $i = 1$); 10 (for $i > 1$)	7816	7816	21	59
Linear $N = 30$	7 (for $i = 1$); 10 (for $i > 1$)	25121	25121	31	89
Herman $N = 15$	10 (for $i = 1$); 8 (for $i > 1$)	810	810	626	3090
Herman $N = 17$	10 (for $i = 1$); 8 (for $i > 1$)	1053	1053	927	4704
Herman $N = 19$	10 (for $i = 1$); 8 (for $i > 1$)	1328	1328	1377	6672
Herman $N = 21$	10 (for $i = 1$); 8 (for $i > 1$)	1635	1635	1730	8810
Tree $L = 4$	9	3547	3688	44	193
Tree $L = 5$	9	178855	185884	92	3549
Tree $L = 6$	9	TO	MO	188	
Sensor $K = 4$	44	75206	83885	511	21191
Sensor $K = 5$	44	TO	MO	1436	
Sensor $K = 6$	44	TO	MO	4300	

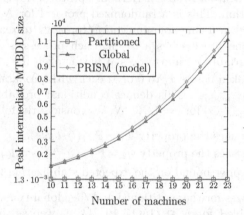

Fig. 1. Results for verification task (2) for the linear topology benchmark.

respective property the peak MTBDD sizes are essentially equal for the two approaches. For $N = 23$ in verification task (3) our approach runs out of memory, and the classical algorithm based on the global transition relation exceeds the time limit of 10 h at $N = 19$. Regarding the execution time, while for verification task (2) all instances complete in under 0.1 s, for (3) we see in Fig. 2 that our approach has better performance.

Since for verification task (2) the peak size of the MTBDD does not increase with N, our approach can verify this property even in cases when the MTBDD for

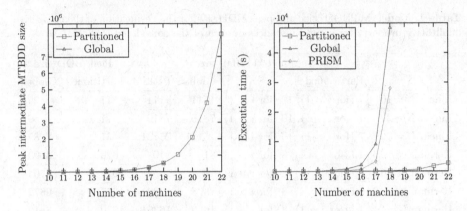

Fig. 2. Results for verification task (3) for the linear topology benchmark.

the global transition system cannot be constructed. This is the case for example for $N = 100, 200, 300$, where our approach completes successfully, but PRISM exceeds even a 20 GB memory limit while building the model.

Herman's Self-stabilization Protocol. Herman's protocol [11] is a distributed self-stabilization algorithm. This is a randomized protocol for N processes (where N is odd) organized in a ring communication topology to reach a stable state, in which exactly one process has a token. Each process is associated with a random Boolean variable x_i, and process i has a token if $x_i = x_{((i-1) \mod N)}$. If process i has a token it sets x_i to 0 or 1, each with probability $\frac{1}{2}$. Otherwise, it sets x_i to $x_{((i-1) \mod N)}$. This defines conditional probability distributions $Pr(x_i' \mid x_i, x_{((i-1) \mod N)})$ for $i = 1, \ldots, N$. We consider the following properties:

(1) Every state satisfies the property $\Phi_1 = \mathbb{P}_{=1}(\lozenge stable)$.
(2) Every state satisfies the property $\Phi_2 = \mathbb{P}_{\geq \frac{1}{2}}(\lozenge^{\leq hN^2} stable)$, where hN^2 with $h = \frac{4}{27}$ is the upper bound on the expected stabilization time [4].

The MTBDD sizes for the partitioned and the global transition relations are shown again in Table 1 for $N \in \{15, 17, 19, 21\}$, as well as the peak BDD size for the qualitative property. Regarding the peak MTBDD sizes, the situation is similar to property (3) in the linear topology case: we do not observe a significant difference between the partitioned and the global versions. For $N = 15$ we have 25179 nodes in both cases, increasing to 400370 (respectively 401543) for $N = 19$. For $N = 21$ the partitioned approach runs out of memory, while the global one exceeds the timeout (PRISM successfully verified the property, in more than 11 h). Here, our approach does not exhibit significantly better running time.

Network with a Tree Topology. Next we consider a network of machines organized in a full binary tree with L levels, consisting of $2^L - 1$ machines. Again, each machine i can be up or down and is associated with a Boolean random variable up_i. A machine at a leaf node can at each step be down with probability p and up with probability $1 - p$. A machine i at a non-leaf node is only in use if both of its children, machines $2i + 1$ and $2i + 2$ are down, and can only then fail, again with probability p. In our experiments we let $p = 0.6$ and analyze the probability of the system going down (i.e., the machine at the root going down):

(1) The property $\mathbb{P}_{=1}(\lozenge$ "the root is down") holds in every state.
(2) Compute the probability of $\lozenge^{\leq 1000}$ "the root is down", for the initial state in which all machines are up.

We show the results for the quantitative case for trees with $L = 4, \ldots, 10$ levels in Fig. 3. Here we observe a significant difference in terms of the peak intermediate MTBDD size. For $L = 5$ the factored representation results in more than 60 times smaller peak MTBDD, and for $L = 6$ the global approach reaches the time limit, while PRISM runs out of memory (given 20 GB of memory PRISM also runs past the 10 h mark). Our approach does not reach the timeout even for the tree with 10 levels, as shown in the right plot in Fig. 3.

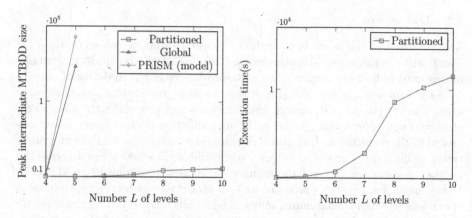

Fig. 3. Results for verification task (2) for the tree topology benchmark.

Sensor Grid. Our final benchmark is a sensor network model described in [9]. We consider a simplified setting where we do not model power consumption and lost nodes. The sensor network models a forest fire alarm system which consists of $K \times K$ sensors organized in a grid. The purpose of the system is to detect fires and carry the alerts to the boundary of the forest (grid), while each sensor communicates directly only with its four neighbours. At each time point each sensor is in one of four possible states: sleep, sense, listen and broadcast. From the sleep state a sensor goes with probability $\frac{1}{2}$ to sense and with probability $\frac{1}{2}$ to listen. If a sensor in state sense detects fire it goes to state broadcast and stays there forever. Otherwise it goes to state listen where it checks if one of its neighbours is broadcasting. If this is the case, it starts broadcasting in state broadcast forever, and otherwise it goes back to state sleep. In the initial state there is a fire at a fixed single cell (F_x, F_y). We analyze the probability of reaching a state in which there is fire still only at (F_x, F_y) (i.e., we assume that the fire does not spread), and the alarm is successfully propagated to the grid's boundary:

(1) Verify the property that if there is a fire only at a fixed cell (F_x, F_y), then with probability 1 the alarm reaches the boundary.
(2) Compute the probability that if there is a fire only at a fixed cell (F_x, F_y), then the alarm reaches the boundary within b time steps.

We consider grids of size $K \in \{4, 5, 6\}$ and fix $(F_x, F_y) = (2, 2)$. For $K = 4$ we set $b = 20$, for $K = 5$ and $K = 6$ we set $b = 5$. For $K = 4$, the peak MTBDD size for our approach is 3783, while for the verification using the global transition relation this is 69893 (the size of the global MTBDD is actually larger and is 75206) and the size of the PRISM model MTBDD is 83885. For $K = 5$ we have peak size of 6718952, while the construction of the global MTBDD times out, and PRISM runs out of memory during the model construction.

5.1   Discussion

The objective of this work is to evaluate factored symbolic representations for quantitative verification. We observe that the use of the partitioned symbolic representation leads to negligible or no improvement in the majority of cases.

As it can be expected, the size of the model representation is considerably smaller in the partitioned version, and for *qualitative* properties the advantages of partitioned representation and early quantification do carry over from non-probabilistic verification. Unfortunately, the same cannot be said about *quantitative* verification. The reason is that early variable elimination can decrease the number of variables, but not the number of different terminals in an MTBDD. For example, for Herman's protocol with 15 processes we observe multiplication operations where the maximum number of terminals reached during the sequence of early variable elimination steps is 12362, while the result of the multiplication has 612 terminals. For the same operation, with the same end result, the intermediate result when using the global transition matrix has 2880 terminals.

For very simple quantitative properties and systems, such as property (2) in the linear topology benchmark, which only refers to the last machine in the linear network, we do observe notable effects on the peak MTBDD size. However, in these cases already the classical symbolic verification methods are quite efficient, and the performance improvement is not dramatic.

For quantitative properties that refer to all the variables in the DBN or where intermediate verification steps require more global reasoning, the partitioned approach does not perform better than the standard one. Indeed, for property (3) in the linear topology benchmark and the quantitative stabilization property for Herman's protocol the peak MTBDD size using the factored representation is comparable to the size of the MTBDD for the global transition relation.

These observations extend also to the benchmarks with more complex dependence graphs. While factorization is beneficial for the simple property that refers only to the root node of the tree, the analysis of the sensor network benchmark is prohibitively hard even for the partitioned approach. For size of the grid $K = 5$ our method succeeds, reaching a peak MTBDD size of more than 6 million nodes, while the other two run out of time and memory respectively, during model construction. However, already for $K = 6$ our approach exceeds the timeout as well, and thus also does not scale beyond small values of K.

6 Conclusion

We presented and evaluated a symbolic model checking approach based on a partitioned symbolic representation of Markov chains induced by DBNs. Our experimental results indicate that known techniques for exploiting model structure in symbolic verification are not efficient in the quantitative setting. While factorization proves to be efficient for model checking qualitative PCTL properties, we conclude that achieving scalability in quantitative reasoning for DBNs requires exploring different avenues.

References

1. Bahar, R.I., Frohm, E.A., Gaona, C.M., Hachtel, G.D., Macii, E., Pardo, A., Somenzi, F.: Algebraic decision diagrams and their applications. In: Proceedings of the IEEE/ACM International Conference on Computer-Aided Design, ICCAD 1993, pp. 188–191 (1993)
2. Baier, C., Clarke, E.M., Hartonas-Garmhausen, V., Kwiatkowska, M., Ryan, M.: Symbolic model checking for probabilistic processes. In: Degano, P., Gorrieri, R., Marchetti-Spaccamela, A. (eds.) ICALP 1997. LNCS, vol. 1256, pp. 430–440. Springer, Heidelberg (1997)
3. Baier, C., Katoen, J.-P.: Principles of Model Checking (Representation and Mind Series). The MIT Press, Cambridge (2008)
4. Bruna, M., Grigore, R., Kiefer, S., Ouaknine, J., Worrell, J.: Proving the Herman-protocol conjecture (2015). CoRR, abs/1504.01130
5. Bryant, R.: Graph-based algorithms for Boolean function manipulation. IEEE Trans. Comput. $\mathbf{C-35}$(8), 677–691 (1986)
6. Burch, J.R., Clarke, E.M., Long, D.E.: Representing circuits more efficiently in symbolic model checking. In: Proceedings of the 28th ACM/IEEE Design Automation Conference, DAC 1991, pp. 403–407. ACM (1991)
7. Burch, J.R., Clarke, E.M., McMillan, K.L., Dill, D.L., Hwang, L.J.: Symbolic model checking: 1020 states and beyond. Inf. Comput. $\mathbf{98}$(2), 142–170 (1992)
8. Clarke, E.M., McMillan, K.L., Zhao, X., Fujita, M., Yang, J.: Spectral transforms for large Boolean functions with applications to technology mapping. In: DAC, pp. 54–60 (1993)
9. Demaille, A., Peyronnet, S., Sigoure, B.: Modeling of sensor networks using XRM. In: Second International Symposium on Leveraging Applications of Formal Methods, Verification and Validation, ISoLA 2006, pp. 271–276, November 2006
10. Fujita, M., McGeer, P.C., Yang, J.C.-Y.: Multi-terminal binary decision diagrams: an efficient data structure for matrix representation. Formal Methods Syst. Des. $\mathbf{10}$(2), 149–169 (1997)

11. Herman, T.: Probabilistic self-stabilization. Inf. Process. Lett. **35**(2), 63–67 (1990)

12. Hermanns, H., Meyer-Kayser, J., Siegle, M.: Multi terminal binary decision diagrams to represent and analyse continuous time Markov chains. In: 3rd International Workshop on the Numerical Solutions of Markov Chains, NSMC 1999, pp. 188–207 (1999)

13. Kwiatkowska, M., Norman, G., Parker, D.: PRISM 4.0: verification of probabilistic real-time systems. In: Gopalakrishnan, G., Qadeer, S. (eds.) CAV 2011. LNCS, vol. 6806, pp. 585–591. Springer, Heidelberg (2011)

14. Langmead, C.J., Jha, S.K., Clarke, E.M.: Temporal-logics as query languages for dynamic Bayesian networks: application to D. melanogaster embryo development (2006)

15. Palaniappan, S.K., Thiagarajan, P.S.: Dynamic Bayesian networks: a factored model of probabilistic dynamics. In: Chakraborty, S., Mukund, M. (eds.) ATVA 2012. LNCS, vol. 7561, pp. 17–25. Springer, Heidelberg (2012)

16. Parker, D.: Implementation of symbolic model checking for probabilistic systems. Ph.D. thesis, University of Birmingham (2002)

17. Ruijters, E., Stoelinga, M.: Fault tree analysis: a survey of the state-of-the-art in modeling, analysis and tools. Comput. Sci. Rev. **15**, 29–62 (2015)

18. Somenzi, F.: CUDD: BDD package, University of Colorado, Boulder. http://vlsi.colorado.edu/~fabio/CUDD/

Program Analysis

A Sketching-Based Approach
for Debugging Using Test Cases

Jinru Hua[⊠] and Sarfraz Khurshid

The University of Texas at Austin, Austin, USA
{lisahua,khurshid}@utexas.edu

Abstract. Manually locating and removing bugs in faulty code is often tedious and error-prone. Despite much progress in automated debugging, developing effective debugging techniques remains a challenge. This paper introduces a novel approach that uses a well-known program synthesis technique to automate debugging. As inputs, our approach takes a program and a test suite (with some passing and some failing tests), similar to various other recent techniques. Our key insight is to reduce the problem of finding a fix to the problem of program sketching. We translate the faulty program into a sketch of the correct program, and use off-the-shelf sketching technology to create a program that is correct with respect to the given test cases. The experimental evaluation using a suite of small, yet complex programs shows that our prototype embodiment of our approach is more effective than previous state-of-the-art.

1 Introduction

The last few years have seen much progress in two related but traditionally disjoint areas of research: automated debugging [10,23] and program synthesis [12]. Automated debugging is the problem of locating and removing faults in a given faulty program with respect to some expected correctness properties, which may be written as individual tests [14,19] or specifications [10,18,21]. Existing debugging techniques try to correct the faulty program by mutating suspicious statements [5], applying evolutionary algorithms to search for repair candidates [16], inferring conditional substitutions systematically [17], or leveraging symbolic analysis and constraint solving to find repairs [20]. Program synthesis is the problem of synthesizing implementations typically using specifications [24] with some recent work using abstract input/output scenarios [7,12].

While innovation in each of these two research areas has been impressive, the techniques developed within one area have largely been confined to that area itself with just a handful of recent approaches looking at the synergy between the areas [15,20]. Our key insight is to exploit this synergy by reducing the problem of automated debugging to a sub-problem in program synthesis, namely *program sketching* [26], in which the user writes a *sketch*, i.e., an incomplete program that has *holes*, and automated tools complete the sketch with respect to given specification, reference implementation, or abstract execution scenarios.

© Springer International Publishing AG 2016
C. Artho et al. (Eds.): ATVA 2016, LNCS 9938, pp. 463–478, 2016.
DOI: 10.1007/978-3-319-46520-3_29

We present SKETCHREP, our program repair approach that translates the given faulty program to a sketch and leverages the program sketching tool-set Sketch [26] to fill in the holes of the incomplete program with respect to the given test suite. The code fragment synthesized by Sketch, which satisfies all given test assertions, provides the repair to the faulty program.

For more efficient repair, we rank suspicious program locations using the relative statement order and spectra-based fault localization [13]. We further prioritize program locations in relation to failing test assertions, which allows SKETCHREP to keep as much of the original implementation as possible and reduce the size of expressions given to subsequent more expensive technique of completing the sketch.

For each suspicious location, SKETCHREP introduces non-deterministic expression sketches based on pre-defined repair skeletons called "repair hypotheses", which are similar in spirit to Feser et al. [7]. For example, the repair hypothesis for an assignment statement is a partial statement with expression sketches for left-hand-side and right-hand-side, and the assignment operator "=". Each expression sketch is a set of expression candidates that can appear in the resulting program. We collect all candidates based on relevant types. The candidates are computed using visible variables and a small number of field dereferences. For example, using up to two field dereferences, the expressions of the type int derived from the variable l that represents a linked list are {l.size, l.head.element} where size is the number of nodes in the list, head is the first list node, and element is the integer value that the node contains. To fix bugs at multiple locations, SKETCHREP incrementally eliminates failing test assertions and generates new hypotheses based on the updated program.

We show the results of applying SKETCHREP on 35 faults derived from students' solutions for 7 data structure subjects. We employ bounded exhaustive test suites [2] in the experiments. The experimental results show that SKETCHREP can generate program repairs for missing conditions and statements. The experiments also show that these faults are hard to fix using two state-of-the-art program repair tools, SPR [17] and Genprog [16]. For our subjects, SPR generates no correct fix while GenProg generates two correct fixes using bounded exhaustive test suites. In contrast, SKETCHREP successfully generates 30 correct fixes using bounded exhaustive test suites and 14 correct repairs using subsets of test suites.

In summary, we make the following contributions:

- **Repair as Sketching**. We introduce the first technique that provides a solution to the problem of program repair by reducing it to the problem of program sketching.
- **Fault Localization**. We introduce a fault localization technique that considers both the relative statement ordering and the spectra-based suspiciousness value [13]. Our experiments show that this technique can save calls to the Sketch backend and prune repair candidates.
- **Repair Hypothesis Generation**. We introduce two repair hypotheses to fix faulty assignments and if-conditions followed by return statements that return

true or false. The expression sketch in a hypothesis are replaced by expression candidates within a given bound. Therefore, SKETCHREP is not confined to generating repairs at the expression level [15,19], rather, it creates new statements that do not exist in the current program. It can also incrementally fix faults at multiple locations based on the test suite.

- **Experimental Evaluation.** We demonstrate SKETCHREP's efficacy to repair faulty assignments and if-return statements with a benchmark of 35 faults derived from students' solutions. The results show that for these small but complex programs, SKETCHREP can repair errors due to missing statements and faults in multiple locations. The comparison with two well-known repair tools illustrates that SKETCHREP is more effective for addressing these faults.

While the focus of our work in this paper is on program repair using test suites—a common form of the program repair problem—our reduction of repair to sketching can be generalized to repair other forms of correctness criteria, e.g., specifications.

2 Motivating Example

To illustrate our SKETCHREP approach for program repair, we use a program (in the Sketch language) that performs destructive updates on a doubly-linked list data structure. The program is small and conceptually simple, but repairing this faulty version is hard. It contains two missing assignment statements. Our approach successfully repairs it but existing state-of-the-art techniques GenProg [16] and SPR [17] are unable to repair (the C version of) this program using the same tests we use.

Figure 1 presents an implementation of the `addFirst` method for the subject `DoublyLinkedList` in the Sketch language [1]. The implementation of this `DoublyLinkedList` is adapted from `java.util.LinkedList` in `openjdk-6-b27`. The list has a sentinel header whose `previous` field points to the last element of the list, and its `next` field heads to the first element of the list. The `addFirst` method first creates a new `Entry` object with the given value `v` and resets `next` and `previous` fields for the header and the new object `Entry e`. Finally, this method should increase the size of the list by one. The faulty program shown in Fig. 1 (A) forgets to update the field `e.previous.next` and the size of the list.

SKETCHREP tries to identify suspicious types and program statements based on failing test assertions. It ranks the type `int` as the most suspicious type based on the failing test assertion at line 13 in Fig. 1(A). As to suspicious statements, each statement in this program has the same suspiciousness value of the spectra-based fault localization technique. To minimize the change impact introduced by the repair hypothesis, we prioritize program locations that are called later during executions.

After ranking suspicious types and locations, SKETCHREP generates an assignment repair hypothesis of the most suspicious type—`int`. SKETCHREP enumerates all expressions derived from local variables with no more than two

---

(A) DoublyLinkedList.addFirst() that adds an element at the beginning of the list

```
1. void addFirst(LinkedList l, int v) {
2.    Entry e = new Entry();
3.    e.element = v;
4.    e.next = l.head.next;
5.    e.previous = l.head;
6.    //e.previous.next = e; /* Missing this assignment */
7.    e.next.previous = e;
8.    //l.size = l.size +1; /* Missing this assignment */
9. }
   /* one test case: add element 5 into an empty list. */
10. void test1() {
11.    LinkedList l = newList();
12.    addFirst(1,5);
13.    assert l.size ==1;
14.    assert l.head.next.previous == l.head;
15.    assert l.head.next.next == l.head;
16.    assert l.head.next.element == 5;
17.    assert l.head.element == 0;
18. }
```

(B) Repair hypothesis generated by SKETCHREP that finds the repair

```
1. void addFirst(LinkedList l, int v) {
2.    Entry e = new Entry();
3.    e.element = v;
4.    e.next = l.head.next;
5.    e.previous = l.head;
6.    e.next.previous = e;
7.    {|l.size|l.head.element|e(.next|.previous)?(.element)|} =
       {|l.size|l.head.element|e(.next|.previous)?(.element)|??|}(+|-|*|/)??;
8.    {|(l.head|e(.next|.previous)?)(.next|.previous)?|} =
       {|(l.head|e(.next|.previous)?)(.next|.previous)?|null|};
9. }
```

(C) Synthesized repair by Sketch

```
1. void addFirst(LinkedList l, int v) {
2.    Entry e = new Entry();
3.    e.element = v;
4.    e.previous = l.head;
4.    e.next = l.head.next;
5.    e.previous = l.head;
6.    e.next.previous = e;
7.    int _tmp_s = l.size +1;
8.    l.size = _tmp_s; //equivalent to l.size = l.size +1
9.    e.previous.next = e; //correct fix
10. }
```

Fig. 1. *DLLAF6*: a bug that requires to change two statements.

field dereferences and picks expressions whose type is `int`. Specifically, the assignment repair hypothesis at line 7 in Fig. 1(B) contains an *assignment* combinator "=" that glues left-hand-side and right-hand-side together. In Sketch programming language, `e(.next | .previous)?(.element)` represents {`e.element`, `e.next.element`, `e.previous.element`}. The left-hand-side includes all expressions of the type `int` that can be derived from local variables `1` and `e`. The right-hand-side contains all these expressions and a constant value hole "??" that can be replaced by any constant `int` values. For primitive types, SKETCHREP uses four primitive type operators $(+, -, \times, \div)$ to connect two expression sketches together. Similarly to the assignment hypothesis of the type `int`, SKETCHREP generates an assignment repair hypothesis of the type `Entry` based on the failing test assertion at line 14 in Fig. 1(A). This assignment repair hypothesis contains all field dereferences of the type `Entry` at the left-hand-side, and has a `null` value together with these expressions at the right-hand-side.

This partial program shown in Fig. 1(B) is sent to the Sketch synthesizer. The synthesizer finds a concrete replacement that satisfies all test assertions for this non-deterministic program, and this replacement is returned as a correct repair for the faulty program. We present this repair in Fig. 1(C).

3 Approach

In this section, we first describe the overall repair procedure, followed by the fault localization technique and the approach of generating repair hypothesis.

3.1 Overview

Our repair follows the spirit of the synthesis procedure of Feser et al. [7] and maintains a priority queue Q of repair tasks in the form of (p, ℓ, t, ω, E), where p is the faulty program, ℓ is a label for the statement location, t is a suspicious type, ω is a repair hypothesis, and E is the test suite. The repair task is:

> Find a replacement of δ for the hypothesis ω at the location ℓ for program p such that the program $p[\delta/\omega]$ obtained by substituting ω by δ satisfies the test suite E.

Algorithm 1 presents the pseudocode of the overall repair procedure. Our tool first executes the program p with the test suite E to obtain failing test assertions ε. Based on failing test assertions, SKETCHREP uses a fault localization technique to rank suspicious locations and types. For each suspicious type, we add repair tasks (p, ℓ, t, ω, E) to the queue Q with ranked suspicious locations and a repair hypothesis ω.

Given a repair task, SKETCHREP generates expression candidates to fill in the repair hypothesis ω. These expression candidates are derived from local variables with no more than n field dereferences. We use n to represent the bound for repair candidates. The repair hypothesis is further applied to the faulty program, and this faulty program with non-deterministic expression candidates is sent to the

---

Algorithm 1. Overall Repair Procedure

    Input   : Faulty program p, Test suite E, Repair Candidate bound n,
              Hypotheses H
    Output: Repaired program δ

1 **Function** *repair* (p, E) **is**
2 | $\varepsilon \leftarrow run(p, E)$; // `failing assertions`
3 | $T \leftarrow FaultType(p, \varepsilon, E)$;
4 | $L \leftarrow FaultLoc(p, \varepsilon, E)$;
5 | $Q \leftarrow \varnothing$;
6 | **foreach** $\omega \in H$, $t \in T$, $\ell \in L$ **do**
7 | $\lfloor$ $Q \leftarrow Q \cup \{p, \ell, t, \omega, E\}$;
8 | **while** $Q \neq \varnothing$ **do**
9 | | $(\delta, \varepsilon') \leftarrow synthesize(Q.poll(), n)$; // `invoke the Sketch synthesizer`
10 | | **if** $\varepsilon' = NULL$ **then**
11 | | $\lfloor$ **return** δ ;
12 | | **else if** $\varepsilon' \subset \varepsilon$ **then**
13 | | | $T \leftarrow FaultType(\delta, \varepsilon, E)$;
14 | | | $L \leftarrow FaultLoc(\delta, \varepsilon, E)$;
15 | | | $Q \leftarrow \varnothing$;
16 | | | $\varepsilon \leftarrow \varepsilon$;
17 | | | **foreach** $\omega \in H$, $t \in T$, $\ell \in L$ **do**
18 | | | $\lfloor$ $Q \leftarrow Q \cup \{\delta, \ell, t, \omega, E\}$;

19 | **return** $FAIL$;

Sketch synthesizer. The synthesizer will try to complete this partial program based on the test suite. Shown in Algorithm 1, the *synthesize* function returns a program replacement δ and failing assertions ε. A repair is found if all test assertions are satisfied ($\varepsilon = NULL$). If this replacement removes some failing test assertions ($\varepsilon' \subset \varepsilon$), we replace the original program with this new program, clear the queue of repair tasks, and regenerate repair tasks based on the new program. Our repair procedure incrementally evaluates repair tasks in a best-first manner until the synthesizer finds a repair or there is no task left in the queue Q.

3.2 Fault Localization

To speed up our repair approach, we rank suspicious locations and types to save the subsequent expensive synthesizing cost.

Location Ranking. SKETCHREP first calculates spectra-based Tarantula [13] suspiciousness value for each statement in the execution trace. To minimize the change impact introduced by the repair hypothesis, we prioritize statements that are called later during executions leading to failing assertions. This technique allows us to reuse as much of the original implementation as possible. Specifically, the fault localization function *FaultLoc* can be interpreted as below:

$FaultLoc(p, \varepsilon, E) = \lambda_1 S_{spectra} + \lambda_2 S_{order}$, where

$S_{spectra} = \frac{pass(s)/total\ pass}{pass(s)/total\ pass + pass(s)/total\ pass}$, representing the Tarantula suspiciousness value,

$S_{order} = \frac{\#current\ stmt}{\#total\ stmts}$, representing the relative location in the execution leading to the failing test assertion,

λ_1, λ_2 are parameters, which are set to 1 by default.

Type Ranking. To identify which types of objects might lead to the failure, we rank object types by the same spectra-based approach, and prioritize "later" types based on the invocation order used in the first failing test assertion. For instance, based on the failing test assertion "`assert l.size==1`", SKETCHREP prioritizes the type `int` over the type `LinkedList` according to the invocation order. This strategy might not always rank first for the faulty type. For example, based on the assertion "`l.head.element==22`", SKETCHREP will rank type `int` as the most suspicious type while the fault might be on the type `Entry`. To understand whether this ranking strategy is sufficient to reduce search space and synthesizing cost, we conduct an evaluation in Sect. 4.2. Note that we consider exceptions (e.g., `NULLPointerException`) as a special failing assertion and rank types that trigger the exception using the same approach.

3.3   Hypothesis Generation

We define two hypotheses to handle bugs in assignments and conditions. Based on the hypothesis, we generate repair candidates with the type t using no more than n field dereference.

Hypothesis Definition. Fig. 2 presents our definition of repair hypotheses in the style of inference rules [7,17]. The first inference rule describes the *assignment* hypothesis we use to repair faulty assignments with non-primitive types and primitive types. The second and third rules describe the *condition* hypothesis that introduces a new if-condition followed by a return statement which returns a boolean value. We use the annotation of $\sigma \vdash (x, n, t) \Rightarrow e$ to represent all expressions e with the type t in the program σ, which are derived from the variable x using no more than n field dereferences. $p(\ell)$ represents the statement at the location ℓ. $c(x)$ is a conditional expression which is either true or false. $primT$ represents primitive types, such as `int` and `bit`.

Specifically, Fig. 3 shows a condition repair hypothesis that contains an if-condition followed by a return statement that returns a boolean value. Our tool introduces a new method called `_condition` which returns either a boolean value, or an expression combined with a relational operator ("$==$" or "$\neq$"). The return value of the method `_condition` will decide if the condition statement at line 10 will return a boolean value by the following return statement (line 11).

For primitive types, we introduce four basic primitive type operators `op` $\{+, -, \times, \div\}$ to connect the expression e_1 and the constant value hole "`??`".

$$\frac{\sigma \vdash (x,n,t) \Rightarrow e,\ e \in t,\ t \notin primT}{p(\ell) = e\text{=}e_1,\ e_1 = e \cup null} \qquad \frac{\sigma \vdash (x,n,t) \Rightarrow e,\ e \in t,\ t \in primT}{p(\ell) = e\text{=}e_1 \text{ op } ??,\ e_1 = e \cup (??)} \qquad (1)$$

$$\frac{c(x) = \{e\text{==}e_1, e \neq e_1, 0, 1\},\ \sigma \vdash (x,n,t) \Rightarrow e,\ e_1 = e \cup null,\ t \notin primT}{p(\ell) = \text{if } (c(x))\ return\ \{1,0\}} \qquad (2)$$

$$\frac{c(x) = \{e\text{==}(e_1 \text{ op } ??), e \neq (e_1 \text{ op } ??), 0, 1\},\ \sigma \vdash (x,n,t) \Rightarrow e,\ t \in primT}{p(\ell) = \text{if } (c(x))\ return\ \{1,0\}} \qquad (3)$$

Fig. 2. The **assignment** and **condition** repair hypotheses

Repair hypothesis generated from SKETCHREP

```
1.  bit hasLoop(LinkedList l) {
2.    Entry ln1 = l.head;
3.    Entry ln2 = l.head;
4.    while (1)  {
5.      ln1 = ln1.next;
6.      if (ln2.next ==  l.head || ln2.next.next == l.head)
7.        return 0;
8.      ln2 = ln2.next.next;
9.      /* Omission error: miss if (ln1==ln2) return 1;*/
10.     if (_condition(l, ln1, ln2))
11.       return ??;
12.   }
13. }
14. bit _condition(LinkedList l, Entry e1, Entry e2) {
15.   Entry lhs={|l.head (.next)?|(e1 | e2)(.next)?(.next)?|};
16.   Entry rhs={|null|l.head(.next)?|(e1|e2)(.next)?(.next)?|};
17.   bit _out = {| lhs == rhs | lhs != rhs | 1 | 0 |};
18.   return _out;
19. }
```

Fig. 3. *LLOOP3*: a bug that misses a condition statement.

Candidates Generation. After introducing repair hypothesis, SKETCHREP generates candidates for the hypothesis based on the suspicious type. For each visible variable at a program location, SKETCHREP enumerates all expressions within a bound of field dereferences derived from this variable and collects expressions of the suspicious type. These expressions are filled into the hypothesis to create a program sketch—a non-deterministic program as the input of the Sketch synthesizer. We set the default bound for generating candidates as two considering the performance of the synthesizer. In Fig. 3, all bounded candidates of the type `Entry` are `l.head(.next)?` and `(e1|e2)(.next)?(.next)?`. These candidates are used to complete the assignment repair hypothesis of the type `Entry` at line 15.

Hypothesis Prioritization. Each invocation to the synthesizer comes with a cost. Intuitively, the more non-deterministic expression sketches are introduced by the repair hypothesis, the higher synthesizing cost is for the synthesizer. We define the cost of the repair hypothesis as the number of "holes" introduced by the hypothesis. Therefore, an assignment hypothesis of non-primitive type has a synthesizing cost of 2, while a condition hypothesis of this type has a synthesizing cost of 4 (e.g., the condition hypothesis in Fig. 3 has 4 expression sketches at line 15, 16, 17, and 11. SKETCHREP prioritizes less-cost hypotheses considering the performance of the synthesizer. The generated repair skeleton ("hypothesis") filled with non-deterministic candidates are sent to the Sketch synthesizer, searching for a replacement that satisfies the test suite.

4   Evaluation

We evaluate SKETCHREP on a benchmark of 35 faults derived from students' solutions for 7 data structure subjects, which were originally written in Java. The subjects are: SortedLinkedList.insert ($LLINS$), SortedLinkedList.reverse (LL REV), SortedLinkedList.hasLoop ($LLOOP$), DoublyLinkedList.addFirst (DLL AF), DoublyLinkedList.addLast ($DLLAL$), DoublyLinkedList.remove ($DLLRM$), and BinarySearchTree.insert ($BSTIN$). The subject DoublyLinkedList.addFirst and DoublyLinkedList.addLast are programs without branches or loops, while the rest contain both loops and if-conditions. The implementation of the DoublyLinkedList is adapted from java.util.LinkedList while the SortedLinkedList and the BinarySearchTree are implemented based on the book [4].

From the students we received 49 answers for each Java subject, and we manually graded the answers. On average, 10 answers were correct for each subject. For the faulty programs, we manually classified them into 35 different kinds of faults. We manually translated each faulty program from Java to Sketch (to apply SKETCHREP) and to C (to apply GenProg and SPR).

We address the following research questions in the evaluation:

– How effective is SKETCHREP to fix faulty programs using tests?
– How does the fault localization technique affect the ability of SKETCHREP to generate repairs?

4.1   Comparison with GenProg and SPR

To study SKETCHREP's efficacy of repairing faulty program, we execute it, GenProg [16], and SPR [17] on the 35 defects using the same test suites.

Methodology. Considering that the quality of the test suite impacts the performance of program repair tools [22,25], we compare the performance of three tools with two test suites—one based on ideas from bounded exhaustive testing and one consisting of just 3 tests.

We use Korat [2], an input generation tool that uses given constraints which define properties of desired inputs to guide our generation of bounded suites. To illustrate, Fig. 4 (top) presents the input lists with up to 3 nodes, which we use to form test cases for SortedLinkedList.hasLoop(), and Fig. 4 (bottom) presents

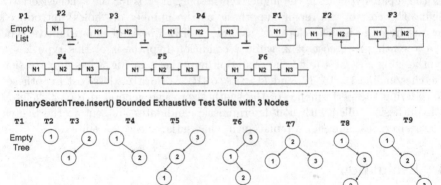

Fig. 4. Bounded exhaustive test suite with 3 nodes.

the different tree structures with up to 3 nodes, which we use to create method sequences that repeatedly invoke the faulty `insert` method, e.g., tree $T5$ represents the sequence "`t=new Tree(); t.insert(3); t.insert(2); t.insert(1);`". To account for repetitions in insertions (or removals) we add a test case that has one insertion (or removal) with a repeated element.

It is conjectured that repair tools are more likely to generate overfitting repairs if used with a few test cases [25], therefore, we create a test suite with a subset of bounded exhaustive tests to investigate the plausibility of repairs generated by SKETCHREP with a few test cases. We randomly pick one passing test, one failing test, and one other test that can be either passing or failing.

Using test suites alone as the criterion for correctness can lead to erroneous repairs [22]. We validate the correctness of generated repairs using an exhaustive test suite with a larger bound (four nodes) than the bound used to create suites. In addition, we manually inspect repairs based on the implementation of `java.util.LinkedList` and a standard textbook [4].

We use the default configuration for SPR and use two search strategies in GenProg: the default brute search strategy (*Brute*) and the genetic algorithm (*GA*). We set a 10-second timeout threshold for the Sketch synthesizer as our experiments show that it is sufficient to generate correct fixes.

Results. Table 1 presents the experiment result for three tools. The first three columns describe the information of the faults: The column LOC shows the lines of code for the method under test, the column *Type* represents that the expected fix is an assignment (A) or a condition (C), and the column *Bug* shows the number of statements that need to be changed. The fifth to eighth column present the number of calls to the Sketch synthesizer (*#Calls*) as well as the number of repair candidates at the statement level (*#Cands*). The rest columns show the comparison result by running SKETCHREP, GenProg, and SPR on the same test suite. The column T_3 represents the result of a subset of exhaustive test cases and the column T_e represents the result of the bounded exhaustive test

Table 1. Comparison with GenProg and SPR

Name	LOC	Type	Bug	Ranking				SKETCHREP				GenProg				SPR	
				#Calls		#Cands		Time		Fix		Brute		GA			
				on	off	on	off	T_3	T_e	T_3	T_e	T_3	T_e	T_3	T_e	T_3	T_e
LLINS1	11	A	1	1	19	168	1,358	1.18	1.14	✓	✓	×	×	×	×	×	×
LLINS2	11	A	1	1	5	72	360	1.08	1.10	✓	✓	×	×	×	×	×	×
LLINS3	11	A	1	1	35	72	360	1.43	1.43	✓	✓	×	×	×	×	×	×
LLINS4	11	A	2	2	24	240	1,718	5.36	70.12	—	✓	×	×	×	×	×	×
LLINS5	11	A	2	2	10	144	720	6.28	34.34	—	—	×	×	×	×	×	×
LLREV1	14	A	1	1	3	210	630	4.38	3.24	—	✓	×	✓	×	×	—	×
LLREV2	14	A	1	1	3	210	630	1.54	1.54	—	✓	×	✓	×	×	—	×
LLREV3	14	A	1	5	3	1,050	420	4.52	2.52	—	✓	×	×	×	×	×	×
LLREV4	14	A	1	5	2	1,050	420	0.71	1.29	—	✓	—	×	×	×	—	×
LLREV5	14	A	2	3	5	630	1,050	4.11	2.29	—	✓	×	×	×	×	—	×
LLREV6	16	A	2	4	6	840	1,260	10.62	10.90	✓	✓	×	×	×	×	—	×
LLREV7	16	A	2	4	6	840	1,260	6.96	9.68	—	✓	×	×	×	×	—	×
LLREV8	16	A	2	7	3	1,470	630	10.49	20.00	—	✓	×	×	×	×	×	×
LLOOP1	19	A	1	3	2	216	144	14.03	82.61	✓	✓	—	×	—	×	×	×
LLOOP2	19	A	1	3	2	216	144	12.57	3.63	—	✓	×	×	×	×	—	×
LLOOP3	19	C	1	31	33	2,564	2,852	14.73	4.58	—	✓	—	×	×	×	×	×
LLOOP4	19	A,C	2	60	60	7,260	7,260	11.58	20.01	—	×	—	×	—	×	×	×
DLLAF1	9	A	1	1	15	168	952	0.93	1.00	—	✓	×	×	×	×	×	×
DLLAF2	9	A	1	1	4	110	440	1.12	1.18	—	✓	×	×	×	×	×	×
DLLAF3	9	A	1	1	4	110	440	1.11	1.20	—	✓	×	×	×	×	×	×
DLLAF4	9	A	1	4	4	440	440	0.66	0.87	✓	✓	×	×	×	×	×	×
DLLAF5	9	A	2	2	8	220	880	2.82	3.03	✓	✓	×	×	×	×	×	×
DLLAF6	9	A	2	2	17	278	1,280	2.82	5.85	—	✓	×	×	×	×	×	×
DLLAF7	9	A	2	2	5	220	550	0.88	11.85	✓	✓	×	×	×	×	×	×
DLLAL1	9	A	1	1	15	168	952	0.78	0.98	✓	✓	×	×	×	×	×	×
DLLAL2	9	A	1	1	4	110	440	1.67	1.42	✓	✓	×	×	×	×	×	×
DLLAL3	9	A	1	4	4	440	440	0.46	0.42	✓	✓	×	×	×	×	×	×
DLLAL4	9	A	1	3	4	330	440	2.63	2.04	—	✓	×	×	×	×	×	×
DLLRM1	15	A	1	3	17	504	1,288	4.14	3.54	—	✓	—	×	—	×	×	×
DLLRM2	15	A	1	3	3	330	330	13.13	11.46	✓	✓	×	×	×	×	×	×
DLLRM3	15	A	2	6	6	660	660	3.41	4.00	—	—	×	×	×	×	×	×
DLLRM4	15	A	2	6	17	834	1,288	4.69	10.18	—	—	×	×	×	×	×	×
BSTIN1	28	A	1	1	52	440	24,076	0.42	10.21	✓	✓	×	×	×	×	×	×
BSTIN2	28	A	1	20	2	18,600	1,860	9.99	10.20	✓	✓	×	×	×	×	×	×
BSTIN3	28	C	1	75	75	34,300	34,300	17.16	14.81	×	×	×	×	×	×	—	×

✓ represents correct fix, — represents plausible fix, × represents not generating fix

suite. The column *Fix* states if SKETCHREP generates correct fix, plausible fix, or no fix. The column *Time* states SKETCHREP's performance time in seconds.

Based on the bounded exhaustive test suite, GenProg is able to generate two correct repairs while SPR can generate none. GenProg and SPR cannot generate correct fixes at multiple locations. Note that GenProg fails to generate repairs for *LLREV1* and *LLREV2* with a subset of test cases, but successfully generates fixes with bounded exhaustive test suite. It is probably because GenProg relies on the spectra-based fault localization technique to identify faulty statements, and the bounded exhaustive test suite helps GenProg prioritize suspicious statements.

SKETCHREP is able to generate 33 repairs for the program repair benchmark and 30 of them are correct based on higher-bound exhaustive test suite and manual inspection. Based on a subset of test cases, SKETCHREP generates more correct repairs compared to other tools as well. While other tools cannot generate repairs at multiple locations, SKETCHREP relies on failing test assertions to incrementally repair the program.

SKETCHREP fails to find the repair for the fault *BSTIN3* because the condition repair hypothesis only generates an `if` condition followed by a return statement that returns either true or false. It does not support conditions which have multiple statements in the condition block. SKETCHREP cannot handle the multiple-location fault *LLOOP4* because the failing test assertion can only be eliminated by changing an assignment and a condition statement together. SKETCHREP generates plausible fixes for *LLINS5*, *DLLRM3*, and *DLLRM4*. In these plausible fixes, apart from repairing errors, SKETCHREP sets values to unreachable objects, such as the removed entry in the subject `DoublyLinkedList. remove()`. This behavior cannot be observed simply using more inputs. We regard these repairs as plausible by checking their semantic behaviors with the manual inspection. As for performance, SKETCHREP takes between 0.4 and 82.6 seconds (10.4 seconds on average) to perform the repair using bounded exhaustive test suites, and between 0.4 and 17.2 seconds (5.2 seconds on average) to perform the repair using subsets of exhaustive test suites.

In summary, SKETCHREP is able to fix a number of faults at the statement level. It can also fix some multi-location faults by incrementally searching for repairs based on tests and failing assertions. We also show that SKETCHREP outperforms previous state-of-the-art repair tools in fixing these faults.

4.2   Efficacy of Fault Localization

To evaluate if our fault localization technique can effectively reduce the number of invocations to the synthesizer and prune the search space of repair candidates, we count the number of calls to the synthesizer and the number of repair candidates at the statement level. The column *off* shows these numbers without ranking suspicious locations and types. The column *on* shows these numbers with fault localization technique. We describe how these numbers are calculated using an example.

The error *DLLAF6* shown in Fig. 1(A) has a failing test assertion at line 13. Based on the invocation order, SKETCHREP prioritizes the type `int` over the type `LinkedList`. For the type `int`, SKETCHREP generates 6 expressions with no more than two field dereferences from local variables: `v, l.size, l.head.element, e.element, e.next.element, e.previous.element`. At the right-hand-side, there are 7 expressions including a constant value hole "??". When we calculate the number of repair candidates, we regard the constant value hole "??" as a simple expression, although in practice it represents a large search space for the SAT solver. SKETCHREP then creates repair hypotheses with 4 primitive type operators $(+, -, \times, \div)$, thus the total search space for fixing this failing assertion is: $6 \times (6 + 1) \times 4$. Based on our fault localization technique,

SKETCHREP puts the partial statement at line 8 in Fig. 1(A), and this replacement removes the failing assertion "`assert l.size==1`" with a concrete implementation "`l.size=l.size+1`". The next failing test assertion at line 14 helps SKETCHREP prioritize the type `Entry`. There are 10 expressions with the type `Entry` in Fig. 1(B), thus the search space for the assignment repair hypothesis at line 8 in Fig. 1(B) represents a search space of $10 \times (10 + 1)$. Therefore, the total search space for fixing this multiple-location bug is 278, with 2 invocations to the synthesizer.

If we turn off the ranking strategy for suspicious types and locations, our tool will search from the first-defined type to the last one followed by primitive types, and check from the first statement to the last one based on the execution trace that invokes the failing assertion until it finds a repair. After checking the location from line 3 to 5, SKETCHREP places an assignment hypothesis of the type `Entry` at the line 6, which fixes the failing test assertion "`assert l.head.next.previous==l.head`". For the failing test assertion "`assert l.size==1`", SKETCHREP checks each location with repair hypotheses of the type `Entry` and `LinkedList`, before it generates a repair hypothesis with the type of `int`. Therefore, the total search space without ranking is $10 \times 11 \times 4 + 6 \times (10 \times 11 + 1 \times 2) + 6 \times 7 \times 4 = 1,280$, and the synthesizer is invoked by 17 times.

On average, SKETCHREP makes 7.7 calls to the synthesizer with fault localization strategy, and makes 12.8 calls without it. The average search space of repair candidates with ranking is 2157.5, and the space is 2642.3 without it. We perform Mann-Whiney test to measure if one dataset is significantly larger than the other and use Cliff's delta effect size to measure how large this difference is. Both numbers with and without ranking strategy are statistically significant ($p < 0.01$, effect size (*medium*): -0.47 and -0.40).

In summary, our experiment demonstrates that our fault localization technique has significantly reduced the calls to the synthesizer and the search space of repair candidates.

4.3   Threads to Validity

Construct Validity. SKETCHREP can fix multiple-location faults incrementally based on the assumption that one change in a statement can remove some failing assertions. However, this assumption may not hold because the fault may require multiple changes to eliminate a single failing assertion.

Currently SKETCHREP only supports two repair hypotheses: assignments and if-conditions followed by return statements that return true or false. SKETCHREP can be extended to support more intricate faults in conditions with abstract condition value similar to SPR [17].

We use off-the-shelf Sketch synthesizer as a basis for repair. Sketch uses counter-example-guided inductive synthesis (CEGIS) for synthesis [26]. Our repair is limited to what Sketch can synthesize.

In our evaluation, we manually translate Java programs to Sketch programs and to C programs to apply SKETCHREP, GenProg, and SPR. While our subjects are small and simple to translate, our manual translation may have inadvertently introduced behavioral differences.

Internal Validity. Using test suites alone as the criterion for correctness may lead to erroneous repairs. Therefore, we manually inspect generated repairs to validate their correctness.

External Validity. The experimental evaluation using a set of small but complex subjects does not necessarily generalize to other programs. Moreover, our repair hypotheses cover only a specific kind of real faults. We investigate the efficacy of SKETCHREP by comparing it with more general purpose tools that have been evaluated against other real faults [16]. Extension of repair hypotheses is future work.

SKETCHREP only works for programs in the Sketch programming language – a small imperative language with loops and recursion, and syntax similar to Java. Limited translations from Java and Python to Sketch exist [11,24] and can provide a basis to apply SKETCHREP to other languages. Our experiment also shows that the Sketch programming language can be applied to a number of real faulty programs using manual translation.

5   Related Work

Program Repair. Search-based repair tools leverage genetic programming [16] and human patch templates [14] to search for a repair that let all test cases pass. Mutation based repair [5] is a popular approach that applies a set of simple mutations to suspicious statements and validates each mutant with the test suite. Yet these tools are confined to reusing existing statements or mutating expressions only.

Other repair tools introduce non-deterministic values to help search for repair candidates. SPR introduces symbolic values for conditions [17] and tries to infer a concrete value for the condition based on the test suite. Similarly, SemFix [20] uses symbolic analysis and leverages constraint solving to generate repairs. The idea of looking for an angelic value [3] is similar to our approach. Yet we make it one step further—we introduce non-deterministic statements and repair the program at the statement level.

Program repair based on specifications has shown its promise as well. AutoFix-E [21] is able to handle some intricate defects in complex data structure for Eiffel program, but it relies on human-written contracts to generate fixes. Gopinath et al. [10] use pre- and post- conditions written in Alloy specification language to identify defects and repair the program, and were the first to conjecture the reduction of program repair to program sketching. Singh et al [24] use detailed specifications to generate feedback for students' faulty python program. We do not require such specifications to fix the program.

Gopinath et al. [9] use machine learning to repair incorrect "Where" clauses in database statements without requiring formal specifications. Gopinath's dissertation extends this idea to a broader class of imperative programs [8].

Demsky et al. [6] use Daikon to learn specifications for data-structure programs, and the specification is used to perform data-structure repair. However, their program invariants are only learnt from passing test cases, which may be different from the specification leading to failing test assertions.

Kneuss et al. [15] fix faulty Scala programs using deductive program synthesis, but they focus on expression-level synthesis and not on generating new statements or fixing multiple-location faults.

Program Synthesis. Program Synthesis techniques such as Program Sketching [26] are able to synthesize code in small but complex programs yet it requires users to provide a partial program as the input of the synthesizer. Other program synthesis tools use input-output examples [7] or oracles [12] to synthesize programs in domain-specific languages. We are different from these techniques in the purpose of debugging an existing faulty program, and translate it to a partial non-deterministic program as the input of the synthesizer.

6 Conclusion

This paper introduces a new approach for automated debugging, specifically for repairing faulty statements with respect to given tests. Our key insight is to reduce the problem of program repair to program sketching and leverage off-the-shelf sketching technology to repair the faulty program. Experimental evaluation using our prototype SKETCHREP shows that our approach is more effective than two previous state-of-the-art techniques for repairing faults in our small but complex subjects.

We believe the close relation between the problem of program repair and the problem of program synthesis holds a key to developing novel approaches that are well-founded, systematic, and scalable for repairing complex faults in code. We hope our work provides a promising start towards realizing such approaches.

Ackowlegement. We thank Armando Solar-Lezama and Rishabh Singh for helpful comments and encouragement. This work was funded in part by the National Science Foundation (NSF Grant No. CCF-1319688).

References

1. The Sketch Programmers Manual. https://people.csail.mit.edu/asolar/manual.pdf. Accessed 07 05 2016
2. Boyapati, C., Khurshid, S., Marinov, D.: Korat: automated testing based on Java predicates. In: ISSTA, pp. 123–133 (2002)
3. Chandra, S., Torlak, E., Barman, S., Bodík, R.: Angelic debugging. In: ICSE (2011)
4. Cormen, T.H., Leiserson, C.E., Rivest, R.L., Stein, C.: Introduction to Algorithms, 3rd edn. MIT Press, Cambridge (2009)
5. Debroy, V., Wong, W.E.: Using mutation to automatically suggest fixes for faulty programs. ICST **2010**, 65–74 (2010)

6. Demsky, B., Ernst, M.D., Guo, P.J., McCamant, S., Perkins, J.H., Rinard, M.C.: Inference and enforcement of data structure consistency specifications. ISSTA **2006**, 233–244 (2006)

7. Feser, J.K., Chaudhuri, S., Dillig, I.: Synthesizing data structure transformations from input-output examples. PLDI **2015**, 229–239 (2015)

8. Gopinath, D.: Systematic techniques for more effective fault localization and program repair. Ph.D. thesis, University of Texas at Austin (2015)

9. Gopinath, D., Khurshid, S., Saha, D., Chandra, S.: Data-guided repair of selection statements. ICSE **2014**, 243–253 (2014)

10. Gopinath, D., Malik, M.Z., Khurshid, S.: Specification-based program repair using SAT. TACAS **2011**, 173–188 (2011)

11. Jeon, J., Qiu, X., Foster, J.S., Solar-Lezama, A.: JSketch: sketching for Java. ESEC/FSE **2015**, 934–937 (2015)

12. Jha, S., Gulwani, S., Seshia, S.A., Tiwari, A.: Oracle-guided component-based program synthesis. ICSE **2010**, 215–224 (2010)

13. Jones, J.A., Harrold, M.J.: Empirical evaluation of the tarantula automatic fault-localization technique. In: (ASE 2005), pp. 273–282 (2005)

14. Kim, D., Nam, J., Song, J., Kim, S.: Automatic patch generation learned from human-written patches. ICSE **2013**, 802–811 (2013)

15. Kneuss, E., Koukoutos, M., Kuncak, V.: Deductive program repair. In: Kroening, D., Păsăreanu, C.S. (eds.) CAV 2015. LNCS, vol. 9207, pp. 217–233. Springer, Heidelberg (2015)

16. Le Goues, C., Nguyen, T., Forrest, S., Weimer, W.: GenProg: a generic method for automatic software repair. IEEE Trans. Softw. Eng. **38**(1), 54–72 (2012)

17. Long, F., Rinard, M.: Staged program repair with condition synthesis. ESEC/FSE **2015**, 166–178 (2015)

18. Malik, M.Z., Ghori, K., Elkarablieh, B., Khurshid, S.: A case for automated debugging using data structure repair. In: ASE, pp. 620–624 (2009)

19. Mechtaev, S., Yi, J., Roychoudhury, A.: Angelix: scalable multiline program patch synthesis via symbolic analysis. In: ICSE 2016 (2016)

20. Nguyen, H.D.T., Qi, D., Roychoudhury, A., Chandra, S.: SemFix: program repair via semantic analysis. ICSE **2013**, 772–781 (2013)

21. Pei, Y., Furia, C.A., Nordio, M., Wei, Y., Meyer, B., Zeller, A.: Automated fixing of programs with contracts. IEEE Trans. Softw. Eng. **40**(5), 427–449 (2014)

22. Qi, Z., Long, F., Achour, S., Rinard, M.C.: An analysis of patch plausibility and correctness for generate-and-validate patch generation systems. In: ISSTA (2015)

23. Saha, R.K., Lease, M., Khurshid, S., Perry, D.E.: Improving bug localization using structured information retrieval. ASE **2013**, 345–355 (2013)

24. Singh, R., Gulwani, S., Solar-Lezama, A.: Automated feedback generation for introductory programming assignments. In: PLDI 2013, pp. 15–26 (2013)

25. Smith, E.K., Barr, E.T., Le Goues, C., Brun, Y.: Is the cure worse than the disease? overfitting in automated program repair. ESEC/FSE **2015**, 532–543 (2015)

26. Solar-Lezama, A.: Program sketching. STTT **15**(5–6), 475–495 (2013)

Polynomial Invariants by Linear Algebra

Steven de Oliveira[1](✉), Saddek Bensalem[2], and Virgile Prevosto[1]

[1] CEA, LIST, Software Reliability and Security Lab,
CEA Saclay - Nano Innov - Bât 862 - PC 174, 91191 Gif Sur Yvette Cedex, France
{steven.deoliveira,virgile.prevosto}@cea.fr
[2] Université Grenoble Alpes, Saint-martin-d'hàres, France
saddek.bensalem@imag.fr

Abstract. We present in this paper a new technique for generating polynomial invariants, divided in two independent parts: a procedure that reduces polynomial assignments composed loops analysis to linear loops under certain hypotheses and a procedure for generating inductive invariants for linear loops. Both of these techniques have a polynomial complexity for a bounded number of variables and we guarantee the completeness of the technique for a bounded degree which we successfully implemented for C programs verification.

1 Introduction

When dealing with computer programming, anyone should be aware of the underlying behavior of the whole code, especially when it comes to life-critical projects composed of million of lines of code [11]. Manual code review cannot scale to the size of actual embedded programs. Testing allows to detect many vulnerabilities but it is never enough to certify their total absence. Indeed, the cost of generating and executing sufficient test cases to meet the most stringent coverage criteria [4] that are expected for critical software becomes quickly prohibitive as the size of the code under test grows. Alternatively, formal methods techniques based on abstraction allow us to prove the absence of error.

However, since a program can, at least in theory, have an infinite number of different behaviors, the verification problem is undecidable and these techniques either lose precision (emitting false alarms) and/or require manual input. One of the main issue of such approach is the analysis of loops, considered as a major research problem since the 70 s [2]. Program verification based on Floyd-Hoare's inductive assertion [10] and CEGAR-like techniques [7] for model-checking uses loop invariants in order to reduce the problem to an acyclic graph analysis [3] instead of unrolling or accelerating loops [12]. Thus, a lot or research nowadays is focused on the automatic inference of loop invariants [17,22].

We present in this paper a new technique for generating polynomial invariants, divided in two independent parts: a *linearization* procedure that reduces the analysis of solvable loops, defined in [22], to the analysis of linear loops; an *inductive invariant generation* procedure for linear loops. Those two techniques are totally independent from each other, we aim to present in this article their

C. Artho et al. (Eds.): ATVA 2016, LNCS 9938, pp. 479–494, 2016.
DOI: 10.1007/978-3-319-46520-3_30

composition in order to find polynomial invariants for polynomial loops. We also add an extension of this composition allowing to treat loops with complex behaviors that induces the presence of complex numbers in our calculation. The linearization algorithm has been inspired by a compiler optimisation technique called *operator strength reduction* [8]. Our invariant generation is completely independent from the initial state of the loop studied and outputs parametrized invariants, which is very effective on programs using a loop multiple times and loops for which we have no knowledge of the initial state. In addition to being complete for a certain class of polynomial relations, the invariant generation technique has the advantage to be faster than the already existing one for such loops as it relies on polynomial complexity linear algebra algorithms.

Furthermore, a tool implementing this method has been developed in the Frama-C framework for C programs verification [15] as a new plug-in called PILAT (standing for **P**olynomial **I**nvariants by **L**inear **A**lgebra **T**ool). We then compared our performances with ALIGATOR [17] and FASTIND [5], two invariant generators working on similar kinds of loops. First experiments over a representative benchmark exposed great improvements in term of computation time.

Outline. The rest of this paper is structured as follows. Section 2 introduces the theoretical concepts used all along the article and the kind of programs we focus on. Section 3 presents the application of our technique on a simple example. Section 4.1 presents the linearization step for simplifying the loop, reducing the problem to the study of affine loops. Section 4.2 presents our contribution for generating all polynomial invariants of affine loops. Section 4.3 extends the method with the treatment of invariants containing non-rational expressions. Finally, Sect. 5 compares PILAT to ALIGATOR and FASTIND. Due to space constraints, proofs have been omitted. They are available in a separate report [9].

State of the Art. Several methods have been proposed to generate invariants for kinds of loops that are similar to the ones we address in this paper. In particular, the weakest precondition calculus of polynomial properties in [20] is based on the computation of the affine transformation kernel done by the program. This method is based on the computation of the kernel of the affine transformation described by the program. More than requiring the whole program to be affine, this method relies on the fact that once in the program there exists a non-invertible assignment, otherwise the kernel is empty. This assumption is valuable in practice, as a constant initialization is non- invertible, so the results may appear at the end of a whole-program analysis and highly depend on the initial state of the program. On the other hand, our method can generate parametrized invariants, computable without any knowledge of the initial state of a loop, making it more amenable to modular verification.

From a constant propagation technique in [19] to a complete invariant generation in [22], Gröbner bases have proven to be an effective way to handle polynomial invariant generation. Such approaches have been successfully implemented in the tool ALIGATOR [17]. This tool generates all polynomial invariants of any degree from a succession of p-solvable polynomial mappings in very few steps. It relies on the iterative computation of Gröbner bases of some polynomial ideals, which is a complicated problem proven to be EXPSPACE-complete [18].

Attempts to get rid of Gröbner bases as in [5] using abstract interpretation with a constant-based instead of a iterative-based technique accelerates the computation of invariants by generating abstract loop invariants. However, this technique is incomplete and misses some invariants. The method we propose here is complete for a particular set of loops defined in [22] in the sense that it finds all polynomial relations P of a given degree verifying $P(X) = 0$ at every step of the loop, and has a polynomial complexity in the degree of the invariants sought for a given number of variables.

2 Preliminaries

Mathematical Background. Given a field $\mathbb{K}$, $\mathbb{K}^n$ is the vector space of dimension n composed by vectors with n coefficients in $\mathbb{K}$. Given a family of vector $\Phi \subset \mathbb{K}^n$, $Vect(\Phi)$ is the vector space generated by Φ. Elements of $\mathbb{K}^n$ are denoted $x = (x_1, ..., x_n)^t$ a column vector. $\mathcal{M}_n(\mathbb{K})$ is the set of matrices of size $n * n$ and $\mathbb{K}[X]$ is the set of polynomials using variables with coefficients in $\mathbb{K}$. We note $\overline{\mathbb{K}}$ the algebraic closure of $\mathbb{K}$, $\overline{\mathbb{K}} = \{x | \exists P \in \mathbb{K}[X], P(x) = 0\}$. We will use $\langle ., . \rangle$ the linear algebra standard notation, $\langle x, y \rangle = x \cdot y^t$, with $\cdot$ the standard dot product. The kernel of a matrix $A \in \mathcal{M}_n(\mathbb{K})$, denoted $\ker(A)$, is the vector space defined as $\ker(A) = \{x | x \in \mathbb{K}^n, A.x = 0\}$. Every matrix of $\mathcal{M}_n(\mathbb{K})$ admits a finite set of eigenvalues $\lambda \in \overline{\mathbb{K}}$ and their associated eigenspaces E_λ, defined as $E_\lambda = \ker(A - \lambda Id)$, where Id is the identity matrix and $E_\lambda \neq \{0\}$. Let E be a $\mathbb{K}$ vector space, $F \subset E$ a sub vector space of E and x an element of F. A vector y is *orthogonal* to x if $\langle x, y \rangle = 0$. We denote $F^\perp$ the set of vectors orthogonal to every element of F.

Programming Model. We use a basic programming language whose syntax is given in Fig. 1. *Var* is a set of variables that can be used by a program, and which is supposed to have a total order. Variables take value in a field $\mathbb{K}$. A program state is then a partial mapping $Var \rightharpoonup \mathbb{K}$. Any given program only uses a finite number n of variables. Thus, program states can be represented as a vector $X = (x_1, ..., x_n)^t$. In addition, we will note $X' = (x'_1, ..., x'_n)^t$ the program state after an assignment. Finally, we assume that for all programs, there exists $x_{n+1} = x'_{n+1} = \mathbb{1}$ a constant variable always equal to 1.

The i OR i instruction refers to a non-deterministic condition.

Each i will be refered to as one of the *bodies* of the loop.

Multiple variables assignments occur simultaneously within a single instruction. We say that an instruction is affine when it is an assignment for which the right values are affine. If not, we divide instructions in two categories with respect to the following definition, from [22].

$$
\begin{array}{ll}
i ::= i;i & exp ::= \quad cst \in \mathbb{K} \\
\quad | \quad (x_1,..,x_n){:=}(exp_1,...,exp_n) & \quad | \; x \in Var \\
\quad | \quad i \textbf{ OR } i & \quad | \; exp + exp \\
\quad | \quad \textbf{while } (*) \textbf{ do } i \textbf{ done} & \quad | \; exp * exp
\end{array}
$$

Fig. 1. Code syntax

Definition 1. *Let $g \in \mathbb{Q}[X]^m$ be a polynomial mapping. g is solvable if there exists a partition of X into subvectors of variables $x = w_1 \uplus ... \uplus w_k$ such that $\forall j,\ 1 \leqslant j \leqslant k$ we have*

$$
g_{w_j}(x) = M_j w_j^T + P_j(w_1, ..., w_{j-1})
$$

with $(M_i)_{1\leqslant i\leqslant k}$ a matrix family and $(P_i)_{1\leqslant i\leqslant k}$ a family of polynomial mapping.

An instruction is solvable if the associated assignment is a solvable polynomial mapping. Otherwise, it is unsolvable. Our technique focuses on loops containing only solvable instructions, thus it is not possible to generate invariants for nested loops. It is however possible to find an invariant for a loop containing no inner loop even if it is itself inside a loop, that's why we allow the construction.

3   Overview of Our Approach

Steps of the Generation. In order to explain our method we will take the following running example, for which we want to compute all invariants of degree 3:

```
while (*) do
    (x, y) := (x + y*y,  y + 1)
done
```

Our method is based on two distinct parts:

1. reduction of the polynomial loop to a linear loop;
2. linear invariant generation from the linearized loop.

We want to find a linear mapping f that *simulates* the behavior of the polynomial mapping $P(x,y) = (x + y^2, y + 1)$. To achieve this, we will express the value of every monomial of degree 2 or more using brand new variables. Here, the problem comes from the y^2 monomial. In [20], it is described how to consider the evolution of higher degree monomials as affine applications of lower or equal degree monomials when the variables involved in those monomials evolve affinely. We extend this method to express monomials transformations of the loop by affine transformations, reducing the problem to a simpler loop analysis. For example here, $y' = y + 1$ is an affine assignment, so there exists an affine representation of $y_2 = y^2$, which is $y_2' = y_2 + 2.y + 1$. Assuming the initial y_2 is correct, we are sure to express the value of y^2 with the variable y_2. Also, if we want to find invariants of degree 3, we will need to express all monomials of degree 3, i.e. xy and y_3 the same way. (monomials containing x^i with $i \geqslant 2$ are irrelevant as their expression require the expression of degree 4 monomials). Applying this method to P gives us the linear mapping $f(x, y, y_2, xy, y_3, \mathbb{1}) = (x + y_2, y + \mathbb{1}, y_2 + 2.y + \mathbb{1}, xy + x + y_2 + y_3, y_3 + 3.y_2 + 3.y + \mathbb{1}, \mathbb{1})$, with $\mathbb{1}$ the constant variable mentioned in the previous section.

Now comes the second part of the algorithm, the invariant generation. Informally, an invariant for a loop is a formula that

1. is valid at the beginning of the loop;
2. stays valid after every loop step.

We are interested in finding *semi-invariants* complying only with the second criterion such that they can be expressed as a linear equation over X, containing the assignment's original variables and the new ones generated by the linearization procedure. In this setting, a formula satisfying the second criterion is then a vector of coefficients φ such that

$$\langle \varphi, X \rangle = 0 \Rightarrow \langle \varphi, f(X) \rangle = 0 \tag{1}$$

By linear algebra, the following is always true

$$\langle \varphi, f(X) \rangle = \langle f^*(\varphi), X \rangle \tag{2}$$

where f^* is the dual of f. If φ happens to be an eigenvector of f^* (i.e. there exists λ such that $f^*(\varphi) = \lambda \varphi$), the Eq. (1) becomes

$$\langle \varphi, X \rangle = 0 \Rightarrow \langle f^*(\varphi), X \rangle = 0 \text{ by (2)}$$
$$\langle \varphi, X \rangle = 0 \Rightarrow \langle \lambda.\varphi, X \rangle = 0$$
$$\langle \varphi, X \rangle = 0 \Rightarrow \lambda.\langle \varphi, X \rangle = 0$$

which is always true. We just need to *transpose* the matrix representing f to compute f^*. It returns $f^*(x, y, y_2, y_3, \mathbb{1}) = (x, y + y_2 + y_3, x + y_2 + 3.y_3, y_3, y + y_2 + y_3 + \mathbb{1}, y + y_2 + y_3 + \mathbb{1})$. f^* only admits the eigenvalue 1. The eigenspace of f^* associated to 1 is generated by two independants vectors, $e_1 = (-6, 1, -3, 2, 0)^t$ and $e_2 = (0, 0, 0, 0, 1)^t$. Eventually, we get the formula $F_{k1,k2} = (k_1.(-6.x + y - 3.y_2 + 2.y_3) + k_2.\mathbb{1} = 0)$ as invariant, with $k_1, k_2 \in \mathbb{Q}$. By writing $k = -\frac{k_2}{k_1}$ and replacing $\mathbb{1}$ with 1, we can rewrite it with only one parameter, $F_k = (-6.x + y - 3.y_2 + 2y_3 = k)$. In this case, information on the initial state of the loop allows to fix the value of the parameter k. For example if the loop starts with $(x = 0, y = 0)$, then $-6.x + y - 3.y^2 + 2.y^3 = 0$, and F_0 is an invariant. The next section will show how the work done on our example can be generalized on any (solvable) loop. In particular, Sect. 4.1 will deal with the linearization of polynomial assignments. Then we will see in Sect. 4.2 that the eigenspace of the application actually represents all the possible invariants of f and that we can always reduce them to find a formula with only one parameter.

Extension of the Basic Method. The application's eigenvector may not always be rational. For example, applying the previous technique on a mapping such as $f(x,y) = (y, 2.x)$ will give us invariants with coefficients involving $\sqrt{2}$. Dealing with irrational and/or complex values raises some issues in our current implementation setting. Therefore, we propose in Sect. 4.3 a solution to stick with rational numbers. Eventually, we treat the case when a condition occur in loops in Sect. 4.4.

4   Automated Generation of Loop Invariants

4.1   Strength Reduction of Polynomial Loops

Lowerization. Let P be a program containing a single loop with a single solvable assignment $X := g(X)$. In order to reduce the invariant generation problem for solvable polynomial loops to the one for affine loops, we need to find a linear mapping f that perfectly matches g. As shown in Fig. 2, the first loop L1 is polynomial but there exists a similar affine loop, namely L2, computing the same vector of values plus and thanks to an extra variable xy.

```
L1 :

while (*) do
  (x, y, z) := (x + 1,  y + 2,  z + x*y)
done

L2 :

xy = x*y
while (*) do
  (x, y, xy, z) := (x + 1,  y + 2,  xy + 2x + y + 2,  z + xy)
done
```

Fig. 2. Polynomial and affine loop having the same behavior

Definition 2. *Let g be a polynomial mapping of degree d using m variables. g is linearizable if there exists a linear mapping f such that $X' = g(X) \Rightarrow (X', P(X')) = f(X, P(X))$, where $P : \mathbb{Q}^m \to \mathbb{Q}^n$ is a polynomial of degree d.*

By considering polynomials as entries of the application, we are able to consider the evolution of the polynomial value instead of recomputing it for every loop step. This is the case in the previous example, where the computation of xy as $x * y$ is made once at the beginning of the loop. Afterwards, its evolution depends linearly of itself, x and y. Similarly, if we want to consider y^n for some

$n \geq 2$, we would just need to express the evolution of y^n by a linear combination of itself and *lower degree monomials*, which could themselves be expressed as linear combinations of lower degree monomials, until we reach an affine application. We call this process the polynomial mappings *lowerization* or *linearization*.

Remark. This example and our running example have the good property to be linearizable. However, this property is not true for all polynomials loops. Consider for example the mapping $f(x) = x^2$. Trying to express x^2 as a linear variable will force us to consider the monomials x^4, x^8 and so on. Thus, we need to restrain our study to mappings that *do not polynomially transform a variable itself*. This class of polynomials corresponds to solvable polynomial mappings, defined in Definition 1.

Property 1. *For every solvable polynomial mapping g, g is linearizable.*

For example, let $g(x, y) = (x + y^2, y + 1)$. g is linearized by $f(x, y, y_2) = (x + y_2, y + 1, y_2 + 2y + 1)$. Indeed with $(x', y') = g(x, y)$, we have $(x', y', y'^2) = f(x, y, y^2)$

Linearization Algorithm. The algorithm is divided in two parts: the solvability verification of the mapping and, if successful, the linearization process. The solvability verification consists in finding an appropriate partitioning of the variables that respects the solvable constraint. It is nothing more than checking that a variable v cannot be in a polynomial (i.e. non linear) assignment of another variable that itself depend on v. This check can be reduced to verifying the acyclicity of a graph, which can be computed e.g. by Tarjan's [23] or Johnson's [13] algorithms.

The linearization process then consists in considering all monomials as new variables, then finding their linear evolution by replacing each of their variables by the transformation made by the initial application. This may create new monomials, for which we similarly create new variables until all necessary monomials have been mapped to a variable. Since we tested the solvability of the loop, the variable creation process will eventually stop. Indeed, if this was not the case, this would mean that a variable x transitively depends on x^d with $d > 1$.

Elevation. We saw how to transform a polynomial application into a linear mapping by adding extra variables representing the successive products and powers of every variable. This information can be useful in order to generate invariants but in fact, most of the time, this is not enough. In our running example of Sect. 2, $g(x, y) = (x + y^2, y + 1)$, the degree of the mapping is 2 but there exists no invariant of degree 2 for this loop. In order to deal with higher-degree invariants, we need not just to linearize g, we also have to add more variables to our study. As we can represent monomials of variables of a solvable mapping as linear applications, we can extend the method to generate higher degree monomials such as y^3 for example : we *elevate* g to a higher degree. The process of elevation is described in [20] as a way to express polynomial relations on a linear program.

Property 2. *Every solvable polynomial mapping g using n variables is lineariz-able by a linear mapping f using at most $\binom{n+d}{d}$ new variables, where d is the degree of P, the polynomial linearizing g as in Definition 2.*

Note. The complexity of the transformation is *polynomial* for d or n fixed. The lowerization algorithm can be used as shown above by adding variables computing the high degree monomials we want to linearize. Moreover, $\binom{n+d}{d}$ is an upper bound and in practice, we usually need much less variables. For instance, in our running example, we don't need to consider $x.y^2$. Indeed, if we tried to linearize this monomial, we would end up with $x.y^2 = x.y^2+x.y+x+y^4+2y^3+y^2$, a polynomial of degree 4. Detecting that a monomial m is relevant or not can be done by computing the degree of its transformation. For example, the assignment of $\dot{x}$ is a degree 2 polynomial, so x^2 associated transformation will be of degree 4. Here, there is actually only two interesting monomials of degree 3, which are xy and y^3. Though those variables will be useless for the linearized mapping, they are still easily computable: $y'_3 = y_3+3.y_2+3.y+1$ and $xy = xy+x+y_2+y_3$. This limits the necessary variables to only 6 $(x, y, y_2, y_3, xy, \mathbb{1})$ instead of $\binom{5}{2} = 10$. This upper bound in only reached for affine transformations when searching for polynomial invariants, as all possible monomials need to be treated.

4.2   Invariant Generation

The transformation described previously doesn't linearize a whole program, but only a loop. Polynomial assignments must be performed before the loop starts to initialize the new monomials. The method we present only focuses on the loop behavior itself, allowing any kind of operation outside of the loop.

Eigenspace. Loop invariants are logical formulas satisfied at every step of a loop. We can characterize them with two criteria: they have to hold at the beginning of the loop (initialization criterion) and if they hold at one step, then they hold at the next step (heredity criterion). Our technique is based on the discovery of linear combinations of variables that are equal to 0 and satisfying the heredity criterion. For example, the loop of Sect. 3 admits the formula $-6.x + y - 3.y_2 + 2y_3 = k$ as a good invariant candidate. Indeed, if we set k in accordance with the values of the variables at the beginning of the loop, then this formula will be true for any step of the loop. We call such formulas *semi-invariants*.

Definition 3. *Let $\varphi : \mathbb{K}^n \mapsto \mathbb{K}$ and $f : \mathbb{K}^n \mapsto \mathbb{K}^n$ two linear mappings. φ is a semi-invariant for f iff $\forall X$, $\varphi(X) = 0 \Rightarrow \varphi(f(X)) = 0$.*

Definition 4. *Let $\varphi : \mathbb{K}^n \mapsto \mathbb{K}$, $f : \mathbb{K}^n \mapsto \mathbb{K}^n$ and $X \in \mathbb{K}^n$. φ is an invariant for f with initial state X iff $\varphi(X) = 0$ and φ is a semi-invariant for f.*

The key point of our technique relies on the fact that if there exists $\lambda, f^*(\varphi) = \lambda\varphi$, then we know that φ is a semi-invariant. Indeed, we can rewrite Definition 3 by $\langle \varphi, x \rangle = 0 \Rightarrow \langle \varphi, f(x) \rangle = 0$. By linear algebra, we have $\langle \varphi, f(x) \rangle = \langle f^*(\varphi), x \rangle$, with f^* the dual of f. If $\exists \lambda, f^*(\varphi) = \lambda\varphi$, then we can deduce that $\langle \varphi, x \rangle = 0 \Rightarrow$

$\lambda\langle\varphi, x\rangle = 0$. This formula is always true, thus we know that φ is a semi-invariant. Such φ are commonly called *eigenvectors* of f^*. We will not adress the problem of computing the eigenvectors of an application as this problem have been widely studied (in [21] for example).

Recall our running example $g(x, y) = (x + y^2, y + 1)$, linearized by the application $f(x, y, y_2, xy, y_3, \mathbb{1}) = (x + y_2, y + \mathbb{1}, y_2 + 2y + \mathbb{1}, xy + x + y_2 + y_3, y_3 + 3y_2 + 3y + \mathbb{1}, \mathbb{1})$. f^* admits $e_1 = (-6, 1, -3, 0, 2, 0)^t$ and $e_2 = (0, 0, 0, 0, 0, 1)^t$ as eigenvectors associated to the eigenvalue $\lambda = 1$. It means that if $\langle k_1.e_1 + k_2 e_2, x\rangle = 0$, then

$$\begin{aligned}
\langle k_1.e_1 + k_2 e_2, f(X)\rangle &= \langle f^*(k_1.e_1 + k_2 e_2), X\rangle \\
&= \langle \lambda(k_1.e_1 + k_2 e_2), X\rangle \\
&= 0
\end{aligned}$$

In other words, $\langle k_1.e_1 + k_2 e_2, X\rangle = 0$ is a semi-invariant. Then, by expanding it, we can find that $-6.x + y - 3.y_2 + 2y_3 = k$, with $k = -\frac{k_2}{k_1}$ is a semi-invariant. In terms of the original variables, we have thus $-6.x + y - 3.y^2 + 2y^3 = k$.

Being an eigenvector of f^* does not just guarantee a formula to be a semi-invariant of a loop transformed by f. This is also a necessary condition.

Theorem 1. $\varphi : \mathbb{K}^n \mapsto \mathbb{K}$ *is a semi-invariant if and only if* $\exists \lambda \in \mathbb{K}, \exists \varphi \in E_\lambda$, *where* $E_\lambda = ker(f^* - \lambda Id)$.

It is now clear that the set of invariants is exactly the union of all eigenspaces of f^*, i.e. a vector space union (which is not a vector space itself). An element φ of E_λ of basis $\{e_1, ... e_n\}$ is a linear combination of $e_1, ..., e_n$:

$$\varphi = \sum_{k=1}^{n} k_i e_i$$

The parameters k_i can be chosen with respect to the initial state of the loop.

Expression of Eigenvectors as Invariants. More than a syntactic sugar, the variable $\mathbb{1}$ brings interesting properties over the kind of invariants we generate for an application f. The vector e_1 such that $\langle e_1, X\rangle = \mathbb{1}$ is always an eigenvector associated to the eigenvalue 1. Indeed, by definition $f(\mathbb{1}) = \mathbb{1}$, hence $f^*(e_1) = e_1$. For example, let's take the mapping $f(x, y, xy, \mathbb{1}) = (2x, \frac{1}{2}y + 1, xy + 2x, \mathbb{1})$. This mapping admits 3 eigenvalues : 2, $\frac{1}{2}$ and 1. There exists two eigenvectors for the eigenvalue 1 : $(-2, 0, 1, 0)$ and $(0, 0, 0, 1) = e_1$. We have then the semi-invariant $k_1.(-2x + xy) + k_2 = 0$, or $-2x + xy = \frac{-k_2}{k_1}$. This implies that the two parameters k_1 and k_2 can be reduced to only one paramter $k = \frac{-k_2}{k_1}$, which simplifies a lot the equation by providing a way to compute the parameter at the initial state if we know it. For our example, $\frac{-k_2}{k_1}$ would be $-2x_{init} + x_{init}.y_{init}$, where x_{init} and y_{init} are the initial values of x and y. More generally, each eigenvector associated to 1 gives us an invariant φ that can be rewritten as $\varphi(X) = k$, where k is inferred from the initial value of the loop variables.

We can generalize this observation to eigenvectors associated to any eigenvalue. To illustrate this category, let us take as example $f(x, y, z) = (2x, 2y, 2z)$. Eigenvectors associated to 2 are $e_1 = (1, 0, 0)$, $e_2 = (0, 1, 0)$ and $e_3 = (0, 0, 1)$, thus $k_1 x + k_2 y + k_3 z = 0$ is a semi invariant, for any k_1, k_2 and k_3 satisfying the formula for the initial condition of the loop. However, if we try to set e.g. $k_1 = k_2 = 1$, using $x + y + kz = 0$ as semi invariant, we won't be able to find a proper invariant when y_{init} or $x_{init} \neq 0$ and $z_{init} = 0$. Thus, in order to keep the genericity of our formulas, we cannot afford to simplify the invariant as easily as we can do for invariants associated to the eigenvalue 1. Namely for every e_i, we have to test whether $\langle e_i, X_{init} \rangle = 0$. For each e_i for which this is the case, $\langle e_i, X \rangle = 0$ is itself an invariant if $\langle e_i, X_{init} \rangle = 0$. However, if there exists an i such that $\langle e_i, X_{init} \rangle \neq 0$, then we can simplify the problem. For example, we assume that $z_{init} \neq 0$. Then $k_1 x_{init} + k_2 y_{init} + k_3 z_{init} = 0 \Leftrightarrow \frac{k_1 x_{init} + k_2 y_{init}}{z_{init}} = -k_3$. We know then that $k_1 x + k_2 y = \frac{k_1 x_{init} + k_2 y_{init}}{z_{init}} z$ is a semi-invariant. By writing $g(k_1, k_2) = \frac{k_1 x_{init} + k_2 y_{init}}{z_{init}}$, we have

$$\begin{cases} x = g(1, 0)z \\ y = g(0, 1)z \end{cases}$$

As g is a linear application, these two invariants implies that $\forall k_1, k_2, k_1 x + k_2 y = g(k_1, k_2)z$ is a semi-invariant.

Property 3. *Let $\mathcal{F}$ a semi-invariant expressed as $\mathcal{F} = \sum\limits_{i=0}^{n} k_i e_i$.*

If $\langle e_0, X_{init} \rangle \neq 0$, then we have that

$$\bigwedge_{i=1}^{n} (\langle e_i, X \rangle = -\frac{\langle e_i, X_{init} \rangle}{\langle e_0, X_{init} \rangle} \langle e_0, X \rangle) \text{ is an invariant} \Leftrightarrow \langle \mathcal{F}, X_{init} \rangle = 0$$

We are now able to use pairs of eigenvectors to express invariants by knowing the initial condition.

Algorithm. As we are restricting our study to solvable loops, that we know can be replaced without loss of generality by linear loops, we assume the input of this algorithm is a family of linear mappings. We can easily compose them via their matrix representation. We end up with a new matrix A. Computing the dual of A is computing the matrix A^T. Then, eigenvectors of A^T can be computed by many algorithms in the linear algebra literature [21]. As the eigenvalue problem is known to be polynomial, our invariant generation algorithm is also polynomial.

4.3   Extension of the Method

Let $A \in \mathcal{M}_n(\mathbb{Q})$. In the general case, A admits irrational and complex eigenvalues and eigenvectors, which end up generating irrational or complex invariants. We cannot accept such representation for a further analysis of the input program because of the future use of these invariants, by SMT solvers for example which hardly deal with non-rational numbers. For example, let us take the function $f(x, y) = (y, 2x)$. This mapping admits two eigenvalues: $\lambda_x = \sqrt{2}$ and

$\lambda_y = -\sqrt{2}$. In this example, the previous method would output the invariants $k.(x + \sqrt{2}y) = 0$ and $k'.(x - \sqrt{2}y) = 0$. With x and y integers or rationals, this would be possible iff $k = k' = 0$. However, by considering the variable xy the invariant generation procedure outputs the invariant $k.(xy) = 0$, which is possible if x or y equals 0. This raises the issue of finding a product of variables that will give us a rational invariant. We aim to treat the problem at its source: the algebraic character of the matrix eigenvalues. A value x is algebraic in $\mathbb{Q}$ if there exists a polynomial P in $\mathbb{Q}[X]$ such that $P(x) = 0$. Assuming we have a geometric relation between the complex eigenvalues λ_i (i.e. a product q of eigenvalues that is rational), we will build a monomial m as a product of variables x_i associated to λ_i such that the presence of this monomial induces the presence of a rational eigenvalue, namely q. Moreover, a rational eigenvalue of a matrix is always associated to a rational eigenvector. Indeed, the kernel of a rational matrix is always a $\mathbb{Q}$-vector space. If $\lambda \in \mathbb{Q}$ is an eigenvalue of A, then $A - \lambda.Id$ is a rational matrix and its kernel is not empty.

Definition 5. *Let $A \in M_n(\mathbb{Q})$. We denote $\Psi_d(A)$ the elevation matrix such that $\forall X = (x_1, ..., x_n) \in \mathbb{Q}^n, \Psi_d(A).p(X) = p(A.X)$, with $p \in (\mathbb{Q}[X]^k)$ a polynomial associating X to all possible monomials of degree d or lower.*

For example, if we have $A = \begin{pmatrix} a & b \\ c & d \end{pmatrix}$ as a transformation for $X = (x, y)$, we have as transformation for the variables (x^2, xy, y^2, x, y) the matrix

$$\Psi_2(A) = \begin{pmatrix} a^2 & 2ab & b^2 & 0 & 0 \\ ac & ad + bc & bd & 0 & 0 \\ c^2 & 2cd & d^2 & 0 & 0 \\ 0 & 0 & 0 & a & b \\ 0 & 0 & 0 & c & d \end{pmatrix}$$

Property 4. *Let $A \in M_d(\mathbb{Q}), \Lambda(M)$ the eigenvalue set of a matrix M and d an integer. Then for any product p of d or less elements of $\Lambda(A), p \in \Lambda(\Psi_d(A))$.*

We can generalize this property for more variables. After working with two variables, we get a new matrix with new variables that we can combine similarly, and so on. Thanks to this property, if we have a multiplicative relation between eigenvalues we are able to create *home-made* variables in the elevated application whose presence implies the presence of rational eigenvalues.

Though we could brute-force the search of rational products of irrational eigenvalues in order to find all possibilities of variable products that have rational eigenvalues, we could search for algebraic relations, i.e. multiplicative relations between algebraic values. This subject is treated in [14] and we will not focus on it. However, we can guarantee that there exists at least one monomial having a rational eigenvalue. Indeed, it is known that the product of all eigenvalues of a rational matrix is equal to its determinant. As the determinant of a rational matrix is always rational, we know that the product of all variables infers the presence of the determinant of the matrix as eigenvalue of the elevated matrix.

Coming back to the previous example, we have the algebraic relation $\lambda_x.\lambda_y = -2$. If we consider the evolution of xy, we have $(xy') = 2xy$. Note that the eigenvalue associated to xy is 2 and not -2. Indeed, we know that $A = P^{-1}JP$, with

$$P = \begin{pmatrix} 1 & -1 \\ \sqrt{2} & -\sqrt{2} \end{pmatrix}$$

and J an upper-triangular matrix, which means the eigenvalues of A are on the diagonal of J. xy in the base of J would be $(x + \sqrt{2}y)(x - \sqrt{2}y) = x^2 - 2y^2$, and we have well $\lambda_x^2 - 2\lambda_y^2 = -2$.

Finally, by knowing that $\lambda_x^2 = 2$, $\lambda_y^2 = 2$ and $\lambda_x\lambda_y = -2$, we will consider the variables x^2, y^2 and xy in our analysis of f. We can deduce new semi-invariants from these variables: $k_1(xy) + k_2(2x^2 + y^2) = 0$ with the eigenvectors associated to 2 and $k.(y^2 - 2x^2) = 0$ with the eigenvector associated to -2.

4.4 Multiple Loops

In this short section, we present our method to treat non-deterministic loops, i.e. loops with non-deterministic conditions. At the beginning of each iteration, the loop can choose randomly between all its bodies. This representation is equivalent to the definition in Sect. 2.

Definition 6. *Let $F = \{A_i\}_{1 \leqslant i \leqslant n}$ a family of matrices and $Inv(F)$ the set of invariants of a loop whose different bodies can be encoded by elements of F.*

$$Inv(F) = \{\varphi | \forall X, \varphi.X = 0 \Rightarrow \bigwedge_{i=1}^{n} \varphi.A_i.X = 0\}$$

Property 5. *Let $F = \{A_i\}_{1 \leqslant i \leqslant n}$ a family of matrices.*

$$Inv(F) = \bigcap_{i=1}^{n} Inv(A_i)$$

As the set of invariants of a single-body loop are a vector spaces union, its intersection with another set of invariants is also a vector space union. Although we do not consider the condition used by the program to choose the correct body, we still can discover useful invariants. Let us consider the following example, taken from [22], that computes the product of x and y in variable z:

```
while (*) do
    (x, y, z) := (2x, (y−1)/2, x + z)
    OR
    (x, y, z) := (2x, y/2, z)
done
```

We have to deal with two applications: $f_1(x, y, z) = (2x, (y - 1)/2, x + z)$ and $f_2(x, y, z) = (2x, y/2, z)$. The elevation to the degree 2 of f_1 and f_2 returns applications having both 10 eigenvectors. For simplicity, we focus on invariants associated to the eigenvalue 1.

f_1^* has 4 eigenvectors $\{e_i\}_{i \in [1,4]}$ associated to 1 such that

- $\langle e_1, X \rangle = -x + xy$
- $\langle e_2, X \rangle = x + z$
- $\langle e_3, X \rangle = xz + x^2 + z^2$
- $\langle e_4, X \rangle = \mathbb{1}$

f_2^* also has 4 eigenvectors $\{e_i'\}_{i \in [1,4]}$ associated to 1 such that

- $\langle e_1', X \rangle = xy$
- $\langle e_2', X \rangle = z$
- $\langle e_3', X \rangle = z^2$
- $\langle e_4', X \rangle = \mathbb{1}$

First, we notice that $e_4 = e_4'$. Then, we can see that $\langle e_1 + e_2, X \rangle = xy + z = \langle e_1' + e_2', X \rangle$. Thus, $e_1 + e_2 = e_1' + e_2'$. Eventually, we find that $e_1 + e_2 + k.e_4 \in (Vect(\{e_i\}_{i \in [1,4]}) \cap Vect(\{e_i'\}_{i \in [1,4]}))$. That's why $(\langle e_1 + e_2 + k.e_4, X \rangle = 0)$ is a semi-invariant for both f_1 and f_2, hence for the whole loop. Replacing $\langle k.e_4, X \rangle$ by $k = -k'$ and $\langle e_1 + e_2, X \rangle$ by $xy + z$ gives us $xy + z = k'$.

Algorithm. The intersection of two vector spaces corresponds to the vectors that both vector spaces have in common. It means that such elements can be expressed by elements of the base of each vector space. Let B_1 and B_2 the bases of the two vector spaces. If $e \in \text{Vect}\{B_1\}$ and $e \in \text{Vect}\{B_2\}$, then $e \in \ker\{(B_1 B_2)\}$. To compute the intersection of a vector space union, we just have to compute the kernels of each combination of vector space in the union.

5 Implementation and Experimentation

In order to test our method, we implemented an invariant generator as a plugin of Frama-C [15], a framework for the verification of C programs written in OCaml. Tests have been made on a Dell Precision M4800 with 16 GB RAM and 8 cores. Time does not include parsing time of the code, but only the invariant computation from the Frama-C representation of the program to the formulas. Moreover, our tool doesn't implement the extension of our method and may output irrational invariants or fail on complex eigenvalues. Benchmark is available at [6]. The second column of the Table 1 represents the number of variables used in the program. The third column represents the invariant degree used for PILAT and FASTIND. The last three columns are the computation time of the tools in *ms*. O.O.T. represents an aborted ten minutes computation and – indicates that no invariant is found.

All the tested functions are examples for which the presence of a polynomial invariant is compulsory for their verification. The choice of high degree for some functions is motivated by our will to show the efficiency of our tool to find high degree invariants as choosing a higher degree induces computing a bigger set of relations. In the other cases, degree is choosen for its usefulness.

For example in Fig. 3 we were interested in finding the invariant $x + qy = k$ for eucli_div. That's why we set the degree to 2. Let X be the vector of variables $(x, y, q, xq, xy, qy, y_2, x_2, q_2, \mathbb{1})$. The matrix A representing the loop in Fig. 3 has only one eigenvalue: 1. There exist 4 eigenvectors $\{e_i\}_{i \in [1;4]}$ associated to 1 in A, so $\langle \sum_{i=1}^{4} k_i e_i, X \rangle = 0$ is a semi-invariant. One of these eigenvectors, let's

Table 1. Performance results with our implementation PILAT

| Program | | | Time (in ms) | | |
Name	Var	Degree	ALIGATOR [16]	FASTIND [5]	PILAT
divbin	5	2	80	6	2.5
hard	6	2	89	13	2
mannadiv	5	2	27	6	2
sqrt	4	2	33	5	1.5
djikstra	5	2	279	31	4
euclidex2	8	2	1759	10	6
lcm2	6	2	175	6	3
prodbin	5	2	100	6	2.5
prod4	6	2	13900	–	8
fermat2	5	2	30	9	2
knuth	9	3	O.O.T.	347	192
eucli_div	3	2	13	6	2
cohencu	5	2	90	5	2
read_writ	6	2	82	–	12
illinois	4	2	O.O.T.	–	8
mesi	4	2	620	–	4
moesi	5	2	O.O.T.	–	8
petter_4	2	10	19000	37	3
petter_5	2	10	O.O.T.	37	2
petter_6	2	10	O.O.T.	37	2

Input : degree = 2

```
int eucli_div(int x, int y){
    int q = 0;
    while (x > y) {
        x = x−y;
        q ++;
    }
    return q;
}
```

Frama-C output :

```
int eucli_div(int x, int y){
    int q = 0;
    int k = x + y*q;
    // invariant x + y*q = k;
    while (x > y) {
        x = x−y;
        q ++;
    }
    return q;
}
```

Fig. 3. Euclidean division C loop and generation of its associated invariants.

say e_1, correspond to the constant variable, i.e. $e_1.X = \mathbb{1} = 1$, thus we have $\langle \sum_{i=2}^{4} k_i e_i, X \rangle = -k_1$ as invariant. In our case, $\langle e_2, X \rangle = y$, $\langle e_3, X \rangle = x + yq$ and $\langle e_4, X \rangle = y_2$. We can remove $(y = k)$ and $(y_2 = k)$ that are évident because y does not change inside the loop. The remaining invariant is $x + yq = k$.

6   Conclusion and Future Work

We presented a simple and effective method to generate non-trivial invariants. One of its great advantages is to only rely on linear algebra theory, and generate modular invariants. Still our method has some issues that we are currently investigating. First, it is incomplete for integers: invariants we generate are only correct for rationals. Perhaps surprisingly, this issue does not come from the invariant generation, but from the linearization procedure which badly takes into account the division. For example in C, the operation $x' = \frac{x}{2}$ with x uneven returns $\frac{x-1}{2}$. This behavior is not taken into account by the elevation, which can freely multiply this x by a variable y with $y' = 2y$. This returns the assignment $xy' = xy$ which is false if x is odd. Next, we do not treat interleaving loops as we cannot yet compose invariants with our generation technique. The tool has been successfully implemented as an independent tool of Frama-C.

Our next step is to use those invariants with the Frama-C tools Value (a static value analyser) and WP (a weakest precondition calculus API) to apply a CEGAR-loop on counter-examples generated by CaFE, a temporal logic model checker based on [1]. Also, we want the next version of the tool to handle irrational eigenvalues as decribed in Sect. 4.3.

References

1. Alur, R., Etessami, K., Madhusudan, P.: A temporal logic of nested calls and returns. In: Jensen, K., Podelski, A. (eds.) TACAS 2004. LNCS, vol. 2988, pp. 467–481. Springer, Heidelberg (2004)
2. Basu, S.K., Misra, J.: Proving loop programs. IEEE Trans. Softw. Eng. 1(1), 76–86 (1975)
3. Beyer, D., Henzinger, T.A., Majumdar, R., Rybalchenko, A.: Path invariants. In: ACM SIGPLAN Conference on Programming Language Design and Implementation, pp. 300–309 (2007)
4. Botella, B., Delahaye, M., Ha, S.H.T., Kosmatov, N., Mouy, P., Roger, M., Williams, N.: Automating structural testing of C programs: experience with PathCrawler. In: 4th International Workshop on Automation of Software Test, AST, pp. 70–78 (2009)
5. Cachera, D., Jensen, T.P., Jobin, A., Kirchner, F.: Inference of polynomial invariants for imperative programs: a farewell to Gröbner bases. Sci. Comput. Program. 93, 89–109 (2014)
6. Carbonell, E.: Polynomial invariant generation. http://www.cs.upc.edu/erodri/webpage/polynomial_invariants/list.html
7. Clarke, E.M., Grumberg, O., Jha, S., Lu, Y., Veith, H.: Counterexample-guided abstraction refinement. CAV 2000, 154–169 (2000)

8. Cooper, K.D., Simpson, L.T., Vick, C.A.: Operator strength reduction. ACM Trans. Program. Lang. Syst. **23**(5), 603–625 (2001)
9. de Oliveira, S., Bensalem, S., Prevosto, V.: Polynomial invariants by linear algebra. Technical report 16–0065/SDO, CEA (2016). http://steven-de-oliveira.perso.sfr.fr/content/publis/pilat_tech_report.pdf
10. Hoare, C.A.R.: An axiomatic basis for computer programming. Commun. ACM **12**(10), 576–580 (1969)
11. Hoare, C.A.R.: The verifying compiler: a grand challenge for computing research. J. ACM **50**(1), 63–69 (2003)
12. Hojjat, H., Iosif, R., Konečný, F., Kuncak, V., Rümmer, P.: Accelerating interpolants. In: Chakraborty, S., Mukund, M. (eds.) ATVA 2012. LNCS, vol. 7561, pp. 187–202. Springer, Heidelberg (2012)
13. Johnson, D.B.: Finding all the elementary circuits of a directed graph. SIAM J. Comput. **4**(1), 77–84 (1975)
14. Kauers, M., Zimmermann, B.: Computing the algebraic relations of C-finite sequences and multisequences. J. Symb. Comput. **43**(11), 787–803 (2008)
15. Kirchner, F., Kosmatov, N., Prevosto, V., Signoles, J., Yakobowski, B.: Frama-C: a software analysis perspective. Formal Aspects Comput. **27**(3), 573–609 (2015)
16. Kovács, L.: Aligator: a mathematica package for invariant generation (system description). In: Armando, A., Baumgartner, P., Dowek, G. (eds.) IJCAR 2008. LNCS (LNAI), vol. 5195, pp. 275–282. Springer, Heidelberg (2008)
17. Kovács, L.: A complete invariant generation approach for P-solvable loops. In: Pnueli, A., Virbitskaite, I., Voronkov, A. (eds.) PSI 2009. LNCS, vol. 5947, pp. 242–256. Springer, Heidelberg (2010)
18. Mayr, E.: Membership in polynomial ideals over Q is exponential space complete. In: Monien, B., Cori, R. (eds.) STACS 1989. LNCS, vol. 349, pp. 400–406. Springer, Heidelberg (1989)
19. Müller-Olm, M., Seidl, H.: Polynomial constants are decidable. In: Hermenegildo, M.V., Puebla, G. (eds.) SAS 2002. LNCS, vol. 2477, pp. 4–19. Springer, Heidelberg (2002)
20. Müller-Olm, M., Seidl, H.: Precise interprocedural analysis through linear algebra. POPL **2004**, 330–341 (2004)
21. Pan, V.Y., Chen, Z.Q.: The complexity of the matrix eigenproblem. In: Proceedings of the Thirty-First Annual ACM Symposium on Theory of Computing, May 1–4, Atlanta, Georgia, USA, pp. 507–516 (1999)
22. Rodríguez-Carbonell, E., Kapur, D.: Generating all polynomial invariants in simple loops. J. Symbolic Comput. **42**(4), 443–476 (2007)
23. Tarjan, R.E.: Depth-first search and linear graph algorithms. SIAM J. Comput. **1**(2), 146–160 (1972)

Certified Symbolic Execution

Rui Qiu[1]([✉]), Corina S. Păsăreanu[2], and Sarfraz Khurshid[1]

[1] University of Texas at Austin, Austin, TX 78712, USA
{ruiqiu,khurshid}@utexas.edu
[2] CMU/NASA Ames, M/S 269-2, Moffett Field, CA 94035, USA
corina.s.pasareanu@nasa.gov

Abstract. We propose a certification approach for checking the analysis results produced by symbolic execution. Given a program P under test, an analysis *producer* performs symbolic execution on P and creates a certificate C that represents the results of symbolic execution. The analysis *consumer* checks the validity of C with respect to P using efficient symbolic *re*-execution of P. The certificates are simple to create and easy to validate. Each certificate is a list of *witnesses* that include: *test inputs* that validate path feasibility without requiring any constraint solving; and *infeasibility summaries* that provide *hints* on how to efficiently establish path infeasibility. To account for incompleteness in symbolic execution (due to incompleteness of the backend solver), the certificate also contains an *incompleteness summary*. Our approach deploys constraint slicing and other heuristics as performance optimizations. Experimental results using a prototype certification tool based on Symbolic PathFinder for Java show that certification can be 3X to 370X (on average, 75X) faster than traditional symbolic execution. We also show the benefits of the approach for the reliability assessment of a software component under different probabilistic environment conditions.

1 Introduction

Certification plays an important role in the development of reliable software systems. For example, a certifying compiler [19,25] produces a proof that the compiled code has specific safety properties or is semantically equivalent to its source-code—which enables component re-use from untrusted parties, aggressive compiler optimizations, etc. As another example, a certifying model checker [31] produces a proof that it indeed performed exhaustive exploration of the program's state space and produced the correct overall checking result—which enables search pruning, optimization heuristics, load balancing etc.

This paper introduces a certification approach for *symbolic execution* [7,15]. Symbolic execution is a classic program analysis technique that has received much attention in the last decade [11,17,22,27,36]. The technique performs a systematic exploration of the program's paths and for each path, it builds a path constraint using a logical formula that represents all inputs that execute that path. Off-the-shelf solvers are used to determine feasibility of path constraints (when possible); solutions to feasible path constraints represent test inputs that

© Springer International Publishing AG 2016
C. Artho et al. (Eds.): ATVA 2016, LNCS 9938, pp. 495–511, 2016.
DOI: 10.1007/978-3-319-46520-3_31

drive the execution of corresponding paths. Symbolic execution has many applications, including automatic test input generation, error detection, regression and security analysis, continuous testing, program repair etc. [5,21,33]. Our approach aims to provide a simple but rigorous examination of the symbolic execution results, and can thus benefit all these applications.

Given a program P the analysis producer in our certification approach symbolically executes P and creates a certificate C that represents *succinctly* the result of symbolic execution. The analysis consumer checks that the results of symbolic execution are correct by checking the validity of C with respect to P using an *efficient* symbolic re-execution of P. Our key insight is that certification for symbolic execution is possible using certificates that are manageable in size and simple to validate without incurring a high cost. Our approach follows the spirit of proof-carrying code [19]. However, our focus is on certifying analysis results produced by symbolic execution.

Each certificate is a list of *witnesses* that include: *test inputs* that directly validate path feasibility; and *infeasibility summaries* that provide *hints* on how to efficiently establish path infeasibility. If for some path, the producer is unable to determine feasibility (due to incompleteness of the solver), the certificate also contains an *incompleteness summary*, similar to the infeasibility summary.

A test input is a set of concrete input values that can be executed against P. Certification establishes path feasibility by checking that test inputs in the certificate satisfy their respective path constraints. An infeasibility summary consists of two elements: (1) a *sliced path constraint* that contains a subset of clauses of the corresponding path's full path constraint, akin to unsatisfiable cores in propositional satisfiability (SAT) formulas [3]; and (2) a *strategy* to deploy for efficiently establishing constraint infeasibility. These strategies specify constraint solving optimizations that we describe in this paper based on logical rules to enable efficiently establishing constraint unsatisfiability and can be naturally extended to include proofs of unsatisfiability such as those produced by SMT solvers, e.g., Z3 [8], which can be verified independently using theorem provers such as Isabelle. Certification utilizes the infeasibility summaries for efficiently validating path infeasibility. The consumer may also utilize the incompleteness summary to enhance the symbolic execution results (say using a different solving strategy or solver). However, certification does not require the consumer to validate the producer's solver's incompleteness.

The cost of certification is determined by validating feasible and infeasible paths. To validate feasible paths (that are executed by the tests), our approach does not require constraint solving—which is often the most expensive operation in symbolic execution. To validate infeasible paths, our approach has the following steps: checking that a sliced constraint (in the certificate) is included in the candidate infeasible paths, which requires no constraint solving; and either applying the strategy (if present) for quickly validating infeasibility without invoking an external solver, or invoking the solver for the sliced constraints that do not have an applicable strategy. Overall, certification performs re-execution of symbolic analysis using *minimal* (for many paths, 0) calls to external constraint solvers and has a much lower cost than full symbolic execution.

The result of certification is either that the certificate is valid (confirming the results of the producer's symbolic execution analysis) or that the certificate is invalid, indicating an error (or unstated assumption) in the symbolic execution engine or in the constraint solver that was used. Thus, our approach enables debugging symbolic execution engines and constraint solvers, which can be very complex systems. Our approach also benefits probabilistic reliability assessment of source code, which is a recent application of symbolic execution for extracting failure and success paths to calculate a reliability value against relevant probabilistic usage scenarios [9]. By storing the probabilities of path conditions in our certificate, we can facilitate the integration of a certified component into bigger systems that define different usage scenarios, obtaining the reliability estimation at a significantly reduced cost.

We illustrate these applications in detail, but note that our approach has many other applications that we can not include for space reasons. For example, our approach enables the efficient verification of new properties on the same code base, since the certificate includes the key elements that are necessary to re-run the analysis efficiently. Furthermore, the certificate enables incremental symbolic execution where the certificate for one program version can be re-used to efficiently check the next program version. Even if the certification fails (e.g. due to some program changes) the certificate still likely contains valid information (test inputs) that reduce the cost of re-application of symbolic execution. Finally, since our approach produces evidence that the software has been thoroughly analyzed, it can be used to aid software certification, which is known to be a costly manual process.

We believe our approach to certification based on symbolic execution holds promise and hope our work will help develop new ways to utilize the power of this classic program analysis.

2 Example

We illustrate certified symbolic execution on the simple example depicted in Listing 1. Method *example* takes three integers x, y, and z as input and returns an integer according to the relations between x, y, and z.

Assume we perform a symbolic execution over the example (in general the execution needs to be bounded to deal with possibly infinite loops). Figure 1 shows the explored execution paths, organized in a symbolic execution tree where tree nodes are symbolic program states and tree edges are program transitions. The analysis maintains a path condition i.e., a conjunction of constraints that the program inputs must satisfy to drive the execution along that path. Initially, *path condition* (PC_0) is true, and input variables x, y, and z have symbolic values X, Y, and Z respectively. Program variables are initialized with symbolic values X, Y, and Z. For each conditional statement in the program, PC is updated with the possible choices from the branch condition so that both true and false valuations are considered. For example, in the first conditional statement (Line 2), PC is updated to PC_1 and PC_{10} for true and false branches of the condition

```
1          int example(int x, int y, int z) {
2            if( z > 0) {
3              if (x <= y) {
4                if (x > y) {
5                  return 1;
6                } else {
7                  return 2;
8                }
9              } else {
10               if (x + 1 == 0) {
11                 if (x != 3) {
12                   return 3;
13                 }
14                 return 4;
15               } else {
16                 return 5;
17               }
18             }
19           }
20           return 6;
21         }
```

Listing 1. Method *example*

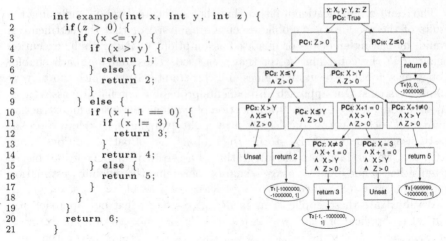

Fig. 1. Symbolic execution tree for method *example*

respectively. Whenever PC is updated, it is checked for satisfiability by calling an off-the-shelf constraint solver. If PC becomes false (unsatisfiable), meaning that the corresponding path is infeasible, symbolic execution does not continue for that path. For example, in Fig. 1, there are two paths that are infeasible due to the unsatisfiable path conditions (PC_3 and PC_8).

To certify symbolic execution of method *example*, one should verify both feasible and infeasible paths. Intuitively, a test input serves as a witness of feasibility of a specific path. These test inputs are obtained by invoking the constraint solver for each satisfiable path condition. For example, in Fig. 1 test input $T_1[-1000000, -1000000, 1]$ (meaning that both inputs x and y are -1000000 and input z is 1) is a solution to path condition PC_4 and it drives the program along the path that leads to return 2.

For infeasible paths, we certify the unsatisfiability of their corresponding path conditions. As mentioned a certificate contains a set of unsatisfiable path conditions from the program. In symbolic execution, every branch introduces a new constraint to be added to the existing satisfiable path condition. Thus, for the unsatisfiability checks, we can slice a path condition to include only the constraints that relate to the last added constraint, as only they can become unsatisfiable. The remaining un-related constraints can be dropped, thus reducing the cost of solving them and the size of the certificate. For example, we slice PC_3 and PC_8 with respect to their last added constraints $X > Y$ and $X = 3$ respectively. Since value Z is not related to X and Y, constraint $Z > 0$ can be dropped. We only store the sliced path conditions $PC'_3 : X > Y \wedge X \leq Y$ and $PC'_8 : X = 3 \wedge X + 1 = 0 \wedge X \geq Y$.

For the symbolic execution of method *example*, the certificate is an ordered list of test inputs, i.e., $\{T_1, T_2, T_3, T_4\}$, and a list of unsatisfiable sliced path conditions, i.e., $\{PC'_3, PC'_8\}$. In this simple example we have no incompleteness summaries. To check this certificate, we re-run symbolic execution for method *example* with the same search order as the previous analysis (e.g., depth-first search). Note that during this re-run, constraint solving is not needed for feasible paths as the test inputs from the certificate serve for validation. We only need constraint solving for the infeasible paths, to re-check that the corresponding path conditions are indeed unsatisfiable and they are in the certificate. This check can be done using a constraint solver that is different than the one used in the original analysis. We can relax this assumption on search order, but then the validation of feasible path constraints is slightly more involved as it should be done against all the test inputs stored in the certificate.

The certification process of method *example* only makes two calls to the constraint solver for checking PC'_3 and PC'_8, while in traditional symbolic execution it makes 10 constraint solving calls (from PC_1 to PC_{10}). Checking if a concrete input satisfies a given path condition is much cheaper than using a constraint solver to check the satisfiability of a PC. Therefore, certifying symbolic execution is computationally cheaper than the original analysis.

To further reduce the cost of certification we also implemented five heuristics (*H1–H5* in Sect. 3) to quickly check the unsatisfiability of path conditions without using a constraint solver. By using the heuristics we reduce the total number of constraint solver calls needed from 10 to 0 (for this example).

In principle both the path slicing and the heuristics can be part of the work performed by an SMT solver that is used for certification, and then checking the unsatisfiability of path conditions amounts to re-checking the results produced by an SMT solver. Our approach can naturally accommodate such a scenario since we provide a clear separation between path exploration and constraint solving. Thus, for an unsatisfiable path condition, the certificate can store a proof for the unsatisfiability from a constraint solver. There are only a few solvers that can produce proofs for unsatisfiability for verification purposes. These proofs can be checked independently using theorem proving [4, 30]. Although this technique is not mature to be used in certified symbolic execution, our certificate can fully integrate these proofs from solver.

3   Certified Symbolic Execution

Certified symbolic execution has two participants: a symbolic execution *producer* and a symbolic execution *consumer*. The *producer*'s symbolic execution analyzes the input program using traditional symbolic execution (up to a specified depth) to generate test inputs and to check given safety properties (e.g., absence of assert violations, run-time exceptions, bounded temporal properties, etc.). At the same time the producer also generates a symbolic execution *certificate*, which succinctly represents the essential information of the analysis process. In our approach, the certificate consists of the test inputs generated by the symbolic execution (for the feasible paths) and the *infeasibility/incompleteness summaries* (for unsatisfiable or unknown path conditions). Here incompleteness is introduced due to the current limitations of existing solvers or due to the inherent incompleteness of certain theories, such as non-linear integer constraints. As a result, some paths in the program would not be explored by symbolic execution (these paths are treated similarly to infeasible paths).

The test inputs are the solutions (obtained with an off-the-shelf constraint solver) to the feasible path conditions corresponding to the terminating program paths. During certification, the *consumer* reconstructs the path conditions of the program by using traditional symbolic execution, but without utilizing a constraint solver. Instead, the consumer's analysis is *guided* by the test inputs in the certificate. These test inputs form "witnesses" for the feasibility of the corresponding path conditions, which obviates the need for constraint solving.

The certificate also contains infeasibility and incompleteness summaries containing sliced path conditions and small scripts encoding the optimizations performed over the path conditions. Note that the feasible paths implicitly characterize the infeasible or incomplete paths in the program. Thus, the reconstructed paths that are not executed by any test inputs are candidate infeasible/incomplete paths, provided that the certificate is valid. The consumer then checks syntactically whether the infeasible/incomplete path conditions contain any of the sliced paths from the certificate and re-applies the optimization steps in the order encoded in the certificate (if such steps are present). Often this is enough to re-check the full certificate. If this is not the case, the consumer uses a constraint solver to re-check the unsatisfiability or undecidability of the (sliced) path conditions. The result of the consumer's analysis is that either the certificate is valid (confirming the correctness of the properties provided by the producer) or that it is invalid, signaling incorrectness in analysis results.

Note that the producer and consumer analysis can be performed with different symbolic execution tools and can use different solvers that may run on different platforms. This is an important characteristic of certified symbolic execution as it is often the case that off-the-shelf solvers are platform specific. Also note that the burden of performing full-blown symbolic execution is on the producer, whereas the consumer (cheaply) re-checks the program. Thus the key to *certified symbolic execution* is for the consumer to efficiently certify the analysis process using the test inputs to validate the feasible path constraints, while using a constraint solver only for (some of) the candidate infeasible/incomplete paths. Slicing of path conditions and heuristics are employed to further reduce the cost of certification, up to the point that no constraint solving may be needed.

Certificate Construction. For a program P with symbolic input $I = \{I_1, I_2, ..., I_m\}$, a *test input* $T = \{i_1, i_2, ..., i_m\}$ contains the concrete input values for each symbolic input in I. A *certificate* C contains a list $\{T_1, T_2, ..., T_n\}$ of test inputs of all feasible (bounded) paths for program P under symbolic execution. The program P takes two different paths for any two test inputs T_i and T_j in C ($i \neq j, 1 \leq i, j \leq n$). The certificate C also contains information for infeasible paths and undecided paths. We mark a path as undecided if the constraint solver cannot determine whether its path condition is satisfiable or not, i.e., the solver returns "unknown" result for a path condition. Specifically, the certificate contains two sets of path conditions, PC_{unsat} for unsatisfiable path conditions and $PC_{unknown}$ for unknown path conditions. Let $PC_1, PC_2, ...$ be infeasible path conditions. In PC_{unsat}, we store in the certificate PC'_1, PC'_2, etc., where PC'_i is the sliced version of PC_i as explained below. Note that a simple solution would be to include directly all the infeasible path conditions in the certificate, and to re-check that on the consumer side. However, unsatisfiability checking using constraint solvers such as CVC3 [2], Z3 [8] or Coral [29] is computationally expensive and we would like to avoid using a constraint solver as much as possible. Towards this end we employ path constraint slicing and several heuristics. Similarly, for unknown path conditions, we store the sliced versions in $PC_{unknown}$.

Consider a path condition $PC_i = c_0 \wedge c_1 \wedge ... \wedge c_n$ (which is unsatisfiable). The last added constraint (c_0) causes PC_i to be infeasible since $c_1 \wedge ... \wedge c_n$ should be satisfiable from the previous check (otherwise the symbolic execution would have not reached that point). Thus the (un)satisfiability of PC_i only depends on the constraints that have common variables with c_0. We can therefore "slice" PC_i to keep only the constraints that are related to c_0 and to eliminate the irrelevant constraints. The slicing is similar to Green [32] and to other optimizations used in constraint solvers (a slice is akin to an unsat core but cheaper to compute). To slice PC_i, we build a constraint graph $G(V,E)$ of PC_i, in which the vertices V are variables of PC_i and edges E indicate whether two variables are part of the same constraint. In G, we find all variables R that are reachable from the variables in c_0. Then the conjunction of the constraints that contain variables in R is the sliced path condition ($PC'_i = c_0 \wedge c_p \wedge ... \wedge c_q$). It is this smaller path condition that is stored in the certificate. Note that the sliced path conditions are cheaper to re-check and also result in smaller certificates. Note also that this sliced path condition may not contain the smallest set of constraints that makes it unsatisfiable. If another sliced path condition $PC'_j = c_p \wedge c_q$ from another path is already in the certificate, PC_i is no longer needed since the certificate contains a smaller sliced path condition. Similarly, if the certificate consists of an unsatisfiable path condition that is a super-set of PC'_i (e.g., $c_0 \wedge c_p \wedge ... \wedge c_q \wedge c_m$), we replace this longer path condition with the smaller one. Thus the certificate always maintains a set of smallest unsatisfiable path conditions.

To further reduce the use of constraint solving for re-checking the unsatisfiability, we apply five heuristics to each of the sliced unsatisfiable path conditions. These heuristics serve as a faster way to check if a path condition is indeed unsatisfiable without using a constraint solver. If a heuristic can be applied to a sliced path condition, the certificate stores it as a script so analysis consumer could directly apply the heuristic to check unsatisfiability. These heuristics are implemented as syntactic simplifications and checks, thus avoiding the cost of constraint solving.

- **H1**: For any constraint c_i ($1 \leq i \leq n$) in PC'_i, if c_i is same as $\neg c_0$, PC'_i is unsatisfiable. For example, c_0 is $x > 0$ and PC'_i contains $x \leq 0$.
- **H2**: If a linear transformation of constraint c_0 satisfies H1, PC'_i is unsatisfiable. The transformation of c_0 includes moving its left hand side expression into right hand side and vice versa, or exchanging left hand side expression with

right hand side expression. For example, if c_0 is $x > y$, its simple linear transformation can be $y < x$, $x - y > 0$, or $y - x < 0$.

– **H3**: If any constraint c_i in PC_i' contains one variable var and it has the form $var = ct$, where "ct" is a constant, we can simply replace all variables var in other constraints c_j $(0 \leq j \leq n, j \neq i)$ in PC_i' with the constant ct. After variable replacement, each of constraints c_j must hold. Otherwise, if one of c_j is unsatisfiable, PC_i' is unsatisfiable. For example, if c_0 is $x == 5$ and PC_i' contains a constraint $x + 3 < 0$, we replace variable x with integer constant 5 in the constraint and obviously it is evaluated to be false.

– **H4**: Constraint c_0 contains a symbolic expression exp and it is of the form "$exp\ op\ ct$", in which op belongs to one of $>, <, \leq, \geq$, and "ct" is a constant (i.e. "ct" is used to define the ranges for the expression). PC_i' is unsatisfiable if it contains another constraint that conflicts the range defined in c_0. For example, c_0 is $x + 3 > 400$ and PC_i' contains another constraint $x + 3 < 200$.

– **H5**: Path condition PC_i' is unsatisfiable if the set of constraints in PC_i' contains the set of constraints of another PC, where the path condition PC is already known to be unsatisfiable. For example, if PC_i' is $(x > 0) \wedge (y < 10) \wedge (x + y < 0) \wedge (y > 0)$ and PC is $(x > 0) \wedge (x + y < 0) \wedge (y > 0)$ which is already known to be unsatisfiable, PC_i' is also unsatisfiable. This heuristic requires storing and accessing previously checked path conditions.

We apply these five heuristics in order from H1 to H5. If any one of them is applicable to quickly validate the unsatisfiability of a sliced path condition PC_i', we encode the applicable heuristic to the certificate along with PC_i'. Despite their simplicity, these heuristics make a significant difference to the number of constraint solver calls made during certification (as shown in Sect. 4). Moreover, one could add other more sophisticated heuristics in our framework.

The consumer has the option to apply the five heuristics for unknown path conditions. If any of the heuristics is applicable, the consumer would conclude that the path condition is unsatisfiable instead of unknown.

During certificate construction, we use a *listener* [23] to non-intrusively monitor traditional symbolic execution and to add test inputs and infeasibility/incompleteness summaries to the certificate. The listener initializes a new certificate after execution enters the target symbolic method of the program. If a terminating return instruction is executed or the search depth limit is reached, we solve the current path condition to generate a test input and add it to the certificate. If an "if" instruction is executed and an unsatisfiable or unknown path condition is returned by the solver, we slice the path condition and check if the certificate maintains the smallest subset of the unsatisfiable/unknown conjunction of constraints. Then we apply the heuristics to the sliced path condition and store it along with the applicable heuristic to the certificate. At the end of symbolic execution, the certificate contains inputs for all explored feasible terminating paths (up to the bound) plus the information about the infeasible or incomplete paths.

Certificate Validation. For certification, the consumer re-runs symbolic execution on the same target program, checking the analysis results. Any discovered discrepancy causes the validation to fail. Discrepancies include:

1. The certificate contains more than one test input for the same feasible program path.
2. The certificate omits a test input, corresponding to a feasible program path.
3. The certificate contains a sliced path condition corresponding to none of infeasible or unknown paths in the program.
4. The optimizations steps for a candidate path do not apply.
5. The sliced unsat path condition in the certificate is found to be satisfiable during certificate validation.

The first type of discrepancy is detected by checking if more than one test input from the certificate satisfies a path condition for a terminal path. The second type of discrepancy is detected by re-checking the unsatisfiability of the path conditions that are not satisfied by the certificate's test inputs. Discrepancies 3 and 4 can be checked syntactically. The last case may happen due to discrepancies between different solvers.

Note that if a sliced unknown path condition is found to be actually satisfiable by consumer due to the differences of constraint solvers, we do not consider the certification process to fail as the analysis results are still correct yet incomplete. However this case is signaled to the user.

Similar to certificate construction, certificate validation is implemented as a *listener* which monitors and guides the symbolic execution of a program using the provided certificate. Whenever a conditional instruction is executed, the listener checks the satisfiability of the current path condition over the test inputs from the certificate. Naturally, if a path condition does not satisfy any test input, this path should be infeasible or incomplete. We therefore re-check the unsatisfiability (undecidability) of the corresponding path condition and, if it is confirmed, we force symbolic execution to backtrack. To check the unsatisfiability (undecidability) of a path condition, we search over the stored sliced path conditions in the certificate to find one that is a subset of the current path condition. Also, if a heuristic is associated with this sliced path condition, we apply that heuristic to check the unsatisfiability. If no heuristic is associated, we invoke a constraint solver to solve the sliced path condition. Furthermore, if a return statement or the search depth limit is reached, we certify that the current path can be executed by only one test input from the certificate.

To check if a path condition is satisfied by one of the test inputs in the certificate, we follow different approaches based on the search order of the producer and consumer. If the search order is the same for both producer and consumer, the test inputs are generated in the same order and the program paths are explored in the same order as well. Thus the validation listener can check the test inputs one by one, as the paths are explored: an iterator indicates the position of the last explored path in the list of tests. Every time a new path is explored, we simply move the iterator to the next input in the list. On the other hand, if the producer and the consumer use different search orders, the listener is more involved as it has to search for a satisfiable test input over the entire list of tests from the certificate. This introduces more overhead for certification, as shown in Sect. 4. Further optimizations for this case, such as reordering the list of test inputs in the certificate [28], are left for future work.

The consumer validates that the program is free of errors (e.g., violations of producer's assertions, run-time exceptions etc.) during symbolic re-execution. Since the certificate is independent of the producer's properties, the consumer may choose to also verify additional properties of interest. In this case, the certificate has the side benefit of speeding up the verification of these additional properties. Certification can also be used to quickly confirm the structural testing coverage achieved by the tests.

Note that we have assumed that both the certificate construction and the certificate validation use the same exploration bound. This means that the consumer can not trust what the program does beyond that exploration bound and if she wants further guarantees she must continue using full-blown, classical symbolic execution up to a further bound. Still we believe that our technique is beneficial since the results stored in the certificate can be re-used to speed-up the analysis at the larger bound. For instance, both the test cases and the sliced paths may be applicable beyond the initial bound and thus can be re-used to reduce the number of constraint solver calls.

Symbolic Execution with Incomplete Search. The producer's analysis results may have two common sources of incompleteness: incompleteness of the back-end solver; and incompleteness of the symbolic execution search, e.g., when a heuristic is used to prune certain paths from exploration. Our certification approach directly supports incompleteness of the back-end solver (using incompleteness summaries) assuming that the symbolic execution was incomplete but systematic, up to a user-specified bound. Furthermore, our certification approach can be extended to handle incomplete search strategies that symbolic execution engines may employ for faster (yet incomplete) analysis. Specifically, we can integrate *memoization trees* [36] with our certificates to define a richer structure that captures the partial search performed by the producer and allows the consumer to validate those results and moreover, to extend the search and make the analysis more complete if the consumer so desires. The non-leaf nodes of the tree encode information of symbolic conditional statements, including method name, instruction offset, and the choice taken by the execution. The leaf nodes of the tree contain either concrete tests (for feasible paths) or sliced path conditions (for the other paths). Overall, the tree encodes the explored space and the key results of symbolic execution performed by the producer. Figure 2 illustrates the tree-based certificate that captures partial search for our example program from Sect. 2. Specifically, the producer explored only 3 out of 6 paths in the program, one infeasible path and two paths that return integer 2 and 6 respectively. Non-leaf nodes that have only one child node shows that only one branch of a conditional statement is executed. For instance, "example:4:1" shows that in method *example*, only true branch of conditional statement in line 4 is executed while the false branch is skipped (1 for true branch and 0 for false branch).

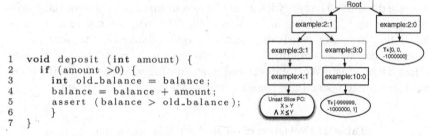

```
1  void deposit (int amount) {
2    if (amount >0) {
3      int old_balance = balance;
4      balance = balance + amount;
5      assert (balance > old_balance);
6    }
7  }
```

Listing 2. Method *deposit*

Fig. 2. A partial tree for method *example*

4   Implementation and Applications

Implementation. We implemented certified symbolic execution in the Symbolic PathFinder (SPF) tool [23], using two listeners. One listener monitors the symbolic execution in SPF and generates a certificate while the other one takes the certificate and validates it while re-running symbolic execution. For convenience, we implemented both certificate generation and validation within the same system. However, in practice, these two tasks could be performed with separate tools, increasing the confidence in the results. We evaluate and discuss here different application scenarios for our certification approach.

Debugging Symbolic Execution Engines or Constraint Solvers. When the analysis producer and consumer have different symbolic execution engines or constraint solvers, certification could help debug these complex systems. Consider a Java method *deposit* shown in Listing 2. The method has three execution paths: one path that is executed for input *amount* less than 0, one path that leads to assertion (Line 5) evaluating to true, and one path that leads to assertion violation.

Assume the analysis producer's symbolic execution engine (or constraint solver) does not consider integer overflow. The path that leads to assertion failure will be considered infeasible since *balance* + *amount* cannot be smaller than *balance* when *amount* > 0 (unless numeric overflow is considered). Thus, the certificate produced would contain an (erroneously classified) unsatisfiable path condition. Assume the consumer employs a more rigorous engine that models overflow. The consumer would detect the erroneously classified path, which is actually feasible. Thus, the certifying process would fail as the consumer finds that an unsatisfiable path condition in the certificate is actually satisfiable. Our certified symbolic execution could reveal this problem.

Evaluation of Certification Cost. We evaluated certified symbolic execution on the following 8 Java programs: *WBS, ASW, Rational, TCAS, BankAccount (BA), MerArbiter (Mer), JDK 1.5 Sorting Algorithms and Red-Black Tree Data Structure,* and *Apollo*. All of these artifacts were used before for evaluating symbolic execution techniques [1,6,14,21,24,26,29,35,36]. These subjects contain rich programming constructs, such as complex non-linear constraints, recursion, etc. that are difficult to handle with symbolic execution. The largest of these artifacts is *Apollo* with 2.6 KLOC in 54 classes [29]. The program contains complex non-linear floating-point constraints and it is quite challenging to analyze. To symbolically execute a configuration with two iterations, traditional SPF takes more than 4 h to finish. We are interested in evaluating whether the certification can be significantly faster than running full-blown symbolic execution.

Table 1. Evaluation of certified symbolic execution

Subject	Method	Time (h:m:s)					# Solver Calls				Cert Size (KB)	# Feasible Paths	# Infeasible /Unknown Paths	Tree Size (KB)
		SPF	Build Cert	Validate(same order) Plain	H1–H5	Validate Rand	SPF	Build Cert	Validate(same order) Plain	H1–H5				
WBS	update	<00:01	00:01	<00:01	<00:01	<00:01	46	46	0	0	1.3	24	0/0	2.3
	main3	00:03	00:04	<00:01	<00:01	<00:01	718	718	7	0	5.1	24	336/0	31.2
	launch	09:33	13:45	00:03	00:03	01:11	27646	27646	0	0	857.9	13824	0/0	1100
ASW	Main0	00:08	00:11	<00:01	<00:01	<00:01	858	858	10	4	19.2	192	254/0	31.2
	mainBody	00:49	00:53	00:03	00:03	00:04	5850	5850	12	2	22.1	192	2942/0	251.9
Rational	simplify	00:01	00:01	<00:01	<00:01	<00:01	92	92	15	1	6.8	14	46/0	3.2
	simp	06:08	07:14	00:12	00:10	00:40	19412	19412	54	3	171.8	2744	9706/0	616
TCAS	startTcas	01:01	01:01	00:01	<00:01	00:01	2348	2348	19	0	12.0	68	1107/0	101.4
	tcasTwice	01:06:31	01:10:10	00:17	00:16	01:52	46782	46782	22	0	864.5	4624	18768/0	2000
BA	main1	00:33	00:36	00:01	<00:01	00:01	736	736	22	0	31.6	258	111/0	32
	main2	07:35	11:36	01:58	01:44	02:58	9294	9294	1228	1206	767.2	2677	1971/0	400
Mer	run3	02:00	03:07	00:44	00:43	00:54	5568	5568	0	0	512.8	2645	0/0	239.8
	run4	17:32	23:27	05:50	03:58	08:33	38944	38944	560	11	2662.4	18283	241/0	1600
JDK 1.5	mergeSort	07:37	08:50	00:06	00:03	00:51	10366	10366	144	0	504.9	5040	144/0	446.1
	quickSort	19:46	22:03	00:48	00:35	04:08	25920	25920	1218	245	1433.6	11743	1218/0	1100
	heapInsert	01:54	02:24	00:01	00:01	00:03	2590	2590	0	0	126.4	1296	0/0	111.7
	rbTree	14:31	16:37	00:19	00:10	02:30	20462	20462	497	43	953	9360	872/0	163.7
Apollo	main1	02:30	02:59	00:06	00:06	00:08	348	348	20	20	107.6	81	0/152	5.1
	main2	04:07:05	04:24:00	00:40	00:40	02:05	12381	12381	45	45	5700	1869	0/1375	4900

Table 1 shows the results of our experiments. For each subject, certificate validation was successful. No pre-specified search depth was needed as no program constructs drive symbolic execution infinite. To evaluate the cost of certificate construction, we first ran traditional symbolic execution using SPF and then we ran the analysis again with the listener to construct a certificate ("Build Cert"). Next, we ran the certificate validation with the same search order as used in certificate construction ("Validate (same order)"). To evaluate the performance of the proposed heuristics, we certify symbolic execution twice. One run does not use heuristics ("Plain") while the other one uses heuristics ("H1–H5").

Furthermore, to evaluate certificate validation in the case that the consumer has a different search order than the producer, we randomly reordered the test inputs in each certificate and validated them using heuristics for unsatisfiable or unknown path condition checking (denoted as "Validate (rand)"). This validation process only introduces an overhead during the satisfiability checking while the number of constraint solver calls is the same as in "Validate (same order) H1–H5", since the number of infeasible or unknown path conditions that need to be re-checked is the same.

We report the number of constraint solver calls and execution time for each analysis. Table 1 also shows the size of the generated certificate and the number of feasible paths and infeasible/unknown paths for each analyzed method. A method that contains more feasible paths would take longer for analysis and its certificate is certainly larger. We also report the size of the full memoization tree for each method. Parts of such memoization trees could potentially be added to the certificate, to account for a partial exploration during symbolic execution as described in Sect. 3. This size does not include the size of leaf nodes that are either test cases or sliced unsat/unknown path conditions as they are already measured in the size of certificate. We include these results to assess the trade-off for supporting incompleteness in search strategies. The certificate would be larger but the exact size of the certificate combining with a partial tree depends on the number of paths explored.

The results show that certificate construction has some overhead on the time of execution on large methods, from about 6 % (*tcasTwice* in TCAS) to 55 % (*run3* in Mer) more time (on average about 20 % more time). However, the certificate validation is significantly faster than re-running the symbolic execution, ranging from about 3X (*run3* in Mer) to 370X (*main2* in Apollo) faster than traditional symbolic execution. On average, certificate validation achieves a speed-up of 75X over 19 methods in 8 subjects. The certificate validation using heuristics is either more efficient or same as not applying heuristics. In some cases the heuristics reduce the number of constraint solver calls to 0 (methods in TCAS, *main3* in WBS, and *main1* in BA, etc.). Methods *update, launch* in WBS, *run3*, and *heapInsert* are special cases since they do not contain any infeasible paths.

Our approach still achieves significant savings for the cases where the construction and validation of a certificate take different search orders, from about 2.1X (method *run4* in Mer) to 118X (method *main2* in Apollo) faster than traditional SPF (about 20X faster on average). However, as expected, it has less savings compared to the validation process with the same search order.

Apollo contains unknown path conditions due to the solver used, Coral, a heuristic based solver that can handle arbitrary complex (non-linear, containing trigonometric functions etc.) constraints [29]. Coral may return unknown result after a number of iterations (algorithmic time out). We found that after slicing, 10 and 23 sliced unknown path conditions are actually satisfiable in method *main1* and *main2* respectively. This is because when slicing a path condition with respect to its newly added constraint, the number of constraints in the path condition is reduced, and Coral may no longer time out. Thus Coral may give inconsistent satisfiability results on path conditions before and after slicing. This case hints to an interesting potential usage scenario for our approach in the future, namely to validate the constraint solvers themselves.

Reliability Analysis. We extended our certification framework to accommodate a recent application of symbolic execution for estimating the reliability of a software component [9] under different probabilistic usage profiles. A *usage profile* (*UP*) describes the environment conditions (i.e. physical environment conditions or interactions with other components) or the different usages of the component in the context of a bigger system in which the component is integrated and evaluated. In [9] the usage profile is defined as a set of pairs $[c_i, p_i]$

where c_i's represent disjoint constraints over input variables and p_i is the probability of satisfying the constraint $Pr(c_i)$. The reliability Rel is computed as follows:

$$Rel = \sum_j Pr(PC_j^S | UP) = \sum_j \sum_i Pr(PC_j^S | c_i) p_i = \sum_j \sum_i \frac{\#(PC_j^S \wedge c_i)}{\#(c_i)} p_i \quad (1)$$

In Eq. 1, PC_j^S's denote the path conditions for successful termination (i.e. no assert violations or uncaught exceptions) and $\#(C)$ denotes the number of elements satisfying the constraint C (assuming a finite, possibly very large, input domain). This value can be obtained using model counting techniques [10, 16]. Furthermore, a value of *confidence* on reliability estimation is defined by $Confidence = 1 - Pr^g(P)$, where $Pr^g(P)$ quantifies the ratio of elements in the input domain that cannot be determined due to the bounded analysis. As the search depth bound increases, the confidence value increases as well.

We have analyzed the flap controller component from [9], that controls the wings of an aircraft under different wind conditions, yielding different reliability values. A random variable profiles wind effect, with two distributions that is either strong or weak. A strong wind profile has higher probability to produce extreme wind strength while a weak wind distribution is more centered around small wind strength [9]. To evaluate the reliability of the actuator program in two different wind effect settings, the analysis from [9] symbolically executes the program twice, loads two usage profiles and calculates reliability values based on Eq. 1 respectively.

We have used our approach to build a component certificate under weak-wind usage profile UP_1 that is then validated and re-used under a different (strong-wind) usage profile UP_2. This corresponds to a more general scenario where a certified component is efficiently integrated into a larger system, that provides different environment conditions, and hence results in different reliability values. We show that our certification framework enables faster reliability analysis and hence faster integration of the same component under different usage profiles. Specifically, to analyze UP_2, we verify the path conditions of the component using concrete test inputs from the certificate without any constraint solving. The analysis for UP_2 is faster as we only need solvers for infeasible paths. Moreover, note that often the constraints c_i in Eq. 1 remain the same for different usage profiles and only the probabilities p_i change, as it is the case for the wind profiles that were obtained from discretizations of Gaussian distributions (with same discrete step). We can thus further reduce the analysis time by storing in the certificate a list of conditional probabilities $\#(PC_j^S \wedge c_i)/\#(c_i)$ ($0 \le i \le N$, where N is the number of constraints in UP) for each path condition PC_j^S in our certificate. Re-calculating Rel for UP_2 only requires to insert a new set of p_i into Eq. 1, without calling model counting [16], which is expensive. By storing and reusing results of previous analysis, our framework achieves significantly faster analysis time than recalculating reliability from scratch.

Table 2 shows our experimental results; "Orig" denotes the original reliability analysis [9] and "Build Cert" denotes certificate construction for weak-wind UP.

Table 2. Evaluation for reliability analysis

Depth	Time (s)				Weak wind		Strong wind	
	Orig	Build Cert	Rerun	Rerun (with P_c)	*Rel*	*Conf*	*Rel*	*Conf*
10	8	9	4	1	0.062600	0.227885	0.060045	0.405127
20	39	40	17	6	0.180638	0.725122	0.129490	0.794932
30	82	86	33	15	0.217204	0.836973	0.145161	0.876152
50	155	161	64	38	0.229749	0.937720	0.150538	0.946407
70	227	231	102	73	0.229749	0.943096	0.150538	0.957160

Two certificate validation runs, one reusing solver results only ("Rerun") and one reusing both solver and probability results ("Rerun (with P_c)"), were performed for strong-wind UP. We report the analysis time and the reliability value with corresponding confidence level. The overhead of constructing the certificate is not much as shown in Table 2. By reusing our certificate, the analysis can be significantly faster than original analysis. For example, in depth 70, reusing solver results and conditional probabilities speeds up original analysis about 3.1X.

5 Related Work

We have already discussed the relationship between our work and proof-carrying code (PCC) [19,25] and "search-carrying code" [31]. Other related approaches [13,34] use model checking and predicate abstraction to obtain the verification conditions that define a certificate. Both these approaches work at the code level while other model checking based techniques [18,20] work on high-level transition models. The work on "explicating symbolic execution" [12] applies to the verification of software contracts and focuses on capturing the over- and under-approximations introduced by bounded symbolic execution with incomplete constraint solving. That work targets the certification of safety-critical systems and it is not in the spirit of proof-carrying-code, in the sense that the evidence provided is not meant to be used to re-run the verification and confirm the results. As such our work here is complementary and it should be possible to use it in conjunction with explicating symbolic execution.

6 Conclusion

We described a certification technique for symbolic execution that is based on compact, easy to check certificates. We implemented the technique in Symbolic PathFinder and showed its merits. Our method is general and could be easily implemented in other symbolic or concolic execution tools. In the future we plan to focus on the application of our technique in a compositional setting, where certificates of components are (re)used for fast reliable component integration with probabilistic guarantees.

Acknowledgments. This material is based on research sponsored by NSF under grants CCF-1319688, CCF-1319858 and CCF-1549161.

References

1. Albert, E., Gmez-Zamalloa, M., Rojas, J.M., Puebla, G.: Compositional CLP-based test data generation for imperative languages. In: LOPSTR 2011 (2011)
2. Barrett, C.W., Tinelli, C.: CVC3. In: Damm, W., Hermanns, H. (eds.) CAV 2007. LNCS, vol. 4590, pp. 298–302. Springer, Heidelberg (2007)
3. Belov, A., Janota, M., Lynce, I., Marques-Silva, J.: On computing minimal equivalent subformulas. In: Milano, M. (ed.) CP 2012. LNCS, vol. 7514, pp. 158–174. Springer, Heidelberg (2012)
4. Böhme, S., Weber, T.: Fast LCF-style proof reconstruction for Z3. In: Kaufmann, M., Paulson, L.C. (eds.) ITP 2010. LNCS, vol. 6172, pp. 179–194. Springer, Heidelberg (2010)
5. Brumley, D., Caballero, J., Liang, Z., Newsome, J., Song, D.: Towards automatic discovery of deviations in binary implementations with applications to error detection, fingerprint generation. In: SS, pp. 15:1–15:16 (2007)
6. Burnim, J., Juvekar, S., Sen, K.: WISE: automated test generation for worst-case complexity. In: ICSE, pp. 463–473 (2009)
7. Clarke, L.A.: A program testing system. In: ACM 1976, pp. 488–491 (1976)
8. de Moura, L., Bjørner, N.S.: Z3: an efficient SMT solver. In: Ramakrishnan, C.R., Rehof, J. (eds.) TACAS 2008. LNCS, vol. 4963, pp. 337–340. Springer, Heidelberg (2008)
9. Filieri, A., Păsăreanu, C.S., Visser, W.: Reliability analysis in symbolic pathfinder. In: ICSE 2013, pp. 622–631. IEEE Press, Piscataway (2013)
10. Geldenhuys, J., Dwyer, M.B., Visser, W.: Probabilistic symbolic execution. In: ISSTA 2012, pp. 166–176. ACM, New York (2012)
11. Godefroid, P., Klarlund, N., Sen, K.: DART: directed automated random testing. In: PLDI, pp. 213–223 (2005)
12. Hatcliff, J., Robby, Chalin, P., Belt, J.: Explicating symbolic execution (xsym-exe): an evidence-based verification framework. In: ICSE 2013, pp. 222–231 (2013)
13. Henzinger, T.A., Jhala, R., Majumdar, R., Necula, G.C., Sutre, G., Weimer, W.: Temporal-safety proofs for systems code. In: Brinksma, E., Larsen, K.G. (eds.) CAV 2002. LNCS, vol. 2404, p. 526. Springer, Heidelberg (2002)
14. Inkumsah, K., Xie, T.: Improving structural testing of object-oriented programs via integrating evolutionary testing and symbolic execution. In: ASE, pp. 297–306 (2008)
15. King, J.C.: Symbolic execution and program testing. Commun. ACM **19**(7), 385–394 (1976)
16. Loera, J.A.D., Hemmecke, R., Tauzer, J., Yoshida, R.: Effective lattice point counting in rational convex polytopes. JSC **38**(4), 1273–1302 (2004)
17. Ma, K.-K., Yit Phang, K., Foster, J.S., Hicks, M.: Directed symbolic execution. In: Yahav, E. (ed.) SAS 2011. LNCS, vol. 6887, pp. 95–111. Springer, Heidelberg (2011)
18. Namjoshi, K.S.: Certifying model checkers. In: Berry, G., Comon, H., Finkel, A. (eds.) CAV 2001. LNCS, vol. 2102, p. 2. Springer, Heidelberg (2001)
19. Necula, G.C.: Proof-carrying code. In: POPL, pp. 106–119 (1997)
20. Peled, D.A., Zuck, L.D.: From model checking to a temporal proof. In: Dwyer, M.B. (ed.) SPIN 2001. LNCS, vol. 2057, p. 1. Springer, Heidelberg (2001)

21. Person, S., Yang, G., Rungta, N., Khurshid, S.: Directed incremental symbolic execution. In: PLDI, pp. 504–515 (2011)

22. Păsăreanu, C.S., Mehlitz, P.C., Bushnell, D.H., Gundy-Burlet, K., Lowry, M., Person, S., Pape, M.: Combining unit-level symbolic execution and system-level concrete execution for testing NASA software. In: ISSTA, pp. 15–25 (2008)

23. Păsăreanu, C.S., Rungta, N.: Symbolic PathFinder: symbolic execution of Java bytecode. In: ASE, pp. 179–180 (2010)

24. Qiu, R., Yang, G., Pasareanu, C.S., Khurshid, S.: Compositional symbolic execution with memoized replay. In: ICSE, pp. 632–642 (2015)

25. Rinard, M., Marinov, D.: Credible compilation with pointers. In: Workshop on Run-Time Result Verication (1999)

26. Rojas, J.M., Pasareanu, C.S.: Compositional symbolic execution through program specialization. In: BYTECODE 2013 (ETAPS) (2013)

27. Sen, K., Agha, G.: CUTE and jCUTE: concolic unit testing and explicit path model-checking tools. In: Ball, T., Jones, R.B. (eds.) CAV 2006. LNCS, vol. 4144, pp. 419–423. Springer, Heidelberg (2006)

28. Siddiqui, J.H., Khurshid, S.: Scaling symbolic execution using ranged analysis. In: OOPSLA, pp. 523–536 (2012)

29. Souza, M., Borges, M., d'Amorim, M., Păsăreanu, C.S.: CORAL: solving complex constraints for symbolic pathfinder. In: Bobaru, M., Havelund, K., Holzmann, G.J., Joshi, R. (eds.) NFM 2011. LNCS, vol. 6617, pp. 359–374. Springer, Heidelberg (2011)

30. Stump, A., Oe, D., Reynolds, A., Hadarean, L., Tinelli, C.: SMT proof checking using a logical framework. Form. Methods Syst. Des. **42**(1), 91–118 (2013)

31. Teleghani, A., Atlee, J.M.: Search-carrying code. In: ASE 2010, pp. 367–376

32. Visser, W., Geldenhuys, J., Dwyer, M.B.: Green: reducing, reusing and recycling constraints in program analysis. In: FSE, pp. 58:1–58:11 (2012)

33. Whalen, M.W., Godefroid, P., Mariani, L., Polini, A., Tillmann, N., Visser. W.: FITE: future integrated testing environment. In: FoSER, pp. 401–406 (2010)

34. Xia, S., Hook, J.: Certifying temporal properties for compiled C programs. In: Steffen, B., Levi, G. (eds.) VMCAI 2004. LNCS, vol. 2937, pp. 161–174. Springer, Heidelberg (2004)

35. Yang, G., Khurshid, S., Person, S., Rungta, N.: Property differencing for incremental checking. In: ICSE, pp. 1059–1070 (2014)

36. Yang, G., Pasareanu, C.S., Khurshid, S.: Memoized symbolic execution. In: ISSTA, pp. 144–154 (2012)

Tighter Loop Bound Analysis

Pavel Čadek[1]([✉]), Jan Strejček[2], and Marek Trtík[3]

[1] Faculty of Informatics, Vienna University of Technology, Vienna, Austria
pcadek@forsyte.at
[2] Faculty of Informatics, Masaryk University, Brno, Czech Republic
[3] LaBRI, University of Bordeaux, Bordeaux, France
trtikm@gmail.com

Abstract. We present a new algorithm for computing upper bounds on the number of executions of each program instruction during any single program run. The upper bounds are expressed as functions of program input values. The algorithm is primarily designed to produce bounds that are relatively tight, i.e. not unnecessarily blown up. The upper bounds for instructions allow us to infer loop bounds, i.e. upper bounds on the number of loop iterations. Experimental results show that the algorithm implemented in a prototype tool LOOPERMAN often produces tighter bounds than current tools for loop bound analysis.

1 Introduction

The goal of *loop bound analysis* is to derive for each loop in a given program an upper bound on the number of its iterations during any execution of the program. These bounds can be parametrized by the program input. The loop bound analysis is an active research area with two prominent applications: *program complexity* analysis and *worst case execution time* (WCET) analysis.

The aim of program complexity analysis is to derive an asymptotic complexity of a given program. The complexity is commonly considered by programmers in their everyday work and it is also used in specifications of programming languages, e.g. every implementation of the standard template library of C++ has to have the prescribed complexities. Loop bound analysis clearly plays a crucial role in program complexity analysis. In this context, emphasis is put on large coverage of the loop bound analysis (i.e. it should find some bounds for as many program loops as possible), while there are only limited requirements on tightness of the bounds as asymptotic complexity is studied.

A typical application scenario for WCET analysis is to check whether a given part of some critical system finishes its execution within an allocated time budget. One step of the decision process is to compute loop bounds. Tightness of the bounds is very important here as an untight bound can lead to a spuriously negative answer of the analysis (i.e. 'the allocated time budged can be exceeded'), which may imply unnecessary additional costs, e.g. for system redesign or for hardware components with higher performance. The WCET analysis can also be used by schedulers to estimate the run-time of individual tasks.

© Springer International Publishing AG 2016
C. Artho et al. (Eds.): ATVA 2016, LNCS 9938, pp. 512–527, 2016.
DOI: 10.1007/978-3-319-46520-3_32

The problem to infer loop bounds has recently been refined into the *reachability-bound problem* [8], where the goal is to find an upper bound on the number of executions of a given program instruction during any single run of a given program. One typically asks for a reachability bound on some resource demanding instruction like memory allocation. Reachability bound analysis is more challenging than loop bound analysis as, in order to get a reasonably precise bound, branching inside loops must be taken into account.

This paper presents a new algorithm that infers reachability bounds. More precisely, for each instruction of a given program, the algorithm tries to find an upper bound on the number of executions of the instruction in any single run of the program. The bounds are parametrized by the program input. The reachability bounds can be directly used to infer loop bounds and asymptotic program complexity. Our algorithm builds on *symbolic execution* [10] and *loop summarisation* adopted from [14]. In comparison with other techniques for reachability bound or loop bound analysis, our algorithm brings the following features:

- It utilizes a loop summarisation technique that computes precise values of program variables as functions of loop iteration counts.
- It distinguishes different branches inside loops and computes bounds for each of them separately.
- If more different bounds arise, it handles all of them while other techniques usually choose nondeterministically one of them.
- It can detect logarithmic bounds.
- Upper bounds for nested loops are computed more precisely: while other techniques typically multiply a bound for the outer loop by a maximal bound on iterations of the inner loop during one iteration of the outer loop, we sum the bounds for the inner loop over all iterations of the outer loop.

All these features have a positive effect on tightness of produced bounds.

We can explain the basic idea of our algorithm on the flowgraph on the right. The node a is the entry location, d is the exit location, and locations b, c form a loop. An initial value of x represents program input. We symbolically execute each path in the loop and assign an iteration counter to it. Then

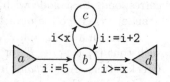

we try to express the effect of arbitrarily many iterations of the loop using the iteration counters as parameters. The loop in our example has just one path bcb that increments i by 2. Hence, the value of i after κ iterations is $\underline{i}' + 2\kappa$, where $\underline{i}'$ denotes the value of i before the loop execution starts. We combine this loop summary with the program state just before entering the loop, which is obtained by symbolic execution of the corresponding part of the program. In our example, we get that the value of i after κ iterations of the loop is $5 + 2\kappa$. To enter another iteration, the condition i<x must hold. If we replace the variables i and x by their current values, we get the condition $5 + 2\kappa < \underline{x}$, where $\underline{x}$ refers to the initial value of x. This condition is satisfied only if $\kappa < \frac{x-5}{2}$. As κ is an iteration counter, it has to be a non-negative integer. Hence, we get the bound on the number of loop iterations $\mathbf{max}\{0, \lceil \frac{x-5}{2} \rceil\}$, which is assigned to all edges in the loop. Edges outside the loop are visited at most once. The situation is more complicated if we have loops with more loop paths, nested loops, or loops where a run can cycle forever. The algorithm is described in Sect. 3.

We have implemented our algorithm in an experimental tool LOOPERMAN. Comparison with several leading loop bound analysis tools shows that our approach often provides tighter loop bounds. For example, our tool is currently the only one that detects that the inner cycle of the BubbleSort algorithm makes $\frac{n \cdot (n-1)}{2}$ iterations in total (i.e. during all iterations of the outer loop) when sorting an array of n elements, while other tools provide only the bound n^2 or $\mathcal{O}(n^2)$. Section 4 presents the comparison with the best performing tool LOO-PUS [12]. Experimental comparison with more tools, a detailed description of the algorithm, and discussion of the BubbleSort example can be found in [15].

2   Preliminaries

For simplicity, this paper focuses on programs without function calls, manipulating only integer scalar variables a, b, ... and read-only multidimensional integer array variables A, B, ... As usual in the context of loop bound analysis, integers are interpreted in the mathematical (i.e. unbounded) sense.

Flowgraph, Backbone, Loop, Induced Flowgraph. An analysed program is represented as a *flowgraph* $P = (V, E, l_{beg}, l_{end}, \iota)$, where (V, E) is a finite oriented graph, $l_{beg}, l_{end} \in V$ are different *begin* and *end nodes* respectively, and $\iota : E \to \mathcal{I}$ labels each edge e by an *instruction* $\iota(e)$. The out-degree of l_{end} is 0 and out-degrees of all other nodes are positive. We use two kinds of instructions: an assignment a:=*expr* for some scalar variable a and some program expression *expr* over program variables, and an assumption assume(γ) for some quantifier-free formula γ over program variables. For example, a statement if γ then... corresponds to a node with two outgoing edges labelled with assume(γ) and assume($\neg\gamma$). We often omit the keyword assume in flowgraphs.

A *path* in a flowgraph is a (finite or infinite) sequence $\pi = v_1 v_2 \cdots$ of nodes such that $(v_i, v_{i+1}) \in E$ for all v_i, v_{i+1} in the sequence. Paths are denoted by Greek letters. A *backbone* in a flowgraph is an acyclic path leading from the begin node to the end node.

Let π be a backbone with a prefix αv. There is a *loop* C with a *loop entry* v along π, if there exists a path $v\beta v$ such that no node of β appears in α. The loop C is then the smallest set containing all nodes of all such paths $v\beta v$.

Each *run* of the program corresponds to a path in the flowgraph starting at l_{beg} and such that it is either infinite, or it is finite and ends in l_{end}.[1] Every run follows some backbone: it can escape from the backbone in order to perform one or more iterations in a loop along the backbone, but once the last iteration in the loop is finished (which need not happen if the run is infinite), the execution continues along the backbone again. We thus talk about a *run along* a backbone.

---

[1] We assume that crashes or other undefined behaviour of program expressions are prevented by safety guards, e.g. an expression a/b is guarded by assume(b $\neq$ 0).

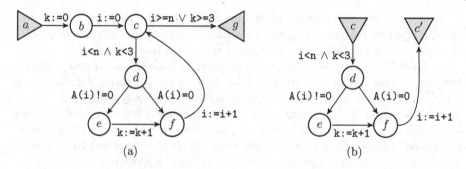

Fig. 1. (a) A flowgraph representing a program that gets an array A of size n and counts up to three non-zero elements in the array. (b) Its induced flowgraph $P(\{c, d, e, f\}, c)$.

For a loop C with a loop entry v along a backbone π, a *flowgraph induced by the loop*, denoted as $P(C, v)$, is the subgraph of the original flowgraph induced by C, where v is marked as the begin node, a fresh end node v' is added, and every transition $(u, v) \in E$ leading to v is redirected to v' (we identify the edge (u, v') with (u, v) in the context of the original program). Each single iteration of the loop corresponds to a run of the induced flowgraph. Figure 1(b) shows the flowgraph induced by the loop $\{c, d, e, f\}$ of the program in Fig. 1(a).

The program representation by flowgraphs and our definition of loops easily handle many features of programming languages like `break`, `continue`, or `goto`.

Symbolic Execution. *Symbolic execution* [10] replaces input data of a program by *symbols* representing arbitrary data. Executed instructions then manipulate symbolic expressions over the symbols instead of exact values. *Symbolic expressions* are terms of the theory of integers extended with functions **max** and **min**, rounding functions $\lceil \cdot \rceil$ and $\lfloor \cdot \rfloor$ applied to constant expressions over reals, and

- for each scalar variable a, an uninterpreted constant $\underline{a}$, which is a *symbol* representing any initial (input) value of the variable a,
- for each array variable A, an uninterpreted function $\underline{A}$ of the same arity as A, which is a *symbol* representing any initial (input) content of the array A,
- a countable set $\{\kappa_1, \kappa_2, \dots\}$ of artificial variables (not appearing in analysed programs), called *path counters* and ranging over non-negative integers,
- a special symbol $\star$ called *unknown*, and
- for each formula ψ build over symbolic expressions and two symbolic expressions ϕ_1, ϕ_2, a construct $\mathbf{ite}(\psi, \phi_1, \phi_2)$ of meaning "if-then-else", that evaluates to ϕ_1 if ψ holds, and to ϕ_2 otherwise.

For symbolic expressions ψ, ϕ and a symbol or a path counter x, let $\psi[x/\phi]$ denote the expression ψ where all occurrences of x are simultaneously replaced by ϕ. Further, $\psi[x_i/\phi_i \mid i \in I]$ denotes multiple simultaneous replacements. We sometimes write ψ^κ to emphasize that ψ can contain path counters $\kappa = (\kappa_1, \dots, \kappa_n)$. An expression is κ-*free* if it contains no path counter.

Symbolic execution stores variable values in *symbolic memory* and all executable program paths are uniquely identified by corresponding *path conditions*. Here we provide brief descriptions of these terms. For more information see [10].

A *symbolic memory* is a function θ assigning to each scalar variable a a symbolic expression and to each array variable A the symbol $\underline{A}$ (array variables keep their initial values as we consider programs with read-only arrays). We overload the notation $\theta(\cdot)$ to program expressions as follows. Let *expr* be a program expression over program variables $a_1, \ldots, a_n$. Then $\theta(expr)$ denotes the symbolic expression obtained from *expr* by replacement of all occurrences of the variables $a_1, \ldots, a_n$ by symbolic expressions $\theta(a_1), \ldots, \theta(a_n)$ respectively.

Symbolic execution of a path in a flowgraph starts with the initial symbolic memory θ, where $\theta(a) = \underline{a}$ for each variable a. The memory is updated on assignments. For example, if the first executed assignment is a:=2*a+b, the initial symbolic memory θ is updated to the symbolic memory θ' where $\theta'(a) = \theta(2*a+b) = 2\underline{a} + \underline{b}$. If we later update θ' on a:=1-a, we get the memory θ'' such that $\theta''(a) = \theta'(1-a) = 1 - 2\underline{a} - \underline{b}$.

If ψ is a symbolic expression over symbols $\{\underline{a}_i \mid i \in I\}$ corresponding to program variables $\{a_i \mid i \in I\}$ respectively, then $\theta\langle\psi\rangle$ denotes the symbolic expression $\psi[\underline{a}_i/\theta(a_i) \mid i \in I]$. For example, if $\theta(a) = \kappa_1$ and $\theta(b) = \underline{a} - \kappa_2$, then $\theta\langle 2\underline{a} + \underline{b}\rangle = 2\theta(a) + \theta(b) = 2\kappa_1 + \underline{a} - \kappa_2$. Note that $\theta_1\langle\theta_2(a)\rangle$ returns the value of a after a code with effect θ_1 followed by a code with effect θ_2. For example, if $\theta_1(a) = 2\underline{a}+1$ represents the effect of assignment a:=2*a+1 and $\theta_2(a) = \underline{a}-2$ the effect of a:=a-2, then $\theta_1\langle\theta_2(a)\rangle = \theta_1\langle\underline{a} - 2\rangle = (2\underline{a} + 1) - 2$ represents the effect of the two assignments in the sequence. We apply the notation $\theta\langle\varphi\rangle$ and $\varphi[x/\psi]$ with analogous meanings also to formulae φ built over symbolic expressions.

Given a path in a flowgraph leading from its begin node, the *path condition* is a formula over symbols satisfied exactly by all program inputs for which the program execution follows the path. A path condition is constructed during symbolic execution of the path. Initially, the path condition is set to *true* and it can only be updated when an assume(γ) is executed. For example, if a symbolic execution reaches assume(a>5) with a path condition φ and a symbolic memory $\theta(a) = 2\underline{a} - 1$, then it updates the path condition to $\varphi \wedge (2\underline{a} - 1 > 5)$.

Upper Bound. An *upper bound* for an edge e in a flowgraph P is a κ-free symbolic expression ρ such that whenever P is executed on any input, the instruction on edge e is executed at most ρ' times, where ρ' is the expression that we get by replacing each variable symbol by the input value of the corresponding variable.

3   The Algorithm

Recall that every program run follows some backbone and the run can diverge from the backbone only to loops along the backbone. The algorithm first detects all backbones. For each backbone π_i and each edge e, it computes a set of upper bounds $\beta_i(e)$ on the number of visits of the edge by any run following the considered backbone. As all these bounds are valid, the set $\beta_i(e)$ can be interpreted as a single bound $\mathbf{min}\,\beta_i(e)$ on visits of edge e by any run along π_i. At the end, the overall upper bound for an edge e can be computed as the maximum of these bounds over all backbones, i.e. $\mathbf{max}\{\mathbf{min}\,\beta_i(e) \mid \pi_i \text{ is a backbone}\}$.

The algorithm consists of the following four procedures:

executeProgram is the starting procedure of the whole algorithm. It gets a flowgraph and computes all its backbones. Then it symbolically executes each backbone and computes for each edge a set of upper bounds on the number of visits of the edge by a run following the backbone. Whenever the symbolic execution enters a loop entry node, the procedure processLoop is called to get upper bounds on visits during loop execution.

processLoop gets a loop represented by the program induced by the loop. Note that each run of the induced program corresponds to one iteration of the loop and it follows some backbone of the induced program (the backbones are called *loop paths* in this context). The procedure then symbolically executes each loop path by recursive call of executeProgram (the nesting of recursive calls thus directly corresponds to the nesting of loops in the program). The recursive call of executeProgram produces, for each loop path, a symbolic memory and a path condition capturing the effect of a single iteration along the loop path. The procedure processLoop then calls computeSummary, which takes the symbolic memories after single loop iterations, assigns to each loop path a unique path counter κ_i, and computes a *parametrized symbolic memory* θ^κ describing the effect of an arbitrary number of loop iterations. This symbolic memory is parametrized by path counters $\kappa = (\kappa_1, \ldots, \kappa_k)$ representing the numbers of iterations along the corresponding loop paths. From the parametrized symbolic memory and from the path conditions corresponding to single loop iterations (received from the recursive call of executeProgram), we derive a *parametrized necessary condition* for each loop path, which is a formula over symbols and path counters κ that has to be satisfied when another loop iteration along the corresponding loop path can be performed after κ loop iterations. Finally, processLoop infers upper bounds from these parametrized necessary conditions with the help of the procedure computeBounds.

computeSummary is a subroutine of processLoop that gets symbolic memories corresponding to single loop iterations along each loop path and it produces the parametrized symbolic memory θ^κ after an arbitrary number of loop iterations (as mentioned above).

computeBounds is another subroutine of processLoop. It gets a set I of loop paths and the corresponding parametrized necessary conditions, and derives upper bounds on the number of loop iterations along loop paths from I.

We describe the four procedures in the following four subsections. The procedure processLoop is described as the last one as it calls the other three procedures. We demonstrate the procedures and finally the whole algorithm on the programs of Fig. 1. Descriptions of symbolic memories related to these programs omit the variables n and A: these variables are never changed and hence the value of n and A is always $\underline{n}$ and $\underline{A}$, respectively.

Algorithm 1. executeProgram

Input:
    P // a flowgraph

Output:
    $\{(\pi_1, \theta_1, \varphi_1), \ldots, (\pi_k, \theta_k, \varphi_k)\}$ // backbones π_i (with symbolic memory θ_i and
                                           // path condition φ_i after execution along π_i)
    β // for each edge e of P, $\beta(e)$ is a set of upper bounds for e

1   states $\longleftarrow \emptyset$;
2   Compute the set of backbones $\{\pi_1, \ldots, \pi_k\}$ of P.;
3   **foreach** $i = 1, \ldots, k$ **do**
4   Initialize θ_i to return $\underline{a}$ for each (scalar or array) variable **a.**;
5      $\varphi_i \longleftarrow true$;
6   Initialize β_i to return $\{0\}$ for each edge.;
7   Let $\pi_i = v_1 \ldots v_n$.;
8   **foreach** $j = 1, \ldots, n-1$ **do**
9   **if** v_j *is a loop entry* **then**
10   Let C be the loop with the loop entry v_j along π_i.;
11             $(\beta_{loop}, \theta_i) \longleftarrow$ processLoop$(P(C, v_j), \theta_i, \varphi_i)$;
12   **foreach** *edge* e *of* $P(C, v_j)$ **do**
13                 $\beta_i(e) \longleftarrow \{\rho_1 + \rho_2 \mid \rho_1 \in \beta_i(e), \rho_2 \in \beta_{loop}(e)\}$;
14   **if** $\iota((v_j, v_{j+1}))$ *has the form* assume(ψ) *and* $\theta_i(\psi)$ *contains no* $\star$ **then**
15             $\varphi_i \longleftarrow \varphi_i \wedge \theta_i(\psi)$;
16   **if** $\iota((v_j, v_{j+1}))$ *has the form* **a** := *expr* **then**
17             $\theta_i(\mathbf{a}) \longleftarrow \theta_i(expr)$;
18             $\beta_i((v_j, v_{j+1})) \longleftarrow \{\rho + 1 \mid \rho \in \beta_i((v_j, v_{j+1}))\}$;
19   Insert $(\pi_i, \theta_i, \varphi_i)$ into states.;
20   **foreach** *edge* e *of* P **do**
21      $\beta(e) \longleftarrow \{\max\{\rho_1, \ldots, \rho_k\} \mid \rho_1 \in \beta_1(e), \ldots, \rho_k \in \beta_k(e)\}$;
22   **return** (states, β)

3.1   Algorithm executeProgram

The procedure executeProgram of Algorithm 1 takes a flowgraph as input, determines its backbones, and symbolically executes each backbone separately. For a backbone π_i, symbolic execution computes symbolic memory θ_i, path condition φ_i, and *bound function* β_i assigning to each edge e a set of symbolic expressions that are valid upper bounds on the number of visits of edge e during any single run along the backbone. Each such a set $\beta_i(e)$ of bounds could be replaced by a single bound $\min \beta_i(e)$, but we prefer to keep it as a set of simpler expressions to increase the success rate of expression matching in the procedure processLoop (we point out the reason in Sect. 3.4).

    The symbolic execution proceeds in the standard way until we enter a loop entry (line 9). Then we call procedure processLoop on the loop, current symbolic memory and path condition. The procedure returns function β_{loop} of upper bounds on visits of loop edges during execution of the loop, and a symbolic memory after execution of the loop. We add these bounds and the former bounds in the **foreach** loop at line 12 and continue the execution along the backbone. If the `processLoop` procedure cannot determine the value of some variable after the loop, it simply uses the symbol $\star$ (unknown).

Another difference from the standard symbolic execution is at line 14 where we suppress insertion of predicates containing $\star$ to the path condition. As a consequence, a path condition of our approach is no longer a necessary and sufficient condition on input values to lead the program execution along the corresponding path (which is the case in the standard symbolic execution), but it is only a necessary condition on input values of a run to follow the backbone.

After processing an edge of the backbone, we increase the corresponding bounds by one (line 18). At the end of the procedure, the resulting bounds for each edge are computed as the maximum of previously computed bounds for the edge over all backbones (see the **foreach** loop at line 20). Besides these bounds, the procedure also returns each backbone with the symbolic memory and path condition after its execution.

Example 1. When `executeProgram` is called on the flowgraph of Fig. 1(b), it finds two backbones $\pi_1 = cdefc'$ and $\pi_2 = cdfc'$. Since there are no loops along these backbones, their symbolic execution easily ends up with the corresponding symbolic memories and path conditions

$$\pi_1 : \quad \theta_1(\mathtt{i}) = \underline{i} + 1 \qquad \theta_1(\mathtt{k}) = \underline{k} + 1 \qquad \varphi_1 = \underline{i} < \underline{n} \ \wedge \ \underline{k} < 3 \ \wedge \ \underline{A(i)} \neq 0$$
$$\pi_2 : \quad \theta_2(\mathtt{i}) = \underline{i} + 1 \qquad \theta_2(\mathtt{k}) = \underline{k} \qquad\quad \varphi_2 = \underline{i} < \underline{n} \ \wedge \ \underline{k} < 3 \ \wedge \ \underline{A(i)} = 0$$

and a bound function β assigning $\{1\}$ to each edge of the flowgraph.

3.2 Algorithm `computeSummary`

The procedure `computeSummary` gets loop paths $\pi_1, \ldots, \pi_l$ together with symbolic memories $\theta_1, \ldots, \theta_l$, where each θ_i represents the effect of a single iteration along π_i. Then it assigns fresh path counters $\boldsymbol{\kappa} = (\kappa_1, \ldots, \kappa_l)$ to the loop paths and computes the parametrized symbolic memory $\theta^{\boldsymbol{\kappa}}$ after $\boldsymbol{\kappa}$ iterations of the loop, i.e. after $\sum_{1 \leq i \leq l} \kappa_i$ iterations where exactly κ_i iterations follow π_i for each i and there is no assumption on the order of iterations along different loop paths. If we do not find the precise value of some variable after $\boldsymbol{\kappa}$ iterations (for example because the value depends on the order of iterations along different loop paths), then $\theta^{\boldsymbol{\kappa}}$ assigns $\star$ (unknown) to this variable.

Due to the limited space, we do not provide any pseudocode or intuitive description of the procedure `computeSummary` here. Both can be found in [15]. It follows the ideas of the procedure of the same name introduced in [14].

Example 2. Assume that `computeSummary` gets symbolic memories θ_1, θ_2 corresponding to loop paths π_1, π_2 as computed in Example 1. It assigns path counters κ_1, κ_2 to π_1, π_2 respectively, and computes the parametrized symbolic memory $\theta^{\boldsymbol{\kappa}}$ describing the values of program variables after $\boldsymbol{\kappa} = (\kappa_1, \kappa_2)$ iterations of the loop that induces the flowgraph of Fig. 1(b). Note that $\underline{i}, \underline{k}$ here represent the values of `i, k` just before the loop is executed.

$$\theta^{\boldsymbol{\kappa}}(\mathtt{i}) = \underline{i} + \kappa_1 + \kappa_2 \qquad \theta^{\boldsymbol{\kappa}}(\mathtt{k}) = \underline{k} + \kappa_1$$

Algorithm 2. computeBounds

Input:

    I // *indices of backbones*

    φ // *a necessary condition to perform an iteration along a backbone*

      // *with an index in I after κ iterations*

Output:

    B // *upper bounds on the number of iterations*

      // *along backbones with indices in I*

1 **if** $\varphi[\kappa_i/0 \mid i \in I]$ *is not satisfiable* **then** **return** $\{0\}$ $B \longleftarrow \emptyset$;

2 **foreach** inequality $\sum_{j \in J \supseteq I} a_j \kappa_j < b$ implied by φ, where each a_j is a positive integer and b is κ-free **do**

3     $B \longleftarrow B \cup \{\max\{0, \lceil b/\min\{a_i \mid i \in I\}\rceil\}\}$

4 **return** B

3.3   Algorithm computeBounds

The procedure computeBounds of Algorithm 2 gets a set I of selected loop path indices, and a necessary condition φ to perform an iteration along some loop path with an index in I (we talk about an *iteration along I* for short) after κ previous loop iterations. From this information, the procedure infers upper bounds on the number of loop iterations along I.

We would like to find a tight upper bound, i.e. a κ-free symbolic expression B such that there exist some values of symbols (given by a valuation function v) for which the necessary condition $\varphi[\underline{a}/v(\underline{a}) \mid \underline{a}$ is a symbol$]$ to make another iteration along I is satisfiable whenever the number of finished iterations along I is less than $B[\underline{a}/v(\underline{a}) \mid \underline{a}$ is a symbol$]$ and the same does not hold for the expression $B + 1$. An effective algorithm computing these tight bounds is an interesting research topic itself.

The presented procedure infers some bounds only for two special cases. Line 1 covers the case when even the first iteration along any loop path in I is not possible: the procedure then returns the bound 0.

The other special case is the situation when the necessary condition implies an inequality of the form $\sum_{j \in J \supseteq I} a_j \kappa_j < b$, where each a_j is a positive integer and b is κ-free. To detect these cases, we transform the necessary condition to the conjunctive normal form, look for clauses that contain just one predicate and try to transfer the predicate into this form. Each such inequality implies the following:

$$\sum_{j \in J \supseteq I} a_j \kappa_j < b \implies \sum_{i \in I} a_i \kappa_i < b \implies \min\{a_i \mid i \in I\} \cdot \sum_{i \in I} \kappa_i < b.$$

Hence, $\sum_{i \in I} \kappa_i < \lceil b/\min\{a_i \mid i \in I\}\rceil$ has to be satisfied to perform another iteration along I after κ previous iterations including $\sum_{i \in I} \kappa_i$ iterations along I. As all path counters are non-negative integers, we derive the bound $\max\{0, \lceil b/\min\{a_i \mid i \in I\}\rceil\}$ on iterations along I.

Example 3. We call `computeBounds({1}, φ)` to get bounds on κ_1 from the condition $\varphi = \kappa_1 + \kappa_2 < \underline{n} \wedge \kappa_1 < 3 \wedge \underline{A}(\kappa_1 + \kappa_2) \neq 0$. Since $\varphi[\kappa_1/0]$ is satisfiable, the procedure uses inequalities $\kappa_1 + \kappa_2 < \underline{n}$ and $\kappa_1 < 3$ implied by φ to produce bounds $B = \{\mathbf{max}\{0, \underline{n}\}, \mathbf{max}\{0, 3\}\} = \{\mathbf{max}\{0, \underline{n}\}, 3\}$.

3.4 Algorithm `processLoop`

The procedure `processLoop` of Algorithm 3 gets a flowgraph Q representing the body of a loop, i.e. each run of Q corresponds to one iteration of the original loop. We symbolically execute Q using the recursive call of `executeProgram` at line 2. We obtain all loop paths $\pi_1, \ldots, \pi_k$ of Q and bounds β_{inner} on visits of each edge in the loop during any single iteration of the loop. For each π_i, we also get the symbolic memory θ_i after one iteration along π_i and a necessary condition φ_i to perform this iteration. The procedure `computeSummary` produces the parametrized symbolic memory θ^κ after κ iterations. Symbols $\underline{a}$ appearing in θ^κ refer to variable values before the loop is entered. If we combine θ^κ with the symbolic memory before entering the loop θ_{in}, we get the symbolic memory after execution of the code preceding the loop and κ iterations of the loop. We use this combination to derive necessary conditions φ_i^κ to perform another iteration along π_i and upper bounds β^κ on visits of loop edges in the next iteration of the loop.

The **foreach** loop at line 6 computes upper bounds for all edges of the processed loop on visits during all its complete iterations (incomplete iterations when a run cycles in some nested loop forever are handled later). We already have the bounds β^κ on visits in a single iteration after κ preceding iterations. For each edge e, we compute the set I of all loop path indices such that iterations along these loop paths can visit e. The `computeBounds` procedure at line 8 takes I and a necessary condition to perform an iteration along I after κ iterations and computes bounds B_{outer} on the number of iterations along I. If there is 0 among these bounds, e cannot be visited by any complete iteration and the computation for e is over. Otherwise we try to compute some overall bounds for each bound ρ_{inner} on the visits of e during one iteration (after κ iterations) separately. If ρ_{inner} is a κ-free expression (line 13), then it is constant in each iteration and we simply multiply it with every bound on the number of iterations along I. The situation is more difficult if ρ_{inner} contains some path counters. We can handle the frequent case when it has the form $\mathbf{max}\{c, b + \sum_{i=1}^{k} a_i \kappa_i\}$, where $a_1, \ldots, a_k, b, c$ are κ-free (see line 15 and note that this is the reason for keeping the bounds simple). First we get rid of path counters κ_j that have some influence on this bound (i.e. $a_j \neq 0$), but e cannot be visited by any iteration along loop path π_j. Let J be the set of indices of such path counters (line 16). We try to compute bounds B_J on the number of iterations along J (line 17), which are also the bounds on $\sum_{j \in J} \kappa_j$. Note that if $J = \emptyset$, we call `computeBounds(∅, false)`, which immediately returns $\{0\}$. If we get some bounds in B_J, we can overapproximate $\sum_{i=1}^{k} a_i \kappa_i$ as follows:

$$\sum_{i=1}^{k} a_i \kappa_i = \sum_{j \in J} a_j \kappa_j + \sum_{i \in I} a_i \kappa_i \leq \mathbf{max}\{0, a_j \mid j \in J\} \cdot \mathbf{min}\, B_J + \mathbf{max}\{a_i \mid i \in I\} \cdot \sum_{i \in I} \kappa_i$$

Algorithm 3. processLoop

Input:

   Q // a flowgraph induced by a loop

   θ_{in} // a symbolic memory when entering the loop

   φ_{in} // a path condition when entering the loop

Output:

   β_{loop} // upper bounds for all edges in the loop

   θ_{out} // symbolic memory after the loop

1 Initialize β_{loop} to return $\emptyset$ for each edge e of Q.;

2 $(\{(\pi_1, \theta_1, \varphi_1), \ldots, (\pi_k, \theta_k, \varphi_k)\}, \beta_{inner}) \longleftarrow \texttt{executeProgram}(Q)$;

3 $\theta^\kappa \longleftarrow \texttt{computeSummary}(\{(\pi_1, \theta_1), \ldots, (\pi_k, \theta_k)\})$;

4 $\varphi_i^\kappa \longleftarrow \varphi_{in} \wedge \theta_{in}\langle \theta^\kappa \langle \varphi_i \rangle \rangle$ for each $i \in \{1, \ldots, k\}$;

5 $\beta^\kappa(e) \longleftarrow \{\theta_{in}\langle \theta^\kappa \langle \rho \rangle \rangle \mid \rho \in \beta_{inner}(e)\}$ for each edge e of Q;

6 **foreach** edge e of Q **do**

7     $I \longleftarrow \{i \mid e$ is on π_i or on a loop along $\pi_i\}$;

8     $B_{outer} \longleftarrow \texttt{computeBounds}(I, \bigvee_{i \in I} \varphi_i^\kappa)$;

9   **if** $0 \in B_{outer}$ **then**

10        $\beta_{loop}(e) \longleftarrow \{0\}$

11   **else**

12   **foreach** $\rho_{inner} \in \beta^\kappa(e)$ **do**

13   **if** $\rho_{inner} \equiv c$ where c is κ-free **then**

14              $\beta_{loop}(e) \longleftarrow \beta_{loop}(e) \cup \{c \cdot \rho_{outer} \mid \rho_{outer} \in B_{outer}\}$

15   **else if** $\rho_{inner} \equiv \max\{c, b + \sum_{i=1}^k a_i \kappa_i\}$ where c, b and all a_i are κ-free **then**

16              $J \longleftarrow \{j \mid j \notin I \wedge a_j \neq 0\}$;

17              $B_J \longleftarrow \texttt{computeBounds}(J, \bigvee_{j \in J} \varphi_j^\kappa)$;

18   **if** $B_J \neq \emptyset$ **then**

19                 $b' \longleftarrow b + \max\{0, a_j \mid j \in J\} \cdot \min B_J$;

20                 $a \longleftarrow \max\{a_i \mid i \in I\}$;

21   **foreach** $\rho_{outer} \in B_{outer}$ **do**

22                    $\beta_{loop}(e) \longleftarrow \beta_{loop}(e) \cup \{\sum_{K=0}^{\rho_{outer}-1} \max\{c, b' + a \cdot K\}\}$

23 **foreach** edge e of Q **do**

24   **if** an edge e' of Q such that $\beta^\kappa(e') = \emptyset$ is reachable from e in Q **then**

25        $\beta_{loop}(e) \longleftarrow \{\rho_1 + \rho_2 \mid \rho_1 \in \beta_{loop}(e), \rho_2 \in \beta^\kappa(e)$, and ρ_2 is κ-free$\}$;

26 $\theta_{out}(\mathbf{a}) \longleftarrow \theta_{in}\langle \theta^\kappa(\mathbf{a}) \rangle$ for each variable $\mathbf{a}$;

27 Eliminate κ from θ_{out}.;

28 **return** $(\beta_{loop}, \theta_{out})$

Using the definitions of b' and a at lines 19–20, we overapproximate the bound ρ_{inner} on visits of e during one iteration along I after κ loop iterations by

$$\rho_{inner} = \max\{c, b + \sum_{i=1}^k a_i \kappa_i\} \leq \max\{c, b' + a \cdot \sum_{i \in I} \kappa_i\}.$$

As K-th iteration along I is preceded by $K - 1$ iterations along I, the edge e can be visited at most $\max\{c, b' + a \cdot (K - 1)\}$ times during K-th iteration. For each bound ρ_{outer} on the iterations along I, we can now compute the total bound on visits of e as $\sum_{K=0}^{\rho_{outer}-1} \max\{c, b' + a \cdot K\}$.

Until now we have considered visits of loop edges during *complete* iterations. However, it may also happen that an iteration is started, but never finished because the execution keeps looping forever in some nested loop. For example, in the program `while(x>0){x:=x-1;while(true){}}`, we easily compute bound 0 on the number of complete iterations of the outer loop and thus we assign bound 0 to all loop edges at line 10. However, some edges of the loop are visited. These incomplete iterations are treated by the **foreach** loop at line 23. Whenever an edge e can be visited by an incomplete iteration (which is detected by existence of some subsequent edge e' without any bound and thus potentially lying on an infinite nested loop), we add the (κ-free) bounds on visits of e during one iteration to the total bounds for e. If there is no such κ-free bound, we leave e unbounded to be on the safe side.

Finally, the lines 26 and 27 combine the symbolic memory before the loop with the effect of the loop and eliminate loop counters from the resulting symbolic memory θ'_{out}. Roughly speaking, the elimination replaces every expression that is not κ-free by $\star$. In fact, the elimination can be done in a smarter way. For example, after the loop in the program `i:=0;while(i<n){i:=i+1}`, the elimination can replace κ by $\max\{0, \theta_{out}(\mathbf{n})\}$.

Example 4. We demonstrate the whole algorithm on the program of Fig. 1(a). We follow calls to individual procedures and we present the current state of the computation in terms of variables of the procedure at the top of the call stack.

The execution starts by calling `executeProgram` with the flowgraph at Fig. 1(a). The flowgraph has only one backbone $\pi_1 = abcg$. The node c is the loop entry to the loop $\{c, d, e, f\}$ along the backbone. Symbolic execution of π_1 up to c is straightforward and leads to the symbolic memory $\theta_1(k) = \theta_1(i) = 0$, the path condition $\varphi_1 = true$, and the bound function β_1 maps each edge to $\{0\}$ except $\beta_1((a,b)) = \beta_1((b,c)) = \{1\}$. At the entry node c we build an induced flowgraph $P(\{c, d, e, f\}, c)$ depicted in Fig. 1(b). Then we call `processLoop`$(P(\{c, d, e, f\}, c), \theta_1, \varphi_1)$.

`processLoop` calls `executeProgram` with the flowgraph at Fig. 1(b), as we did in Example 1. Recall that `processLoop` receives the following

$$\pi_1 = cdefc' \quad \theta_1(\mathbf{i}) = \underline{i} + 1 \quad \theta_1(\mathbf{k}) = \underline{k} + 1 \quad \varphi_1 = \underline{i} < \underline{n} \wedge \underline{k} < 3 \wedge \underline{A}(\underline{i}) \neq 0$$
$$\pi_2 = cdfc' \quad \theta_2(\mathbf{i}) = \underline{i} + 1 \quad \theta_2(\mathbf{k}) = \underline{k} \quad \varphi_2 = \underline{i} < \underline{n} \wedge \underline{k} < 3 \wedge \underline{A}(\underline{i}) = 0$$

and a bound function β_{inner} assigning $\{1\}$ to each edge of the flowgraph. Now we call `computeSummary` for the symbolic memories θ_1 and θ_2 and we get the parametrized symbolic memory θ^κ described in Example 2:

$$\theta^\kappa(\mathbf{i}) = \underline{i} + \kappa_1 + \kappa_2 \qquad \theta^\kappa(\mathbf{k}) = \underline{k} + \kappa_1$$

Next, at line 4 of `processLoop` we compute necessary conditions to perform another iteration along backbones π_1 and π_2 respectively:

$$\varphi_1^\kappa = \kappa_1 + \kappa_2 < \underline{n} \ \wedge \ \kappa_1 < 3 \ \wedge \ \underline{A}(\kappa_1 + \kappa_2) \neq 0$$
$$\varphi_2^\kappa = \kappa_1 + \kappa_2 < \underline{n} \ \wedge \ \kappa_1 < 3 \ \wedge \ \underline{A}(\kappa_1 + \kappa_2) = 0$$

The next line produces bound function β^κ which is the same as β_{inner}, in this case. Now we have all data we need to start the computation of resulting bounds for all five edges of the passed flowgraph.

The main part of this computation is performed in the loop at line 6. We show the computation for the edge (e, f). First we call computeBounds$(\{1\}, \varphi_1^\kappa)$. As shown in Example 3, we obtain the set $B_{outer} = \{\max\{0, \underline{n}\}, 3\}$. Since $0 \notin B_{outer}$ and $\beta^\kappa((e, f)) = \{1\}$, we get to the line 14 in processLoop, where we receive $\beta_{loop}((e, f)) = \{\max\{0, \underline{n}\}, 3\}$. The computation proceeds similarly for other edges, but for (c, d), (d, f), (f, c) it produces only one bound $\{\max\{0, \underline{n}\}\}$. The difference originates in the calls of computeBounds. For (c, d) and (f, c), we call computeBounds$(\{1, 2\}, \varphi_1^\kappa \vee \varphi_2^\kappa)$ and get only the bound $B_{outer} = \{\max\{0, \underline{n}\}\}$. For (d, f), we call computeBounds$(\{2\}, \varphi_2^\kappa)$ and get the same single bound. Since, the condition at line 24 is false for all edges, the resulting β_{loop} returns $\{\max\{0, \underline{n}\}, 3\}$ for (d, e) and (e, f), and $\{\max\{0, \underline{n}\}\}$ for the others. The resulting symbolic memory θ_{out} assigns $\star$ to i and k.

The control-flow then returns back to executeProgram where we update β_1 according to received β_{loop}. Then we symbolically execute the remaining edge (c, g). The computation in the loop at line 20 computes maximum over all bounds for a considered edge. The algorithm then terminates with the bound function β assigning $\{1\}$ to edges (a, b), (b, c), (c, g), the set $\{\max\{0, \underline{n}\}\}$ to edges (c, d), (d, f), (f, c), and the set $\{\max\{0, \underline{n}\}, 3\}$ to (d, e) and (e, f).

We can conclude for the flowgraph at Fig. 1(a) that the loop can be executed only if the program is called with some positive integer $\underline{n}$ for the parameter n. In that case the loop is executed at most $\max\{0, \underline{n}\}$ times (according to $\beta((c, d))$), but the path following the if branch can be executed at most $\min\{\max\{0, \underline{n}\}, 3\}$ times. So the asymptotic complexity for the program is $\mathcal{O}(\underline{n})$, but $\mathcal{O}(1)$ for the if branch inside the loop.

4   Experimental Evaluation

We implemented our algorithm in an experimental program analysis tool called LOOPERMAN. It is built on top of the symbolic execution package BUGST [17] and it intensively uses the SMT solver Z3 [21].

We compared LOOPERMAN with state-of-the-art loop bound analysis tools LOOPUS [12], KOAT [5], PUBS [1], and RANK [3] on 199 simple C programs used in previous comparisons of loop bound analysis tools [19,20]. We focused on two kinds of bounds: asymptotic complexity bounds for whole programs and *exact* (meaning non-asymptotic) bounds for individual program loops. The comparison of asymptotic complexity bounds and other details about our experimental evaluation can be found in [15]. Here we present only the comparison of exact bounds, which was restricted to LOOPERMAN and LOOPUS as the other tools use input in a different format and (as far as we know) they do not provide any mapping of their bounds to the original C code. Note that LOOPUS is a strong competitor as it achieved the best results in the asymptotic complexity bounds.

The presented experiments run on a machine with 8 GB of RAM and Intel i5 CPU clocked at 2.5 GHz. We apply the 60 s time limit to the analysis of

Table 1. Comparison of loop bounds inferred by LOOPERMAN and LOOPUS

	LOOPERMAN	LOOPUS
Correctly bounded loops	227	267
Incorrectly bounded loops	0	3
Loops with no bound found	86	43
Bounded loops, not bounded by the other	11	51
Asymptotically tighter bounds	16	11
Tighter bounds, but not asymptotically	44	2

one program by one tool. The LOOPERMAN tool (both sources and Windows binaries), the 199 benchmarks, and all measured data are available here [18].

The 199 benchmarks contain 313 loops. Table 1 provides for both tools the numbers of correctly and incorrectly bounded loops, and the number of loops for which no bound is inferred. The second part of the table compares the inferred loop bounds. It presents the number of loops where one tool produces a correct loop bound while the other does not, the number of loops where one tool provides an asymptotically tighter loop bound than the other, and the number of loops where one tool infers a tighter bound than the other tool, but the difference is not asymptotic (e.g. n versus $2n$). To complete the presented data, let us note that both tools inferred exactly the same bound for 143 loops.

The results show that LOOPUS can infer bounds for slightly more loops than LOOPERMAN. However, there are also loops bounded by LOOPERMAN and not by LOOPUS. The biggest advantage of LOOPERMAN is definitely the tightness of its bounds: LOOPERMAN found a tighter bound for 28 % of 216 loops bounded by both tools, while LOOPUS found a tighter bound only for 6 % of these loops.

5 Related Work

Techniques based on recurrence equations attempt to infer a system of recurrence equations from a loop (or a whole program) and to solve it. PUBS [1] focuses primarily on solving of the system generated by another tool, e.g. [2]. R-TuBOUND [11] builds a system of recurrence equations by rewriting multi-path loops into single-path ones using SMT reasoning. The system is then solved by a pattern-based algorithm. In ABC [4], inner loops are instrumented by iteration counters (one counter for a whole loop). Recurrence equations are then constructed over program variables and counters. SPEED [7] instruments counters into the program (one counter for each back-edge) as artificial variables. Then it computes their upper bounds by a linear invariant generation tool. In our approach, we use recurrence equations and counters to summarise loops. We compute upper bounds from necessary conditions for executing backbones. In contrast to [4,7], we introduce a counter for each loop path and counters are not instrumented.

RANK [3] applies an approach based on ranking functions. It reuses results from the termination analysis of a given program (i.e. a ranking function) to get an asymptotic upper bound on the length of all program executions. KoAT [5] uses ranking functions of already processed loops to compute bounds on values of program variables, which are then used to improve ranking functions of subsequent loops. LOOPUS [16] uses several heuristics to transform a program in particular locations so that variables appearing there represent ranking functions. Program loops are then summarised per individual paths through them. The approach was further improved by merging nested loops [12] and by computation of maximal values of variables [13]. Our algorithm does not use ranking functions. However, the passing of information from a preceding to a subsequent loop we see in [5] or [13] happens also in our approach, through symbolic execution. The loop summarisation per individual loop paths presented in [16] is similar to ours. However, while [16] computes summary as a transitive hull expressed in the domain of a size-change abstraction, we compute precise symbolic values of variables after loops. In contrast to [12], we do not merge nested loops.

There are other important techniques computing upper bounds, which are, however, less related to our work. For instance, SWEET [9] uses abstract interpretation to derive bounds on values of program variables and a pattern matching of loops of predefined structure. In [8], a program is transformed with respect to a given location: preserving reachability from the location back to itself. Loops are summarised into disjunctive invariants from which upper bounds are computed using a technique based on proof-rules. WISE [6] symbolically executes all paths up to a given length in order to infer a branching policy for longer paths. Then it symbolically executes all paths satisfying the policy. The longest path represents the worst-case execution time of the program.

6   Conclusion

We presented an algorithm computing upper bounds for execution counts of individual instructions of an analysed program during any program run. The algorithm is based on symbolic execution and the concept of path counters. The upper bounds are parametrized by input values of the analysed program. Evaluation of our experimental tool LOOPERMAN shows that our approach often infers loop bounds that are tighter than these found by leading loop bound analysis tools. This may be a crucial advantage in some applications including the worst case execution time (WCET) analysis.

Acknowledgement. P. Čadek has been supported by the Austrian National Research Network S11403-N23 (RiSE) of the Austrian Science Fund (FWF) and by the Vienna Science and Technology Fund (WWTF) through grant ICT12-059, J. Strejček by the Czech Science Foundation grant GBP202/12/G061, and M. Trtík by the QBOBF project funded by DGCIS/DGA.

References

1. Albert, E., Arenas, P., Genaim, S., Puebla, G.: Automatic inference of upper bounds for recurrence relations in cost analysis. In: Alpuente, M., Vidal, G. (eds.) SAS 2008. LNCS, vol. 5079, pp. 221–237. Springer, Heidelberg (2008)
2. Albert, E., Arenas, P., Genaim, S., Puebla, G., Zanardini, D.: Cost analysis of Java bytecode. In: De Nicola, R. (ed.) ESOP 2007. LNCS, vol. 4421, pp. 157–172. Springer, Heidelberg (2007)
3. Alias, C., Darte, A., Feautrier, P., Gonnord, L.: Multi-dimensional rankings, program termination, and complexity bounds of flowchart programs. In: Cousot, R., Martel, M. (eds.) SAS 2010. LNCS, vol. 6337, pp. 117–133. Springer, Heidelberg (2010)
4. Blanc, R., Henzinger, T.A., Hottelier, T., Kovács, L.: ABC: algebraic bound computation for loops. In: Clarke, E.M., Voronkov, A. (eds.) LPAR-16 2010. LNCS, vol. 6355, pp. 103–118. Springer, Heidelberg (2010)
5. Brockschmidt, M., Emmes, F., Falke, S., Fuhs, C., Giesl, J.: Alternating runtime and size complexity analysis of integer programs. In: Ábrahám, E., Havelund, K. (eds.) TACAS 2014 (ETAPS). LNCS, vol. 8413, pp. 140–155. Springer, Heidelberg (2014)
6. Burnim, J., Juvekar, S., Sen, K.: Automated test generation for worst-case complexity. In: ICSE, pp. 463–473. IEEE (2009)
7. Gulwani, S., Mehra, K.K., Chilimbi, T.: SPEED: precise and efficient static estimation of program computational complexity. In: POPL, pp. 127–139. ACM (2009)
8. Gulwani, S., Zuleger, F.: The reachability-bound problem. In: PLDI, pp. 292–304. ACM (2010)
9. Gustafsson, J., Ermedahl, A., Sandberg, C., Lisper, B.: Automatic derivation of loop bounds and infeasible paths for WCET analysis using abstract execution. In: RTSS, pp. 57–66. IEEE (2006)
10. King, J.C.: Symbolic execution and program testing. Commun. ACM **19**(7), 385–394 (1976)
11. Knoop, J., Kovács, L., Zwirchmayr, J.: Symbolic loop bound computation for WCET analysis. In: Clarke, E., Virbitskaite, I., Voronkov, A. (eds.) PSI 2011. LNCS, vol. 7162, pp. 227–242. Springer, Heidelberg (2012)
12. Sinn, M., Zuleger, F., Veith, H.: A simple and scalable static analysis for bound analysis and amortized complexity analysis. In: Biere, A., Bloem, R. (eds.) CAV 2014. LNCS, vol. 8559, pp. 745–761. Springer, Heidelberg (2014)
13. Sinn, M., Zuleger, F., Veith, H.: Difference constraints: an adequate abstraction for complexity analysis of imperative programs. In: FMCAD, pp. 144–151. IEEE (2015)
14. Strejček, J., Trtík, M.: Abstracting path conditions. In: ISSTA, pp. 155–165. ACM (2012)
15. Čadek, P., Strejček, J., Trtík, M.: Tighter loop bound analysis (Technical report) (2016). CoRR, abs/1605.03636
16. Zuleger, F., Gulwani, S., Sinn, M., Veith, H.: Bound analysis of imperative programs with the size-change abstraction. In: Yahav, E. (ed.) SAS 2011. LNCS, vol. 6887, pp. 280–297. Springer, Heidelberg (2011)
17. Bugst. http://sourceforge.net/projects/bugst/
18. Looperman, benchmarks, and evaluation. https://sourceforge.net/projects/bugst/files/Looperman/1.0.0/
19. http://aprove.informatik.rwth-aachen.de/eval/IntegerComplexity
20. http://forsyte.at/static/people/sinn/loopus/CAV14/index.html
21. Z3. https://github.com/Z3Prover/z3

Author Index

Printed in the United States
By Bookmasters